ADVENTURING IN
NEW ZEALAND

MARGARET JEFFERIES

ADVENTURING IN
NEW ZEALAND

◆ ◆ ◆ ◆ ◆ ◆ ◆ ◆ ◆ ◆ ◆ ◆ ◆ ◆ ◆ ◆ ◆ ◆

THE SIERRA CLUB
TRAVEL GUIDE
TO THE
PEARL OF THE PACIFIC

Sierra Club Books
San Francisco

The Sierra Club, founded in 1892 by John Muir, has devoted itself to the study and protection of the earth's scenic and ecological resources—mountains, wetlands, woodlands, wild shores and rivers, deserts and plains. The publishing program of the Sierra Club offers books to the public as a nonprofit educational service in the hope that they may enlarge the public's understanding of the Club's basic concerns. The point of view expressed in each book, however, does not necessarily represent that of the Club. The Sierra Club has some sixty chapters coast to coast, in Canada, Hawaii, and Alaska. For information about how you may participate in its programs to preserve wilderness and the quality of life, please address inquiries to Sierra Club, 730 Polk Street, San Francisco, CA 94109.

Library of Congress Cataloging-in-Publication Data

Jefferies, Margaret.
    Adventuring in New Zealand : the Sierra Club travel guide to the
  Pearl of the Pacific / Margaret Jefferies.
    p. : ; cm.
    Includes bibliographcal references (p.) and index.
    ISBN 0-87156-571-4 : $15.00
    1. New Zealand—Guidebooks.   I. Title.
  DU405.5.J44 1993
  919.304'37—dc20   93-12366
                              CIP

Production by Robin Rockey
Cover design by Bonnie Smetts
Book design by Abigail Johnston
Maps by Tine F. Ningal

Printed in the United States of America on acid-free, recycled paper.

10 9 8 7 6 5 4 3 2 1

CONTENTS

ACKNOWLEDGMENTS

Many people contributed to the production of this book, in hundreds of different ways. All deserve credit but who to thank first is difficult. Perhaps I should start with my parents, who introduced me to the outdoors and the wonderful New Zealand bush at a tender age, and later, during my teenage years, encouraged my interest in hiking. My mother showed infinite patience and understanding when each week she washed and dried my muddy socks and grubby hiking clothes so they would be ready for another weekend in the local hills.

Jim Cohee, editor of Sierra Club Books, deserves thanks for suggesting to my husband, Bruce, that we might be interested in writing an "Adventuring" guide to New Zealand. Bruce then handed the job to me, but my thanks go to him for his support and encouragement during the book's gestation, for putting up with my long absences from home, for his company during our many adventures, and for taking me to places I might never have gone to alone.

Others who shared adventures with me also deserve special credit. They are Sue Webb, for her unflagging enthusiasm, practical support, and the energy she inspired me with on long walks; Pat Casey, for her cheerfulness, great humor, superb hospitality, and untiring conversation as she took me along her favorite tracks; my sister, Adrienne Jeffs, for her companionship and for sharing her pleasure at rediscovering the outdoors; my daughter, Lynda, for finding time in her busy life to come journeying with me and for infecting me with her enthusiasm for caves. Without her company, researching materials for this book would not have been half the fun it was.

To the many friends and colleagues whose help with accommodation, information, and transport was invaluable, thank you — particularly Dave and Marion Bamford, Pat and Maureen Devlin, Murray and Pat Reedy, Alex and Sue Miller, Kerry and Marie Mawhinney, Mike and Karen Clare, Ron and Robin Peacock, Brian and Rosemary Ahern, Pete Simpson, Craig Murdoch, Geoff and Helen Rennison, John and Kathy Ombler, Malcolm Smith, Dave and Barbara Wilson, Tim Jackson, and Nevil Jones. There are others too, whose names I do not know — the women who look after New Zealand's many information centers, the proprietors of motorcamps, fellow hikers and travelers — who offered information through casual conversation and made the adventuring more interesting and enjoyable.

Last but not least are all the staff of the Department of Conservation, who not only were helpful to me but also look after New Zealand's splendid conservation estate. Without their efforts there would not be such a superb country to adventure in.

1 INTRODUCTION TO NEW ZEALAND

• •

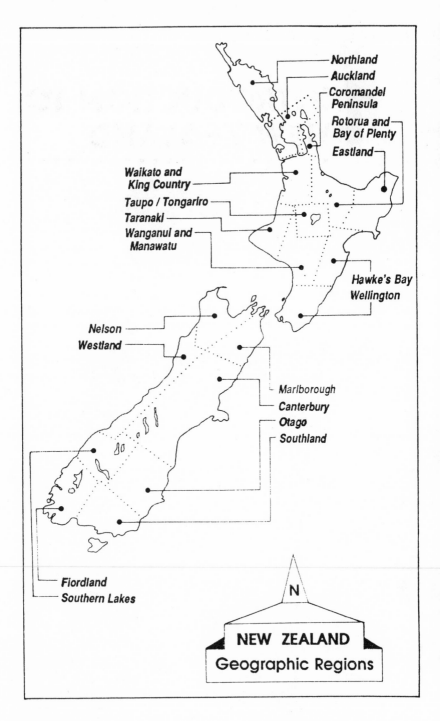

Northland
Auckland
Coromandel
Peninsula
Rotorua and
Bay of Plenty
Eastland

Waikato and
King Country
Taupo / Tongariro
Taranaki
Wanganui and
Manawatu

Hawke's Bay
Wellington

Nelson
Westland

Marlborough
Canterbury
Otago
Southland

Fiordland
Southern Lakes

N

NEW ZEALAND
Geographic Regions

Stretching north and south for over 1,500 kilometers, with a bank of cloud clinging to its long mountain backbone, New Zealand was a welcome sight to early Polynesian navigators at the end of their long and often dangerous voyages across the Pacific. They named it *Aotearoa* – Land of the long white cloud. Dutch navigators later christened it *Staten Landt*, then renamed it *Niew Zeeland*. Since then the country has been given many labels: the Last Great Paradise, Jewel of the Pacific, Land of Milk and Honey, Godzone, to name a few. Most Kiwis (New Zealanders) would these days disagree with the last two names as changes in world trade and radical restructuring of the country by its own government force a less complacent lifestyle on them. Despite the pain and disenchantment that come with economic reform, the majority of Kiwis still enjoy comparatively good lifestyles nurtured by modern conveniences, diverse sporting activities, and the best ingredient of all, the great outdoors.

Jewel of the Pacific and Last Great Paradise are names that still apply, even in these rapidly changing times, and it is doubtful whether any other country of comparable size can boast of the diversity of magnificent scenery that New Zealand can. Similar in size to Japan or Great Britain, New Zealand holds vast tracts of dense rainforest, glaciated mountains, wild rivers, numerous crystal-clear lakes, and rich rolling farmlands. Its long coastline is as varied as any seaboard could possibly be. There are sandy beaches that sweep unbroken for tens of kilometers; on others, steeply shelving banks of rounded pebbles rattle noisily with the surge of the sea. The coastline is deeply notched with convoluted inlets, coves, and bays; dramatic cliffs, some pale and crumbling, others dark and resistant, buffer the pounding of waves born vast distances away.

Human occupation began with the arrival of Polynesians a mere 1,200 years ago. Europeans came only within the last 200 years. The stories of the changes that people wrought – upon the land, its flora and fauna, and themselves – lend a special character to the country and add to the visitor's interest and enjoyment.

Almost a quarter of the New Zealand countryside has some form of protected status. Given its twelve national parks, three maritime parks, twenty forest parks, numerous scenic and scientific reserves, eight coastal farm parks, and many protected offshore islands, visitors to New Zealand could be forgiven for thinking that the country is one great wilderness. It has, in fact, been described as one great national park, and although that may be a slight exaggeration, those large areas of untamed, uninhabited country are New Zealand's greatest asset. With only 3.4 million inhabitants, it is possible to find peaceful solitude within a few kilometers of every town and city. Popular destinations are well peopled at times, but the crowds are minuscule compared to those at other tourist spots around the world.

Adventure means different things to different people. For tour bus travelers, or those who prefer the comfort of five-star hotels, and those who choose not to stray off the main highway, scenery may be enough. Others will want to follow the lure of excitement to the mountains, valleys, and coastline they see. Byways and backcountry roads offer chances of interesting unexpected encounters. For the outdoor person, New Zealand probably is the Last Great Paradise. The mountains and valleys offer innumerable walking opportunities, from gentle strolling to serious mountaineering. There are caves to explore. At the coast there are swimming, surfing, sailing, diving, and fishing; on the rivers and lakes, rafting, canoeing, and angling. It is all here.

As I collected material for this book I was amazed at how much there was to see and do—and I had thought I knew my own country. It became obvious, however, that I could not include everything there was to see and do in one volume and, of necessity, I have had to be selective. My goal is to help you, the adventurous visitor, discover some of New Zealand's obvious and hidden attractions. The book is divided into geographical areas as New Zealanders know them, working more or less from North to South. For each area I have tried to describe a wide variety of places to adventure in and enjoy, to cater to the do-it-yourself tourist who doesn't want to burn unlimited dollars but wishes to see and do as much as possible. I have also tried to provide insights into the things that make the areas I have described interesting—their wildlife, vegetation, history, geology, and other special features. I have included some telephone numbers and addresses of commercial adventure operators, fully aware that such things are always subject to change, partly to give a clearer picture of the adventuring possibilities available, and also to facilitate forward planning and prebooking. Because this book is only an introduction to things to see and do, I have listed sources of more detailed information for you to use as you follow your interests and your own sense of fun. Good luck—and happy adventuring.

1 ◆ THE LAND AND ITS INHABITANTS

GEOLOGY, PLANTS, AND ANIMALS

Spawned by the supercontinent Gondwanaland, New Zealand has not always been three islands in the shape we know them today. Over 500 million years ago, the edges of Gondwanaland projected northward into the Northern Hemisphere, connecting it with what we know as China and Southeast Asia. Eventually, Gondwanaland began to swing south into the Southern Hemisphere, and by the Devonian period, between 410 million and 350 million years ago, New Zealand was developing coastal links with South America via Antarctica. The land masses continued to drift southward during the Carboniferous and Permian periods (350 million to 235 million years ago) toward the South Pole.

Part of present-day New Zealand and New Caledonia became part of a huge, broad, slowly sinking depression (a geosyncline) in the sea floor. For the next 150 million years, lava and ash from volcanic activity on both land and sea, along with sand, mud, and gravel eroded from Gondwanaland, accumulated in this depression, which was situated between the coasts of Antarctica and eastern Australia. The layers of sediment were gradually compressed to form huge bands of hard sandstones and siltstones (greywackes and argillites), measuring 10 km deep in places.

The long period of underwater deposition ended abruptly between 140 million and 120 million years ago, and about this time (late Jurassic and early Cretaceous periods) a major collision between the Indian-Australian and Pacific plates thrust a huge portion of the sea floor out of the ocean. This substratum, along with volcanic material, became the original landmass of New Zealand. The rotation of Gondwanaland placed southern Africa, New Zealand, New Caledonia, and Australia in middle latitudes. The tropical, subtropical, and temperate climates allowed life to flourish, and with the continents closely grouped, terrestrial and marine organisms were able to spread across Gondwanaland. Early migrants included the ancestors of present-day New Zealand reptiles, frogs, insects, snails, and ferns. Some interesting relics of that ancient time are the tuatara and geckos, which have many primitive features; Hochstetter's, Archey's, and Hamilton's frogs (genus *Leiopelma*), which have no tadpole stage and no webbing between their toes and can live in habitats without running water; and large land snails, such as *Paryphanta*, with its beautiful polished shell over 8 cm in diameter. The antecedents of some of New Zealand's distinctive flora—the kauri, rimu, totara, kahikatea, silver beech, rewarewa, and many ferns—also came at this time. Several curious plants, such as *Psilotales* and *Tmesipteris* species, are living fossils of an ancient division of the plant kingdom.

About 110 million years ago the days of Gondwanaland were drawing to a close. Several rifts began to crack the Earth's crust. New Zealand began to break away from the Australian parts of Gondwanaland by the formation of what is now the Tasman Sea, about 80 million years ago. As the rift widened, migration by animals that needed a land bridge ceased, but birds and bats were still able to cross the widening gap. It is thought that the ancestors of some of New Zealand's distinctive native birds and its only mammals, two species of bat, crossed the infant Tasman Sea before the distance became too great.

The Tasman Sea had reached its greatest width sometime between 80 million and 60 million years ago, but it was not until about 55 million years ago that the sea between Antarctica and Australia commenced to form. The new sea floor joined the one already forming between New Zealand and Antarctica, and the land masses started drifting apart—Antarctica to the south and Australia, with New Zealand attached to it, to the north. As it moved southward, Antarctica became colder. Ice fields and glaciers began to form and cold marine currents started to encircle the continent. As the oceanic gaps widened and cyclonic conditions were spawned from the Antarctic Ice Cap, the development of the Circum–Antarctica current commenced—a system of winds and ocean currents that today dominates the meteorology and oceanology of the Southern Hemisphere. The westerly winds at latitudes 40, 50, and 60 degrees south are known, because of their power, as the Roaring Forties, Furious Fifties, and Screaming Sixties.

Meanwhile, the land was undergoing considerable change. Erosion commenced immediately, and by the time uplift slackened, the sharp young mountains had been ground down to broad lowlands. The next 50 million years brought a series of uplifts and submergences, volcanic activity, and earthquakes, all of them changing the outline of New Zealand. Over time, uplift has won out against erosion.

The general northeasterly alignment of the coasts and ranges of New Zealand are the result of more recent geological activity along the line of contact between the Indian-Australian and Pacific plates. New Zealand sits astride these two plates—or more correctly, the junction of the plates cuts across New Zealand. The North Island and the northern and western areas of the South Island are part of the Indian-Australian plate; the southern and eastern South Island are part of the Pacific plate. Movement of these two plates, as they slide alongside each other, has created the Alpine Fault. It runs the length of the Southern Alps and extends northward as a system of branching faults across Cook Strait and up into the Bay of Plenty and beyond. As the Pacific Plate is subducted below the Indian-Australian Plate, off the east coast of the North Island, it is subjected to increasing heat and pressure until the crust melts back into magma. The magma rises, and when it finds suitable fractures in the crust above, rises to the surface as lava. This process has formed the line of volcanoes around the edge of the Pacific Plate known as the Pacific Ring of Fire, and includes those in the North Island. In the South Island, as a result of movement of the land in opposite directions along the Alpine Fault, rocks that once adjoined have slid almost 500 km apart.

It was perhaps during the Pliocene (5 million to 2 million years ago), after the onset of a major mountain-building period when most of the axial mountain ranges were formed, that the New Zealand environment saw the most changes. What followed were the Pleistocene Ice Ages (2 million to 14,000 years ago), when a series of climatic oscillations produced cold periods alternating with warmer periods. During the severe glacial periods many temperate organisms that had survived the steady deterioration of climate throughout the Miocene and Pliocene times were restricted to the northernmost regions of New Zealand and a few coastal areas, where the influence of the sea moderated the cold glacial climate. Other, more warmth-loving creatures and plants did not survive.

At the peak of the last glaciation, 20,000 to 18,000 years ago, glaciers and snowfields covered the young mountain ranges. At this stage, with the sea 100 m lower than it is at present, the three islands of New Zealand were one and the land about 25 percent greater. As temperatures warmed again 14,000 to 10,000 years ago, the glaciers started to retreat. Sea levels rose again slowly, flooding many previously low lying areas until New Zealand became the three islands we know today.

With more favorable temperatures, the new habitats opened by the retreating glaciers were quickly colonized by surviving plants and animals. In the course of time, lichens covered bare rocks and finer sands and gravels, eventually supporting mosses and short grasses, cushion plants, and hardy herbs. Within two hundred years, as soil formed, these were replaced by shrubs, which were eventually succeeded by a forest of small trees. After several hundred more years, the climax forests of tall podocarps—rimu, totara, kahikatea, miro, and matai—were established.

Some areas had not been glaciated or subject to volcanic activity: the far north, eastern parts of the South Island, and Stewart Island. These still had forests, shrubs, and grasslands. Two mountainous areas of the South Island, Fiordland and northwest Nelson, although widely separated, were geologically similar and provided important refuges for alpine plants and beech forests.

Although some landforms were young, others had existed long enough to have a good cover of soils and vegetation. This variation of topography and soils, along with rocks of varying chemical composition, accounted for the vast range of plant and animal communities present when the first Polynesians arrived on the shores of New Zealand at the end of the eighth century. Eighty percent of the country was forested then, and the remainder included small arid parts of central Otago, the grasslands of red tussock around the central North Island volcanoes and the Southland plains, and the peatlands of the Waikato and Hauraki plains. By the time the first Europeans arrived, the Polynesians had burned off about 50 percent of the forest cover. In only 150 years, this next wave of settlers further reduced the forests to about 23 percent.

Besides destroying the forests, humans introduced elements that caused ecological changes. The early Polynesians killed the huge, flightless moa for meat, eventually hunting them to extinction. The introduction of a rat (the kiore) and a dog probably led to the extermination of at least forty other species of lesser-known birds, including an eagle, the New Zealand coot, several rails, a pelican, a crow, and two harriers.

The European settlers introduced plants and animals from their home countries, with devastating effects. In a short time, rabbits, possums, deer, and goats had multiplied so much that they were declared pests. The indigenous New Zealand flora and fauna, which had evolved with no threat from predatory or grazing mammals, had no defense mechanisms against these new occupants. Rodents and stoats decimated bird populations. (Parasites and diseases introduced by exotic species probably contributed to the demise of many native birds also.) Gorse, broom, nasella tussock, briar roses, and heather also thrived and overwhelmed native plants.

As well, the removal of forest by burning, and later overgrazing of these same lands, has led to widespread soil erosion in many hill areas and consequent loss of many unique plant communities and habitats for native fauna. The draining of swamps, clear-cutting of forests, and burning of tussocklands has had the same effects. The indigenous forests and shrub cover have largely been replaced by pine forests or pasture, where only a minimal number of native plants and animals can survive.

New Zealand birds that have become extinct since the arrival of Europeans include the New Zealand thrush, the huia, the New Zealand quail, the laughing owl, and many subspecies of rail, snipe, and wren. Many others—takahe, kakapo, black petrel, New Zealand brown teal, black stilt, New Zealand shore plover, orange-fronted parakeet, New Zealand bush wren, stitchbird, South Island kokako, and the Chatham Islands black robin—are endangered. Sadly, many of these birds are found nowhere else in the world. In fact, most of New Zealand's plant and animal species that still exist today are found nowhere else. Of the higher plants, 51 percent are endemic, as are 57 percent of the sixty-five species of terrestrial birds, 85 percent of the twenty-five or twenty-six species of freshwater fish, over 90 percent of the insects, and 100 percent of the approximately thirty-eight reptiles, three amphibians and two mammals. Those that are left are found mainly in more remote, uninhabitable areas—steep bushed gullies, wetlands, or windswept mountain ranges—or in national or forest parks.

On the brighter side are some notable successes in retrieving species from the brink of extinction. For example, the Chatham Islands black robin was once the world's rarest bird, with only five individuals left. By foster-parenting the eggs and chicks of the one surviving female and moving the birds to a predator-free habitat, conservationists were able to increase the population to the point where this bird is now out of danger. Attempts are currently underway to save the flightless takahe, which was once thought to be extinct, and the kakapo, a large ground-dwelling parrot. Both have been bred in captivity and some birds have been relocated to safe habitats.

THE PEOPLE: A BRIEF HISTORY

The First New Zealanders

In the beginning there were two people—Rangi, the sky-father, and Papa Tu-anuku, the earth-mother. They lay together in a tight embrace, so close that their many children were trapped between them. Craving light and freedom, the strongest child, Tane Mahuta, pushed and struggled, finally managing to push his parents apart. Taking pity on his naked mother, Tane clothed Papa with trees and plants and so became the father of all living things. Still saddened by their forced separation, Rangi's tears are the rain that falls on the land and its plant coverings; the morning dews are Papa's own sighs of grief.

In Polynesian legend there was also Maui, half god–half human, who fished up the islands of the Pacific. It was Maui, seated in his huge canoe (the South Island), which was anchored by a massive rock (Stewart Island), who hauled a giant fish from the depths of the ocean. This fish became the North Island of New Zealand and is known in Maori as Te Ika a Maui, the fish of Maui. Perhaps it is no coincidence that modern geology confirms that New Zealand was raised from the sea floor.

Humans came later, "like fish in the sea, gliding through the currents of the oceans." Whatever legend tells us, what is known is that the first Polynesians arrived on the shores of New Zealand between A.D. 600 and 800. They came from the Tahitian area, most likely from Raiatea (formerly known as Havaiki), and could possibly have been recent Marquesan immigrants. Their arrival at New Zealand was probably not by chance but by conscious navigation toward the southwest. The Tahitians were skilled navigators and also a sharp-eyed people who must have observed the direction taken by the long-tailed cuckoo on its annual migration. A land bird, the cuckoo could only have been making for a land to the southwest. From Rarotonga, the 2,700 km to New Zealand is favored by winds and currents, and the target is large.

The canoes that made these long sea voyages were laden with dogs, pigs, chickens, and the tubers and rhizomes of food plants so that the people on board could start a new life wherever they landed. Kumara, taro, gourd, and paper mulberry could grow in the cool climate of New Zealand, but it is probable that plants such as breadfruit, bananas, and sugarcane did not survive. Also, pigs and chickens were unknown to the Maori when the first Europeans arrived, which suggests that no return visits to the homeland were made. Earlier theories, supported by legend, of a voyage of exploration followed by a return home and a setting out of a "Great Fleet," have now been discounted. Archaeological evidence does, however, point to one or more independent migratory groups from the same region. They may have left their lands of origin because of overcrowding and consequent scarcity of food resources, or to escape war and hostility from other groups.

The new land was unlike anything the Polynesian settlers were used to. It was much cooler and much larger than the islands of the Pacific, and had dense forests of tall trees. Ferns carpeted the forest floor. There were dozens of bird species, the most useful being the flightless moa (*Dinornithidae*), which offered a food supply on a scale not previously encountered.

The canoes landed in several places along New Zealand's coast, and their occupants set about claiming the land and settling in the most favorable areas, such as the coasts or near river mouths where food was plentiful. This gave rise to the tribes as we know them today. Although there were local variations, the main features of their culture were similar throughout the country. The basis of life was competitive tribalism. Over time, the new settlers adapted to the environment by using their cultural resources and skills. Remains of their earliest settlements and carbon dating have given clues to the growth and spread of populations.

Extensive horticulture was practiced. The forests were cleared using traditional slash and burn methods. Then soil improvements such as mulching, drainage, and water control were carried out. At certain times of the year, temporary huts were built for workers who gave the crops continuous attention. Year-round food production was not possible, as it had been in the tropics, and it became important to store food for the cold months. The kumara, or sweet potato, which matured in only five months, became an important staple. Roots of the bracken fern, which quickly sprang up after the forest was cleared by fire, became another. Berries of some native plants could also be eaten, but only after lengthy processing to remove poisons.

The bounty of the sea and rivers was important to the food supply. Shellfish, fish, crayfish, sea eggs, porpoises, seals, and eels were always available. Hunting and gathering supplemented horticulture to a large extent but was regulated to prevent overexploitation. The system of *rahui* (temporary bans) provided for any particular food, either plant or animal, to be taken only when its quantities or stage of growth ensured that some would be left for the future.

Population expansion was accompanied, even preceded, by a thorough exploration of the country—a country that was not easy to travel through. Rivers were deep and swift, forests were dense with undergrowth, and stretches of wild coastline were almost impassable. Over time, routes were established across alpine passes and down river valleys. They were often complemented with extended canoe voyages. A network of trade routes enabled the people of Northland to use obsidian and basalt from the Bay of Plenty area, and for all to obtain the prized greenstone (Nephrite jade) from remote parts of Westland.

When Captain James Cook arrived in New Zealand, he found the Maori a people who venerated their ancestors and their gods, who represented the natural elements of earth, sky, sea, and wind. All aspects of life—whether religion, war, food gathering, art, or death—were related and regulated by concepts of *tapu* (sacredness), *mana* (spiritual authority), *utu* (satisfaction), *mauri* (life force), and a belief in sorcery. Society was organized around the family and *hapu* (subtribe) and was divided into *rangatira*, the chiefly families, and *tutua*, the commoners. Because all families in a community were descended from a common ancestor they were controlled by the rangatira families, whose authority was partly hereditary and partly based on past achievements. Decisions were made by the *kaumatua*, or elders, who were family heads.

Each community, based on membership of a single hapu, lived in a *kainga* (village) close to water, food supplies, and cultivations. There could be few or many households on each kainga. Fortified villages called *pa* were often constructed on hilltops where they could be easily defended. Families living in adjacent kainga would retreat to the pa when threatened by a raid or war. The interior stronghold of a pa was encircled by ditches, banks, and palisades.

Weak hapu were often annihilated, but generally war was not totally destructive. That is until the Europeans introduced muskets. Nonetheless, the chances of being killed in war were high, and those who did not die were often tortured by their captors and enslaved. Cannibalism was widely practiced. The concept of mana, both for individuals and tribes, was of utmost importance. Mana was increased by victory and lost through defeat. It was particularly important for chiefs to gain their mana through strength and courage in combat, as they needed to establish their authority over other males. Overall, life for pre-European Maoris was not easy, and medical examination of remains has shown that few lived much more than thirty years. The staple of their diet, fern roots, would not have been conducive to longevity.

In spite of the hardships of living, artistic ability was nourished. The carving of bone, wood, and stone developed to a degree not often found elsewhere. House gables, door lintels, and canoe prows were all intricately carved in wood;

personal ornaments, such as *tiki* and pendants, were made from bone or the prized *pounamu*, or greenstone. Tattooing was also a feature of Maori art, with intricate patterns being worked on mens' faces and buttocks, and on women's lips and chins.

European Newcomers

The first of the European explorers to investigate the South Pacific region was Abel Janzoon Tasman. He led an expedition in the ships *Heemskirk* and *Zeehaen* to discover the great southern continent. After sighting the snow-capped peaks of the Southern Alps on December 13, 1642, Tasman sailed north along the west coast of the South Island and six days later anchored in a bay on the northern side of what eventually became Cook Strait. The Maori discouraged Tasman's attempts at landing, and when a small boat traveling between his two ships was rammed by a canoe, fighting broke out and both sides lost men. Called Murderers' Bay by Tasman, the place is now known as Golden Bay. Tasman named the country Staten Landt, the Dutch name for the southern tip of South America, because that is where he believed he was. Not long afterward, however, another Dutch navigator, Henrick Brouwer, discovered that Tasman's Staten Landt was not part of a huge continent and it was renamed Niew Zeeland. As the newly discovered land did not appear to offer anything profitable, it held no further interest for the Dutch.

It was not until New Zealand was rediscovered by James Cook, a captain in the British Royal Navy, that was it was found to be at least two islands. Cook's main objective on this voyage in the bark *Endeavour* was to observe, from the island of Tahiti, the transit of Venus over the sun in June 1769. After this his instructions called for him to sail as far as 50 degrees south. First sighting of the new land was made on October 6, 1769, by Nicholas Young, a ship's boy, and to commemorate this a prominent headland was named Young Nick's Head. Two days later they sailed into an inhabited bay to a hostile reception, even though Cook had on board with him a Tahitian chief, Tupaea, who could converse with the Maori. Unable to replenish food and water there, Cook named the place Poverty Bay. He obtained fresh supplies near Tolaga Bay, where the Maori were friendlier, and from there he sailed north to Mercury Bay, staying ten days while the transit of Mercury was observed. At Mercury Bay, Cook, in the tradition of the time, formally took possession of New Zealand.

During the six-month circumnavigation of the country, several weeks were spent in Ship Cove in the Marlborough Sounds while the *Endeavour* was cleaned and restocked with water, food, and wood. During this time, the expedition's two botanists, Joseph Banks and Daniel Solander, were able to study the flora and fauna of the area. Before he began his return voyage to England, Cook charted the New Zealand coastline. His work was brilliantly accurate except for mistaking Stewart Island for a peninsula and Bank's Peninsula for an island.

Cook returned to the South Pacific two more times, once from 1772 to 1775, and again from 1776 to 1780. His ships on these expeditions were the *Resolution* and the *Adventure*. During the first of these voyages, Cook ventured further south than anyone was known ever to have been before. Although he came within 112 km of Antarctica, he was unlucky and did not sight it. On his return north from the cold, storm-lashed southern oceans, Cook anchored the *Resolution* for six weeks in the calm waters of Dusky Sound to allow his weary crew time to recover from the hardships they had endured. During this time they set up an observatory, charted every part of Dusky Sound, and made valuable notes on the flora and fauna. They were also able to repair their health by brewing spruce beer from the native podocarp trees, which provided much-needed vitamin C, and by consuming plenty of fresh seal meat, which made "excellent eating." From Dusky Sound they sailed once more to Ship Cove to rendezvous with the *Adventure*, from which they had become separated in bad weather.

The second expedition took Cook northward into the Arctic Circle in search of the long-sought Northwest Passage to the east. Like many explorers before him, he did not find a route, but on the return south he discovered Hawaii. The islanders' hospitality was overwhelming, but by the time he departed, Cook, a man always sensitive to the culture of the native people he encountered, felt his crew had worn their welcome thin. When a storm damaged one of the ships shortly after their departure, he was reluctant to return to the same place. His instinct proved valid. When he tried to take a hostage in exchange for a ship's boat that had been stolen, Cook was pushed into the water and stabbed to death.

Cook's accurate charts and accounts of his voyages encouraged other navigators to follow in his path. Among them was George Vancouver, who had been a midshipman on the *Resolution* and who became an explorer in his own right. Vancouver returned to Dusky Sound in 1791 for replenishments. Two years later, a Spanish expedition led by Malaspina anchored at the entrance to Dusky Sound while one of its boats sailed up into Malaspina Reach.

One of the last of the great navigator-explorers to arrive off New Zealand's coast was Dumont d'Urville. His first visit was as executive officer of the *Coquille* in 1824; his second, in 1827, was as commander of the same ship, which had been renamed the *Astrolabe*. A daring sailor, d'Urville skillfully navigated through the dangerous waters of French Pass and continued on to chart the east coast of the North Island.

Cook's accounts of the abundance of whales and seals in the southern waters interested the whaling and sealing industry, and within a year of Vancouver's visit to Dusky Sound a sealing gang was landed there from the *Britannia*. Several other ships arrived in Dusky Sound over the next few years to land sealers, who commenced the slaughter of the animals for their fur. By the 1830s the seal populations of the Southern Ocean had been almost destroyed.

The sealers were followed by the whalers, and by the mid-nineteenth century, whale populations were also declining, their demise hastened by shore stations set up around the New Zealand coast. Other traders also came, to procure supplies of flax and timber, which the Maori were happy to provide. Contact with Europeans became more frequent but the relationship between the two peoples, although relatively peaceful, was never easy. The Europeans frequently offended the Maori by not observing their customs or by ill-treating and tricking them. Retaliation was often harsh and violent, and in 1809 the brig *Boyd* was burnt in Whangaroa Harbour—and its crew eaten.

Establishment of a Colony

British colonization of Australia began in 1788, when Port Jackson, now Sydney, was developed as a penal colony, but the early whalers and sealers who visited New Zealand were in no way colonists. Until the legislation of the colony of New South Wales was extended in 1817 to include New Zealand, there was no jurisdiction. Actual implementation of legislation did not begin until 1823, and meanwhile New Zealand was a lawless outpost.

In 1814 the Reverend Samuel Marsden, a dedicated evangelist, arrived from New South Wales, where he had been magistrate. His mission was to convert the Maori people to Christianity and to develop their skills in carpentry, farming, and technology. With him Marsden brought the first horses and cattle, gifts from Lachlan Macquarie, the governor of New South Wales. Six years later, John Butler, another missionary, introduced the first plough and demonstrated its use on the soils of Kerikeri in the Bay of Islands.

Not all the missionaries of the time were as zealous as Marsden and Butler. Many were involved in drunkenness, adultery, gunrunning, and even pagan rites. It is not surprising therefore that only two Maori were converted to Christianity in the first twenty years of missionary activity. Some good things were accomplished, however, in spite of the missionaries' shortcomings. The first grammar and dictionary of Maori language was compiled by Thomas Kendall, and in 1834 William Colenso established the first printing press—two things that helped develop Maori literacy. Other less benevolent settlers—such as the Norwegian rat and several sorts of weeds—had also established themselves by the mid-1830s.

Back in the "home country," as Britain was regarded, there was continuing debate as to whether New Zealand should be settled officially or not. The missionaries, on the whole, fought against it, believing that the Maori would be better off if left uncontaminated by the immoralities that would inevitably be introduced by European settlers. Others felt that if settlement were well organized and managed by responsible people, tragedies that had occurred when other new lands had been settled could be forestalled. While the British government dithered, land was quickly being taken up by those Europeans already in the country.

A major influence in the eventual British decision to gain sovereignty over New Zealand was a preliminary expedition in 1839 by Edward Gibbon Wakefield's New Zealand Company to buy land for colonists. On January 29, 1840, Captain William Hobson arrived in the Bay of Islands, carrying with him official instructions to conclude a treaty with the Maori people that would give the British government official standing. Hence the Treaty of Waitangi was drawn up and the Maori version was duly signed by about fifty northern Maori chiefs on February 6, 1840. The document was then carried around the country and signed by the chiefs in other districts. Although the first group of New Zealand Company settlers had already arrived at Port Nicholson (Wellington Harbour) on the *Aurora* by the time the Treaty of Waitangi was signed, the official colonization of New Zealand did not begin until May 21, 1840, when Hobson proclaimed Queen Victoria's sovereignty over the whole of the country. The pace of colonization then quickened, with three more ships—the *Arrow, Whitby,* and *Will Watch*—arriving in October 1841 and more settlers of the offshoot Plymouth Company landing in New Plymouth the next month. By 1850, the European population—perhaps 2,000 before the Treaty of Waitangi—had risen to over 20,000.

Along with the settlers came more explorers, some keen to find out about the people and nature of the country and others to find usable land. Of the more notable were John Bidwell, Ernst Dieffenbach, William Colenso (who established the first printing press), Thomas Brunner, and Charles Heaphy. The names of Bidwell, Dieffenbach, and Colenso are immortalized in the scientific names of many of New Zealand's native plants, as are those of M. E. Raoul, a surgeon based at Akaroa to service two French ships; John Sinclair, who had been Colonial Secretary; David Lyall, a surgeon-naturalist on the *HMS Acheron;* and Joseph Dalton Hooker. These men all made extensive botanical collections and notes during their travels. Brunner's epic 550-day return journey from Nelson down the Buller Gorge to South Westland was a saga of hardship matched by few other expeditions. Two other men, Arthur Dudley Dobson, a surveyor, and the geologist Julius von Haast, are both remembered for their exploratory work by the names of Arthur's Pass and Haast Pass.

By the early 1860s the North and South Islands presented very different pictures of development. The South Island was prosperous owing to sheep, abundant grasslands, and the important discovery of gold. In contrast, the North Island settlers were still trying to establish claims to the land, a task that was proving very difficult. When arrivals on the first ships came to Wellington they found that the New Zealand Company did not own the land it had promised them and neither could they purchase it directly from the Maori owners. The government had a preemptive right to purchase and resell, and besides, the supply of land did not meet the demand. Meanwhile, the Maori were becoming disenchanted with the Treaty of Waitangi and increasingly concerned at the loss of their lands, for which they were paid a pittance. They had not failed to notice that their land was often resold for up to twenty times what they had been paid for it.

The Maori attitude hardened steadily and tensions over land problems climbed to a critical level, particularly in Taranaki, culminating in the Land Wars, which lasted from 1860 to the end of the decade. The frequent battles waged across different parts of the North Island were often bitter and bloody. With the defeat in 1869 at Te Porere, close to Mt. Tongariro, of Te Kooti Rikirangi, a talented but ruthless leader, guerrilla-type attacks on settlers became sporadic and eventually the wars ended. Confiscation of land followed, along with other less legal methods of acquisition, opening the way for European-style development of the North Island.

The New Colony Develops

The 1870s saw an economic boom initiated by Sir Julius Vogel, then Colonial Treasurer, who borrowed heavily overseas to fund major public works such as a railway and road system in both islands. Construction of the railway opened up country that had previously been almost inaccessible. Forests that were once approachable only from the coast could be reached from the interior, and they became an overexploited resource. Not only were the trees used for railway sleepers, telegraph poles, and houses in the towns that sprang up along the new railway, but many were milled and made into fence posts to contain stock on the newly cleared land. Several farsighted politicians of the day were already concerned about changes wrought by the building of the railway and by the introduction of exotic plants and animals. They advocated forest conservation measures. Some success was met when the New Zealand Forests Bill was passed in 1874, allowing for state forests to be set aside in each province, the appointment of a Conservator of Forests, and allotting £10,000 per year for forest management. The most positive outcome of this legislation was the setting aside in 1875 of Mt. Egmont, with an 8-mile radius of forested land. Other than that, the first Forests Act was a failure.

The idea of conservation was kept alive and pushed constantly before the assemblies until a second Forests Act was passed in 1885, again setting aside state forests and providing for their conservation and management. The newly appointed chief conservator, Thomas Kirk, reserved over 140,000 ha of forest in his first week in office.

Tourism was also starting to pick up by the 1870s, with the thermal area at Rotorua being the most popular attraction. New accommodations, improved services, and more attractions were promoted every year. At this stage the idea of forming a national park, such as the new Yellowstone National Park in the United States, had not quite occurred to the New Zealand government.

It was not until September 1887 that the nucleus of New Zealand's first national park, Tongariro, was designated when the summits of Tongariro, Ngauru-hoe, and Ruapehu were gifted to the Crown by Horonuku Te Heuheu, then chief of the Ngati Tuwharetoa Maori. The gift was a generous one, as the volca-noes were among the most feared and revered of all the sacred mountains in the land, and ownership conferred great mana to the Tuwharetoa people. There was, however, another reason for this action. Ownership of the three volcanoes had already been debated in 1881 during sittings of the Land Court in Taupo, but the Tuwharetoa were able to successfully maintain their claim to the terri-tory, particularly the summits of Tongariro and Ngauruhoe. Most of Ruapehu also belonged to them except for the southwest corner, which came under the domain of Wanganui tribes. At a further sitting of the Land Court early in 1886, again near Taupo, further claims to ownership of the mountains and land sur-rounding them were heard.

As with the earlier court sittings, the threat of sale to Europeans loomed over the whole hearing, and it was to prevent this possibility, and with it the consequent loss of mana to the tribe, that Te Heuheu finally offered the sum-mits to the Crown to be protected for all New Zealanders.

The original gift of 2,400 ha covered only the very tops of the mountains and as such formed only the nucleus of a possible park. It was not until 1907, after further years of wrangling over ownership, that enough land had been pur-chased by the government for Tongariro National Park to be officially registered. Mt. Cook National Park also had an early beginning when the Hooker Valley was reserved for recreation purposes in 1885. The Tasman Valley was added two years later.

Bird life had declined rapidly with the introduction of stoats and weasels and with the continued destruction of forests. In response, eminent scientists pressured the government to establish preserves for natural flora and fauna. For-tunately the advice was heeded, and in 1892 Resolution Island was set aside and the purchase of Little Barrier Island commenced. By 1897, Kapiti Island had been added to the list. Kapiti and Little Barrier are still the main preserves of New Zealand's bird life.

The original Egmont reserve was declared a national park in 1900, and by the following year Arthur's Pass had also been set aside. The reserve at Mt. Cook was expanded by 7,000 ha one year later, and by 1905 nearly a million ha of Fiordland had become the Sounds National Park. By 1920 the nucleus of Abel Tasman National Park and reserves in Westland, including the Franz Josef Glacier area and 120 ha at Punakaiki, were also set aside, bringing pro-tected land to 174,000 ha. Although this record was admirable, it is important to note that the emphasis had been placed on scenic areas only. Science had little to do with deciding which areas would be preserved. Unfortunately, many areas of lowland forest and plant associations that were representative of district or regional ecologies were destroyed, and only land that was not useful for running sheep or cattle was preserved. In attempts to redress this imbalance, Paparoa National Park and Whanganui National Park have been established as recently as 1987.

By the end of the 1870s the economic boom sparked by Sir Julius Vogel was waning. The heavy borrowing that had financed public works schemes was now costing the fledgling country more than it could afford and it was almost bankrupt. Depression set in with high unemployment, causing more than 9,000 settlers to leave the country for economically greener pastures in Australia.

An event that was to shape the economic future of the country was the sailing, in 1882, of the refrigerated ship *Dunedin,* with a load of frozen sheep carcasses. When the *Dunedin* arrived in England, after three months at sea, its cargo fetched much higher prices than it would have in New Zealand. This set the stage for the new and burgeoning frozen meat industry and the export of dairy products, which increased prosperity for farmers by the early years of the twentieth century.

In spite of its very British beginnings, New Zealand is now a cosmopolitan country whose ethnic communities hail from around the world. The gold rushes of the 1860s drew Irish and Chinese immigrants, and the next decade brought 100,000 new settlers from Europe. Of these, the Scandinavians tended to live in the central North Island, where they founded towns such as Dannevirke and Norsewood. Many Dalmatians came to dig kauri gum in Northland and eventually established the country's wine industry. Greeks and Italians favored Wellington, giving the capital city a distinct Mediterranean flavor. Italians still operate a fleet of fishing boats from the suburb of Island Bay. In the 1920s immigrants from India arrived, many of whom set up and still run fruit and vegetable shops.

The end of World War II brought more newcomers—first Polish children in 1944, fleeing Nazi-occupied Europe, and later Jews, Czechs, Lithuanians, Ukrainians, Latvians, Russians, and Estonians escaping from Soviet forces. Thirty thousand Dutch immigrants made a big impact during the late 1940s and early 1950s, with their hardworking ways. Last to arrive have been more than three thousand refugees from Indochina. Pacific Islanders arrive almost daily, many of them coming to join relatives already established. They see New Zealand as offering more opportunities than their small island homes can provide. Auckland is now considered to be the largest Polynesian city in the world.

Determination to succeed and sheer hard work are helping many of the new settlers achieve a lifestyle they could never have dreamed of in their own countries. All of the groups who have come have melded together and integrated successfully into their new nation, each one adding to the prosperity and culture in subtle ways and helping to produce today's "Kiwi" citizen.

WEATHER AND SEASONS

In New Zealand the weather is a much discussed subject for good reason. It is fickle – sometimes wet and windy, sometimes gloriously and unexpectedly good, but almost reliably unpredictable. The reason for this is New Zealand's island character and position. Situated between latitudes 34 and 47 degrees south and running roughly north-south for over 1,500 km, the country's weather is dominated by the westerly trade winds that swirl around the Southern Hemisphere. These winds draw low-pressure areas northward from their origins in the southern oceans, rolling them over Australia then onto New Zealand. Frontal systems spiralling northward from these lows sweep up the length of New Zealand. Preceded by mild northwesterly winds, a cold front usually brings rain, especially along western coasts. The rain is then followed by cooler west to southwest winds and clearing weather. Between the depressions come the anticyclones or highs, bringing settled weather with light winds and brilliant clear skies that allow visibility of 100 km and more. The unusual clarity of light during sunny weather can lead to severe sunburn, a fact not easily appreciated by anyone used to a polluted Northern Hemisphere sky.

Although New Zealand's climate is described as temperate, with little variation between summer and winter temperatures, it does have definite seasons. Surrounding oceans have an ameliorating effect on the weather, but New Zealand winters can be very cold at times and the summers very hot. Generally, the northern half of the North Island has the least variation, and Northland is often described as being winterless. Southern and central districts are usually the coolest regions of the North Island all year round. The Central Volcanic Plateau, Mt. Egmont, and other ranges of the North Island experience regular snowfalls during winter, and these are heavy enough at times to close roads. Both Mt. Ruapehu and Mt. Egmont have ski areas. East of the ranges the weather tends to be much drier and warmer.

Extending to lower latitudes, and being more mountainous, the South Island is understandably cooler, with harsh winters in the central, mountainous areas. Coastal areas are more equable, but at times there are snowfalls almost to sea level. The one region that does have markedly contrasting summers and winters is central Otago. Divided by the Southern Alps, the South Island has distinct climatic zones. First to receive moisture as it sweeps in from the Tasman Sea, the west coast has record-breaking rainfalls. Twenty-five mm (1 in.) of rain an hour, falling for up to twelve hours, is not uncommon; Milford, in Fiordland, received more than 9 m (350 in.) in 1988. This unrestrained precipitation nourishes the country's luxuriant forests and abundant rivers and streams. In contrast, the land east of the Southern Alps, from Marlborough down to central Otago, tends to be drought prone. At times in winter, air in the wake of a cold front is drawn directly from the Antarctic, bringing cold, snowy weather to eastern Otago and Canterbury. During these winter storms, with the winds coming from the south or southeasterly quarter, Westland and Fiordland experience long spells of cool clear weather.

For anyone contemplating a lot of outdoor activity, the best times to visit New Zealand are summer and autumn (December to the end of April). Unsettled spring weather can extend well into December, but by then temperatures are usually mild and daylight hours are long. New Zealand practices daylight saving from October to March, with clocks set forward one hour to make the most of daylight hours. January normally ushers in the settled summer weather that is ideal for outdoor life. Christmas through to New Year is a traditional holiday time for the majority of Kiwis. The long summer school break commences around mid-December and schools do not reopen until the beginning of February. Consequently, the cities empty out as people head for their favorite holiday spot, and camping grounds and beaches become crowded. In this antipodean land, Christmas is almost synonymous with summer. Snowy white Christmas scenes are a figment of the imaginations of traditional, Northern Hemisphere Christmas card designers, and a New Zealand Christmas dinner is often a barbecue at the beach.

Once the schools reopen, midweek visitors to the beaches are mainly the seagulls. Temperature soar and most people acquire good suntans. Spells of rainy weather occur throughout summer, particularly in western districts, but they are usually of little consequence. Eastern regions often have a parched appearance by the time March rolls in.

As March passes, mornings and evenings are noticeably cooler, and by April autumn has definitely arrived. There are frosts in some areas, and exotic, deciduous trees are turning color. Otago and Southland are particularly beautiful at this time. Daylight temperatures are mild, but only the hardy still swim enthusiastically. The first autumn storms bring a sharp reminder that winter isn't far off.

May can bring a mixed bag of weather—sunshine, wind, rain, possibly snow, but still the occasional warm day. Night comes early and mornings become steadily colder. June ushers winter in with short, cold, damp days and those storms that skiers pray for but that farmers despair of. July and August bring more of the same, with winter reluctant to relinquish its grip. Although the first day of September is officially the beginning of spring, it often seems wrongly designated. Spring flowers are out and the days are warming and lengthening rapidly, but bursts of miserable weather persist.

October days bring much more credibility to the idea that summer is coming, and it often seems to already have arrived, early. It's warm again, the sun rises early, but with the equinox come strings of westerly gales to blow away fantasies of swimming and barbecues. Then comes November, a disappointing month when the promising days of October seem swept away by more gales and cloudy skies. Will summer never come, winter never end? But as surely as the sun gets up each day, the seasons change, and by December, although the skies are somewhat changeable, it is definitely summer.

2 ✦ PRACTICALITIES

VISAS AND VISITOR PERMITS

Bonafide tourists with onward tickets and sufficient funds, from the following countries, can travel to New Zealand without a visa, provided their intended stay is less than three months: Austria, Belgium, Canada, Denmark, Finland, France, Germany, Great Britain, Greece, Iceland, Indonesia, Ireland, Italy, Japan, Kiribati, Liechtenstein, Luxembourg, Malaysia, Malta, Monaco, Nauru, Netherlands, Norway, Portugal, Singapore, Spain, Sweden, Switzerland, Thailand, Tuvalu, and the United States.

On arrival, a visitor permit is applied for. It is usually readily given but can be refused if the applicant has been convicted for immigration or other offenses, is suspected of being a terrorist, or is likely to be carrying out criminal activities while in New Zealand. Visitor permits can be extended a further three months to applicants who have viable means of support, are genuine tourists, or cannot leave for valid reasons. Travelers who know that they will be staying longer than three months should apply for a visa for the length of their visit (up to twelve months) before traveling to New Zealand.

Citizens of countries not listed above, and people who wish to visit for any purpose other than as tourists, need two documents: a visa to travel to New Zealand and a visitor permit to enter the country.

As of November 1991, a visitor permit cost NZ$50. Married couples and families pay only one fee if one application is made for all members, they are visiting for the same reason, and all are accompanying the main applicant.

MONEY MATTERS

At time of writing, the exchange rate for New Zealand and American dollars was around NZ$1.00 to US$0.54. Money exchange facilities are available at international airports (Auckland, Wellington, and Christchurch) and in downtown

Auckland. Travelers' checks are best cashed at banks; even small towns have at least one bank. Opening hours are 9 A.M. to 4 P.M., Mondays to Fridays. Larger hotels in major tourist areas should be able to cash travelers' checks, but don't expect smaller places to do this. Visa, Mastercard, Diner's Club, and American Express cards are widely accepted. Tipping is not expected, but it is appreciated as a gesture that service or food has been good.

Because the exchange rate is so favorable to the U.S. dollar, visitors from the United States will find New Zealand prices for accommodation and food more than reasonable. Rental cars will work out to be slightly more expensive; gasoline prices are high, at around NZ$1.02 to $1.05 per liter.

HEALTH

Should health problems arise while you are in New Zealand, finding a doctor is usually easy. Hospitals maintain high standards and you will get emergency treatment regardless of whether you have health insurance or not. Treatment is not free to visitors, however, so it's a good idea to carry insurance. Medical drugs can only be obtained from pharmacies with a doctor's prescription.

There are no serious insect-borne diseases in New Zealand, and you can safely drink tap water throughout the country. It used to be safe to drink from streams in bush areas, but the intestinal parasite giardia, which causes diarrhea, has recently been found in water supplies in high-use areas of some national parks. Notices advising people to treat drinking water are posted in these areas.

Almost all towns, even small ones, have public conveniences. These are often AA signposted. Otherwise you will find toilets in public bars, rail and bus stations, service stations, and major department stores.

COMMUNICATIONS

Telecommunication services are top class. All New Zealand phone numbers have been changed in the last two years so that there are now nine area codes, and all new numbers have seven digits. You will still find many outdated numbers on printed material, however, and if you use an old number you will get a recorded message advising you of Telecom's help line, where you'll get the new number.

New Zealand is twelve hours ahead of Greenwich Mean Time. During Standard Time periods, when it is midday in New Zealand on a Monday it will be 12 A.M. in London (Monday), 4 P.M. in Los Angeles (Sunday), and 7 P.M. in New York (Sunday). Daylight saving is practiced from October to March.

GETTING AROUND

Buses

InterCity is the major transport operator, with buses connecting all cities, major towns, and smaller centers. Booking offices will be found in most towns; travel passes are available.

Mt. Cook Line and **Newmans Buses** provide services on major routes only, in both islands. Bookings can be made through travel agencies or travel centers in major towns. Travel passes are available for both.

Regional Bus Services. Many exist. Check at information centers for routes and timetables.

Backpacker Buses

A fairly new phenomenon are buses catering for the growing number of back-packing tourists. They service all major tourist areas in both islands, and travelers can stop off when, where, and for as long as they like on any route. Prices, routes, and timetables are usually advertised in backpacker lodges and hostels, backpacker newspapers, and information centers. Bookings are made through backpacker hostels and booking agents. In 1991 the following backpacker buses were operating:

Kiwi Experience. Auckland–Wellington via Rotorua and Ohakune; Nelson–Queenstown via Blackball, Greymouth, Fox and Franz Joseph glaciers, and Makarora; Queenstown–Christchurch and Christchurch–Picton.

North Cape Shuttle. Auckland–North Cape.

East Coast Fun Bus. Auckland–Rotorua–Gisborne via East Cape, with connections to Wellington.

Flying Kiwi Bus. One of the more novel ways of touring the South Island. Eighteen-day tours depart Picton every month. Overnight camps are made in beautiful but less touristy locations; sleeping is on board or in tents. Time is allowed on the trip for visiting tourist attractions, hiking tracks in Mt. Aspiring National Park, cycling, canoeing, fishing, and skiing (winter only). A complete kitchen is carried on board, food is bought en route, and costs are shared. Mountain bikes, a Canadian canoe, all windsurfer, and fishing gear are carried, or you can bring your own. No age limit. The cost in 1991 was NZ$580 for 18 days (NZ$32 per day), excluding food. For information or bookings, write or phone Lucy or Micha, 2 Canterbury St., Picton, phone (03)5738-126.

Trains

In the North Island the Main Trunk Railway runs between Auckland and Wellington, servicing Hamilton, Taumarunui, Taihape, Palmerston North, and places in between. Day and overnight trains run in both directions. Branch lines connect Wellington with Napier and the Wairarapa.

In the South Island, the Main Trunk Railway connects Picton, Christchurch, Dunedin, and Invercargill with services daily. Branch services also operate daily between Christchurch, Arthur's Pass, Hokitika, and Greymouth.

Bookings are made at railway stations or at InterCity offices.

Air Services

Air New Zealand flies between cities and major towns, while two subsidiary airlines, **Eagle Air** and **Air Nelson,** provide connections between smaller centers. **Mt. Cook Airlines** also services major towns and tourist centers. Bookings for all the above are made at any Air New Zealand travel center or through travel agents.

Ansett New Zealand is the other major carrier providing services between main centers. Bookings are made through travel agents, at Ansett desks at airports serviced by them, and at Ansett offices in major centers.

Rental Vehicles

Larger car rental companies, such as Avis, Hertz, and Budget, have depots at all major airports and in most main towns. Listings of smaller companies will be found in the Yellow Pages of telephone directories. Drivers must be 21 years old and have a current driving license. In New Zealand, cars are right-hand drive and travel on the left-hand side of the road.

Campervans have become very popular in recent years and are an ideal way of touring. They come with 2, 4, or 6 berths, and contain all cooking equipment, sleeping bags, and linen. In winter, some are equipped with ski and drying racks. While not inexpensive, they solve the problem of accommodation and give greater flexibility to travel plans. Rates depend on the size of the van and season and are higher over summer (Oct.–Dec.). Bookings should be made in advance, direct, or through travel agents. Following is a list of major companies:

Maui Campers, Private Bag, Auckland, phone (09)2753-013, Fax (09)2759-690; 530–544 Memorial Ave., Christchurch, phone (03)3584-159, Fax (03)3587-519.

Bluesky Motorhomes, 41 Veronica St., New Lynn, Auckland, phone (09)8276-399, Fax (09)8274-302; 96 Papanui Road, Christchurch, phone (03)3552-364.

Gypsy Hire Campervan Rentals, 62 Tonar St., Northcote, Auckland 9, phone (09)4805-098, Fax (09)4430-485; 17 Princess Place, Kaiapoi, Christchurch, phone (03)3276-230.

Horizon Holidays, 530–544 Memorial Ave., Christchurch, phone (03)3535-600; 164 Parnell Road, Auckland, phone (09)3078-226.

Suntrek Campervans and Cars, Box 74-121, Market Road, Auckland, phone (09)5201-404, Fax (09)5206-756; 4 Norton's Road, Avonhead, Christchurch, phone (03)3428-262, Fax (03)3428-246.

Buying a Car

If you intend to stay a while and do a lot of touring, buying a car could be a good investment. Buy only from a reputable dealer, make sure the car has a current Warrant of Fitness (WOF), and check whether you can get a buy-back guarantee. It is worthwhile belonging to the Automobile Association (AA) for discounts on tires, motor camps, and other things, and for their excellent road maps, which are free to members. They will also check vehicles before you make a purchase. Offices and agencies can be found in most towns and cities.

ACCOMMODATION

Finding accommodation to suit your pocket should not be a problem in New Zealand. Almost every town, no matter how small, has at least one hotel or campground, and most have motels. Motels often cost around the same as hotel rooms but have more space and kitchens, so you can cook your own meals. The Automobile Association (AA) has signposted most motor camps on highways, so they are easy to find. They vary in standard, but almost all have kitchens and laundries and many have cabins, trailer homes, and tourist flats. Campgrounds and camping areas are generally more basic, often with only cold-water taps and pit toilets, but they are usually superbly sited. They are also a little harder to find, and for this reason, good ones are noted in the text. Camping is usually permitted in picnic areas on the edges of national and forest parks, recreation reserves, and sometimes scenic reserves, where toilets are provided, except where there are No Camping signs.

Budget accommodation is available in motor camp cabins, in the many backpacker hostels springing up everywhere, and in youth hostels. All charge NZ$10–15 per night. Backpacker hostels are similar to youth hostels, with dormitories and shared bathrooms and kitchens, but you don't have to participate in the cleaning chores. Some lodges in resort areas offer rooms at youth hostel rates during their low season.

Farm and homestay accommodations provide ideal ways to meet New Zealanders and to experience the New Zealand way of life. Over fifteen hundred rural properties are listed, including dairy farms, high-country sheep farms, orchards, deer farms, and horse studs. Tariffs usually include meals and range from NZ$70 to NZ$100 per person per night. For further information contact the Secretary, **New Zealand Assn. of Farm and Home Hosts,** Box 51-252, Wellington.

The following accommodation guides are available from information centers and bookshops:

Jasons Guide to Motels and Motor Lodges.

Jasons Guide to Budget Accommodation: Lists motorcamps, campgrounds, hotels, and lodges with budget rooms.

Automobile Association Outdoor Guide: Available to members only; lists motorcamps, cabins, and tourist flats.

NZ Budget Backpackers Hostels: Free pamphlet listing hostels; available from information centers or write to Foley Towers, 208 Kilmore St., Christchurch.

Youth Hostels Association Good Bed Guide: Free pamphlet available from information centers or Box 436, Christchurch. You need to be a member of YHA to use their accommodation but can join on arrival at a hostel. Membership is valid at all YHA hostels internationally.

INFORMATION

Almost every town of reasonable size has an information center of some sort, signposted with a large green or blue (i) sign. Make the information center your first port of call to find places to stay and eat and things to do. Many centers take bookings for local sightseeing and tourist attractions. In larger towns they will have copies of free backpacker newspapers, which are also good sources of information for travelers. You can write to information centers for lists of boat charter companies, dive tour operators, and hunting, fishing, and tour guides in their areas.

Another excellent source of names and addresses is *New Zealand Outdoor Holidays,* a booklet published annually by **New Zealand Tourism Department,** Box 95, Wellington. Copies are available in the United States from the New Zealand Tourism Department Office, 501 Santa Monica Blvd., #300, Santa Monica, CA 90401, phone 1-800-388-5494.

Information on national and forest parks is best obtained from Department of Conservation offices or park visitor centers. Addresses of information centers and Department of Conservation (DOC) offices are included in each section.

MAPS

Good maps are readily available. The AA produces the best range of maps for motoring. On their regional maps all roads are clearly named and motor camps, campgrounds, and places of interest are indicated. They are free to members and can be purchased by nonmembers at main AA offices.

Infomaps, published by the Department of Survey and Land Information

(DOSLI), include holiday, national and forest park, touring, topographical, walking-track, and streetfinder maps. They can be purchased at DOSLI offices in cities and towns, at information centers and at national and forest park visitor centers. A free Infomap catalogue can be obtained by writing to **Infomap Centre,** Private Bag, Upper Hutt.

WHAT TO BRING

New Zealand is a modern country, and even if you arrived with only an overnight bag you could purchase everything you need on arrival. Some of the world's best-quality outdoor equipment and clothing is readily available in most towns. The following suggestions may therefore help you decide on what to bring and what to leave at home.

First and foremost, if you contemplate engaging in a lot of outdoor activities, bring good-quality, wet-weather gear. The New Zealand mountains are notorious for their unpredictable weather, and it can get cool in coastal areas even in summer.

Lightweight hiking boots will also be invaluable, as many bush tracks tend to be wet, if not muddy, and running shoes are not suitable. A small daypack for carrying your wet-weather gear, extra warm clothing, lunch, drink, camera, map, and other hiking necessities can double as hand baggage for traveling and is useful for shopping.

A sleeping bag will enable you to make use of youth or backpacker hostels and cabin accommodation in motor camps. It will also be necessary if you plan to stay in the backcountry huts that abound in New Zealand. If you plan on camping a lot, either to cut accommodation costs or just because you enjoy it, make sure the tent you bring has a built-in floor and insect netting. You will also need some sort of waterproof sleeping mat.

A range of clothing, some warm and some lightweight, will be useful for the variations in weather and temperature. Kiwis tend to be fairly casual about dress, and jeans and shorts are acceptable in most places. Some bars and restaurants in larger hotels will, however, insist on a reasonable standard of dress.

Last but not least—although it almost goes without saying—bring a camera. Film and film processing are readily available.

3 ✦ ADVENTURING OPTIONS

HIKING AND MOUNTAINEERING

In New Zealand, hiking is called tramping and mountaineering is climbing. Whatever the name, the activity remains the same. Tramping can mean anything from a gentle stroll to days of "going bush" in remote backcountry. All national and forest parks have extensive networks of tracks and huts, and there are also many walkways over private and Crown land. Tracks vary in standard from well-maintained paths, bridged and stepped where necessary, to rough routes where you find your own way by following markers tacked onto trees (usually strips of white plastic or orange disks) or small rock cairns in open country, and everything in between.

Tracks are graded on a scale of 1 to 4 as follows:

Grade 1: Easy to follow, well-formed, benched, and graded, with bridges over all major streams and rivers. Many short nature walks and major tourist tracks are in this category.

Grade 2: Marked, cut, and partly formed tracks, with bridges only where necessary. Most backcountry tramping tracks are this standard.

Grade 3: Marked, cairned, poled, or obvious routes, with no cut or formed track. Popular routes over alpine passes are usually this standard.

Grade 4: Routes with no markers, poles, or cairns, usually following ridges, stream or river beds, and crossing alpine passes.

Unless noted otherwise, the tracks described here are all in the grade 1 and 2 categories. Track descriptions in this book, and in others you will come across in New Zealand, use the expressions "true left" and "true right," which mean the left or right side when facing downstream or downhill. The Department of Conservation currently has plans to charge a fee for use of the more popular tracks in national parks. This includes the Kepler, Routeburn, Mt. Tongariro, Lake Waikaremoana, and Abel Tasman Coastal tracks, and possibly others.

At present, most huts are equipped with bunks and mattresses and a stove or fireplace. Some, but not all, in high-use alpine areas, where wood is scarce or nonexistent, have gas or other fuel for cooking. Many huts in remote areas have an ax for cutting firewood, but this may be blunt from misuse. You may not cut live trees. Firewood has to be collected, and, when wet, is difficult to burn. The hut stove can be very slow for cooking on, and you may have to compete with others for its use. Also, current Department of Conservation policy is to phase out stoves in huts because of the high cost of maintenance and fuel. Given all of this, you should carry your own small portable stove and your own cooking equipment. The Department of Conservation charges a fee for the use of huts; it varies according to the standard of hut. Annual hut passes are available, but these cannot be used for huts on the Routeburn, Kepler, and Milford tracks.

While novice trampers should experience few difficulties with the more popular, well-used tracks, several points should be kept in mind. You need to be totally self-sufficient in food and clothing, and whatever you bring into the hills must be taken out with you. This means all rubbish, including tins, bottles, and packaging. Conditions in the New Zealand mountains are different from those in other countries. There are no poisonous snakes, spiders, or dangerous animals, but the weather is unpredictable, and can pose a significant threat. Warm clothing, preferably woolen or polypropylene, including a hat and mittens, and a complete windproof layer, should always be carried on longer tramps, even in summer. The hat and mittens can be omitted in coastal areas and on short walks in the bush, but you should still carry some warm and waterproof clothing.

Always obtain up-to-date weather forecasts and as much information about the track you intend to use before setting out. Avoid tramping alone; help may be a long time coming if you get lost or injure yourself. Always let someone know where you are going and when you intend coming back. National park visitor centers have logs (intentions books) that hikers should fill in before going tramping or climbing; books are also located at popular track ends and major entry points to forest parks. Always fill in hut log books and remember to sign out or let someone know you have returned safely. Unnecessary searches for people who don't sign out are a waste of time, money, and energy, and you may be billed for the cost.

Never underestimate rivers. Even the smallest stream can become uncrossable after heavy rain. If in any doubt, go another way or camp and wait until the level falls. Always wear boots when crossing. The safest method of crossing a river is by three or more people grasping a stout pole, with the heaviest person at the upstream end, and everyone moving together across the flow.

Snow and ice climbing is concentrated around Mt. Cook, Westland, and Mt. Aspiring national parks; easier peaks are found in Arthur's Pass and Nelson Lakes national parks. The Darran Mountains in Fiordland also offer good mixed climbing and have some excellent routes on superb granite. Elsewhere, the grey-colored sedimentary rock called greywacke, found throughout the mountains, is very crumbly and does not offer good rock climbing. Guided climbing is available in Mt. Cook and Westland national parks.

For addresses of tramping clubs throughout New Zealand, write to Federated Mountain Clubs of New Zealand, Box 1604, Wellington.

SKIING

In general, the New Zealand ski season commences in June in the South Island and sometimes as late as mid-July in the North Island, finishing around the end of October. The North Island commercial areas, Whakapapa and Turoa, are both located on Mt. Ruapehu in Tongariro National Park. Another eleven commercial areas are located in the South Island near Christchurch, Queenstown, and Wanaka. Most have ski schools, equipment hire and repair, good cafeterias or restaurants, and ski patrols. Heliskiing is available at Mt. Hutt, Mt. Cook, Wanaka, and Queenstown. At present there is only one area for nordic or cross-country skiing, near Wanaka.

In addition, there are twelve established club skifields, one on the eastern side of Mt. Ruapehu, one on Mt. Egmont, and the rest in the South Island. These are open to the public, and while facilities are not as well developed as in commercial areas, they still offer some good skiing. Most have good on-field accommodation.

HUNTING

New Zealand is a paradise for hunting, and there are no seasons or limit bags. Red, fallow, sika, wapiti, sambar, and rusa deer, chamois, thar, wild goat, and wild boar are all exotic imports that have thrived on the native vegetation, much to its detriment. Red deer are found in forests in both islands, sika deer occur in North Island beech forests, wapiti occur in Fiordland, white-tail deer are only on Stewart Island. Chamois and thar are found in the Mt. Cook region. In the past, deer numbers were so high that government hunters were employed to cull them. These days the use of helicopters makes the job a lot easier.

Because of the ruggedness of New Zealand's mountain and bush country, and unpredictable weather, it is recommended that visitors use a registered hunting guide. Two types of hunting are offered: free range 'fair chase' hunts and safari ranch hunts, where there are managed game herds and a fee is charged for a trophy. March and April are the best months for hunting deer; May and June are best for thar and chamois. Most professional guides will provide suitable firearms and ammunition. All firearms must be registered, and any brought into the country must be presented to the police for inspection on arrival.

FISHING

You will need a license to fish for trout and salmon. Licenses are available from fishing tackle and sports shops throughout the country for a day, month, or season. Special tourist licenses, which allow visitors to fish all over New Zealand

Ski touring on Mt. Ruapehu, Tongariro National Park. *Photo by Bruce Jefferies.*

for one month, are available from InterCity Travel Offices in Auckland, Rotorua, Wellington, Christchurch, Dunedin, and Queenstown. There are two fishing seasons—the summer season, which runs from October to April in most districts, and the winter season, from May to October. Winter is the best time for the Rotorua-Taupo district, the main fishing area in the North Island. Regulations and seasons for all areas are printed on the back of the license.

The rivers of the east coast of the South Island, principally the Waimakariri, Rakaia, Rangitata, Ashburton, and Waitaki, are outstanding salmon fishing waters. The season runs from October to April; best months are January to March. Guides for both trout and salmon fishing are available.

Big game fishing for swordfish, marlin, tuna, and shark tends to be concentrated on the east coast of the North Island around Northland and the Bay of Plenty. There are bases at the Bay of Islands, Tutukaka, Whangaroa, Whitianga, Mayor Island, and Whakatane, where charter boats supplying all equipment are available. No license is required, and the best months are January to May.

Surfcasting or fishing from boats or rocks is popular everywhere, and equipment can often be hired. Fishing competitions, with some good prizes, are held in coastal areas throughout summer and are usually well advertised locally. Most campgrounds and stores in coastal areas sell bait, or you can use shellfish gathered on the spot. Regulations as to the size and number of fish allowed to be taken are posted in popular areas.

Further information on all types of fishing is available from F. W. Murphy, President, New Zealand Professional Fishing Guides Assn., Box 16, Motu, Gisborne, phone or Fax (06)8635-822.

CYCLING

Cycle touring is rapidly gaining popularity, particularly with the new multigeared cycles. Main highways are not busy by world standards, and there are many back roads and four-wheel drive tracks that are ideal for cycling. Standard road rules apply to cyclists using public highways, remembering that New Zealanders drive on the left side of the road. It is compulsory to wear cycling helmets. At present, mountain-biking is not permitted in national parks, but it is allowed on some tracks in forest parks. Check with local Department of Conservation staff as to which tracks you can use. You can be fined if you get caught riding on a walking-only track. Most towns have good cycle shops for repairs and spare parts. Ten-speeds and tandems can be rented in most cities for sightseeing, and some resort areas have mountain bikes for exploring and long-term rental. Unfortunately, theft of bicycles is common, particularly in towns and cities. Never leave unattended cycles unlocked. Two handbooks, *Cycle Touring in the North Island* and *Cycle Touring in the South Island*, are available from the Southern Cyclist, Box 5890, Auckland. Another, *Classic New Zealand Mountain Bike Rides*, by Paul Kennett, Patrick Morgan, and Jonathon Kennett, is available from NZ Adventure Magazine, Box 31, Gisborne, for NZ$24.95. Also useful is the *Guide to Cycle Touring in New Zealand* by Bruce Ringer, available in most bookshops.

Guided cycle tours, from six to eighteen days, are available in both islands. These leave you free to travel unencumbered by baggage, and give back-up service on long hills or when you are tired. For more information on these contact **Pedal Tours,** Box 49-039, Auckland, phone (09)3020-968, Fax (09)3030-967; and **Unravel Bike Tours,** David Irvine, Square Edge Building, Palmerston North, phone or Fax (06)3565-500; U.S. agent is Cathy Newman Travel Spot, phone (408)425-7822.

BOATING

"Bare boat sailing" means you rent a boat and do your own thing. It is becoming a popular way of cruising the waters of the Hauraki Gulf, Bay of Islands, and Marlborough Sounds. Both yachts and launches are available. Boat charters are available at Auckland; in Northland at Paihia, Russell, Whangarei, Whangaroa, Tutukaka, Mangonui, and Doubtless Bay; in the Marlborough Sounds at Picton and Havelock; and at Nelson. A fully equipped vessel appropriate to your level of expertise is supplied, and all you need to do is organize your own provisions, although some operators will do this for you. If you don't feel capable of sailing a boat by yourself, skippers can be hired. Prices vary according to season and boat size. Peak times are late October and mid-February, off-peak rates apply mid-February to Easter, and low-season rates run from Easter to mid-October.

RAFTING

Rafting has become very popular in New Zealand over the last decade, with half-day trips favored. Longer trips of up to five days are available, and helicopters are often used to fly to remote and otherwise inaccessible upper regions of some rivers. In the central North Island, the Tongariro, Rangitikei, Rangitaiki, Wairoa, Mohaka, and Motu rivers are the most popular and exciting. Good South Island rivers are the Buller and Karamea in Nelson, Clarence and Wairau in Marlborough, and Rangitata and Waiau in Canterbury. At Queenstown, short trips are offered on the Shotover and Kawarau rivers, or you can arrange longer trips on the Landsborough River in Westland. Rafting operators usually supply safety helmets, life jackets, and wet suits for short trips, and full camping equipment and food on multiday expeditions.

The following rafting companies run several rivers:

The Rafting Company, Box 2392, Rotorua, phone (07)3480-233; Fax (07)3662-748.

Whakatane Raft Tours, Box 2124, Kopeopeo, Whakatane, phone (07)3087-760.
Woodrow Rafting Expeditions, 58 Paine St., Tauranga, phone (07)5762-628.
Action in Marlborough Rafting, 59 Lakings Road, Blenheim, phone (03)5784-531.
Danes Shotover Rafts, Box 230, Queenstown, phone (03)4427-318; Fax (03)4426-749.
Buller Adventure Tours, State Highway 6, Westport, phone (03)7897-286 or Fax (03)7898-104.
Rangitikei River Adventures, Main Road, Mangaweka, phone or Fax (06)3825-747.
Kawarau Raft Expeditions, Box 266, Queenstown, phone (03)4429-792; Fax (03)4427-876.

HORSE TREKKING

Horse trekking is becoming an increasingly popular way of traveling through rural areas, and throughout the country you'll find stables offering short treks ranging from a couple of hours to a full day. Many rides are through bush, along beaches, often over farmland, often combining all three. Overnight and multi-day treks are available, with camping, farm, and hotel accommodations. The open, dry Canterbury backcountry is ideal for horse travel, and there is some challenging riding in the central North Island and on the west coast of the South Island.

For information on multiday treks contact:

South Kaipara Horse Treks, RD 1, Helensville, phone (09)4202-835 or 4202-850.
Plateau Guides, Box 29, National Park, phone (07)8922-740.
Hurunui Horse Treks, Hawarden RD, North Canterbury, phone (03)3144-204.
Ashley Gorge Horse Treks, Ashley Gorge Road, Glentui RD, Oxford, phone (03)3124-211.
South Westland Saddle Safaris, Peter and Ruth Salter, Waitaha Valley, RD Ross, South Westland, phone (03)7554-182.
The Farm House, Central Road, RD 2, Ngongotaha, Rotorua, phone (07)3323-771 or 3323-334.

CANOEING AND KAYAKING

Experienced kayakers will find challenging water in the Mohaka, Motu, Rangitikei, Tongariro, and Rangitaiki rivers. Guided kayak trips of several days' duration are available. The most popular flat-water river is the Wanganui River, which can be tackled by complete novices. Commercial guides for the Wanganui River are listed under Wanganui and Manawatu.

Two South Island rivers, the Buller in Nelson/Westland and the Clarence in Marlborough, offer exciting kayaking. The Buller has several grade 3 sections close to Murchison that are good for short trips, while the Clarence requires around five days. Westland's many lakes are ideal for gentle canoeing and two commercial operators offering Canadian canoe trips are listed under Westland.

For information on other rivers contact:

New Zealand Canoe Assn., Box 3768, Wellington.
Plateau Guides, Box 29, National Park, phone (07)8922-740.
Bruce Webber Kayak Adventures, Box 792, Taupo, phone (07)3784-715.
Ray Button, 23 Coroglen Ave., Birkenhead, Auckland, phone (09)4190-796.
Topsport Kayaking, 459 Cashel St., Christchurch, phone (03)3891-789.

Sea kayaking is also gaining in popularity and can be done through commercial operators around Banks Peninsula, the Marlborough Sounds, Bay of Islands, and Abel Tasman National Park.

DIVING

Diving is good around much of the New Zealand coastline, and PADI dive shops can be found throughout the country. The coast of Northland, Hauraki Gulf, the Bay of Plenty, and Marlborough Sounds are the most popular areas. The Bay of Islands offers clear, sheltered water, and offshore are the Poor Knights Islands, Cavalli Islands, and wreck of the *Rainbow Warrior.* Mayor Island and White Island, off the Bay of Plenty coast, are also considered good. The clear but cold waters of Cook Strait have different marine life from the warmer northern waters, and another attraction is the wreck of the *Mikhail Lermantov,* a Russian cruising ship that ran aground off Point Jackson in the Marlborough Sounds in 1986. The south of the South Island also has some good diving. In Fiordland, deep-water red and black coral can be seen in as little as 6 m of water, and off Stewart Island are huge kelp beds and giant crayfish and paua.

For more information, contact the **New Zealand Underwater Assn.,** Box 875, Auckland 1.

Major diving operations are:

Aqua Adventures, Adrian Van Dooren, 36 Havelock Street, Vogeltown, Wellington, phone (04)3893-727.
Divers World, 57 Rugby Street, Wellington, phone (04)3858-533.
Aquarius Charters, Box 34-092, Birkenhead, Auckland, phone (07)4447-626, Fax 4442-337.

The Diving Network, Box 38-023, Howick, Auckland, phone (09)3675-066.
Dive Center, 128 Wairau Road, Takapuna, Auckland, phone (09)4447-698,
4446-948, or 4449-351.

4 ◆ DECIDING
WHERE TO GO

New Zealand's two main islands offer such contrasting scenery that deciding
which to visit, or if you have sufficient time, which to visit first and how much
time to allocate to each, can be difficult. In many ways the outdoor recreation
opportunities of each island are similar but the locations are often vastly different.

If you like high mountains, then you will love the South Island. Its long
rectangular shape, divided by the Southern Alps, makes it easy to tour by traveling down one side and returning up the other without the need to backtrack
or miss out too much. South Island roads are good, and noticeably uncrowded
since only about 27 percent of the total population of 3.4 million lives there.
Each of the eight national parks in the South Island (Nelson Lakes, Abel Tasman, Mt. Cook, Paparoa, Westland, Mt. Aspiring, Arthur's Pass, and Fiordland) and the Marlborough Sounds Maritime Park offers a different experience.
As well, there are seven forest parks (Northwest Nelson, Mt. Richmond, Hanmer, Victoria, Lake Sumner, Craigieburn, and Catlins) and numerous state forests where hiking and trout fishing are superb. Stewart Island, New Zealand's
least populated third island, has been included under the South Island. Bird life
is prolific there, and almost all of its vast wilderness has conservation status.

Although more heavily populated and intensely farmed, the North Island
does not lack wilderness. Its intricate coastline and the superb islands of Hauraki
Gulf Maritime Park and Bay of Islands Maritime and Historic Park will appeal
to those who like beaches, swimming, boating, or anything else to do with the
sea. The North Island mountain ranges may lack the grandeur of the Southern
Alps, but they are just as rugged in a different way and offer equally challenging
hiking. Within the fourteen forest parks (Northland, Coromandel, Kaimai-
Mamaku, Pirongia, Whakarewarewa, Whirinaki, Raukumara, Pureora, Kaimanawa, Kaweka, Ruahine, Tararua, Rimutaka, and Haurangi) are hundreds of
kilometers of tracks, dozens of camping areas, and some excellent rivers for fishing
or rafting. There are thermal areas and active volcanoes, as well, which you won't

find in the South Island. When snow-clad in winter, the volcanic peaks of Tongariro and Mt. Egmont national parks are impressive mountains. Urewera and Whanganui national parks offer lake and river experiences combined with the history of Maori and of European settlement. Because of its complicated shape, effort, planning, and a commitment to following back roads are needed to see the best of the North Island.

History buffs will find the North Island rich with Maori culture. Land, with its food and forest resources, was important to tribes for their survival. It was, therefore, fiercely defended, and battles over ownership were often long and bloody. The European newcomers also saw the land's potential and acquired it from the Maori, sometimes legally but more often by less legitimate means, causing more bitter conflict. The story of European settlement is one of determination, hard work, and difficulties as the pioneers cleared the forests for timber and to make way for farms, searched for gold and kauri gum, and built roads and railways.

The South Island, because of its smaller Maori population, saw far less conflict, particularly between the Maori and white settlers, but its history is no less interesting. Battles fought there were more against the land and elements as Europeans hunted seals and then whales, and later searched for gold and staked out grazing country for sheep. Tales of hardship and endurance abound. Today the altered landscapes and the remains of abandoned mines, water races, machinery, and towns are visible reminders of the gold rush years.

Although New Zealand may appear on world maps as a small country, the impression is deceptive. There is so much to see and do that a month in either island is barely sufficient. Allow as much time as possible for your visit. You won't regret it.

2 THE NORTH ISLAND

5 ◆ NORTHLAND

LANDSCAPE

The winterless north of the North Island is an area of rugged charm, where there are few flat areas except along rivers, many rocky hills, dense forests of ancient kauri trees, and hundreds of wonderful bays and beaches. Some beaches are surf-raked, stretching flat and golden for tens of kilometers into a haze of sea mist, while others lie tranquil and clear, sheltered by headlands hung with ancient, contorted pohutukawa trees. Inland the hills are patched with farmland and forest, all of it lush and intensely green, and studded with evocative outcrops of rock. Offshore are islands—the Poor Knights, the Cavallis, and the Hen and Chicken group—where some of New Zealand's rarest birds, animals, and plants are found. Around them the sea teems with fish and other marine life not found elsewhere on the coasts.

At a quick glance of a map the western coast of Northland seems to form a clean, smooth line. Appearances are deceptive though. Behind the long, straight coastal edge, with its vast sandy beaches, are some untidy, muddy inlets, concealed by narrow entrances. Southernmost is the Kaipara Harbour, a vast waterway covering millions of hectares. Next is the Hokianga, stretching more than 50 km inland and almost halfway across the Northland Peninsula. Its twisting, intricate shape is said to have been formed by the eleven offspring of a taniwha, a mythical monster. After their birth in a cave, the baby taniwha began digging their way out, shovelling back the land with their snouts and forming a dozen fresh channels for the sea to enter. The Hokianga's entrance is perilous. Guarded by rocks and crashing surf, it was called Kaiwaka, the canoe devourer, by the Maori—a title Europeans also found appropriate. On the south side a mosaic of bright green farmland and dark forest mottles the steep hills. The north side glows golden with high, curving sand hills that march inland, driven by the ceaseless beat of the westerly wind. The dunes extend north along the coast before giving way to jagged black rocks near the narrow, dangerous entrance of Whangape Harbour, slicing fiordlike through high hills before opening out to a broad shallow basin. Smaller Herekino Harbour forms a similar neighboring haven from the blustering westerly winds.

The eastern coast has more obvious origins. Eroded black volcanic rocks form peninsulas, headlands, islands, bays, and rocky inlets. There are harbors here too, but they have a different feel. Parengarenga, in the far north, reaches long fingers of water into the Aupouri Peninsula. The sand of its glittering white beaches contains so much silica it is used for making glass. Quiet Houhora Harbour, guarded by Mt. Camel, makes a sheltered base for fishing boats, while

Rangaunu seems fit only for sand crabs. To the south, the green waters of beautiful Whangaroa Harbour reach deep between wooded hills and imposing rocky bluffs. It provides a serene contrast to the more open, blue waters of the aptly named Bay of Islands, with its sheltered inlets and dozens of coves and beaches. Nowhere are the volcanic origins of Northland more obvious than around the entrance to Whangarei Harbour.

Northland can be considered a very stable part of New Zealand, geologically speaking. Its rocks are old, most of them formed 30 million to 40 million years ago. The oldest ones are in the east, and the remainder are a mix of volcanics and marine sandstones, forming ranges of hills and outcrops of sculpted bluffs. In more recent geological times, when the Ice Ages were causing fluctuations in sea levels, more than twenty volcanoes erupted between Kawakawa and Whangaroa. Some formed scoria cones and others spread sheets of basaltic lava across the landscape, filling newly excavated valleys where they now form waterfalls, such as the Haururu Falls at Paihia and Rainbow Falls at Kerikeri. Rivers were carved across the new landscape; then, when seas rose again ten thousand years ago, after the last ice Ice Age, the valleys were flooded, leaving the dramatic harbors seen today.

The northern extremity of Northland is also a cluster of volcanic rocks, but these are much older. They erupted under the sea about a hundred million years ago. They once formed an island, but general uplift of the land and an accumulation of sand carried up the western coast by northerly inshore currents connected them to the mainland. The continued transport of sand by prevailing westerly winds has built huge sand dunes, some up to 120 m high, and as vegetation became established, some of the sand changed to soil. Cook described this northern extremity, the Aupouri Peninsula—or the Far North, as it is more commonly called—as a "desert coast," but for those who take the time to explore, it is a region of unusual beauty. For the Maori, Ninety Mile Beach was the highway the spirits of the dead traveled to the final departure point, an aged pohutukawa tree clinging to the rocks at Cape Reinga. Below the tree, the kelp would part to reveal the way to the hereafter and the submarine journey to the lost Polynesian homeland of Hawaiki. This vast beach is also a departing point for thousands of bar-tailed godwits, or kuaka, to breeding grounds in the arctic tundras of Alaska and Siberia.

HISTORY

To the early Polynesian inhabitants of New Zealand, Northland was a storehouse of food riches and timber for mighty canoes. The climate was kind and the sea bounty was plentiful. The many early occupation sites indicate that Northland was probably one of the earliest areas of settlement. The main tribe in

Northland today, the Ngapuhi, trace their ancestry to Rahiri, who came on the Mamari canoe sometime before the traditional Great Fleet left Hawaiki. The Ngapuhis' most infamous son was Hongi Hika. In 1820 he was taken to England to assist a professor with Maori grammar and the writing of a dictionary. Hongi was received well, feted, and lavished with many gifts. On returning to Sydney and hearing that his tribe was at war with the Hauraki Maori, Hongi promptly sold all his gifts, except one, and purchased three hundred muskets and a supply of powder and bullets. Having heard of Napoleon Bonaparte, he thought he could do better and caused almost as much trouble. Hongi's first attack was on Totara Pa, near Thames, which he took by trickery, and this was followed by the slaughter of most Auckland tribes. Armed only with stones, clubs, tomahawks, and spears, Hongi's enemies were easily vanquished. Between 1821 and 1826 whole districts were wiped out, and those who weren't shot were enslaved by the thousands and eaten by the hundreds. He moved on to the Waikato, where he massacred about ten thousand people at Matakitaki Pa. Not satisfied, he attacked the central North Island, where he annihilated many Arawa, and then the East Coast, where the Ngati Porou pa were cut down one by one.

Hongi's cruelty deprived him of allies and the small size of his army gave his enemies a chance. The Waikato tribes rallied under Te Whero Whero to cut off more than one Ngapuhi war party, and Te Waharoa, a Hauraki chief as bloodthirsty as Hongi, also withstood his attacks. When Hongi returned to Northland there were more feuds with northern neighbors, ending in a battle with Whangaroa tribes. During this fight, Hongi neglected to wear his suit of chain armor—the one gift from King George IV that he hadn't sold in Sydney. It had saved his life before, and this time, without it, he was fatally shot through the back and lung. Being as tough as he was ruthless, Hongi lived for fifteen months, and it was said that he entertained select friends by letting them hear his breath whistle through the bullet hole.

The Bay of Islands became a major population center and today has many archaeological sites. Almost every headland was a pa site, and there are numerous old garden sites and middens. The archaeological digs have shown that seals, dolphins, dogs, rats, moa, birds, and fish were eaten. The presence of bones from seal pups also indicates that seals once bred in Northland, whereas now they do not breed north of the southern South Island. The moa were also wiped out, and the emphasis turned more to cultivation, mainly of kumara, and to gathering bracken fern root, berries, and other wild plants for food. Some pa were occupied only seasonally, others only one or two times. While not in a pa, the people would live in temporary shelters in locations where they could fish, hunt, or garden. Kainga, which were undefended villages, were not common until after Europeans arrived.

The first fortified settlements appeared by about A.D. 1500, whether in response to increased population pressure or merely because of changes in fighting tactics is not known. Early pa were defended by means of ditches and open palisades backed with a fighting platform from which weapons, stones, and insults could be hurled. This worked well when both sides were armed only with clubs and spears, but not when one side had the advantage of muskets. Men on the fighting platforms made good targets, and muskets could be fired through the gaps in the palisades. What the Maori learned during early fights with the British, they used to revolutionize traditional forms of defense. Instead of serving as obstacles, ditches became trenches for men to shoot from, and palisades were constructed more strongly and covered with leaves to hide the warriors inside. The technique of digging food storage pits was used to construct bombardmentproof cellars.

As James Cook sailed up the east coast of the North Island in 1769, the French explorer Jean de Surville was sailing up the west coast. De Surville was on his way to Tahiti and, hearing of the land Tasman had discovered, made his way to New Zealand in the hope of finding fresh food and water. They passed within a hundred kilometers of each other. Like Cook, de Surville had discovered that wild cress and celery were good for curing scurvy, and at the time his crew were dropping like flies from the disease. De Surville discovered the part of New Zealand's coast between Cape Reinga and Kerr Point, but Cook and Tasman preceded him everywhere else. Only one place name bestowed by de Surville remains, Surville Cliffs, on the northernmost part of the North Island.

Three years later, in 1772, Marion du Fresne sailed into the Bay of Islands and anchored his ships, the *Mascarin* and *Maquis de Castris,* between Moturua Island and Orokawa Peninsula. His crew were ill and his ships needed refitting. Their three-month stay began with friendly relations between the French and Maori, but sadly, ended with tragedy. While cutting new spars for the ships, du Fresne and twenty-five of his crew were killed, possibly because they had breached some law of tapu. The remaining crew retaliated by destroying Paeroa Pa on Moturua Island, killing hundreds of Maori, and by burning Tangitu Pa on the mainland.

Not many years elapsed before the first whalers arrived in the Bay of Islands and anchored in the Oihi-Te Puna Inlet area. They were supplied with wood, water, pork, vegetables, and women in exchange for European commodities and iron—and later, muskets. The birth of the first half-caste child was recorded in 1804, and the following year local chief Te Pahi and four of his sons traveled to Norfolk Island and Sydney. Whangaroa Harbour was discovered in 1807 by Captain Wilkinson of the sealer *Star,* and when it sailed away it had on board a young Maori boy, Te Aara. When Te Aara returned two years later on the *Boyd,* he complained of ill treatment. As a consequence, his brother, the chief

Te Puhi, killed the captain and crew. This caused a disintegration of the good relations between the whalers and chief Te Pahi of the Te Puna area. Believing Te Pahi to be involved in the massacre at Whangaroa, the whalers destroyed his village, and Te Pahi himself was killed in later fighting.

Missionaries also arrived on the scene early in their bid to convert heathen souls to Christianity. A reconnaissance was made by Samuel Leigh for the Wesleyans in mid-1809, and in 1814 Samuel Marsden arrived with two lay readers, Thomas Kendall and William Hall, and set up the first Anglican mission at Rangihoua for the Church Missionary Society. Marsden also brought horses and cattle, the size of which amazed the Maori, as they had never seen anything larger than a pig before. On his second visit, in 1819, he established a mission at Kerikeri.

The Wesleyans established their mission at Kaeo in 1821, and there was then great competition for souls, with the women teaching sewing, baking, and other homemaking skills, and the men teaching gardening, forestry, and building. The Roman Catholics entered the scene relatively late, when Bishop Jean Baptiste François Pompallier established a mission at Kororareka (Russell) in 1839. Pompallier House, built about 1841 on the site of the old mission, still stands.

By the end of the 1820s the number of Europeans in the Bay of Islands had grown to about two hundred. Many of them were engaged in procuring spars for ships, shipbuilding, and pit-sawing, as well as whaling and sealing. The general behavior of all had become unruly, with liquor and drunkenness the major cause of brawls. In response, the British appointed James Busby as governor in 1833, but like a man-o-war without guns, he had no police to maintain law and order. Busby could act only under the jurisdiction of the Governor of New South Wales, and he was a long journey away across the Tasman Sea.

Land purchases in Northland took place earlier than elsewhere in New Zealand, and one of the first was by Frenchman Baron Charles de Thierry, who bought a large block of land in the Hokianga in the 1820s. In 1835, fancying himself a sort of head of state, de Thierry wrote to Governor Busby stating his intention of sailing to New Zealand from Papeete with armed ships and a following of several hundred settlers. This alarmed Busby and others, who signed a declaration of independence. Although the incident is amusing now, it wasn't at the time. When de Thierry did arrive in 1837, it was on a brig from New South Wales with about ninety settlers. They arrived in the Hokianga to take up their 9,000 ha of land, only to find that the deal had gone sour. The chiefs who had sold the land had since died, and it had dwindled to 122 ha. The settlers stayed, however, and were well treated by the Maori, but it was a tough existence with no means of support.

With the signing of the Treaty of Waitangi in 1840, several small settlements sprang up around the Bay of Islands, and for a short time Okiato was the government capital of New Zealand, and Kororareka its commercial capital. In spite of the treaty there were problems over land sales, and it was not only the Europeans who were dissatisfied. The Maori were also disgruntled, and in defiance of the government, Hone Heke, a young, missionary-educated Ngapuhi chief of influence and standing, cut down the flagstaff at Russell. It was reerected, but Heke felled it again — three more times. On the last occasion, during the ensuing battle between government loyalists and Heke's forces, Russell was sacked. The trouble spread to other areas, and many settlers fled to Auckland. Armed forces were called in, and Heke and a friend, Kawiti, led the Maori troops across Northland, fleeing from pa to pa. In spite of superior weapons, the British were rebuffed each time and eventually retreated after forty soldiers were killed.

Heke was by now wounded in the thigh, and, anticipating a further attack, he and his followers stole away once again, this time by night, to Ruapekapeka Pa. By now, having defeated the British three times, Heke's mana was very high. This made the British even more determined to subdue their quarry, and a force of a thousand British and over four hundred loyal Maoris gathered around Ruapekapeka, dragging twelve heavy guns into position on hills overlooking the pa. On Sunday, January 11, 1846, they succeeded at last. Believing there would be no fighting on a Sunday, the pa defenders were outside the walls holding a religious meeting. Discovering this, the British rushed in and took the pa by surprise, easily capturing Heke and Kawiti. The pair later requested an honorable peace, which was granted, but, in spite of not creating any further trouble, Heke never resumed friendly relations with the government.

With Hone Heke subdued, peace returned to Northland and settlement started to go ahead. In the 1850s and 1860s, large areas of land were made available under the forty-acre system. On payment of his own fare, an adult immigrant was entitled to a grant of 40 acres (approximately 16.27 ha), plus 40 acres for his wife and 20 acres for each child between the ages of 5 and 18. There were only a few simple conditions, and many settlers with little capital but plenty of grit and determination made a go of it. Other land was acquired on deferred payment or by fulfilling certain requirements. The groups of settlers were of various nationalities and religions. Waipu, near Whangarei, was settled by Nova Scotians who had originally come from the Scottish highlands in the early 1800s. This religious group built their own ships and sailed first to Australia then on to New Zealand.

The Puhoi area was settled by Bohemians, led by Captain Martin Krippner, most of whom took 40-acre blocks. The soil at Puhoi was terribly poor, and the land covered in scrub and impenetrable bush. Many settlers survived only by supplying firewood, posts, charcoal, and shingles to Auckland, which at the time was not connected by road. It was a life of extreme hardship, with the women assisting the men as well as raising the children. Nevertheless, the settlement grew, but for many years it remained isolated by barriers of language and a lack of roads.

Another group known as the Albertlanders, from the Nonconformists Association, in the 1860s founded Port Albert on the edge of Kaipara Harbour. They were the last of three church emigration enterprises promoted in England, the other two being the Scottish Presbyterians to Otago in 1848 and the English Churchmen to Canterbury in 1850. The new settlement, named after Prince Albert, who had died a few months before the settlers sailed from England, had been laid out on paper but was not quite what they expected. Again, many difficulties were experienced in breaking in the land, but the soil was better than at Puhoi, and people were soon able to grow good crops. Matakohe was another Albertland settlement.

Northland's wealth lay in the vast kauri forests, which almost covered the land, but unfortunately the early settlers did not realize their full potential. They knew the timber was good for ships' spars, boat building, and houses, but the immensity of the forests must have given the impression that they were inexhaustible. From the 1820s, many ships crossed the treacherous bar at Hokianga and sailed with cargoes of kauri from the hills in the upper harbor. Dense forests at Kaipara and Whangaroa were also felled, and for almost twenty-five years Kaipara had a larger export trade than any other port in the country. Forests were often fired, not to clear the land but just to get a few logs out. Often more timber was wasted than was used. Fires would get out of control and forests would burn. Many of the logs sent down creeks in floods of water were shattered. And wood was wasted when logs were squared to prevent their rolling about in ships' holds. In 1840, Ernst Dieffenbach warned against needless destruction of the forests, and the next year Governor Hobson issued a proclamation that kauri could only be taken for the British navy. For a while, little was felled but, as time progressed, kauri again became available for a pittance. Public recognition of the kauri's destruction was slow, and it was not until 1913 that 80 ha of Waipoua Forest and the whole of Warawara Forest were protected. Eventually, after more protests by concerned citizens, another 8,000 ha were preserved as a forest sanctuary.

The kauri, a giant of the vegetable world, had another value in the golden gum it secreted. Cook had found kauri gum in a mangrove swamp at Mercury Bay in 1769 and concluded it came from a tree. It was also discovered by de Surville, who noted that it burned with a bright flame and sweet odor. The Maori burned and powdered the gum and then used it as a pigment for tattooing, but its greatest value was realized as an ingredient of varnish. At first the gum lay abundantly on the ground, and so was easily obtainable. When that ran out, it had to be dug for.

Kauri diggers, many of them Dalmatians or Yugoslavs, gathered in camps near water and firewood. It was hard work, but they were able to save money for land and eventually became prosperous settlers. Fossil gum was the most sought after and was found either by probing the ground with a long spear or by paddocking with a spade. Any gum collected was dropped into a sack tied around the digger's waist and later washed free of dirt. Other men climbed trees by means of ropes and spiked boots to collect the fresh gum from the forks of branches. The practice of bleeding the trees damaged them and was finally stopped by an act of Parliament. Earliest exports were in the 1830s, and by 1856, almost 1470 tons were shipped out. By the end of the century 10,200 tons had been shipped. Parengarenga yielded 4,080 tons a year for forty years.

Between 1890 and 1920 about seven thousand diggers were concentrated in the Houhora, Waihopo, and Pukenui areas, all of them in tent camps. One of the most famous gum fields was the Ahipara, at the southern end of Ninety Mile Beach, where a thousand men once lived. Today it is an arid, windswept plateau of hard, leached land, covered only with scrappy fern and scrub. Never ploughed or enriched with fertilizer, it is now a historic site — a reminder of past times and labors.

Today Northland's wealth lies in tourism, farming, and a small amount of fruit growing, mainly oranges, around Kerikeri. The first orange tree was grown from seed planted by Mrs. Kemp, wife of the missionary, at Kerikeri in 1819. When Northland's whaling industry ran out of whales, it was replaced by big game fishing, made famous by novelist Zane Grey's world-record catches. Adherents of this sport still go out regularly off the Northland coast, and Northland now has dozens of hotels and motels for luxury holidaying. Many travelers visit only the Bay of Islands in Northland, and while it has a great deal to offer, in both ready-made and do-it-yourself adventures, it is only a small part of a region of amazing beauty and diversity.

✦PLACES TO VISIT AND THINGS TO DO

THE EAST COAST

Mangawhai

Not far north of Wellsford, on SH 1, at a small and insignificant settlement called **Kaiwaka**, a road branches right to Mangawhai. It can be followed as an alternative route to Whangarei. Before taking this road, sample the tasty Dutch cheeses and salamis made at Kaiwaka. The factory and shop are on the main road. The sleepy settlement of Mangawhai, at the head of the Mangawhai estuary, and nearby Mangawhai Heads are both well known to Aucklanders as pleasant places for holidays. There are good motor camps at both places, boating fishing, and swimming, and, as a bonus, the estuary and sandspit are **wildlife** reserve and good for birdwatching. From the back of Mangawhai River Camp in Black Swamp Road, Mangawhai, you can walk around the edge of the estuary at low tide and out onto the sandspit. It is also accessible from Mangawhai Heads at low tide. The estuary provides good swimming at half tide – or for something wilder, try the surf at beautiful **Ocean Beach.** The **Mangawhai Cliffs Walk,** with its superb mix of coast, bush, and farm scenery, starts by the surf club building on Ocean Beach and follows the beach north for about 1 km before climbing onto the hills and sea cliffs. From a high point, the track descends steeply to a rocky foreshore. Close by is a shag colony in a pohutukawa tree. If the tide is low enough, and you'll know this if you can get past the first few rocks without getting wet, you can return along the beach and, with luck, see dolphins playing in the offshore surf. The return walk takes about 3.5 hours.

From Mangawhai Heads the road continues north over the hills, passing the Robert Hastie Scenic Reserve and start of the **Brynderwyn Hills Walkway,** before descending to beautiful **Langs Beach.** The Robert Hastie reserve has good examples of kauri, totara and puriri, and from a lookout point on the Brynderwyn Hills track (2 to 3 hours return) there are magnificent views up and down the coast and out to the Hen and Chicken Islands.

Bream Bay

The long gentle scoop of Bream Bay to the south of Whangarei Harbour entrance is another place often overlooked by visitors as from SH 1 there is little to see of it. There are some magnificent surf beaches here, good motor camps, and two interesting wildlife reserves, one at **Waipu Cove** and the other at Ruakaka. The reserve at Waipu Cove, accessible from Johnson Point Road off the Waipu-Mangawhai Heads Road, is important as one of the last breeding sites of the fairy tern, once a common bird around New Zealand's shores but now extremely rare. The nest is merely a scoop in the sand dunes.

Don't be put off visiting **Ruakaka** by the uninteresting facade presented from SH 1. The wildlife reserve is at the mouth of the Ruakaka River and backs the large and very pleasant Reserve Motor Camp. One of the best times to visit is November, when the New Zealand dotterel and variable oystercatchers are nesting. To prevent disturbance during this time, nesting areas are roped off, but the birds are easily seen. Other birds present in large numbers feeding around the estuary are banded dotterels, godwits, knots, caspian terns, reef herons, and wrybills. A total of forty-five bird species have been recorded at Ruakaka, either roosting or feeding.

For more casual camping or picnicking, go to **Uretiti Beach** a few kilometers south of Ruakaka on SH 1. It is marked by the AA sign Camping Reserve as well as a Department of Conservation sign. You can pick your own site beneath shady pines and enjoy a long, uncrowded beach. Toilets and cold showers are provided.

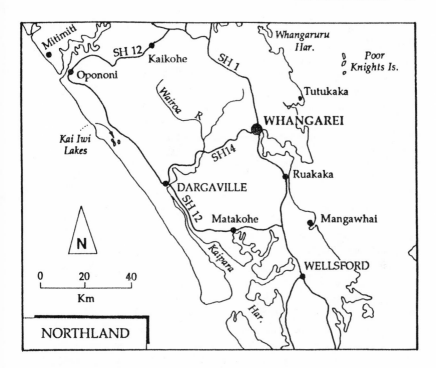

Around Whangarei

Whangarei city has several pleasant walks through bush reserves and parks. A brochure describing them is available from the Whangarei Visitor Centre. The **Northland Regional Museum** is located at Maunu, SH 14, on the edge of the city, and attractions include a nocturnal house for kiwis, the Clarke Homestead built in 1885, and an exhibition center. On the eastern side of the city, the **Wairaka Walkway** (4 hours return) climbs from the Onerahi Domain to the Wairaka Scenic Reserve on Mt. Tiger, where there are magnificent views over the harbor and coast. The Onerahi Domain is at the end of Cartwright Road opposite the Onerahi shops. Mt. Tiger can also be reached via a scenic drive along Owhiwha Road from Parua Bay, returning via Whareora Road and the A. H. Reed Memorial Kauri Park.

    Parahaki Scenic Reserve, dominated by Mt. Parahaki, is also on the eastern side. The summit can be reached via Parahaki Memorial Drive, off Riverside Drive, or you can walk. There are three main tracks: two of them leave from **Mair Park** on the banks of the Hatea River, and the third starts at the end of Dundas St., off Riverside Drive. All routes take about 2 hours return. Parahaki reserve has an abundance of ferns, many interesting plant associations, and several rare plant species.

The **Coronation Scenic Reserve** in the western hills overlooking the city has several well-maintained walkways that lead to old pa sites and Maori workings, lookouts over the city, and other places of interest. In the bush are a number of unusual plants. Entrances are at Kauka Road, Selwyn Ave., and Russell Road, all off Western Hills Drive.

Northwest of Whangarei is **Pukenui Forest,** which has a 10-km loop track taking 3 to 4 hours. It is reached by turning left into Three Mile Bush Road at the Kamo post office. The dominant tree in Pukenui Forest is taraire, but there are also nikau palms, kauri, rimu, miro, kahikatea, and a few puriri and pukatea. Birdwatching is particularly good, with kaka, yellow-crowned parakeet, pied tit, and kiwi being found here as well as the usual pigeons, tui, and long-tailed and shining cuckoos.

Whangarei Heads is another interesting place. The road passes several picturesque bays where good swimming, picnic areas, fishing places, and several walks are to be found. The most obvious point on the heads is the dramatic, castellated summit of **Mt. Manaia,** reached by a stiff 1.5-hour haul, ending with an exciting rock climb. This is not for the fainthearted. An easier climb for less adventurous souls can be made to the top of **Mt. Aubrey,** from Tiller park on Reotahi Road. From **Woolshed Bay,** at the far end of **Urquarts Bay,** there is a 30-minute walkway to **Smugglers Cove,** an idyllic, white-sand beach fringed with pohutukawa trees. **Ocean Beach,** at the end of the road, has magnificent surf, clear water, and sparkling sand. There are miles of beach for walking and rocky outcrops to fish from. Another option is to walk out from Bream Head to Peach Cove where there is an old hut (2 hours one way).

The Tutukaka Coast

North of Whangarei, around Tutukaka Harbour and the small town of Ngunguru, is an area of spectacular scenery known as the Tutukaka Coast. Ngunguru — which has two motor camps, two motels, a motor lodge, shops, and service stations — sits near the mouth of the Ngunguru River and is protected from the ocean swells by a long sandspit. Small boats can be rented from both motels and the lodge to cross over to the spit where there is good walking or you can do some rough camping. The ocean beach has good surfing. You can also walk from the north end of Ngunguru around to **Whangaumu Bay** or drive to it via Block Road on the way to Tutukaka. **Tutukaka** is a complete contrast, with its deep harbor and bush-fringed bays. Here you'll find the Whangarei Deep Sea Anglers Clubhouse and boats that go out to the Poor Knights Islands for diving.

Remnants of vast lava domes that have been eroded and perforated by the sea, the **Poor Knights Islands** and the Pinnacles and Sugar Loaf Rock to the south, are renowned for their scenic splendor; the range and number of endangered plants, animals, and birds they provide a refuge for; and for the amazing marine life in the surrounding waters. Here, in the lucid waters of a subtropical current, 1.5°C to 2.5°C warmer than the adjoining coastal waters, are spectacular shoals of blue makomako, yellow and black butterfly fish, golden snapper, yellow-banded parrotfish, and kingfish, which feed on the abundant plankton and other minia-ture marine life forms of sheltering reefs. The underwater scenery is a dramatic spectacle of cliffs, caves, archways, domes, and tunnels. Since 1981 the islands and all water and seabed within 800 m have been protected as a marine reserve. Swimming, boating, and diving are permitted around the islands, but landing on them is strictly prohibited. Some recreational fishing for certain species is permitted except in two closed areas. No commercial fishing is allowed. The islands are also home to eight species of petrels, five species of skinks, two geckos, and the tuatara. They are the only known nesting site of Buller's shearwater, and the burrows of over 2 million birds make walking hazardous. Another special inhabitant is the red-flowered Poor Knights lily (*Xeronema callistemon*), which the Maori named raupo taranga, a relic of prehistoric flora. The only other place it is found is on Hen Island in the Hen and Chickens group.

North of Tutukaka are beautiful **Matapouri Bay, Whale Bay, Woolleys Bay,** and **Sandy Bay.** Whale Bay is only accessible by walking, and there are other good walks on the hills between it and Matapouri Bay. The lighthouse at the northern headland of Tutukaka Harbour can be reached by walking from the marina or from a road along the top.

AROUND THE BAY OF ISLANDS

The Bay of Islands' main commercial and tourist center is **Paihia.** It offers a range of accommodation from motor camps and backpackers' hostels to luxury motels and hotels. During off-peak times many places cut their rates to attract custom, and some of these are good value. The town has a good shopping center, but unfortunately, goods are priced to extract the maximum number of tourist dollars. Close by is Waitangi, which consists mainly of the Waitangi Hotel and the historic **Treaty House** and **National Marae,** set in beautiful grounds over-looking the Bay of Islands. The Treaty House and Marae are administered by the Waitangi National Trust, and stopping at these and the visitor center is es-sential in any tour of Northland. It was here that the Treaty of Waitangi was signed, legally welding the Maori and European inhabitants into a nation with allegiance to Britain. The Treaty House, surrounded by old English gardens, had been revamped several times and now has modifications to show how it was originally constructed.

From Paihia there are daily bus tours to Cape Reinga and the sand hills of Ahipara, and launch trips out on the bay. The most famous of these are Fullers Cream Trip—originally started as a delivery service, carrying mail and goods to the islands by launch—and the cruise to Cape Brett and the hole in Piercy Rock. Either cruise is a good way to see the Bay of Islands if you have limited time. You can also rent catamarans, windsurfers, canoes, sea kayaks, pedal boats, water taxis, and U-drive boats for a bit of fun on the water. Check at the information center on the waterfront at Paihia for details about these. More serious boaties can rent yachts, launches, and runabouts to cruise around the bay at their leisure. People who dive and fish are also well provided for. The **Shipwreck Museum** on the barque *Tui* at Waitangi has some fascinating relics, including gold, silverware, coins, and jewelery, salvaged from shipwrecks around New Zealand by diver Kelly Tarlton.

Historic **Russell** has a quieter and slightly less commercial atmosphere. It can be reached by passenger ferry from Paihia or by road and car ferry from **Opua**. The old-world atmosphere of Russell has been carefully preserved along its beautiful waterfront, where there are genuine historic buildings—Pompallier House and the Police Station—and newer buildings, such as the visitor center and the headquarters for the Bay of Islands Maritime and Historic Park. A visit to the latter should not be missed. Yachts and launches for charter and rent are also available here. Opua has a large yacht marina and is a port of entry to New Zealand. All overseas vessels arriving here must be cleared by customs. There are several small scenic reserves with short walks close to Opua, or you can take a ride on the vintage railway to **Kawakawa**. The train departs from the station near the wharf. The 2-hour round trip is fun and a great way to see the countryside. Opua Store, by the car ferry, has a schedule of departure times and costs.

BAY OF ISLANDS MARITIME AND HISTORIC PARK

The Bay of Islands Maritime and Historic Park encompasses various historical and archaeological sites, bush reserves, and islands between Whangaroa Harbour in the north and Mimiwhangata Marine Park in the south. It is simply not possible here to describe all of them fully. Indeed, you could spend an entire holiday here and still not see everything. There are historic walks, bush walks, beautiful bays, and islands for exploring, picnicking, and back-to-nature camping. The park headquarters and visitor center are located at Russell, where you can obtain the park handbook, *The Enduring Land: The Story of the Bay of Islands Maritime and Historic Park*, which gives good background information, and several other pamphlets on walks and places of special interest. The small booklets *Walking in Bay of Islands Maritime and Historic Park* and *Huts and Camping* are particularly useful.

The following is a brief outline of some of the park's more easily accessible attractions.

Camping

There is one camping area with facilities at Puriri Bay, **Whangaruru North Head Scenic Reserve,** with 65 sites, fresh water, cold showers, toilets, and rubbish disposal. Part of the reserve is a farm park, and it has several safe, sandy beaches and coastal and bush walks with superb views out to the Poor Knights Islands and over Whangaruru Harbour. No bookings are taken for the campground, and campers must provide their own food and fuel. At the back-to-nature camping areas at **Urupukapuka Island Recreation Reserve** and **Whangamumu Scenic Reserve,** too, campers need to provide their own food and fuel. There is water but no toilets, and all rubbish must be carried out. Urupukapuka Island has an archaeological walk (about 5 hours), with sites of interest marked. Whangamumu is the site of an old whaling station and is reached by boat or by an hour's walking.

Historic Sites

Visitors should try to see Tapeka Point and Maiki (Flagstaff) Hill Historic reserves at Russell, Ruapekapeka Pa, the Stone Store, Kemp House, and Kororipo Pa at Kerikeri, Akeake Historic Reserve at the entrance to Kerikeri Inlet, Marsden Cross Historic Reserve, and any of several other pa sites. The Stone Store at Kerikeri was built about 1832 and now houses a shop downstairs (snacks and souvenirs) and a museum upstairs. The museum is not professional, but it has some fascinating old household and farming implements, including the first plough used at Kerikeri and a map made in 1858 on which New Zealand is shown as New Ulster and New Munster. Kemp House is the oldest house in the country, and Kororipo Pa was the stronghold from which Hongi Hika launched his vicious attacks.

Bush Reserves and Walks

The park includes several bush reserves where good stands of kauri can be seen. One of the best is **Manginangina Scenic Reserve,** adjoining Puketi State Forest, which is easily accessible by road from either Paihia or Kerikeri. It has easy paths and viewing platforms within a stand of particularly fine, tall-boled kauri. Another area of beautiful bush, the **Ngaiotonga Scenic Reserve,** can be seen 20 km from Russell on the back road to Whangarei. There are two short walks here, both clearly signposted on the road. The 20-minute Kauri Grove Loop passes through a grove of spectacular kauri and another 10-minute walk leads to an unusual twin-boled kauri. Further along the road from the two short walks is the start of the 21-km **Russell Walkway.** A shorter walk can be made along the first section of the walkway to Te Ranga Trig for views over the Bay of Islands and Whangaruru Harbour.

For coastal scenery, **Oke Bay Scenic Reserve** and **Kaimarama Bay Recreation Reserve** at Rawhiti are hard to beat. Oke Bay Reserve has a 1.5-hour loop walk, beautiful beaches with clear water, and a good shore for tidepooling. The rocks at Te Hue Point, around from Kaimarama Bay, are good for fishing. The walking track to **Cape Brett** also begins at Rawhiti. This is a marvelous but strenuous 8-hour hike over rugged terrain to the lighthouse at the end of the Cape Brett Peninsula. During summer it can be a hot, dry walk, and water should be carried. The track—only lightly marked—follows the ridge top, with magnificent views down either side, particularly along the last windswept section. About halfway, the track descends to **Deep Water Cove,** once the site of a game fishing settlement. There is a stream here, making it a good place to stay overnight if 3 days are taken for the trip. Alternatively, you can stay at Cape Brett Hut (12 bunks), a converted lighthouse keeper's house. Cape Brett and sheer-sided **Piercy Rock,** with their jagged black cliffs pounded by the foaming, surging, clear green sea have a stunning, wild beauty that imparts a marvelous feeling of isolation. The waters are renowned for diving. The track to Cape Brett passes through private land, so permission must be obtained from the owners. You can get details about this and make hut bookings at the park headquarters before you set out.

On the south side of the Cape Brett Peninsula is tranquil **Whangamumu Harbour,** with its relics from whaling days. The scenic walk to the harbor from the Rawhiti road takes about an hour and passes through native bush. It's a beautiful spot for picnicking, swimming, diving, and snorkeling, and as mentioned earlier, it has a back-to-nature camping area.

Harrison Scenic Reserve at Opua contains a fine example of Northland coastal forest. It can be reached either from the Opua Car Ferry or from Broadview Road (signposted on the Opua–Paihia Road). From the car ferry a signpost points the way to the track around the coast to Cherry Bay (about 30 minutes' walk). From there the track ascends through the reserve to Broadview Road. The return walk takes about 1.5 hours.

Rainbow Falls Scenic Reserve, located about 5 km along Waipapa Road from Kerikeri, is well signposted. The 1–1.5-hour walk between the 27 m high Rainbow Falls and Kerikeri, which can be started at either the falls or the ranger station, follows the course of the Kerikeri River through stands of young kauri, totara, and other native bush.

Mimiwhangata Marine Park

Mimiwhangata lies about half way between Whangarei and the Bay of Islands and is reached by a side road from Helena Bay on the back road between Russell and Whangarei. If you drive from Whangarei, turn off SH 1 at Whakapara. The last section of road from Helena Bay is very narrow and winding and unsuitable for caravans. Parts of Mimiwhangata are farmed, but within the park, archaeological sites, coastal forest, wetlands, dunes, and marine areas are protected. The rare brown teal is found here. The main attraction is the coast. Two magnificent beaches separated by a headland can be reached on foot. Both are good for swimming; spear and line fishing are permitted, with certain restrictions. Rental accommodations, in either a cottage or an 8-bed lodge, are available, but must be taken for at least a week. Bookings are made through the Bay of Islands Maritime and Historic Park, Box 134, Russell.

PUKETI, OPUA, AND RUSSELL FORESTS

Puketi, Opua, and Russell Forests are parts of Northland Forest Park, which comprises seventeen separate forest areas administered by the Department of Conservation, Box 249, Kaikohe. For the casual visitor, the main attractions of **Puketi Forest** are its fine bush and the chance of seeing the rare kokako. The forest headquarters are just off Waiare Road, skirting the eastern side of the forest. This is easily reached via Puketotara Road from Kerikeri. Manginangina Scenic Reserve is close by. There is an excellent campground next to the headquarters and several short walking tracks. The longest is the nature trail, which takes about 2 hours and passes through a variety of forest types. Markers identify many trees, and an explanatory booklet describes the natural processes at work in the forest. Another beautiful camping area is located beside the **Waipapa River** at the end of Forest Road, off SH 1 about 9 km north of Okaihau. There are good pools for swimming and walks up the Waipapa River and along the Forest Pools Bushwalk.

Russell Forest adjoins the southern end of Ngaiotonga Scenic Reserve and lies adjacent to the back road from Russell to Whangarei. The main recreation area is the **Punuruku Valley**, accessed by a side road 3 km north of Oakura, where there are picnic and camping areas with toilets, tables, and fireplaces. The 1- to 2-day **Russell Walkway** starts here, and there are other shorter and easier tracks. Much of the forest was logged in the past and now has large stands of regenerating kauri. The Hori Wehi Wehi Track leads to a giant specimen that escaped the axmen.

Opua Forest in the hills behind Paihia and Opua has some easily accessible short walks to mature stands of kauri and lookout points over the Bay of Islands. From School Road, Paihia, there is a 40-minute walk to a lookout point, or you can continue for another 2 hours up ridges to join the Opua–Oromahoe Road. Short walks from Oromahoe Road include a delightful 15-minute stroll to kauri trees of various ages, some 400 to 500 years old, and a 1.5-hour loop through beautiful stands of rimu, kauri, and hardwoods.

WHANGAROA HARBOUR

Many people claim that Whangaroa Harbour is more beautiful than the Bay of Islands, and while that may be so in some respects, the comparison is invalid. It's a bit like comparing peaches with pineapples. Both are good. Whangaroa is quieter, less touristy, and has a serenity not seen in the Bay of Islands. Both Whangaroa and nearby Kaeo townships have an old-world feel, with many buildings over 100 years old. Whangaroa has a hotel, motel, youth hostel, and motor camp, and is the base for the Swordfish and Big Gamefish Club. Nestled in utter seclusion near the entrance to the harbor is Kingfish Lodge, with its licensed restaurant and boat-only access. Kaeo has a small information center.

The beauty of Whangaroa Harbour can only be truly appreciated by a cruise on the tranquil waters. This gives a much better perspective of the massive outcrops of ancient volcanic rock, the waterfalls descending from vertical cliff faces, the bush-clad coves and bays, and the deep, narrow entrance to the harbor. Harbor tours can be booked at the Boyd Gallery on the waterfront at Whangaroa or at the information center at Kaeo. The alternative is to climb to the top of **St. Paul's Rock** behind Whangaroa township. Views over the harbor from this dome of rock are panoramic. The way is signposted in town, and if you drive up the very steep road first, the climb is short. If walking from town, allow about 2 hours round trip. Near the entrance to the harbor are **Pekapeka Bay** and **Ranfurly Scenic Reserve.** At Lane Cove, on the southern side of Pekapeka Bay, the 12-bunk **Lane Cove Hut** makes a good base for exploring. You'll need a boat to get there and to reach three marked walks in Ranfurly Scenic Reserve.

Close to Whangaroa are the superb beaches of **Taupo Bay** and **Matauri Bay,** both of which have large motorcamps. If you take the coastal road between the two you'll find the **Mahinepua Peninsula Scenic Reserve.** The peninsula pokes fingerlike into the sea, with open ocean on the northern side and many sheltered bays and beaches on the southern side. These can be reached from a walking track along the length of the peninsula. The round trip takes about 1.5 hours, and the coastal views are outstanding. (The wreck of the *Rainbow Warrior,* the Greenpeace ship sunk at Auckland by French terrorists, has its final resting place off Matauri Bay and is a popular dive site.)

Four kilometers northeast of Matauri Bay are the **Cavalli Islands.** The largest of these, **Motukawanui Island,** is part of the Bay of Islands Maritime and Historic Park and, as a scenic reserve, is open to the public. It was farmed until 1974 but is now being left to regenerate into native vegetation. The rare saddleback bird has been liberated here now that the island appears to be free of the

Norway rat, and it is important that all visitors help to keep it that way. The waters around the island are particularly good for diving, and accommodation is available at the renovated farmhouse at Papatara Bay. Bookings must be made at the park headquarters. Camping is not permitted because of the fire risk. A walking track traverses the top of the island from the hut.

THE WEST COAST

The west coast of Northland is very different from the east coast. The scenery is no less amazing and it has a wonderful ambience of isolation and abandonment. Walking on the beaches you may feel as though you are the only person on this planet. The longest beach stretches 85 km between the entrance to Kaipara Harbour and Maunganui Bluff. At low tide the hard, flat sand makes a highway for the locals. The only town of any size is **Dargaville,** on the banks of the Wairoa River at the northern end of Kaipara Harbour. Dargaville has hotels, motels, a youth hostel, a motor camp in the town and another at **Bayleys Beach,** about 15 minutes' drive west.

There are three places of interest along SH 12 on the way to Dargaville. At **Bushmens Memorial,** a magnificent grove of very tall kauri and tanekaha trees 1 km off the road just north of Paparoa, you'll find picnic tables and toilets. One of the most interesting museums in Northland is the **Matakohe Pioneer and Kauri Museum,** a short detour off the main highway at Matakohe. The displays on the kauri logging industry, gum digging, and pioneer life are excellent, as are the wood turnings and other souvenirs made from fossilized kauri, which are for sale. North of Ruawai, **Tokatoka Hill,** the central plug of an ancient andesitic volcano, makes a distinctive landmark. You can climb to the top for good views via a track starting a few kilometers up the side road by the Tokatoka Hotel.

In the region north of Dargaville, known as the Kauri Coast, the real kauri giants are found. Before reaching them there is another place worth stopping to see.

Kai Iwi Lakes

The Kai Iwi Lakes are freshwater dune lakes formed in unconsolidated sand laid down approximately a million years ago. Beneath them an almost impermeable ironstone pan prevents the water from draining away. They have no inlets or outlets, and Lakes Taharoa and Waikare (at 30 m and 37 m) are the deepest dune lakes in New Zealand. The water is crystal clear, and Lake Taharoa is surrounded by white sand, pines, and grassy picnic and camping areas. They are popular in summer and at weekends, and if you don't like crowds you'll do better to avoid them then. A walking track follows the northern shore of Lake

Taharoa and links with a vehicle track across the isthmus between it and Lake Waikare. There are more superb picnic sites here. Popular activities on the lakes are trout fishing (with a license), waterskiing, windsurfing, yachting, and swimming.

Near the end of Kai Iwi Lakes Road, markers point the way across farmland to the coast and the start of the 2- to 3-day walkway to Hokianga Harbour. The total distance is approximately 50 km, but road access at several points means sections of it can be walked separately. It's a beach lover's walk, sometimes along the flat, hard sand, sometimes over farmland or dunes or along the tops of cliffs, but always within sight of the sea. The first section from Kai Iwi Lakes to **Maunganui Bluff** is a good leg stretcher. It takes about 30 minutes to reach the beach, where your eyes are immediately drawn to the huge Maunganui Bluff rearing 460 m above the mist of pounding surf, like the nose and back of a gigantic stranded whale. The walk to Aranga Beach at the foot of the bluff takes another 1 to 1.5 hours, over smooth, hard sand with only the wind, surf, blowing sand, and pied shags for company. There are a few beach cottages at Aranga Beach, public toilets, and road access to SH 12. Most people retrace their steps from here, but it's worth climbing even part way up the bluff.

The track climbs up and around the steep side of the bluff, at first through scrub and flax and then bush, before coming out on farmland for the final bit along an old vehicle track to the summit where the views are breathtaking. The track continues down a grassy ridge to a prominent hill, then along the cliff-top ridge to a low saddle. From a junction here it is another hour to a campsite at Waikara Beach or 20 minutes inland to another entrance/exit point. The walk from Aranga Beach to Waikara Beach takes about 3 hours.

The Kauri Forests

From the Kai Iwi Lakes turnoff its only another 6 to 7 km north to the side road that runs through **Trounson Kauri Park** where there is a pleasant Department of Conservation Campground and short walking tracks. The side road continues through Donnellys Crossing and rejoins SH 12 just south of **Waipoua Forest**. The first road on the left after the junction leads past a lookout point over the forest before returning to SH 12 near the forest headquarters and visitor center, where you can get information on walking tracks. **Tane Mahuta** and **Te Matua Ngahere,** the two biggest trees in New Zealand, are well signposted further along the highway. Te Matua Ngahere is massive, with a girth of 16.1 m. It seems to be a smooth grey cliff face rather than a living tree. Less bulky but taller, Tane Mahuta is 51.5 m high and just as impressive. As well as the famous kauri trees, Waipoua Forest contains about three hundred other tree and plant species.

The Hokianga

From Waipoua Forest the road descends to the Waimamaku Valley, where attempts to farm the land have mostly failed and have left little impact. There is raw beauty here among the rugged, partially tamed hills and rustic, tumbledown farm buildings. A short side road leads to remote Waimamaku Beach and access to the coastal walkway. At the crest of the next hill the breathtaking panorama of Hokianga Harbour is suddenly revealed. Below is the small settlement of Omapere and the surging waters of the harbor entrance; to the east the tranquil waters ripple away into the hinterland, and northward, high golden dunes merge with farmland and the distant dark smudge of Warawara Forest. The regional visitor and information center is located at Omapere, as well as a general store, campground, and motel. Neighboring Opononi also has a campground and hotel.

The best views of the harbor entrance are seen from the end of Signal Station Road on the South Head. Here, on the top of an outcrop of rock with cliffs dropping abruptly to the water, are the remains of equipment used to signal to incoming ships. The **Hokianga Heads Walkway** starts here, descending initially to the ocean beach below, then following the coast south to Waimamaku Beach. The first hour along the grassy cliff tops to a small beach gives breathtaking views along the coast to the mountainous dunes of the North Head and surf-pounded beach stretching northward to Mitimiti and Whangape Harbour. Below, in a magical mix of contrasting colors and textures, the turquoise sea surges and foams over dark, rocky reefs and pounds relentlessly at the base of cliffs separating tiny, inaccessible coves with smooth pale beaches.

Bush lovers will enjoy the **Waiotemarama Bush Walk** in the Waipa Forest. The well-graded track starts about 10 km from either Omapere or Opononi, along Waiotemarama Gorge Road off SH 12. After following the pretty Waiotemarama Stream to a waterfall, the track climbs to a lookout over a fine stand of mature kauri. The lush, damp forest is a good place to find kauri snails, and, in November, the tiny, ground-hugging spider orchid, with purply, heart-shaped leaf, and green hooded flower, is prolific. The walk to the lookout and back takes 1.5 to 2 hours. The enthusiastic can continue climbing from the lookout for another hour or two on a very steep, unforgiving track to Hauturu Trig.

From Opononi, SH 12 wends eastward to Kaikohe and later rejoins SH 1. If you are heading for the Far North, the shorter alternative to Kaitaia is to take the side road to **Rawene**, the commercial and administrative center for the Hokianga district, and the vehicular ferry across the harbor to **Kohukohu**. Picturesque Rawene, sited on a narrow headland separating two deep inlets, was once a thriving timber town. It has many historic buildings worth visiting and a range of accommodation, including a campground with a million-dollar view. The ferry runs hourly and provides an important link to Kohukohu and other isolated communities on the northern side of Hokianga Harbour. Kohukohu was also a timber town, with one of the largest and busiest mills in the country, built on land reclaimed by the tons of sawdust it produced. Around the turn of the century up to seven ships at a time moored at the two wharves, awaiting cargoes of kauri logs. By 1914 most of the kauri was gone and Hokianga Harbour filled with silt washed down from the denuded hills. Several devastating fires over the decades and the postwar depression combined to reduce Kohukohu to the quiet village it is now.

A left turn after the ferry crossing will take you through the settlements of Motukarara and Panguru and out to **Mitimiti** on the west coast. Now only a scattering of houses along a wild, isolated coast below the hills of Warawara Forest, Mitimiti in the 1830s was a bawdy timber town. Situated between the entrances to Whangape and Hokianga harbors, the 22-km-long beach once provided a highway for men and cattle. Today Mitimiti provides a retreat from all civilization. You can camp on a grassy area near the end of the road, opposite the sign marking the track through Warawara Forest to Pawarenga. This is a very muddy track, quite steep in places, which reaches an old kauri slab hut in about 1.5 hours, then traverses a ridge through mature kauri forest to reach the old Warawara logging road in another hour or so. It's a 14-km walk along the road to Pawarenga. About 2.5 km along, a short side track climbs steeply to Maungapohatu Lookout (653 m), giving magnificent views over the Hokianga and surrounding countryside.

Mitimiti's main attraction is the beach, for walking, beachcombing, and good fishing from the rock reefs. The walk to Whangape Harbour is superb. Apart from terns, gannets, pied stilts, oystercatchers, dotterels, and some cattle, you'll most likely have the beach to yourself. Allow about 2.5 hours to walk the beach and climb to a high point overlooking Whangape Harbour. From here the **Golden Stairs Walkway,** an old cattle track, descends to the harbor and follows the shoreline to historic St. Gabriel's Church at **Pawarenga** (2.5–3 hours). In its gorge, Whangape Harbour is less than 100 m wide, and the waters swish vigorously along the shoreline as the tides rise and fall. The narrow, dangerous entrance claimed many ships in the past and can only be negotiated in calm conditions. Timber ships sometimes waited up to six weeks to enter. A two-day round trip through Mitimiti and Pawarenga can be made via the beach, Golden Stairs Walkway, and the Warawara Forest logging road. Pawarenga is also reached by road from Broadwood.

THE FAR NORTH

Kaitaia, Doubtless Bay, and Karikari Peninsula

The Far North is another world again and one that cannot really be appreciated during a one-day bus tour. As a place to stay, Kaitaia lacks appeal, but it has all services and a good information center. There are hotels and motels here, but much better beach motor camps are located at **Ahipara** and **Waipapakauri**.

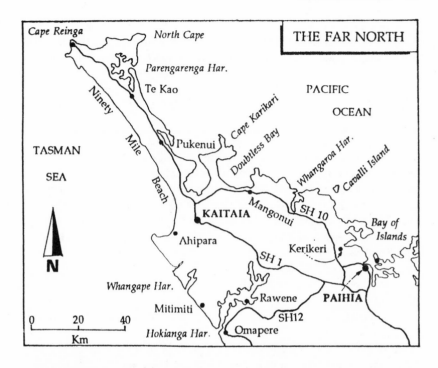

Doubtless Bay on the east coast has superb scenery and a string of golden-sand beaches, with good motor camps and motels at **Taipa, Cable Bay,** and **Coopers Beach.** The main cente for Doubtless Bay is the historic town of **Mangonui.** It is easy to spend time here and well worth the short detour off the main road. The town, built along the edge of the waterfront, has an excellent fish shop and grocery store standing on stilts above the sea. Many old buildings have been faithfully restored and the town retains a peaceful feeling of bygone times. There are two craft shops selling a wide range of high-quality goods, most of them locally made, a bank, service station, cafe, barber, draper, bookshops, bakery, and fruit and vegetable shop. For accommodation, you can choose between the hotel, motels, and the Old Oak Inn, built in 1861 and now a popular back-packers' hostel, with a restaurant and craft shop.

The northern end of Doubtless Bay is formed by the **Karikari Peninsula,** where there are more long, sparkling beaches. Karikari Bay and Tokerau Beach both have campgrounds, and Rangiputa has two motels. The main settlement on the peninsula is at Whatuwhiwhi, where there is a licensed motor inn and information center. The pick of the beaches is **Matai Bay,** where the Department of Conservation has a large and very pleasant campground. Much of the surrounding land is scenic reserve, containing some rare plants, and the endangered

New Zealand dotterel also nests on some of the beaches. Good views over the bays and peninsula can be had from the high point at the southern end of Matai Bay, reached by walking around the beaches and following a track through the scrub.

NORTH OF KAITAIA

North of Kaitaia and Awanui the main road runs straight for 107 km to **Cape Reinga.** The first place of interest is the **Wagener Museum** and historic **Subritsky Homestead** at **Pukenui,** near the entrance to peaceful Houhora Harbour. Right opposite the museum is a very pleasant camping area with many tranquil views across to Mt. Camel and out to the harbor entrance. A little further up the road is **Pukenui Wharf,** where you can watch shags swimming under the water in pursuit of herring. Fishing boats tie up at the wharf and locals fish from it, with good results. You may even be lucky enough to see a dolphin here. There is another campground at Pukenui, backpackers' accommodation, and a huge general store that sells everything from food to building materials, baby clothing, and camping equipment.

About 13 km north of Pukenui, a short side road leads to **Rarawa Beach,** a fabulous strip of dazzling white sand backed by sand hills. The beautiful Department of Conservation campground, just before the road end, has many shady sites under pines at the side of a shallow stream. There are tracks down to the beach, and at low tide you can walk around the headland at the southern end to fish or explore in other bays.

The next settlement is tiny **Te Kao,** with its historic Ratana church. Like all Ratana churches it has the two distinctive domed towers flanking the front entrance. Te Ahu Road at the south end of Te Kao leads out to **The Bluff** on Ninety Mile Beach, a flat outcrop of volcanic rock pounded by the huge waves sweeping relentlessly across the Tasman Sea. Many people have been drowned here while fishing. Northward, the sand stretches unbroken to Scott Point and Cape Maria van Diemen, with Motupia Island standing offshore. This distinctive rock pinnacle, pierced with a round hole, is said to be an anchor stone of Maui's canoe. Te Kao is the last dependable place to buy gasoline; don't count on Waitiki Landing, 21 km further north, to have any.

Te Paki Farm Park

Most of the land north of Waitiki Landing, the northern tip of the Aupouri Peninsula, forms the Te Paki Farm Park, one of New Zealand's most unusual and ecologically interesting areas. The 23,000 ha of Te Paki, administered by the Department of Conservation, comprise four separate reserves: Te Paki Recreation Reserve, North Cape Scientific Reserve, Motuopao Island Nature Reserve, and Mokaikai Scenic Reserve. North Cape Scientific Reserve and Mokaikai Scenic Reserve both contain important archaeological sites and rare plants and animals. These include two extremely rare varieties of hibiscus, a prostrate pittosporum, good populations of the northern green gecko and the New Zealand flax snail (*Placostylus*). Access to these areas is restricted and permission must be gained to cross Maori-owned land to reach them. Motuopao Island, off the tip of Cape Maria van Diemen, has breeding colonies of fairy prion, white-faced petrel, and black-winged petrel.

The recreation reserve includes beaches, campgrounds, dunelands, Cape Reinga, a rugged hinterland of scrub-covered hills, and 2,900 ha of farmland. The public has access over the farmland; there are also several marked walking tracks. Much of the area was at one time covered by a rich forest of kauri, rimu, and totara trees, but for unknown reasons, at some early stage most of this disappeared, leaving a barren scrubland. Remnants of forest still remain in some of the deeper valleys, including a stand of kauri just below Te Paki Trig. In early spring the scrubland is transformed by a haze of flowering manuka in varying shades of pink.

Waitiki Landing marks the junction of the road out to **Spirits Bay,** an 8-km-long sweep of crushed pink and gold shell, sloping steeply into the Pacific from a border of high dunes. A large camping area at the eastern end of the bay has basic facilities for self-sufficient campers. You must carry your own cooking fuel; fires are not permitted. Dramatic **Hooper Point** at the eastern end of the bay plunges steeply to the ocean, and from the high cliffs there are breathtaking views northeast across Tom Bowling Bay to Kerr Point. Southwest, the gentle curve of Spirits Bay gives way to steep hills and rugged cliffs leading to Cape Reinga.

There is another superb camping and picnic area at **Tapotupotu Bay,** reached by a short side road just before Cape Reinga. The facilities include cold showers, toilets, and a small cookhouse with benches and sinks. As with the campground at Spirits Bay, campers must carry in cooking fuel. Insect repellant is another essential, to ward off the mosquitoes. From sheltered Tapotupotu Bay there are excellent hikes along the cliff tops in both directions. The coastal scenery is wonderful. The 6-km walk to Cape Reinga takes 2 to 3 hours, with two uphill sections; the reverse direction, starting from the radio masts near the lighthouse, is a little easier, with only one uphill section.

The 22-km track to Spirits Bay can be a long hot haul, and you'll need to carry water and sunscreen. The track crosses the stream by the campground (easiest at low tide), then climbs steeply to the seaward ridge. From a high point, reached after about an hour, it turns inland and follows Darkies Ridge to connect with a farm track not far from the summit of Te Paki (310 m). Follow the farm track downhill and you'll come to Pandora, an idyllic little beach separated from Spirits Bay by a low, grassy headland. If the tide is low enough, continue around the rocks to the lagoon and sand hills behind Spirits Bay. The beach is not safe for swimming, but the tea-colored lagoon is good for a dip and it's warmer, too. From here you either walk along the beach or follow a rough vehicle track at the back of the dunes to the campground. Both are soft walking.

Cape Reinga is a major attraction visited daily by several tourist buses on one-day excursions from the Bay of Islands, Kaitaia, and Kerikeri. As well as a lighthouse, it has a souvenir shop, post office, and refreshment shop, which will be most welcome if you've walked there. If you don't have your own transport, the tour buses are a good way to visit this northernmost part of New Zealand. Most buses will stop for you at prearranged points and will bring you back on a different day from the one you travel up on. Cape Reinga is a dramatic place, where the waters of the Tasman Sea and Pacific Ocean meet in a maelstrom of waves and spray. Physically, this really is the top of New Zealand, despite the fact that geographically, North Cape to the east is 4.6 km further north. On the western side, the Cape Reinga Walkway heads south along dramatic, wave-lashed black cliffs hung with wind-twisted pohutukawa trees and scrub before descending to **Te Werahi Beach.** Ahead, across vast pale dunes is **Cape Maria van Diemen,** named by Abel Tasman in 1642.

The walk to Cape Maria van Diemen, via Te Werahi Beach and Twilight Beach to the south, is a never-to-be-forgotten experience over an unusual and dramatic landscape of high, hard-packed sand hills, huge dunes, swampland, smooth beaches, black cliffs, and crashing surf. It takes a full day, and you need to prepare for sun (sunscreen and dark glasses), wind, and thirst. The round-trip is best started at the Te Werahi farm gate, about 2 km south of the side road to Tapotupotu Bay.

At the southern end of the park the **Te Paki Stream Road** leads to a picnic area and out to Ninety Mile Beach, following the trickling stream as it wends between farmland and great sand dunes. The stream has its beginnings in two small lakes. Tourist buses use this access for the drive along Ninety Mile Beach, which becomes broad and concrete-hard at low tide, but it is not recommended for the public. Many vehicles have been trapped in soft sand by rising tides.

USEFUL ADDRESSES

Department of Conservation, Northland District Office, Box 842, 12 Kaka St. Whangarei, phone (09)4380-299; Bay of Islands Maritime and Historic Park, Box 134, Russell, phone (09)4037-685.

Tourism Northland, Box 365, Paihia, phone (09)4027-683, Fax (09)4027-672.

Whangarei Visitors Bureau, Tarewa Park, phone (09)4381-079, free phone 0800-675-474 (24 hours), Fax (09)4382-943.

Bay of Islands Information Centre, Waterfront, Paihia, phone (09)4027-426.
Kaitaia Public Relations and Information Office, South Road, Kaitaia, phone (09)4080-879.
Hokianga Visitor Information Centre, Omapere Beach, Hokianga, phone (09)4058-869.
Dargaville Information and AA Office, Normanby Street, Dargaville, phone (09)4398-360.

6 ◆ AUCKLAND AND THE HAURAKI GULF

LANDSCAPE

Wasp-waisted Auckland straddles the narrow isthmus between two drowned river systems: the huge Manukau Harbour to the west and smaller Waitemata Harbour to the east. South of the Waitemata Harbour the long, narrow, contorted estuary of the Tamaki River also reaches into the isthmus, threatening to bisect the city and the entire North Island.

Guarding the entrance to the Waitemata Harbour are some of the Hauraki Gulf's many islands, the gently sloping cone of Rangitoto being the most obvious. It lies near the harbor entrance, close to the busy port and the city's inner heart, centered around Queen St. From Queen St. the suburbs fan out over the isthmus, spreading around and beyond the edges of the Waitemata Harbour and up the eastern coast, engulfing a string of beaches known as the East Coast Bays, which were only weekend retreats until the advent of the harbor bridge in 1959. North of these pleasant beaches the straight coastline is interrupted by the knobbed finger of Whangaparaoa Peninsula poking straight out into the Gulf, with Tiritiri Matangi Island off its end. Suburbia has sneaked in here, too, surrounding the many sheltered bays and coves of the peninsula with houses and creeping up and around the coast as far as Waiwera, where hot springs mix with sun and sand.

Beyond Waiwera, suburbia gives way to farmland and the coastline becomes an intricate maze of harbors, bays, and headlands. From Warkworth, the center for this prosperous farming and orcharding area, roads lead out to the Mahurangi and Tawharanui peninsulas, with their many beautiful beaches and sheltered coves,

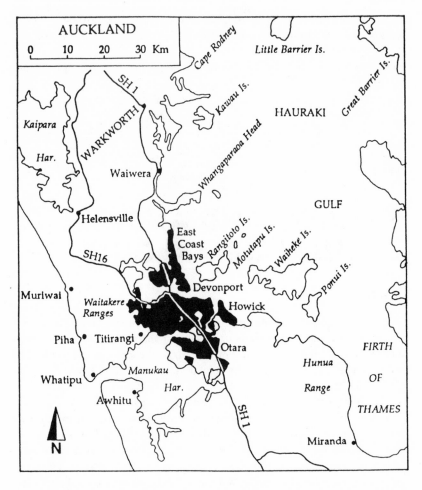

and to Sandspit, the takeoff point for ferries to Kawau Island. Largest of a cluster of islands off this part of the coast, Kawau is famous for its historic Mansion House and is a popular destination for boaties and day trippers from Auckland. At Cape Rodney to the north is Goat Island Marine Reserve, the first of its kind on New Zealand's coasts, and, since its establishment in 1975, a resounding success in terms of marine life conservation.

To the south, the eastern coast is guarded by sprawling Waiheke Island, now an outer suburb, and smaller Ponui Island. Suburbia clutters the eastern edges of the Manukau Harbour, too, spreading toward the rolling farmlands where wealthy business people seek a rural lifestyle to offset the city rat race.

Gradually the farms give way to the bush-clad slopes of the Hunua Ranges, which rise to 688 m before falling away to the western edge of the Firth of Thames. There are volcanic rocks around Auckland and the Coromandel Peninsula on the opposite side of the Firth of Thames, but those of the Hunua Ranges are an uplifted block of 100-million-year-old greywackes. Most of the Hunua Ranges are used as water reserve for the city and are closed to the public.

Auckland's western coast presents a very different picture. Flanked by the Tasman Sea, the land's edge sweeps smoothly northwestward from the mouth of the Waikato River and is characterized by mineral-rich, black-sand beaches (known as ironsands in New Zealand) and thumping surf. Towering sand dunes form a band of mild, undulating country behind. There is one anomaly in this regularity. On the northern side of the narrow, treacherous entrance to Manukau Harbour, steep forest-covered hills rise dramatically from a wild, salt-misted shore where sheer, eroding cliffs and headland-entrapped beaches break the relentless march of the Tasman's great waves. These are the Waitakere Ranges, the eroded remains of a chain of volcanoes that were extruded beneath the sea 26 million years ago. Mountain-building processes have since raised the ancient lava flows and volcanic rubble above sea level, and the fertile volcanic soils now support a rich variety of plants and animals. The kauri tree once flourished here, but a century's logging after 1835 left only the trees that were too difficult to reach and mill. Today the rugged ridges, rising to 474 m at the southern end, bush-choked gullies, and untamed beaches provide Aucklanders with a superb recreation area. North of the Waitakeres, the low dune country resumes once more, with paler sand now, along the 50-km stretch of Muriwai Beach ending at the mouth of the vast Kaipara Harbour.

Auckland is often called the City of Sails, and on a fine summer's day it seems as though most of the population is out on the sparkling blue waters of the Waitemata Harbour and Hauraki Gulf in some kind of boat. With more than a hundred islands and islets, the gulf is a marvelous and extraordinary aquatic recreation and scientific area. Almost half the islands are included within the **Hauraki Gulf Maritime Park**, which covers 13,600 sq km of the Pacific, from Rangitoto Island to Cuvier and The Aldermen Islands off the east coast of the Coromandel Peninsula. Established in 1967, the park is administered by the Department of Conservation. Many of the inner islands were farmed in the past and are now either recreation or scenic reserves used entirely for public recreation, but with conservation of wildlife the main objective. The less accessible outer islands, such as Little Barrier, the Poor Knights, Hen and Chickens, and Aldermen islands, are nature reserves, and access to them is restricted. Many are the last hope for several rare and endangered species of birds and animals.

Within the gulf are a variety of marine habitats. The sediment-laden shallow waters of inlets and harbors and the Firth of Thames retreat at low tide to expose extensive mudflats—not a particularly beautiful sight to us, but to birds, a gourmet's delight. The mangrove forests and salt marshes are valuable as primary producers for marine organisms. In contrast the deeper, oceanic waters of the outer gulf are clear. Influenced by the warm East Auckland Current, which originates in the Tasman Current off Australia, the sea around the Poor Knights and other outer islands sustains an amazing variety of marine life. The islands themselves are both volcanic and sedimentary in origin.

The gentle cone of Rangitoto Island, like the many other cones around Auckland's suburbs, is entirely basaltic. Those in the city's metropolitan area erupted during the last 60,000 years, with the youthful Rangitoto appearing less than 1,000 years ago. Although Rangitoto last erupted only 200 years ago, the wide apron of rough scoria boulders encircling a 259-m-high central cone already supports more than 200 species of native plants, including 40 species of ferns. The island is a living museum of plant regeneration. There are some unique pohutukawa forests, with many unusual hybrids, epiphytes that grow from the ground, and subalpine moss cushions at sea level. All this growth is in spite of there being no running water and exceptionally high temperatures on the dark rocks during summer.

In contrast, the 722-m-high hogback of Little Barrier rises almost vertically from the surrounding, crystal clear seas. Its rugged, ravine-torn slopes are covered in indigenous forests that include diverse habitats ranging from coastal to subalpine. Above 600 m, subalpine species, ferns, and mosses flourish in the near-perfect, cool, damp conditions provided by an ever-present cloud cap. Little Barrier Island is one of the world's most important scientific reserves. No introduced animals live there. A five-year program launched in the 1970s eliminated over a thousand feral cats, and none have been seen since 1980. The prolific bird life is an example of how New Zealand once was. The tiny short-tailed bat is also found on the island, but has become very rare on the mainland. It has a body structure unlike that of any other bat and spends more time crawling on the ground than flying.

HISTORY

The gentle terrain, rich volcanic soil, and mild climate around the Waitemata and Manukau harbors enabled the Maori to cultivate kumara easily, while they reaped an abundance of seafood from the sheltered waters. Many islands of the gulf are archaeologically rich in Maori history, and the sites of fortified pa and kumara pits can be easily seen. According to legend, the Tainui canoe, which first landed at Whangaparaoa near East Cape, sailed north along the Bay of Plenty and around the tip of the Coromandel Peninsula. After exploring the Firth of

Thames, the Tainui entered the Tamaki estuary. Manukau Harbour was sighted and reached after a portage across the narrow isthmus. Although short, the portage was difficult because Marama-Kikohua, wife of Hoturoa, the captain, had committed adultery with a slave and this made canoe-hauling chants ineffective. Descendants of the disgraced Marama-Kikohua and others, who were left behind when the canoe sailed on across the Manukau Harbour and down the west coast to eventually rest at Kawhia, established the Nga Marama tribe.

The fertile isthmus, coveted by many other tribes, was subjected to a number of invasions. Several Ngapuhi war parties from Northland passed through it, and epidemics of European diseases decimated the population, so the area was almost deserted when it was chosen in 1840 as the site of the new colony's permanent capital. The name Auckland was bestowed in 1840 by Governor Hobson in honor of his former commander, Lord Auckland, who was at that time Viceroy of India and a popular British hero. Although Auckland was not a planned settlement with regular arrivals of immigrants, the town soon grew with the influx of officials, tradespeople, and laborers from the Bay of Islands. Before long its citizens were casting hungry eyes over the rich Maori-owned lands to the south. The outbreak of conflict over land in the Taranaki in 1860 raised fears for Auckland's safety, and by 1864 the entire male population had been enlisted for service. Imperial troops were stationed in Auckland, and a chain of fortifications was built across the isthmus to protect against invasion from the south. Invasion never happened, however, as the war was carried south into the Waikato.

By 1865, with the end of hostilities and the title of "capital" now transferred to Wellington, Auckland became a depressed settlement with little work for new arrivals. Eventually, increased activity in the Thames goldfields and increasing agricultural development aided the town's recovery. By the turn of the century Auckland was growing rapidly and hasn't stopped since. The present population of over 911,000 is more than 27 percent of New Zealand's total population. Employment opportunities have brought many Pacific Islanders to Auckland, and they, in combination with the large Maori population, make it the largest Polynesian city in the Pacific region. This Polynesian character is reflected in the huge outdoor market held every Sunday at Otara.

Most of Auckland's recreational opportunities center around marine pursuits, which is understandable considering the omnipresent sea, but these can be easily combined with land-based activities, such as camping and bush walking. As well as the islands of the Hauraki Gulf Maritime Park, the city has several regional parks scattered around its periphery. Some of these parks, administered by the Auckland Regional Council, are working farms to which the public has free access. Almost all have superb beaches and offer walking and camping opportunities.

CITY TRANSPORT

Buses

Several different bus companies service the city, and most have terminals in the downtown area. The **Auckland Regional Transport Guide,** which covers all operators, is available from bus terminals and visitor centers. **Auckland Regional Council (ARC)** is the largest operator. Special day passes and organized tours are available. The Downtown Bus Centre is close to the wharves and the lower end of Queen St. For timetable and route information, phone 3797-119, 6 A.M. to 11:30 P.M. Mon.–Sat., and 7:30 A.M. to 10:30 P.M. Sun.

    Airporter Bus Service. Connects Auckland Airport with the Downtown Airline Terminal, located near the bottom end of Queen St. Every day departs approximately every 30 minutes, from either end, between 6:45 A.M. and 8 P.M. Phone 275-9396 for departures later than 8 P.M.

    United Airlines Explorer Bus. Every day departs hourly, 10 A.M. to 4 P.M., from the Downtown Airline Terminal, for a circuit of main tourist attractions, stopping at Victoria Park Market, Oriental Market, Mission Bay Beach, Kelly Tarlton's Underwater World, bungee jumping at Freemans Bay, Auckland Museum, and Parnell Village.

Trains

The suburban train service, **Cityrail,** runs from the Central Railway Station (close to the Downtown Bus Centre) to Waitakere in the west and Papakura in the south, with numerous stations in between. It operates on weekdays only, between 6:30 A.M. and 5:30 P.M. Phone 3794-600.

Ferries

North Shore Ferries. Ferry Building, Quay St., downtown Auckland. Phone 303-3319 or 303-3318. A shuttle service between Queens Wharf and Devonport operates weekdays, 6:30 A.M. to 11 P.M., and weekends, 7 A.M. to 10 P.M. Ferries connect with buses for Stanley Bay, Cheltenham, Narrowneck, and Takapuna.

◆PLACES TO VISIT AND THINGS TO DO

ISLANDS OF HAURAKI GULF

Great Barrier Island

Great Barrier Island, 80 km from Auckland to the northeast of the Coromandel Peninsula, is the largest island in the Hauraki Gulf. About half of the 40-km-long island is privately owned; the rest is forest park. The rugged topography— rising to 621 m from an irregular coastline of sheltered harbors, coves, and surf beaches—makes Great Barrier a superb place for snorkeling, diving, surfing, fishing, hiking, and just plain holidaying. Other attractions are historic sites, shipwrecks, and hot pools. With only about 500 permanent residents and not much in the way of roads, it's a place for those who favor a self-sufficient lifestyle and are prepared to do a bit of walking.

The island's forests, which are similar to those of the Coromandel Peninsula, were heavily logged for kauri early this century, and some large, well-preserved dams can be seen on the climb to Mt. Hobson. Fortunately, the kauri is now regenerating quickly, but it will be centuries before the forests return to their former richness. The Department of Conservation maintains a network of walking tracks through the forests, and there are huts and campsites at some fabulous beaches. These are basic camping areas, with water and pit toilets only, so you need to take all other equipment (including fuel) with you. More information can be had from the Department of Conservation, Private Bag, Auckland, phone (09)3079-279. If you intend doing a lot of hiking, Fitzroy is the best place to base yourself.

Accommodations around the southern half of the island range from luxurious guest houses to basic cabins, to bunkrooms, and a youth hostel at Tryphena. Most of these will help guests with transport. Rental cars, taxis, minibus tours, campervans, and mountain bikes are available, but there is no regular bus service. More information on accommodation and transport around the island can be had from the **Great Barrier Island Travel and Information Centre**, Princess Wharf, Queen St., Auckland, phone (09)3771-235 or **Great Barrier Travel Line**, RD 1, Great Barrier Island, mobile phone (025)923-678.

Getting to Great Barrier is relatively easy. You can fly or go by ferry, or you can take a leisurely 3- to 4-day cruise on the *Te Aroha*, a historic schooner that takes tourists on its regular round of the gulf islands. Bookings are made through **Adventure Cruising Co.**, Adventure Centre, Box 338, Auckland, phone (09)444-9342.

Kawau Island

Kawau lies 8 km off the Rodney Coast and is reached by ferry from Sandspit, near Warkworth, or from Auckland. As well as the historic Mansion House of Governor Sir George Grey, the island has pleasant walks, secluded beaches to enjoy, the ruins of old coppermine works, many pa sites to explore, and good views across the gulf and back to the mainland. Governor Grey had his gardens planted in exotic trees and shrubs and the surrounding hillsides planted with pines. These provide good habitat for native bush birds and the survivors of Grey's exotic-wildlife liberations: abundant wallabies and a few kookaburras, rosella parakeets, and peafowl. The five species of wallaby on the island are protected. One of them, the white-throated or parma wallaby, is almost extinct in Australia, its homeland.

If you want to stay on Kawau Island, the Department of Conservation has two holiday houses available for rent. Bookings can be made by phoning the Mansion House at (09)4228-882.

Rangitoto Island

Well-defined walking tracks lead around the perimeter of Rangitoto and up to the summit cone, where extensive views of the city and neighboring islands can be had. Most of the tracks were made by convicts stationed on the island between 1925 and 1936. The walk to the summit from Rangitoto Wharf takes just over an hour (one way), and if you detour to some lava caves on the way up you'll need to allow another 30 minutes. Longer tracks can be taken back to Rangitoto Wharf, to make an interesting loop. From the summit to Islington Bay Wharf takes about 1 hour and 40 minutes, and you can catch the ferry here on its return trip. Wear boots or very strong shoes, as the scoria is very tough on anything flimsy. The only good beaches for swimming are Whites Bay and Mckenzie Bay at the northern end. Boulder Bay, about one hour's walk from Islington Bay, is pleasant, with a small sandy beach, good rocks for fishing, and several shipwrecks to explore further along the coast.

Winter and spring—when the black-backed gulls are nesting and kowhai trees, Kirk's daisy, and orchids are flowering—are perhaps the best times to visit. Late November and December, when the pohutukawa and rata trees are a blaze of red, are also pleasant. In summer you'll need a good sun hat, sun screen, and plenty to drink, as the heat off the scoria can be blistering.

Motutapu Island

Motutapu, the sacred island, is connected to Rangitoto Island by a causeway but is totally different from its neighbor. It is run as a farm park, and because of grazing by the sheep, the many archaeological sites can be easily seen. Military installations built during World War II are a reminder of the island's strategic position. A walkway, less than 3 hours return, crosses the island from Islington Bay on Rangitoto Island to **Home Bay** on the eastern side, where there is an area for camping.

Motuihe Island

Unlike the young, volcanic, bush-clad Rangitoto, Motuihe Island is of ancient sedimentary rock covered in rolling grassland. Its long sandy beaches are favorites with Aucklanders at all times of the year. Most of the eastern end of the island is farmed, but there are many walking tracks that will take you to a few patches of native forest and many archaeological sites of Maori habitation. Signs mark the locations of whare, storage pits, and defensive ditches. At low tide, the intertidal marine reefs make for interesting exploration.

The island has had a checkered history since it was bought by the Crown in 1872 and set up as a quarantine station. During World War I it was used as a prisoner-of-war camp and later converted to a children's health camp. It was used as a naval training base from 1941 until 1963. In 1967, it was ceded by the Auckland City Council to become part of the newly formed Hauraki Maritime Park. The two main beaches have toilets and changing sheds, and during summer, from the end of October until Easter, a canteen operates.

Rakino Island

Most of Rakino is privately owned and used for grazing, but 10 ha adjacent to Sandy Bay and Woody Bay are part of the Hauraki Gulf Maritime Park. Sandy Bay is sheltered from the open sea by Tuatara Island, which you can walk to at low tide, and there is good fishing and snorkeling in the crystal clear waters at Woody Bay. The rest of the coast is rocky and fringed with pohutukawa trees. There are several pleasant walking tracks. Take water with you, as there is none available on the island.

Waiheke Island

With a population of around six thousand, Waiheke is really part of the city, although the locals think otherwise. There are shops, restaurants, and a regular bus service that meets all ferries and runs to Onetangi. Accommodations range from hotels and motels to cottages, hostels, and campsites. The **Waiheke Island Tourist Association,** P.O. Box 266 Ostend, Waiheke Island, phone (09)372-7568, can help you find a place to stay.

Long sandy beaches on the ocean side of Waiheke are all on the bus route. Onetangi Beach has good surf in northeasterly winds, and the 45-ha Onetangi Reserve behind the beach offers refreshing shady bush and pleasant picnic sites. Palm and Oneroa beaches are smaller and you can rent canoes, windsurfers, dinghies, catamarans, surfboards, and snorkeling gear here.

At the undeveloped eastern end of the island is the **Stony Batter Walkway.** Access is through the Man o' War Station along the road of the same name. The reserve is named for the strange andesitic boulders, some 3 m across, which lie scattered across the landscape as if tossed there by some giant hand. It takes about 45 minutes to reach the historic reserve, where the remains of three World War II guns remain. If you take a good flashlight, you can explore the tunnels and stairs connecting a maze of rooms beneath the gun sites. From the gun sites, tracks descend to Hooks Bay and Opopo Bay, both taking about 45 minutes one way. Views from the high point, just before the gun sites are reached, are panoramic, taking in the islands of the gulf, the Firth of Thames and Coromandel Peninsula, the Hunua Ranges, and Auckland.

Waiheke Island is an ideal place for cycling, and bikes can be brought over on the ferries or you can rent them on the island from **Waiheke Rental Cars,**

13 Tahi Road, Ostend, Waiheke, phone (09)372-8635 or, after hours, 372-8386. If you call ahead, they'll have a bike or car waiting when you arrive. They also rent sailing and fishing gear.

Pakatoa Island
Pakatoa is a small resort island off the eastern end of Waiheke Island. Trimmings and entertainment are provided for those who stay there, but day-trippers can visit and use the facilities. For more information contact **Hideaway Resorts Ltd.**, Box 9023 Newmarket, Auckland, phone (09)520-5636, 520-5154, or 372-8089.

Little Barrier Island
Little Barrier Island is a mecca for bird lovers. Parakeets feed in flocks on the ground here and the air is filled with sound of tui, whiteheads, bellbirds, and tomtits. The shy stitchbird survives here and the saddleback is also making a comeback since being reintroduced after the removal of feral cats. Blue penguins nest around the coast, and Cook's petrels and the rare black petrels nest in burrows on high forested ridges. Landing on Little Barrier is by permit only, from the Department of Conservation, and is possible at one place only, a bay sheltered by a point of flat land formed by ocean currents. At times, rough seas make it impossible to get on or off the island for days. There is a bunkhouse for accommodation, but you must bring all your own bedding and food. A department officer is stationed permanently on the island.

Transport to the Gulf Islands
Fullers Cruise Centre, Ferry Building, Quay St., Auckland, phone (09)3774-074. Open daily for ferries to Rangitoto, Motutapu, Motuihe, Rakino, Waiheke, Great Barrier, Kawau, and Pakatoa islands.

Sea Flight Cruises, Ferry Building, Quay St., Auckland, phone (09)3661-421. Day and stopover cruises to Great Barrier Island; day cruises to Kawau Island.

The Ferryboat Co., phone (09)4258-006; regular sailings to Kawau Island from Sandspit, and charters to Little Barrier, Great Barrier, and Tiritiri Matangi islands.

Rangitoko/Rakino Express, opposite Princes Wharf, Quay St., Auckland, mobile phone (025)927-337; regular service daily from 9 A.M.

Subritsky Shipping Service, Half Moon Bay, Bucklands Beach, phone (09)534-5663 or 534-7855; regular vehicular ferry to Waiheke Island.

Gulf Trans, Wynyard Wharf, Auckland, phone (09)3734-036; passenger, vehicle, and freight service to Great Barrier Island.

Great Barrier Airlines Ltd., Box 53-091, Auckland Airport, phone (09)275-9120 or 275-6280; twice-daily service to Great Barrier Island.

REGIONAL PARKS

The largest area administered by the Auckland Regional Council lies within the Waitakere Ranges, while several smaller parks and farms give the public access to some superb areas of coastline. Three lie on the east coast, washed by the warm waters of the Hauraki Gulf, and a fourth, very different one is on the exposed western seaboard. Others lie on the sheltered edges of the Manukau Harbour and Firth of Thames. Camping with tents or light campervans is permitted in most of the farm parks from late December until Easter. Information on camping and permits is available from the **Auckland Regional Council,** Private Bag, Auckland, phone (09)3662-151 or 3794-420, Fax (09)3662-027.

The **Waitakere Ranges Regional Parklands** covers 8,600 ha that are open to the public for hiking and recreation. The remaining 6,000 ha of forest in the Waitakere Ranges has restricted access as it is part of the city's water catchment area. Within the park are 135 tracks covering over 200 km. These are impossible to describe in this small space, and the first port of call for anyone contemplating a visit to the Waitakeres is either the Regional Parks Department or the **Arataki Park Information Centre** on Scenic drive, 5 km from Titirangi. It's open weekdays from 1 to 4:30 P.M., and weekends and public holidays from 10 A.M. to 5 P.M., or you can phone (09)8177-134. The **Walking and Tramping Guide to the Waitakeres** is a map showing all tracks, with times and short descriptions. Another useful booklet, **Waitakere Walks** by Graeme Foster (Wilson and Horton, 1985), is also available from city bookshops. Both are probably essential if you don't want to get lost. The ranges are rugged and have a high rainfall, so wear strong shoes or boots and take waterproof clothing.

Many good walks start near Piha and Huia on the coast. Piha is served by ARA buses from the Downtown Bus Centre. A weekdays-only commuter bus, run by Commercial Buses, leaves Huia Bridge at 6:40 A.M. and departs from the Downtown Bus Centre at 4:50 P.M., but this is not much use to day-trippers.

Long Bay Park, the closest coastal park to the city, is reached by ARA Buses 839, 858, and 878 from Victoria St. West. It has a large recreational sports and picnic area, and from the northern end of the beach, a track taking about 1.5 hours leads over farmland to Okura Creek, passing two secluded bays on the way. If you prefer a shorter walk through some delightful bush, then the Awaruku Reserve in the valley behind Long Bay could be the place to go.

Shakespear Farm Park, at the tip of the Whangaparaoa Peninsula, is reached by ARA buses 898 and 899, to Whangaparaoa or Hibiscus Coast, from the Downtown Bus Centre. It's a pleasant place for bush, farm, and cliff-top walks, hang-gliding, swimming, snorkeling, picnicking, and camping, and as the park is a working farm, you can also view many farming activities.

Wenderholm Regional Park occupies a grassy, tree-studded peninsula at the mouth of the Puhoi River just north of Waiwera. On one side is a beautiful sandy ocean beach and on the other a tidal estuary. Unfortunately, the only public transport, ARA bus 895 for Waiwera, runs only on weekends and public holidays from Labour Weekend to Easter.

Tawharanui Regional Park, at the end of the Tawharanui Peninsula near Warkworth, is another superb recreation reserve. The 588 ha of farmland are bounded by a rocky, indented coast that provides excellent swimming, picnicking, and camping opportunities. There are walking tracks across the farmland, and for marine life enthusiasts there is good snorkeling and diving off the northern shoreline, which is extended out for 800 m as a marine reserve. There is no public transport.

Muriwai Beach Regional Park occupies 183 ha at the southern end of the 50-km-long Muriwai Beach. The main beach is good for surfing and swimming, between the surf patrol's flags, and there are walking tracks in the nearby pine forests. A pleasant camping ground with all facilities is situated behind the sand dunes; phone (09)4118-076 for bookings. The headland and two offshore stacks at the south end of the beach are the nesting sites of gannets, best seen during the breeding season between November and April. A track around the headland gives excellent views. Rock platforms below the headland are popular fishing sites.

The 8-km-long coastal **Muriwai-Te Henga Walkway** and the track to **Goldie Bush** both start from Constable Road to the south of Muriwai Beach. Most of the walkway to Bethells Beach (3 to 4 hours one way) crosses farmland, but there are outstanding sea views from the cliffs. Tracks in Goldie Bush and neighboring Motutara Scenic Reserve provide walks of up to 4 hours.

Awhitu Farm Park is north of Waiuku on the shores of Manukau Harbour. It's a good base from which to explore the South Manukau Head, with its lighthouse at the end of Lighthouse Road. Other possibilities are birdwatching, swimming when the tide is in, coastal walks, and camping (caravans are permitted here).

Ambury Regional Park, also on the shores of Manukau Harbour, is a good spot for watching wading birds. Such rare seasonal visitors as royal spoonbills, white herons, cattle and little egrets, whimbrels, and curlews have been recorded here. High tide is best, as the birds tend to be closer inshore then. The park can be reached by taking an ARA bus to Mangere from the Downtown Bus Centre and walking along Kiwi Esplanade to the entrance.

Small **Omana Farm Park** at Maraetai, facing the south side of Waiheke Island, has a quiet, gentle landscape of rolling pastures fringed by low cliffs hung with pohutukawa trees. There are walking tracks along the cliff tops, good fishing from the rocks, and good places to swim, picnic, or camp (caravans are permitted).

Waharau Regional Park lies north of Miranda and Kaiaua on the western side of the Firth of Thames. The narrow 169-ha strip of parkland extends from the sea up into the hills, providing a variety of very pleasant picnic settings ranging from coastal to bush, and walks through farmland and bush. Some tracks lead to the heights of the Hunua Range, where there are great views of the Coromandel Range and Hauraki Gulf.

Miranda has large thermal baths and also an important bird sanctuary. Huge flocks of godwits, knots, and turnstones are seen from October to March, and in winter, wrybills and oystercatchers make their annual visit. Other species seen are curlews, whimbrels, red-necked stints, and curlew sandpipers.

BEACHES

Auckland has several pleasant beaches close to the city center. Judges Bay, Okahu Bay, Mission Bay, Kohimarama Bay, and St. Helier's Bay are all popular inner-harbor beaches, accessible from Tamaki Drive, and serviced frequently by buses from the Downtown Bus Terminal. Karaka Bay at Glendowie is also popular. On the North Shore there are excellent beaches along the east coast from Cheltenham to Long Bay and along the Whangaparaoa Peninsula. These can be reached by bus from Takapuna, North Shore, or the Downtown Bus Terminal.

The west coast beaches are all good for surfing, but you'll need your own transport to reach most of them. Some have dangerous rips and holes, so swimming should only be done in patrolled areas. Anyone who is fishing should also be wary of freak waves, particularly during spring tides; many people have been swept off the rocks and drowned while fishing along this coast.

Whatipu Beach, on the northern side of Manukau Harbour entrance, has a feeling of remoteness in spite of being so close to the city. There are long walks along the sand, rambles in the bush above the cliffs, caves to explore, and excellent fishing. One of the nicest walks is to Parahaha, to the north, via the track, and returning along the beach. In the lee of Paratutae Rock are the remains of a jetty where cutters and schooners once tied up to load timber. **Whatipu Lodge,** an old farmhouse behind the beach, has self-catering accommodation in bunkhouses and a campsite with basic facilities. Contact Whatipu Lodge, c/o Huia Post Office, Auckland 7, phone (09)8118-860, for more details.

Piha is a fabulously wild beach dominated by a huge crouching islet appropriately named Lion Rock. Somehow the scenery has escaped being tamed by popularity and habitation. As well as fishing and surfing, you can climb Lion Rock and walk around the cliffs and headlands at either end of the beach or up toward the Waitakere Ranges behind the Piha Domain Motor Camp. The camp is open all year and has all facilities. Write to **Piha Domain Camp,** c/o Post Office, Piha, or phone (09)812-8815, for bookings and details. There is bus service to Piha from the Downtown Bus Centre, but it only runs two or three times a week, depending on the season. Access by car is via Scenic Drive and Piha Road.

Karekare, south of Piha, is a much shorter beach but lacks none of the wildness characteristic of this coast. The sand is flanked at either end by high promontories that give scope for wind-blown cliff-top walking. Tracks to the north, toward Te Ahu Ahu Road, traverse the cliffs and offer spectacular views, or you can head south at low tide and follow the remains of an old tramline to Parahaha. The beach and barbecue/picnic area is reached via Karekare Road off Piha Road; you can get there by bus (to Piha) and by walking.

Between Piha and Muriwai beaches is another exciting stretch of surf-raked sand—**Te Henga,** or **Bethells Beach.** It is reached via Te Henga Road, off the north end of Scenic Drive west of Swanson. There are no shops, facilities, or bus transport here. At the south end of the beach are some huge caverns worth exploring, and beyond the sand dunes lies an unusual wetland, the **Lake Wainamu Scenic Reserve.** A walking track that follows the northern shore to the head of the lake starts near the road bridge over Waiti Stream, about 1 km before the road end. The walkway north, along the cliffs to Muriwai Beach, also starts here (see Muriwai Beach Regional Park), with some breathtaking views near the start.

CITY WALKS

Check at the visitor center in Aotea Square for brochures on a number of walks in the city area. If you're interested in buildings and history, then the **Heritage Trail** (about 2 hours) could suit. The 13-km **Coast to Coast** trail across Auckland is fine for those who don't mind a bit of pavement pounding.

To observe marsh, wading, and seabirds, visit **Tahuna Torea** on the Tamaki River estuary. The name means "gathering place of the oystercatcher," and the bird is common here between March and August. Godwits and knots also gather in February and March before flying off to breeding grounds in the Northern Hemisphere. Access is from West Tamaki Road, Vista Crescent, or Riddell Road in Glendowie, by taking ARA buses with numbers commencing with 75- or 76- for Glendowie from the Downtown Bus Centre.

There are walking tracks up all of Auckland's volcanoes, but **One Tree Hill** is recommended, not just for the view but because it is one of the best pa sites in New Zealand. It has been estimated that as many as two thousand people could have lived here at one time. Ditches and banks that would have been topped by wooden palisades formed the outer defenses, and beyond these are terraces where the whare and storehouses stood, where food was cooked and kumara were stored in pits. Another row of inner defense works protected the crater rim, where the chief and tohunga lived. The 183-m-high volcano, which is part of **Cornwall Park,** is topped by one lone pine and a young sacred totara tree standing next to an obelisk and the grave of John Logan Campbell, a settler regarded as the city's founding father.

Campbell donated 220 ha of farmland to the City of Auckland and stipulated that it be kept in a rural state. Today that farsighted gift provides the citizens recreational space within the metropolitan hurly-burly. The park was named for the Duke and Duchess of Cornwall, who were visiting when the land was designated. The park has entrances in Manukau Road, Greenlane Road, Maungakiekie Avenue, and Campbell Road, and can be reached by any ARC bus whose number starts with 30 or 31 for Onehunga or Favona, from Victoria St. East.

For grand harbor views, take the ferry to Devonport on the North Shore and walk up onto **North Head.** The maze of old tunnels here is good for exploring. On a fine day, a walk along the waterfront and **Tamaki Drive** from the lower end of Queen St. can be fun, especially in summer if you take a bathing suit. You can include Victoria Market, the Oriental Market, Parnell Pool, the Rose Gardens, the Savage Memorial, Bastion Point, with its views, and Kelly Tarlton's Underwater World. There are lots of places to eat and beaches where you can rent windsurfers. You'd be exhausted by the time you got to St. Helier's, but you could catch a bus back.

MUSEUMS, MARKETS, AND OTHER PLACES

Auckland Museum in the Auckland Domain is open daily and admission is free. Access is from Stanley St., Park Road, or Parnell Road. The museum shop has excellent craft work if you are looking for souvenirs.

Motat (Museum of Transport and Technology), Great North Road, Western Springs, is also open daily. On weekends, demonstrations include steam-driven machinery and horse and buggy rides. From Motat, you can take a tram ride to the Auckland Zoo to see kiwis, kea, and other exotic creatures.

Kelly Tarlton's Underwater World is a huge marine aquarium where you travel by conveyor belt through a perspex tunnel to view sealife from within the tank.

The **Victoria Park Market,** in Victoria St. West, is an exotic bazaar located in an old red-brick building where the city's rubbish was once burned to generate electricity.

Visit the **Oriental Market** at the corner of Quay St. and Britomart Place for European and Asian wares and foods.

Otara Flea Market, in the Otara shopping center carpark and community hall, has a distinctive Polynesian atmosphere. Clothing, produce, and just about everything else is sold every Saturday from 6 A.M. to midday.

Also in the suburbs is **Howick Colonial Village,** Bells Road, Pakuranga, a restored military settlement of the 1840–1880 period.

WATER SPORTS

Takapuna Beach is popular with local windsurfers, and you can rent boards from several surfing/windsurfing shops along Barrys Point Road. You can also rent windsurfers at Tamaki Beach and by the yacht club at Mission Bay.

Fishing, sailing, and launch cruising are very much part of the Auckland scene. Numerous operators provide skippered and bare-boat charters for day trips or longer on the Hauraki Gulf. Contact the **Boat Charter Booking Centre** (agents for all boat rentals), 1st Floor, Pier 21, Westhaven Drive, phone (09)3098-784 for information, or look in the Yellow Pages of the telephone directory.

The best places for diving are around the outer islands of the Hauraki Gulf. On the mainland, **Goat Island Marine Reserve,** at Cape Rodney north of Warkworth, is particularly good. You'll only need a mask, snorkel, and fins. The fish are almost tame. Maps and brochures on the local marine habitat and species are available from the Marine Research Laboratory at the edge of the reserve. All species within the reserve, which extends from Cape Rodney to Okakari Point and 800 m offshore from high-water mark, are fully protected.

USEFUL ADDRESSES

Auckland Visitors' Bureau, Aotea Square, 299 Queen St., Auckland, phone (09)3666-888. Open weekdays, 8:30 A.M. to 5:30 P.M., weekends and public holidays, 9 A.M. to 4 P.M.

Auckland Regional Council, Regional Parks Central Office, Regional House, corner of Pitt and Hopetoun streets, Auckland, phone (09)3662-166 or 3794-420.

Department of Conservation, corner of Liverpool St. and Karangahape Road, Auckland, phone (09)3079-279, or write: Private Bag, Newton, Auckland.

Tourism Auckland, 87 Queen St., or write: Box 5561 Wellesley St., Auckland, phone (09)3077-999. Open Mon.–Fri., 8:30 A.M. to 4:45 P.M.

Automobile Association, 99 Albert St., Auckland, phone (09)3774-660, Fax (09)3094-563. Open Mon.–Fri., 8:30 A.M. to 5 P.M.

7 ✦ THE COROMANDEL PENINSULA

LANDSCAPE

With its spine of rugged hills, the Coromandel Peninsula pokes out into the Pacific Ocean like a protective thumb, forming a high-walled boundary to the Hauraki Gulf and flat plains to the south. Only toward the north does the central range lose height briefly, with softer, less dramatic contours than before, rising steeply again from a rocky, wave-washed shoreline to culminate as a final pointing gesture in Moehau, the highest point at 892 m. Shallow inlets reach in toward the very base of the range's crenellated walls. The eastern coastline is a delightful mix of sheltered harbors, bays, coves, and long sweeps of pale, glistening sand separated by pohutukawa-hung headlands and cliffs. Offshore islands guard the coastline. The Slipper and Shoe islands stand at the mouth of Tairua Harbour, with The Aldermen group in attendance farther out; islets and rock stacks lie sprinkled off Mercury Bay and farther north are the Mercury Islands, while Cuvier, Great Barrier, and Little Barrier islands are arranged around the tip. The western shoreline is smoother, indented only around Coromandel and Colville. Scattered around the entrances to these inlets are innumerable islands, some little more than a hectare in size. They are the high points of land not inundated by the sea. The beaches are different in character, too—darker, more bouldery, and overhung by giant pohutukawa with their roots almost in the sea.

The many bluffs, pinnacles, and jagged ridges of the Coromandel Range are a legacy of ancient volcanism beginning about 20 million years ago. The first period of activity, lasting nearly 15 million years, buried the older, underlying sedimentary rocks with andesitic lava. Then followed a period of quiet and erosion. Another round of volcanism followed, this time producing more acidic rhyolitic lava accompanied by silification, hydrothermal alteration, and base metal mineralization, which left gold-bearing quartz veins and rocks prized by lapidaries and rockhounds. Accompanying the final stages of this volcanic activity, major earth movements raised the ranges about 1,500 m above the sea.

All volcanic activity ceased about 1 million years ago, and since then erosion has worn away the softer rock, leaving the harder rhyolitic domes and plugs as a dramatic landscape of bluffs and pinnacles jutting from steep slopes. Nourished by a mild damp climate, lush, near-tropical vegetation clothes the precipitous hills in a thick, dark mantle. In general the forests are similar to those found north of Auckland—associations of kauri, podocarp, and broadleaved species—

but they have a character of their own, due almost entirely to the peninsula's islandlike nature. Latitude is also an important factor. The kauri grows well here but is nearly at its southern limit. More extraordinary is the number of mountain-loving plants found on higher points of the range, plants more typical of the central volcanic plateau and southern ranges, some of which reach their northern limit here.

HISTORY

Huge stands of kauri once occurred throughout the peninsula's forests, but logging, mining, and gum digging have all taken their toll. Logging of the kauri began in 1832 with the building of a sawmill at Mercury Bay, where shipbuilding and repairs were carried out. The industry grew and spread to Tairua, Coroglen, and the Kauaeranga Valley behind Thames, all of which supplied logs to Auckland mills. By the mid 1880s they were producing 60,000 cu m of sawn timber annually. A century of exploitation later, these wonderful forests had been plundered of their most precious bounty and huge kauri were a rarity.

Not only were the forests stripped, but much of the valuable timber was wasted by the methods used to extract it. After being felled, the huge logs were shifted with jacks, with three men moving thirty to forty logs at a time. As logging moved further inland, bullock teams were used to drag the logs along cleared tracks. Later, skid roads were constructed. In more inaccessible areas, the logs were jacked or slid into creek beds for what were known as river drives. Wooden dams were constructed in the headwaters of small creeks, and during rainstorms or when enough water had collected, they were tripped to release their water. The resulting flood would carry the logs downstream to the main valley below. Some drives were incredibly large. In one, recorded in 1882, 15,000 logs containing 57,000 cu m of timber thundered down the Tairua Valley. Many logs were smashed to pulp when they were driven over waterfalls or down stream beds that were too steep.

The dams were perhaps the loggers' greatest engineering feat. Some took up to two years to build. As they were constructed in stream beds of solid rock, vegetation, soil, and rock had to be cleared away first. The timber to build them had to be felled and pit sawn, usually close to the site. They were constructed with a trigger mechanism that released the gate planks holding back the water and logs, and as these were attached to the stringer beams by wire cables, they weren't swept away, allowing the dam to be reassembled and the process repeated.

The loggers were followed by gum diggers, prospectors, and farmers. During the boom years of the 1890s, kauri gum headed Auckland's exports, with an annual total of over 8,160 tons. Thousands of men of all nationalities searched the hillsides for lumps of gum, which ranged from the size of a walnut to that

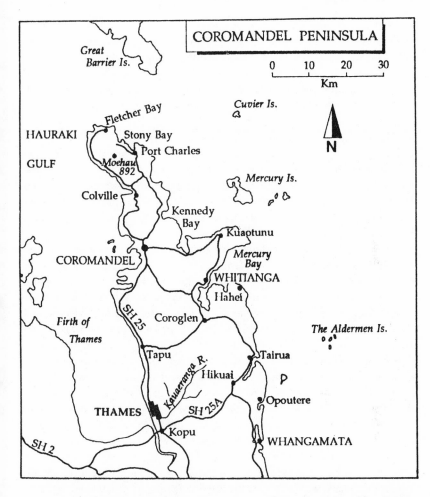

of a pumpkin. Fossil gum, deposited centuries earlier, was retrieved by digging or by probing the ground with long spears, while fresh gum, lodged high in the forks of branches, could only be taken by climbing the huge tree trunks with the aid of ropes, spike-toed boots, and hand picks.

The gum diggers and farmers often burned what was left of the logged forests, and it is thought that the heat of these fires destroyed the seeds of the kauri and other trees. In places, poor soil made regeneration slow, and much of the peninsula still remains covered in manuka scrub. If left alone, the manuka provides a nursery for forest trees but, not content, humans, in their wisdom, have replaced much scrubland with exotic forests.

Gold was the peninsula's other bonanza. Discovery of the precious metal in 1852 at Driving Creek near Coromandel lured nearly 3,000 men to work the area, but there was little to show for their efforts. It was not until the Thames goldfields were discovered in 1867 and the Waihi and Karangahake areas were opened up in the 1870s that the industry really got going. More than 1,100 mining companies were formed, but although they moved more than 15 million tons of rock and obtained almost 1,250 tons of bullion, very few fortunes were made.

Unlike the logging industry, mining left few scars on the landscape. Last century, the hills behind Thames and Coromandel were devoid of forest, their steep slopes pitted with tunnel entrances, criss-crossed with tracks and tramways, and dotted with tents, makeshift houses, poppet heads, batteries, and pump houses. Today, apart from several carefully preserved mine entrances and other relics, there is little evidence of all this activity, as the benign climate has helped vegetation to return and cover the scars.

Fortunately, large tracts of forest were left untouched, mainly because they grew in places too steep to mill or farm, and these now form the various blocks of the Coromandel Forest Park. Despite the ravages of industry, wildlife is still prolific in and around forested areas and along the coasts. Along with the more common species of bush birds — pigeons, bellbirds, tui, and fantails — you will quite likely see fernbirds, or hear their double *tic-tic* sound in scrub areas. Moreporks call frequently at night. Kingfishers are a common sight, perched on powerlines or pohutukawa trees overhanging the sea or streams, and shags congregate on rock stacks, often with wings outstretched to dry. In tidal estuaries and on sandy beaches, terns, white-faced herons, pied stilts, and oystercatchers — and the ubiquitous gulls — search the shoreline for snails, crabs, and other tasty morsels.

Of special interest are the two species of native frog that are found in higher, wet areas of forest. *Leiopelma hochstetteri* was discovered in 1852 by gold prospectors, but when a specimen was shown to Maoris, they denied ever seeing such a creature before. *Leiopelma archeyi* was not discovered until 1942. Both species are tiny and have very primitive characteristics, such as no tadpole stage and an ability to inhabit areas without running water.

Today the beautiful beaches and coastal scenery of the Coromandel Peninsula attract thousands of holidaymakers and an increasing number of tourists who find its history of gold mining and logging fascinating. Owing to the nature of the country they traverse, the peninsula's roads are narrow and winding, but most have been improved in the last decade, and access and travel to all but the remotest corners is relatively easy. Now the main coastal roads, from Waihi to Whitianga on the eastern side and from Thames to Colville along the west coast, are good highways. Apart from the relatively new Kopu–Hikuai road (SH 25A), cross-range roads still have gravel surfaces and require careful driving, but no longer do travelers need to stop or even back their vehicles to allow another car to pass. A few roads, such as that between Tapu and Coroglen, are as rough, tortuous, and narrow as they have always been.

For most visitors to the Coromandel Peninsula, Thames is the first port of call. From here you can head directly north along the western coast to Coromandel, or alternatively, take SH 25A across the range to Hikuai and Tairua before following the eastern coast to Whitianga.

◆PLACES TO VISIT AND THINGS TO DO

AROUND THAMES

The first place to visit should be the excellent information center on Queen St., where you will get plenty of helpful advice. They can tell you the opening times of the **Mineralogical Museum,** the adjacent **School of Mines** (at the corner of Cochrane and Brown sts.), and the **Historical Museum**—three places that will give you an insight into the trials, tribulations, and workings of the gold mining industry. Important gold mine sites are scattered around the town and are marked by yellow signs giving brief details of their significant features. The visitor center may be able to help you locate these. In summer the Hauraki Prospectors Association gives guided tours through the **Moanataiari Mine** workings and nearby stamper battery, which is located on the outskirts of the town beside the main road. Several other important sites are also signposted along the main road, just to the north.

Thames retains many buildings from the gold mining era and perhaps the most famous is the **Brian Boru Hotel,** built in 1868. Exciting, action-packed **murder and mystery weekends,** when guests and actors enact and solve a murder, are held at this hotel. Saturday's activities include rafting, wine tasting, visits to gold mines, and tours of Mercury Bay. The cost at time of writing was NZ$355, which includes everything from Friday night to Sunday noon. If you guess "who done it" and why, you receive a prize; if you are the "victim," you get a refund. Further information can be obtained from **Brian Boru Hotels,** 200 Richmond St., Thames, phone (07)8686-523, Fax (07)8689-760.

COROMANDEL FOREST PARK

Kauaeranga Valley
The main area of activity in the Coromandel Forest Park is the Kauaeranga Valley near Thames, the site of intense kauri milling until the 1920s. The valley has many lovely camping and picnic areas and good tracks to sites of historical interest. The Coromandel Forest Park Headquarters and Visitor Centre is located 12 km up Kauaeranga Valley Road, which leaves the main highway at the

north side of the Kauaeranga River Bridge, which you cross as you enter Thames. Displays, photographs, maps, and brochures give information on the history and natural features of the valley, and a few minutes' walk from the visitor center is a working model of the type of dam used during logging operations.

All campsites and many short walks are clearly marked beside the road, which extends another 10 km up the valley from the park headquarters. Of the longer walks, those to **Table Mountain,** the obvious flat-topped giant to the north of the valley, or to **Pinnacles Hut** and the **Billy Goat Stream,** where many relics remain, are the most interesting. Overnight hikes can also be made from here along the crest of the range or across to the eastern side.

Table Mountain

The track commences at the back of the Wainora Camping Ground, 7 km past the park headquarters, and can be done as a 6-hour circuit. It involves some steep climbing up to and down from the ridge and usually a very muddy walk through the goblin forest along the mountain's flat, swampy top. A shorter walk of 2 to 3 hours can be made to a large kauri near the top, with good views across to Billy Goat Falls. There are several stream crossings along the first part of the track, so be prepared for wet feet.

Pinnacles Hut and Billy Goat Stream

A 6- to 7-hour loop walk can be made to Pinnacles Hut, with a return via the Billy Goat Stream, or you can make separate, shorter trips to each. Billy Goat Stream drops 200 m in several spectacular leaps, and early attempts to drive logs over the falls resulted in a loss of 90 percent of the timber. Eventually a tramline was built and logs were winched down the incredibly steep incline on trucks whose braking mechanisms were operated by men standing on the back. The track, which follows the old incline, will help you appreciate the steel nerves of those men. The remains of some of the tramline trestles can still be seen.

The pleasant 20-bunk Pinnacles Hut is situated near the top of the range, close to some spectacular rock formations. There are exciting views across to Table Mountain and down into the Tairua Valley below, and about 50 m from the hut are the well-preserved remains of Dancing Camp Dam, named for the men-only dances held at a nearby gum diggers camp.

The track starts at the road's end. After about 15 minutes beside the river, it turns right and climbs alongside Webb Creek, often up steps cut into stone for packhorses. A junction at a clearing known as the Hydro Camp is reached in 1 to 1.5 hours, and from here it takes about 45 minutes to the hut. A side track (1.5 to 2 hours return) from the hut leads to the cluster of rock spires known as the Pinnacles, or you can make a longer hike by continuing along the main track to the end of Rangihau Road near Coroglen.

From the Hydro Camp the right-hand track traverses the hillside and ridge top, with great views over the range, before descending to the headwaters of Billy Goat Stream in about 1.5 hours. After crossing the stream and passing the junction of tracks to Hihi, Motutapere, and Tarawaere Dam, the Billy Goat Track heads downstream, crossing twice more before sidling to the left. Below here the stream makes its spectacular plunge to the Kauaeranga Valley. There are some good views of the falls before the track descends the steep stone staircase of the old incline, finishing about 500 m before the road's end.

NORTH OF THAMES

North of Thames the road hugs the coastline tightly, passing the small settlements of **Tararu, Te Puru,** and **Waiomu** before reaching **Tapu.** The streams flowing into the Firth of Thames at these places were all scenes of past mining activity. Rapid regrowth of the bush has covered much of the evidence, but the old pack tracks still offer some short, pleasant bush rambles. Tracks start from the ends of the short side roads leading up all the streams. About an hour up the **Waiomu Stream Track** is a grove of large kauri trees and several big totara. Be prepared for wet feet as there are many stream crossings.

At Tapu, the old **road to Coroglen** and Whitianga turns right and follows the stream into the hills, twisting and turning as it climbs over the range. This is a very scenic route, but is not recommended for nervous drivers. There are, however, some interesting sights along the way. The privately owned **Rapaura Water Gardens,** 6 km from Tapu, is a pleasant 26-ha park with a mixture of exotic and native plants. There are picnic sites, a craft shop, and tearooms, and a short walk through native bush to the beautiful three-tiered Rapaura Falls.

Follow the road for another 3 km and you will come to the **Square Kauri,** a huge specimen with an unusual rectangular bole, estimated to be about 1,200 years old. There are good views from here across to the hunched peaks of **Maumaupaki,** the Camel's Back. The track to the top of the Camel's Back leaves from the road summit and is part of the track system running the length of the range. It's a long climb – allow about 4 hours (return) – but the views are superb, even if you don't go all the way. The track is rugged and guaranteed to get you muddy.

AROUND COROMANDEL

North of Tapu the road continues to hug the shoreline as far as Kereta and then climbs steeply to the summit of the Manaia Hill, where a superb panorama of islands, inlets, and the Hauraki Gulf across to Auckland unfolds before your eyes. Coromandel, still hidden from view at this point, has a peaceful atmosphere, unhurried by tourism. Placid waters sprinkled with islands, boats, and oyster and mussel rafts stretch out from the wharf toward the Hauraki Gulf. Dark hills rising steeply behind the town are crossed by the snaking lines of two roads, one to Kennedy Bay and the other to Kuaotunu on the other side of the peninsula. It's a place where potters, artists, and other craftspeople revel in the peace and quiet, and where their alternative lifestyle is accepted—a far cry from the population of 12,000 who crammed the streets a hundred years ago.

Coromandel was first known for its kauri, logged as early as 1795 and shipped to England for use as spars and masts on the British naval ships. Once the logging industry got underway, a billion feet of timber was taken from the area in twenty years. Relics of the gold mining days can be seen at the **School of Mines,** located in Rings Road. Built in 1898 to teach all aspects of mining and mine engineering, it is now a memorial to the era. The **Coromandel Stamper Battery,** a fully operational quartz-crushing machine, is located in Buffalo Road. Phone (07)8668-765 for more information and operating times.

The richest reefs around the town were the **Tokatea Mines** located near the summit of the **Kennedy Bay Road.** From the summit, where a large hotel once stood, a loop track, taking about 15 minutes, climbs to **Lucas Lookout** on the top of the windswept ridge. There are superb views from here over both sides of the peninsula. As the area is riddled with mine drives and shafts, you are advised to keep to the track.

On the other side of the road summit a steep vehicle track leads to a radio relay station. From this road, just before the mast, a walking path leads south along the ridge to **Kaipawa Trig** (586 m) in 45 to 60 minutes, for more good views. The path continues, with some meandering, to a vehicle track that can be followed to the Coromandel–Whangapoua Road. There are many mine shafts and drives around here, too, which walkers straying off the track have inadvertently fallen into.

If you're not interested in gold mines, there is a very pleasant 20-minute stroll through the bush reserve behind the motor camp at **Long Bay.** A kauri of impressive size and a grove of beautiful young trees are passed before the track rejoins the road connecting Long Bay with the delightful camping area at **Tucks Bay.** There is also a track around the promontory between the two bays. Long Bay is signposted and is a few kilometers past the Coromandel wharf.

The **309 Road** is the shortest route between Coromandel and Whitianga. It is winding and unsealed and branches off about 3 km south of Coromandel. From near the turnoff, the fascinating bulwark of **Castle Rock** rises on the skyline. An easy track to the top starts a few kilometers along Forestry Road 37, which turns off the 309 Road 5 km from the junction, taking about 40 minutes to reach the summit rocks through stunted bush that is thick with nikau palms. About 3 to 4 km further along the 309 Road, a sign and parking area mark the start of a short track to a spectacular **Kauri Grove**. A good viewing platform, before the trees are reached, and a boardwalk beneath them give a superb perspective of the trees. The main purpose of the boardwalk is to protect the trees' root systems from damage by trampling. A short loop track leads past another grove containing a strange specimen known as the Siamese kauri.

THE TOP OF THE PENINSULA

Between Coromandel and Colville the road skips inland, only skirting the coast at Oamaru Bay, Papa Aroha, Amodeo Bay, and Waitete Bay, where there are good campgrounds. Like many other peninsula settlements, Colville was once a bustling town but now has only a store and is the last place you can get petrol. Captain Cook named the place Cabbage Bay, as it was here that his men had to eat the native milk thistle to ward off scurvy.

The top end of the peninsula is for those who like remoteness. It feels isolated, and is, in a sense, as the only settlement of any size is at Port Charles on the eastern side. On the western side, the road is at first undemanding, following the rocky shoreline through groves of ancient, gnarled pohutukawa. It's simple but dramatic scenery, heightened in December when the trees are in full crimson bloom. Because much of the land here is administered by the Department of Conservation as the **Cape Colville Farm Park,** the public has access to some beautiful areas that might be closed if the farms were privately owned. Within the park are four informal camping areas; a small fee is charged for their use. The first is at **Fantail Bay** on the western side. Beyond here the road narrows and climbs over a headland before descending to **Port Jackson,** where there is another campground. Little more than a name on a map these days, Port Jackson was once a bustling timber port. The road leaves this long bay and climbs again above the sea with exciting views below and out to Little and Great Barrier islands, before descending to the camping area at beautiful **Fletcher Bay.**

From Fletcher Bay, the 7-km **Coromandel Walkway** leads over the farmland and around the coast to Stony Bay, where the road on the eastern side of the peninsula ends. This superb walk, taking about 3 hours one way, has outstanding bush and coastal scenery. An alternative walk is to climb to the top of the **Sugarloaf,** a prominent hill at the end of a more eastern headland. There is no marked track and the easiest route is from the track to Stony Bay, leaving it at a prominent ridge reached after about 35 minutes. A walk around the coast to the **Needles,** the spectacular rock pinnacles at the base of the Sugarloaf, is also worthwhile. At low tide, the broad platform at the base provides a great spot to fish from.

To climb **Moehau** (892 m) you have a choice of two routes, from either the western or eastern coast. The track on the western side starts near the mouth and bridge of **Te Hope Stream,** 13 km north of Colville. The first part of the walk is over private farmland to the forest park boundary. After crossing the Te Hope Stream twice, the track climbs a bushed spur to emerge into open subalpine vegetation below the rocky knob of Little Moehau. This is traversed before crossing a boggy saddle and making the final ascent to the trig on the summit.

The twisting gravel road to **Stony Bay, Port Charles,** and **Waikawau Bay** turns right a few kilometers north of Colville. There are a few houses beside beautiful, sheltered Port Charles Harbour and more at Sandy Bay, a little further up the coast. From Sandy Bay the road narrows and snakes around the hills for another 7 km before descending to Stony Bay, where the Department of Conservation provides another camping area. Isolated as it may seem, this beautiful secluded bay, rimmed by spreading pohutukawa trees, is crowded with campers during the Christmas–New Year holiday.

The eastern track to Moehau starts at **Stony Bay,** and although steeper than the Te Hope Stream route, the climbing distance is exactly the same. Like the other route, the track at first climbs over farmland, up a grassy spur behind the farmhouse, with superb views down to Stony Bay. The first bush encountered is tall kanuka, but as elevation is gained along the steep, narrow ridge many young totara, rimu, and occasional kauri appear. Epiphytic orchids are prolific, with *Earina autumnalis* flowering profusely in May. Scarlet rata blossoms are also seen at this time. As the subalpine region is neared, the ground becomes much wetter, with sphagnum moss, cushion plants, stunted podocarps, and mountain toatoa forming the cover. Small, dark-green kaikawaka dot the alpine bog like miniature Christmas trees. The rare native frog *Leiopelma archeyi* is found in this region.

The summit of Moehau is sacred to Maori people as the legendary burial place of Tama te Kapua, leader of the Arawa canoe. There are tremendous views down both sides of the peninsula and across the Hauraki Gulf to Auckland. Either route to the top will take about 3 hours. Carry along food, drink, and warm clothing, as the summit can be very cool and breezy.

If you don't have time to walk all the way to Fletcher Bay, a stroll part way along the track and out onto some of the headlands reveals some outstanding views. The coastal forest along the first part of the track is beautiful, with nikau palms, tall tanekaha, pohutukawa, and some kauri.

Waikawau Bay Farm Park also has large camping areas and provides access to the beautiful long sandy beach. The Kawetoto rocks, a reef at the mouth of the Waikawau River, is a popular spot for fishing. From Waikawau Bay the road winds over the hills to Tuateawa and Kennedy Bay, then back over the range again to Coromandel. The views are spectacular.

AROUND WHITIANGA

Whangapoua and Kuaotunu

There's another hill to negotiate between Coromandel and Te Rerenga at the head of Whangapoua Harbour, but it's not too big an obstacle. Turn left at Te Rerenga and you will come to the main beach at **Whangapoua**, a beautiful stretch of pale sand. From the northern end of the sealed (paved) road running behind the beach there is access to the Pungapunga River estuary. You can wade across if the tide is less than full, and by following the rocky coast toward the headland you will find a track across a low point. In about 20 minutes you'll go through a delightful grove of nikau palms and pohutukawa to **New Chums Beach**, or Wainototo Bay. Fortunately, this superb beach with pink-tinged sand has not yet been developed as a holiday resort, making it a prime spot for secluded picnicking.

The right-hand road at Te Rerenga brings you around Whangapoua Harbour to another junction. Turn left for the newly developed resort of **Matarangi**, with its long dune-backed beach, or right for **Kuaotunu**. The short but very narrow winding road that traverses the Matarangi Bluff Recreation Reserve between these two beaches is not recommended for large vehicles or nervous drivers. From Kuaotunu the road continues out along the subpeninsula, crossing the Black Jack Hill and descending to the 2-km-long white sands of **Otama Beach** and **Opito Bay**'s long sparkling beach. From the road end it is a short walk to **Opito Point Historic Reserve** on the steep headland enclosing the southern end of the bay. Old fortification terraces and trenches from a pa that once stood here can still be seen. From the top there are excellent views out to the Mercury Islands and the many islets off Opito Bay.

The hills behind Kuaotunu were the scene of gold mining activity after a Maori prospector, Charles "Coffin" Kawhine, discovered the rich Try Fluke reef. **Kuaotunu Walks and Gold Trails,** led by Grant Simpson, go through the old workings every Monday morning, leaving from the Kuaotunu Hall at 9 A.M. Bookings and extra tours can be arranged through the Whitianga Information Centre or Kuaotunu Stores, or by phoning (07)8665-555. You'll need sturdy footwear and a flashlight for these interesting trips.

Whitianga

The main road south from Kuaotunu crosses more hills and skirts **Wharekaho** and **Buffalo Beaches** before reaching **Whitianga**, a bustling fishing and tourist town. It is the home of the Mercury Bay Boating Club, which in 1987 launched the controversial challenge to the San Diego Yacht Club to race for the America's Cup. As well as having a history of kauri logging and gum digging, Whitianga has a claim to fame from the days of Captain Cook. It was at Cook's Beach, in November 1769, that Cook watched the planet Mercury move across the sun, an event that enabled him to fix the exact longitude of New Zealand. It was also where he planted a British flag in the sand to claim the new land for King George III.

Mercury Bay was previously known as Te Whanganui-o-Hei (the great bay of Hei), after Hei, a chief who came with the legendary Arawa canoe around 1350 and settled in the area. Nearby Hahei had a coastal landform that Hei thought resembled his nose.

The narrow entrance to Whitianga Harbour is crossed by a pedestrian ferry that operates continuously between 7:30 A.M. and 6:30 P.M. every day. From the historic **Ferry Landing** (built in 1837) on the eastern side, there are several short walks. **Whitianga Rock,** a pohutukawa-covered point of land to the right of the wharf, is one of the oldest fortified pa sites in the country, and remains of the deep defense ditch and terracing can still be seen. A short way along the road from the wharf you will come to **Front Beach** and, at its far end, the high-bluffed promontory that Cook named **Shakespeare Cliff.** A maze of tracks leads to a lookout at the top and on down to **Lonely Bay,** a beautiful, secluded little beach tucked between cliffs, and the much longer **Cook's Beach.**

The road to **Cook's Beach, Hahei,** and **Hotwater Beach** turns off SH 25 at Whenuakite, a 25-km-drive from Whitianga around the extensive estuaries and mudflats of Whitianga Harbour. The 309 Road to Coromandel is passed about 7 km out of town, and the road to Tapu turns off beside the lonely pub and store at **Coroglen.** In its heyday, around the turn of the century, Gumtown, as Coroglen was then known, had three stores, a 25-bedroom hotel, two boarding houses, a butcher, a bakery, a boot maker, and a billiards room. It was serviced three times weekly by a small steamer from Whitianga, and each day teams of fifty packhorses left the town for lumberjacks' and gum diggers' camps in the hills behind.

Gold was discovered in 1898 in the head of the Rangihau Stream south of Coroglen. Several claims were worked over the following thirty years, but none yielded a fortune. **Rangihau Road,** just south of Coroglen, leads up the Rangihau Valley. At the road end, about 10 km from Coroglen, are an informal camping area at the edge of the forest park and the start of the track across the range to the Kauaeranga Valley via Pinnacles or Moss Creek Huts. The road-end area is very scenic, with high black cliffs rising from bush-clad slopes beside the deep pools and boulders of the stream. The top end of Rangihau Road has several fords to cross and is very rough and unsuitable for low-slung vehicles.

Hahei

Modern developments lend a certain suburban quality to Hahei, but the beautiful pink-tinged beach, lapped by clear waters and sheltered by a chain of island gems, still has its charm. The excellent campground adjacent to the beach is

Cathedral Cove, Coromandel Peninsula. *Photo by Bruce Jefferies.*

very popular over summer. At the southern end of the beach, terracing of the once heavily fortified Te Mautohe Pa can be seen on the grassy headland of Hereheretaura Point. Hahei's best attraction, however, is **Cathedral Cove,** one of the loveliest places on the peninsula. Two exquisite pink-sand beaches, backed by pale cliffs hung with pohutukawa trees, are linked by a huge cavern. In the clear waters off these beaches, strangely sculptured rock stacks stand like ships at anchor. It's the perfect place to spend a day swimming and picnicking. The track starts from a lookout (with outstanding views) at the end of Grange Road, which branches left at the Hahei Store to wind up the hillside. It takes 30 to 40 minutes to walk to Cathedral Cove, but if you allow 2 hours for the round trip, you'll have time to explore a magnificent grove of huge puriri and karaka trees and for side trips to Gemstone and Stingray Bays.

Hotwater Beach

With no sheltering offshore islands, long, dune-backed Hotwater Beach often has good surf and is popular with local surfing enthusiasts. It gets its name from hot springs at the southern end of the beach. These are found by digging in the sand, between low- and mid-tide, near some rocks off a pohutukawa-studded headland about 200 m along the beach from the road end. Small bubbles in the sand or a feeling of warmth between your toes will indicate where to start digging. If the tide is in, you can still have a hot swim at the enclosed pools run by the shop at the motor camp. To get onto the beach from the road end you need to ford the stream. This can be avoided by taking a short side road about 1.5 km back from the road end.

AROUND TAIRUA

South of Whenuakite the road climbs into the hills again. Before the highest point is reached, about 8 km north of Tairua, a parking area and signs indicate the start of a well-formed loop track to a **kauri grove.** This takes about 1.5 hours. A much longer hike, taking the best part of a day, can also be made from here down to the coast. Near the summit, **Sailors Grave Road** leads down to **Te Karo Bay.** A 15- to 20-minute walk along the beach will bring you to the grave of William Simpson, a sailor who drowned in the bay in 1842 when the jolly boat of *H.M.S. Tortoise* capsized while landing to collect kauri spars. The grave lay hidden in the bush until the 1890s; recent restoration has provided a white picket fence.

Tairua flourished during the kauri milling days, then dwindled in size after a disastrous fire destroyed most of the uncut timber. It remained a small farming town until the highway from Kopu was opened in 1967, giving easy access. The twin peaks of **Paku** guard the entrance to Tairua Harbour and provide wonderful views along the coast. You can drive almost to the top, and a walking track to the highest of the summits leaves from the end of Tirinui Crescent, off Paku Drive. Across the harbor is **Pauanui,** a recently developed resort town covering what was once a barren sandspit. By road, Pauanui is 27 km from Tairua, but a 5-minute pedestrian ferry service now connects the two towns.

Pauanui Trig

Pauanui's ocean beach is almost 3 km long, with road access to each end and picnic areas in between. About 100 m south of the southern road end a sign-posted track leaves the beach and climbs through magnificent pohutukawa groves, coastal flax, shrubbery, and pines to **Pauanui Trig** (387 m). It takes about an hour to reach the top, where the view sweeps from the coast and offshore islands to the rugged and spectacular hinterland behind Hikuai.

Broken Hills Gorge

Extensive gold mining was carried out in the **Broken Hills Gorge** behind Hikuai around the turn of the century, and many of the mines, stampers, water-race trenches, and other relics can be seen from a network of signposted tracks. You can walk through the Collins Drive if you have a good flashlight, sturdy foot-wear, and some head protection. The slightly curving drive runs almost level for 500 m through a hill. Apart from the interesting ruins, the scenery around Broken Hills is spectacular and the spot is good for gemstone fossicking. There is a very pleasant forest park campground beside the river near the road end. Access is by **Puketui Valley Road** off SH 25, just south of Hikuai by the Tairua River bridge.

Kopu–Hikuai Road

From Kirikiri Saddle, the highest point on the Kopu–Hikuai Road (SH 25A) a walking track leads to the **Devcich Kauri** and on to the summit of **Kaitarakihi** (852 m). The Devcich Kauri, estimated to be the fourteenth largest known in New Zealand, has a superb bole rising 12.5 m to the first branch and an overall height of 47 m. The fern- and grass-edged track follows the main ridge, un-dulating gently through bush dominated by tawa. After about 45 minutes, the track to the kauri branches to the right and descends through less luxuriant growth, coming to the mighty tree quite suddenly. From the track junction it takes another 1 to 1.5 hours through wind-stunted podocarp and broadleaf forest to reach the top of the sharp, rocky peak of Kaitarakihi. The last section is very steep and is climbed with the aid of a wire rope.

AROUND WHANGAMATA

Like other towns along the eastern coast of the peninsula, Whangamata has boomed recently as a coastal resort—and for good reason. It's a scenic place that offers plenty of opportunities for safe swimming, surfcasting, line fishing, diving, surfing, sailing, walking, and gemstone collecting.

Sheltering the harbor is the long, pine-covered **Whangamata Peninsula,** a part of Tairua State Forest, which has been developed as a recreation reserve. From a lookout at the end of the headland, short walking tracks lead around the tip and down to a sheltered beach, with good views over the town and harbor entrance. Other tracks lead to **Te Ananui Ocean Beach** and **Pokohino Beach,** both popular places for swimming, fishing, and picnicking. Te Ananui Beach often has good surf, whereas Pokohino Beach, guarded by cliffs, is more scenic and secluded.

Wharekawa Valley
Tairua State Forest covers much of the country inland from the main road north of Whangamata, mainly around the headwaters of the Wharekawa River. Within it are tracks to old gold mine ruins, some beautiful native forest, and some huge kauri specimens. Of the mines in the Wharekawa Valley, the **Luck At Last** was the most productive, and remains of battery, cyanide tanks, and other relics still litter the forest. It is worth calling at the forest headquarters (3 km north of Whangamata) for a map of the area and up-to-date information on tracks and logging operations. The main access to the area is **Taungarata Road,** which turns left off SH 25 a few kilometers north of the forest headquarters.

Oputere
About halfway between Hikuai and Whangamata, a side road follows the broad estuary of the Wharekawa River to the quiet little settlement of **Oputere.** Just past the small collection of houses a small sign on the left marks a steep track to **Wharekawa Lookout,** a 15- to 20-minute climb that will reward you with views over Wharekawa Harbour and The Aldermen and Mayor islands. The Oputere Youth Hostel is just along the road. Beyond it is a picnic area and a track through the lupin, marram grass, and pine-covered dunes of Oputere Beach Recreation Reserve to the surf-raked ocean beach. Most of the sandspit stretching out toward the harbor mouth is wildlife reserve and is particularly important as a breeding ground for the New Zealand dotterel, which is now a threatened species. Oystercatchers, terns, gulls, and other waders also gather here in large numbers.

Wentworth Valley and Falls
The Wentworth Valley, 3 km south of Whangamata, was once mined for gold, and the old village site near where the road ends is now a beautiful grassy camping and picnic area. The old route used by miners in the 1800s to cross the ranges to Whangamata provides a pleasant walking track to the **Wentworth Falls,** which descend 50 m over a bush-hung cliff in two dramatic leaps (2 hours return). The track continues through dense forest to the top of the range where

it meets the wide trailbike track and the old **Wires Track** from the end of Maratoto Road on the western side. The Wires Track was the route of the telegraph line between Auckland and Wellington, diverted this way to avoid troubled areas during the Waikato Land Wars. Loggers' kauri-cutting and later activities by gum diggers, gold prospectors, and farmers destroyed the area's original bush cover. The remains of an old settlement, kauri dam, mill, and portable steam engine still lie on the plateau at the top of the track.

Royal Standard Gold Mine

Known locally as the Royal Sovereign, this gold mine was a flop, producing only 500 g of gold. It did, however, have an 8-km horse-drawn tramway from the mine site to the sea, built before the reef had been thoroughly tested. The tramway is now a pleasant walk beside the Wharekirauponga Stream, taking an hour or more to the battery site and a short tunnel through the hill. It starts at the end of **Quarry Road,** off SH 25 by the Otahu River Bridge, 6.5 km south of Whangamata. The old quarry site has some fascinating volcanic rock formations.

Whiritoa Beach

The beach at Whiritoa, 15 km south of Whangamata, is a favorite spot with surfcasters but also offers short rambling opportunities. From the lagoon at the northern end of the beach a short track through bush and farmland leads around the cliffs to **Waimama Bay,** an idyllic little beach backed by shady pohutukawa trees. The cliffs at the southern end of Whiritoa Beach are also traversed by a rough track leading to **Otonga Point,** which gives good coastal views. Along the way you pass a blowhole that can give some great displays in rough weather during the right tide.

THE ARTS, CRAFTS, AND ALTERNATIVE LIFESTYLE TRAIL

The peninsula attracts many artisans and others wishing to pursue a more relaxed, back-to-nature lifestyle than is possible in the bigger cities. Crafts vary from pottery- and jewelery-making to silk weaving, wood turning, glassblowing, and wool spinning to wine making and canning preserves. Lists of craftspeople, their specialties, and their locations are available from the information centers at Whitianga and Coromandel. Two very interesting places near Whitianga are **309 Honey Cottage,** a few kilometers along the 309 Road, and **Purangi Winery,** on the road to Cooks Beach. At 309 Honey Cottage you'll find accommodation and a small farm where everything is grown organically. Free transport is provided to Purangi Winery from Ferry Landing and can be arranged through the Whitianga Information Center or by phoning (07)8663-724.

TRANSPORT

InterCity Buses provides a service to and around the Peninsula on weekdays. You will need to check an up-to-date timetable for specifics. **Whangamata Buses** provides a service to Waihi on weekdays, departing from Whangamata Post Office at 8:45 A.M. and returning from the InterCity Bus Depot, Waihi, at 12:30 P.M. On Mon., Wed., and Fri. buses run between Whangamata and Oputere, departing Oputere at 7:55 A.M. and Whangamata at 2:30 P.M.

Air Coromandel, phone (07)8664-016 or Fax (07)8664-017, operate an air taxi service from Thames, Whitianga, Pauanui, Coromandel, and Matarangi to Auckland and Hamilton, and also do scenic flights.

Local services to the ends of walking tracks are lacking. The only exception is **Aotearoa Adventures,** Aotearoa Lodge, RD, Whitianga, phone (07)8663-808. They will pick up hikers from the end of Rangihau Road, Coroglen, or the Tapu Road summit.

USEFUL ADDRESSES

Thames Information Centre, 405 Queen St., Thames, phone (07)8687-284.
Whitianga Information Centre, Box 61, Whitianga, phone (07)8665-555.
Coromandel Information Centre, Kapanga Road, Coromandel, phone (07) 8668-598.
Department of Conservation, Box 78, Thames, phone (07)8686-381.

8 ◆ THE WAIKATO AND KING COUNTRY

LANDSCAPE

Lying between the high jumbled volcanic pile of Pirongia Mountain and the dark, steep wall of the Kaimai Range is some of the most productive pastoral land in the world—and it was created by people. This 5,000-sq-km green heart of the Waikato, the center of New Zealand's dairy industry, supports the world's densest concentration of free-grazing domestic livestock. The lush green pastures of today are vastly different from the swamps of peat and standing water lying between low hills of ash and scrub that the first missionaries and settlers faced.

With typical zeal and backbreaking labor those settlers drained the swamps and cut back the bush to all but the most rugged or elevated terrain. Now conservationists fight to save the few remaining swamp areas as habitat for a dwindling number of birds.

On the northern edge of this cow paradise is the trough of the Hauraki Plains, once a vast peat swamp and now treeless flat pasture, and the low-lying hills and swamplands around Huntley, where coal is mined. To the south-east, where the Kaimai Range dwindles and broadens, the dairy lands give way to the pine forests of the high ignimbrite plateau. Southward is the King Country. In the west this broken hill-country is distinguished by outcrops of hard, cream-colored limestone; many streams flow through the narrow gorges between these steep bluffs, disappearing underground and reappearing elsewhere. It is here that the famous Waitomo caves lie. More rugged areas of this hilly region still retain some of their bush cover or are recovering from farmers' futile attempts to work the steep slopes.

Through this landscape the broad Waikato River winds a sinuous course northward from Lake Taupo, its birthplace. The upper reaches, green and swift, cut a narrow channel through the volcanic rocks of the central high country. Here the river's power has been harnessed by a series of dams to provide hydro-electricity, causing it to form the long, narrow lakes of Ohakuri, Atiamuri, Whakamaru, Maraetai, Waipapa, Arapuni, and Karapiro. On reaching the Wai-kato basin its character changes. Less contained, it becomes murky, and nearing its journey's end, it turns west and broadens to sweep silently between swampy, willow-lined banks and islands before washing through high coastal dunes to the Tasman Sea.

The present landscape has its origins far back in time. About 40 million years ago New Zealand was a low-lying land, with sluggish rivers, extensive flood plains, and many swamps. The vegetation accumulated and decayed in the swamps and formed thick coal-bearing deposits. In time these were flooded by shallow seas and covered with deposits of pale muds, sands, and the shells of small sea creatures. This quiet period of sedimentation ended abruptly about 20 million years ago when massive earth movements, along predominantly north-south faults, buckled the land. Some parts of the sea floor were lifted to form new hills and ranges while others sank to form deep marine troughs. The uplifted parts now form the western hills of the Waikato and King Country and the coal-bearing deposits in the north around Huntly. More recently, a spate of volcanic activity formed the mountains of Pirongia, Karioi, Mangatautari, Mangakawa, and Kakepuku. This was followed by the Ice Ages, when sea levels shrank, and interglacial periods, when they rose again, forming high, level beach terraces and sand dunes and flooding river valleys to form harbors at Raglan, Kawhia, and Aotea. Inland, the young Waikato River carried down vast quantities

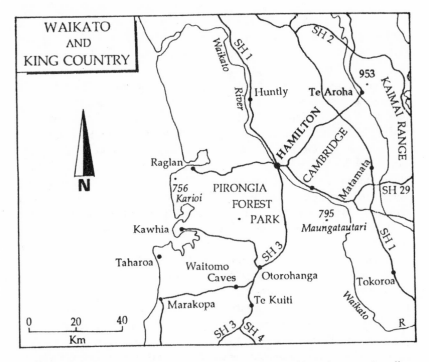

of volcanic material from the central North Island to build up the extensive alluvial plain of the Hamilton basin.

Guarding the entrance of Raglan Harbour to the northwest of Pirongia Mountain is Karioi (755 m), basaltic and part of the same volcanic chain. Raglan Harbour's proximity to Hamilton makes it a popular holiday resort, but the two other harbors to the south are both quiet and comparatively undeveloped. Aotea, the smaller of the two, lies almost cradled beneath the slopes of Karioi and Pirongia, while Kawhia Harbour spreads its shallow, watery fingers far into the hills to the south.

The Kawhia region is a center of geological interest; the first ammonite discovered in New Zealand was found here by the Austrian geologist Ferdinand Hochstetter. In 1977 a huge ammonite, measuring 1.4 m across, was found near Taharoa in rocks about 142 million years old. It took a year to unearth it, and it is now in the Auckland Museum. Taharoa is the site of ironsand mining. An estimated 300 million tons of titanomagnetite lie within this ironsand resource, the largest in the country. Ironsand occurs along the west coast of the North Island between Wanganui and Muriwai north of Auckland. It is thought to be the remnants of ancient Taranaki volcanoes, swept along by coastal currents as sea levels fluctuated. The ironsand is dredged, upgraded, and stockpiled. At shiploading time the concentrate is mixed with water to form a slurry that is pumped to a mooring buoy offshore and from there to bulk ore carriers from Japan.

HISTORY

The rich, peaceful Waikato farmlands saw many bloody conflicts in years past — first between Maori tribes vying for dominance, and later between Maori and *pakeha* over land. Kawhia is the homeland of all Maori people of Tainui descent, and its links with the past are strong. It was here that the great Tainui canoe finally came to rest and was tied to a pohutukawa tree. Called Tangi te Korowhiti, this majestic tree, revered by the Tainui people for generations, is still alive and is believed to be one of the largest in New Zealand. When the Tainui people arrived, the land around Kawhia belonged to the Kahu–punga-punga tribe, who for about three hundred years held most of the land around the northern parts of the central North Island, particularly the upper Waikato toward Lake Taupo. By the mid-sixteenth century, the Tainui tribes had expanded and consolidated their position and had begun to take over the lands of the Kahu–punga-punga, driving them back to the borders of the Arawa people at Rotorua.

Beginning with the Tainui people's takeover of Kahu–punga-punga lands, the Waikato and King Country regions had a long history of intertribal warfare. About 1725, a war party of Tuwharetoa from Taupo invaded the Waikato, but news of their coming preceded them. The crafty Waikato chief, Te Putu, at first joined battle with them and then feigned a retreat, leading the Tuwharetoa into an ambush in which they suffered a crushing defeat. The Tuwharetoa never again invaded the Waikato.

A petty quarrel in 1804 over a catch of fish sparked more fighting, this time between several tribes. A huge force of Ngati Toa of Kawhia and their allies gathered over the next three years and then moved slowly northward from near Otorohanga to seek revenge on the Maniapoto (King Country) and Waikato tribes. Although outnumbered 7,000 to 1,600, the well-organized and better-led Waikato and Maniapoto drove off their attackers near Te Awamutu in one of the biggest battles fought before muskets were introduced. The defeated Ngati Toa continually sought revenge over the next fourteen years, but were finally forced to migrate south to Kapiti Island under their leader, Te Rauparaha.

As the Ngati Toa-Waikato conflict ended, a war with the Ngapuhi of Auckland began that lasted for almost four years. Hongi Hika of the Bay of Islands had acquired muskets and used them against his old rivals, the Tainui tribes.

After defeating some Tainui south of Auckland, Hongi marched across the Hauraki Plains and by trickery captured and burned the great Totara Pa just south of Thames in 1821. The next year he invaded the Waikato and scattered the lower Waikato tribes. Ten thousand men, women, and children waited for him at Matakitaki but, in spite of high palisades and a strong natural position, they were defeated by Hongi's muskets. Soon after, peace between the two tribes was ensured by the marriage of Hongi's daughter to a cousin of the Waikato chief.

Further conflict between subtribes of the Tainui followed, with raids and counterraids over the next seven years. A truce was called in 1830. Then from 1831 to 1834, combined Waikato and Ngati Maniapoto war parties under the chieftainship of Te Whero Whero invaded Taranaki. Following their victory at Pukerangiora Pa near Waitara, they met very strong opposition when attacking Otaka (New Plymouth), where the defenders had help from eight pakeha armed with four ship's guns. While these raids were in progress, the Ngapuhi sent more war parties to the lower Waikato. Near Rangiriri, they surprised and slaughtered fifty men. The Waikato hastily organized retaliatory war parties and pursued the Ngapuhi, eventually overtaking and defeating them at Kawau Island in the Hauraki Gulf. Elated by their success, the Waikato continued up the coast, subduing a large pa at Whangarei and laying waste as far as Ngunguru before returning home satisfied.

Almost thirty years of peace followed, during which the teachings of the missionaries brought an end to cannibalism and lessened intertribal warfare. One of the first to come was the Reverend William Williams in 1833, followed a year later by James Hamlin and A. N. Brown. All described the countryside as devoid of human life because of Hongi Hika's raids. Through necessity the first missionaries were also farmers, and they encouraged the Maori to plant crops and fruit trees and also taught them to read and write. From 1835, trade along the Waikato River increased steadily, as the Maori were happy to provide scraped flax in exchange for European goods, particularly muskets. Eventually the founding of Auckland, with its open markets, changed this; the traders took their wares there to sell.

Further conflict began brewing in 1840, when the chiefs Te Whero Whero and Wiremu Tamehana refused to sign the Treaty of Waitangi and commit the Waikato and King Country tribes to British sovereignty. The idea of having a Maori king was first raised in 1853 at a gathering of central North Island tribes, but was not well received. At another gathering the next year it was resolved that no more land would be sold to the government and there would be no roads. It was further decided that a king should be elected, and during meetings in 1857, the powerful Waikato chief Potatau Te Whero took the title. Potatau I was by then already an old man, and when he died in 1860 he was replaced by his son Tawhiao (Potatau II).

Dislike of the government hardened to opposition when conflict arose over the sale of land at Waitara, and before long the unrest spread to the Waikato. Alleging that the Waikato people were about to invade the growing township of Auckland, government troops occupied the Waikato in 1862, and after several skirmishes, the Kingite capital at Ngaruawahia was abandoned and the Maori withdrew toward Te Awamutu and Kihikihi. By 1864, the government troops reached the fortified pa of Orakau, and here Rewi Maniapoto, a supreme chief by common consent, and his men held out against overwhelming odds. Short of food and tormented by thirst, they were subjected to a continual barrage of shells, bullets, and hand grenades from the 1,800 British troops who surrounded the pa. In spite of severe casualties, the fight continued, with the Maori saving their few bullets for daylight firing and hurling grenades back at the British before they could explode. When offered the chance to surrender, Rewi cried out, "Peace shall never be made—never, never." The defenders then broke out in a mass and, armed only with tomahawks and their last few rounds of ammunition, dashed through the British troops, who hesitated to fire for fear of hitting each other. Of the 300 Maori defending the pa, about 160 were killed and at least half of the survivors were wounded.

By the time Wiremu Tamehana made peace a month later, relations between the two races had been badly damaged. Waikato land was confiscated and the Kingite Maori were forced to retreat south of the Puniu River, near Kihikihi. The area became known as the King Country, and for ten years no attempts were made by either side to negotiate. Settlers quickly moved onto the confiscated lands, and towns grew at the garrison settlements of Ngaruawahia, Pirongia, Cambridge, and Kihikihi. In contrast, Kawhia township, which had been a busy timber and flax trading center from the early 1800s, and a port from which grain and vegetables where shipped to the California gold fields, suffered a reversal in fortunes. Its commercial heyday came to an abrupt end as the wars gained momentum and white people were barred from the entire King Country.

By 1875 the growing colony needed access to the central part of the North Island through the King Country. Generous offers were made by the government to restore tribal lands in exchange for Tawhiao giving up his kingship, but these were rejected because they would cause a loss of mana. Eventually agreement was reached without the Maori kingship being abandoned, and Waikato people were allowed to leave the King Country and return to their own territory. Although they did not regain confiscated lands, a capital for the Kingite movement was reestablished at Turangawaewae Marae, Ngaruawahia, and this is still the focus of spiritual and cultural life for Maori of the region.

Even when peace was restored in 1881, the reopening of Kawhia as a port was opposed by the Kingites, and lacking good rail and road links, it remained small and comparatively undeveloped. The rest of the King Country was gradually opened up as the Main Trunk Railway was pushed slowly south and the towns of Te Kuiti and Taumarunui were established to serve the line.

◆PLACES TO VISIT AND THINGS TO DO

Hamilton

The city of Hamilton is not exactly a center for adventure tourism, but outlying areas offer plenty of scope for walking, swimming, fishing, caving, and exploring. Within the town there are walkways along the banks of the Waikato River and around Hamilton Lake behind the main shopping area. You can also cruise the river on the **Waipa Delta,** a paddle steamer cum licensed restaurant. Not far north of the city and west of Ngaruawahia are the **Waingaro Hot Springs,** with New Zealand's largest open waterslide. The pools are open daily from 9 A.M. to 10 P.M. The Waikato Visitor Centre is located in Ward St., Hamilton, if you need directions, advice, or to book tours within the region.

Around Raglan

The popular resort town of Raglan has all shopping facilities, a motor camp, and a motel. One of its main attractions is the surf at the harbor entrance, and devotees of surfing are offered a variety of low-cost accommodations. Even if you don't surf yourself, it's easy to spend time watching those who do. One of the most spectacular drives in the Waikato is from Raglan around the seaward flank of **Mt. Karioi.** From Whale Bay the narrow road twists and turns, with spectacular views, down to the sea. About halfway around the mountain is the **Te Toto Gorge,** and a short distance farther are the carpark and the start of the track to the summit. The track ascends farmland through manuka then wind-blasted bush, and from a grassy knob, reached after about 45 minutes, there are extensive views up and down the coast to the entrances to Raglan, Aotea, and Kawhia harbors. Ahead, along a sawtooth ridge, is the lookout point at the seaward summit of Karioi (716 m). It's a steep climb, but the many tree roots for foot- and handholds make it relatively easy. Unfortunately the thick bush limits the views, but they are still worth the effort. Most people are content to reach the lookout, but you can continue along the ridge for another hour to the true summit, through stunted, wind-shorn bush carpeted with the fallen leaves of mountain neinei. Allow about 3 hours for the return walk to the lookout, and 5 hours if you go to the summit.

South, around the base of the mountain, you'll encounter dramatic coastal views before you reach Te Mata, where you can return to Raglan or continue on toward Makomako and Kawhia. The beautiful **Bridal Veil Falls,** which plunge 55 m over a sheer, bush-hung cirque, is not far along the road to Kawhia. A viewing platform at the top is reached by a 10-minute walk along a wide, easy track, and the more ambitions can continue down steps to the base of the falls.

Maungatautari Mountain

The ancient andesitic cone of Maungatautari to the southwest of Cambridge is believed to have formed almost 2 million years ago. Its two summits, Pukeatua and Maungatautari (795 m), are densely forested and traversed by a north-south trail. The most popular walk to Maungatautari summit, taking around 3 hours return, starts from the end of Hicks Road on the south side of Lake Karapiro. From Cambridge, take SH 1 toward Rotorua for 7 km, then turn right over the Karapiro Dam. Turn left at the next intersection and continue past the Karapiro Lake Domain (you can camp here) to Maungatautari Village. Hicks Road branches right opposite the school.

From the road end, the route is over farmland for about 15 minutes to a well-defined track in the bush. The ascent is gradual at first, through attractive, tall tawa forest; then it steepens toward the stop, where stunted kamahi, tawari, and horopito are dominant. Views from the top extend eastward over Matamata to the Kaimai Range and Mt. Te Aroha. Below are the elongated lakes of Karapiro and Arapuni, and westward, the town of Te Awamutu can be seen at the base of Mt. Pirongia.

Kawhia

If you are looking for a quiet, peaceful spot, the gentle, unassuming, sleepy Kawhia may be just the place. It has motel and hotel accommodations in town and motor camps to the north and south. The fishing is good from the wharf during the hour before and after high tide, particularly if it falls at early morning or dusk, or you can try your luck for snapper by surfcasting along the harbor entrance channel. For flounder, try the shallow sandy flats along the foreshore.

Fed by five rivers and covering over 6,000 ha, much of the harbor's bed is exposed at low tide. Despite this, the harbor entrance is deep, scoured daily by the massive volume of water that flows out with each low tide. It has been estimated that average tidal flow through the entrance is almost 200,000 cu m of water a minute, with the maximum flow of almost 340,000 cu m occurring at two-thirds ebb tide.

Ocean Beach, just north of the harbor, has good surf, or you can dig in the sand between low- and half-tide for the hot and cold water that bubbles up. Both the beach and Te Puia Springs are signposted. The walk from the wharf along the foreshore to Karewa, passing the historic pohutukawa tree, Tangi te Korowhiti, on the way, and continuing around the beach to the point south of the marae at Maketu is pleasant. Across the harbor entrance is the tiny fishing village of Te Maiki, accessible only by boat.

The drive around Kawhia Harbour through Kinohaku and Te Waitere is long and tortuous, through country dominated by impressive towers of rock. Next to Kawhia, these were two of the harbor's major settlements. Te Waitere, a pleasant village with a wharf that's popular for fishing, can be reached by small boat from Kawhia, a much quicker trip than via the road. The road to Taharoa branches off between Te Waitere and Kinohaku, or you can turn off at Kinohaku for Te Anga. At Te Anga you have a choice of turning inland to Waitomo, passing the beautiful Marakopa Falls, the Piripiri Caves, and the Mangapohue Natural Bridge on the way, or continuing to Marakopa and on down the scenic back route to Awakino and SH 3.

Otorohanga Kiwi House and Bird Park

This excellent bird park, set among pleasant gardens, is one of the best places to view some of New Zealand's endangered bird species. As well as an excellent kiwi house, where kiwis can be watched going about their normal business in night time gloom, it has the country's largest walk-through aviary, housing the rare stitchbird, saddleback, and other less frequently seen species in a very natural setting. They also have tuatara and geckos. The park is open daily from 10 A.M. to 5 P.M.

Te Kuiti

The railway running down one side of the main street makes Te Kuiti's origins immediately apparent. The town's name is an abbreviation of Te Kuititanga, meaning "the narrowing in," which may refer either to the constriction of the Mangaokewa Valley here or to the Maori land confiscations after the Waikato War. After the battle of Orakau, fought near Te Awamutu in 1864, followers of the Maori King Movement sought refuge here, and Te Kuititanga became home to King Tawhiao for seventeen years. Europeans dared not enter the King Country during this time, but for Te Kooti, fleeing from government troops after his unsuccessful campaigns in the Urewera country, it was a sanctuary until he was pardoned.

The town has a pleasant walk along the Mangaokewa Stream, from Redwood Park at the southern end to the railway bridge at the northern end. Only 3 km out of town, along SH 30, is the pleasant **Mangaokewa Gorge Scenic Reserve,** reached by a short narrow side road under the Waitete Viaduct. At the road end is a pleasant picnic and camping area, with toilets, picnic tables, and barbecue sites, set in a grove of eucalyptus, conifers, and deciduous trees among bush and limestone bluffs. The stream has good swimming holes, and there are tracks on both sides of the stream.

Pirongia Forest Park

Bush-mantled Pirongia Mountain lies directly west of Te Awamutu and is easily reached from Hamilton. The name, meaning "the scented presence of Kahu," is an abbreviation of Pirongia-Te Aroao-O-Kahu. Kahupeka, the wife of a chief, once stopped on the mountain slopes and anointed her body with the oil of crushed leaves.

Pirongia was formed about 2.5 million years ago from several centers of activity along a deep-seated northwest-to-southeast fracture in the earth's crust. Successive eruptions of basaltic lava and ash built up cones around the main centers of Pirongia and Karioi, and these eventually combined to form the present mountain. Much of the forest on the lower slopes was logged when the Waikato was settled, but untouched areas within the park are dense and lush, dominated by rimu and totara, with an understory of tawa and kamahi. At higher levels the podocarp and broadleaf forest becomes more stunted and includes mountain flax, *Dracophyllum* species, Hall's totara, and kaikawaka.

The headquarters for the 1,700 ha Pirongia Forest Park is located at **Pirongia Village,** 15 km from Te Awamutu. Known originally as Alexandra, the military settlement grew around a redoubt topping a small hill to the south. To the north, at a small roadside and picnic area near the Mangapiko Stream, is a plaque commemorating the major battle at Matakitaki Pa, when the musket-bearing Ngapuhi Maori slaughtered the locals. At the small visitor center at Pirongia you can see a model of the park, with tracks marked on it, and displays and maps on the geology, flora, and fauna. Check with the Department of Conservation in Hamilton, phone (07)8383-363, or at Pirongia, phone (07)8719-646, for days and times the visitor center is open.

Many tracks climb spurs to the two main summits, Mt. Pirongia (959 m) and The Cone (945 m), and to lesser summits, and traverse the ridges in between. Of the easier walks in the park, one of the most popular is the climb to **Rua Pane** (723 m) along the **Tirohanga Track,** from the end of Corcoran Road. From the turn-off to Te Pahu on the Hamilton–Pirongia Road, it is about 5 km to Corcoran Road, which ascends the northern slopes. The hour-long climb starts in beautiful tawa forest, enriched with a lush undergrowth of kiekie and ferns. The ascent is steady, and toward the top, just past the intersection of the route from Waite Road, the tall tawa forest is replaced with low rewarewa, mahoe, and kamahi as the track ascends a narrow rocky section. Views from the top extend over the Waikato basin and along the ridges to other summits of Pirongia Mountain. The track continues to a second summit (Rua Pane means "two heads") in about 5 minutes and on to Mt. Pirongia, another 3 hours away.

Several tracks start at the pleasant **Kaniwhaniwha Stream** picnic and camping area, reached by a 30- to 40-minute walk across farmland. The access track starts along Limeworks Loop Road, near Te Pahu, and is marked alongside the Kaniwhaniwha Stream to the bush and the park boundary. Here a notice board shows the layout of the many tracks in the area. The path continues through dense bush of kahikatea, rimu, tawa, pukatea, and rewarewa, crosses the stream by a high swing bridge, and about 10 minutes later emerges at a bush-flanked clearing with picnic tables.

Waitomo Caves and Beyond

The King Country's pride and joy is undoubtedly the **Waitomo Caves,** and with good reason. The main Glowworm Cave is spectacular, and the glowworm grotto has to be seen to be believed. There is an admission fee to view the caves, and visitors are taken through in guided groups. No bookings are necessary for individuals or small groups, and the 45-minute tours leave every hour on the hour, from 9 A.M. to 4 P.M. There is more to do at Waitomo than just visit the tourist caves, and it's worth spending more than just a day in the area. The **Caves Museum,** run by the local community, has excellent displays on how limestone caves are formed and explored, an exciting "cave crawl," and a superb 28-minute audiovisual show. Also in the locality is **Rabbit World,** an angora rabbit farm, where you can watch the fluffies being shorn.

A range of accommodations, from hotel, motel, motorcamps, and farm stays, is available at Waitomo and nearby Otorohanga and Hangatiki. The small motor-camp at Waitomo, although pleasant enough, was rather run-down at time of writing. Backpackers or anyone wanting to meet cavers can arrange to stay at the Hamilton Tomo Club's hut, about 1 km along the road from the caves, by phoning (07)8787-442. **Waitomo Horse Trekking** offers budget accommodation as well as 2-hour to full-day or overnight horse treks. They are located 6 km from Hangatiki on the road to Waitomo. Phone (07)8787-649.

For real excitement you can go **black water rafting,** a unique experience of floating through underground passages on an inflatable tube. You wear a wet suit and get a hot shower afterward to warm up after this amazing 3-hour trip. It's very popular, particularly at weekends, so book in advance at the Museum of Caves by writing to Box 12, Waitomo Caves, or by phoning (07)8787-640.

For a genuine caving experience, you can go underground with **Lost World Adventure Caving Trips.** They have an easy 2.5-hour "Taste of Caving" trip for youngsters, oldies, and those with limited time, and two other trips of one and two days. Even the easy trip involves some wading in streams, so you need to wear shoes you don't mind getting wet. On the longer trips, you spend 5 hours underground, following the Mangapu Stream to and from the spectacular Lost World Cavern. The 2-day trip is held on weekends and includes a day's instruction in abseiling, or rappeling, as you start your caving with a 100-m descent into a huge limestone shaft. All equipment is provided, but you need a swimsuit, boots, and a change of warm, dry clothing. Book at least a week in advance at the Museum of Caves, Box 12, Waitomo Caves, phone (07)8787-640, or write to Lost World Adventures, Box 29, Waitomo Caves.

There are several walks in the Waitomo area that take you through this fascinating terrain with its patches of bush, limestone outcrops, and sinkholes. The 5-km-long **Waitomo Walkway** (2.5 hours), starting by the Museum of Caves, has been divided into three sections, each with road access at both ends so that they can be treated as separate walks. One section includes the 1-hour **Ruakuri Caves Walk**, following the Waitomo Stream's course through some spectacular caverns and arches. Do this section at night (take a flashlight), as the glowworms along the river banks are a sight to rival the famous grotto of the main Waitomo Caves. If you go to the Ruakuri Caves Walk by road, continue 500 m past the Glowworm Cave, turn left across the Waitomo Stream, and after 2 to 3 km a signpost will direct you to a parking area and picnic ground at the start of the walk.

For something different, try the **Opapaka Pa Bush Walk** (45 minutes) at **Ohaki Maori Village** 2 km from Waitomo. Information boards along the track describe forest lore and traditional Maori medicinal and utilitarian use of the forest. In the opposite direction, continuing past Waitomo on the scenic road to Marakopa, are more walks. The first is to the **Tawarau Double Waterfall**, a 1.5-hour walk starting from Alpiger Hut at the end of Appletree Road, which takes in native bush, pine plantation, rivers, limestone and, of course, a double waterfall. There are several other tracks in the **Tawarau Forest**, and a pamphlet on these can be obtained from the Department of Conservation in Te Kuiti.

The track to the picturesque **Mangapohue Natural Bridge**, a huge double arch overhung with ferns and trees with a stream flowing beneath, is about 5 km on from Appletree Road. The walk takes about 30 minutes and returns above the arch over pleasant green farmland studded with fluted limestone outcrops. Continue another 4 km to the short track to the Piripiri Caves hidden in the bush. If you want to explore the main cave and its inner cavern containing huge fossil oyster shells, you will need boots, a good flashlight, and clothes you don't mind getting dirty. The return bush walk takes less than 30 minutes, but allow extra time to explore the cave. You can view the **Marakopa Falls** from the road a few kilometers farther on. The river thunders over a spectacular broad leap into a bush-filled valley. A 30-minute return walk through the bush to the base of the falls starts a short distance down the road from the lookout.

Beyond the three houses and pub of Te Anga the countryside opens out into a wide, flat valley flanked by seaward hills. The last 15 km to the coast and Marakopa run through the valley. The small beach settlement of Marakopa, with its row of small houses behind dunes of black sand and a wild sea, is a popular place for catching whitebait and for surfcasting. Although the beach is not very safe for swimming, it attracts surfers. Apart from a couple of places offering casual accommodation there is only a small, uninspiring campground at the old school. It has power sites and a camp store.

If you like backcountry roads and have plenty of time, take the road from **Marakopa to Awakino,** but make sure you have plenty of gasoline; there are no service stations beyond Waitomo on this scenic drive through rugged inland bush country. The first 5 km to the black sands of **Kihitere Beach** are paved but very steep and narrow and are not recommended for caravans. Beyond here there are no difficulties, the road now twists up and down through the lovely bush of the Wharekino Forest, passing a pleasant camping and picnic area beside a stream in the Mangatoa Scenic Reserve. **Waikawau Beach,** about halfway between Marakopa and Awakino, is worth visiting. The last 500 m of road are very narrow, ending abruptly at an even narrower tunnel beside a small picnic and camping area. Walk through the tunnel and you'll find yourself on a wild black beach backed by high cliffs and raked by a pounding surf. The tunnel was dug by hand early this century to allow stock to be driven along the beach rather than across the rugged inland hills.

Western Kaimai Range

The steep escarpment of the Kaimai Range, which extends from the Karangahake Gorge near Paeroa southward to the Mamaku Plateau, forms the eastern boundary of the Waikato. Much of the range is included within the **Kaimai-Mamaku Forest Park,** administered by the Department of Conservation from Tauranga and Rotorua. Some tracks in the eastern side of the park are described in the Rotorua–Bay of Plenty section of this book. The western side also has some interesting and scenic walks including the ascent of Mt. Te Aroha. All the following walks are easily reached from Matamata or Te Aroha, or you could base yourself at the motor camp at Okauia Hot Springs and take advantage of the hot pools.

Te Aroha Mountain

The 953 m summit of Te Aroha Mountain, highest point in the Kaimai Range, rises steeply behind the small town of Te Aroha and, as would be expected, provides outstanding views over the Waikato, Hauraki Plains, and Kaimai Ranges. A television transmitter on the summit is linked to the town by a steep winding road, but this is not open to the public. If you want to drive to the summit, you can go with a locally conducted tour, booked through the Te Aroha Public Relations Office at the southern end of town near the Te Aroha Domain gates. The only other way to reach the top is by walking.

Two routes lead to the summit. The **Mountain Tracks** network is the longest. It can be started from Tui Road, from a parking area a short distance farther on up the mountain road, or from the end of Hamilton St. The **Domain Track,** taking about 2.5 hours one way, starts in the Domain, beside the Mokena Geyser and hot spa baths. The partly benched, well-worn track climbs through pines and regenerating bush, which give way to kanuka and more mature bush as height is gained, to reach Whakapipi or Bald Spur viewpoint (349 m) in about 50 minutes. The summit is another 1.5 hours away, and after an easy section through a connecting saddle the climb steepens through forests of tawa and tawari, then neinei and gnarled, moss-hung silver beech to emerge by the transmitting tower and building. The best views are had from the highest point on the other side of the transmitter. The return can be made by the Mountain Tracks network, which begins on the south side, opposite the transmitter station door. There are several side tracks, but by turning left at each junction you should come around the back of the mountain, pass the old Tui Mine workings, and eventually return to the Domain.

Wairongomai Valley Tracks

The Wairongomai Valley on the south side of Te Aroha mountain was once the scene of intense gold mining activity. It is reached by continuing south from Te Aroha along the Gordon–Shaftsbury Road for 3 km, turning left into Wairongomai Loop Road, then left again along a short side road. Within the valley a network of tracks, mainly along the remains of tramlines, pack tracks, and water races, leads to scenes of past activity. The first traces of gold were found in 1880, and the main reef was discovered the following year. Initial assays were promising, but in spite of large investments of capital there was little return. The gold was difficult to extract, and a lack of water to drive the battery machinery, especially at dry times, was another problem. Around 1884, the town of Wairongomai, sited near the present carpark, had a population approaching four thousand people, twelve shops, and three hotels. The booklet *A Guide to the Wairongomai Valley*, describing the area's history and tracks, is available from the Department of Conservation office at Waharoa or the Te Aroha Public Relations Office.

Tracks into the valley start just above the concrete bins beside the carpark; a signboard map shows their layout. The easiest walk is to the **Bendigo Battery** along the **Water Race Track** running above and parallel with the stream. After 30 to 40 minutes, a junction is reached near a short tunnel. One side track leads down to the large, corrugated-iron cyanide tanks, concrete hopper foundations, and scraps of timber, iron, and wire of the Bendigo Battery site beside the stream; another climbs very steeply for a short distance to connect with the tramline at the foot of Butler's Incline. The main track continues up the valley for another 20 to 30 minutes to another junction.

A 2.5-hour loop walk can be made by following the **Bulldozer Track** (left from the carpark sign) to near the top of **Butler's Incline,** then returning down the incline and connecting track to the Bendigo Battery. At the top of Butler's Incline are the remains of the winding gear. The circuit can be extended to 4 or 5 hours by continuing to the head of the valley via the **Tramline** and **May Queen Incline,** or via the **Pack Track** to **Hardy's Hut** and a campsite with toilets and fireplaces on a terrace where a miners' camp and store once stood.

Dilapidated Hardy's Hut was miner Edwin Hardy's residence and is now a protected historic building.

Wairere Falls

The magnificent Wairere Falls, plunging 153 m in two leaps from the crest of the Kaimai Range, can be seen from many places between Matamata and Te Aroha but can only be truly appreciated from close up. A detour to view them is well worth the time, and as a bonus, the walk is one of the most beautiful along the western side of the Kaimai Range. The track to the falls, following an old route used by the Maori to cross the Kaimai Range from the Bay of Plenty, begins from a carpark at the end of Goodwin Road, signposted on Old Te Aroha Road about 15 km from Matamata via Okauia Springs. After crossing an attractive boulder-strewn terrace, the track ascends through dense bush beside the swift Wairere Stream, tumbling and cascading between huge boulders in a narrow bush-lined gorge. The track then climbs an impressive flight of wooden steps to a lookout over the falls. To reach the top of the falls, backtrack a short distance from the lookout and continue zig-zagging upward to a three-way junction. Downstream is another breathtaking viewpoint from the edge of the escarpment. A stroll back up the stream, slow-moving here and silent, will bring you in about 20 minutes to an area of majestic kahikatea and rimu trees. Allow about 45 minutes to reach the first lookout and another 45 minutes to climb to the top of the falls.

Rapurapu Kauri Grove

If you don't mind getting wet feet, you'll find this walk at the southern end of the Kaimai Range delightful. The track access is AA signposted on SH 29 (Hamilton–Tauranga) where the road starts to climb to the top of the range. It's on the right, almost 7 km past Te Poi and 2 km past Rapurapu Road. The walk starts along a farm track, then enters bush and descends to Rapurapu Stream after 30 to 40 minutes. From here the wide, boulder-strewn stream is followed for about the same time again, with eight crossings, to a grove of three large kauri and many young rickers. The streamside scenery of towering kahikatea and rimu is refreshingly cool and beautiful.

As another diversion, if you drive 1 km along Rapurapu Road, you'll find a large picnic area under shady poplars beside the Rapurapu Stream. It's a popular spot in summer for swimming and has toilets, changing sheds, and barbecue sites.

USEFUL ADDRESSES

Waikato Visitor Centre, Box 970, Hamilton, phone (07)8393-360.
Department of Conservation, Private Bag, Hamilton, phone (07)8383-363.
Museum of Caves, Box 12, Waitomo Caves, phone (07)8787-640.

9 ✦ ROTORUA AND THE BAY OF PLENTY

LANDSCAPE

First impressions of Rotorua are that it is a slick tourist town where everything is aimed to separate visitors from their hard-earned dollars in the shortest possible time. There are numerous souvenir shops selling some good things, but also a lot that is high on the kitsch scale. The main road south is lined with motels, each one advertising itself with garish neon signs designed to lure customers, and the information office seems more interested in booking you on something to somewhere than actually dispensing information. But don't let all this put you off. Behind the brash promotion is a region of wonderfully diverse scenery—hot springs, mud pools, volcanoes, lakes, islands, golden surf beaches, forests—and many things to do. Rotorua and the Bay of Plenty were seemingly designed for lovers of the outdoors, as well as for farmers, foresters, and horticulturalists.

The first thing most visitors notice in Rotorua is the all-pervasive smell of eggs—hydrogen sulphide from the numerous thermal areas—but that quickly fades as the olfactory sense adjusts. Lying as it does along the Taupo Volcanic Zone, the region's history of violent eruptions goes back to ancient eras and includes very recent times. Unlike the large, active andesitic volcanoes of Ruapehu, Ngauruhoe, and White Island, the volcanic centers around Rotorua have created a landscape of high plateaus and sunken basins. Instead of building mountains, these eruptions produced vast quantities of superheated rock fragments and gases that flowed outward from several vents to solidify as huge sheets of ignimbrite, a welded rock of rhyolitic composition.

Formed at shallower levels in the earth's crust than andesitic lava, rhyolitic lava has a higher silica content and is less dense. Being more buoyant, it tends to rise, and eventually protrudes through the overlying crust. Associated with the pyroclastic flows that form the ignimbrite sheets is the formation of calderas, the extrusion of lava domes, and explosive eruptions of pumice tephra. Following a massive outpouring of lava, the roof of the magma chamber tends to collapse, forming a caldera. The Rotorua basin is one such caldera, formed about 170,000 years ago, after the outflows of ignimbrite that produced the Mamaku Plateau to the west. These flows covered about 3,000 sq km. Rotorua's hot springs, mud pools, and geysers are another result of shallower magma bringing heat sources closer to the earth's surface.

Adjacent to the Rotorua basin is the Haroharo Caldera, containing Lakes Rotoma, Rotoehu, eastern Rotoiti, Okataina, and Tarawera. It lies within the Okataina Volcanic Centre, which produced at least four eruptions between

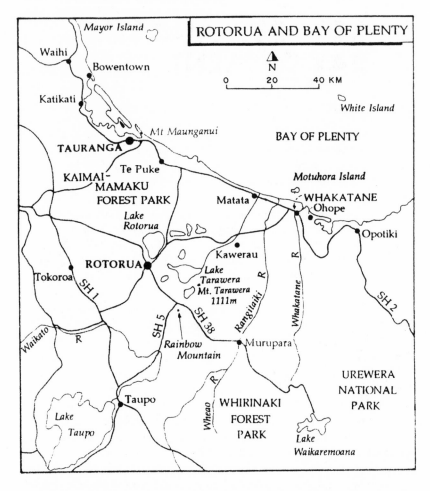

260,000 and 40,000 years ago. The earliest of these eruptions produced the Matahina Ignimbrites, which reached the coast at Matata and extended west to Pikowhai. In places, this rock has been overlain by younger sheets, such as the Kaingaroa Ignimbrites, which formed the Kaingaroa Plateau. Once all the magma has been discharged and the chamber has collapsed, new but less volatile magma starts to collect again, raising the caldera floor. Being more viscous, this new lava is extruded slowly. Steep-sided domes grow as the outside layers cool and solidify, while new lava continues to be injected from below.

There are about 150 rhyolite domes within the Taupo Volcanic Centre. Most spectacular of these is Mt. Tarawera, whose three domes formed only about 900 years ago. The mountain then lay dormant for 800 years, and Maori and

Europeans alike stopped regarding it as a volcano. That complacency was shattered one winter night in 1886, when Tarawera erupted violently. Tremors felt shortly after midnight increased steadily until 1:30 A.M., when there was a tremendous explosion accompanied by a blinding flash of light. The noise was heard as far away as Auckland. By 2:30 A.M. the activity had increased along the whole length of the three summits, producing a huge ash cloud charged with electricity. About an hour later, the bed of Lake Rotomahana was torn apart, throwing steam and mud skyward. Intense eruptions continued for another two hours and then gradually died down.

Accompanying the tremendous upthrust of gases and steam was a tornado-like inrush of air that destroyed the forests around Blue Lake. The village of Te Wairoa was buried and twenty-eight Maori residents died. At first, buildings withstood the rain of airborne debris, but as mud thrown up from Rotomahana accumulated, the weight of it eventually crushed them. Within a few hours an estimated 500 million cu m of ash had been ejected and spread over 15,000 sq km. As well, masses of scoria and rock fell close to the mountain and lay heaped to depths of over 60 m in some places.

By 6 A.M. the eruptions were lessening in violence, but the huge cloud of ash hung over Rotorua, keeping all in darkness, until 9 A.M., when the wind changed and moved it toward Tauranga. The clear dawn here reverted quickly to darkness as the cloud moved over the land and out to sea. In the late morning, daylight returned to reveal the whole district blanketed in thick grey mud.

At the northeastern end of the Taupo Volcanic Zone, where it meets the sea at the Bay of Plenty coast, the land is flat. Once a vast swampland where flax grew in abundance, it has since been drained and its rivers diverted to produce the fertile dairy land of the Rangitaiki plains. Here the Matahina Ignimbrite Sheet has been downtilted to form the Whakatane graben. Twenty kilometers wide at the coast, this depression becomes narrower inland. Its western boundary fault crosses the coast at Matata. Elsewhere, low rolling hills reach to the edge of the coast, in places forming high cliffs edged with fine sand beaches. Westward, around the huge sweeping bay, is Te Puke, the center for kiwi fruit growing. Then comes the city of Tauranga, sprawling around the shores of its harbor. Originally a mission station and military settlement, Tauranga stayed a quiet farming town until an expanding horticulture industry and the maturing of neighboring pine forests turned it into an important port. At Tauranga, low hills are replaced by the steep, bush-covered Kaimai Ranges, which form a western boundary to sprawling, indented Tauranga Harbour. Containing the harbor waters are huge sandbars, the southern one joining Mt. Maunganui to the mainland.

Tauranga Harbour has two entrances, the southern one at Mt. Maunganui being the main one. Between the two entrances is flat, pine-covered Matakana Island.

HISTORY

That Rotorua and the Bay of Plenty are steeped in Maori tradition and legend is not surprising, as it was here that two canoes carrying settlers from Hawaiki were said to have made landfall. The Arawa canoe, under the chieftainship of Tama-te-Kapua, is said to have beached at Maketu. Ihenga, a grandson of the chief, first discovered Lake Rotoiti, which he named Te-Roto-iti-kite-a-Ihenga (the little lake seen by Ihenga). On reaching Lake Rotorua, which he named Roto-rua-nui-a-Kahu (the second big lake of Kahu), he found that there were already people there. By trickery he managed to lay claim to the land around Rotorua and here the Arawa people settled.

Between Lakes Rotoiti and Rotoehu is a short isthmus covered in tall tawa forest. The short walking track here is known as Hongi's Track, as it was through here in 1823 that Hongi Hika, a Ngapuhi chief from the Bay of Islands, portaged his canoes from the coast to Rotorua. His intention was to attack the Arawa people. Forewarned, the Arawa had taken refuge on Mokoia Island in the center of Lake Rotorua, but they had only traditional spears and clubs, and Hongi's men were armed with muskets. The gulls that circle the island are said to be the spirits of the slain Arawa chiefs and are therefore sacred.

Mokoia Island is also the setting of a love story. Hinemoa, a beautiful maiden of high birth, fell in love, against her family's wishes, with Tutanekai, a young warrior who lived on Mokoia. At night Tutanekai would play his flute to guide Hinemoa, should she come to the island by canoe. To prevent this, her family had beached all the canoes, so in desperation Hinemoa swam to the island. Arriving cold and shivering she warmed herself in a hot pool before being found by Tutanekai.

The Ngati Awa people of Whakatane trace their ancestry to the Mataatua canoe, which landed near the present town. Legend tells how the men went ashore, leaving the women to guard the canoe, but when it started to drift away the women were powerless to stop it because paddles were *tapu*. Eventually, Wairaka, the captain's daughter, seized a paddle and cried out, "I will act like a man." Other women helped her and brought the canoe safely back to shore. In recognition of this act the place was named Whakatane, meaning "to be manly." A statue of Wairaka stands on the rocks at Whakatane Heads.

Early settlement of the Bay of Plenty and Rorotua was hampered by the wars in the Waikato, where Maori loyal to the government fought those siding with the Kingite movement. Once the wars ended, the thermal areas around Rotorua attracted many visitors, and eventually the government developed the place as a spa town and visitor center. Like many other North Island towns, Tauranga began as a mission station and expanded to become a military settlement. For many years it was a quiet place to retire to, but with the growth of agriculture and timber shipping, the population expanded dramatically.

Whakatane, a prosperous little town serving the plains farmers and now the center for regional government, stands at the mouth of the Whakatane River, whose source lies deep in the heart of the Urewera Ranges to the south. Considered a rough frontier town a century ago, it now wears an air of respectability. Early European visitors were probably whalers, but the first recorded ship's visit was that of the mission schooner *Herald* from Northland in 1828. Although the town served last century as a port for the flax trade, all ambitious plans since then to increase shipping activity have come to nought because of the treacherous bar at the entrance. Today the wharf serves commercial fishing boats and charter vessels for sightseeing, game fishing, and diving trips.

Inland, along the eastern edge of the Rangitaiki plains, where the Tarawera River leaves the hills, is the region's newest town, Kawerau, built in 1953 to serve the huge pulp and paper mills using logs from the Kaingaroa forest. When it was discovered that the high volcanic plateau was unsuitable for raising cattle (the animals died of "bush sickness" caused by a lack of cobalt in the soil), it was planted in pine forests, which flourished. By 1936, the trees covered more than 100,000 ha, making Kaingaroa the largest planted forest in the world at that time. Looming over this industrial scene stands Mt. Edgecumbe, or Putauaki, a cone of andesitic lava thought to be last active about A.D. 950.

◆PLACES TO VISIT AND THINGS TO DO AROUND ROTORUA

Whakarewarewa Forest

Almost at the back door of some of Rotorua's largest hotels is the Whakarewarewa State Forest Park (3,860 ha), which plays the dual roles of wood production and public recreation area. Numerous tracks criss-cross the park, providing varied routes for walking and jogging. There are also pony trails and areas set aside for trail and mountain bikes. The entire forest—except for small, isolated pockets of native bush around Blue Lake—is planted in exotic trees. In autumn, golden larches break up the somber green. Most of the longer trails start from the main park entrance behind the Forest Research Institute on Long Mile Road. You can obtain maps there, showing the various tracks, their times and distances.

Two very scenic lakes within the forest, Green Lake (Rotokakahi) and Blue Lake (Tikitapu) named for their contrasting colors, have pleasant picnic areas and walking tracks. Green Lake, 13 km south of Rotorua on SH 5, is privately owned and cannot be used for fishing or swimming, whereas Blue Lake, beside SH 32 to Lake Tarawera, is probably one of the most popular recreation spots close to the city. During summer weekends its shores are packed with picnickers, swimmers, and boaties enjoying the crystal clear waters and the neighboring campground is packed with campers.

Lake Okataina

For unspoiled beauty, Lake Okataina is unsurpassed. Completely surrounded by native forests its deep, clear waters are renowned for their excellent trout fishing. Lake Okataina was an important lacustrine route for the Maori people of the area, as canoes could be portaged across the narrow strips of land separating it from Lakes Tarawera and Rotoiti. The old trails used are still followed today by motorists and walkers. The narrow, 7-km-long access road from Ruato Bay at Lake Rotoiti hints at the beauty to come as it climbs through a tunnel of overhanging bush.

The bush surrounding Lake Okataina has undergone change, with the original podocarp and hardwood forest being destroyed when Mt. Tarawera erupted. Regeneration since then has been swift, and surrounding hillsides are now clothed in tall kamahi, kanuka, and rewarewa. Several walking tracks start at or near Lake Okataina and a pamphlet and map describing these (*A Guide to Lake Okataina Scenic Reserve*) is available from the Department of Conservation. Of these walks perhaps the best are the Eastern Okataina Walkway, the Ngahopua Track, and the ascent of Mt. Whakapoungakau on the Western Okataina Walkway.

Eastern Okataina Walkway is a 20-km return walk along the eastern side of Lake Okataina and across to Lake Tarawera. The scenery is superb and in summer there are refreshing swimming opportunities. As the southern end of the lake is approached, the views down to the water are breathtaking. Pohutukawa trees hang out from the steep slopes over the water which, depending on the depth, and amount of light and shade, varies in color from light turquoise through kingfisher blue to deep green. In December the pohutukawa are ablaze with crimson blooms. Normally a coastal tree, the pohutukawa grows well here in the volcanic soil. From Otangimoana Bay at the southern end, the track continues south, crossing a low ridge and descending to Lake Tarawera at Humphries Bay in about 20 minutes. The scenery is equally impressive here, with views across the lake to Mt. Tarawera, looming bulkily on the skyline. Allow a full day for the trip.

From Humphries Bay it is possible to continue around the northern shore of Lake Tarawera to the outlet, a distance of 7 km, taking 2 to 3 hours. Camping is permitted at Humphries Bay, but there are no facilities.

Mt. Whakapoungakau and the Western Okataina Walkway

The complete Western Okataina Walkway is 22.5 km long, starting at Ruato Bay on Lake Rotoiti, and finishing at Millar Road on Lake Okareka, but it can be broken into shorter sections. The most interesting part is the ascent to Whakapoungakau Trig (758 m) located on a spur track that gives sweeping views. Mayor Island and steaming White Island stand out in the Bay of Plenty, while to the south the the volcanic trend is continued with the brooding masses of

Tarawera and Mt. Tauhara on the shores of Lake Taupo. Westward and immediately below are the shining waters of Lakes Rotorua and Rotoiti.

The walkway can be gained at the Okataina Recreation Centre, on the Lake Okataina access road. From the carpark at the education centre the track climbs steadily to the south up a leading spur with views down to Lake Rotoiti. The turnoff to the trig (to the north or right) is signposted, and the summit is reached in about 1.5 hours. The mown grass effect around the trig is created by wallabies, Australian imports that inhabit the reserve.

Ngahopua (Crater Lakes) Walk

Followed in a counterclockwise direction, this 45-minute loop track climbs gently through tawa and rimu forest to the rim of Rotoatua (Lake of the Gods) set in a deep, steep-sided pit. There are spectacular views down to its green waters 100 m below. Rotongata (Mirror Lake), a smaller lake with more bluish-colored water, is visible in its reed-fringed bowl-like depression before the track returns to its starting point. These lakes and three other craters to the west were formed simultaneously about 3,500 years ago by explosions that blew out an estimated 500 million cu m of material.

Rainbow Mountain and Kerosene Creek

Maungakakaramea (mount of colored earth), or **Rainbow Mountain,** a dacite volcano formed about 900 years ago, is named for the multicolored clays in its steaming cliffs. It lies 28 km south of Rotorua between the junction of SH 5 and SH 38. The summit is crowned with a forestry fire lookout for the very reason that the view from here is spectacular. You can either drive or walk to the fire lookout, and there is also a walking track around the mountain. To drive up, take SH 38 to the Waiotapu Forestry Village for a permit and directions. The forestry road climbs steeply to a parking area on a high shoulder of the mountain, and from here it is a 10-minute walk to the lookout.

Walking around Rainbow Mountain takes about 4 hours, but a shorter walk can be made on the same track to view the vivid green Lake Rotowhero and two small explosion craters beneath the steaming red, orange, and brown cliffs, all of which are close to the road. The track starts on SH 5, about 1 km south of the junction with SH 38, at a grassy parking area on the left, immediately before a gravel road (Old Waiotapu Road) and small bridge with white railings. A sign at the parking area indicates the start of the Crater Rim Walk. At a junction reached in about 5 minutes, turn left to view the explosion craters and right for views of Lake Rotowhero. You can also view Lake Rotowhero by going a short distance down Old Waiotapu Road.

Kerosene Creek (Hakereteke Stream) is one of the very few places around Rotorua where you can have a hot swim for free. The only improvements made to this natural hot swimming hole are a good access track and a punga-walled changing shed to protect your modesty. You might find the water too hot in summer, but it's a great place when days are cooler. Follow Old Waiotapu Road for 2.6 km and look for the track leading from an ill-defined parking area on the right. The track may not be signposted. The swimming pools are reached in a couple of minutes.

Mt. Tarawera

Whether you walk, drive, or fly up Mt. Tarawera, you're sure to get a bit of an adrenalin buzz. From a distance the summit gives no hint of the deep craters that rend its rounded domes in an awe-inspiring, jagged fissure several kilometers long. Steam vents around the rim of the westernmost crater, Lake Rotomahana, were active for several years after the eruption in 1886. During the blast, the world famous Pink and White Terraces — beautiful, vast sinter formations that had taken thousands of years to form on the lake edge — were not just buried but were completely blown apart.

There is more than one route up Tarawera. Two tracks branch off Tarawera Road, and the start of one of these is described in the section on Tarawera Outlet and Falls. The easiest route is from Ashpit Road, Rerewhakaaitu. Take SH 38 (toward Murupara) past the Waiotapu Forestry Headquarters and turn into either of the next two roads on the left. At the next intersection take Brett Road and follow it until you reach Ashpit Road. Turn right onto Ashpit Road, and continue about 2 km to the Tarawera access road on the left. It is narrow and rough but it will take you about 5 km to a small parking area. A sign at the bottom warns of the dangers you will subject your car to. You'll need four-wheel drive on the road from the parking area up through the forests and scrub that have regenerated since the eruption. Most people walk to the open, stony, summit plateau rent by its enormous crater. There is no sheltering scrub here, and it can be a cold windy place.

It is well worth continuing upward around the crater to the trig on Ruawahia dome, the highest point at 1,104 m. From here the views over the Rotorua and Bay of Plenty districts, the Urewera mountains, Tongariro volcanoes, and Lake Taupo are magnificent. The crater is a great chasm at your feet. In clear weather, when you can see where you are going, take the steep path off the summit and continue around the rim to a well-worn track descending to the right through a gap in the black lava walls. Once through the short steep part, it's an exhilarating run down deep, loose scoria to the track at the bottom. You'll need to empty your boots here before walking along the bottom of this and the next crater and making the climb out to where you first peered over the edge.

Allow a whole day for the return trip — an hour's driving each way, 1.5 to 2 hours for the ascent, 2 hours around the top, and another 1 to 1.5 hours to descend. Wear boots or very strong shoes, and take warm, windproof clothing, food, camera, and plenty to drink. If you don't want to walk to the top, there are four-wheel-drive tours to the summit and scenic flights that land on the plateau. These can be arranged through the information centers in Rotorua and Kawerau.

Lakes Tarawera and Rotomahana and Waimangu Thermal Valley

One commercial tour that is recommended covers all three of the above scenic attractions. Waimangu Thermal Valley, located about 20 km south of Rotorua off SH 5, is an extension of the line of craters running across the summits of Mt. Tarawera. It has some spectacular hot lakes and craters that are visible during a walk down to the shores of Lake Rotomahana. From here you can travel by boat around the lake and then walk across a narrow isthmus to Lake Tarawera. Another boat will transport you across Lake Tarawera to Tarawera Landing, a few kilometers past Te Wairoa, the Buried Village. The trip takes a full day and bookings can be made at **Waimangu Thermal Valley**, P.O. Box 1149, Rotorua, phone (07)3666-137; **Intercity Travel Centre**, phone (07)3490-590; and **Tourism Rotorua**, phone (07)3485-179.

A half-day trip can be done covering either the Lake Tarawera or Waimangu ends of the above tour. From Tarawera Landing there is a one-hour cruise around the shores, a one-hour lunch break that allows time to walk across to Lake Rotomahana and back, then an hour's cruise back to the jetty. The Waimangu trip includes a cruise on Lake Rotomahana after a walk down the valley. Inquiries about these shorter excursions should be made to the agencies listed above. If you have less than half a day, a visit to Waimangu alone is worthwhile.

Airborne Thrills

If you are keen for a bit of excitement in the air, Rotorua might be the place to find it. As well as the usual sightseeing flights over the district you can take a flight in a hot air balloon or go for a spin in an open-cockpit de Havilland Tiger Moth, the sort used for training British pilots before World War II. You even get to wear the goggles and leather flying helmet and jacket, just to make it feel more authentic. In suitable weather, you can not only fly over Mt. Tarawera but also land on the summit plateau only a short distance from the crater. All flights leave from Rotorua Airport or you can make bookings at Tourism Rotorua.

WHIRINAKI FOREST PARK

Whirinaki Forest Park lies about 100 km southeast of Rotorua, sandwiched between Urewera National Park and the vast Kaingaroa pine forests. Here, on lowland river terraces, are some of the country's most magnificent stands of podocarp forest. Huge rimu, matai, miro, kahikatea, and totara trees form a dense, towering canopy that dwarfs its understory of ferns and smaller hardwood species. Not so very long ago these ancient, gigantic trees were under the threat of the forester's ax. Only through the concerted efforts of conservationists, with backing from such well-known people as Britain's Dr. David Bellamy, were logging operations in the Whirinaki Forest halted. Some of Whirinaki has been planted in exotic species, but most of the forest cover is indigenous. Within the 54,130 ha of forest park are several ecological areas that have been set aside for special protection and also a 163-ha forest sanctuary that is legally protected in much the same way as a national park.

Rugged, higher altitude regions toward the eastern and southern boundaries of the park contain mostly pure beech forest. With decreases in altitude, the beech becomes mixed with hardwoods and rimu until it phases out entirely and podocarp and hardwood species take over completely. Within the forest is a network of tracks linking huts for use by walkers, hunters, and anglers. Some of these tracks are well maintained and easy to follow; others are less so and are for experienced hikers only. The easiest and most popular of these is the track down the Whirinaki River. Near Minginui are shorter walks through some of the very best areas of podocarp forest. Minginui was a thriving mill settlement until the conservationists got their way. Now it is almost a ghost town, inhabited mainly by Ngatiwhare people whose family ties lie here and for whom the forest has cultural and traditional significance.

To reach Whirinaki Forest Park, take SH 38, and turn off at Te Whaiti, 17 km east of Murupara. The Park Visitor and Information Centre is located at Minginui. Murupara—the only town of any significance along SH 38, which traverses Urewera National Park on the way to Wairoa—is a good place to replenish food and gasoline supplies, if you haven't already done so. There is little available at Minginui. About 1 km before Minginui a sign indicates the **Mangamate Waterfall,** where there is a very pleasant camping area beside the Whirinaki River. Another camping area is located along the **Okahu Valley Road,** which leaves SH 38 at Ngaputahi, about 10 km east of Te Whaiti. From the end of this 11-km gravel road a good track leads to Whangatawhia and Te Wairoa Huts. Mid Okahu Hut (9 bunks) is located about halfway along the road on the true left of Okahu stream and is reached by a short track.

If you want help with transport to and from road or track ends, or would like your car looked after during an overnight or extended tramp, contact Ken or Anne Looney of **Whirinaki Forest Lodge.** You will find them just off the Minginui Road, about 1 km from Te Whaiti. A sign will direct you to their comfortable, countrystyle accommodation and genuine Kiwi hospitality. Not only do the Looneys offer a range of very reasonably priced accommodation (from backpacker, self-contained motel, to fully serviced), they also provide guide services for hikers, anglers, hunters, horse trekkers, and any other personalized outdoor holiday you could wish for.

Whirinaki Valley Track

This can be walked either as an easy two-day hike, staying overnight at **Mid Whirinaki Hut,** or as a long, one-day leg stretcher. The total distance is 27 km, but the track is very easy and mostly downhill if you start from Plateau Road at the southern end of the park. Total walking time is 7 to 8 hours if you are carrying gear for an overnight stay and less with a light daypack.

From Plateau Road the well-graded and benched track descends through beautiful beech forest to the Whirinaki River in about 1 hour. There are some huge old beech trees along this section, all of them supported by massive buttressed roots and hung with epiphytic ferns and perching lilies. Flocks of chattering whiteheads inhabit this area, and you may also see the rare blue duck on the river if you approach quietly. Mid Whirinaki Hut, set in a large grassy clearing beside the river, is about another hour down the valley. The track continues down the true right side of the river, passing in two places beneath high bluffs of pumice deposited during the Taupo eruption 1,800 years ago. The forest is dominated by towering rimu and kahikatea and beautiful groves of tawa. The loop track leading to the impressive Whirinaki Falls marks another change in the forest structure, and tall podocarp species become more dense and towering. Birdlife is prolific. About 10 minutes from the road, in fitting finish to what must be one of the most beautiful bush walks in the country, the track crosses the river at Te Whaiti nui-a toi Canyon, a spectacular tunnel-like slot with walls of columnar lava.

Whirinaki Falls Loop

This is a 3-hour return walk along the lower section of the Whirinaki River track, traveling up one bank of the river, crossing at the Whirinaki Falls, and returning down the other side. Spectacular stands of podocarps, the falls, and Te Whaiti nui-a toi Canyon are seen on the way.

H-Tree Walk

Some of the best tree specimens in the park can be seen on this 30- to 35-minute walk. There is an unusual double rimu—an older tree joined to a younger one to form the letter H—and some huge rimu and totara veterans that tower above the subcanopy of tall tawa trees and dense understory of tree ferns. Many trees are labeled. The track starts 1.5 km along Fort Road. From Minginui, take the first road to the left almost immediately after crossing the Whirinaki River, then the next road on the right.

Sanctuary Walk

To reach the Forest Sanctuary, take the dirt road behind the Minginui school grounds. It leaves Rimu Crescent between the second and third houses on the left of the school entrance and passes beneath an avenue of pine trees. Take the right-hand road at a junction about 500 m along. There is a pleasant picnic area beside Minginui Stream at the road end. The walk through the sanctuary is a 45- to 60-minute loop through a mix of podocarp species, including some massive totara trees. As the track is unformed and there are a few unmarked side trails, follow the white markers on the trees to avoid confusion.

Arahaki Lagoon

From the Whirinaki River Track carpark on River Road, continue along the narrow road through dense forest for a few more kilometers to another parking area. The track, marked by white tags on trees, follows an old road line through cut-over scrub for the first 10 minutes. Then, after crossing a stream it climbs steeply to a ridge and follows it for some distance. Here the forest is fairly open and consists mainly of tawa trees, with a carpet of filmy ferns (*Hymenophyllum* spp.), short grasses, and mosses. The descent is short to the lagoon, a shallow body of water ringed by reeds and tall kahikatea trees. To support itself in the wet ground, the kahikatea develops large buttressed roots, many of which are twisted like corkscrews. During dry times there may be no water in the lagoon; when full there may be waterfowl on it. Allow about an hour each way.

UREWERA NATIONAL PARK

The vast forests of Urewera lie on either side of SH 38, which snakes its way along valleys and over ridges, passing beautiful Lake Waikaremoana en route and finally descending to the coast at Wairoa. Although the western side of the park lies close to Rotorua and Bay of Plenty, its heartland and center of activities lie within the provincial boundaries of the East Coast. Information is therefore included in the section on Eastland. It is worth noting here, however, that there is a park information center located 2 km east of Murupara on SH 38. A number of walking tracks into the park start along the eastern side of the Rangitaiki Valley or off SH 38, and information on these is best gained from the Murupara Visitor Centre.

AROUND WHAKATANE

Kohi Walkway

The Kohi Walkway, traversing about 7 km of coastline between Whakatane and Ohope Beach, has marvelous scenery and passes through some interesting pa sites, one of which is reputedly the oldest in the country. Informative panels interpret the layouts of these pa. As it is not a loop track, return transport should be arranged. Behind the rock opposite the post office at Whakatane are steps that lead to Puketapu Lookout and to a track to Kohi Point Lookout. Kohi Point

Lookout can also be reached from Otarawairere Road off the Whakatane-Ohope Beach Road. Coastal views from here take in most of the Bay of Plenty.

From Kohi Point Lookout the track descends gradually through bush, passing the pa sites on the bluffs above Whakatane. The town, river mouth, and port all lie below you, almost like a map, as you follow the track along the cliff line to Whakatane Heads. After you pass above rocky coves, headlands, and rock stacks set in surging seas, you'll come to steps leading down to beautiful Otarawairere Bay, fringed by pohutukawa trees. Swimming is safest at the western end of the beach, which can also be reached by a walking track from the end of Otarawairere Road. Continuing around the beach the main track climbs up and around the cliffs before descending to the western end of Ohope Beach. Allow 2.5 to 3 hours one way if you start from Whakatane Post Office, or about 2 hours from Kohi Point Lookout. In summer, take food, drink, and swimming gear for a very enjoyable day.

Ohope and Ohiwa

At the western end of Ohope Beach, where the road to Whakatane starts to climb, is a scenic reserve protecting a magnificent example of coastal pohutukawa forest. It's a cool, calm place in which to escape the summer heat or to get away from the beach for a while. A loop track through the forest, taking 50 to 60 minutes to walk, starts behind the Ohope Hall and climbs to a lookout point with good views over Ohope Beach.

The eastern end of the beach is a long sandspit enclosing tranquil Ohiwa Harbour, a good place to observe wading birds. Most of the original sand dunes of Ohope Spit have been converted to suburban ugliness, but at the end is a wildlife reserve, excellent for beachcombing and birdwatching. If you visit in March, you may see hundreds of kuaka or godwits assembled before they lift skyward on their long flight to the Northern Hemisphere. Ohiwa Harbour is a popular windsurfing venue and during summer months, windsurfers and catamarans can be rented at Otao Domain, opposite the Port Ohope Store.

Mt. Edgecumbe

Dark and forbidding, Putauaki (Mt. Edgecumbe) dominates the town of Kawerau and much of the Bay of Plenty skyline. Like the young, active vent of Ngauruhoe to the southwest, Putauaki has the classical steep-sided cone shape of a volcano built up by successive layers of scoria and lava. Being relatively low, Putauaki is clothed in forest. The top has two craters, one of which holds a small reedfringed lake, and from a high point on the rim there are extensive views over Rotorua and the Bay of Plenty, marred in some directions by unsightly transmitter aerials.

There are two routes to the top. One is a rough, overgrown track going straight up the western side. This I would not recommend to anyone except a masochist. The other is the road to the television repeater, which makes a pleasant 1-hour climb through pine forest and bush that is thick with tall mamaku, the black tree fern, then pleasant tawa forest. From the crater, a side track on the left, just before the short climb to the television buildings on the rim, leads to the high point on the southeast rim.

Private vehicles cannot be taken up the mountain road but are allowed on the lower forestry roads if a permit is obtained from Tasman Forests Ltd., phone (07)3234-599, or stop at the forest headquarters on Waterhouse St. in Kawerau. To reach the mountain access road, turn left immediately after crossing the Tarawera River as you enter Kawerau, then left again into Waterhouse St. Continue past the forest headquarters turnoff and workshop compound, then left into Tarawera Road. At the next junction, about 1 km on, turn right into McKee Road and follow it for 4 km to Putauaki Road. There is a small parking area about 500 m up Putauaki Road just before a locked gate.

Kawerau Mountain Safaris take four-wheel-drive trips to the top, and bookings can be made at the **Kawerau Information Centre**, phone (07)3237-550 or, after hours, (07)3238-755. They also do trips to Mt. Tarawera and the Tarawera Falls.

Lake Tarawera Outlet and Tarawera Falls

While the western end of Lake Tarawera is a well visited tourist destination, the beautiful eastern end, drained by the crystal clear Tarawera River, receives scant attention except from locals who know about its attractions. At the outlet is an extensive, informal camping area maintained by the Department of Conservation. It's a delightful spot where you can fish, swim, and hike, or just laze about. From the outlet, one track follows the northern lakeshore to Humphries Bay to join with the Eastern Okataina Walkway.

Another track, to the **Tarawera Falls,** follows the Tarawera River downstream to where it disappears underground through cracks and holes in the ancient lava flows that blocked the valley about 5,000 years ago and caused the lake to form. The track passes some wonderful swimming pools, the only exception being the one with a hole through which the river drains—and this is clearly signposted. From the top of high bluffs above the falls there are views over the forested valley below before the track descends the escarpment. At the bottom the river gushes from a hole in the towering cliffs and dashes down a boulder-strewn slope before continuing as a deep, quiet flow beneath overhanging trees. Unless you can arrange pick-up transport to meet you here, the walk from the outlet to the falls and back will take 3 to 4 hours. The falls can be reached from below by a shorter track (20 to 30 minutes one way) from the carpark at the end of Fenton Mill Road. There are also some good swimming holes on that route.

Mt. Tarawera can also be climbed from near the lake outlet. Just before the campground is reached, a sign pointing down a side road indicates the way to the start of the track. After climbing through regenerating forest of kanuka and rewarewa, the track ascends steep scoria slopes to the crater rim. You will need boots or very strong footwear, warm clothing, and plenty to drink. Allow a full day if you wish to spend time exploring around the top.

Another interesting climb in this area, taking about 5 hours return, is the ascent of **Maungawhakamana,** a distinctive conical peak above the Tarawera Valley. The track is signposted off Fentons Mill Road before you reach the Tarawera Falls. It's quite a steep climb over ground covered with cinders from Mt. Tarawera, through regenerating kamahi and rewarewa forest. From the 727-m summit, there are good views.

To reach the Tarawera Outlet and Falls, turn left into River Road immediately after crossing the Tarawera River as you approach Kawerau from Whakatane. Turn left again into Waterhouse St., then right into Tarawera Road and follow signs.

Matata

Matata, 19 km west of Whakatane on SH 2, could easily be overlooked by travelers hurrying to the better-known attractions of Tauranga and Mt. Maunganui. This small, relaxed, and somewhat sleepy seaside settlement was once a busy port where scows and steamships came regularly to load up with flax from a nearby mill. Today it is hard to imagine the town bustling until you realize that both the Tarawera and Rangitaiki rivers once entered the sea here. A drainage scheme, implemented in 1914, diverted the Rangitaiki River to its present position, and three years later moved the mouth of the Tarawera River, effectively ending all port activities. What remains today is a lagoon providing a sanctuary for many waterfowl. On the seaward side of the lagoon is a pleasant camping area, sheltered from ocean winds by high sand dunes. By walking along the dunes between the sea and the lagoon to the present mouth of the Tarawera River, you can observe several species of ducks, swans, geese, pied stilts, herons, pukeko, fernbird, and others. The area is a wildlife reserve administered by the Department of Conservation.

Behind the town is a steep bush- and scrub-covered escarpment, the blunt seaward edge of hills bordering the river floodplains. The views from this high land are outstanding, an important factor in the siting of the many ancient pa that were once built along here. The **Matata Skyline Walk,** which crosses the top of the escarpment, starts across the railway line at the end of Mair St. and finishes at the quarry at the western end of the town. Old earthworks can still be seen around the highest point of the track. Allow 2.5 to 3 hours for the round trip.

AROUND TAURANGA

Mt. Maunganui, famous for its surfing beaches, is a mecca for surfers. In summer it is also a popular holiday destination for many New Zealand families who just like to be beside the sea. There are picnic areas and many motor camps and motels here, plus commercial entertainment, if that is what you are seeking. "The Mount" (Mauao, 232 m), as it is locally known, was originally an island, but has been joined to the mainland by progressively widening sandbars. Several tracks and a four-wheel-drive road lead to the summit and circle the base of the hill. From the top there are good views over Tauranga Harbour toward the Kaimai Range and Coromandel Peninsula, Matakana Island, and the coastline south. It takes at least an hour to walk to the top and back, and a little less to walk around the base.

KAIMAI-MAMAKU FOREST PARK

West of Tauranga and its spreading shallow harbor, the dark bush-covered spine of the Kaimai Range rises steeply above lush, rolling orchard lands. Until 1970 the forests of the Kaimai Range were logged for native timber (podocarps and tawa), an industry that followed gold mining to provide timber for houses. Dams were constructed on streams and rivers, and when sufficient water had built up the logs were floated downstream. Elsewhere, extensive tramlines were laid to drag the trees out. The relics of these industries remain, providing the basis for many walking tracks.

Access to tracks in the Forest Park is usually by side roads off the main highways, and these are signposted. Many of the tracks link huts, and it is also possible to walk along the spine of the range. The map of the Kaimai-Mamaku Forest Park (Infomap 274-08) will give plenty of ideas for possible walks and overnight hikes. Check with the Department of Conservation in Rotorua or Tauranga for further information. Below are a few of the more interesting tracks on the eastern side of the range.

Eliza Mine

Sited high on the slopes of Mt. Eliza, the Eliza Mine was worked from the 1890s until about 1905, but it never produced any substantial quantities of gold. Several shafts were sunk into the side of the mountain, some of them several hundred meters long. The path to the main shaft entrance starts off **Thompson's Track,** a partly formed road across the Kaimai Range that is popular with trailbike and mountain bike enthusiasts. Thompson's Track Road leaves the Tauranga-Katikati Road (SH 2) about halfway between Aongatete and Katikati.

Follow the muddy Thompson's Track for a few hundred meters to a large orange-painted post on the right at a corner. The Eliza Mine track descends steeply to the Waitekohe Stream, crosses and then follows the bank on an old benched packtrack used to bring in supplies when the mine was working. Where a section of this old track has been destroyed by landslides, a prominent sign marks a detour up a steep spur to a grassy clearing where the mine's camp and ore testing plant once stood. At a second sign, the left-hand track leads to the mine entrance while the right-hand track continues up to a short prospecting drive and the top of Mt. Eliza. The main entrance is a horizontal drive about 200 m long, with two short side drives. Old sleepers and rails for the ore cart can still be seen under the ankle-deep water on the floor. The drive is reasonably safe to enter, but you will need a flashlight. Allow 2 to 2.5 hours for the return walk.

Tracks Starting from Hot Springs Road

Several walks can be made from the end of Hot Springs Road, a few kilometers south of Katikati on SH 2. Sapphire Springs is a very pleasant hot pools and camping ground complex along this road. The pools, especially the spas, are great for soaking in after you've been on a hike.

The track to the **Kauri Grove** and **Te Rere-a-Tukahia Hut** starts about 100 m back from the end of Hot Springs Road. A few minutes walk brings you down to a beautiful stream. On a terrace on the far side are about twenty kauri, averaging about 1 m in diameter. The track continues up a ridge, climbing steadily through more kauri and large kohekohe and puriri trees, to reach a dense grove of young kauri rickers mixed with larger trees, some of which are beginning to develop their large crowns. It takes about 35 to 45 minutes to reach this point, and a return can be made from here.

The reach Te Rere-a-Tukahia Hut, continue up the ridge. The comfortable 20-bunk hut has mattresses but no cooking utensils or stove, so you will need to take a portable cooker with you if you want hot food. It sits in a clearing near the top of the ridge, and from the hill above there are good views over Tauranga Harbour and the surrounding country. Allow 2 to 2.5 hours one way from the road. A longer return can be made by continuing along the ridge and descending to Hot Springs Road by the Tuahu Track.

The large obelisk of **Sentinel Rock,** on a subsidiary ridge to the east of the main Kaimai Range, is an obvious landmark in this area. From the road end, the flat, benched **Tuahu Track,** which eventually leads to the main north-south track and the western side, is followed for about 20 minutes to a junction. Sentinel Rock Track climbs to the left and, in a few minutes, to two **large kauri** trees. One is a magnificent specimen, with a large girth and crown festooned with astelia and the epiphytic orchid *Dendrobium cunninghami.* Above the kauri trees the track climbs very steeply for another 5 to 10 minutes to gain a spur, which it follows to reach Sentinel Rock in about 2 hours.

AROUND WAIHI

Waihi, famous at the beginning of this century for the amount of gold produced from the Martha Hill Mine, sits a short distance inland at the base of the Coromandel Range. In its heyday the Martha mine was one of the richest in the world, but dwindling outputs forced it to close in 1952. It was reopened in 1988 as an opencast mine, and the town now hopes for a small comeback. Other mines were located in the Karangahake Gorge and surrounding hills. The local information center and museum are good places to find out more of the town's history. Nearby **Waihi Beach** is popular for surfing and swimming and has motels, campgrounds, and backpacker accommodation. It runs for 8 km to **Bowentown Heads** at the northern entrance to Tauranga Harbour. Shell middens and stepped terraces dropping to the sea tell a story of human occupation at Bowentown Heads. Called Te Kura o Maia by the Maori, this pa saw many battles. The grassy picnic area with shady pohutukawa trees and the sheltered sands of Anzac Bay at the base of the hill make for a delightful spot.

Orokawa Bay

In complete contrast to Waihi's long surf beach backed by sand dunes and suburbia, Orokawa Bay is a secluded, unspoiled gem of white sand rimmed by shady pohutukawa veterans. It can only be reached by walking. The track starts at the northern end of Waihi Beach and climbs around the cliff face and bushy ridges at an easy grade, with grand views along the coast and out to offshore islands. Two small streams enter the bay, and a rough track leaving the beach beside the northernmost one leads up the stream, crossing frequently, to the **William Wright Falls,** which descend a high amphitheatre of smooth rock. It takes 35 to 45 minutes to walk to Orokawa Bay and about another 50 minutes to go to the falls and return. Be careful swimming here; the beach shelves steeply.

Karangahake Walkway

From Waihi, SH 2 follows the Ohinemuri River through the Karangahake Gorge to Paeroa on the edge of the Hauraki Plains. At the turn of this century, two townships in the gorge, Karangahake and Mackaytown, were the scene of intense gold mining activity. A railway line built through the gorge to ensure that mining machinery and coal could be quickly and easily transported now forms a 4.5-km walkway along the banks of the river, where old batteries and relics of the mining industry can be seen. Part of the walk is through a 1,086-m-long tunnel, an eerie place that requires a flashlight. Interpretive panels along the walk explain places of significance. The track starts at Karangahake, about 7 km east of Paeroa, and finishes at Owharoa Falls, about 9 km from Waihi, taking about 1.5 hours one way.

OFFSHORE ISLANDS

One of the features of the Bay of Plenty is the offshore islands that the public can visit. Mayor Island (Tuhua), White Island (Whakaari), and Whale Island (Motuhora) are all of volcanic origin and are all conservation areas. White Island is the tip of an active volcano and its plume of steam can be easily seen from many inland areas.

Whale Island

Whale Island, lying close to Whakatane, is a wildlife reserve, and landing is by permit only from the Department of Conservation. Considerable efforts have gone into removing all the rabbits and cats that once roamed the island, and it is hoped that all the rats have also been eliminated. During the Christmas–New Year holiday period the Department of Conservation runs guided trips to the island. It's an enjoyable half-day trip, with time for swimming and lunch. To the west of Whale Island are the Rurimas, rocky islets popular for diving.

White Island

Legends tells us that when Maui stepped on the North Island, which he had just fished out of the sea, he accidently caught up some of its fire. He shook this off into the sea where it remains today as White Island. Although the island is a scenic reserve, the protection is as much for the bird life as for the mineral resources. From 1885 the large sulphur deposits were mined and shipped to Tauranga and Sydney for processing until an eruption in 1914 destroyed the factory and killed all the workers. The remains of a new factory built in the early 1930s can still be seen. Mining ceased in 1934. The waters around White Island, which lies 48 km from Whakatane, are popular for both scuba diving and game fishing. Record-breaking hapuka and yellowtail have been hooked there. The warm Auckland Current, the warming effect of the volcanic activity, plus the island's proximity to the deep waters of the White Island trench bring an abundance and variety of marine life.

You must have a permit to land on White Island, and the Whakatane Information Office can tell you how to obtain one. Several charter boats take full-day or overnight trips to the waters off the island, and lists of these are available from the Tauranga and Whakatane information offices. You can also fly there by helicopter and land if you go with **White Island Tours,** Box 10, Waima, phone (07)3084-188, or Fax (07)3123-111.

Mayor Island

Mayor Island was once occupied and there are at least twelve pa sites, many of them fortified. Obsidian obtained here was very important to the Maori for making tools and has since been found in places many thousands of kilometers away from its source. Like the other islands, Mayor Island is a wildlife reserve. There are several walking tracks to bays, pa sites, and the crater, but to visit them all you will need more than one day. A map of tracks and attractions is available from the Tauranga Public Relations Office. Bird life in the bush is prolific, and many unusual species can be seen.

The island is a popular destination for sightseers, scuba divers, and fishermen during summer, and you can go just for the day or stay overnight in the Tauranga Game Fishing Club's lodge. Accommodation is in cabins using your own bedding or in self-contained units with bedding and linen supplied. Meals are bought in the lodge dining room. Bookings are made through the management on the island, phone (07)577-0533, or through the Mayor Island Trust Board, Box 501, Tauranga.

During the height of the summer holidays, the *Te Kuia* and *M.V. Manutere* make daily trips to the island from Coronation Pier, Tauranga, taking about 3 hours each way. (Take sea-sickness medicine if you are a bad sailor.) The boats leave early in the morning and return in the evening, giving visitors about 6 hours ashore. The fare includes a landing fee, which gives visitors access to all parts of the island, and also a club association fee, which allows use of the club's facilities.

RAFTING AND JET BOATING

Several rivers in the Rotorua–Bay of Plenty region offer good rafting opportunities. The most exciting is the **Wairoa River,** close to Tauranga, but because the waters are used for electricity generation and flow is controlled, rafting is possible on only 26 days a year. You need to book early for this one. Day trips are also run on the **Rangitaiki River** and are a fast and exciting ride. **The Rafting Company** runs both the Wairoa and Rangitaiki rivers in a weekend. Phone (07)3480-233 for bookings.

The main jet-boating river in the area is the Rangitaiki, which offers an exciting ride, or you can do short trips, combined with rafting, on the **Kaituna River** near Te Puke.

TROUT FISHING

Rotorua's many lakes offer good fishing for the keen angler and are open all year, but streams are closed from July until the end of November. Check your license for local regulations. Popular rivers are the Tarawera, Whirinaki, and Rangitaiki. Access to the **Tarawera River** is from a 4-km walking track starting close to the Tarawera Road bridge, about 6 km from Kawerau. The **Whirinaki River** is accessible from the road to Minginui and from Okui Hut, reached by turning off SH 38 about 2 km before Te Whaiti. The upper part of the **Rangitaiki** and its tributary the **Wheao River** offer wonderful fishing, pristine surroundings, and wily trout. Access is through the Kaingaroa Forest from Murupara. A permit can be obtained from the forest headquarters at Kaingaroa Village or Murupara. Leave SH 38 at Murupara before crossing the Rangitaiki River; turn right and gain Kiorenui Road via the forestry yard. From Kiorenui Road, signs will direct you to the junction of the Wheao and Rangitaiki rivers.

Fishing licenses can be obtained from sports shops, or the Department of Conservation on the corner of Tutanekai and Pukakai streets, Rotorua, and they may also be able to help with free advice on good areas to try your luck. **Tourism Rotorua,** at 67 Fenton St., Rotorua, has a fishing advisory officer who can help, and they can also supply names and contacts for local guides.

DIVING, BIG GAME FISHING, AND LINE FISHING

The Bay of Plenty is renowned for the size of the yellowtail (kingfish), yellowfin and bluefin tuna, marlin, and hapuka caught in the waters around the offshore islands. The same warm current that brings the big fish also allows a wide variety of other marine species to live in the waters around White Island, Whale Island, and Mayor Island. Many of these species are usually found only in more tropical waters to the north. Charter boats run game or line fishing and diving trips from Tauranga and Whakatane. Tauranga and Whakatane information offices can provide lists of these.

RECOMMENDED TOURIST ATTRACTIONS

Waiotapu Thermal Wonderland is 29 km south of Rotorua on SH 5.

Waikite Thermal Baths features crystal clear hot pools in a bush setting and tent or caravan sites. Turn off SH 5, 29 km south of Rotorua.

Te Wairoa (The Buried Village) holds the remains of the Maori village buried during the eruption of Mt. Tarawera in 1860. Tarawera Road, Lake Tarawera.

Kiwi Fruit Country displays the insides and outsides of the kiwi fruit industry. Open daily; 6 km east of Te Puke on SH 2.

Tauranga Historic Village is a living history exhibit of an early New Zealand township. On 17th Avenue, Tauranga.

USEFUL ADDRESSES

Department of Conservation: Information Centre, Longmile Road, Rotorua, phone (07)3461-155; corner of McLean and Anson sts., Box 1026, Tauranga, phone (07)5787-677; 28 Commerce St., Whakatane, phone (07) 3087-213.

Tourism Rotorua, 67 Fenton St., Rotorua, phone (07)3666-137.

Tauranga Public Relations Office, The Strand, Tauranga, phone (07)5788-103.

Whakatane Information Centre, Boon St., Whakatane, phone (07)3086-058.

10 ◆ TARANAKI

LANDSCAPE AND CLIMATE

Rising smoothly and steeply to a sharp point, the 2,518-m-high cone of Mt. Taranaki, also called Mt. Egmont, dominates this western province of the North Island. When seen from the north or south the isolated, dormant volcano appears to have almost perfect symmetry and is often compared with Japan's Mt. Fuji. Eastern and western perspectives reveal different profiles, with the southern slopes interrupted by a subsidiary cone called Fantham's Peak in honor of Fanny Fantham, who, in 1887, was the first woman to climb it.

Egmont is the largest and youngest of a short chain of volcanoes; oldest are the eroded stumps of the Sugar Loaf Islands, which lie just off the coast of New Plymouth. On the coast is Paritutu, a spine of lava estimated to be around 1.75 million years old. Between these and Egmont are the Kaitake and Pouakai ranges, both remnants of volcanoes that were once almost as high as the present dominant cone. Now eroded to a height of 683 m, Kaitake was active about 500,000 years ago while the younger Pouakai, 10 km to the southwest, had its heyday around 250,000 years ago. As Pouakai was dying, probably around 125,000 years ago, a new cone began to form, and by 35,000 years ago had grown to an estimated height of 2,700 m. It would have carried a cap of ice during the last ice ages. Explosive eruptions and natural collapse reduced this summit to about 1,200 m, sending avalanches of stones and mud out onto the surrounding plains and into the sea beyond the present coastline. The lumpy remains of these enormous lahars can be seen today as hillocky farmland.

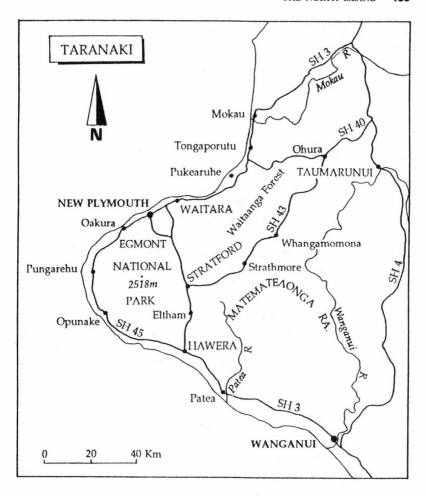

Subsequent ashfalls covered the ring plain, giving rise to the Taranaki Province's fertile soils.

Around 20,000 years ago, a new cone began to rise above the remains of its predecessor, building itself upward with successive layers of lava and ash. Heavy rainstorms and further eruptions sent more layers of mud and tephra surging down the slopes again, obliterating many earlier geologic features. Egmont's last devastating eruption occurred about A.D. 1500, with hot gas clouds destroying much of the forest. With no trees to bind the unstable soils, rainstorms once again set off landslides. Another fiery but less catastrophic eruption 150 years later covered the slopes with ash. According to Maori legend, the mountain grew tall during this time because it was proud of a successful invasion of Atiawa territory by local people. The tholoid in the present crater is thought to have formed at this time. The last known eruption appears to have been in 1755, but this was a minor affair, scattering only 5 to 12 cm of ash over the upper slopes.

The rest of Taranaki Province is made up of sedimentary rocks. On the coastal side of Egmont, between New Plymouth and Hawera, a narrow belt of very young rocks, less than 2 million years old, ring the mountain. The inland high country, east of the mountains, has older, Tertiary rocks up to 20 million years old. These soft mudstones once formed a vast plateau sloping gently westward from the Tongariro volcanoes. Erosion has reduced this to flat-topped ridges separately by narrow, steep-walled valleys. Most famous of these is the Wanganui River, which begins on the slopes of Mt. Tongariro and enters the sea at Wanganui after a journey of approximately 250 km.

Mt. Egmont not only dominates the landscape but also the lives of the people who live in Taranaki. Their main topic of conversation is likely to be the weather, mainly because they must plan their days around it. There is truth to the saying "If you can't see the mountain it's already raining; if you can see it, then it must be going to rain." As the high point on an otherwise relatively flat piece of land, Egmont has a magnetic effect on bad weather and is frequently obscured by moisture-laden clouds carried across the Tasman Sea by the prevailing westerly winds. The absence of rain for longer than a fortnight is considered a drought by Taranakians. New Plymouth's lowest recorded rainfall was 1,120 mm in 1963! Rain falls on an average of 166 days each year, but this is offset by warm summers and mild winters, with a high dose of sunshine.

The result of all this precipitation is lush vegetation. When Europeans first came to Taranaki, 75 percent to 80 percent of it was covered in bush, but this has been replaced by rolling pastureland, green with juicy grasses favored by the dairy cattle. Dairy farming and Taranaki are almost synonymous to New Zealanders. Most of the milk is made into butter, cheese, casein, and milk powder. The province's other major industries are oil, liquid petroleum gas, and methanol.

Oil was known to pre-European Maori, who considered it to be a drowned spirit that was undergoing decomposition. European settlers were not slow in digging for the black gold, and five wells were built between 1865 and 1897. The first British oil field, at Moturoa near Port Taranaki, began yielding crude oil in March 1866, but it did not become economically viable until the late 1880s. Unfortunately, there being no refinery, no means of export, and no local market, the owners had a problem knowing how to use the oil they did produce. However, the last well at Moturoa did not close until 1972. By then the more lucrative gas fields at Kapuni and off the coast at Maui had been discovered.

HISTORY

Egmont must have been under its customary cloud cap when Abel Tasman sailed up the west coast of the North Island, as he did not mention it. James Cook was luckier and did sight the mountain in January 1770, although it remained partially cloaked most of the time. A note in Cook's log book, dated January 14, "saw for a few minutes Mount Egmont," is a sentiment echoed by many visitors since. Two years later, on March 25, 1772, Marion du Fresne sighted the peak and named it Le Pic Mascarin. Cook named the mountain in honor of the Earl of Egmont, once a First Lord of the Admiralty. Today many New Zealanders feel that the Maori name Taranaki is more appropriate for such a noble mountain. Opinion was so divided over this that now either name is officially correct.

To the Maori the higher slopes of Taranaki were and are sacred, but they did venture onto the lower slopes for red ochre, used as a pigment, and to bury chiefs and tohunga (priests). When Ernst Dieffenbach, a young geologist of the New Zealand Company, and James Heberly, a whaler, climbed to the top in 1839, the Maori were not impressed and relieved them of the rocks and plants they had collected so they could be returned to the mountain. The stones are considered to be part of the mountain's skull and the plants its hair.

Maori legend tells that Mt. Taranaki once fought a fierce battle with Mt. Tongariro for the favors of Pihanga, a female mountain at the southern end of Lake Taupo. Taranaki was defeated. Expelled by Tongariro, he fled westward, gouging out the path of the Wanganui River in his anger and despair. Perhaps bent on suicide, he was prevented from drowning in the sea by a spur, which threw out a restraining arm as he rested, binding him to the land.

Early history of the area is obscure, but it is known to have been inhabited around A.D. 600, and the remains of feasts and moa hunting sites dating between A.D. 1000 and A.D. 1400 have been found. Tribal and oral tradition go back to around A.D. 1300. As intertribal warfare became more of a way of life during the seventeenth and eighteenth centuries, fortified pa sites proliferated. A pattern of tribal expeditions, invasions, and retreats, left many parts of the province almost deserted. When Europeans first made contact with the Maori inhabitants, their population was estimated to be about ten thousand. Along a 6-km-wide coastal strip were about 500 pa sites, most of them built to take advantage of easily defended natural barriers such as cliffs, rivers, and hill tops. Most Taranaki Maori trace their ancestry to three canoes—the Aotea, Kuruhaupo, and Tokomaru. Major tribes today are the Ngati Awa in the north, Ngati Ruanui in the south, Ngati Maru in the east, and Taranaki, who are centered at Parihaka on the western slopes of the mountain.

Ships bringing around two thousand settlers arrived at the embryo New Plymouth between March 30, 1841, and January 20, 1843. To many settlers, owning land in the new paradise, as they thought New Zealand would be, was compensation for the long and often irreversible voyage. That the land would be available to them was regarded as a fait accompli. Unfortunately, it was not so simple. To the Maori, land belonged to the tribe and was secured by occupation, cultivation, and burial, even if only by token practice. There was no concept of individual title.

Many adaptations and compromises were demanded by both races in too short a time, so settlement was bound to be fraught with problems. Tension deteriorated into outright war at Waitara in 1861, and New Plymouth became a fortified military garrison. Military skills of both parties were as diametrically opposed as their feelings on land issues. Traditional military maneuvers used by the British were often useless against the Maoris' guerrilla warfare, and their pa proved surprisingly impregnable. There were no decisive victories, and the skirmishes finally ended with exhaustion on both sides and the land returning to encroaching weeds.

Although the Maori were demoralized, resistance was revived by the people of Parihaka, led by Te Whiti and Tohu, who preached human rights. In 1879, still bristling against the occupation of their lands, they staged a passive resistance by pulling out survey pegs, digging up roads, removing fences, and plowing European-held land. The plowmen were arrested, only to be replaced by an endless supply of new workers until the number of prisoners became an embarrassment to the British. Eventually, Te Whiti and Tohu were expelled and draconian laws enacted that allowed Parihaka to be sacked and its people driven away. When the militia marched into the pa in November 1881 they were met with lines of children singing and dancing. Today Parihaka flourishes again as a place of learning and meditation, but it is a place many Pakeha would prefer to forget.

Despite the protests, settlement of Taranaki went ahead, with land cleared back toward the eastern hills. By 1901 the dairy industry was fully established. It was helped along in the 1880s by an astute Chinese merchant named Chew Chong. The ex-gold miner set up stores in New Plymouth and Inglewood and established one of the first butter factories near Eltham, paying farmers cash for their milk. Chew Chong also paid itinerant workers to pick an edible fungus that grew on the decaying trees left after land was cleared. The fungus was dried and exported to China. In the early days, New Plymouth's development was hampered by lack of a port. The breakwater built in 1881 enabled Port Taranaki to grow in importance while the river ports of Waitara and Patea steadily declined. Port Taranaki is now the only deep-water port on the west coast. Today New Plymouth's population is about 47,000.

◆PLACES TO VISIT AND THINGS TO DO

MT. EGMONT NATIONAL PARK

Taranaki's pride and joy is undoubtedly its mountain and the land surrounding it, preserved in a national park. As land around Mt. Egmont was cleared, there were fears that even the slopes of the mountain would eventually be stripped. With some foresight, in 1875 the government placed all forests on the mountain within an 8-km radius of the summit under protection. Six years later, the area was extended to include all land within a 9-km radius, a total of more than 29,000 ha, and by the time Mt. Egmont was declared a national park in 1901, another 24,000 ha of the Kaitake Range had been added.

Well before then, the mountain had attracted climbers and walkers—people who appreciated the aesthetic values of scenery and forest. A track from New Plymouth through the Pouakai Range and up the lower slopes of Mt. Egmont was cut as early as the 1850s, giving access to the summit. In the 1880s, the first Round the Mountain track was cut during topographical surveys of the mountain. Today a network of tracks and huts gives access to all sides of the mountain, and there are a variety of short walks and overnight or longer hikes.

With its steep slopes runneled by the many streams and rivers radiating outward, plenty of up-and-down walking is necessary to cross some of the deep gorges that score Egmont's sides. The popular Round the Mountain walk takes about three days in summer, when a high-level route can be used, but in winter, the same trip, via the lower tracks, can take up to a week. In summer many people make the straightforward climb to the summit. An ascent in winter is a different matter, however, and should only be undertaken by people who are experienced in mountaineering and properly equipped. Mt. Egmont has claimed more lives than any other mountain in New Zealand. The upper slopes have many bluffs created by old lava flows, which are extremely dangerous when snow covered. Wet, windy conditions in winter can create an armor of "boilerplate ice" overnight, and even during the day the slopes can ice over rapidly when clouds form. This, combined with poor visibility, has trapped many unwary climbers.

Egmont's abundant rainfall brings to its forests an almost unreal lushness of mosses, ferns, liverworts, and lichens. They cover boulders, tree trunks, and branches in a soft, absorbent blanket, while epiphytic lilies and orchids crowd branches and the crowns of canopy trees, drawing nutrients from leaves decaying in pockets and hollows. These forests are also unusual in their lack of beech trees and other common species of plants. The reason is not known, but is thought to be related to the mountain's long history of volcanic disturbance and its isolation from other high mountain ranges. The forests are typical of those that once covered much of Taranaki; watered by over 5,000 mm of rain annually, they are true rainforest. The dominant tree species is kamahi, overtopped by emergent rimu and rata, which grow to 50 m and 30 m respectively. Other common shade-tolerant species are mahoe and tree fuchsia. Stunted goblin forests grow on the higher slopes, the trees gnarled and festooned with mosses, the light low, and the air damp.

Above 900 m, on steep slopes, totara and windblasted kaikawaka rise above the canopy of tree fuchsia and five-finger, giving way above 1,100 m to a dense scrub of tough leatherwood. Tussock gradually takes over at higher elevations, but above 1,400 m the barren slopes are left to hardy, low-growing herbs, mosses, and lichens. Many plants in these beautiful alpine herb fields are highly specialized to survive in the difficult environment. Long taproots or creeping runners help them hold on in the loose scree, and thick leathery leaves and layers of silvery hairs or white tomentum reduce water loss to the constant wind and to the high summer temperatures that the dark scoria retains.

Vegetation on the Kaitake Range is different from that of Mt. Egmont and the Pouakai Range because of the lower altitude. Here tawa, rewarewa, hinau, and pukatea flourish, with warmth-loving species such as nikau palms, kohekohe, and karaka near the coast. On higher ridges, where heavy rainfall has leached nutrients from the soil, stunted kamahi forests similar to those on Egmont are found.

Between Egmont and Pouakai is the Ahukawakawa Swamp, formed when debris flows from Egmont blocked the Stony River. This bog's unusual microclimate is colder than is normal at 920 m above the sea. Over 260 plant species are found here among the large red tussocks that thrive at this lower-than-normal altitude.

Three access roads—to Dawson Falls Tourist Lodge, Stratford Mountain House, and the North Egmont Visitor Centre—climb to around 1,000 m, and many tracks start here. Both the Dawson Falls Tourist Lodge and Stratford Mountain House provide hotel-style accommodation. There is also a visitor center at Dawson Falls and a ranger station on Pembroke Road, Stratford.

Walking Tracks

Round the Mountain Track, a 55-km-long track, can be joined at any of the main mountain roads. Huts are situated roughtly 4 to 5 hours apart so that the walk can be done in easy stages. Much of the walking is either up or down, into and out of the numerous valleys and gorges. There are many short side tracks to view waterfalls and an ever-changing variety of vegetation, from scrubland to dense forest and alpine swamp, combined with the many moods that the mountain above offers each day. Allow at least 5 days for the complete circuit. You will need good boots and warm and waterproof clothing. Visitors are requested to make their intentions known at visitor centers before setting out on this walk and to fill in hut log books en route.

Summit Routes

The following are recognized summer routes to the summit. On the **northern side,** from the North Egmont road end and visitor center, take the Translator Road to Tahurangi Lodge, then climb the "stairway to the stars," steps built to prevent damage to the fragile moss fields. Above here the route is up a scoria slope west of Snow Valley to a prominent rocky ridge, the Lizard, which leads up to the crater entrance. Allow 4 to 6 hours for the ascent and 3 hours for the descent.

On the **southern side,** the track starts just above the visitor center at Dawson Falls and climbs first to Hooker Shelter, at 1,140 m, then up steps to the junction of the track to Lake Dive and Kapuni Lodge, at 1,400 m. Above here is the Knoll (1,674 m), from which a long zig-zag route up steep scoria slopes leads to the top of Fantham's Peak (1,962 m). There is a short descent to Rangitoto Flat, the saddle between Fantham's Peak and the main peak, and a further climb up the scoria to the south entrance of the crater, which is crossed to reach the final scoria slopes and summit rocks. Allow 5 to 7 hours to reach the summit and 3 to 4 hours to descend.

Mountain guides approved by the Department of Conservation can help you make a safe ascent of this notorious mountain. Both Chris Prudden and John Jordan are experienced mountaineers who offer guided climbs and skiing on Egmont. They can be contacted by writing to **Mountain Guides Mt. Egmont,** Box 783, New Plymouth, or by phoning Chris, at (06)7588-261, or John, at (06)7624-752.

Short Walks

Many short walks, taking from 15 minutes to 4 hours return, start at the three major road ends. From the **North Egmont** road end good examples of high-altitude forest, with its stunted, windshorn trees are seen on the Connett, Ngatoro, and Veronica walks, or you can climb higher to subalpine areas along the Translator Road and Round the Mountain Track. The Veronica and Ngatoro tracks descend to lower-altitude forests.

On the eastern side, at **Stratford Mountain House,** the Manganui Skifield and Curtis Ridge tracks give access to alpine herb fields. The small, club-operated Manganui Skifield opens when there is sufficient snow and can be a fun place on the right day. The lower slopes are suitable for beginners, but the upper slopes are steep and often icy. Skis can be rented from Stratford Mountain House.

Examples of the effects of volcanic activity on forests can be seen along the Patea Track, a 1.5-hour loop, and on the short Kamahi and Potaema walks.

While the track to Curtis Falls on the Manganui River would be of interest to fern lovers, a longer excursion (5 hours return) can be made by following the Waingongoro Track around to Dawson Falls on the south side and returning via the high-level route to the Manganui Plateau.

At **Dawson Falls** road end, on the south side, are tracks to Psyche's Bath and Wilkies Pool on the Kapunui River and to Dawson Falls where it plunges over the lip of an old lava flow. Alternatively, you can climb Hasties Hill for views of Fantham's Peak.

Access to the **Stony River** area on the western side is from the end of Puniho Road. The Puniho and Stony River tracks lead to Holly Hut, or the Puniho and Waiweranui tracks can be used for a full-day or overnight round trip to Kahui Hut. Parts of the Puniho, Stony River, and Maero tracks can be combined to make a half-day loop walk.

Pouakai Range

From the top of the Pouakai range there are spectacular views toward Mt. Egmont and over the coastline and hinterland. Being an older volcano than Egmont, Pouakai has some plants not found on the younger peak. The main path across the top of the range from Pouakai Trig (1,400 m) to Henry Peak (1,200 m) is the **Pouakai Track**. There are five access routes to this track, all taking around 2.5 to 3 hours, which can be combined to make trips of varying lengths. They are the **Kaiaua Track** from North Egmont Road, the **Maude Track** from Maude Road, **Mangorei Track** from the end of Mangorei Road, the **Dover Track** from Carrington Road opposite Dover Road, and the **Ahukawakawa Track** across the swamp from Holly Hut.

Kaitake Range

A full day is needed for the round trip to **Patuha Trig** (684 m), the highest point on the Kaitake Range. The easiest access is via the **Waimoku** or **Sefton Ridge tracks** (both 3 to 4 hours) from **Lucy's Gully,** a delightful picnic area at a grove of magnificent redwood trees planted in the 1930s. Lucy's Gully, named after an old lady who lived in the area for many years, is just off SH 45, a few kilometers south of Oakura. The short access road opposite Ahu Ahu Road is easily missed.

Transport to the Park

There is no public transport to road ends, but two companies run regular excursions and sightseeing tours to the mountain, and one of them will drop off and pick up at road ends and track ends. This is John Morton of **Mountain Excursions,** 133 Mangorei Road, New Plymouth, phone (06)7582-315. Inquiries can also be made at the North Egmont Visitor Centre, phone (06)7522-710. The other operator is **Neuman's Sightseeing Tours,** 23a Devon Mall, New Plymouth, phone (06)7584-622. For access to the Stratford Mountain House, check with the **Taranaki Pioneer Village,** Main Road South, Box 401, Stratford, phone (06)7655-399, or with local taxi companies.

AROUND NEW PLYMOUTH

City Walks

New Plymouth has several official city walks that take in many parks and bush reserves. A pamphlet showing these routes is available from the city's information center.

The 5.5-km **east coastal walk** from the Mt. Bryan Domain to Waiwhakaiho Park, is mainly along coastal reserves, passing Lake Rotonamu Wildlife Refuge en route, while the 6-km **west coastal walk** starts at Paritutu Beach, passes the power station and wharves, and then traverses Ngamotu Beach and Kawaroa Park to the historic Richmond Cottage.

The **Huatoki Valley** walk follows the Huatoki Valley for 5 km from the Sir Victor Davies Park to the outskirts of the city, taking in a number of pleasant bush areas, including Pukekura Park.

Five pa sites, the historic Te Henui Vicarage, which dates from Taranaki's early days of colonization, and a variety of native and exotic flora and birds are seen in the pleasant 5-km **Te Henui Walkway** along the banks of the Te Henui Stream. The walk, extending from the coast at East End Reserve and finishing at the city's southern boundary, is particularly pleasant in spring, when the golden kowhai and *Clematis paniculata* are flowering.

Parks and Reserves

Barrett Domain, a 36-ha blend of native bush, plantations, open spaces, and wetland, is a wildlife refuge. Several walking tracks start at the main entrance, on Roto St. in Westown.

Ratapihipihi Scenic Reserve, on the outskirts of New Plymouth, contains 20 ha of bush rich in tawa, kohekohe, pukatea, rewarewa, nikau, puriri, and titoki. The name Ratapihipihi comes from the name of the rata tree and the sound *pihipihi,* which kaka hunters used to make by blowing through a leaf to attract the birds to the rata trees in which the hunters were hiding. Access is from the suburb of Westown via Tukapa St. and Cowling Road.

Pukeiti Rhododendron Trust, set in 340 ha of native bush, lies cradled in a saddle between the Pouakai and Kaitake ranges. More than eight hundred different varieties of rhododendrons and azaleas can be viewed from a maze of easy paths. The peak flowering time for the rhododendrons is September to November, but the variety of other plants in the garden makes it attractive at any time of the year. The entrance to the garden is 20 km from New Plymouth on Carrington Road.

AROUND NORTH TARANAKI

Whitecliffs Walkway

The towering face of Paraninihi, the White Cliffs, is approximately 50 km north of New Plymouth. From the top are magnificent views along this wild stretch of coast, used first by the Maori as a highway for trading and raiding and later by European newcomers. The dense forest and dissected mudstone country behind was almost impregnable and offered a more fearsome obstacle than the tides and waves below. The 9.6-km Whitecliffs Walkway runs between Pukearuhe and Tongaporutu, following the Maui gas pipeline much of the way through native forest and across farmland. The full walk takes about 5 hours, and return transport would need to be arranged as there is no public transport to Pukearuhe. To avoid this problem, most people do the more interesting southern end of the walk only, making a loop by walking along the tops of the cliffs and descending to the beach at either Waipingau Stream or via the old stock route tunnel at Tamurenui Stream. If the tide is low, the return can be made along the beach beneath the cliffs.

The coast is exposed to strong westerly winds and weather, so take adequate clothing and wear boots if you have them, as the track can be slippery when wet. You will also need food and drink. Note also that the track can be closed in September for lambing.

Mt. Messenger

Today Mt. Messenger (310 m) is no more than a steep section of SH 3 between Ahititi and Urenui, but before 1916 it was an obstacle to all vehicle traffic. People not only traveled by foot or on horseback but also drove sheep and cattle along the beach between Pukearuhe and Tongaporutu at low tide. It was named after William Bazire Messenger of No. 6 Company, Taranaki Military Settlers, who was based at the garrison at Pukearuhe, which was built in 1863 to protect the northern end of the confiscated Maori lands. From SH 3 a steep 30-minute climb will bring you to the summit, with its views over the coast and rugged hinterland. If traveling north from New Plymouth, the track is signposted on the left about 1 km from the base of the southern side of Mt. Messenger. Tracks continue from the summit over Waipingau Trig to connect with the Whitecliffs Walkway in about 4 hours (one way).

Mokau and Tongaporutu

The drive along the North Taranaki coast is very scenic and there are several things worth stopping to see. Mokau, which means "winding river," is reputed to have been the resting place of the Tainui canoe. It's a good spot for fishing, and you can take boat trips up the picturesque river if you contact the folk at the local **Holiday Inn Motel** (phone (06)752-9725). You can also do leisurely

2-day trips in Canadian canoes with **Camp 'n Canoe**, RD 29, Kaponga, phone (06)7646-738. The Mohakatino River, about 5 km south of Mokau, is often claimed to have been the landing place of the Tokomaru canoe. If you visit Tongaporutu at low tide, be sure to take a look at the Maori carvings in the sea caves near the river mouth. The northern end of the Whitecliffs Walkway starts here, and even if you haven't time for walking, it's worth driving to the track end for the breathtaking views from the cliff tops. The amazing high white cliffs shine to the south, while below, the sea foams and hisses over a black sand beach.

AROUND EASTERN TARANAKI

Waitaanga Forest and Te Rerepahupahu Falls

Waitaanga Forest lies to the west of Ohura within a rough triangle formed by SH 40, SH 43, and Mangapapa Road. Although parts of the mixed podocarp and beech forest were logged between 1936 and 1968, there is still some magnificent bush to be seen in this area. Rivers have eroded the soft mudstone landscape and left rugged steep-sided ridges and some remarkable waterfalls, one of which is beautiful Te Rerepahupahu Falls. Lying in the center of the forest, the falls can be reached by three marked routes, two of which can be linked to make an interesting and varied overnight trip. Pamphlets describing these routes in more detail can be obtained from the Department of Conservation in New Plymouth. Note that they are fairly strenuous and require some experience in tramping.

One route, taking about 3.5 to 4 hours one way, starts 14 km southwest of Ohura from the Tatu Mine Site at the end of Waro Road off SH 43. The Tatu Mine opened in 1940 and until 1971 provided coal for many of the dairy factories in the district. The track climbs to the top of Tatu (606 m) before descending steeply to the junction of the Tangarakau and Waitaanga rivers. The Waitaanga River is then followed upstream for about an hour to the falls, passing a campsite about 15 minutes before reaching them.

The second route, which takes 4 to 4.5 hours, starts at the end of Waitaanga South Road off SH 40. After crossing farmland, follow an old tramline down the Waitaanga Valley, crossing the river four times. After about 3 hours, the track leaves the river and climbs steeply before plunging back to the valley floor about 10 minutes' walk below the falls.

Matemateaonga Track

The Matemateaonga Track traverses 40 km of the Matemateaonga Range in eastern Taranaki between Makahu and the Wanganui River. There are three huts and three shelters along the track, and the walk usually takes 3 to 4 days. From vantage points along the ridge there are views across broken country clothed in dense forest, with glimpses of the Tongariro volcanoes and Mt. Egmont. The track is almost entirely in tall forest, and much of it follows an old road that was started in the 1920s but never completed. The Taranaki end of the track starts at Kohi Saddle, about 15 km east of Makahu on Mangaehu Road. Makahu is reached by Brewer Road, which turns off SH 43 at Strathmore. The Wanganui end is only accessible by boat, and arrangements must be made prior to setting out. A number of boat operators are listed under Whanganui National Park in "Wanganui and Manawatu."

For transport to the Taranaki end of the track, contact any of the following operators:

Midhurst Motors, RD 24, Stratford, phone (06)7628-772.

Mrs. Francis Ford, Strathmore, phone (06)7623-895.

Pioneer Jet Boat Tours, Box 399, Taumarunui, phone (07)8958-074 for mini-bus to Kohi Saddle and jet boat pickup on the river.

Camp 'n Canoe, RD 29, Kaponga, phone (06)7646-738, provide transport to both ends, with a choice of canoe, kayak, or jet boat transport down the Wanganui River. They also do guided trips on the track by arrangement.

Macanz Tours, Box 36, Wanganui, phone (06)3444-194, also do 4-day guided trips, with a jet boat return to Wanganui.

Lake Rotorangi

Lake Rotorangi, formed by a hydro dam built on the Patea River in 1984, follows the valley's long sinuous course for 46 km. It is reached by Ball Road, off SH 3 south of Hawera, which provides a very scenic 35-km drive into the backcountry. Recreational opportunities created by the lake's formation include fishing, canoeing, houseboating, jet boating, and waterskiing. There is also a short walk around a promontory near the dam. Evidence of human intrusion on the scenery is quickly left behind as the track climbs through beautiful black beech forest, with many lovely views down to the still, green waters filling bush-rimmed inlets. A small camping area with toilets and showers makes it possible to stay overnight at this tranquil spot.

The houseboats are based at the top end of the lake, reached by following Anderson and Rawhiti roads from Eltham. There are two boats, sleeping four and six people, and both are fully equipped for overnight accommodation. Off-season rates apply from May to November. For more information, contact **Houseboat Holidays,** Box 26, Stratford, phone (06)7656-978 or 7647-523, or after hours, R. Petrie at (06)7657-858.

If you want to fish on the lake or take a cruise, contact the Hawera Information Centre or any of the following:

Lake Rotorangi Scenic Tours, Gary Brown, 91 Turuturu Road, Hawera, phone (06)2783-227 or 2786-125.

Hawera Marine and Sports, Hawera, phone (06)2787-187 for boat rental.
Camp 'n Canoe, RD 29, Kaponga, phone (06)7646-738, for rental of motorized kayaks and dinghies, sailing dinghies, and Canadian canoes.

PLACES OF HISTORIC INTEREST

Taranaki, with its rich Maori traditions, sites of conflict and stories of the white settlers' endeavors to tame the land, has much to interest history buffs. **Taranaki Pioneer Village,** on SH 3, just south of Stratford, is open daily. It has more than thirty-six buildings under restoration, including a jail and a railway station. Two **Heritage Trails** have been set out to enable visitors to learn more of this history, and these are described in a very informative booklet obtainable from information and visitor centers. Heritage Trail sites are signposted with distinctive green and gold signs, and there is additional on-site information.

One trail follows the very scenic **Stratford–Taumarunui Road** (SH 43) as it winds through farmland and rugged bush country, passing the now almost deserted settlements of Whangamomona, Tangarakau, and Tahora. In the late 1800s, before the line of the Main Trunk Railway was finally decided on, consideration was given to running it from Taumarunui through to Stratford. There was already a line in place between New Plymouth and Stratford, and this would avoid the then largely unknown central plateau. Work started at the Stratford end, but progress was slow, and after several years the line only reached 60 km to Whangamomona. No further construction was done until 1929, when the government decided to hire unemployed men to do the job. A huge work camp was set up at Tangarakau and it became a bustling town with more than 2,000 residents. Once the line opened and workers were no longer needed, Tangarakau was left to the bush and birds once more. Closure of the rail service between Taumarunui and Stratford in the late 1970s isolated the tiny communities along the line even more, and only farmers and the hardy have stayed on. If you choose this route to the central North Island, allow a full day. As well as forgotten towns, there are old coal mining sites, forest walks, and several detours to waterfalls.

Macanz Tours, Box 36, Wanganui, phone (06)3444-194, take guided tours to Tangarakau and other places in the district. For those who want to spend more time in the area, **Bushlands Farm Campground** (phone (06)7625-546) at Tangarakau has cabins and a self-contained farm cottage for rent, and Whangamomona has hotel and campground accommodations.

The **Taranaki Trail** takes in places of interest along the main highways encircling Mt. Egmont, including Pukerangiora, Koru, and Turuturu Mokai Pa sites. **Pukerangiora Pa,** where the land wars began, is 8 km up Waitara Road from Waitara. Here, high on a cliff above a bend in the Waitara River, a Waikato war party under Te Whero Whero besieged the local Ngati Awa people for three months in 1832. The attackers eventually captured the pa, and many of its defendants threw themselves over the cliffs. Some were crushed, but some survived by landing on the bodies of others. Te Whero Whero killed 150 of those who remained with his own *mere* (club), and at the cannibal feast that followed, some Waikato are said to have died of gluttony. Later, in 1861, the Waikato and local tribes combined to defend the pa against the British.

Koru Pa was a stronghold of the Nga Mahanga people, and although it is now clothed in vegetation, the complex stone ramparts can still be seen. It is close to Oakura, following Wairau Road, then Surrey Hills Road, and can be reached by a 15-minute walk over farmland.

The ancient and massive **Turuturu Mokai Pa** was restored extensively in the 1930s and is now the focal point of a historic reserve on Turuturu Road, Hawera. All that is left are the triple lines of trenches and the remains of many dug-in hut sites and food storage pits on the summit. Each trench once had a high rampart surmounted by a stockade that was practically impregnable. The remains of five satellite pa lie close by, and one of these can be seen in the reserve. Another was connected to the main pa by a tunnel under the Tawhiti Stream. Turuturu Mokai was the scene of a massacre of Ngati Tupea people by the Taki Ruahine in a time now lost to history. Afterward, the smoke-dried heads of the slain were impaled on stakes thrust into the ground and the pa was given its present name—Turuturu, "the stakes," and Mokai, "the dried heads." An intense battle between the military settlers and Titokowaru's forces also took place here in 1868. The dissident Titokowaru conducted a guerrilla campaign against settlers who moved onto confiscated land around military garrisons.

Tawhiti Museum, in Ohangai Road, Hawera, is one of those special places that should be on everyone's itinerary, whether they are keen on history or not. It is privately owned and is housed in an old dairy factory. Excellent dioramas and lifelike models recreate events and incidents from Taranaki's past, while a detailed miniature bush tramway illustrates aspects of timber milling. There is also a model of nearby Turuturu Mokai Pa and a "live dunny" (pit toilet), which is guaranteed to shock and amuse. The museum is open Fri.–Mon., 10 A.M. to 4 P.M., but Sundays only in June, July, and August.

Opunake has a pleasant coastal walkway that traverses two hundred years of history. Near the northern end of the walk is the important Te Namu Pa site, where a small group of Taranaki Maori held out successfully for a month against attacks by a strong force of 800 Waikato invaders. Remains of the old Armed Constabulary Cemetery, with the poignant headstone of one Mary Doble, who was murdered in 1880, stand on a small headland jutting out into Opunake Lake. Nearer the beach is the Cottage Hospital, built in 1922. The walkway has several access points from adjoining streets and also passes the town's sheltered beach, where there is good swimming and a pleasant motor camp.

Parihaka Marae, where Te Whiti and his followers staged a passive resistance against the government, is a few kilometers from Pungarehu, up Parihaka Road. You can view it from the road, or you may be shown around if you ask permission.

SURFING AND WINDSURFING

Taranaki coast is considered the most exciting place in the country for surfing and windsurfing—better, some say, than Hawaii's Hookipa. And the good thing is that not a lot of people know this, so it's never crowded. The coast is exposed to the prevailing westerly winds, and for almost 60 percent of the time, winds exceed 11 knots. For nearly 20 percent of the time the wind comes from the southwest, the best direction for sailing, by local reckoning. An easterly wind, bringing the worst conditions, occurs only 4 percent of the time. The hardest thing is knowing which is the best location on any day, but the locals are very helpful. Call in at **Sirocco** in Oakura to find out where all the action is.

Popular **Oakura Beach,** close to New Plymouth, has a pleasant campground right beside the black sand, so you don't need to go far to find out what conditions are like. Other good beaches are at the end of **Ahu Ahu Road** and **Weld Road,** a short distance down the coast. There are three beaches close to **Opunake:** Green Meadows, Sky Williams, and Kina Road. They are favorites, and the town also has a good campground. Other good locations, which you'll need a car to reach, are at the ends of **Stent Road** and **Bayley Road,** both turning off SH 45 between Puniho and Pungarehu.

USEFUL ADDRESSES

Department of Conservation, Atkinson Building, Devon St., Box 462, New Plymouth, phone (06)7580-433.

New Plymouth Public Relations Office, 81 Liardet St., New Plymouth, phone (06)7586-086.

Taranaki Pioneer Village, Main Road South, Box 401, Stratford, phone (06) 7655-399.

Hawera Information Centre, High St., Box 5, Hawera, phone (06)2788-599.

11 ◆ LAKE TAUPO AND THE TONGARIRO REGION

LANDSCAPE

Occupying the heart of the North Island are Lake Taupo and Tongariro National Park. To the west the lake is bordered by the low, gently undulating Hauhungaroa Range, and to the east the rugged Kaimanawa Ranges stretch southward in a distinct barrier. It is a region rich in geologic and human history, legend, and diverse scenery. On a crisp, clear winter's day the view south from Taupo, across the sparkling blue waters of the lake to the three snow-capped volcanic peaks, Tongariro, Ngauruhoe, and Ruapehu, is one that must have stirred the hearts and quickened the imaginations of the first Maori visitors and then of the early European explorers and settlers, as much as it excites and beckons today's climbers and skiers. On such a day, looking across the expanse of Taupo-nui-a-Tia (the great cloak of Tia), as the lake is known, it is difficult to appreciate that these peaceful waters fill the collapsed caldera of an ancient volcano with a history of producing some of the most violent and devastating eruptions ever to occur on this planet. The last eruption, around A.D. 186, is believed to have been the biggest volcanic event ever recorded. Fine volcanic dust emitted during the blast would have filled the atmosphere and circled the globe, reaching far into the Northern Hemisphere. Confirmation of this is provided by both Chinese and Greek scholars of the time, who commented on the vivid red sunsets and darkened daytime skies.

During that eruption, an estimated 60,000 to 100,000 cu km of tephra were spewed out, an amount 15,000 times that emitted by the 1980 eruption of Mt. Saint Helens. The first material ejected was a column of pumice that reached heights of more than 50 km; then a pyroclastic flow of hot material traveled radially away from the vent at tremendous speeds. Forests lying in the path of this flow, within a radius of 80 km, were flattened by the blast, and logs were carbonized by the tremendous heat. Remnants of these forests can be seen today in the form of charcoal and charred logs buried in deep layers of pumice. It has been estimated that the pyroclastic flow must have been traveling at least 600 km per hour through the Turangi area to have been able to pass over the summit of Mt. Tongariro (1,968 m) and to slurp up the sides of Ruapehu to a height 1,000 m above the present lake level.

Lake Taupo and the Tongariro volcanoes form the southern part of the Taupo Volcanic Zone, which extends from White Island in the Bay of Plenty through the thermal centers of Rotorua and Taupo to Mt. Ruapehu. The summits of

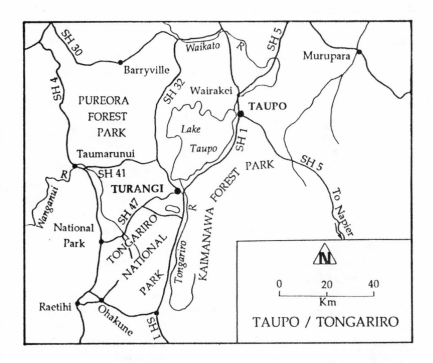

Tongariro, Ngauruhoe, and Ruapehu at the southern extremity stand in line with the more northern cones of Tauhara and Putauaki (Mt. Edgecumbe); far to the west is the isolated cone of Taranaki (Mt. Egmont). Maori legend tells how once all these male mountains stood close together; all were enamored of the beautifully adorned Pihanga (the forested mountain immediately south of Turangi). A fierce battle over who should lay claim to Pihanga was won by the gallant old warrior Tongariro. He stands close to her today, separated only by the waters of Lake Rotoaira. Defeated, the other mountains had to move away quickly, before the next dawn. Putauaki hurried toward the warmth of the rising sun, but the dejected Tauhara dallied, reluctant to leave Pihanga. By dawn he had only reached the northern shores of Lake Taupo, where he stands, watching his beloved forever. Taranaki fled westward toward the setting sun, and during his furious departure formed the path of the Wanganui River.

Neither did the mountains always belch forth fire and hot rocks as they do today. Legend also tells us that it was Ngatoro-i-rangi, a *tohunga* (priest or person with special powers) and navigator of the great canoe Te Arawa, who created the volcanic activity in the North Island. On sighting the peak of Tongariro at the southern end of Lake Taupo, Ngatoro vowed to reach its summit. Commanding his men to fast until his return, he set off with his female slave

Auruhoe. During the ascent a blizzard descended upon them, sent by the gods who were angry because Ngatoro's men had broken their fast. The force and cold of the storm were unlike anything Ngatoro had ever experienced before, so he prayed to his sisters in Hawaiki to send fire to warm them. His prayers were answered; the sisters sent fire underground. But it rose too soon, first at White Island, then at Rotorua, Tarawera, Orakei Korako, and Taupo. By the time the fire burst forth at Tongariro, Auruhoe was already dead from the cold. Ngatoro, now saved, was so grateful that he hurled her body into the newly formed crater, which has since been known as Ngauruhoe.

The eruption of Taupo 1,800 years ago not only devastated the surrounding forests but changed the character and composition of the future vegetation. Before the blast, much of the forests was red and silver beech, with podocarp species occupying only the lower, warmer areas. At higher altitudes and in poorer sites the tough mountain beech would have predominated. The only areas untouched by the flows of hot pumice were high alpine zones, the southwestern slopes of Ruapehu, and odd pockets of vegetation tucked into the lee sides of ridges and gullies away from the blast. Revegetation of the raw, new covering would have started soon after the eruption, from seed supplied by lone plants that survived, and the podocarps would have had the advantage over the beech species.

Forest birds are attracted by the fleshy receptacle that cups the seed of podocarp trees, and as the seeds can survive passage through a bird's gut, they are carried long distances. The heavy, lightly winged beech seed is only effectively transported by water. Without it, beech forests extend their boundaries very slowly by seeds that drop from the outermost trees. Today, in the Lake Taupo and Tongariro region, podocarp forests are found at altitudes that would normally be occupied by red and silver beech. Small pockets of beech seen today probably originated from a few survivors in sheltered sites.

HISTORY

The volcanic wonders of the central North Island have always found favor with both Maori and European peoples. The Maori revered the peaks for their power and held them sacred. Natural steam vents and hot pools at Taupo and Tokaanu supplied warmth and easy cooking; the first Europeans were more interested in their tourist potential. Ngauruhoe was first climbed in 1839 by John Bidwell, who made the ascent alone. His Maori companions refused to go with him, first because the mountain was sacred and second because it had been noisy during the night. At the top, Bidwell peered into "the most terrific abyss I ever looked into or imagined." His illegal ascent so angered Chief Te Heu Heu Tukino that many other would-be summiteers were turned back from the mountain. Ruapehu was ascended in 1853, but the crater lake was not discovered until 1879.

In 1857, the Reverend T. S. Grace arrived in the area and decided that the extensive tussocklands surrounding the volcanoes would be ideal for sheep. His twin sons set up the Kariori Company in 1874, and by 1880 had almost 10,000 sheep grazing the northern parts of Tongariro, the Rangipo Desert, and the Waimarino Plains. Because the sheep found the tussock unpalatable, the tussocklands were burned to promote the growth of other grasses. Although there appeared to be good grazing, many sheep died of "bush sickness," a malady later found to be caused by a deficiency of cobalt in the volcanic soils. This, combined with stock losses and transport costs for the wool, spelled the end of early sheep farming attempts in the region.

By the time writer-explorer J. H. Kerry-Nicholl journeyed through the central North Island in 1883, tourism was already becoming well established. Settlement of Taupo began in 1869 with the establishment of an armed constabulary post during the campaign against Te Kooti, and a coach service from Taupo to Rotorua became established 1875. By then there were already modest hotels at Wairakei and Taupo.

The new Tongariro National Park, the core of which was established by the gift of the summits of Tongariro and Ngauruhoe in 1887 from the Tuwharetoa people, saw few visitors at first. With the opening of the Desert Road in 1893, the park became more easily accessible to visitors, but it was not until Waihohonu Hut was built in 1901 that there was any accommodation for them. This tiny building on the eastern side of the park became the center for activities and was the base from which the first skiers, William Mead and Bernard Drake, set out to try the new sport. Once the Main Trunk Railway was completed in 1909 the western side of the area was opened up, but it did not become very popular until a road was built from Tokaanu through to Waimarino (now National Park township) in 1919. At the same time, a cart track was formed through the bush to Whakapapa and an accommodation hut was built there. As skiing and hiking became more popular, more accommodations were built until a sizeable village began to grow, culminating in the opening of the Chateau Tongariro in 1929. The career of this large Georgian building has been checkered and colorful, and although it may seem a building that is out of place in the wild setting of volcano, bush, and tussockland, it is one of the few grand places left in New Zealand to remind of an English heritage.

Skiing continued to attract enthusiasts, and a large village of lodges, built entirely with funds and labor of tramping and ski club members, mushroomed at the base of Whakapapa Skifield. In 1953 a public company, Ruapehu Alpine Lifts, was formed from subscriptions from skiers and others and the first chairlift was installed and running the following winter. Development has continued apace since then, and Whakapapa is now the biggest ski area in the country. On the southern slopes of Ruapehu, above Ohakune, Turoa Skifields opened their first ski lifts in 1978.

◆PLACES TO VISIT AND THINGS TO DO

AROUND TAUPO

The attractive town of Taupo, set on the northern edge of Lake Taupo, is one of the North Island's most popular holiday destinations, in summer for water-based activities, and in winter for trout fishing and skiing. There is good shopping, all facilities, and a vast range of accommodation, with numerous motels to choose from, hotels, backpacker and fishing lodges, and campgrounds. Boats can be chartered for fishing on the lake or you can cruise on the *Taupo Cat*, a luxury catamaran, the *Ernest Kemp*, a replica steam ferry, or *The Barbary*, a 40-ft. yacht. If the weather is inclement, the **De Brett Thermal Pools** are a great place to while away some time. Tourist attractions just north of town along SH 1 include the **Wairakei Geothermal Power Station** and natural thermal valley, the replica historic **Huka Village,** the thundering **Huka Falls,** and **Craters of the Moon** thermal area, which is as good as anything around Rotorua and has no entry fee. In summer you can rent catamarans for fun sailing or join a growing number of windsurfers. SH 1 runs along the eastern side of Lake Taupo and because much of the lake edge is public reserve there are numerous places for picnicking and swimming. **Motutere Bay,** about halfway between Taupo and Turangi, has a pleasant campground and is very popular over the Christmas–New Year period.

Both the Kaimanawa Range, to the east and south of the lake, and the Pureora forests, on the western side, are good for hunting and hiking. The Kaimanawa Range is particularly popular for fly-in fishing and hunting trips. Guides and flights can be organized in Taupo and Turangi. Several walkways and tracks close to town are good for more leisurely walking, and pamphlets giving details of access are available from information centers.

Panoramic views over the Taupo region are gained from the summit of **Mt. Tauhara** (1,088 m), rising steeply behind Taupo township. Most of the 1.5-hour climb is steep, and passes through scrubby brush until it enters the sheltered 40,000-year-old crater, which is filled with an unusual association of broadleaf trees. The trail starts at the end of Mountain Road, about 7.5 km along SH 5 (Taupo-Napier) from the lakefront.

Waipahihi Botanical Reserve is another delightful place to amble in September and October, when rhododendrons and camelias are in full bloom. This well-kept bush reserve, covering rolling hilltops at the eastern edge of the town, has a charming mix of native vegetation planted with over 2,000 species of rhododendrons, camelias, and azaleas. The entrance to the reserve is at the top end of Shepherd Road, off SH 1 (the second street on the left, south of the junction of Highway 5).

The **Lions Walk**, starting at 2 Mile Bay by the boat ramp at the end of Mapou St. (southern end of town), offers a very easy ramble along the lake edge to Wharewhaka Point (4 Mile Bay). Parts of the walk pass through groves of kowhai trees, which in spring are festooned with glorious yellow blossoms. The return can be made via streets a short distance back from the lake edge.

You can also walk to the **Huka Falls**, and on to **Aratiatia Rapids**, from town along the right bank of the Waikato River. The well-defined track starts at **Spa Thermal Park**, at the end of County Avenue off Spa Road. Huka Falls is reached in about an hour, and from there it's another 7 km, taking around 2 hours, through pine forest to the rapids. As the flow of the river is controlled for hydroelectricity generation, the Aratiatia Rapids (meaning "Staircase of Tia") are not the spectacular sight they once were—except when the flood gates are opened at 10 A.M. and 2:30 P.M. It is worth timing your walk to coincide with this spectacle.

NORTHERN END OF KAIMANAWA FOREST PARK

The more gentle northern end of the Kaimanawa Range, with its magnificent beech forests and easy valleys, offers pleasant hiking and good rivers for trout fishing. The most popular hike at this end of the park is to **Boyd Hut** via **Te Iringa Hut** and **Oamaru Hut**, taking 2 days one way. Airstrips at Oamaru and Boyd huts make it possible to fly in or out if you don't want to retrace your steps. Maps of the park are available from the Taupo Information Office or from the Department of Conservation at Wairakei and Turangi. Access to the park and the start of the track to these huts is off SH 5, turning right into Taharua Road 27.5 km from Taupo (toward Napier) at an AA Kaimanawa Forest Park sign. Follow Taharua Road and then direction signs for another 16 km.

From the carpark, the well-defined track climbs steadily through magnificent beech forest for 1.5 to 2 hours to Te Iringa Hut (6 bunks) a short distance below the top of Mt. Te Iringa. From the top there is a steady descent to the Tiki Tiki Stream, which is followed to its junction with the Kaipo River, then easy travel down the right bank of the Kaipo to reach Oamaru Hut (12 bunks) on a terrace above the junction of the Kaipo and Oamaru rivers in another 4 hours.

Oamaru Hut to Boyd Hut takes 5 hours or more. River flats on the true left are followed upstream to a sign marking the start of the cut track. High pumice cliffs on the opposite bank give some idea of the amount of pumice thrown out of Lake Taupo when it erupted 1,800 years ago. The track continues beside the Oamaru River, crosses several side streams, reaches Waitawhero Stream, then climbs steadily to Waitawhero Saddle on the edge of the broad, open Ngaruroro Valley. Boyd Hut (16 bunks) set at the edge of beech forest above the river terrace on the far side has views down the open tussock-covered river flats. This section of Ngaruroro Valley is open, so walking is easy, or you can climb to the ridge above the hut for views.

PUREORA FOREST PARK

Small Pureora Forest Park on the western side of Lake Taupo is better known to hunters and conservationists than hikers. The Pureora forests, which cover the Hauhungaroa and Rangitoto ranges, had been logged from the 1920s, and when it was realized that some of the country's best stands of lowland forest were scheduled for destruction, protests and direct action by some dedicated conservationists saved them. Within the park are dense stands of podocarp forest under a tight canopy of rimu, matai, miro, and totara mixed with occasional kahikatea and tanekaha. Some of the giants here reach 45 m in height and 1.5 m in girth and are 500 to 1,000 years old.

The park is divided into southern and northern blocks on either side of SH 30 between Te Kuiti and Taupo. The northern block, which has been extensively logged, is a recreational hunting area; it is the southern area which is of most interest, as it is here that the endangered kokako (*Callaeas cinera*) may be seen. The bluish-grey kokako, with its distinctive bright blue wattles, has a slow, melodious, flutelike song that it sings loudly for long periods in the early morning, causing early settlers to call it the organ bird. Being a poor flier, it loses altitude as it glides or flies from tree to tree and must therefore hop back up through the vegetation to gain elevation for the next flight. Often, instead of flying, the kokako runs and hops along branches from tree to tree, and it needs reasonably dense vegetation to do this. The kokako's diet consists of leaves, fruits, and flowers from a variety of trees, particularly the succulent berries of podocarp species; in summer it also consumes insects, especially a scale insect, *Ctenochiton viridis*. It often holds its food in its foot, parrot fashion. Destruction of lowland forests, competition for the same foods by possums, and the introduction of predators such as stoats and ferrets have led to the kokako's decline in the last century.

Maps and information on the park are available from the Department of Conservation, Taupiri St., Te Kuiti, and from the park headquarters located at Pureora on a short side road signposted a few kilometers from Barryville on SH 30. There is a small visitor center here and nearby is the pleasant, grassy Ngaherenga camping area. Other camping areas are at Kakaho on the eastern edge of the park and Piropiro Flats on the western side. Kakaho picnic and camping area can be reached via Link Road, which runs from the headquarters across the northern end of the block or from Kakaho Road, which connects with SH 32 along the western side of Lake Taupo.

Close to the headquarters is the 30-minute **Totara Walk** through podocarp forest, the **Buried Forest** where large tree trunks lie buried under deep layers of pumice, and the **birdwatching tower** (on Bismark Road). The high tower takes you into the canopy of the forest among the dense crowns of huge rimu, matai, and tawa hung with lianes, ferns, and perching lilies. Below is a subcanopy of tree fern crowns. It's an amazing experience, being up in the trees, and a few minutes of patient waiting will reward you with the kokako's haunting call. With luck and good binoculars you will also see these rare birds. Other birds you'll quite likely see are kaka, long-tailed cuckoo (in spring and summer), grey warbler, and whitehead.

The two highest points on the Hauhungaroa Range, **Mt. Titiraupenga** and **Mt. Pureora,** have tracks to their summits. The shortest (3 hours return) to Titiraupenga's distinctive thumblike summit is from the end of Arataki Road, and a longer route starts from a carpark on Link Road. To reach Arataki Road, follow Link Road from the park headquarters or Kakaho Road from SH 32, to Waimona Road. One kilometer along Waimona Road turn right into Titiraupenga Road (signposted "YMCA Camp") and follow it for 4 km. Mt. Pureora can also be reached in an hour from the carpark on Link Road.

Another pleasant walk is to **Waihaha Hut** (6 bunks), set in a clearing in towering podocarp forest toward the southern end of the park. The 9-km walk takes less than 3 hours and is one of surprising variety, with a mix of river scenery, regrown forest, scrubland, and virgin podocarp forest. The track starts at the north end of the Waihaha River Bridge on SH 32 and follows the true left bank upriver. The extensive scrub-covered **Pokaiora Clearing,** about half way along, has some excellent campsites beside the river, and in summer, the deep pools offer a refreshing respite from walking. Near the hut, giant rimu, matai, and totara trees tower above dense groves of tree fern, and the forest silence is broken only by the call of tui and the noisy flight of plump wood pigeons as they make their way heavily between tree tops. With luck, you may also hear the haunting call of the rare kokako.

If you are in the Pureora area it's worth walking 15 minutes to the gigantic **Poukanui Totara,** reputed to be the largest in New Zealand with a diameter of 3.63 m. It's around 1,700 years old and contains enough timber for two houses. This last fact, recorded on a sign by the tree, must have been written in preconservation days! The track is signposted on the eastern side of SH 30. If traveling toward Taupo, watch for the sign, set back from the road on the right, about 8 km past Barryville and 1 km before Ranginui Road.

AROUND TURANGI

Turangi is a much smaller center than Taupo, but it has most services and hotel, motel, backpacker, and motorcamp accommodation. For many years it was a quiet fishing retreat, but this changed when the Tongariro Hydroelectric Power Scheme was built and a new town was constructed to cater for the workers. Many of these were Italian tunnellers, imported to dig the massive tunnels required to redirect the flow of rivers on the western side of Tongariro National Park to Lake Taupo. Once the power scheme was completed many workers moved away and the town went into decline for some years. It remained popular as a base for fishing on the Tongariro River and more recently has seen a small comeback as a center for tourists visiting Tongariro National Park, both in summer and winter. The information office has excellent displays on the Tongariro power scheme and Tongariro National Park and can help with transport and queries on local walking tracks. If you'd like to know more about trout, visit the **National Trout Centre,** just south of Turangi on SH 1. The **Tokaanu Hot Pools** are another popular attraction, particularly during winter after a hard day skiing or fishing. If you find there is a queue for the private pools, take a walk through the thermal area behind the baths complex. It has some beautiful bubbling hot pools set among tall manuka scrub.

Pleasant walking close to town can be had along the **Tongariro River Walkway,** which follows the true right bank of the Tongariro River, giving access to fishing pools. The track starts at the Major Jones Pool footbridge at the end of Koura St. and ends at the Red Hut Pool footbridge, 4.5 km south of Turangi on Highway 1. Allow about 1.5 hours to walk between the two footbridges.

Views over Turangi and the delta of the Tongariro River are good from the top of **Mt. Maunganamu,** an isolated conical hill on the northern side of the Tokaanu power station tailrace. The track starts about 1 km along the dirt road on the north bank of the tailrace and climbs around the flank of the hill through tall kanuka forest to reach a viewing platform in 20 to 25 minutes.

Pristine podocarp forest—ideal habitat for pigeons, tui, and small bush birds—surrounds **Rotopounamu** (Greenstone Lake), which nestles in a basin on the western slopes of Mt. Pihanga. The 8-m-deep lake has several streams flowing into it but no visible outlet, and its other unusual feature is that in spite of being so accessible, the water is free from exotic plants. The lake edge is reached in about 20 minutes by a well-graded track that leaves Highway 47 just below the top of Te Ponanga Saddle, 8.3 km from Turangi. Walking around the lake can take another hour or more. Small beaches on the western and northern shores and a longer one at the eastern end are good places for picnicking.

Other Points of Interest

Along SH 47 between Turangi and National Park township are **Hinemihis Track,** a short section of the old Maori trail across Te Ponanga Saddle, the reconstructed

Opotaka Pa site on the shore of Lake Rotoaira at the base of Te Ponanga Saddle, and **Te Porere Redoubt,** the site of Te Kooti's last battle against government troops in 1869, just south of the junction of SH 47 and SH 47a.

SOUTHERN END OF KAIMANAWA FOREST PARK

The southern end of the Kaimanawa Range is much more rugged than the northern end, with steep bush faces and high open ridges of rock and tussock. Until 1991 the main access to tracks was from Kaimanawa Road, about 10 km south of Turangi on SH 1. This road has since been closed to the public by the Maori landowners, but negotiations are in process to allow public access to the park. Tracks starting from Kaimanawa Road lead to **Umukarikari** and **Urchin,** two easily reached vantage points, and on to Waipakihi Hut in the beautiful upper Waipakihi Valley. The valley has extensive grassy flats in its upper reaches, and, with its beech forest, is similar to many South Island valleys. If you are keen to visit this area, check with the Department of Conservation in Turangi. Access to the lower end of the Waipakihi Valley is from Waipakihi Road off SH 1, 38 km south of Turangi. There are pleasant picnic and camping sites here, beside the river. Waipakihi Hut can be reached in about 8 hours by traveling up the river, with many crossings.

Tree Trunk Gorge and Pillars of Hercules

Spectacular Tree Trunk Gorge, where the Tongariro River is funnelled into a terrifying roaring cataract plunging between dark slimy walls, is reached by Tree Trunk Gorge Road, off Highway 1 approximately 23 km south of Turangi. From the gorge a walking track follows an overgrown survey road (put in when the Rangipo Power Scheme was being constructed) down the river to the Pillars of Hercules. Here the river flows silently and deeply, with barely a ripple, through a narrow, straight-walled constriction in the hard andesitic rock. The pleasant walk between these impressive features takes 1 to 1.5 hours one way, through mixed podocarp and beech forest, with several small ups and downs and one stream crossing. It's a good walk when the weather is too miserable for the open country in neighboring Tongariro National Park.

Kiko Road Tracks

Kiko Road turns off SH 1 approximately 10 km north of Turangi; follow the forest park access signs for 18 km to a carpark at the road end. A very pleasant **Forest Loop Walk,** taking 2 to 2.5 hours, follows a well-graded, benched track through magnificent beech forest, or you can climb to the top of **Ngapuketurua** for magnificent views over Lake Taupo. The latter is a steady 3.5-hour climb up a long ridge onto the open tussock-covered top of the range. Take warm clothing, food, and drink if heading up there.

TONGARIRO NATIONAL PARK

Being an active volcanic area, Tongariro National Park has features and scenery found in few other places in the world. Where else are there ski areas on the side of a volcano whose active crater is a large, hot lake set in permanent snowfields? And this same volcano, Ruapehu, has dense rain forests on one flank while another is desertlike and treeless. The youngest volcano of the group, Ngauruhoe, is still growing and displays its recent past in a series of lava flows. Tongariro's numerous craters, some now water-filled, provide a fascinating landscape almost moonlike in texture and quality, etched in raw earth colors.

The peak of Tongariro probably began to form at least 1.5 million years ago with numerous vents adding layers of new rock at different times to build a sprawling volcanic complex. Extensive glaciation during the last Ice Age wore away much of the original mountain, but subsequent activity over the past 50,000 years built up the present scarred and torn arena of peaks and craters. Two of the older vents, Red Crater and upper Te Maari Crater, have been active within living memory. Red Crater erupted ash in 1897 and again in 1926, and Upper Te Maari Crater formed as recently as 1868. Activity in this crater in 1896–97 scattered ash over the Desert Road to a depth of 50 mm and spread a dusting as far as Napier. The only active vent now is Mt. Ngauruhoe, which only began to form about 2,500 years ago. It is believed that another large peak once stood where the present Ngauruhoe now stands, but that it was eroded away. Evidence of this "Proto-Ngauruhoe" is visible as old glacial valleys that radiate from the base of the present peak.

Ruapehu, like Tongariro, is a stratovolcano with a complex history dating back 500,000 years. Eruptions from numerous vents built up the 2,797-m-high massif, and the site of current activity is known as Crater Lake. Situated at an elevation of 2,550 m, this roughly circular lake with a diameter of 500 m provides an amazing contrast between two forces of nature—volcanic heat and glacial ice. On occasion the surface of the lake has frozen over, but most of the time it is warm and at times reaches 60°C, even when surrounded by snow and ice. The water is also extremely acidic, with a pH of 0.8–1.5. In the past it was less so, and there are photographs of people swimming in the water—a practice not recommended today.

In spite of its serene appearance, Ruapehu can be an unpredictable and dangerous volcano. From time to time minor eruptions occur when superheated water flashes to steam and rises to the surface of Crater Lake like a giant bubble, bursting forth as a geyser. There is usually no ash or other debris ejected. Larger eruptions occur when molten magma beneath the lake comes in contact with the overlying water. The magma chills and contracts on contact with the water or wet sediments, then shatters in a series of violent explosions. During these phreatomagmatic eruptions, steam may rise in a column hundreds of meters above the crater and water, and lake sediments and fresh lava are ejected outward from the base. This hot material has the potential to melt the surrounding ice and snow, creating lahars, or mud flows, which race down the mountainsides with devastating force.

Massive lahars have thundered down Ruapehu's slopes many times over the centuries, pouring forth in all directions to build up the ring plain that surrounds the volcanoes for 20 km. Two recent lahars, in June 1969 and April 1975, while comparatively small, were still very destructive and had the potential to be lethal, as both flowed through the major skifield on the mountain. Fortunately they occurred at night, but if they hadn't, many people could have been killed. Eruptions occur with little warning, and scientists are still learning to understand Ruapehu's moods. The size of the crater and temperature of the lake are monitored regularly to glean clues that might forewarn of future bursts of activity. Seismographs make continuous recordings of all tremors, and at a certain level a lahar warning is triggered. This will give people 5 to 10 minutes to move to higher ground, out of the path of any flow of water or mud that may descend the mountain.

Many areas around the mountains are free of forests, and it is thought that this has been caused by fires started by eruptions from Ngauruhoe, and later by humans. Each time the forests were destroyed they would have been replaced by the hardy tussocks that now clothe most of the western slopes of Tongariro and Ngauruhoe. The eastern slopes of Ruapehu and the summit of the saddle between Turangi and Waiouru were swept by repeated fires, so much so that even the tussocks have given up their battle to survive. Vicious winds sweeping down from the mountains have eroded the layers of tephra to create the barren landscape known as the Rangipo Desert. Although rainfall on the eastern side of Ruapehu is much lower than on the western side, it is not a lack of rain that has created the Rangipo Desert but the desiccating effects of strong winds combined with an alpine environment.

Since the beginning of this century, the tussocklands have undergone further change, solely through the actions of John Cullen, the first ranger, known as the Honorary Caretaker. Cullen envisioned Tongariro National Park as a place where the wealthy could come to shoot grouse, as they had done in England. In spite of protests from a well-informed public, between 1912 and 1920 Cullen lit many fires, broadcast imported seed, and planted seedlings of Scottish heather (*Calluna vulgaris*) to replace the burnt tussock. Several pairs of grouse were also imported and liberated. The grouse did not survive but the heather did, and thrived on the volcanic soils. Today the heather smothers the lower northwestern slopes of Tongariro and Ruapehu in a haze of purple. The dominance of the tussock has been broken, and now, as the heather becomes taller and more spindly, it provides a nursery for native shrubs of five-finger, mountain toatoa, coprosmas, and hebes—the forerunners of future forests.

Rising majestically above the ring plain and serried ranks of lesser ridges to the west, the three volcanoes tend to attract any bad weather that drifts across the Tasman Sea. If you are unlucky enough to strike murky weather, remember that the mountains form a weather barrier. In west or northwest wind conditions, the weather will be better on the eastern side of the park. When a south to southeasterly wind comes in, usually with cold temperatures, the northwestern side will be clear of cloud. The mountains also produce a katabatic effect on wind flows. A northwesterly wind is almost unnoticeable at Whakapapa on the northwestern slopes of Ruapehu but becomes a howling demonic force at Turoa on the southern slopes. Conversely, a southeasterly wind is a force to be reckoned with at Whakapapa but fades to a gentle zephyr at Turoa. Weather changes can be dramatic and sudden, and as most of the tracks in the park are across high open country with almost no shelter, warm clothing and wet-weather gear, including hats and mittens, should always be carried. Winter weather is usually cold, with snow to well below the bushline, making conditions miserable for hiking but good for skiing.

The park headquarters is located at Turangi, and there are visitor centers at Whakapapa on SH 48 and at Ohakune, where you can obtain current weather reports, maps, and track information. A network of tracks encircles Ruapehu and Ngauruhoe and traverses Tongariro, with large comfortable huts located an easy day's walk apart for overnight hikes. These are equipped with bunks and mattresses, sink benches, wood stoves, and fuel (to protect the local vegetation). Food and all equipment for cooking, eating, and sleeping must be brought with you. A fee is charged for the use of huts. Access to the tracks is from SH 1, SH 47 and SH 47A, the Ohakune Mountain Road, and SH 48.

Accommodation at Whakapapa includes the luxury Chateau Tongariro, the slightly less pricey Skotel, and the Whakapapa Motor Camp. There are several lodges and a hotel in National Park township and another lodge with cabins close to the junction of SH 47 and SH 48. Ohakune has several lodges and motels, a motor camp, and a hotel. Informal camping is permitted at **Mahuia Camp** located between National Park township and the SH 47/48 junction, and at **Mangawhero Camp,** sited about 2 km up Ohakune Mountain Road from Ohakune Visitor Centre. During the ski season (July–Oct.) accommodation is often fully booked and can be particularly difficult to find during the August and September school holidays. Many people stay in motels and cabins at Taupo and Turangi, where they have a choice of other activities if the weather precludes skiing.

Skiing

Many people are surprised to learn that New Zealand's largest ski areas are in the North Island and in a national park. This is mainly because of publicity about the main South Island areas, many of which have package deals for overseas visitors. At present, Whakapapa Skifield on the northwestern slopes of Mt. Ruapehu has more skiers per day than any ski area in the country—more than 8,000 at peak times—and the facilities to cope with them. Around 70 percent of New Zealand's population lives north of Tongariro National Park, so there is no shortage of customers and potential new skiers. Turoa Skifield, on the southern slopes of the mountain, attracts around 2,000 to 3,000 skiers at peak times.

The North Island ski season does not usually get under way until early- or mid-July, but in a good year it will last until early November. October is considered to be local time—when the locals have the snow to themselves. Many traditional summer sports are under way before the end of October, and Aucklanders, who make up the bulk of skiers, have given up skiing for the year. Consequently, the ski slopes are crowd-free. On a good day in October you can ski yourself to exhaustion by the time the snow gets too mushy, around midday.

Weather, snow, and road conditions for both skifields are broadcast over local radio stations from early in the morning each day during the ski season. There are regular updates during the day. Information centers in Taupo, Turangi, Ohakune, and Whakapapa also provide regularly updated information, as do most ski lodges.

Whakapapa Skifield is unusual in having a village of club lodges right at the base of the facilities. The lodges are reserved for club members and friends and accommodation is arranged directly through the club. The varied terrain of basins, ridges, and bluffs gives challenging runs for experienced skiers, gentle slopes for beginners, and everything in between for intermediates. It has a serviced vertical rise of 615 m from the end of Bruce Road at 1,500 m, with a further 250 m of skiing above the lifts available by walking. When there is sufficient snow, the run down from Crater Lake, about one hour's walk above the highest lift, to the road end is magnificent. Check with the ski patrol about weather and snow conditions on the upper mountain before heading above the highest lifts. A free guide service to some of the lesser-known trails is offered by the ski patrol.

Facilities at Whakapapa include four double chairlifts, one quad express chairlift, one quad chairlift, six T-bars, three platter lifts, and eight beginners' rope tows. Uphill capacity is 23,000 skiers per hour. There are six cafeterias, parking for 1,500 cars (with a free courtesy coach from the lower carparks), ski patrol, ski school, ski and clothing rental, a ski shop, and a children's crèche.

Access to Whakapapa Skifield is by SH 48, the upper 7 km of which are known as Bruce Road. Signs at Whakapapa Village advise whether chains or four-wheel drive are necessary to get up the road, and a chain fitting and rental service is available. Public transport operates from the village to the ski area.

Compared to Whakapapa, **Turoa Skifield** is a relatively new area. Although it also lies within Tongariro National Park its development has been very different and there are no club lodges on its slopes. The nearest accommodation is at Ohakune, and this can be booked through the Turoa Accommodation Bureau, Box 46, Ohakune, phone (06)3858-456, Fax (06)3858-992. You will need to prebook accommodation during the August school holidays.

Where Whakapapa's slopes are broken by bluffs and basins, Turoa's are more open and undulating. Facing southwest, and therefore on the colder side of Ruapehu, the snow cover tends to stay firmer until later in the day, a definite advantage in warm spring weather. The field has a vertical rise of 700 m, with its highest lift rising to 2,322 m. Uphill facilities include one triple and two quad chairlifts, three T-bars, and four platter lifts, with a capacity of 10,000 skiers per hour. There are three cafeterias, a licensed bar, carparking for 800 vehicles, ski school, ski rental and repair, ski patrol and medical clinic, a children's crèche, and a small accessories shop. Public transport to the ski area leaves from the Turoa Information Centre in Ohakune. Snow chains can be rented from several outlets in Ohakune if they are required to get up the Ohakune Mountain Road.

Long Hikes

Round the Mountain Track (RMT), encircling Mt. Ruapehu, has 6 huts that allow the walk to be done in 4 to 5 days. Much of the track is at or above the bushline, giving good views of the countryside below and the mountain above, with its changing skyline and moods. One of the features of this walk is the dramatic changes of terrain and vegetation encountered on the different sides of the mountain, from the barren, wind-sculpted eastern slopes, where only the hardiest alpine plants can survive, to beech forests on the southern and western slopes and tussocklands on the gentle Tama Saddle between Ruapehu and Ngauruhoe. Unlike the huts on the track around Tongariro and Ngauruhue, those on the RMT are rarely crowded. The walk can be done in either direction and commenced at Whakapapa Village, Ohakune Mountain Road, or from SH 1 by joining the track at Waihohonu Hut.

The Tongariro Crossing and Circuit is probably the most popular walk in the park, so it is rare for the four huts along the track to be unoccupied. At times, sleeping space is at a premium. The complete circuit of Ngauruhoe and Tongariro usually takes 3 to 4 days, but hikers often choose the shorter 2- to 3-day crossing over the spectacular summit of Tongariro. This can also incorporate an ascent of Ngauruhoe as a side trip. The Tongariro Crossing can be done in one long day (7 to 8 hours) if transport to the track ends is arranged ahead of time. It is often acclaimed as the best one-day walk in the world—and probably is when the weather is favorable. In bad weather it can be a miserable experience. Although Tongariro is not particularly high, it can be extremely windy and cold across the open top.

The volcanic scenery is as dramatic as it is contrasting—from the gentle Mangatepopo Valley, with its lava flows, alpine shrubbery, and flowers, to the flat sandy pan of South Crater, where the few plants that can survive surprise with the delicacy of their flowers; steaming Red Crater, with its velvety red and black walls and the brilliant Emerald Lakes sprinkled like jewels at its base; Central Crater, with its fan of young black lava rippling outward from a tiny obscure vent; the circular bowl of Blue Lake; alpine gardens on the slopes of North Crater; views over Lake Rotoaira; and the hissing steam vents and boiling mud pools of Ketetahi Hot Springs—an amazing kaleidoscope of color, texture, and nature at its best.

A full circuit of the mountains also includes the fascinating moonscape of Oturere Crater, with its sandy basins and weird outcrops of jagged lava. Oturere Hut, set among tussock-covered mounds at the end of the lava flow, has sensational views of Ngauruhoe, particularly when it is silhouetted against an evening sky. Between here and Waihohonu, the landscape is different again; barren slopes dotted with clumps of alpine vegetation, each one a miniature garden, give way to the lush Waihohonu Valley where the river emerges from beneath the scoria slopes of Ngauruhoe, and finally to the cool, sheltered beech forests at Waihohonu Hut.

Close to Waihohonu, the icy cold, crystal clear Ohinepango Springs well silently from beneath the beech-clad toe of an ancient lava flow. A pair of blue ducks are sometimes seen here if you approach quietly. Historic Old Waihohonu Hut stands at the edge of a copse of beeches close to the main track across the Tama Saddle, a reminder of early times when coaches traveling the new Desert Road stopped here for the night. In its day the hut was a refuge of warmth and comfort, with double-skinned corrugated iron walls filled with pumice to provide insulation and an open fire for cooking and warmth. Women must have been deemed very hardy, as their quarters were separate and without a fireplace. Visitors who stayed here over the early years have carved and written their names on the walls, ceiling, and beams of the hut, leaving a fascinating history. Nowadays that would be considered vandalism, but the record left by old-time visitors is far more interesting than today's hut log book.

Climbing the Volcanoes

Ngauruhoe is usually climbed from the saddle at the head of the Mangatepopo Valley. In summer this is relatively easy as the slopes will be snow free and it is really only a matter of putting one foot in front of the other and trying not to slide backward in the loose scoria. The main danger lies more in being hit by a rock dislodged by someone above than from a volcanic eruption, unless you deliberately ascend during an active phase. A winter ascent is a different matter, requiring an ice ax, crampons, and some climbing experience. The 30° slopes can be very icy and there is nothing to stop you if you slip. **Mt. Tongariro**

can also be difficult in winter. Even when there is little snow, the gravel slopes can be frozen and very slippery, making boots and ice axes essential. **Ruapehu** is an easy mountain to climb from Whakapapa, but it should not be underrated. Sudden weather changes can turn the summit plateau into a death trap. Several people have had very lucky escapes after being caught up there in prolonged and vicious storms and whiteout conditions. Others have perished. Most people climb only to the **Dome**, a high point above Crater Lake, and in winter, when the ski area is operating, this takes only about an hour from the top of the highest tows, providing a great ski run down. If walking from the road end, the climb will take 3 to 4 hours. The chairlifts are sometimes run during peak visitor times in summer (Christmas–New Year) and guided trips to the crater are organized by park staff. A small shelter hut on the top of the Dome also houses seismic equipment used to monitor the mountain's activity.

The true summit of Ruapehu stands directly above Turoa Skifield, on the opposite side of Crater Lake from the Dome. If ascending from the Ohakune side, the last section is steep and can be icy. Good views of Crater Lake can be gained from the saddle to the south of Paretetaitonga Peak, and this is reached by traversing left from the top of Turoa Skifield. There is another small shelter, below the saddle. Always check current snow conditions and weather forecasts before setting out, and heed the advice of park staff.

For guided climbs, contact **Plateau Guides**, Box 29, National Park, phone (07)8922-740, or **Powderhorn**, Ohakune Junction, phone (06)3858-888.

Short Walks from Whakapapa

All the short walks from Whakapapa include a mixture of beech forest, with its wonderful mosses, filmy ferns, lichens, and liverworts, and colorful subalpine scrub and tussocklands. The **Taranaki Falls Loop** follows the Wairere Stream, which plunges over the lip of an ancient lava flow. At **Silica Rapids** the rushing Waikare Stream wells from the base of another lava flow and, owing to chemical changes in the water, deposits layers of creamy-white allophane 50 m down the stream bed. Along the **Whakapapanui Track** are palmlike mountain cabbage trees; tiny rifleman wrens, denizens of the beech forest, search the mossy tree trunks for insects. All three tracks take 2 to 2.5 hours.

If you have time for a longer walk (5 hours or more) and the weather is clear, head out to the **Tama Lakes** on the broad saddle between Ruapehu and Ngauruhoe. Occupying huge explosion craters, the lakes add a colorful contrast to the tawny, tussock-covered landscape. In sunny weather the lower lake is usually a vivid blue, pale where infilling gravels have shallowed one edge, then deepening to turquoise. The upper lake is darker and more sombre, perhaps reflecting its higher altitude and proximity to Ngauruhoe. Black-headed gulls use the lower lake and banded dotterels are occasionally seen scurrying across the gravel.

The **Whakapapiti Valley** on the western flanks of Ruapehu provides a different contrast, with its rampart of guardian bluffs, waterfalls, and bonsai-like beech trees. It is reached from Whakapapa by a track around the lower slopes of the mountain or from **Scoria Flat** near the top of the Bruce Road (SH 48). An enjoyable 5-hour round trip can be taken along those tracks. Whakapapiti Hut is a pleasant place to stay overnight if you want to spend more time exploring or looking for alpine plants.

Although the **Ridge Track** is very short, taking only 15 to 20 minutes to reach a viewpoint at the bush edge, a much longer walk with excellent views can be had by continuing upward to where the ridge becomes more defined. From here there is no track, but in clear weather it is easy to follow the ridge as it climbs gently toward the upper slopes of Ruapehu. Where it starts to steepen sharply you can descend either to the south, into the Whakapapanui Valley, or north, to Wairere Stream. Both valleys offer very easy traveling and are good places in summer for alpine flowers. Wairere Stream flows through some spectacular minigorges, making cascades, and waterfalls in its upper reaches that in summer are good places to see alpine stream vegetation.

Mangatepopo Valley and Mt. Pukekaikiore

A walk up the Mangatepopo Valley to Soda Springs near the head is always pleasant, particularly in November and December when the yellow *Ranunculus insignis* and other alpine plants are in bloom. Lava flows in the valley can be roughly assessed for age from the amount of vegetation they support. Older lava now supports a dense shrub cover, mainly of snow totara and *Dacrydium laxifolium*, both miniature cousins of the giant podocarp species rimu and totara. *Dacrydium laxifolium* is the smallest conifer in the world. The most recent flows, from the 1954 eruption of Ngauruhoe, are still black and fresh looking, and one of the best places to view them is at the right-hand side of the valley where the dark, jagged aa-aa lava abuts the pale, aged, and weathered cliffs of Pukekaikiore. Aa-aa lava is slow moving; a rough, broken crust forms on the outside while the interior of the flow is still moving. The name comes from Hawaii.

If you have the time and energy it is worth climbing to the narrow saddle between Pukekaikiore and Ngauruhoe and then returning to the valley via Pukekaikiore's summit.

The Mangatepopo Valley Road turns off SH 47 about 5 km north of the junction with SH 48. It takes about 20 minutes' walking to reach Mangatepopo Hut, a popular base for school groups and hikers climbing Ngauruhoe or crossing Tongariro, and another hour to reach the head of the valley.

Ketetahi Springs

Filling a crease on Tongariro's northern flanks, the fumaroles, mud pools, and hot springs of Ketetahi are a popular destination for day and overnight hikes.

The **Ketetahi Track** starts at the end of a short side road off SH 47A, climbing very gradually at first through totara forest, then ascending more steeply to the sharply defined bush edge, from where there are unrestricted views across gentle scrub and tussock to the springs and upper slopes of Tongariro. The valley below, which the track crosses, is filled with a massive lava flow from Upper Te Maari crater opposite Ketetahi Hut and is estimated to be about 450 years old.

The lower end of the springs is reached in about 2.5 hours from the road end and the hut is a further 20 minutes on, via a track leading left up the hillside. Another route marked by poles climbs beside gurgling pools and roaring vents, the largest of which discharges superheated steam (about 138°C) at the rate of up to 90 m per second, then continues around the slopes just above the hut. Take care using this route, as the surrounding ground is unstable, with boiling water not far below a thin crust. The springs were valued by the Maori for their medicinal properties, and you'll find the hot, muddy water is good for soaking tired feet. Although the pools are small, a few have been scooped large enough for almost total immersion; don't be surprised to find a few nude bathers.

Walks near Ohakune

Most walks close to Ohakune start on the **Ohakune Mountain Road,** which climbs 17 km, through changing vegetation zones of podocarp and beech forest, subalpine scrub, and tussock, then alpine herb and moss fields, to Turoa Skifield. Particularly noticeable on this side of the mountain are the gaunt, conical mountain cedars (*Libocedrus bidwillii*), which grow near the bushline.

Commencing opposite the Ohakune Ranger Station, the **Mangawhero Forest Walk** (1 to 1.5 hours), part of which is suitable for wheelchairs, makes a circuit through the magnificent podocarp forest, which escaped destruction by Lake Taupo's eruption. Approximately 7 km above the Ohakune Visitor Centre, the **Old Blyth Track** leaves the road and climbs gradually to join the Waitonga Falls track near the bush edge. First surveyed in 1910, this old track from Ohakune to Ruapehu's upper, southern slopes was popular with early park visitors. The use of horses in the early days soon turned the track into a quagmire, and it became necessary to lay pieces of split mountain cedar across the ground to achieve a firm footing. This old construction, termed corduroy, can still be seen in places, and the track still has a reputation for being muddy.

Sections of the **Round the Mountain Track,** which reaches the road about 11 km above the visitor center and continues again from a sharp corner near the bush edge another 4 to 5 km further up the road, make good short walks. The **Waitonga Falls,** tumbling 63 m over the lip of a lava flow, are about an hour's walk from the road, and for more of a leg stretcher you can continue up to **Blyth Hut** at the bush edge for grand views. On a wet day, when the feeder stream is more full than normal, in frosty winter weather when long icicles formed from spray hang from the lava cliffs, or after a fresh fall of snow, the Waitonga Falls are quite spectacular.

With its mosaic of beech forest and open tussocklands ringed by bluffs and cascading waterfalls, the **Mangaturuturu Valley** is a particularly beautiful place. **Mangaturuturu Hut** on the valley floor is reached in about an hour from the road, and if you continue for another hour or so, across the river and up through the obvious break in the line of forbidding bluffs, you'll come upon **Lake Surprise,** a shallow mountain tarn hidden among the beech trees and tussock near the bush edge.

Nestled in forest at the toe of the 14-km-long Rangataua Lava Flow are the two **Rotokuru lakes,** one of which is artificial. The other, a more beautiful lake, is surrounded by a matrix of red and silver beech and podocarp forest. The red and silver beech extends up the lava flow, merging gradually with mountain beech on the upper slopes to form a unique forest not found elsewhere in the park. A quiet approach on the track around the second lake can reward with sightings of the infrequently seen spotless crake and other waterfowl. To reach the lakes, follow SH 49 south from Ohakune to Karioi Station Road. Turn left across the railway line and continue straight ahead, ignoring all side roads. It takes about 10 minutes from the carpark to reach the first lake and another 5 minutes to reach the second one.

AROUND TAUMARUNUI

In spite of being close to Tongariro National Park and the ski areas, Taumarunui doesn't attract tourists heading for the mountains and is better known as a starting point for canoe and jet boat trips down the **Wanganui River.** (See "Wanganui and Manawatu.") Geographically and historically the town belongs to the King Country and was important in the past as a meeting point of several routes through the central North Island. It has all services, hotel, motel, and motorcamp accommodation, and the local hospital even offers rooms in the now disused nurses' hostel. The motor camp is pleasantly situated beside the Wanganui River at the southern end of town. Like other railway towns, Taumarunui has a long street with shops down one side and the railway down the other.

Scenic SH 41 over the **Waituhi Saddle** links Taumarunui with Turangi, while the main road, SH 4, connects with National Park and Te Kuiti. Between Taumarunui and Tongariro National Park are the small townships of Kakahi and Owhango, both with charming scenery and some little-advertised attractions. **Kakahi,** reached by a side road off SH 4, has homestay accommodation and horse trekking, and being close to the confluence of the Wanganui and Whakapapa rivers, is a good spot for fishing. The **Ohinetonga Scenic Reserve** at **Owhango** has superb bush and a loop track giving access to the Whakapapa

River, another good place to cast a lure. Owhango also has a pleasant domain where you can camp. Side roads from Owhango lead to **Whakahoro** on the Wanganui River, another launching place for canoes.

TROUT FISHING

Turangi proudly proclaims itself Trout Fishing Capital of the World, and with the Tongariro River flowing past its back door and several smaller rivers, streams, and lakes in the surrounding district all producing large trout, the claim is not unfounded. Brown trout over 4 kg and slightly smaller rainbow trout are caught regularly. Anything under 1.5 kg is considered not worth taking. Trolling and harling on Lake Taupo are very popular, and there is a plethora of rental boats to take you out on the water. Phone the Taupo Boat Harbour at (07)3783-444 or contact the information centers at Turangi or Taupo. Motel and lodge owners will also be able to help you.

Popular fishing areas close to Turangi are the tailrace below the Tokaanu power station, the Tokaanu wharf and marina, and the Tongariro River. Access to the pools above the bridge on SH 1 is from the Tongariro Walkway. Below the bridge, access is from Grace Road to the north and from Crescent Reserve, off Tautahanga Road in Turangi. Shallow **Lake Otamangakau,** off SH 47, formed as part of the Tongariro Power Scheme, has a reputation for providing large fish.

Trout fishing, Tongariro River. *Photo by Bruce Jeffries.*

Fishing on beautiful **Lake Rotoaira** is controlled by a Maori trust and requires a special fishing license, supplementary to the standard one. These and rental boats are available from the Lake Rotoaira Motor Camp on SH 47A.

The **Hinemaiaia** and **Waitahanui streams** on the eastern edge of Lake Taupo are both very popular. Hinemaiaia Stream enters the lake at Hatepe, 25 km south of Taupo, and access from the road bridge on SH 1 is by a flat easy track through kanuka, five-finger, and kowhai forest. The Waitahanui Stream, 12 km south of Taupo, is famous for its row of anglers standing like a picket fence at the stream mouth. Access to upper pools is from the SH 1 bridge and from Blakes Road at the south end of Waitahanui Village.

OTHER THINGS TO DO

If you have just spent frustrating days sitting out bad weather and the clouds clear as you plan to leave, a scenic flight over the mountains will give a chance to see the spectacular volcanos of Tongariro National Park and lakes of the Taupo area. Flights can be arranged from Turangi and Taupo, or you can fly with Mountain Air from the tiny airstrip at the junction of SH 47 and SH 48. Phone (07)8922-812.

Rafting the Tongariro River is a fun way to fill half a day, and trips leave from Turangi all year round. In winter you wear a wet suit, and you can warm up afterward in the Tokaanu Hot Pools. More difficult rafting is available on the Manganui-a-te-Ao and Whakapapa rivers, flowing off the western side of Ruapehu. Horse trekking can be arranged in Turangi, Taupo, Ohakune, and National Park township; mountain bikes can be rented from Powderhorn at Ohakune Junction, and here you can also bungee jump off the now disused Hapuawhenua Rail Viaduct. The bungee jumping craze in New Zealand started in Ohakune.

If the weather is too bad for any outdoor activities, visit the Army Museum at Waiouru. Even if you don't like wars or anything connected with them, this interesting place is worth visiting. It will take at least two hours to see properly.

LOCAL TRANSPORT

InterCity buses run a thrice weekly service between Turangi, Ketetahi Track, Whakapapa Village, National Park township, and Ohakune. The Turangi Visitor Centre can tell you whether there are private companies operating minibus services to track ends and if a car-minding service still exists so that you don't have to leave your own vehicle at a road end and risk having it vandalized. Macrocarpa Lodge in National Park offers free transport for guests to the start of tracks in Tongariro National Park.

USEFUL ADDRESSES

Department of Conservation, Private Bag, Turangi, phone (07)3868-607.
Whakapapa Visitor Centre, phone (07)8923-729; **Ohakune Visitor Centre,**
   phone (06)3858-575.
Turangi Information Centre, Ngawaka Place, Turangi, phone (07)3868-999.
Taupo Information Centre, Tongariro St., phone (07)3789-000.
Ruapehu Visitor and Information Centre, 54 Clyde St., Ohakune, phone
   (06)3858-427.

12 ◆ EASTLAND

LANDSCAPE AND CLIMATE

Although joined physically to the North Island, the large protuberance known
as Eastland stands apart with an air of detachment and remoteness, as if the
rest of the country had rushed onward and left it in a slower time warp of its
own. Separated from the central volcanic plateau and the Bay of Plenty by the
vast, sprawling ridges of the Urewera and the extremely rugged Raukumara Range,
Eastland has always been difficult to reach. Few roads traverse the interior and
in the past, transport to Gisborne (the area's major city and life support center
for farmers and other small coastal settlements) was often easier by sea than
by land. Today the main highways to Gisborne from the south and west are
good, but they still do not allow for fast travel over Eastland's endless hills and
river gorges. The 330-km coastal route from Gisborne to Opotiki requires a
fair amount of time, not so much because of the ruggedness of the country
it traverses as for the magnificent scenery it presents.

The boundaries of Eastland extend from the Mohaka River, south of Wairoa
in Hawke's Bay, to Opotiki in the Bay of Plenty, encompassing the rugged hinterland of Urewera National Park and Raukumara Forest Park. These protected
areas, combined with the Waioeka and Urutawa state forests and the Waioeka
Gorge Scenic Reserve, form the largest continuous tract of native forest in the
North Island. Most of the hill country east of these ranges was cleared of its
forest cover by the 1900s to make way for the burgeoning sheep and wool trade.
Early warnings that it was unwise to strip the land of its natural mantle went
unheeded, and today many farmers are paying the price for that folly. The problem lies with the nature of the soil and the underlying rocks of easily eroded
sandstones and mudstones. Sheltered from the predominant damp westerly winds,

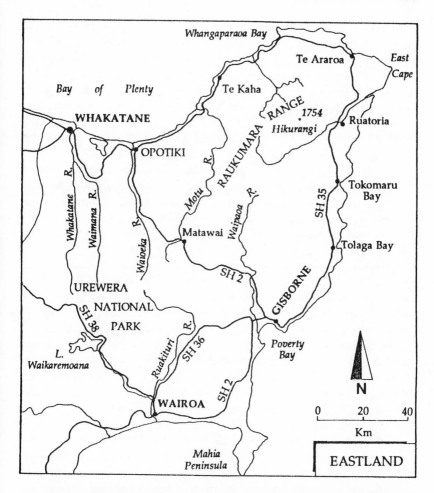

the East Coast has a warm, dry climate, and undergoes long periods of sparse rainfall and even droughts. When heavy rain does come, it can be disastrous. In recent decades more than one devastating cyclone, spawned in the Pacific, has cruised down the eastern edge of the North Island and lashed the coast with southeasterly gales and downpours. With no forest to soften the impact of the rain, the fragile soil turns to mud that flows from the hills, choking rivers and valleys with silt and debris. The most recent of these was Cyclone Bola, in 1988, which left behind it slumping land and scarred hillsides that are almost useless, even for sheepfarming. Now many farmers are faced with the prospect of having to leave their land or of planting it in forest to prevent what remains from sliding seaward.

Further inland the rocks are much older and more stable sedimentaries that have been upthrust to form the Urewera and Raukumara ranges, a continuation of the chain of mountains that starts at Cook Strait. This change in land structure can be clearly seen when driving around the coast from Gisborne to Opotiki.

The eastern coastline is characterized by long sandy beaches alternating with dramatic headlands and cliffs of pale, crumbling mudstones, offshore reefs, and small, steep-sided islands. Marking the eastern end of Hawke Bay is the Mahia Peninsula, a rectangle of hills that was once an island. Gently sloping beaches on either side of the swampy land bridge that now connects the peninsula to the mainland receive the second highest number of whale strandings in the world. It is thought that the huge mammals attempt to swim through what seems to be a gap between the mainland and the peninsula, and as the water becomes increasingly shallow they are unable to turn back.

West of Te Araroa, roughly 20 km from East Cape, there is a sudden change in rock structure. Unlike the soft sandstones that form the cliffs above Te Araroa, the rocks around Hicks Bay are hard, dark-colored volcanics that erupted under the sea and have since been uplifted. They form the Pukeamaru Range, a forbiddingly rugged cluster of dark hills rising to 990 m behind the township and a lower ridge, aligned east to west, extending to Cape Runaway. Evidence of their uplift can be seen in two well-preserved marine benches at Matakaoa Point, north of Hicks Bay. The pale mudstones disappear and the shoreline changes to sheltered coves and bays bounded by hard, dark, jagged rocks. Crowding closely, scrub- and bush-covered hills rise sharply to the Raukumara Range, with the small amount of gentle land along their base farmed out to the margin of the ocean, fringed with pohutukawa and puriri. Clusters of houses, well-tended marae and meeting houses, or small churches mark places of importance to the Maori community, whose ties with the land and sea go back many centuries. Every turn in the road invites closer inspection of the shore below, for fishing, swimming, picnicking, or camping possibilities. At Opape, 17 km from Opotiki, the broken, rocky shoreline ends and the long series of fine-sand beaches that characterize the Bay of Plenty begins.

HISTORY

Much of the East Coast is owned by the Maori tribes who settled the area, and the population is predominantly Maori. Here the marae provides an important focus for a proud people living a mainly rural lifestyle; traditional culture is still alive and flourishing. European and Maori history combined with local legend lend a unique flavor to the small settlements scattered along the coast.

The hills behind Gisborne were probably the first part of New Zealand to be sighted by Nicholas Young when Cook sailed the *Endeavour* into the South

Pacific in 1769. In honor of that historic occasion, the white cliffs at the southern end of Poverty Bay were named Young Nicks Head. Poverty Bay was also named by Cook—to commemorate the unfriendly welcome he received from the Maori residents and his failure to obtain much-needed supplies of food and fresh water. It is a misnomer, however, as the fertile flood plains of the Waipaoa River, which drains into Poverty Bay, are highly productive. High-quality wines, kiwi fruit, citrus, and vegetables are all grown here in large quantities for both the domestic and international markets.

After the none-too-friendly reception at Poverty Bay, Cook sailed north and was pleased to find a more welcoming people at Anaura Bay. He stayed two days there, replenishing water and food supplies until a rising surf made beaching the ship's boats difficult. The Maori directed him south again to Tolaga Bay, and at a small cove tucked behind the southern headland he was able to obtain more supplies. Tokomaru and Tolaga bays were once quite large centers, as the remains of the old wharves and derelict freezing works still testify.

Full settlement of the East Coast was later than in other places and was generally hampered by conflicts with Hauhau Maori and the presence of Te Kooti. Whaling bases had been established around East Cape in the 1830s, and with them came the traders, who established a flax trading base at Tolaga Bay, and a few missionaries. Among the traders was G. E. Read, who opened the first store in Gisborne in 1853, and who is credited with founding the town. As well as being a successful trader, Read had cattle and sheep raising interests and dealt in land sales to new settlers.

The Hauhau movement, which arose in the Taranaki and spread far and wide, reached Poverty Bay in 1865, when the fanatical prophet Kereopa arrived to recruit converts. Although many Ngati Porou, the principal East Coast tribe, sided with the government, a large number joined the Hauhau. There were conflicts throughout the district, ending only after two key battles. In one, five hundred Ngati Porou Hauhau were captured near Ruatoria and released only after vowing allegiance to Queen Victoria. At Waerenga a Hika, the pa was besieged for a week before the four hundred Hauhau defenders were induced to surrender.

Te Kooti Rikirangi was one of the more controversial figures to emerge from these wars. He was involved in the battle at Waerenga a Hika, fighting on the government side, but after this was suspected of treachery and later arrested for supposed antigovernment activities. As punishment he was sent to the Chatham Islands in 1866 without being tried, an act that no doubt embittered him. In 1867 Te Kooti claimed to have received a divine order to form the Ringatu Church, which survives today. Based on the Old Testament, the Ringatu faith compared the plight of the Maori under the English with that of the Israelites under the Egyptians. Following his vision, Te Kooti and others escaped from the Chatham Islands and made their way back to the Urewera, gathering supporters along the way. The rugged country served as a stronghold to retreat to after he made sudden raids on unsuspecting settlers. One of the worst was at Matawhero, on the outskirts of Gisborne, in 1868; thirty-three Europeans and thirty-seven Maori loyal to the government were brutally murdered. Over the next four years, raids were made on Whakatane, Rotorua, and Mohaka. These guerrilla attacks inspired great fear and hatred among the recipients and intense loyalty from Te Kooti's followers. In all these attacks, he proved himself more than a match for the government troops. Constantly pursued by the Armed Constabulary, he was finally defeated in a battle at Te Porere on the slopes of Mt. Tongariro, but he escaped once again to the bush and reached Te Kuiti in the King Country, where he lived under the protection of Tawhiao, the second Maori king, until he was pardoned in 1883. He was granted land at Ohiwa in 1891 and died there two years later. With the menace of Hauhauism and Te Kooti removed, sheep were run on huge tracts along the East Coast and the land rapidly stripped of its bush cover.

◆PLACES TO VISIT AND THINGS TO DO

TE UREWERA NATIONAL PARK

Te Urewera is truly a land of mists. They cling to the valley floors on fine frosty mornings or rise in creeping fingers over the treetops and the crests of ridges, blanketing all in a damp white cover, then parting to reveal darkly folded land. Rainfall can be heavy, and daily falls of over 100 mm occur regularly, but it is the mist and rain that nourish the trees, mosses, and ferns, and that feed the many streams, rivers, and lakes. Snowfalls occur regularly around Lake Waikaremoana during winter months, but the snow does not usually last long at this altitude. Summer temperatures are pleasantly mild, making the park a popular destination during the Christmas–New Year holiday.

At first the forest seems a confusing jumble of species, but it does have a regular pattern, based mainly on altitude. Soils, climate differences, and aspect affect the predominance of certain species, and generally the composition is of podocarp and broadleaf species in warmer, lower altitude valleys, with rimu, rata, and tawa up to about 800 m. Between 800 m and 900 m, rimu and beech species predominate, but above this altitude the hardy beech dominates almost completely. Red beech gives way to almost pure stands of silver beech at 1,200 m, forming mysterious forests of gnarled, stunted trees encrusted with lichens, mosses, and filmy ferns on the higher and most windswept ridges. Only on Mt. Manuoha, the highest point in the park at 1,403 m, does the silver beech reach its altitudinal limit just below the summit, which is capped with dense subalpine scrub.

Lake Waikaremoana (Sea of Rippling Waters) is thought to have been formed about two thousand years ago by a gigantic landslide that blocked the Waikareta-heke River. Among the mass of broken rock is a block of sandstone 3 km long by 1 km wide. The lake's outlet was originally through gaps between the blocks of stone, but these have been channelled into one flow to a hydroelectric station. Maori legend tells us that the lake was formed by the thrashings of Hau-mapuhia, a taniwha or water monster, who was trying to reach the sea.

More westward ridges of the park, the Huiarau and Ikawhenua ranges, are comprised of greywacke rocks. (Huiarau means "many huia," and refers to the extinct bird, which was once plentiful here.) The ridges around Lake Waikare-moana are younger sedimentaries, laid down 10 to 15 million years ago. Most obvious is the Panekiri Range, which rises 600 m above the eastern side of the lake in a formidable scarp of sheer bluffs. Hikers walking around the lake must traverse the top of this ridge.

Clear streams, spectacular waterfalls, lush forests of tall podocarp and beech trees, ferns and mosses, dramatic bluffs, and rich bird life characterize Te Ure-wera. It has always been remote and isolated, and even the road that crosses the park from Murupara to Wairoa is only a tenuous thread of civilization.

The people of Te Urewera are the Tuhoe (Children of the Mist), whose homeland centers around Ruatahuna, a small enclave of cleared land within the forest. The Tuhoe trace their ancestry to Toroa, commander of the Mata atua canoe that landed near Whakatane. Life for the Tuhoe was harsh, as the climate was cold and damp and they were far from the sea with its bounty of fish and shellfish. Their food consisted of fern roots and shoots, berries, birds, and kiore (a small rat), a few eels, and the small native fish they called kokopu.

The first European to travel through the Urewera forests was the Reverend William Williams, who had established a mission at Turanga (now Gisborne) in 1840. He was followed the next year by Father Claude Baty, a Roman Catholic priest, and the Reverend William Colenso. Following the visits of Williams, Baty, and Colenso, the Roman Catholic church became active in the area up until 1850.

Conflicts between the Maori and government during the 1860s involved the Tuhoe, and there were skirmishes around Wairoa and Lake Waikaremoana. Afterward, much Tuhoe land was confiscated because they had supported Te Kooti. Poor living conditions and disease combined to reduce the population dramatically, and a lack of money meant they were unable to develop the little land remaining to them. Out of the despair that reigned at the turn of this century there emerged Rua Kenana, a leader who offered the Tuhoe people hope. Rua was a self-acclaimed prophet who said he was the messiah proclaimed by Te Kooti. Through his enthusiasm 800 ha of forest were cleared and a settlement with houses, schools, roads, a courthouse, and a church was formed by 1907 at Maungapohatu. Rua was constantly under police scrutiny for various alleged offenses and was eventually arrested, tried, and imprisoned for "moral resistance." Forced to pay for the defense and trials for Rua and his followers, and for the police raid in which they were captured, the settlement of Maungapohatu went into decline. Rua attempted to rebuild the community in 1927, but the isolation owing to a lack of roads and the forced sale of assets contributed to its eventual collapse. Rua died in 1937, and today there are only ghosts of the former thriving community, but the cleared land is again being worked successfully by descendants of the earlier occupants.

The Tuhoe refused to allow prospecting, surveying, and road making on their land until 1895, when the government was able to persuade them that a road would bring many advantages. Although it was started from both the Wairoa and Murupara ends, the present SH 38 was not opened to motor traffic until 1930. Improvements and widening have been carried out since then, but it is still a narrow, winding gravel road for most of its length.

Early New Zealanders were not slow to appreciate the beauty of Lake Waikaremoana, and a lodging house, built about 1874 at the Armed Constabulary redoubt at Onepoto, was used until the first Lake House was built in 1900. Lake House became an official government tourist hotel in 1909 and remained operational until financial losses forced its closure in 1972. Records of the early 1900s show that the government of the day supported the development of the Urewera forests for settlement. By 1921 public opinion had changed, and the forests were seen to have more value for their natural beauty. The idea of a national park was broached as early as 1925, but it was not until 1954 that 49,000 ha were officially registered as park land. A further 135,000 ha were added in 1959, making Urewera the second largest national park in New Zealand.

Much of Te Urewera's 211,000 ha of hog-backed ridges and primeval forests are infrequently visited, but its scenic jewel, Lake Waikaremoana, attracts many visitors from all over the world for fishing, holiday making, and hiking. The park's most popular walking track follows the lake's shoreline for 40 km. Other tracks follow old Maori trails and provide hunters and experienced trampers with access to some of the more remote interior regions.

Most visitor activities center around the park headquarters at Aniwaniwa, 67 km from Wairoa on the shores of Lake Waikaremoana. Many of the lake's beautiful bays and inlets are accessible from SH 38, which follows the northern shore, and are suitable for camping. There is also a large formal campground at Home Bay, 2 km from the park headquarters, which has cabin and motel accommodation as well as tent and caravan sites, a shop, and gasoline supplies. Information on the park and bookings for the motor camp are available from the Department of Conservation, Private Bag 213, Wairoa, phone (06)8373-803.

The Lake Waikaremoana Area

Lake Waikaremoana Track is one of the most popular walks in the park, and in summer the five huts along the tracks can become overcrowded at times. Boaties also have access to the huts, and because of this the maximum stay at any one hut is two nights. A tent can be a preferable alternative, and it is advisable to take a portable stove, as the hut stoves are not designed for cooking.

Whichever direction the 43 km between Onepoto and Hoporuahine are traveled, the Panekiri Range, which reaches 1,100 m, must be crossed. Some people prefer to get the climb over with on the first day; others like to leave it until the end, when they hope they will feel fitter and their packs will be lighter. The views from the Panekiri bluffs are breathtaking, as is the wind at times along the exposed cliff edge; the waters, inlets, and bays of the lake are spread at your feet, and forested ridges ripple westward as far as you can see. The rest of the walk follows the lake shore, sometimes close to the water's edge where opportunities for swimming often present themselves, and at other times climbing to avoid small bluffs and steep ground. Always the presence of the water is felt, whether milky calm and reflective, sparkling in bright sunshine and lapping gently against the shore, or curtained in rain and whipped to spume-capped waves by a furious wind.

The Panekiri Range is exposed and all extremes of weather can be experienced in the 3 to 4 days it takes to walk the distance, making warm and waterproof clothes a necessity. Good boots are also preferable, as parts of the track can be wet and muddy.

Lake Waikareiti and **Sandy Bay Hut.** Nestled in beech forest at 900 m, Lake Waikareiti is one of the country's loveliest mountain lakes. Its crystal clear waters contain six small islands, one of which is unique in that it also contains a small lake. Like Lake Rotopounamu in Tongariro National Park, Waikareiti is free from introduced weeds. There is a feeling of timelessness and solitude here that is not found on the much larger Lake Waikaremoana, 300 m below. From the small shelter at the lake edge, reached in about an hour, it takes about 30 minutes to reach the Ruapani Lakes Track, and another 2.5 to 3 hours to reach the 18-bunk hut at Sandy Bay, a popular place for overnight stays. The maximum stay here is two consecutive nights. From Sandy Bay, a 3.5 to 4-hour return walk can be made to the **Kaipo Lagoons,** an extensive swampy area with unusual tundralike vegetation.

If you don't care to walk around the lake you can rent a dinghy and row yourself across. Fishing, particularly trolling, is usually very rewarding here. More details on boat rentals are available at the park headquarters.

Mt. Manuoha. In clear weather the open, scrub-covered summit of Mt. Manuoha affords panoramic views over the lakes and high ridges of the park. Nestled in a sheltered hollow at the bush edge just below the summit is the very cozy and comfortable Mt. Manuoha Hut (6 bunks), which sees few visitors. It's a good place to go for solitude if you don't mind a 4- to 6-hour hike. The track starts where SH 38 crosses the Waiotukupuna Stream and, apart from an initial steep section, climbs at a moderate grade through beech forest, which becomes mossy and stunted as height is gained. Water can sometimes be found about 1 to 1.5 hours before the summit but shouldn't be relied on, especially in summer.

From Mt. Manuoha, a well-marked route leads east over the Pukepuke Range and down to the Kaipo Lagoons. In places a track has formed where people have walked, but it is mostly rough travel. You need to push your way through tangled fern and undergrowth as you follow the markers on the trees. From the lagoons there is a good track to Sandy Bay at Lake Waikareiti. This route takes 6 to 8 hours and is for experienced hikers only. More information and advice on using it are available from the park headquarters.

Short Walks. A number of short walks start close to the park headquarters and visitor center at Aniwaniwa. The **Black Beech Track** follows the old road line to the Motor Camp, passes through stands of black beech trees, and provides good views of the lake. **Hinerau's Track,** a circular walk taking 30 minutes, follows the Aniwaniwa River downstream, past three spectacular waterfalls, then returns above the lake via a headland. A disused coach road up the **Aniwaniwa Valley** can be followed to Wards Hut, a rather rustic edifice set in a delightful grassy clearing at the edge of tall beech forest. Apart from the mud, which can be washed off, it's a pleasant 1.5-hour walk. **Ngamoko Trig,** above Home Bay and Aniwaniwa, is a superb viewpoint. The climb is fairly stiff, through wonderful forest, and takes about 1.5 hours to the top.

The gentle 1-hour climb to **Lake Waikareiti** (see above) can be extended to a 5-hour loop by returning via the **Ruapani Lakes** and **Waipai Swamp,** a series of interesting ponds within the forest. At the eastern entrance of the park you'll find the **Onepoto Caves** within the giant landslide that created Lake Waikaremoana. The track through takes about 1 hour and is fun if you take a flashlight and wear old clothes. Other short tracks to bays and picnic sites beside the lake edge are signposted along SH 38.

Western and Northern Sectors of the Park

Whakatane River Track. Starting at Ruatahuna, the Whakatane River can be followed downstream to Ruatoki in 4 to 5 days. The traditional route used by Tuhoe people to reach the Bay of Plenty coast used the river bed, but now a benched track located close to the river is a safe alternative during flood conditions. There are five huts on the track and many pleasant camping places on the numerous river flats. Land in the lower Whakatane Valley is mostly privately owned, and road access above Ruatoki is limited.

An alternative trip can be made down the Whakatane to its confluence with the Waikare River, returning to Ruatahuna via the Waikare River and Takura Track.

Waimana River. Like the Whakatane River, the Waimana gave the Tuhoe people easy access to the coast. You can drive up the lower end of the valley, where there are several informal camping areas in clearings that were once farmed. There is plenty of scope for anglers and good picnic sites and swimming holes. The Waimana Valley Road is signposted on SH 2 between Taneatua and Opotiki.

Walks around Murupara. Good day-walks can be made on the park's western edge, which rises steeply from the Galatea Plains in the Rangitaiki River valley. Access is from Troutbeck Road (off the Murupara–Te Teko Road), which runs along the base of the hills. The **Horomanga River** has good hunting and fishing and has two huts within a few hours' walk of the road. The track starts at the end of a short side road and crosses the river many times. If you want a hill to climb, **Tawhiuau** and **Hikurangi** trigs on the Ikawhenua Range give good views. Both are steep climbs taking up to 3 hours. The track to Tawhiuau starts from a gravel side road by the Mangamate Stream bridge; the Hikurangi track starts through Clyde Nicholson's farm at the end of Troutbeck Road.

If fishing is the main item on your itinerary, you can drive to within 10 minutes' walk of **Okui Hut** beside the Whirinaki River. Turn off SH 38 about 2 km before Te Whaiti. Full descriptions of these tracks are available from the park visitor center at Murupara.

RAUKUMARA FOREST PARK

The 115,103 ha of Raukumara Forest Park, which were registered in 1979, have few tracks and only four huts. Most of the terrain is extremely rugged and is designated as wilderness, so is undeveloped for recreation. Road access is limited, and this tends to discourage use except by a hardy few. Two areas that are used are the Motu River, for rafting and canoeing, and Mt. Hikurangi.

Motu River

The upper reaches of the Motu River are accessible from the road to Motu, leaving SH 2 at Matawai. From Motu you can drive down Motu Road on the right side of the river to view the **Motu Falls** or take Marumoko Road down the left side. At a saddle 14 km along Marumoko Road there is a carpark and entrance to **Whinray Bush,** a reserve of pre-European podocarp forest. A track through the reserve, following part of the old coach road, leads to the Motu Falls and some picnic areas. The return walk takes about 4 hours. SH 35 crosses the river near its mouth. The 88 km between are extremely remote and inaccessible except for one point reached by Otipi Road, a four-wheel-drive track built for hydro-investigation access. The upper 34 km of the river, between Motu and Otipi Road, are difficult and should only be tackled by very experienced rafters or canoeists. At least 2 days are needed to negotiate this section. The 54 km from Otipi Road to the bridge on SH 35 are a little easier and also take at least 2 days. Usually 5 days are allowed for the full trip, but times vary according to river flow. People have been caught in the gorges—and there is no way out on foot.

Several commercial rafting operators will take trips down the Motu, and a comprehensive guide to the river is available from the Department of Conservation. It is also possible to travel about 30 km upstream from the river mouth by jet boat.

Mt. Hikurangi

Near Ruatoria the abrupt peaks of Hikurangi, Aorangi, and Wharekia rise conspicuously on the skyline. An isolated mass of hard sandstone over 100 million years old, they tower above the surrounding soft and easily eroded mudstone. At 1,752 m, Hikurangi is the highest nonvolcanic peak in the North Island, and is reputed to be the first place on Earth to receive the sun each day.

Many people climb to the summit to greet the sun as it rises over the eastern horizon. The ascent is made from the Tapuaeroa Valley, north of Ruatoria, usually with an overnight stay at the 10-bunk hut maintained by the Gisborne Canoe and Tramping Club on the upper slopes of the mountain. The hut is open to all users and bookings are made through Chris Sharp, phone (06)8625-677. As it is on private land, permission to cross the land is necessary and obtained from the manager of Pakihiroa Station (phone (06)8648-962). It takes about 3 hours to climb to the hut from Pakihiroa Station at the end of the road up the Tapuaeroa Valley, following a four-wheel-drive track over farmland, and then a foot track for the last 20 minutes up a ridge. The summit is another 2 hours away via scree slopes above the hut. In strong winds or when there is much snow and ice around, the narrow summit ridge can be dangerous.

Old Motu Coach Road

At the Waiaua River, 10 km east of Opotiki on SH 35, a road heads inland to Toatoa and eventually to Motu. This is the old coach road to Gisborne, and it is much the same today as it was early this century. It's narrow and tortuous, but on a fine day the scenery is superb. You'll be lucky (or unlucky, depending on how you view solitude) to meet another car, so don't go unless you have a reliable vehicle and a well-developed sense of adventure and self-sufficiency. At Toatoa, which is still farmed, the four-wheel-drive road to Otipi on the Motu River turns off and heads into the backcountry.

URUTAWA AND WAIOEKA FORESTS

Urutawa and Waioeka state forests lie to the south of Opotiki on either side of SH 2. The Waioeka Forest has a common boundary with Urewera National Park. Both forests have a network of tracks and huts, most of them put in during the heyday of government deer culling, and these are now used mainly by private hunters.

Urutawa Forest

If you've had enough of beaches, hot sun, and sand, the Te Waiti Valley in Urutawa Forest is a pleasant place for a bush walk. The main access is from the end of Te Waiti Road, 17 km from Opotiki. Head south from Opotiki on SH 2 and on the outskirts of town take the road veering left that's signposted Urutawa Forest. The last few kilometers up the Te Waiti Valley to a parking and picnic area are very narrow, but not as bad as they first appear. From the road end, a level, benched track above the Te Waiti Stream will bring you to dilapidated Te Waiti Hut in 2 to 2.5 hours. The bush is rather patchy for the first hour but improves to lush tawa forest with many nikau palms higher up the valley. A pleasant alternative in hot summer weather would be to return down the river, which has a good shingle bed and some pleasant pools for swimming.

Waioeka Forest

Along SH 2 through the Waioeka Gorge there are numerous picnic areas, campsites, and pools for swimming and fishing. There is good tramping and fishing in the upper reaches of the Waioeka River, which is gained from a gravel side road leaving SH 2 at Wairata in the Waioeka Gorge. Alternative access is from Moanui Road, which leaves SH 2 at a one-way bridge about 3 km north of Matawai. From the end of Moanui Road tracks lead to Tawa Hut (8 bunks) in about 3 hours and to Koranga Forks Hut (6 bunks) in 2 hours. A round trip can be made taking in both huts, or from Koranga Forks Hut the Waioeka River can be followed down to Wairata. The Department of Conservation offices at Opotiki and Gisborne will be able to help with more information on these areas.

THE EAST COAST—FROM WAIROA TO OPOTIKI

Morere Hot Springs

Between Wairoa and Gisborne are the Morere Hot Springs, an oasis of superb native forest in an otherwise agricultural landscape. As well as facilities for bathing in enclosed public pools and superb private spas that are open to the bush, there are several walking tracks. These range from an easy 30-minute stroll along either the **Cemetery Track** or the **Nikau Loop Track** through some impressive groves of nikau palms, to the 2-hour **Ridge Track** and more demanding and longer **Mangakawa Track.** The Mangakawa Track is not as well formed as the others but offers a variety of scenery as it follows the beautiful Mangakawa Stream and then climbs to a high lookout point before returning down a ridge.

The reserve also has pleasant picnic areas with gas barbecues, and there are tearooms, a motor camp, and a tavern nearby.

Gisborne

Known originally as Turanganui-a-kiwa, then Turanga, the city was renamed in 1870 after a colonial secretary, Sir William Gisborne. Settlers and Maori refused to accept the new name at first, but they saw its virtues when new government buildings, planned for Turanga, were mistakenly erected at Tauranga in the Bay of Plenty. The city straddles the Waimata and Taruheru rivers, which join to form the Turanganui. Flowing only 500 m before meeting the sea, the Turanganui has the dubious distinction of being the shortest river in the world.

With a population of around 31,000 people, Gisborne has good motels, hotels, campgrounds, restaurants, and shops. The city's main attractions are its vineyards, warm sunny climate, uncrowded sandy beaches, and best of all, a very relaxed atmosphere. Waikanae Beach is a 10-minute walk from the city center, while a short drive north brings you to the beautiful, uncrowded, surf-raked expanses of Wainui, Okitu, and Makarori beaches. Many of Gisborne's unemployed are avid surfers, and a surf report is broadcast daily over the local radio. Wilder stretches of beach that are good for swimming, fishing, and rock-pool exploration are found beyond Makarori at **Tatapouri, Turihaua,** and **Pou-awa.** Tatapouri is the base for the local big game fishing club. It has a campground for members, opposite the club rooms, and there is also a tavern that's popular with locals.

From **Kaiti Hill,** above Gisborne's port, there are good views of the city and Poverty Bay. You can either walk up via a network of tracks or drive. **Kaiti Beach,** at the base of the hill, is the site of the local yacht club and a good spot for windsurfing. Other walking opportunities close to the city are limited, but if you have your own transport, it's worth driving the 9.5 km out to **Gray's Bush,** a 12.1-ha reserve of unique forest on Back Ormond Road. Within this remnant of forest, which was once common on the plains, incredibly tall kahikatea overtop huge puriri trees. Two km past Gray's Bush is the **Waihirere Domain,** a pleasant place for bush picnicking. **Eastwood Hill Arboretum,** located at Ngatapa about 30 km from the city, is a beautiful place in spring and autumn. It has a network of tracks wandering through groves of Northern Hemisphere conifers and deciduous trees. On the same road, 48 km from Gisborne, are the **Rere Falls,** a spectacular broad cascade of water and a pleasant place in summer for picnics, swimming, and fishing.

Gisborne to Wairoa via SH 36

SH 36, the alternative route between Gisborne and Wairoa via Tiniroto, takes longer than the same distance on SH 2 because of its more tortuous nature.

About 25 km from Gisborne the road climbs sharply to the **Gentle Annie** summit, which gives panoramic views of Poverty Bay, and at another 25 km a short side road leads to **Doneraille Park** beside the Hangaroa River. This bush and grass reserve is a pleasant place for fishing, picnicking, camping, and just relaxing. Seven km south are the small **Tiniroto Lakes,** where you can fish year-round for trout. At **Te Reinga,** the Hangaroa and Ruakituri rivers combine to form the Wairoa River, which plunges over limestone bluffs, forming the magnificent **Te Reinga Falls.** The Ruakituri River is good for trout fishing and can be followed toward the edge of Urewera National Park by a side road from Te Reinga.

Tolaga Bay, Anaura Bay, and Tokomaru Bay

Not so many years ago at Tolaga Wharf, which stretches out into the bay for over a kilometer, ships called regularly, bringing in fertilizers, petrol, beer, and foodstuffs, and taking out maize, livestock, and wool. Today the wharf is used primarily for fishing. The small township has a hotel, motel, and several shops, and there are two camping areas, an informal one at the northern end of the beach and a formal one at the south end, about 3 km out of town.

Starting near the wharf, **Cook's Cove Walkway** leads to the small bay where Cook was able to land safely and take on fresh water and food supplies. Most important of these were scurvy grass (*Lepidium oleracum*) and wild celery (*Apium prostratum*), which were boiled every morning with "portable soup" (a sort of meat extract made up in thin cakes) and oatmeal for the sailors' breakfast. The track climbs over farmland, with superb views over Tolaga Bay and the coast from the top of the cliff, before descending the small valley at the head of the cove. If you allow 3 hours for the return walk, you'll have time to explore the "hole in the wall," where a small stream flows out to sea through a tunnel, and shores of the cove.

The golden curve of Anaura Bay, one of the most beautiful bays along this coast, lies 7 km off the main road, between Tolaga and Tokomaru bays. There is a formal motor camp or you can pitch your tent in a reserve at the north end of the beach, but this area is prone to flooding. A walking track climbing through the scenic reserve on the hill behind the beach gives lovely views over the bay. From Anaura the road continues north around the coast for a few more kilometers, through a gate (it should be unlocked), and over another headland to **Nuhiti,** a long open beach that offers good swimming and fishing. Don't be deterred by the fence between the road and the beach; it is there to prevent cattle from straying onto the dunes and destroying the native pingao grass. A farmhouse here, Nuhiti Home, can be rented.

Like Tolaga, Tokomaru has a disused wharf, the end of which is distinctly decayed. Remains of the old freezing works and Harbour Board offices near the wharf all add to Tokomaru's air of genteel decline, but in spite of this the place has a peaceful charm that attracts beach lovers, potters, artists, and musicians, many of whom use the old buildings as workshops. There is a camping area by the motel and a backpackers' lodge, but the town's pride and joy is the new tavern, built since the old one was destroyed by Cyclone Bola in 1988.

Te Puia Springs, Ruatoria, and Tikitiki

The small thermal area that gives Te Puia Springs its name is located in the gardens behind the hotel. Hot water rises along a fault line in the mudstones and although visitors are free to wander through the area, the hot pools are for hotel guests' use only. The tiny town also has a small hospital. From Te Puia or Ruatoria a detour can be easily made to **Waipiro Bay**, a lovely remote place steeped in history. The quiet village, with its beautiful marae and meeting house spectacularly sited close to the sea, gives little hint of its former size or importance as a coastal town.

From Ruatoria, the center for Ngati Porou people, there are impressive views across the Waiapu River to mounts Hikurangi, Aorangi, Wharekia, and Taitai. The town has banking, shopping, and motoring services, and one hotel, but no motel or campground. It also has the distinction of having its own radio station, Radio Ngati Porou, which operates from a garage in the main street, playing local music and relaying community and personal messages. More than one gentleman has been requested to hurry home from the pub by an irate wife through the services of Radio Ngati Porou!

Tikitiki sits on the western bank of the Waiapu River, north of Ruatoria and nearer the river mouth. The highway makes a sharp turn here away from the river, and enclosed within the bend is a beautiful Anglican church, which is worth viewing for its Maori architecture. There is little else in the town except a hotel, which has a small caravan park. Roads from Tikitiki lead to Rangitukia and the mouth of the Waiapu River, where there is good surfcasting.

Te Araroa, East Cape, and Hicks Bay

Clustered beneath high cliffs at the eastern end of a broad bay, Te Araroa, at the midpoint between Opotiki and Gisborne, claims to be the most easterly beach resort in the world. A huge pohutukawa tree here is said to be the largest in New Zealand and about six hundred years old. Accommodation is available at the Kawakawa Hotel on the beachfront or at the Te Araroa Holiday Park, an excellent campground with a range of facilities, including a movie theater with armchairs for its patrons, which is claimed to be the smallest in the world.

Between Te Araroa and East Cape the coast is splendidly isolated, and you'll find yourself sharing the road with the cattle and sheep that browse the shore and use the beach as a highway. The few houses along here were only supplied with electricity in 1990. East Cape Lighthouse is reputed to be the most easterly in the world, and it originally stood on East Island, an eroding grassy stack just offshore. Problems with access and crumbling cliffs made life unpleasant for the lighthouse keepers, and after four of them were drowned, the light was removed to its present site. A steep stepped track climbs through coastal forest to the lighthouse, 154 m above the sea on a windswept manuka- and flax-covered headland. Walk out through the scrub to the end of the headland for the best views. For lovers of isolation there are small campsites at the eastern end of the last beach before the lighthouse. Water is obtained by digging holes in the sand at the edge of the grass and letting them fill up.

As the road descends to Hicks Bay, named by Cook after one of his officers, the beautiful sheltered curve of Horseshoe, or Onepoto, Bay is seen below. This idyllic bay has a backpackers' lodge a few meters from the water's edge and a motel, superbly sited for views on a rocky ledge high above. The motel has rooms with and without kitchens and a licensed restaurant. There is a walking track to the beach below and another, starting opposite the entrance, leads to some huge old puriri trees in about 20 minutes.

At the western end of Hicks Bay are the remains of the old freezing works and wharf, reminders of a time when access to the area was easier by sea than by road. Fishing from the wharf and rocks at either end of the bay is said to be good.

Lottin Point

About halfway between Hicks Bay and Whangaparaoa, at Potaka, a gravel side road crosses the hills and descends to Lottin Point. It's a short detour to make to a magnificent place where steep hills descend to a wild rocky shore edged with green farmland and twisted pohutukawa trees grow so close to the sea that their roots are washed by the tide. At low tide the clear, surging seas withdraw to expose a rocky shelf dropping sharply to deep water—a rewarding spot for line fishing and diving. Most of the land here is privately owned, as numerous signs will tell you, but there is public access at the eastern (right-hand) road end, and camping is permitted where a small stream enters a sheltered cove. Watch out for the particularly voracious type of mosquito that breeds in stagnant rock pools around the coast.

Whangaparaoa, Waihau Bay, and Whanarua Bay

Known as the Bay of Whales, Whangaparaoa is where the Arawa and Tainui canoes traditionally landed. Their captains argued over who had arrived first and was therefore entitled to claim the land and a whale stranded on the beach. The prize went to the Tainui people. Nowadays the long, driftwood-littered beach is a favorite with people who camp on the rather barren, shingly dunes near the mouth of the Whangaparaoa River to fish. Across the river the high, prominent point of Cape Runaway, named by Cook, marks the eastern end of the Bay of Plenty. When threatened by five heavily armed canoes, Cook's men fired a warning round of grape shot over the Maoris' heads and they literally ran away. There is no road access to Cape Runaway, but the rocky shore can be gained by fording the river at low tide.

Waihau Bay, with its hotel, service station, and store, is a base for deep-sea game fishing. The foreshore opposite the hotel is rocky, but nearby Orauiti Beach has fine sand and is ideal for swimming and fishing. There is a very pleasant campground here and numerous campsites along the foreshore.

Many claim beautiful Whanarua Bay to be the best on the coast. It has several small secluded beaches ideal for picnicking, swimming, and fishing, and there are good campsites at Waikawa Point and at the mouth of the Kereu River to the west.

Te Kaha to Torere

The community of Te Kaha is spread along several kilometers of lovely coves and beaches. It has a store, motel, and campground, but its center of activity is the Te Kaha Hotel, sited on a headland with million-dollar views along the coast. The flavor of the coast is best gained by spending an hour or two at the hotel bar. Opposite the post office is the Tukaki meeting house, whose intricately carved lintel is one of the best examples of this art in the district. In bygone days Te Kaha was the scene of many fierce intertribal battles and later of intense whaling activity, which continued until the 1930s. Farming and fishing are today's major activities.

Between Te Kaha and the Motu River are many sheltered coves and beaches where attractive campsites can be found. The best camping and picnic sites at Omaio are at the western end of the wide shingle beach toward Pokohinu Point. Access to the Motu River mouth and beach to the southwest are gained from a short side road signposted Maraenui Marae. Line fishing, surfcasting, and diving are all good along here.

Separated by a high headland, Hawai and Torere are similar with their steeply shelving pebble beaches. The deep water close inshore makes them unsuitable for swimming but ideal for fishing.

Opotiki

Opotiki, once the largest of several Maori settlements around the mouth of the Waioeka River, was the scene of a terrible murder in 1865. Hauhau fanatics, led by their prophet, Kereopa, killed the Reverend Carl Volkner, a German

Lutheran missionary. After hanging Volkner, Kereopa gouged out and swallowed his eyes and cut off his head. He then took the severed head to Volkner's church, placed it on the rim of the pulpit, and harangued his Hauhau followers. The communion chalice was then filled with Volkner's blood and passed around in the belief that those who sipped from it would be able to speak English. The town was subjected to several attacks from Hauhau warriors over the next three years, and Kereopa was later captured and executed at Napier.

Today the town is a peaceful place, serving a large farming community. Its miles of sandy beaches, safe for surfing and swimming, and its good motor camps, make it a popular place in summer. There are good swimming holes and some gentle rafting along the Waioeka Gorge and pleasant hiking in nearby Urutawa Forest. The **Hikutaia Domain,** about 7 km out of town along the road heading inland from the Waioeka bridge, is 4.4 ha of superb bush where many plants are labeled for identification. Of particular interest is an immense puriri tree named Taketakerau, which was used as a burial tree by local tribes. It has a girth of 20.5 m and is estimated to be around a thousand years old.

TRANSPORT AROUND THE EAST COAST

Since InterCity stopped its bus services around the East Coast in 1990, a number of private operators now ferry passengers and freight. Check at information centers about the current situation. Operating at time of writing were the following:

Matakaoa Passenger Service: Dick and Aomihi Cook, Te Araroa, phone (06)8644-711; transport between Gisborne and Te Araroa.

Backroad Tours, 319 Titirangi Road, Auckland 7, phone (09)8178-675, run tours that take in East Cape. Their buses are the **North Cape Shuttle** and the **East Cape Fun etc. Bus.** Tours include time for sightseeing, photography, swimming, and fishing and use budget accommodation. Bookings can also be made through backpacker lodges, travel agents, and Tourism Rotorua, 67 Fenton St., Rotorua.

USEFUL ADDRESSES

Department of Conservation, corner of Elliot and John sts., Box 326, Opotiki, phone (07)3156-103; information on Raukumara Forest Park, and Urutawa and Waioeka forests.

Urewera National Park, Private Bag 213, Wairoa, phone (06)8373-803.

Gisborne Information Centre, 209 Grey St., Box 170, Gisborne, phone or Fax (06)8686-139.

13 ✦ WANGANUI AND MANAWATU

LANDSCAPE

After sheltering in Wellington Harbour, the legendary Maori voyager Kupe traveled up the west coast of the North Island, eventually arriving at the mouth of a large river. Strong winds and rough water made a crossing of the river bar impossible, forcing him to wait for better conditions, so the river was named Kai Hau o Kupe—the place where Kupe ate the wind. Once the wind abated, Kupe was able to cross the bar and explore upriver, which, apart from an abundance of birds, was unoccupied. Satisfied that the swampy lower reaches were unsuitable for cultivation, Kupe continued his voyage along the coast to the next large river, where the land appeared more fertile and promising.

The "place where Kupe ate the wind" is now known as the Wanganui River, a magnificent waterway, rising on the slopes of Mt. Tongariro and flowing around 250 km through rugged, forested hills before disgorging itself into the sea. Its catchment covers most of the western side of Lake Taupo and the Tongariro National Park mountains, an area of almost 7,300 sq km, most of which is remote, traversed by few roads, and sparsely populated. The lower reaches of the Wanganui are tidal for 30 km from the mouth, and only the last 16 km of its channel are wide enough to form valley plains.

Away from the volcanic plateau, the Wanganui River landscape is characterized by soft sandstone and mudstone, ranging in age from 10 million years to less than 1 million years. From the air the region appears as a gently sloping plateau carved into myriad flat-topped ridges. They are in fact the remnants of an old erosional surface carved by the sea when the land was lower. The original surface of these tertiary sandstones and mudstones, known as "papa," was reduced to a peneplain in the late Pliocene. Subsequent uplifting by a series of earth movements raised the peneplain to a plateau that sloped gradually from 760 m to 150 m near the coast. Large streams flowing across the plateau formed deep valleys, while smaller streams branched freely in all directions, cutting into the surface of the soft rock to form a maze of symmetrical, razor-backed ridges of near uniform height, separated by narrow gorges.

Along the coast near the mouth of the Wanganui River a narrow belt of lowlands extends inland about 12 km before merging with the dissected hill country. Two broad marine terraces, which represent stages in the successive uplift, are separated by a line of sea cliffs. To the south the coastal plains extend inland to the base of the Tararua Ranges and southern end of the Ruahine Ranges.

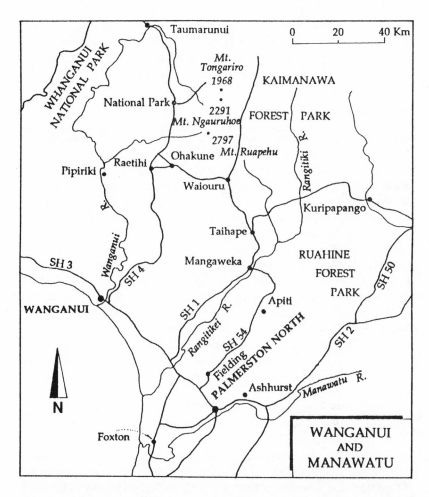

Two other large rivers, the Rangitikei and the Manawatu, cut across these broad plains and enter the sea south of the Wanganui River. Rising in the heart of the Kaimanawa Ranges, east of the Tongariro volcanoes, the Rangitikei flows southward, its passage wild at first, through narrow rocky gorges. On leaving the mountains it calms, cutting a deep trench through the soft mudstone of the lower hill country west of the Ruahine Ranges and creating a legacy of startling white cliffs and broad terraces before reaching the flat coastal plains. The Manawatu River has its beginnings on the eastern side of the Ruahine Ranges, near Norsewood. It flows south for 40 km and then turns northwest through a spectacular 5-km-long, 350-m-deep gorge cut across the southern end of the Ruahine Ranges. On the western side of the ranges, the Manawatu resumes its southwest passage across the coastal plains to the sea. It is thought that the river's course was fixed before the ranges started rising. Patches of marine sediment about 1.5 million years old still cover the hard rock core near the gorge and remind us that the Tasman Sea once covered this area.

HISTORY

Long after Kupe's initial discovery, the Wanganui River valley was settled by Maori tribes who trace their ancestry to Turi, a chief of the Aotea canoe. The valley offered great advantages. It was warm and sheltered, there was enough flat land for cultivation, birds were plentiful, and the river was full of eels. Sea foods could be easily obtained from the coast, and the river provided a highway to the interior. Palisaded pa, cut deep into the ridge tops, were easily defended and gave good protection and security against hostile tribes who might seek to challenge the ownership of the land.

The Wanganui River's importance to the Maori as a highway is hard to imagine nowadays, but in pre-European times it was the southern link in a chain of inland waterways spanning nearly two-thirds of the North Island. As the west coast of the island did not provide safe travel for canoes, the Maori traveled, instead, by the head of the northern Wairoa River, Kaipara Harbour, the Helensville River, Waitemata and Manukau harbours, the Waikato River, Lake Taupo, and the Wanganui River—a distance of more than 600 km—without going into open sea. There were recognized portages over land sections and around difficult sections.

No Europeans visited the area until 1831 when Joseph Rowe, a whaler and trader from Kapiti Island, called in to purchase dried and tattooed heads of Maori chiefs. A ready and profitable market for these existed with the captains of British and American ships, who sold the heads to collectors. Rowe, a black sailor, and another companion named Powers became embroiled in a fight with the Maori, and Rowe was killed. The black sailor was spared because of his color, but Powers was kept captive until ransomed for 25 pounds of tobacco. As final retribution, Rowe's head was dried and later offered for sale.

About the same time that Joseph Rowe met his demise, a flax trading station was established by one David Scott, and another trader, Joseph Nicol, visited him. Nicol was married to a Maori woman from one of the river tribes. In 1836, two Maori preachers from south Taranaki, recent converts to Christianity, came to spread the word. Unfortunately for them, their intentions were misunderstood, and they were killed and eaten. More preachers from the same tribe came and, although they made some impact on the minds of the locals, they met a similar fate.

By this time the Wanganui was known as the Knowsley River, and in 1839

Colonel William Wakefield visited the area in search of land for settlers. He left, thinking erroneously that he had the agreement of the Maori chiefs to sell land. The following year his nephew, Edward Jerningham Wakefield, arrived with a boat load of trade goods to exchange for approximately 16,200 ha. The Maori accepted the goods, understanding them to be a gift in return for their present of thirty pigs and over ten tons of potatoes, but not for the land. When the new settlers arrived, they were at first denied access to the land they thought they had bought from the Wakefields. Many had walked along the coast from Wellington, an arduous 5-day journey that involved many river crossings, because there was insufficient land for them there. With nowhere else to go, the settlers stayed. Over the next few years, resentment among the Maori grew as they saw their lands being taken over. Some settlements were attacked, and in December 1846, armed forces were brought in and a stockade built. It was not until 1848 that the issue was settled when the chiefs signed an agreement to accept £1,000 for 35,100 ha.

Ten years of peace followed, during which the new settlement, named Petre, expanded. It later became known as Whanganui, after the river, but over time the letter *h* was dropped from the name and "Wanganui" was officially adopted as the name of the city. One of its earliest industries was the processing of flax, which grew abundantly in swampy areas around the river, to make good-quality ropes for ships' rigging. Much of the flax was processed by hand by the Maori, and many moved nearer to the swamps to do the work, to the detriment of their health. Mechanical processing was much easier, and water-driven mills were erected on the banks of streams. Two rope factories were also built. Another early industry grew from the demand in Wellington, and on the west coast of the South Island, where the gold rush was in progress, for cured ham and bacon, when it was found that pigs grew fat quickly on the succulent root of the raupo, a native bulrush.

Smaller settlements flourished farther up the river wherever there was enough flat land to grow crops. Many of these—Atene (Athens), Hiruhama (Jerusalem), Ranana (London), and Koroniti (Corinth)—were named by the missionary Reverend Richard Taylor and are still inhabited today. Flour milling became important, and many mills were built on the side streams entering the river. One of these has been restored and can be seen at Kawana.

The 1860s brought more strife between the two races over land, and the wars in Taranaki spilled over to the Wanganui area. The rise of the new Pai Marire faith (or Hauhauism, as it became known) further inflamed the Taranaki tribes, and many isolated homesteads north of Wanganui were attacked, their crops destroyed and stock driven into the bush. Based on old Maori beliefs interspersed with inspired biblical phrases, Pai Marire appealed to the imaginations of the Maori, who were prepared to accept it as a means of driving the

Pakeha away. The first intrusion of the new faith came to Wanganui when Te Ua Haumene, the self-appointed leader, arrived at Pipiriki with three hundred followers, carrying a pole with the head of a murdered Pakeha on it. Te Ua Haumene claimed to possess supernatural powers that he could impart to his followers, making them impervious to bullets. The new faith quickly gained many converts, and at many pa along the river, tall ceremonial poles called *niu*, were erected. Several times daily the Pai Marire followers would gather and perform fanatical ceremonies, chanting battle cries as they marched around the poles, always finishing their incantations by shouting the word *hau*, hence the name Hauhau.

Near Wanganui and at Pipiriki in 1864 and 1865, fierce battles took place between Hauhau and Europeans, aided by Maori loyal to them, before the Hauhau withdrew. More trouble flared in 1868, when tribes of Kai Iwi and Waitotara, led by Taranaki chief Titokowaru, made more raids on outlying settlers. More redoubts were built at Wanganui and volunteer corps formed. Several skirmishes between Titokowaru's men and government forces took place before Titokowaru was finally forced to flee to the Waitotara district, abandoning his stronghold at Taurangaika when faced by over 800 troops armed with guns and mortars. Pursued by government forces, he and his followers were driven deeper into the remote Taranaki backcountry.

By the 1880s there were enough settlers living in the Wanganui Valley to warrant a better means of travel than canoes. A steamer service to Pipiriki was established in 1892, and ran for nearly 50 years. The service was extended to Taumarunui in 1904 by using very shallow-draught boats, and this opened up the scenic middle section of the river. Tourist trips became popular, with the journey between Wanganui and Taumarunui being made in three stages. Overnight stops were made at Pipiriki, and at a floating hotel moored first at the confluence of the Ohura River and later at the Retaruke River. From Taumarunui, people could travel north by train or to Rotorua by coach. Homing pigeons were used to coordinate the various services and announce the number of travelers.

Farming activities and tourist traffic reached their peak in the 1920s. After World War I, the difficult country between Raetihi and the Wanganui River was opened up to provide land for returning soldiers on rehabilitation grants. It was a grand scheme but one doomed to failure. The settlers struggled constantly and in isolation to clear the bush; the soil was poor and stock fared badly because of bush sickness. When overseas prices for primary produce fell in 1921, many people were forced off the land, unable to pay mortgages and rents. The Great Depression caused further financial problems, and all the farms were eventually deserted. Today the remains of old buildings, overgrown tracks, broken fences, and bridge foundations are mute reminders of a hopeless effort to subdue a wild land.

Once the road to Pipiriki was opened in 1930, use of the steamer service declined and finally ended in 1939. A short tourist service 25 km upriver from Pipiriki continued until 1958. Fire destroyed the Pipiriki store and post office the same year, and the following year saw the guest house gutted. Pipiriki seemed destined to become a ghost town, but the development of passenger jet boats supported a return to tourist trips in the 1960s. Today Pipiriki is the center for the Whanganui National Park and once again provides facilities for the tourists who use the river. Most of them come by canoe, paddling down from Taumarunui through the majestic narrow gorges. Quiet stretches of water, beneath towering cliffs dripping with ferns, mosses, and ribbon waterfalls, alternate with mild rapids between steep bush-clad slopes. The only sounds are those of the river and birds. When a light mist hangs over the water, suspended between the valleys walls, it almost seems as though the spirits and ghosts of the past will speak again.

The densely forested coastal plains of the Manawatu, interspersed with swampy low-lying areas in which flax grew prolifically, were rich in birds and eels and were occupied by the Rangitane people, who claim descent from Kupe, Whatonga, and Kuri. Unlike many of their kinsmen, the Rangitane escaped the savage reprisals inflicted by Te Rauparaha, and from the safety of the bush were able to maintain control of their lands. Later, during the Land Wars they fought for the government so they were able to again retain ownership and negotiate land sales to settlers. Palmerston North, the Manawatu district's capital, was founded in 1866 in a 360-ha clearing within dense forest. At the time, Foxton was the center of importance as a port and main outlet for large quantities of dressed flax and timber. The isolated settlement of Palmerston was linked to Foxton and the coast by the Manawatu River. By 1876 a railway through the bush connected the two towns, which then vied for importance. When the decision was made in 1886 to route the main trunk line along the edge of the hills, bypassing Foxton, Palmerston grew in importance. The towns of Levin, Shannon, and Tokomaru, founded as railway settlements, became farming centers as the settlers moved in and cleared the bush. Today Palmerston North services a huge farming district and is home to numerous students who attend Massey University. Once an agricultural college, Massey is also the country's center for extramural studies, serving thousands of people who are unable to attend a university in their own area.

Unlike the history-steeped Wanganui River, the Rangitikei has no great history of battles over land. Its swifter waters did not harbor the eels and lamprey so loved by the Maori nor did they provide an easy passage for canoes. Until the arrival of the railway, the district's only link with the outside world was the tortuous track from the area known as "Inland Patea" (near Ohakune), across the hills to Napier. The "Inland Patea" route was eventually upgraded to a road (see "Hawke's Bay"), but it fell into disuse when the main trunk line progressed through the central part of the country. The towns of Taihape and Mangaweka grew as the railway pushed northward. Hunterville began in 1884 when a store opened to supply workers who were clearing the bush to provide grazing land. Today they are service centers for the district's scattered sheep farming communities.

The hilly country on either side of the river, rising to the high, rolling, tussock-topped Ruahine Ranges in the east, has a certain charm. In winter the range tops are often snow covered, or swept by heavy grey clouds pushed along by brisk westerly winds. Always the air is crisp and the light fractured by dark valleys and pale hills. Tourism has come slowly and quietly to the district in recent time as the Rangitikei River's potential for rafting has been discovered. There have always been opportunities for hiking and hunting in the nearby Ruahine Ranges, but now bungee jumping, the latest craze in adrenalin-producing thrills, has reached this quiet corner where sheep were once the mainstay of the economy.

◆WANGANUI—PLACES TO VISIT AND THINGS TO DO

Wanganui's main attractions are the river and the proximity to Whanganui National Park, but if you have time to spend around the town there are some good places to visit. **Virginia Lake Scenic Reserve** and **Bason Botanical Reserve** are both pleasant spots for a quiet ramble. Virginia Lake is close to the center of town, beside SH 3 to New Plymouth. A circuit of the lake takes about 25 minutes, but the picnic places and maze of other tracks make it easy to spend much longer there. Bason Botanical Reserve is located about 11 km northwest of town on Rapanui Road, off SH 3 at Westmere. There is a small lake here also, but of more interest are the gardens of both exotic and native plants. Further out, at 24 km, is **Bushy Park,** which is run by the Royal Forest and Bird Protection Society. The 98-ha park has a historic homestead that is used for accommodation, and there is also a bunkhouse with kitchen and shower facilities. Day visitors can view the old house, picnic in the grounds, and enjoy leisurely walks in the bush. To reach Bushy Park, take SH 3 to Kai Iwi, then follow a signposted road for 8 km. Accommodation is booked through the manager of Bushy Park Lodge, Kai Iwi, RD 8, Wanganui, phone (06)3429-879.

The **Wanganui Regional Museum** at the civic center in Watt St. is worth visiting for its displays on colonial history, Maori artifacts, and canoes, and there are more beautiful carvings and woven tukutuku panels at **St. Paul's Memorial Church,** Anaua St., Putiki. For views over the city and river, go to the top of **Durie Hill** by the pedestrian tunnel and elevator, located directly opposite City Bridge at the bottom of Victoria Avenue. Local swimming, surfing, and windsurfing beaches are at **Castlecliff,** 9 km west of the city center, and **Mow-hanau Beach,** signposted about 5.5 km north of town on SH 3. There is also swimming at **Lake Wiritoa,** 12.5 km south of the city.

River trips in jet boats, on the paddle wheeler *Otunui,* or on the old river-boats *Wakapai* and *Waireka* are fun ways to see the lower reaches of the river. The *Waireka* served on the difficult stretch of river between Taumarunui and the moored houseboat in the early 1900s, and even when river travel faded from popularity it stayed in service. During summer the *Waireka* does 4-hour cruises up the river from the city, and in winter there are trips downriver from Pipiriki to Jerusalem (Hiruhama). The *Wakapai* does 5-day camping trips from Tau-marunui to Wanganui from November through February.

WHANGANUI NATIONAL PARK

Until 1987 the present national park was a series of scenic reserves along the banks of the river, with the majority of them between Pipiriki and Taumarunui. These reserves contained some of the largest remaining areas of unmodified lowland forest in the North Island, with a fairly uniform cover of podocarp and broadleaf species. The canopy, mainly of kamahi, tawa, hinau, and "pigeon-wood," is broken by emergent crowns of northern rata, rewarewa, rimu, totara, miro, and kahikatea. High rainfall endows this forest with a dense understory of shrubs, lianes, and tree ferns and a proliferation of mosses, lichens, small ferns, and orchids. On higher sandstone ridges, where soils are drier, the understory is open, and the dark, rounded black beech contrast with other vegetation. In the lower reaches of the river, the warm climate allows species more common to coastal areas to extend well inland. The karaka, which becomes common on riverside terraces, was probably introduced by the Maori who used its ber-ries for food.

The berries of the miro and kahikatea trees attract pigeons, and in spring the nectar-loving tui feast on the yellow flowers of the kowhai growing abun-dantly along the riverbanks. Bellbirds, fantails, North Island robins, pied tits, white-eyes, and brown kiwi are common in the bush, and kingfishers, black and little shags, grey ducks, pukeko, white-faced herons, and paradise shelducks are often seen along the river margins and its side streams. The rare native bat is also known to be present in several locations.

Within the park are areas of modified forest where pioneer farmers once attempted to wrest a living from the land. These date back to the riverboat era and rehabilitation schemes for returned servicemen. The efforts of these brave people have largely been reclaimed by the ferns and trees, but reminders of their being here are seen along the Mangapurua Track. Perhaps the most famous relic is the Bridge to Nowhere, a solid concrete structure built in 1936 before settlement was abandoned.

Most of the park covers the scenic stretch of river between Taumarunui and Pipiriki. There is road access along both sides of the river for some distance below Taumarunui and to Whakahoro, but between Whakahoro and Pipiriki the park can only be appreciated by traveling on the river, either by canoe or jet boat.

Although the park's headquarters are in Wanganui, most visitors call at the park information center at Taumarunui (located at Cherry Grove where SH 4 crosses the Ongarue River) or at the main visitor center at Pipiriki, housed in a restored colonial cottage thought to have been built before 1885. The little cottage, surrounded by a garden and white picket fence among deciduous trees, still imparts a feeling of the old days when Pipiriki was a major tourist center and guests stayed at Pipiriki House. This huge hotel, which burned down in 1959, was famous for its comfort and gracious living. It had sixty-five double rooms and eight parlors, a commercial room, billiards room, and ladies' drawing room.

Pamphlets are available on use of the river and the Matemateaonga, Mangapurua, and Atene Skyline tracks. The park handbook (*A Scenic, Historic and Wilderness Experience: The Wanganui River*) and *The Wanganui River Digest*, by Arthur P. Bates, both give more details of the fascinating history of the river and its people.

Canoeing and Jet Boating the River

The extremely gentle gradient of the Wanganui River made it easily navigable in the past, and it can be canoed by complete novices. A trip down the river for either its historic aspects or as a back-to-nature exercise, offers a pleasurable experience. Most river travelers start their journey at Taumarunui, and the first section down to **Whakahoro** at the mouth of the Retaruke River has the greatest fall, with 104 of the 239 named rapids. The scenery alternates between farmland and untouched native bush, and includes the **Maraekowhai** and **Reinga Kokiri falls,** visible at the junction of the Ohura River. Maraekowhai was the stronghold of the rebellious Hauhau, and two niu poles can still be seen here. There is a camping area at Whakahoro, and the old school is maintained as a hut for river travelers and trampers on the Mangapurua Track.

Below Whakahoro there is no further road access until Pipiriki is reached, and the only places where there is foot access are the Mangapurua and Matemateaonga tracks. There are two huts along this stretch, **John Coull** and **Tieke,** and many campsites, both formal and informal. The scenery is sublime—quiet wilderness, where the water flows gently, mirroring the towering bush and the sky, and more open country, where the river runs faster and you can catch occasional glimpses of distant farmland. There are side rivers, waterfalls, caves, old landing sites, and the Bridge to Nowhere to visit and explore. Occasional patches of willow and pine mark places where Maori kainga once stood. Some, perched on the tops of cliffs, were reached only by vine ladders, which could be quickly pulled up if enemies were seen approaching. It is a river reeking with history. Most canoeists take 4 to 5 days to make the journey; some take longer, and those in a hurry go by jet boat.

Walking Tracks in the Park

Mangapurua Track. The Mangapurua and Kaiwhakauka valleys were opened in 1917 as rehabilitation settlements for soldiers returning from World War I, but despite their heartbreaking endeavors the scheme was not a success. Access was by steamer on the river or by road from Raetihi or Whakahoro, all long and time-consuming journeys. Eventually the problems of access, erosion, poor soil, and the hard times of the Depression years forced people off the land. After a devastating flood in January 1942, the government refused to fund further maintenance on the road from Raetihi, and the last three families were ordered out. Parts of the Kaiwhakauka Valley are still farmed, but by May 1942, the Mangapurua Valley was totally deserted.

The 40-km Mangapurua Track follows the old road line from Whakahoro up the Kaiwhakauka Valley, passes Mangapurua Trig (652 m) then descends the Mangapurua Valley to the Wanganui River, 30 km upstream from Pipiriki. River transport from the Mangapurua Landing at the southern end of the walk must be arranged before setting out on the track. Whakahoro is accessible by road from Owhango and Raurimu, south of Taumarunui on SH 4. Average walking time is 20 hours, spread over 3 days, but this depends on fitness and inclination. The only hut on the track is at Whakahoro, but there are many ideal campsites on grassy river flats. An excellent historical map of the Mangapurua Valley, showing the location of house sites and other places of interest, is available from local visitor centers.

Matemateaonga Track. This track and access to the Taranaki end are described more fully in the Taranaki section. The track is popular, and people usually start it at the Taranaki end as this gives them the option of canoeing the Wanganui River down to Pipiriki at the end of the walk. It also avoids the long climb from the river to Puketotara Hut (427 m). Whichever way the track is walked, transport from track ends must be prearranged. Within easy walking distance of the track end at the Wanganui River is the privately owned **Ramanui Lodge,** which offers accommodation and meals to trampers and also operates a jet boat service

Atene Skyline Track. The almost circular Atene Skyline Track is located 36 km from Wanganui at Atene on the River Road. The track ends are less than 2 km apart, and the 18-km walk, which takes 6 to 8 hours, is usually started at the upriver end. The main feature of the walk is Puketapu Hill, which once stood at the end of a peninsula around which the Wanganui River flowed. In time the narrow neck of the peninsula eroded away and the river formed a new course, cutting off the old riverbed. Deposits of partly fossilized shells can be seen in cuttings along the track, and from vantage points there views to the river and mounts Taranaki and Ruapehu are spectacular. The only source of water on the track is at the half-way point, near Taumata Trig (523 m).

Aramoana Walk. This walk is not strictly within the park, but is included here because it is located on the River Road. The 7-km track starts and ends at the Aramoana Lookout, 3 km up the River Road (18 km from Wanganui). Much of the walk is over farmland, with panoramic views over the river, but it also passes through exotic and native forest. In many cuttings and banks there are fossil oyster and cockle shells, reminders that this land was once under the sea. A kainga once stood across the river from Aramoana, and another below the lookout was the site of an early mission called Ramahiku (Damascus), established by the Reverend Richard Taylor. Evidence of early occupation by Maori is found in the karaka trees by the picnic area below the lookout.

Sightseeing by Road

Below Pipiriki many historical places can be seen along the **Wanganui River Road,** which wends its way through the early settlements of **Atene, Hiruhama, Ranana,** and **Koroniti.** All places of interest, such as the restored Kawana flour Mill, are well marked and have interpretation signs that explain their story. As well as being of historical interest, the drive is beautiful. In places the road cuts into sheer bluffs, where layers of sediment and beds of fossilized oyster shells can be plainly seen, and there are magnificent views down to the river. There are picnic and camping areas at Otumaire, near Atene, and at Pipiriki, where there is also a new shop and motel complex.

The upper reaches of the river can be seen by road from Taumarunui. At the northern end of the town, where SH 4 crosses the Ongarue River, the road to Ohura branches left and follows the right bank of the Wanganui River. About 14 km along Ohura Road, the Te Maire Bridge gives access to the left bank. An entrance on the left gives foot access to the **Te Maire** area and picnic areas on the river flats. From the main entrance to this part of the park, 3 km away up Te Maire Road, a loop track taking 2 hours leads to a lookout and down to the river. In the reserve are large specimens of totara, rimu, kahikatea, and matai, and good populations of bush birds, particularly the North Island robin.

The road continues another scenic 27 km down the left side, with many views of bush-clad riverbanks and waterfalls, before ending near Tawata, once the site of a large kainga.

About 8 km along Ohura Road from the Te Maire Bridge, Saddler Road turns left and winds a few kilometers through scenic reserve to the river, passing several pleasant picnic sites. To visit the historic site of **Maraekowhai**, continue along Ohura Road to Tokirima, then turn left and follow Tokirima Road to its end. From here a short walking track leads across farmland, then through forest and across the Ohura River to the old Hauhau pa site with its niu poles. The first pole, raised in 1864, was the war pole, "rongo nui," which has two cross arms with hands pointing in four directions to call the warriors to fight the Pakeha. The second pole, "rere kore," or peace pole, was erected at the end of hostilities to counter the influence of rongo nui.

River Transport

Pioneer Jet Boat Tours, Box 399, Taumarunui, phone (07)8958-074; jet boats and minibus service to Whakahoro, Pipiriki, Ruatiti, and Matemateaonga Track.

Pipiriki Jet Boat Tours, The Secretary, Pipiriki Community Co-op, RD 6, Wanganui, phone (06)3854-733.

Ramanui Lodge and Jet Boat Service, Ken and Raewyn Haworth, Box 192, Raetihi, phone (06)3854-128.

Retaruke Jet Tours, Ivan and Hilary Rusling, RD 2, Owhango, phone (07)8966-233.

River City Tours, Box 4224, Wanganui, phone (06)3472-529.

Waireka River Trip, C/o Vance Crozier, Box 9033, Wanganui, phone (06) 3436-346.

Wakapai River Trip, C/o Winston Oliver, RD 6, Raetihi, phone (06)3854-443.

Canoe Rental and Guided River Trips

Baldwin Canoe Adventures, Box 198, Wanganui, phone (06)3425-729 or 3444-560; 6-day guided trips from Whakahoro, canoe and gear rental.

Canoe Safaris, Box 180, Ohakune, phone (06)3858-758. Five-day and 2-day weekend trips, canoe and kayak rental.

Plateau Guides, Box 29, Whanganui National Park, phone (07)8922-740.

Wades Landing Outdoors, Oio Road, RD 2, Owhango, phone (07)8955-995. Canoe and kayak rentals from Whakahoro or Taumarunui; cost includes return transport. They also do guided horse treks, from half-day to overnight.

Yeti Tours, Box 140, Ohakune, phone (06)3858-197. Six-day guided trips; canoe, kayak, tent, cooking equipment, and sleeping mat rentals; and transport to Taumarunui and return from Pipiriki.

◆MANAWATU AND RANGITIKEI— PLACES TO VISIT AND THINGS TO DO

PALMERSTON NORTH

With its wide flat streets extending from a central square, Palmerston North tends to be a fairly uninspiring city, but it makes a good base for exploring the local countryside. Close by are some good beaches for swimming, surfing, and windsurfing, and dune lakes for birdwatching. The Manawatu and Rangitikei rivers are both good for trout fishing, rafting, canoeing, and jet boating, and the Ruahine Forest Park has camping, walking, hunting, and tramping possibilities. For anyone interested in machinery, the **Tokomaru Steam Engine Museum** has a fascinating collection of steam engines in working order, ranging from horse-drawn fire pumps to locomotives. The museum is 18 km south of Palmerston North on SH 57 to Shannon and Levin and is open daily. Rugby football fans can visit the **National Rugby Museum** on the corner of Carroll and Grey sts., Palmerston North, to view photographs, badges, jerseys, and other exhibits connected with the sport. It's open from 1:30 to 4 P.M. daily.

Within the city there is pleasant walking along the banks of the Manawatu River on the **Riverside Walkway and Bridle Track,** which extends for 9.6 km between Maxwells Line and Dittmer Reserve. There is access to the track from several streets, the city motor camp, and two golf courses. For newcomers a good place to start would be the park beside the Fitzherbert Street Bridge. This is about halfway along the walk, allowing it to be followed either up or down river.

Pohangina Valley

The Pohangina Valley, running northeast from Ashhurst on the western flank of the Ruahine Ranges, has a number of scenic reserves with short walking tracks. Along Pohangina Valley East Road are **Totara Reserve** and **Pohangina Reserve,** which have picnic and barbecue facilities and tracks through kahikatea forest. Camping is permitted at Totara Reserve in summer, and bookings are made through the Palmerston North City Council. The Porewa Walkway also starts off this road, but is not recommended for scenery, good bush, or other interest. On the western side of the valley, just beyond Pohangina, is the 2- to 3-hour **Beehive Creek Walkway.** The track goes along the shallow stream, crossing it many times, and then returns over farmland with good views across the valley to the Ruahine Range.

Beaches and Birdwatching

Side roads from SH 1 between Foxton and Sanson lead to **Himitangi, Foxton,** and **Tangimoana beaches** on the 30-km section of coast between the mouths of the Manawatu and Rangitikei rivers. They are, in fact, one continuous beach of fine grey sand backed by high dunes, and thus provide beachcombers with miles of uninterrupted walking. All these beaches have motor camps. Tangimoana and Foxton beaches have the added advantages of estuaries for fishing and birdwatching, and Tangimoana also has a reputation for being a great spot for windsurfing. Tucked in among the coastal dunes are a number of lagoons and small lakes with associated raupo swamps, which provide excellent habitat for waterfowl. **Lake Kotiata** lies 20 km west of Bulls, among the pines of Santoft Forest, and **Pukepuke Lagoon** is to the southeast of Tangimoana. Pukepuke Lagoon has accommodations and an observation tower for viewing birds. For access and further information contact the Department of Conservation in Palmerston North.

Alternative Roads to SH 1

Two secondary roads through the Rangitikei region provide interesting and scenic alternatives to SH 1 between Palmerston North and Mangaweka. The main one is **SH 54**, which passes through pleasant, productive farmland, with excellent views of the Ruahine Ranges. From hills before Mangaweka, is a superb vista across the Rangitikei Valley to the Tongariro mountains. The beautiful **Cross Hills Gardens** at Kimbolton, which contain over two thousand varieties of rhododendrons and azaleas, are worth a visit. They are open weekdays, 8 A.M. to 5 P.M., from May through September, and 10:30 A.M. to 5 P.M. through October and November, when flowering is at its best. At the Mangaweka end of SH 54 is a delightful domain where you can camp or picnic. It's an informal grassy area under tall trees right beside the Rangitikei River. Although the cookhouse is rather quaint and rustic, the toilet and shower block are new. And the cost—only NZ$5 per night for two people!

A slightly shorter route can be taken by turning left off SH 54 in the middle of the town of Cheltenham. If you follow it you'll join SH 1 at Vinegar Hill, a few kilometers north of Hunterville. There are good views along this route also and where it crosses the Rangitikei River you'll find another beautiful grassy picnic area with access to the water.

The **Taihape-Napier Road** is an interesting route across the high country between Hawke's Bay and the Rangitikei region. It is tar-sealed to well past the Rangitikei River. Then, for a while it becomes narrower and has some short twisting sections that could be difficult with a caravan until it comes to the Ngaruroro River on the Hawke's Bay side. The Rangitikei and Ngaruroro rivers are good for fishing and camping. Views over the Kaimanawa and Ruahine ranges are excellent. (See the section on this road under "Hawke's Bay" for more details.)

RUAHINE FOREST PARK

The best hiking opportunities in the Manawatu and Rangitikei region are within the 93,564 ha of Ruahine Forest Park. The Ruahine Ranges stretch 95 km in a roughly north-south direction, from the Taruarau and Ngaruroro rivers in the north to the Manawatu Gorge, and they form a climatic barrier between the western and eastern areas of the lower North Island. The Manawatu and Tukituki rivers, which flow to the east, originate here, as do several tributaries of the Rangitikei River. At the northern end is a high plateau broken by numerous valleys, and this is traversed by the Taihape-Napier Road. To the south the ridges rise steadily to a rugged central region, with peaks over 1,700 m high, where subsidiary ranges diverge to the northwest and southwest. Of these, the Ngamoko Range, on the western side, for a while forms a higher barrier than the main range, whose prominent ridge extends south to its abrupt end at the Manawatu Gorge.

The shattered greywacke rock that forms the range erodes easily, and higher parts, where there is little vegetation, is crumbling and broken, with scree slides extending down into the valleys. Rain can fall on 180 to 250 days of the year, with the western side receiving around 5,000 mm annually. Wind speeds can exceed 140 km/hour on highest parts of the range. At Wharite Peak on the southern tip of the range, the average daily windspeed is 34 km/hour. Winter snowfalls can lie on the high ridges for weeks at a time. Statistics like these tell why the Ruahine Ranges are no place for novice hikers and why warm and windproof clothing is essential when tramping here.

Variations in rainfall and altitude bring corresponding ranges of vegetation zones, and in many places the plant communities have been severely modified by pre-European fires. Burned areas now carry manuka and kanuka shrublands, which are one of the early stages in forest succession. Introduced deer, goats, and possums have also taken a toll on the forest, weakening the soil structure and opening the way for erosion. Except for the southern end, lower flanks of the ranges are clothed in mixed podocarp, beech, and hardwood forests or beech forests with red beech and rimu the dominant species. The understory is rich in ferns and shrubs. The southern end has similar forests but lacks the beeches, and the understory is more dominated by shrubby trees such as rangiora, mahoe, pepperwood, and toro, with an entanglement of supplejack. Much of the rata and kamahi, which were once dominant, are either dead or are dying off because of damage done by possums. At night they gorge themselves on the young leaves, slowly stripping the trees of their life force. Toward the bushline, mountain beech becomes dominant, and the kaikawaka, or mountain cedar, with its distinctive olive-green spires, is seen.

At higher levels, a band of subalpine scrub gives way to tussocks and small herbs. In northern parts of the park the scrub, which is almost impenetrable in places, is mainly a mixture of dwarf manuka, hebe, and dracophyllum species, and some mountain pines. At the southern end, the hardy leatherwoods (*Senecio* and *Olearia* spp) are dominant and form an even more effective barrier to movement.

Because of its wild nature and generally rough weather conditions, only the hardiest and most experienced trampers and hunters use the inner regions of this park. There are, however, some good tracks on the fringes, which give more average hikers the chance to enjoy a good walk in the bush or a climb to the open tops of the range. As weather changes can be sudden and severe, particularly on the exposed tops, always carry warm and weatherproof clothing. Only access points and tracks on the western side are described here; those on the eastern side are included in the Hawke's Bay section. For guided hiking, fishing, or hunting in the western Ruahine region, contact **Wildtrack Adventure Tours**, Box 5093, Palmerston North, phone (06)3570-865 or (06)3248-434.

The park is administered by the Department of Conservation in Napier, and the field center for the western side is in Ashhurst. Information and the park map (NZMS 274-5) may be obtained here or by writing to the Department of Conservation, Box 644, Napier, phone (06)8350-415, or the Department of Conservation, Pohangina Field Centre, Utuwai Road, Ashhurst, phone (06)3284-732.

Rangiwahia

This is probably the most popular track as it leads reasonably quickly and easily to Rangiwahia Hut, nestled in the tussock on the edge of the Whanahuia Range. In the 1930s the gentle slopes behind the hut were used for skiing. An enthusiastic group formed the Rangiwahia Ski Club, extended a shepherd's shelter for better accommodation, and installed a rope tow. Nowadays a younger breed of enthusiasts use the range for heliskiing or ski touring. It takes 1.5 to 2 hours to reach Rangiwahia Hut, and a much longer walk can be made by continuing on to Mangahuia Trig on the top of the range. In fine weather, there are panoramic views across farmland of the Rangitikei Valley to the mountains of Tongariro National Park. Access is from SH 54, turning right about 1.5 km north of Rangiwahia and following Te Parapara and Renfrew roads to a parking area at the road end.

Orua River

Walks by the river, access to the open range tops, and pleasant campsites make the Orua River Valley a popular place for camping, fishing and hiking. From Apiti, continue northeast along Orua Valley Road; then turn right and travel 10 km along Table Flat Road. There is a carpark on the right, 50 m past a gate. From the carpark a farm track follows the park boundary down to the Umutoi Creek Bridge, then continues through red beech forest on a former logging road to **Heritage Lodge,** owned by the Manawatu Deerstalkers Association. If a red flag is flying on the track, the rifle range to the left is in use. Just before Heritage Lodge there are two track junctions. The track to the left leads down to pleasant grassy flats beside the Orua River, which can be followed for about 30 minutes downriver to **Iron Gate Gorge.** The track to the right climbs to **Umutoi Trig** (948 m) and **Tunupo Trig** (1568 m) on the Ngamoko Range. A third track, from the far side of Heritage Lodge, sidles across steep faces on the true left of the Orua River to **Iron Gate Hut** (6 bunks). From this well-benched track there are impressive views down to the river. The walk from the carpark to Heritage Lodge takes a half hour; from the lodge to Orua River flats, allow 20 minutes. The trek from the lodge to Iron Gate Hut takes 4 to 5 hours, and from the lodge to Tunupo Trig, 2 to 3 hours.

Sixtus Tracks

Sixtus Lodge is a well used educational center, and nearby is the short **Ngahere a Tane Walk,** while **Shorts** and **Deerford tracks** give access to the top of the Ngamoko Range. Access is the same as for the Orua Valley tracks, but continue to the end of Limestone Road from Table Flat Road. From the carpark at the roadend, about 1 km past Sixtus Lodge, public access follows the fenceline for 500 m, crosses Coal Creek, then takes a zig-zagging bulldozed track up a manuka-covered face. About halfway up is the junction of Shorts and Deerford tracks.

Deerford Track turns left and sidles through forest, passing the Ngahere a Tane loop on the left, then descends and crosses Coal Creek. Another track here turns right and joins with Shorts Track, making a pleasant loop walk. After about 30 minutes, the main track veers right and follows what is known as Knights Track up a long ridge. The vegetation changes from red beech forest to pink pine (*Halocarpus biforme*), leatherwood, and mountain flax before reaching **Toka Trig** (1,526 m), the highest point on the Ngamoko Range. From Toka Trig, Shorts Track follows a poled route (marked with poles) southward along the open crest of the range before descending a spur to join the Deerford Track. The walk to Toka Trig from the road end will take 2 to 3 hours if you go via Deerford and Knights tracks, and 3 to 4 hours if you take Shorts Track. If you take the Deerford–Shorts Track loop walk, allow 1 to 2 hours.

RAFTING, CANOEING, AND JET BOATING

The upper reaches of the Rangitikei River offer some very exciting rafting through rugged bush country, often on grade 5 rapids. Some trips start well into the headwaters in the Kaimanawa Ranges, entailing a fly-in by helicopter. For the not-so-adventurous there are more gentle trips through the scenic lower gorges, either by canoe, raft, or jet boat.

River Valley, in the foothills of the Ruahine Ranges, offers a range of rafting trips, three-day Canadian canoe excursions down the lower section, horse trekking, and hunting and fishing trips. They are located about 30 minutes' drive from Taihape in the Pukeokahu District and have lodge accommodations — or you can camp beside the river. For further information contact River Valley, RD 2, Taihape, phone (06)3881-444, or Fax (06)3881-859. **Rangitikei River Adventures,** located on SH 1 at Mangaweka, offers jet boating, one-day whitewater rafting on the Rangitikei, and a 42.5 m bungee jump from the Omatane Bridge. All are exciting. Phone or Fax them at (06)3825-747.

Yeti Tours, 28 Snowdon Ave., Palmerston North, phone (06)3570-202, run two-day kayak trips on the Rangitikei. No previous experience is necessary; instruction is given before setting out.

The narrow, rocky Manawatu Gorge is also exciting in a jet boat. **White Horse Jet** is located at the Woodville end of the gorge. Phone (06)3765-118, or inquire at the Palmerston North Information Centre.

USEFUL ADDRESSES

Wanganui Information Centre, 101 Guyton St., Wanganui, phone (06)3453-286.

Taumarunui Information Centre, Box 345, Taumarunui, phone (07)8957-494.

Palmerston North Public Relations Office, Civic Complex, The Square, Palmerston North, phone (06)3585-003.

Department of Conservation for **Whanganui National Park:** 68 Ingestre St., Box 4065, Wanganui, phone (06)3452-402; Cherry Grove, Taumarunui, phone (07)8958-201; Pipiriki, RD 6, Wanganui, phone (06)3854-631. For **Ruahine Forest Park:** Pohangina Field Centre, Utuwai Road, Ashhurst, phone (06)3284-732.

14 ◆ HAWKE'S BAY

LANDSCAPE AND CLIMATE

Pip and stone fruit orchards, vineyards, clear rivers lined with willows, neat orderly towns, white coastal cliffs, narrow beaches of shingle and sand, clear blue skies, and rolling grassy hills dotted with sheep — a summary of Hawke's Bay today. It was different 150 years ago. Then the hills were clothed in dense forests and bordered by plains of grass, fern and scrub, or low-lying areas of raupo swamp. The coastal cliffs and hills haven't changed much—except perhaps to slump a bit more, and their covering of high fern has been replaced by short grass. The high country to the west—the Ruahine, Kaweka, and Urewera ranges—still has its topcoat of dark beech forest and golden tussock where the slopes are too steep for sheep to graze. The rivers still run clear, but the raupo and flax-filled swamps have gone.

This is geologically young land. Toward the south the soft coastal mud-stone and sandstones are a mere 2 million to 3 million years old, and they've not long been raised above the sea in which they were formed. Wave-cut terraces several thousand years old are now up to 10 meters above the present sea level, and they continue to rise about 2 mm each year. Further inland and toward the north the rocks are older, about 15 million years old. Rocks of the inland ranges are older still. They were a gently sloping plateau until they were carved and altered by rivers draining the mountainous heartland. The rivers brought down endless silt, shingle, and rubble, building new land and changing their own courses to form the landscape we see today.

Protected from the rain-bearing westerly winds by the Ruahine and Kaweka ranges, the region has a mild, dry climate almost free of winter frosts, but the same hills provide an abundance of streams to water the land. With its fertile, rolling hills, it must have been the sort of place every new settler dreamed of arriving at to start a new life. Stretching from near Wairoa in the north to Wood-ville in the south, along the eastern seaboard of the North Island, the province takes its name from the huge bay named by Captain Cook after Sir Edward Hawke, First Lord of the Admiralty. The Maori had another name for the region—Heretaunga.

HISTORY

Little is known of the earliest people who lived here, but the main tribe of the region today, the Ngati Kahungunu have a history. Their ancestor was Kahung-unu, a great grandson of Tamatea, commander of the Takitimu canoe. Kahungunu was reputed to be a traveler and a man irresistible to women. During his travels he married several times, each time leaving behind a clutch of children and a community of people destined to become a branch of the Ngati Kahungunu. Toward the end of the thirteenth century, Taraia, a great grandson of Kahung-unu, and his father fled from their home in the Gisborne district because Taraia's father had killed two chiefs. Attracted by stories of rich food resources at Ahuriri (Napier), they moved south with their followers, conquering the land and its inhabitants, pa by pa, until they reached the mighty pa of Otatara at Taradale.

Even this well-defended fortress fell, and Taraia began permanent occupation of the Heretaunga district.

The Ngati Kahungunu people's first contact with Europeans in 1769 was not a happy occasion. On anchoring near the high promontory that marks the southern end of the great Hawke's Bay, Cook's boat was surrounded by Maori war canoes. Some of the warriors climbed aboard the *Endeavour* and captured Tiata, a young Tahitian boy, perhaps thinking him to be one of their own people. Shots were fired and several Maori were killed. In the confusion that followed, Tiata jumped out of the Maori canoe and was rescued by Cook's crew. The place was called Cape Kidnappers, and today it is famous for the hundreds of gannets that nest there.

Cook continued south along the east coast before the weather forced a halt. At Cape Turnagain he turned north once more, noting many villages and fires inland as he sailed back up the coast. It was a well-populated region then, as the many kumara pits, terraces, and old pa sites attest, but did not remain that way. In the early 1820s, hostile tribes from the north swept down the country, devastating the Heretaunga people with their guns and taking many of those not killed back to the Waikato as prisoners. When, in 1843, Bishop Selwyn and Chief Justice Martin followed the Manawatu River through to Hawke's Bay, then later traveled north, they encountered few Maori because the population had been severely reduced by intertribal wars. The following year, the Reverend William Williams and the lay preacher William Colenso bought 4 ha of land from the Maori. Being well liked and respected by the Maori, Colenso was more successful in converting them to Christianity than the earlier missionaries at the Bay of Islands had been. He was also an avid explorer and botanist, and discovered many plant species that now bear his name.

Preceding the missionaries were a few whalers and traders, one of whom was Captain Rudolphus Kent from New South Wales. Kent set up flax trading stations around Heretaunga, where the flax grew prolifically in the swampy ground. He was typical of the Sydney shipmasters, who would pay 2 muskets for a good dried tattooed head and only one musket for flax, which needed days of preparation and scraping with a sharp shell to produce the fine silky floss. But, with flax being easier to come by than dried heads, the flax trade flourished.

Many of the whalers married high-ranking Maori women when they set up their shore stations, and their relationship with the tribes was generally easy. Land was rented and axes, blankets, cloth, and tobacco were exchanged for food. Peach stones were also used as currency, and before long peach trees were growing around many villages. Today the Heretaunga Plains are the largest fruit growing area in New Zealand. Much of the fruit is exported and many tons are supplied to canneries. Another Hawke's Bay industry, wine making, was started by the Catholic missionary Euloge Reignier when he and his Marist brothers made altar wine from vines planted around their mission station.

More Europeans followed but there was no organized settlement until the 1850s, when land was purchased from the Maori. By then much of Hawke's Bay was already planted in wheat, corn, potatoes, and peaches. Some Maori settlements had their own flour mills and even processed pigs for bacon. Maori owned and sailed their own schooners and traded regularly with other ports, such as Auckland and Wellington, where the many new settlers provided good markets. In 1855, 259 ha of land was bought for the new town of Napier, named after Sir Charles Napier, a military hero of the Indian Campaign. At that time Bluff Hill was almost entirely surrounded by the Ahuriri Swamp, and fresh water was a problem until artesian water was found in the 1870s.

Within twenty-five years, nearly all Maori land had been bought or taken to pay for military protection and tied into unbreakable leases. The potential of the land for farming was quickly realized by one Algernon Tollemache, who was traveling through with Governor Grey and Bishop Selwyn. Tollemache had vast amounts of capital, which he loaned to a few favored settlers, enabling them to buy huge tracts of land and turn them into sheep runs. Swamps were drained, the bush burned, fences erected, and English grasses sown. The small settler with little money could only work for a large landholder or earn a wage in a service industry. During the 1890s these large sheep stations were split up so that smaller farmers could acquire land, and by hard work they also were able to emerge as comfortably off landowners.

Although the usual problems of land ownership did not overly affect the early settlers of Hawke's Bay, troubles in the Bay of Plenty, Taranaki, and Wanganui with the Hauhau did touch the doorstep. Most Hawke's Bay Maori were loyal to the government, and when the Hauhau camped on the far side of the river at Wairoa they were promptly driven away. There were further skirmishes, and during one in 1865, Te Kooti Rikirangi was captured. After his escape from the Chatham Islands in 1868, Te Kooti landed at Whareongaonga and a few months later massacred about thirty men, women, and children. The next year his forces attacked Wairoa but were driven back. A second group attacked a small settlement upriver from the mouth of the Mohaka, while a third group, led by Te Kooti himself, attacked two stockaded villages at the river mouth, killing seven Pakeha. Next, two fortified pa in the same area came under attack. After being repulsed several times, Te Kooti proffered peaceful intentions and succeeded in luring the defenders from one of the pa, whereupon he slew most of them. Guns and ammunition were taken and the pa razed; then Te Kooti turned again to the other pa. Before reinforcements from Napier could reach Mohaka, Te Kooti and his followers had fled into the bush.

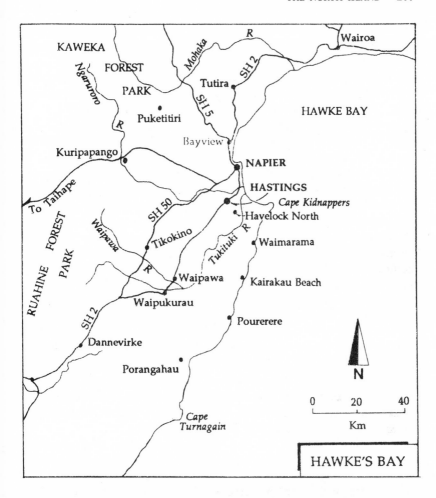

KAWEKA

FOREST

PARK

Ngaruroro

Mohaka

R

Wairoa

Tutira

SH 2

SH 15

Puketitiri

HAWKE BAY

Bayview

Kuripapango

NAPIER

HASTINGS

Cape Kidnappers

To Taihape

SH 50

Havelock North

RUAHINE FOREST PARK

Waipawa

Tikokino

Tukituki R

Waimarama

R

Waipawa

Kairakau Beach

Waipukurau

SH 2

Pourerere

Dannevirke

N

Porangahau

0   20   40

Km

Cape
Turnagain

HAWKE'S BAY

When the threat of war finally receded, the taming of the land began in earnest. Roads were pushed through early, linking Napier with Wellington via the Manawatu Gorge by 1874, but it was a difficult three-day journey. Most travel to the capital was still by sea even in the 1880s, and that was also a rugged voyage along a wild coast frequently swept by gales. A rough road reached Taupo by the 1860s, to supply the Armed Constabulary stationed at the lake. It followed a route used by the Taupo-based Tuwharetoa Maori to carry seafood from Ahuriri Lagoon, and it was still rough when the first coaches were taken through in 1872. Horror stories of coaches and horses bogging down in mud abounded. There is now a good highway, but travelling that same route today, ascending and descending the many long, steep hills, the mind reels at what it must have been like in a horse-drawn coach. The early settlers in this land were definitely hardy people.

Another road was pushed through to Taihape, a distance of 165 km. The first, and easiest, section reached Kuripapango by 1881 and was used to take flocks of merino sheep to the huge runs of Inland Patea. Beyond Kuripapango the route was steep and difficult, and many packhorses were lost over the side of the misnamed Gentle Annie Hill before it was improved enough to take coaches. Two hotels were built at Kuripapango, the meeting place for pack trains and bullock wagons. It was also considered a place with a bracing climate, and from 1893, once coaches could reach Taihape, Kuripapango became the Hawke's Bay's mountain resort. The two hotels were later amalgamated into one, which burned down in 1901. The road also served to convey supplies to Taihape for the construction of the Main Trunk Railway, thus bringing about its own demise. Once the railway was completed, the big inland sheep stations no longer used the tortuous route to Napier and, although motor coaches replaced horse coaches, the tourist trade died.

Many settlements, such as Waipukurau and Waipawa, grew as road making progressed, but others were deliberately planned. About 500 Norwegian and Danish immigrants arrived in 1872 to settle the Seventy-mile Bush in the south of the province. Bungling bureaucrats confused the dairy-farming Danes with the Norwegians and thought they had come from a forested country. The government wanted settlers to clear the bush, so the Danes' first task was to clear a 12-m-wide strip through dense forest for a road. Knowing nothing about logging, they started work in despair as there was no alternative. The only bonus was that they found themselves owners of 16.3 ha plots of land, which they could never have dreamed of owning before the mixup. The forest contained some of the best stands of totara and matai in the country and, as the railway was pushed through, sawmills sprang up until about twenty were in operation. The town founded by the Danes was called Daneverk, in honor of their labors, and after various spellings had been tried, the accepted name became Dannevirke.

The Norwegian settlers were also awarded blocks of land that they could pay off. To meet their debts they had to work at making a path for the railway, at 5 shillings per day. Although the railway bypasses Norsewood, the road bisects it. The small town has a good museum and a well-known factory, Norsewear, which makes woollen wear in distinctive Scandinavian style.

Close to Napier a second city, Hastings, grew and flourished. After a late start in 1873 and a slow beginning on swampy, low-lying ground that was plagued by flies in summer, Hastings is now known as the fruitbowl of New Zealand. In general, the young Hawke's Bay was a prosperous province blessed with good soil and a warm sunny climate, but it was not without its setbacks. The number of sheep in the province grew steadily, from 850,000 in 1867 to 5 million by 1955, and so did the rabbits. By the 1880s they were already a problem. The warm climate and sheltering effect of the western ranges also have their downsides at times, and summer frequently brings drought, causing farmers to destock their pastures. On occasion, the normal weather pattern of warm, dry westerly winds and sunny weather is reversed by severe southeasterly gales and torrential rainfalls. The latest of these devastating storms, Cyclone Bola in 1988, affected the hill country in the north of the province, causing landslides and flooding that irrevocably scarred the land. But by far the greatest disaster was the violent earthquake that broke the calm of a summer morning in February 1931. Over 250 people were killed, and almost every building in Napier and Hastings was destroyed in the initial shake and the fires that followed. The main shake, recorded in England, Egypt, and India, was followed by waves of tremor for ten days. Napier was the worst affected, and the disaster is usually referred to as the Napier Earthquake. Bluff Hill cliffs crumbled and the Ahuriri Lagoon was raised above sea level, providing over 3,000 ha of new land. Today this land is the site of the airport and the suburbs of Marewa, Onekawa, Pirimai, and Maraenui.

◆PLACES TO VISIT AND THINGS TO DO

CENTRAL HAWKE'S BAY

The first thing most visitors do in Napier is stop on Marine Parade. It seems the natural place to gravitate to, and here, along the 2-km beachfront, you will find the main information center for the district and a collection of facilities for pleasure and entertainment that could take a day or so to work through. These include the Nocturnal Wildlife Centre, saltwater swimming pool, the Putt Putt Golf Course, skating rink, a boating lake and Can Am cars, where you can do the sort of driving and paddling not normally possible without inflicting injury, the Hawke's Bay Aquarium, and Napier's pride and joy, Marineland, with its performing dolphins, sea lions, and sea leopards.

A walk to the top of **Bluff Hill** via the walkway from Lighthouse Road is a pleasant way to see the city and views over the harbor and coast. Around the northern side of Bluff Hill is the harbor and Westshore, which is now the city's maritime playground. There are grassy parks, an open beach, a yacht marina, and a motor camp here. Windsurfers, wave skis, surfboards, and canoes can be rented at **West Shore Water Sports Warehouse,** Pandora Road, Westshore, and bikes can be rented from **Napier Cycle World** at 104 Carlyle St., Napier. Continuing north along the main highway is Bay View, with its bargain fruit and vegetable outlets.

After the 1931 earthquake, Napier was virtually rebuilt and now features many art deco buildings. Lovers of this type of architecture can join guided **Art Deco Walks,** which leave the Hawke's Bay Art Gallery and Museum every Sunday at 2 P.M. For arts and crafts enthusiasts, the **Old Napier Woollen Mills** at 32 Main St., Corunna Bay, will be of interest, as it houses the Kane Carding Co. (who card wool for spinners and weavers), a woolcraft studio, an exhibition hall of arts and crafts, a specialty silk shop, and the Hawke's Bay Museum. Arts and crafts can also be found at the **Bay City Bazaar** at the Soundshell on Marine Parade every Saturday morning. A pamphlet listing local artists, galleries, potters, and studios is available from information centers.

Hawke's Bay vineyards range from small boutique to large scale commercial operations, and a list of those on the **Wine Trail,** with opening times, location map, and other information, is available from information centers. As well as providing an opportunity to taste and purchase wines, it's a good way to see the countryside. Tours are available.

Hastings is a neatly laid out town surrounded by apple, peach, and pear orchards. Its major attraction is **Fantasyland,** a storybook playground for both children and adults, with free entry for children. In spring the city hosts a **Blossom Festival,** with many events. There is also an information center here, in Russell St. The satellite town of Havelock North, on the slopes of **Te Mata Peak,** is now almost part of Hastings. From the craggy summit of Te Mata Peak, a tilted block of limestone, there are panoramic views over Hawke's Bay. You can either walk there or drive from Havelock North, on a twisting road that passes **Te Mata Park,** with its network of walking tracks, before reaching the top. As well as being a good viewpoint and destination for a drive, Te Mata Peak is the favorite launching site for hangliders on the occasion when easterly winds blow.

Te Mata Peak Walks

For a long climb, you can start the **Te Mata Peak Walkway** from Waimarama Road beside the Tukituki River on the back side of the hill. A Walkway sign and marker poles indicate the route over farmland and up onto the crest, but be warned, it is steep in places. The walk is much shorter and easier if done from the other side, starting near the Peak House Restaurant on the summit road. If you can arrange return transport, you can start from the summit and walk down to Waimarama Road. From the ridge crest there are some exciting 200-m drops to the farmland below, made even more interesting when a strong wind is blowing. Within the plantations of exotic and native trees of Te Mata Park there are four main walking tracks, the longest taking about 2 hours.

Cape Kidnappers Gannet Reserve

The Cape Kidnappers promontory at the southern end of Hawke's Bay is reserved for the protection of a breeding colony of gannets. Cook did not note that gannets were nesting there, and later records by early travelers suggest that the colony may have begun in the 1850s. The gannets usually begin congregating from late July but do not lay eggs until September and October, with chicks appearing about 43 days later. Migration of the chicks and dispersal of adult birds commence in February and March, and by April the colony is almost deserted. As the reserve is closed from the first of July to the Wednesday preceding Labour Weekend (late Oct.) each year, to prevent disturbance to the birds during the early nesting phase, the best time to visit is between early November and late February.

You can reach the reserve on foot by walking around the coast from Clifton, or you can drive with private transport operators. One runs tractors and trailers along the beach from Te Awanga, and the other runs a four-wheel-drive service over private land. The 8-km walk from Clifton along the sandy beach is a pleasant 1.5- to 2-hour walk beneath high, unstable cliffs to Black Reef, then on a track to the reserve. It can only be done at low tide, so check tide times before setting out at the Department of Conservation, Napier, phone (06)8350-415, or at the information offices in Napier and Hastings.

The **tractor** rides to the colony leave from Sullivan's Motor Camp, Te Awanga, and bookings (essential) can be made through information offices or by phoning (06)875-0400, 835-7182, or 875-0334. **Gannet Safaris,** who run the four-wheel-drive vehicle, can be booked by writing to Andrew Neilson, Gannet Safaris, RD 2, Hastings, or phoning (06)8750-511.

Waimarama and Ocean Beaches

Most beaches close to Napier and Hastings tend to be shingly and unsuitable for swimming, but Waimarama and Ocean beaches to the south of Cape Kidnappers are two exceptions. They are reached by a scenic road that skirts the base of Te Mata Peak beside the Tukituki River and then coasts through pretty, rolling farm country. Ocean Beach is the closest, and the last 2 km of road down to the curving golden-sand beach are unsealed, narrow, and a bit rough. There is no camping here, and the foreshore is a bit bare, but it's a good place for surfing in the right conditions. Waimarama is a larger holiday settlement at another beautiful, long, sandy beach. The foreshore is pleasant for picnics and there is also a campground, tearooms, store, and gasoline pumps. Offshore, the stark white cliffs of Bare Island, rising straight from the sea, provide a dazzling contrast to the blue water on a sunny day. **Bare Island Tours** run boat trips around the island, or can take you diving or sportfishing along the coast here. During weekends and summer holiday periods they have a regular program of fishing trips and tours. At other times trips are by arrangement. Contact Keith Atkins, 200 Harper Road, Waimarama, phone (06)8746-724.

Otatara Pa

Otatara Pa was occupied from around A.D. 1150 and is significant today for the large number of dwelling sites and food pits and for the lack of defensive earthworks. Bounded by cliffs, steep spurs, and the Tutaekuri River, it was well sited for natural defenses, and apart from a 40-m ditch between it and Hikurangi, another pa site higher on the hill, it is thought that the only fortifications must have been palisades. The surrounding area was rich in food resources such as eels, fish, and shellfish, as in earlier times the flat land of Taradale had been a large tidal lagoon. From the high ground there are panoramic views of the coastline and Heretaunga Plains. A walking track through the reserve leads to many archaeological features, and recent restoration work gives an idea of how the pa looked in former times. Access is via Springfield Road, which branches off the main road through Taradale just south of Hawke's Bay Polytechnic. The entrance is immediately on the right.

KAWEKA FOREST PARK

Lying between the Napier–Taihape Road and SH 5, between Napier and Taupo, are the steep, dissected ridges of the Kaweka Range, 67,000 ha of which form the Kaweka Forest Park—a rugged but beautiful recreation area. Northwest of the main range is the rolling country of an old dissected peneplain, which drains northeast into the Mohaka River and southwest into the Ngaruroro River. The Oamaru River, a major tributary of the Mohaka, forms a common boundary with Kaimanawa Forest Park to the west. Most of the range consists of young, moderately soft greywacke that has been folded and contorted. To the south and east the youngest greywackes are overlain by more recent limestones, mudstones, and sandstones. Geological instability and a thin covering of volcanic soils combined with the effects of frost heave, high rainfall, and strong winds, have allowed erosion to gain a hold, and this has been accelerated by fires, sheep grazing, and the introduction of deer and possums. Consequently the eastern flank of the range presents a high scarp scarred by long fingers of scree descending from the bare, rocky tops.

It is known that the Maori had settlements in the eastern Kaweka foothills; the forests were a good source of food and the upper Mohaka contained renowned eeling grounds. Transient camps were established during the eeling season by tribes from as far away as Taupo. The Maori often lit fires that became uncontrollable, but large-scale modification of the forests did not begin until the 1880s, when sheep were grazed in the valleys and along the tops of the range. More huge fires were lit to clear the trees and to burn off grasses unpalatable to stock. Rabbits and hares soon competed with the sheep for food, and before long the steep faces were severely overgrazed. Much of this land has since reverted to manuka, kanuka, and regenerating beech. Extensive revegetation programs have been carried out using mainly the exotic *Pinus contorta*, and today this hardy and invasive species is a problem, as it is displacing natural vegetation, particularly in areas above the bushline. Fortunately, there are still large areas of red and mountain beech at higher altitudes, and at lower altitudes in the river valleys are pockets of podocarp and broadleaf forest. Despite the modification of the bush, bird life is reasonably good, and brown kiwi, fernbird, kaka, New Zealand falcon, and the rare blue duck have all been recorded here.

Red and sika deer are found throughout the park, and the Mohaka, Makino, and Ngaruroro rivers are considered good for trout fishing. Commercial rafting on the upper Mohaka and Ngaruroro rivers is also becoming increasingly popular.

Access to the southern end of the park is from the Napier–Taihape Road; access to the northern end is from the Napier–Puketitiri to Hot Springs Road. The road to Puketitiri is gained from either Puketapu Road from Taradale or Seafield Road from Bay View. A network of tracks and huts gives access to the interior of the park. Pamphlets on tracks are available from the Department of Conservation in Napier or from their Puketitiri Field Station, RD 4, Napier, phone (06)839-8814. The park map (NZMS 274-12) also gives information and you'll want to carry it along if you venture into the park.

Tracks in the Southern Kawekas
(Kuripapango Area)

Blowhard Bush and Lawrence Road. Take the Napier–Taihape Road through the small settlements of Sherenden and Willowford and past the Kaweka Forest Headquarters. **Lawrence Road** turns to the right shortly after the commercial pine forest begins. Immediately on the left is **Blowhard Bush,** a remnant of podocarp/broadleaf forest. A maze of tracks meanders between intriguing weathered limestone rock formations, with their tunnels, caves, and passages, to the top of the reserve, where there are good views. A picnic shelter, Lowry Lodge, is at the southern end of the reserve.

At the end of Lawrence Road, a 10-minute walk down a steep road will bring you to picnic and camping areas, with barbecues, tables, and toilets, by the Tutaekuri River. The track to **Lotkow Hut** (4 bunks) commences here and takes 2 to 3 hours. About 45 minutes along the Lotkow Track, a track to Mackintosh Hut branches left and after a few minutes reaches a rocky viewpoint. From here it descends steeply to the Donald River, which can be easily followed back to the Tutaekuri River just up from the Lawrence swingbridge, making a round trip of about 3 hours.

From Mackintosh and Lakes carparks. Eight km along the main road from

Lawrence Road, **Kuripapango Road** turns right and reaches a T-junction after 5 km. To reach Mackintosh Carpark, turn right, go 1.5 km, and then turn left for a short distance. From a vantage point about 100 m from the carpark, the 2 to 3 hour track to **Mackintosh Hut** (4 bunks) begins its descent to the Tutaekuri River. After crossing the river on a 3-wire bridge, it climbs to the Mackintosh Plateau and continues over flat ground through manuka and beech forest.

To reach **Lakes Carpark**, turn left at the T-junction, then veer right after 500 m. Tracks from here lead to **Kaweka Hut** (18 bunks), a very rustic but cozy abode, to Kuripapango Lakes, or over Mt. Kuripapango. The track to **Kaweka Hut** drops downhill to the right of the carpark through pines to the Tutaekuri River (30 minutes). Across the river the track climbs through kanuka to a ridge where there is a junction. Continue straight ahead and down to a small stream. Follow it upstream for 15 to 20 minutes and then climb up to the hut. A good round trip of about 4 hours can be made via Kaweka Hut by taking the left-hand track at the ridge-top junction and climbing for about an hour up onto **Rogue Ridge**. Northward along the ridge, a large cairn atop a small knob marks the descent down a steep shingly spur to Kaweka Hut. From the hut it is 1 to 1.5 hours back to the carpark.

The climb to **Mt. Kuripapango** and back takes 2 to 3 hours, and although strenuous, rewards with extensive views. The track starts in dark Douglas fir trees, then zig-zags through kanuka forest to the main ridge, with the panorama expanding as height is gained. From the top, one track descends the southern face to Cameron Carpark on the main road; another continues northwest along the ridge to Kiwi Saddle Hut. The **Kuripapango Lakes** at the base of Mt. Kuripapango are reached in 30 minutes by the track to the left from the carpark. The lakes were formed long ago when streams were dammed by a massive landslide. The lakes can be fished for brown trout, and the surrounding vegetation is interesting for the number of species it contains.

Cameron Carpark and **Kuripapango** are another 1.5 km along the main road from Kuripapango Road. From Cameron picnic and camping area, one track leads down to the Ngaruroro River, giving access for fishing and rafting, and from the eastern end an old road descends to a water gauge. The track to **Mt. Kuripapango** starts from this road and climbs steeply through kanuka. After 10 minutes, a benched side track branches off giving an easier and more sheltered option, but both routes take 3 to 4 hours round trip. The route to **Cameron Hut** is up the Ngaruroro River and can only be used when the river is low.

Further along the main road are a Department of Conservation Field Base and two more pleasant picnic and camping areas, all popular for fishing and rafting. One is across the paddock from the Department's base and the other is on the right, a short distance along the main road after crossing the Ngaruroro River.

Tracks in the Northern Kawekas (Puketitiri Area)

There are two main recreation areas in the northern Kawekas: the **Mangatutu Hot Springs/Mohaka River** area and the **Makahu Saddle**. Both are reached via the Puketitiri Road, which branches about 60 km from Napier into Whittle Road and Hot Springs Road.

Hot Springs Road passes **Balls Clearing Scenic Reserve**, which has walking tracks, and after 6 km, Makahu Road turns left and passes through Makahu Station to the Park Boundary. It continues for another 6 km to the **Gums Carpark**. All fords have been bridged, and although the road is usable by two-wheeled-drive vehicles, it can be slippery in wet weather. Just before the Gums Carpark are a number of camping areas among the manuka. The **Mangatutu Hot Springs** are found a short way down the track to the river from the end of the camping area. Hot thermal water passes from a deep, undercut hole on the top terrace and trickles down a bluff to fall into a pool retained by a concrete wall. There is just enough room for two to three bodies to have a good soak. If you intend camping here, take a large water container, as water is obtained from the stream about 50 m along the track from the Gums Carpark.

From "The Gums," the benched track to **Te Puia Lodge** (20 bunks) at first sidles high, then drops to grassy river flats beside the **Mohaka River**. It continues up the river, mostly on easy level ground, but climbs high in places to avoid bluffs. The 2-hour walk is very pleasant, with spectacular gorge scenery of high rocky bluffs and deep river pools. The **Mangatainoka Hot Springs** are about 30 minutes up the river from Te Puia Lodge. Here the hot water trickles over a small cliff and to get a hot dip you must first fill the blue fibreglass tub, using the plastic pipe provided. It's a unique experience to soak in a tub of hot water amid the bush beside a clear, fast-flowing river.

Makino Hut can be reached via a track from the Mohaka River, just above Te Puia Lodge, or from Makahu Road. The latter commences from a saddle on the road a short distance after entering the park. From the road, the track climbs through manuka and then red beech and continues past Makino Bivouac and the tracks to Middle Hut (left) and Te Puia Lodge (right). A long day (6 to 7 hours) or overnight round trip can be made via Makino Hut and Te Puia Lodge.

Makahu Saddle lies between the Black Birch Range and the main Kaweka Range and is reached by taking Whittle Road and Kaweka Road. It's a popular area for day walks, and one of the best is the climb to **Kaweka J** (1,724 m), the highest point on the Kaweka Range. The track ascends through scattered beech and pine from the carpark, then follows marker poles and stone cairns to the top of the ridge. Here it turns south and reaches the trig after another easy 5 minutes. In summer, hardy edelweiss, gentians, and mountain daisies break the barrenness of the scree, and from the top the views are superb. The round-trip walk takes 3 to 4 hours, and care should be taken in misty or winter conditions. Warm and windproof clothing should always be carried.

Makahu Saddle Hut (4 bunks) is only a couple of minutes' walk from the road end, and from here there are two tracks. One climbs up through the trial plantings to Makahu Spur, and the other sidles through beech forest, then manuka, in a northerly direction to **Kaweka Flats**. Both tracks take about 2 hours round trip. Other shorter walks are the **Ngahere Loop Track** and tracks to **Dons Spur** and **Dons Stream**, or you can walk along the top of the Black Birch Range. A few kilometers back from the road end, a short side road to the left leads to **Littles Clearing**, where there is a picnic area and a 20-minute loop track through the beech forest.

NORTHERN HAWKE'S BAY

State Highway 2 may follow a relatively straight path across the gentle southern Hawke's Bay countryside, but north of Napier and the junction of SH 5 to Taupo it takes on a very different character. No longer are there broad, flat plains, but a jumble of hills cut by narrow, steep-sided gorges through which the road snakes, dips, and climbs in accordance with the terrain. Along the way there are several diversions you can make. The first is to Tangoio and Waipatiki beaches. Neither is particularly good for swimming, but they are good for surfcasting. Next is the 6-km-long **Tangoio Walkway**, 25 km north of Napier, which winds up the Tangoio Valley through native bush and pine forest to the **White Pine Bush Scenic Reserve** a few kilometers further up the highway. At White Pine Bush, a remnant of kahikatea forest, you'll find a picnic area and a number of short walking tracks.

At the top of a hill, a few kilometers beyond White Pine Bush, a yellow AA sign marks Aropaoanui Road to the start of the **Hawke's Bay Coastal Walk**. If you like lonely, untamed beaches and coastline you'll probably find this walk appealing. It follows the coast for 16 km to the mouth of the Waikare Stream. The southern end of the walkway, from Aropaoanui, can only be done at low tide, as it crosses a number of reefs and should not be attempted at all during stormy southeast conditions. Much of the first 4 km to the Moeangiangi River is beneath spectacular cliffs. The northern end of the walkway, reached via Waikare Road, turning off SH 2 at Putorino, 59 km north of Napier, follows a wild driftwood-littered stretch of coast south toward more spectacular white cliffs. Last century a pack track followed this coastline, and sheep stations here had to rely on steamers for supplies and to get their wool out. During the 1931 earthquake, which was centered near here, the coastal cliffs slumped badly, blocking several stream outlets and causing dramatic flooding.

After winding down into and back out of a particularly deep valley, the highway suddenly comes out at serene little **Lake Tutira**, 45 km from Napier. Open grassy areas and scattered willows at the southern end of the lake make pleasant picnic or overnight camping sites. Until the middle of last century Lake Tutira was a prime source of food for Maori living in the area and there were three pa sited on its shore. In 1980 the area was classified as a historic reserve and the lake, which has been stocked with trout, is also a wildlife refuge. European development of the surrounding land commenced in 1873 and the bush was stripped from the surrounding hills, leaving them bare as they appear today. Cyclone Bola in 1988 caused the extensive slipping on the hills around the lake. Three connecting loop tracks of the **Tutira Walkway**, lead from the lake to the 494-m-high Table Mountain on the eastern side. You can make a round trip of about 9 km or walk the tracks in shorter combinations. From Table Mountain there are extensive views over the hill country, with the formidable backdrop of the Mangaharuru and Kaweka ranges to the west.

In the hills to the northwest of Lake Tutira is the 8-km-long **Boundary Stream Walkway**. This starts along Pohokura Road, off SH 2 at Tutira Store, and finishes at Heays Access Road, off Matahorua Road, which turns right off Pohokura Road after 5 km. The walkway is also signposted north of Tutira where Matahorua Road rejoins SH 2. The 8-km-long track through the bush of Boundary Stream Scenic Reserve takes about 3 hours and is best walked downhill from Pohokura Road. A feature of the walk is the 59-m-high **Shine Falls**, which cascade over high sandstone bluffs, and a shorter round-trip walk (1.5 hours) can be made to these by starting from the picnic shelter at Heays Access Road. The pleasant track to the falls follows an old stream bench through mainly open forest with some large old kanuka trees and soft grass underfoot. Above are huge bluffs of smoothed and rounded sandstone, while below, Boundary Stream flows through a narrow gorge.

Tiny **Lake Opouahi** is found a few kilometers before the start of the Boundary Stream Walkway on Pohokura Road, nestling in a bush-fringed bowl high in the rolling farmland. The lake was formed by a landslide, and it was been stocked with trout fingerlings and brook char, which can be fished for if you have a license. From a picnic area, one walking track encircles the lake, and another, from the northern end, leads on to a lookout point with commanding views over the countryside from Mahia to Cape Kidnappers. After skirting a swampy area it leads across farmland to Thomas Bush, where there is a choice of two tracks, either of which can be followed to make a circuit. It can be cold and windy up on these hills so take a windbreaker if you plan to go to the lookout, a round trip of about 2.5 hours.

SOUTHERN HAWKE'S BAY

SH 2 and SH 50

Of the two main highways through southern Hawke's Bay, SH 50 is the quieter, running through picturesque farmland nearer the foothills of the Ruahine Ranges. The only villages along here are Fernhill, where the road to Taihape heads into the hills, historic **Onga Onga**, and **Tikokino**, which has an old pub where accommodation and refreshments are available. There's little difference in distance or traveling time between the SH 2 and SH 50, and they join near Takapau. Farther south are the old Scandinavian towns of **Norsewood** and **Dannevirke**. About 2 km north of Norsewood, a short side road leads to **Anzac Park** (signposted), a particularly pleasant grassy domain surrounded by bush, which makes a nice spot away from the main highway for a picnic lunch. Dannevirke also has a very pleasant domain featuring a deer park, aviaries, and the town's campground, which is hard to better for uncrowded peacefulness and good facilities. From Dannevirke you can do a spot of caving and see moa bones at the **Coonoor Caves**. They are on private property, and bookings are essential. Check at the Dannevirke Public Relations Centre or phone (06)374-2721 or 3747-867. Transport is available from Dannevirke.

Beaches

There are some magnificent unspoiled beaches along the southern Hawke's Bay coast, but they are a long way from the main highway and reached by fairly tortuous roads across the coastal hills. Consequently, they are more popular with locals than visitors. Each is different, and all but Mangakuri have motor camps. Dramatic **Kairakau Beach** and **Mangakuri Beach** are reached by leaving SH 2 at Waipawa and driving out through Patangata and Elsthorpe. Long, sandy **Pourerere Beach** is popular in summer and is also reached from Waipawa, but by a road through Omakere. South of Pourerere is sheltered **Aramouna Beach**, with its old historic station homestead. To reach **Blackhead Beach**, take Farm Road from Waipukurau. **Porongahau Beach** can be reached from Blackhead Beach or, more directly, by taking SH 52 from Waipukurau. Southwest of Porongahau is the hill with the longest place name in the world—Taumatawhakatangihangakoauauotamateaturipukakapikimaingahoronukupokaiwhenuakitanatahu. A signpost on adjacent Mangaorapa Road gives the translation. The road continues south from the township of Porongahau and, at Wimbledon, a side road leads back to the coast at **Herbertville Beach,** another long sweep of pristine sand. The southernmost beach is at **Akitio,** reached from Dannevirke. Locals consider all these beaches to be good for fishing as well as swimming.

RUAHINE FOREST PARK (Eastern Side)

See the section "Wanganui and Manawatu" for information on the Ruahine Forest Park and tracks and access to the western side of these hills. Several easy hiking trails on the eastern side of the ranges start from side roads off SH 50 and from SH 2 near Dannevirke. These lead to a number of huts, so both day and overnight hikes are possible. The bush and river scenery is lovely, and from the tops of the range there are superb views over Hawke's Bay. Unlike the western side of the range, the eastern side does not have a broad band of dense subalpine scrub, and the stunted bush either gives way abruptly to open tussock and rock-fields or has a narrow fringe of scrub. Pamphlets describing these tracks in more detail, and the park map (NZMS 274-5), are available from the Department of Conservation in Napier or from the Onga Onga Field Station, P.O. Box 78, Onga Onga, phone (06)8566-808.

North Block Road Tracks

To reach North Block Road from SH 50, take either Makaroro Road 3 km south of Tikokino, or Wakarara Road 2 km north of Onga Onga. After 15 km, Makaroro Road joins Wakarara Road, and 4 km past this junction, North Block Road turns left and continues for another 7.5 km, partly through farmland. Gates should be left as found. Part way along North Block Road a carpark, stile, and signpost mark the track to **Triplex Hut** (12 bunks), reached in 10 minutes. Behind the hut a short track leads to a small side stream and the junction of three tracks. Sharp left is **Swamp Track,** a loop taking 1 hour; left is the track to the fairly new **Sunrise Hut** (8 bunks) and **Waipawa Forks Hut** (12 bunks); right is the **Staircase Track,** a steeper alternative route to Sunrise Hut. From Triplex Hut, allow 2.5 hours to reach Sunrise Hut and 1.5 hours to reach Waipawa Forks Hut.

The gently graded and benched Sunrise Track zig-zags to a low, forested saddle, then continues uphill to emerge from stunted bush into the open. Sunrise Hut sits beside a small tarn just above the bushline in a sheltered basin known as Buttercup Hollow. The alternative route, Staircase Track, joins the main track above the forested saddle. From Sunrise Hut it takes about 30 minutes along an exposed, windy ridge to Armstrong Saddle (great views over the ranges), and a further hour to Top Maropea Hut (4 bunks). Waipawa Forks Hut is reached by turning off at the forested saddle and descending to the Waipawa River. A shorter alternative is to follow the Waipawa River from the end of North Block Road. Allow a full day for this round trip.

Makaroro River Tracks

The Makaroro River is reached by continuing along Wakarara Road (see "North Block Road Tracks," above). After about 5 km it descends through farmland to a parking area beside the river, the site of Yeoman's Mill. The road continues across the river and climbs through commercial pine forest to the forest park boundary. Continue past a turnoff on the right and after 20 minutes' walking there is a signposted junction. Craigs Hut (9 bunks) can be seen to the left along the road, while the **Yeoman's** and **Parks Peak tracks** continue straight ahead. It's a 3 to 4 hour climb to Parks Peak Hut along a high ridge just at bushline level, with extensive views over the ranges. Yeoman's Track is a gently graded lowland forest walk following an old logging road and taking 4 to 5 hours round trip. At the northern end is Ellis Hut, also called Murderers Hut, an old shepherd's hut built in 1884 but better known for the arrest here in 1904 of fugitive murderer James Ellis, who had avoided capture for nine months.

Tamaki West Road

At the end of Tamaki West Road is a large riverside picnic and camping area with barbecues, shelter, toilets, and several tracks through the bush and onto the open tops of the range. Traveling south from Dannevirke on SH 2, turn right into Law Road and right again into Top Grass Road. A left turn along here into Sullivan Road will bring you to Tamaki West Road. From the picnic area, one track heading south leads to **Rokaiwhana Stream** in 1 hour, while another climbs steeply to **A-Frame Hut** (6 bunks) and **Takapari Road** in 2 to 3 hours. Takapari Road is a four-wheel-drive track across the top of the range from the Pohangina Valley on the western side. About 2 hours north along Takapari Road, the steep **Rimu Track** leads, in 1 hour, down to the Tamaki West Stream, which can be followed back to the picnic area. **Stanfield Hut** (6 bunks) can be reached via Tamaki West Stream or by Holmes Ridge Road (no vehicle access), which leaves just before the picnic area and follows the ridge between the Tamaki Stream's east and west branches. Either route takes about 2 hours and the views from Holmes Ridge make it a good round trip.

RAFTING, FISHING, AND JET BOATING

For advice on local fishing spots, phone Les Gillam, secretary of the Central Hawke's Bay Anglers Club, phone (06)8588-528.

Most rivers in Hawke's Bay are good for angling, particularly in their upper reaches, but the best are the Tutaekuri, Mohaka, Tukituki, and Ngaruroro. Access to the Mohaka and Ngaruroro rivers is described under "Kaweka Forest Park."

Commercial rafting is available on both the Mohaka and Ngaruroro rivers.

From Boyd Lodge in the Kaimanawa Forest Park it is a 3- to 4-day wilderness trip down the Ngaruroro River to Kuripapango, then another 1 to 2 days through the lower gorge. Mohaka trips start from the boundary of Kaimanawa Forest Park and Poronui Station and pass through the Te Puia and Mangatutu Hot Springs areas before ending at the Napier–Taupo Highway. Other trips start at SH 5 and tackle the impressive lower Mohaka, well known for its thrills. Many operators run the Mohaka River, but there is only one local rafting company in Hawke's Bay. **Riverland Outback Adventures,** Private Bag, Napier, phone (06)8349-756 or (025)427194 (mobile), Fax (06)8391-713, are located at Riverland Station on McVicar Road, which turns left on the Taupo side of the Mohaka River viaduct on SH 5. They also offer camping, fishing, and horse trekking.

For jet boating on the Ngaruroro River, with fishing and camping options, contact **Jet Tours Hawke's Bay,** Box 1322, Hastings, or local information centers.

USEFUL ADDRESSES

Napier Information Office, Box 722, Napier, phone (06)8357-182 or 8354-949, Fax (06)8357-574.

Hastings Information Centre, Private Bag, Hastings, phone (06)8760-205 or 8769-747.

Department of Conservation, 59 Marine Parade, Box 644, Napier, phone (06)8350-415.

15 ◆ WELLINGTON

LANDSCAPE AND CLIMATE

The southern portion of the North Island—encompassing the Horowhenua and Wairarapa districts, Wellington city, and the Hutt Valley—is a geographically diverse region with a surprising number of opportunities for outdoor recreation. This may seem strange if your first glance at a map has indicated a well-populated region. As the country's capital, Wellington houses more than its share of grey-suited public servants who slave away in drab office blocks, but it also has a high proportion of rugged individuals who love to spend their weekends and spare time hiking or hunting the local hills, zapping the harbor waters under the power of sail, diving or fishing the coastal waters for a sea-bred contribution to the table, or just enjoying the fresh outdoors. Perhaps this comes from living in a maritime city built on hills that are frequently blasted by winds of gale force.

Windy Wellington is not an undeserved epithet. In springtime, equinoxial gales can bowl citizens over as they struggle along the city pavements, and force the airport to close to all but the largest airliners. On such days, Cook Strait attains a deep blue color and white-capped waves are whipped into sheets of foam. This is the weather windsurfers love, and not surprisingly the sport has a strong following here. Being situated close to latitude 40′ south, Wellington cannot escape the Roaring Forties, and prevailing westerly winds are funneled through the narrow gap of Cook Strait with impressive force.

Splitting the southern North Island into two distinct regions are the Tararua Ranges and their southern extension, the Rimutaka Range. Although not spectacularly high, the rugged, tussock-covered tops of the Tararua Range are frequently shrouded in clouds and lashed by strong northwesterly winds sweeping unimpeded from the sea, while southerly storms can coat them with snow even in summer. To the west of the Tararua Range, the flat Manawatu Plains form a widening swath of productive agricultural land bounded by a seaboard of dunes and broad, fine-sand beaches that sweep uninterrupted toward Taranaki. Seen from the air, the sand dunes march in ordered rows oriented to the prevailing northwesterly wind, and in places they extend up to 20 km inland. Trapped between the rows of dunes are many small shallow lakes and lagoons, providing important wetlands for waterfowl.

East of the ranges lies the intensely farmed Wairarapa. South of Masterton the broad floodplains of the Ruamahanga, Waiohine, Waingawa, and Tauherenikau rivers and Lake Wairarapa dominate the landscape. The Waiohine and Waingawa rivers both join the Ruamahanga on its journey south to Lake Onoke and hence to the sea. The Tauherenikau flows directly into Lake Wairarapa, as the Ruamahanga once did before flood control channels diverted its flow. Covering 79 sq km, the shallow waters of Lake Wairarapa and adjoining lagoons and marshes form prime wetland habitat for water birds and an important fishing ground, particularly for eels. In February and March, when the eels are migrating, Maori people come long distances to exercise traditional fishing rights. Lake Onoke, a much smaller body of water, is separated from the sea at Palliser Bay by only a 3-km-long shingle bar. So shallow is the outlet that it often becomes blocked by sand and shingle carried up the steep beach by huge storm-driven waves. To prevent flooding of the surrounding land, the outlet must then be bulldozed open.

Between the Wairarapa Plains and eastern seaboard are extensive coastal hills—rounded, farmed, and almost treeless, except at their southern end, where they rise to form the Aorangi Mountains. Along the east coast there are few

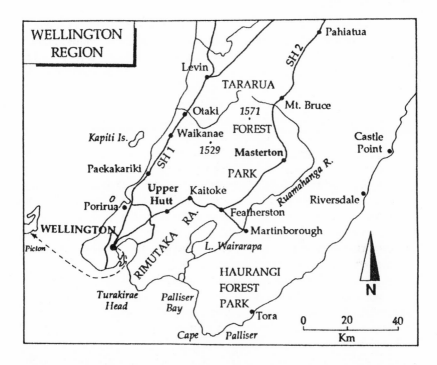

beaches, and the Pacific Ocean pounds relentlessly against cliffs or offshore reefs. Two exceptions are the golden-sand beaches at Riversdale and Castlepoint.

In complete contrast to both the western and eastern coasts, the southern coast, from Cape Palliser westward, around Turakirae Head and Wellington to as far north as Paekakariki, is rocky and bounded by steep hills. Apart from a few city beaches, almost all others are steep and shingly, and wild Palliser Bay has been the scene of many shipwrecks. Two exceptions on the west coast south of Paekakariki are Titahi Bay and Plimmerton.

The rocks that form the Tararua and Rimutaka ranges and southern coastline are very old. Laid down as sands and muds from Permian to Jurassic times, they were later metamorphosed by heat and pressure to form greywacke and argillite. When first raised, these rocks formed New Zealand's long primeval backbone. Progressive erosion by rivers rounded their form. Then in upper Eocene and lower Oligocene times their weathered surface was once more submerged. About 2 million years ago, the greywacke and argillite were again pushed up to form the Rimutaka and Tararua ranges, and farther north again, the Ruahine Ranges. New Zealand is still rising, and nowhere is this more graphically illustrated than at Turakirae Head near Wellington, where a series of raised beaches records the uplift occurring over the past 6,500 years. Wellington Harbour is bordered on its western side by a clearly defined fault line, a continuation of the Alpine Fault, which runs the length of the South Island. The city is built on this fault and, like San Francisco, experiences fairly frequent earthquakes. A severe one in 1855 raised parts of the fledgling city and added more flat land for development.

Much of the region's weather is dictated by its geography. Running roughly northeast to southwest, the Tararua and Rimutaka ranges block the flow of moisture from the west. Clouds build up over the western side of the range, spilling their damp load over the high country and leaving little moisture for the Wairarapa. In the lee of the hills the land is green, but further east it becomes parched and golden by the end of summer from lack of rain. Hot, dry northwest winds sweeping down from the hills add to the dryness. Reflecting local weather conditions, the vegetation varies accordingly. The Aorangi Mountains situated in the southeastern corner of the region are relatively dry compared to the Tararua and Rimutaka ranges.

Around the Wellington hills, and on either side of the Hutt Valley, the shortsightedness of the British settlers is very much in evidence in the form of gorse. Brought in for use as a hedge plant, the gorse flourished in Wellington's blustery climate and thrives all the more for being burned. If left to grow to maturity it can provide a nursery for native plants, but all too often fires, often started by children, sweep up the hillsides, destroying all vegetation, until the gorse comes back. Natural vegetation still survives around the rocky southern shorelines and is often the only thing that can withstand the wind and salt spray. Flattened, tightly knit hummocks of pohuechue (*Muhlenbeckia axillaris*) form springy cushions along stony beaches, and stunted bushes of taupata (*Coprosma repens*) sport firm, glossy leaves that combat the effects of salt spray. Other tenacious plants are the sage-colored tawhinu, or cottonwood (*Cassinia leptophylla*), and dwarf, or mountain, flax with its yellow-green flowers. Among the stones and matted vegetation, skinks and geckos are able to find shelter and hiding places.

On a fair day, with little wind and a bright sun, Wellington is magnificent. The tall buildings of the inner city cluster on the harbor's edge, the wharves to one side and steep suburban hills crowding to the west. Beyond the last houses the hills continue to rise, grass and scrub covered, with occasional gullies and patches of remnant bush. At the northern end of the harbor is Lower Hutt City and the valley of the Hutt River stretching back into the forested Tararua Range, the tops of which form a distant skyline. Across the sparkling blue waters, houses are sprinkled along the eastern harbor edge below steep, bush-covered hills. Behind them the eroded ridges of Mt. Mathews and the Rimutaka Range form a dramatic backdrop.

HISTORY

Kupe, the legendary explorer credited with discovering New Zealand, is said to have visited Wellington Harbour, camping for a time on the island of Motu-kairangi, now Miramar Peninsula. Somes and Ward islands, the harbor's two other small islands, are said to be named after his nieces (or possibly his daughters), Matiu and Makaro, who accompanied him. The first pa was constructed on Matiu (Somes Island) by Tara and Tautoki, sons of Whatonga, one of the earliest explorers. More pa were constructed around the harbor as Tara's descendants increased in number. Over time, other tribes migrated south, settled around the harbor, and intermarried.

In 1840, the first European settlers were unloaded on the beaches at Petone to camp or to sleep under umbrellas. They were sorely disappointed with their new land, which had been represented to them as a true Eden. After experiencing an earthquake and a Hutt River flood, which threatened to destroy their flimsy huts, the settlers moved their township around the harbor to Thorndon. A hotel was quickly erected on the beach front (now Lambton Quay) by the entrepreneurial whaler, "Dicky" Barrett, and this became a center for social, recreational, and cultural activities. It also served as a ballroom, a courthouse, and even as the provincial council's chambers. By the end of the year the new settlement had been named Wellington, after the Duke of Wellington.

Land purchases made for the new settlers by the New Zealand Company came under dispute from the Maori almost immediately. After two years, the Land Commissioner, William Spain, investigated the alleged purchases and awarded the New Zealand Company 28,760 ha, excluding Maori villages and occupied land. Due to the uncertainty of the location of the excluded areas, tension increased and erupted into battle in the Hutt Valley in 1845, but it never reached the proportions of the land wars in other parts of the North Island. An uneasy peace came with the capture of Te Rauparaha at Plimmerton and the departure of his cohort, Te Rangihaeata, to a voluntary exile in the north.

After twenty-five years of frustration and ill will, with the fledgling government trying to run the new nation from distant capitals—first in the Bay of Islands, and later in Auckland—far from many of its citizens in southern regions, the decision was made to move the seat of power to a more suitable location. Wellington was chosen as the place that "presented the best advantage," and in 1865 it finally became the capital. With the title came all the trappings and personnel of government, changing the character of the settlement forever. By 1870 the population of the new capital was almost 8,000 and rapidly increasing, as the advantages of the safe port brought added prosperity. Now, over a century later, most of the original city buildings have gone, many of them replaced with glass and concrete monoliths during a rapid expansion of commercialism during the 1970s and 1980s.

CITY TRANSPORT

Wellington City
All suburbs except Khandallah, Ngaio, and Johnsonville are serviced by the city council's big red buses, which start their runs outside the main railway station. Timetables can be obtained from the railway station or Courtenay Place terminals or by phoning (04)3859-955. Khandallah, Ngaio, and Johnsonville are serviced by Cityline buses and commuter trains. Bus terminals are at Stout St. in Wellington; Ganges Road in Khandallah; and the Johnsonville station. Phone (04)8017-000 for bus timetables. Trains leave from the main railway station.

Hutt Valley, Eastern Bays, and Wainuiomata
Regular commuter trains connect Wellington city with all suburbs in the **Hutt Valley** as far north as Upper Hutt. Cityline buses connect with trains at Waterloo and Upper Hutt stations for **Wainuiomata** and outer areas of the Hutt Valley. Phone (04)5692-933 for timetables. At present, buses to the **eastern bays** and Eastbourne depart from Bunny St., Wellington (by the railway station), and travel via Petone. It is possible that in future they will leave from the Waterloo Interchange in the Hutt Valley. There is also a ferry service across the harbor from Queens Wharf to Days Bay.

Northern Suburbs
Tawa, Porirua, and as far north as Paraparaumu, are serviced by commuter trains. Cityline buses connect at Porirua and Paraparaumu stations for outer areas.

◆PLACES TO VISIT AND THINGS TO DO

AROUND WELLINGTON AND THE HUTT VALLEY

As a capital city, Wellington seems lacking in the usual tourist attractions that cost you money. The **House of Parliament,** where the politicians perform, and the **Dominion Museum and Art Gallery,** which has good displays on Maori culture and local and overseas exhibitions, both have free entry. The **Dowse Art Museum** in Laings Road, Lower Hutt, also has interesting exhibitions. Other places of historic interest are the **Old St. Paul's Cathedral** in Mulgrave St., Thorndon, the **Katherine Mansfield Birthplace** at 25 Tinakori Road, and the **Colonial Cottage Museum** in Nairn St. One of the best ways to see the city and its interesting harbor is to take a cruise or a bus tour; they leave at 2 P.M. daily,

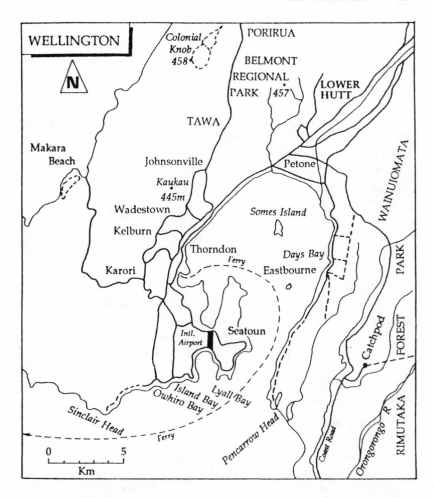

from the Public Relations Office. For folk arts and crafts and goodies in general, visit the **Wakefield Market** on the corner of Jervois Quay and Taranaki St. (open Fri., 11 A.M. to 8 P.M., Sat. and Sun., 10 A.M. to 4:30 P.M.) or the Station Village Market on the corner of Hutt Road and Railway Avenue, Lower Hutt (open Thurs. through Sun., 10 A.M. to 5 P.M.). Lists of other art and craft outlets are available from information centers.

There are many places around the city where you can stretch your legs and enjoy the breezy air. One of the nicest is the **Botanic Gardens,** close to the main downtown area, providing a pleasant haven for flower lovers and city dwellers alike. Covering 26 ha, the gardens are a mixture of exotic and indigenous flora. Wilderness and formal gardens are linked by a network of trails. There are several entrances, and if you want a downhill walk, take the **cable car** from Lambton Quay to the top terminus by the Carter Observatory and Meteorological Office and enter here. The ride on the cable car and view of the city from the top are worthwhile on their own account.

The formal gardens are best from early summer to late autumn, starting with a spring display from 30,000 bulbs. Most of the flower beds are near the Glenmore St. entrances, which can be reached by taking a No. 12 bus from outside the railway station or by walking via Bowen St. If walking, watch for a footpath on your left as you approach the motorway overpass. The footpath leads to the gardens via a footbridge over the motorway and the old Bolton Street Cemetery, with the Seddon Memorial and graves of early settlers and pioneers.

The following short descriptions of parks and walks can be augmented with maps and more detailed information available from the City Information Centre at the Town Hall, Wakefield St., or from the Lower Hutt Information Centre, The Pavilion, 25 Laings Road, Lower Hutt.

Otari Plant Museum

Often called **Wilton's Bush,** this unusual museum is devoted entirely to the cultivation and preservation of indigenous New Zealand flora. Its 80 ha of native bush and 2 ha of cultivated garden contain the largest single collection of native plants in New Zealand. Over 500 species are labeled with their botanic and common names and places of origin, where known. Well-marked trails provide over 8 km of walking. To reach Otari, take a No. 14 (Wilton) bus from outside the main railway station.

Khandallah Park and Mt. Kaukau

Khandallah Park on the western hills behind the suburb of Khandallah is a pleasant recreation area, with over 60 ha of native bush, about 9 km of walking tracks, picnic areas, and an outdoor swimming pool. Spectacular views of the city and harbor, the South Island, Cook Strait, and Rimutaka Ranges are the reward for climbing to the top of Mt. Kaukau behind the park. The summit, topped with a TV transmitter, is open and exposed to strong winds at times, so take a warm, windproof jacket and wear strong footwear. Tracks to the top start from the park entrances off Simla Crescent, Clark St., and Woodmancote Road. These are within easy walking distance of Simla Crescent, Boxhill, and Khandallah stations on the Johnsonville suburban railway. The easiest route is from Simla Crescent.

Southern Walkway

The Southern Walkway covers 11 km along the Town Belt between Oriental Bay on the inner harbor and Island Bay on the south coast. The Town Belt was a concept originally introduced in England in the 1830s by the New Zealand

Company to provide space for public recreation, and between 1924 and 1944 over a million exotic coniferous trees were planted around Wellington. The Walkway begins beside the Park Royal Hotel on Oriental Parade, climbs to the top of Mt. Victoria, then traverses a long ridge behind the suburbs of Newtown, Kilbirnie, and Melrose and the Zoological Gardens before climbing Mt. Albert and descending to Houghton Bay. From here the walkway follows the road around the coast to Island Bay. The views over the harbor, airport, surrounding hills, and Kaikoura Range of the South Island are excellent.

Eastern Walkway

For views of Wellington's hazardous harbor entrance and rugged coastline this walk is a must. Most of the 4.5-km route along part of the Miramar Peninsula is exposed and open, and there are some steeply stepped sections. The Miramar Peninsula was originally an island until earthquakes around 1460 and in 1855 raised the land, leaving the peninsula as it is now. Visible along the walk are a number of military bunkers built during World War II as preparation against invasion by Japan. The line of rocks leading out from Point Dorset at the harbor entrance ends at Barretts Reef, scene of many shipwrecks, the most recent and tragic being the *Wahine* in 1968, when fifty-one lives were lost. Displays of scenes of the Wahine disaster can be seen at Rowan Hatch Pharmacy, Seatoun.

The walk starts at the Pass of Branda, a 10-minute walk from the Seatoun bus terminus, (No. 3 Seatoun bus from the railway station) and ends at Taraki Bay, 30 minutes' walk farther around the coast.

Red Rocks and Sinclair Head

Red Rocks Scientific Reserve protects a small outcrop of ancient lava on the coast 4 km west of Owhiro Bay. Maori legend tells how the rocks were colored by the blood of the daughters of Kupe, who had left them at Sinclair Head. Worried by his long absence and supposing him to be dead, they cut themselves on the rocks in grief. Seals are usually in residence at Sinclair Head between May and September; if you don't see them at first, a strong fishy odor will alert you to their whereabouts. Between Red Rocks and Sinclair Head are a shingly bay and small stream. A grove of wind-blasted karaka trees marks the site of an abandoned pa, Taumata-patiti, one of the earliest occupied sites in the Wellington area. Views across Cook Strait to the Kaikoura Mountains and around the coast are superb from the World War II bunker on the steep hillside above the headland.

The coast is wild and exposed to the elements, so take warm, windproof clothing and wear strong footwear. Buses to Owhiro Bay run only at peak times on weekdays, so you will probably need to walk from Island Bay, which is serviced regularly by No. 1 buses. Allow at least half a day for this walk, more if you are using public transport.

Makara Walkway

Makara Valley, with its small settlement, lies west of the hill suburb of Karori. From Makara beach the walkway leads south around the coast, then up onto the hills to the site of some World War II gun emplacements, with sweeping views across Cook Strait to the Marlborough Sounds. After passing some old defense barracks, the trail descends to the Ohau Stream and returns to the start via the coast. The round trip is 6 km and takes 3 to 4 hours. Although this part of the coast is sheltered from southerly winds, it is very exposed to strong northwesterlies. Take warm, windproof clothing and wear strong shoes, as the beach is stony. Public transport goes only as far as Karori.

Walks on the Eastern Side of Wellington Harbour

The forested hills rising behind the small pockets of houses along the eastern side of the harbor offer several alternatives for keen walkers. Most of the trails start from the bays and climb to the main ridge, which has a track running along most of its length from the Wainuiomata Hill summit. It is possible to do a round trip starting at one bay and finishing at another. Forest species are mainly black beech and hard beech interspersed with kamahi along the ridges, with a variety of broadleaved trees in gullies. The pamphlet *East Harbour Bush Walks* should be available from the city information office. It contains a good map and descriptions of the walks from each entrance. An easy-to-find trail starts at **William Park, Days Bay**, a popular place for swimming, sailing, and wind-surfing.

Butterfly Creek

In a small valley behind Eastbourne is Butterfly Creek, another favorite picnic spot for families and school groups. There are four main routes, making it possible to do a round trip in about 2.5 hours. The first, as you get to Eastbourne, starts at the top of Mckenzie Road, opposite the Eastbourne post office. Others start between numbers 259 and 261 on Muritai Road, from the top of Kowhai St., and at the south end of the Eastbourne bus garage. The shortest and most popular route is from Kowhai St. All tracks start with an initial climb to the top of the ridge before descending to Butterfly Creek. Bush in the valley varies from black beech to lush podocarp and broadleaf forest.

Another popular walk from Eastbourne follows a four-wheel-drive track south along the coast for 8 km to **Pencarrow Head** at the harbor entrance. The first "lighthouse" at Pencarrow was a shed erected in 1849, with an ordinary lamp placed in the seaward-facing window at night. This was replaced in 1859 by the Pencarrow Light, the first lighthouse to be erected in New Zealand. Use of Pencarrow Light ceased in 1935, when Baring Head Light, farther around the coast, became operational. Although roads are generally boring, this can be a pleasant walk on a fine winter day, as it lies to the sun and is not muddy underfoot. There are superb views of the harbor entrance and snow-covered Kaikoura mountains to the south. Remains of numerous shipwrecks can be seen along this strip of coast, and it is also a good place to see seabirds and tide pool life. Behind the lighthouse ridge lie Kohangapiripiri and Kohangatera lagoons. The round-trip walk takes 3 to 4 hours. An alternative on summer weekends is to rent a mountain bike from either Days Bay or the Eastbourne Bus Terminus and ride. The quickest way to reach Days Bay from the city is by ferry from Queens Wharf.

Turakirae Head
If you continue down the Wainuiomata Valley for another 9 km past the Rimutaka Forest entrance, you come to the coast. To the east, where the public road ends, is the mouth of the Orongorongo River, and just beyond that the Rimutaka Range ends abruptly, forming Turakirae Head. Along this wild, barren strip of coast, New Zealand's violent tectonic past is splendidly displayed in a sequence of five raised beaches. The most recent uplift occurred in 1855, when the beach was raised 2.5 m. A second beach ridge was raised to about 8 m above sea level by another violent earthquake around A.D. 1460, and above that is a third beach ridge at about 16 m, estimated to have been uplifted about 3,000 years ago.

Turakirae Head Scientific Reserve is not only of interest geologically but also has some unusual plants growing among the dense scrub and swamp vegetation on the bouldery beach terraces. Here the bleak environment supports the spiny wild spaniard *Aciphylla squarrosa*, a plant usually found in subalpine regions. Even more strange are the bamboo orchids (*Dendrobium cunninghamii*) growing on some of the large boulders. These normally grow on trees in forests. Within the microclimates created by the boulders, mountain flax, coastal tree daisy (*Olearia solandri*), and cottonwood are other small orchids, herbs, and ferns. In more open patches, the yellow horned poppy (*Glaucium flavum*) thrives, its grey, hairy leaves retarding evaporation and a long taproot foiling the wind by reaching deep into the stoney ground for an anchor. Its yellow summer blooms seem too delicate for such a hostile environment.

Three skink species, one of them rare in the Wellington region, and the common gecko can be found here, hiding among the stones. This unusual gecko is the only one known to give birth to live young instead of laying eggs. A colony of up to 500 fur seals, most of them juvenile males, also resides at Turakirae over the winter months, although a few will be seen even during the summer.

Belmont Regional Park
Covering approximately 3,700 ha of hill country between the Hutt Valley and suburban areas of Porirua and Tawa, Belmont Regional Park is a popular recreation area. Although most of the park, managed by the Wellington Regional

Council, is grassed hill country farmed by Landcorp, extensive stands of the original forest cover of northern rata, rimu, tawa, and hinau still remain in the lower Korokoro Valley—the former Petone Water Supply Reserve. One of the most popular places in the park is the **Korokoro Dam**, where the stream has brown trout and eels and there are several good swimming holes. **Belmont Trig**, the highest point locally, at 457 m, offers grand views of the Hutt Valley, Wellington Harbour, the South Island, Rimutaka and Tararua ranges, and the Porirua Basin. The round trip walk takes 3 to 4 hours, and you will probably need warm, windproof clothing. Although the Korokoro Valley is reasonably sheltered, higher regions of the park are often subjected to Wellington's infamous winds.

The main entrances to the park are very close to Lower Hutt City. One is at Cornish St., almost under the Petone Overbridge, where the Korokoro Stream reaches the sea. Others are at Oakleigh St., off Dowse Drive, Maungaraki; Stratton St., which is reached via Dowse Drive or Normandale Road; and the top of Hill Road, Belmont. Dowse Drive, Normandale Road, and Hill Road are all signposted exits from the Western Hutt Motorway. Further information is available from the Wellington Regional Council, P.O. Box 40847, Upper Hutt, phone (04)5264-133.

Colonial Knob Walkway

Overlooking the western coast with extensive views of the Marlborough Sounds, Mana and Kapiti islands, Tararua Range, Porirua Basin, and Wellington Harbour, Colonial Knob offers a good climb for the enthusiastic. About 80 ha of hillside on the eastern side of this 468-m-high point are in bush, with two water reservoirs, forming a scenic reserve. The walk can be started from Tawa, at the Broken Hill Road entrance to the reserve, or from Raiha St., Porirua, near the entrance to the Elsdon Youth Camp. The distance is 7.5 km, taking 3 to 4 hours. In places the route is along the road to the civil aviation radio station on the top, and there are some steep sections. Take warm, windproof clothing, as the top section is exposed to strong winds. A pamphlet describing this walk in more detail is available from the Department of Conservation.

North of Upper Hutt (along SH 2)

Kaitoke Regional Park. Wellington's water comes from the headwaters of the Hutt River in the Tararua Range, with treatment of the supply carried out at Kaitoke, north of Upper Hutt. The deep gorge of the Hutt River below the treatment station, clear pools of the Pakuratahi Stream, which joins the Hutt River here, and dense forests make for pleasant outings, including bush walks, picnicking, camping, fishing, swimming, and white-water activities. Three short walks in the park pass some magnificent specimens of northern rata, rimu, and beech trees, and a longer walk can be made to a lookout on a ridge above the valley.

Rafting, kayaking, or tubing the Hutt River Gorge are popular summer activities, taking from 1 to 6 hours depending on the method of travel and flow of water. Life jackets, wetsuits, and helmets are essential, even in normal conditions, and after heavy rain in the headwaters, the river can be dangerous. Anyone intending to travel down the gorge is requested to telephone the park rangers, at (04)5267-322, to let them know your planned start and finish times and to say you are out safely. Access to the park and camping area is off SH 2; turn left after the Kaitoke Hill into Kaitoke Waterworks Road if traveling north from Upper Hutt.

Rimutaka Summit. For unequalled views of Lake Wairarapa, the Aorangi Mountains, Tararua Range, and Palliser Bay, make the short climb to the top of the ridge above the summit of the Rimutaka Hill on SH 2. The clearly signposted track begins 300 m below the summit on the Wellington side and takes 45 to 60 minutes round trip. The Rimutaka Hill is notoriously windy, and by walking up this track you can experience subalpine conditions at only 725 m above sea level. If a typical nor'wester is blowing you will find yourself propelled along when the wind is at your back, only to be clutching the shrubbery to make headway when facing into it. It's a great experience if you like wind, but the fierce gusts at the top can be dangerous.

RIMUTAKA FOREST PARK

Only 940 m at its highest point, Mt. Mathews in the Rimutaka Range does not have any open, tussock-covered ridges. Being closer to the sea and exposed to strong winds, however, the vegetation along some ridges is so stunted, gnarled, and weatherbeaten as to be almost impenetrable. Beech forest grows on drier slopes, while damper valleys have a mix of rimu, rata, and broadleaf species. The Rimutaka Forest Park's proximity to a large urban population makes it a wonderful recreation area for Wellingtonians, offering superb picnicking and camping opportunities and day or overnight hikes. The main recreation areas are the Orongorongo Valley and Catchpool Stream, and access to these is from the main park entrance 9 km south of Wainuiomata on the Wainuiomata Valley and coast roads. The visitors' information center has interesting displays of the park's natural and human history and the small shop sells mainly light refreshments and barbecue food. Information on the park is also available from Rimutaka Forest Park, Private Bag 2, Wainuiomata.

The **Catchpool Stream** has been developed for day use with picnic sites and a camping area suitable for tents, caravans, or campervans, although there is no electricity. Several loop trails through pleasant beech and mixed forest, each taking about 2 hours, start from picnic areas at the end of the road. There is also a short loop trail through pine forest behind the visitor center and another, through a grove of tawa trees, which is suitable for wheelchair users.

The **Orongorongo Valley** is a favorite weekend destination for many Wellington trampers seeking peace and quiet away from the hustle and bustle of the city. So popular has it always been that there are about fifty private huts hidden away in the dense forest along the valley sides, built before the area was established as a forest park in 1972. No more building is permitted, and the existing huts will eventually be removed. Five huts have been taken over by the Department of Conservation, who manage the park, and these can be rented by the public. All have gas cooking and lighting, kitchen utensils, and a fireplace. One even has a hot shower! The charge for these is currently around NZ$9.00 per adult per night for Friday, Saturday, and Sunday nights, and $5.00 for a weeknight, with a minimum charge of $10.00. For bookings and more information on these huts write to the Rimutaka Forest Park or telephone (04) 5643-066.

The benched and well-graded **Orongorongo Track** from the road end in the Catchpool Valley is a very pleasant, easy walk taking 1 to 1.5 hours to reach the Orongorongo Valley. Apart from the first few hundred meters, the track passes through mature forest, with mixed hardwood species in damper areas and tall beech on drier sites. In summer, sprays of the small white orchid *Earina autumnalis* perfume the air and forest floor greenery is broken by the rich purple or chinablue *Dianella nigra* berries. At the valley edge the track descends the steep "Jacobs Ladder" to the shingly river bed. From here you go either up or downstream, depending on where your hut is. There are many campsites in the valley—the choice is yours. Care must always be taken with fires, and at times during prolonged dry spells there is a complete fire ban. In summer the river shrinks to a small stream but still has small pools that provide a refreshing dip.

AROUND THE WAIRARAPA

The Wairarapa is a rural district, and Masterton, the main town, reflects a certain country charm reinforced by the annual **Golden Shears** competition. This is an international event held the first weekend in March, when shearers compete to strip sheep of their wool in the fastest possible time. Wide streets and pleasant parks tend to give the impression of an unhurried pace, belying Masterton's busy commercial and industrial life. There is a good motor camp and no shortage of hotel and motel accommodation. The information office in Dixon St. has lists of local craftspeople and events in the district. **Greytown, Carterton,** and **Featherston,** strung along SH 2, also have motor camps and limited motel accommodation. The colonial origins of the district are reflected in these quiet communities. At the north end of Greytown, the center for a large orcharding community, you'll find many roadside fruit stands with tempting bargains. **Martinborough** also has a colonial past. It is laid out around a central square with 8 roads radiating outward to represent the British Union Jack. The microclimate here is particularly suitable for growing grapes, and several newly established vineyards close to the town are producing top-quality wines.

Lower Tauherenikau Gorge

Where the Tauherenikau River leaves the Tararua Range there is a pleasant camping and picnic area and access track to pools in the gorge. To get there, take the road signposted Bush Reserve and Tararua Forest Park at the western end of Featherston and turn left at an unsignposted junction after 5.5 km. The next 2 km to the road end are a little rough and narrow. The track up the gorge starts from the picnic area and climbs about 100 m above the river before descending into the gorge. The pools offer great swimming in summer and good fishing.

Cross Creek and Rimutaka Incline

Before the 8.8-km Rimutaka Tunnel was completed in 1955, trains traveling between Masterton and Wellington were hauled from the Wairarapa plains to the Rimutaka Summit by special Fell engines. The line climbed 265 m in less than 5 km and to haul the trains up this 1-in-15 grade, the Fell engines had four extra wheels mounted horizontally so that they placed a sideways grip on a raised central rail. The horizontal wheels also acted as a braking system on the descent. Up to five locomotives, each separated by three carriages, were used at a time, and one of these can be seen in a reserve at Featherston.

Although the railway lines and two tiny settlements that serviced the incline have gone, the bridges, tunnels, and embankments are still there, making an interesting 16-km walk or mountain bike ride. Interpretive panels along the incline feature historic and present-day views of the route along with reminiscences of people associated with the area. The ends of the incline are well separated and to do the whole walk you will need to arrange return transport. Just walking part of the route, however, will give a feel of the steepness of the incline, and the best side for this is the shorter, steeper Wairarapa side, where the old settlement of Cross Creek used to be. Allow about 4 hours for the round trip to the summit, and take warm clothing—it can be very windy. In 1880, several carriages and wagons were blown from the section of line named Siberia! Both ends of the walkway are signposted; the eastern end, about 10 km south of Featherston along Western Lake Road, and the western end, on SH 2 near the top of the Kaitoke Hill north of Upper Hutt.

Ocean Beach

If you like wild coastal scenery you will probably enjoy the western corner of Palliser Bay. Dark, bush-covered slopes of the Rimutaka Range rise straight up from big, storm-tossed beaches fed with shingle from narrow, shattered-rock canyons. Where **Corner Creek** reaches the sea by the fishing shacks at Ocean Beach (marked by a Rimutaka Forest Park sign), there are many sheltered campsites tucked away among the manuka scrub. Corner Creek provides interesting scrambling, and it is possible to travel up the stream bed without getting wet feet. Turn back when the travel becomes too difficult.

To reach Ocean Beach take Western Lake Road from Featherston to the coast and continue another 4 to 5 km along a rough beach road, crossing three shallow streams. Don't go past the Historic Anchor and cairn near the last houses of Ocean Beach, as beyond here the road crosses private property and also rises steeply with no turning places. The anchor is from the *Emerald*, which sank here in 1883, and the cairn is in memory of the sixty-one lives lost from thirty ships that foundered in Palliser Bay between 1841 and 1945. One of the wrecks can be seen on the beach.

Lake Ferry

The tiny settlement of Lake Ferry at the southern end of Lake Onoke is a popular spot for both fishermen and windsurfers. When strong nor'westers blow, the wind helps carry the surfcasters' lines out to sea and at the same time provides ideal windsurfing conditions on the safe, shallow waters of the lake. There is a motorcamp here and a pub with accommodation. The hotel acquired its first license on the condition that the publican maintain a ferry service.

Putangirua Pinnacles

Narrow canyons separate tall turrets and castellations of stones cemented together with mud in the fascinating Putangirua Pinnacles Reserve, the remains of an alluvial fan laid down about 10 million years ago. The entrance to the reserve is just beyond Te Kopi on the Cape Palliser Road, about 500 m past the Department of Conservation field station and information office. You can either walk up the Putangirua Stream to the base of the pinnacles, taking about 40 minutes one way, or take a longer loop walk, which gives better views. The loop track starts about 10 minutes up the stream on the left and climbs steadily through pleasant beech and kanuka bush to emerge on the main ridge above the pinnacles. The views down into the turrets and towers are dizzying. You can either descend to the base of the pinnacles by a steep, slippery track and return via the stream (2 to 3 hours) or continue up the ridge to join a bulldozed track that descends back to the coast (3 to 4 hours). As well as the usual tui, bellbirds, fantails, tom-tits, and grey warblers, the bush falcon is also resident in this reserve.

Cape Palliser

From Te Kopi to Cape Palliser, wild, arid brown hills rise steeply behind broad shingle beaches broken by outcrops of rocks. The fishing village of Ngawhi has a Mediterranean appearance, its houses clustered together above a sheltered beach lined with cradled boats and a rustic collection of tractors and bulldozers. Gasoline and refreshments can be found here. A few kilometers past Ngawhi is the Mangatoetoe Stream, up which there is legal access to the Haurangi Forest Park. The valley appears barren and dry but affords pleasant walking and has good campsites near Mangatoetoe Hut, which is reached in about 1.5 hours. Beyond Ngawhi the coast becomes more rocky, and crayfish and paua (abalone) abound. Just before the red and white tower of Cape Palliser Lighthouse is reached, the distinctive slab of Nga-ra-o Kupe (Kupe's sail) rears above the road. Tradition tells us that Kupe laid his triangular sail (ra) here to dry and departed without it. Near the lighthouse is the largest colony of fur seals in the North Island, easily viewed from the road.

Unless you have a rugged four-wheel-drive vehicle, the road ends at boulder-strewn Rocky Point, a few kilometers beyond the lighthouse. This was once a popular camping area and place to gather paua and crayfish, but a fire in January 1990, destroyed the manuka scrublands that afforded pleasant shelter and had taken so many years to grow. Other campsites can be found along the coast, but locating water can be a problem in summer. The four-wheel-drive track continues around the coast to the road end at Ngapotiki (White Rock).

Tora and White Rock

Tora and White Rock on the southeast coast are reached by a road that seems to wind forever over brown hills, and the last few kilometers of road are rough, but the scenery, when you get there, is worth the long journey. From the road end, a 10-minute walk brings you to Ngapotiki Hut on the edge of the Haurangi Forest Park. The hut is often used by surfers and hunters. The coastline here is wild with heavy seas crashing at the very foot of the Aorangi Mountains as they rise steeply from a haze of spray. White Rock takes its name from a prominent 18-m-high limestone formation in the middle of the beach. The beach is not safe for swimming but is a favorite with surfers when swells are running from the southerly quarter.

Tora is also popular for surfing and a good place for fishing. If you have a wet suit and mask you'll have no trouble finding crayfish, mussels, and paua. Most of the beachfront is on private land, but there is public access just across the bridge at the mouth of the Awhea River. The rusting remains of the *Opua*, a victim of the seas in 1926, can be seen just offshore.

Haurangi Forest Park (Aorangi Mountains)

Unlike the Tararua Forest Park, Haurangi Forest Park does not receive much attention from the many tramping clubs in the Wellington region. This is partly because of the distance from the main centers to park entrances and also, perhaps, because the area is less challenging. The Aorangi Mountains have less rigorous weather than the Tararua Range. Many access points are across private land,

and permission is required to cross. The area is, however, popular with local hunters.

Information pamphlets on hunting and walks can be obtained from the Department of Conservation or the Haurangi Forest Park Headquarters at Te Kopi on the Cape Palliser Road (Te Kopi, R.D. 2, Featherston, phone (06) 3088-230).

Tinui and Castlepoint

It's about an hour's drive from Masterton to Castlepoint on the east coast, passing the "Living Historic Village" of Tinui en route. There is plenty to see here in the way of local crafts and restored historic buildings, and the well-known Tinui Hotel offers liquid refreshments, meals, and accommodation. Close to Tinui is the distinctively bluffed summit of **Tinui Taipo**, or Mt. Maunsell. Permission to climb Tinui Taipo is required and can be obtained from the manager of Pineview Station, which is 500 m past the village on Castlepoint Road; phone (06)3726-815. Further information on the walk and area can also be obtained from the manager of Pineview or from the Department of Conservation, Masterton.

In summer Castlepoint is a popular place for swimming, fishing, and shellfish collecting, and horse races are held on the beach in March each year. The area is interesting geologically, archaeologically, and scenically, is a popular breeding site for sea birds, and is also the habitat for a daisy, _Senecio compactus_, found nowhere else in the world. The daisy colonizes the distinctive crushed, eroded cliffs of young limestone at Castlepoint and Castlerock, the only exposed rock of its age on the Wairarapa Coast. Erosion of the crushed rock behind the limestone outcrop has left a reef that contains many young, well-formed fossils and that encloses a sheltered lagoon. Castlepoint Lighthouse at the northern end of the reef started operating in 1913 to help ships from Panama make their first sighting of New Zealand. Its light can be seen for 26 nautical miles. There are tracks to the lighthouse and to the 160-m summit of Castle Rock, where you can stop for excellent views, or you can walk northward along the coast for about 30 minutes. Weathering and earthquakes have altered the form and height of Castle Rock so that it now bears little resemblance to the landmark that Captain Cook sighted in 1769.

Mt. Bruce Wildlife Centre

Originally established as a place to breed the rare takahe (_Notornis mantelli_) after its rediscovery in the Murchison Mountains of Fiordland, Mt. Bruce National Wildlife Centre now holds New Zealand's largest collection of native New Zealand wildlife. Endangered species are bred and studied here in the effort to prevent their becoming extinct. The center is set in native bush, a remnant of the wide swath that once extended from Mauriceville to Woodville, to which plantings of exotic firs, cypress, and redwood have been added. Paths through the bush allow you to see rare birds in near-natural settings. You can also visit a nocturnal house where kiwi and owls can be seen and view informative displays on other New Zealand wildlife.

Just south of the Mt. Bruce Wildlife Centre, on SH 2, is a pleasant camping and picnic area. Two bush walks start from here, one going to a lookout (1 hour round trip) and the other to **Bruce's Hill** (710 m). The latter is steep in places and takes about 3 hours round trip, but it provides some interesting views toward the Tararua Range.

TARARUA FOREST PARK

Stretching about 80 km along the Tararua Range and covering over 100,000 ha, the Tararua Forest Park is the main "stamping ground" for trampers from the greater Wellington region. The area is so popular that Wellington and Hutt cities alone support more than six tramping clubs whose members use the extensive network of tracks, routes, and huts most weekends—and not because the Tararuas offer easy country. The reverse is more true. There is very little flat walking except along a few river valleys, and to get into these you must first climb an uphill stretch. The open, tussock-clad tops offer superb walking—when the weather is good. Unfortunately, fine days are relatively rare. Weather surveys indicate that there are only about 70 fine days per year; on the remaining days (almost 300) it will either be raining or cloudy! In addition, weather changes are often sudden and severe.

On the damp western side of the Tararua Range, lush broadleaf and beech forests grow to around 1,100 m, and above this almost impenetrable subalpine scrub extends 100 to 200 m. The main scrub plant is leatherwood, or tupare (*Olearia colensoi*), which has stiff, unrelenting branches and leathery serrated leaves. Tall tussock grasses and alpine herbs cover the tops of ridges above about 1,200 m. On the drier eastern side, beech is more dominant from lower levels, the bushline more clearly demarcated, and the scrub zone less extensive, more open, and more varied in species.

Most of the tracks leading from the main access points are well marked and easy to follow, but they can be muddy, particularly during winter. The same cannot be said of tracks going deeper into the range. Most tracks along the highest ridge tops are unmarked and are in reality routes only, making route-finding in thick mist a difficult exercise. Also, many streams and rivers are unbridged, and when flooded, are difficult and dangerous to cross. There are many huts in the park, varying from small 6-bunk structures built by the now-defunct Forest Service when deer culling was in its heyday to larger, basic structures with sleeping platforms only, which were built by tramping clubs to accommodate many. In between there are a few newer, larger more comfortable huts.

There is not room here to describe the multitude of hikes available, but the Tararua Forest Park Map (Infomap 274-02) will give some ideas and more information. A map is essential in the forest park, as are a compass and good equipment. If you want to get into the more remote areas, you should get advice on your proposed trip from a local tramping club. Tramping in the Tararuas is true adventuring, and in general this range is not a place for the inexperienced. There are, however, many relatively easy hikes and walks in peripheral areas that can be undertaken safely. You will still need strong boots and waterproof clothing. There are several major entry points to the park, with the southernmost one at Kaitoke, north of Upper Hutt, and the others from the Wairarapa and Horowhenua.

Kaitoke Entrance

Access is gained by turning off SH 2 at the Pakuratahi Bridge, just north of Kaitoke, and following Kaitoke Valley Road. From here the easiest walk is into the beautiful Tauherenikau Valley. The **Tauherenikau Valley Track** leads off from a stile and reaches a junction after about 10 minutes. Take the right-hand track and climb about 30 minutes to the top of a ridge where four tracks converge. Go to the right, along the ridge, and a few minutes later take the left-hand track, which drops steeply to Smiths Creek. A benched track continues down the creek to the Tauherenikau River. Above the Smiths Creek confluence, the Tauherenikau Valley is broad and open; below it, the river flows through a narrow gorge with many deep pools before it exits the range near Featherston. Allow about 2 hours to reach the river from the carpark. A 2- to 3-day hike finishing at the Mt. Holdsworth entrance can be made by traveling up the Tauherenikau Valley and crossing Cone Saddle to the Waiohine Valley.

Mt. Holdsworth Entrance

Tracks to several huts on the eastern side of the park start at the Mt. Holdsworth entrance, 18 km from Masterton, and many are suitable for day walks. Access is by Norfolk Road, off SH 2 just south of Masterton. The area has good bush and a large grassy camping area. Basic overnight accommodation is available in Holdsworth Lodge at the road end. The presence of a resident caretaker ensures that facilities are well maintained and that cars parked overnight are not interfered with. Maps and other information are available at the caretaker's office.

Donnelly Flat, a pleasant grassy river flat beside the Atiwhakatu Stream, can be reached in 15 to 20 minutes from the road end. It's a good place for picnics and camping. You can continue up the Atiwhakatu Stream to **Mid Atiwhakatu Hut** (2 to 3 hours) or just use the river track for a pleasant amble. About an hour past Donnelly Flat, a side track climbs steeply to **Mountain House,** one of the older huts in the park. This can be used to make a round trip.

From Donnelly Flat, the main track climbs to **Mt. Holdsworth** (1,474 m) which in fine weather gives outstanding views over the Wairarapa and other ridges and valleys of the park. The climb takes 3 to 4 hours, making a long day hike, or you can stay overnight at either Mountain House, at around the halfway mark, or **Powell Hut**, which sits at the bush edge less than an hour below the summit. The views from here are almost as good as from the peak, the subalpine vegetation is interesting, and it's a superb place for sunrises. Make sure you have good weatherproof clothing if you do go to the top. Even though the weather may be reasonable at lower levels, it can be extremely unpleasant once the shelter of the bush is left behind. In winter the top may be snow-covered and icy.

Totara Flats (3 to 4 hours from the road end) in the Waiohine Valley is reached by a track that branches off about an hour along the Mt. Holdsworth Track. There are many grassy campsites on the river flats, or you can stay in **Totara Flats Lodge**. Tracks continue down the true right bank (the bank on your right as you face downsteam) to the Waiohine Gorge road end and across Cone Saddle to the Tauherenikau Valley.

Holdsworth Lookout, about an hour's climb from the road end, is a good spot for views of the Tararua Range and has a compass sighter to help you identify the peaks. The track to the lookout branches off the main trail soon after crossing the Atiwhakatu Stream.

Waiohine Gorge
The Waiohine Gorge is reached by Waiohine Gorge Road, off SH 2 immediately north of the Waiohine River bridge between Greytown and Carterton. The upper section of the road gives access to the river for fishing. At the end of the road is a camping and picnic area, a track down to pools in the gorge and a footbridge across to the track to Totara Flats (3 to 4 hours; see "Mt. Holdsworth" section).

Kiriwhakapapa
The Kiriwhakapapa Road leaves SH 2 about 16 km north of Masterton and leads along an increasingly forested valley to a pleasant picnic and camping area at the edge of the park. The shortest walk from the road end is a 45-minute loop through redwoods and native bush along an old tramway built in the late 1920s. A longer walk (3 hours), for which you would need to arrange return transport, heads south over a low saddle to the Mikimiki Valley road end. If you are feeling very energetic, you can climb to Blue Range Hut (900 m) for views into the Ruamahanga River catchment. The 4-bunk hut is in reality only a corrugated iron shed painted an eye-catching orange, but it serves its purpose in providing shelter to hunters and trampers. Allow 4 to 5 hours for the round trip walk.

ALONG THE WEST COAST

The Horowhenua, or Kapiti Coast, with its long, safe beaches sheltered by Kapiti Island, market gardens, and bush areas of the Tararua Range, has generally sunny weather and is a favorite weekend escape for Wellingtonians. Paraparaumu has developed as the main commercial center, but it is closely followed by Waikanae. Further north are Otaki and Levin, both substantial farming centers serving the widespread market-gardening community. Fruit and vegetable stalls along SH 1 between Otaki and Levin sell produce at much cheaper rates than do shops in the city. Paekakariki, Paraparaumu, Waikanae, Otaki, and Levin all have good motorcamps, and there are numerous motels along SH 1.

Between Paekakariki and Waikanae there are several places worth visiting, all signposted on SH 1. The first is **Queen Elizabeth Park,** which extends along the coast from Paekakariki to Raumati. The park is made up of farmland and an undeveloped coastal strip, with cleared pockets for picnics and barbecues. It also has a **Tramway Museum,** which would interest mechanical types, as would the **Southward Car Museum,** just north of Paraparaumu, with one of the largest collections of vintage and veteran cars in the Southern Hemisphere. At **Lindale Farm Park,** north of Paraparaumu, you can experience the sights, smells, and action of New Zealand farm life. The specialty cheeses and ice creams made by their Farm Kitchen Restaurant are definitely worth sampling.

Nga Manu Sanctuary at Waikanae, a 15-ha park developed by a privately funded charitable trust to help preserve some of New Zealand's native flora and fauna, contains examples of natural sand dune, swampland, and bush. Birds to be seen here include kea, harrier hawk, New Zealand falcon, morepork, pigeon, and kiwi. There are also fish, tuatara, and other reptiles. To reach Nga Manu, take Te Moana Road off SH 1 just south of the Waikanae Shopping Centre, then turn right into Ngarara Road.

There are two short bush walks close to Waikanae that make a pleasant change from beach scenery. Both take 1.5 to 2 hours round trip. One, the **Parata Track** in the **Hemi Matenga Reserve** on the steep hills behind the town, climbs through kohekohe forest to a grassy lookout point where views over the coast, Kapiti Island, and Reikiorangi Valley are excellent. Forests of kohekohe, a member of the Meliaceae family, once covered much of the western coast from Wellington to Waikanae. Signs at the Waikanae traffic lights will direct you to the reserve.

The other walk, along the **Mangaone Walkway,** follows an old logging road for 8 km, at first through pleasant regenerating forest that is thick with tree ferns, then farmland. Many people turn back when they reach the farmland (about 45 minutes). Return transport needs to be arranged if you want to do the complete walk. To reach the walkway, leave SH 1 at the Waikanae traffic lights and follow Reikiorangi Valley Road, turning left into Ngatiawa Road, then left again to the end of Mangaone South Road.

At Te Horo, stop at **Parsonage Hill** and taste some of the fruit wines, or take a look at the excellent pottery and blown glass at **New Zealand Craftworks.** Only 1 km north, the workshop of potter **Mirek Smisek** is open daily.

Otaki Forks (Tararua Forest Park)

The confluence of the Otaki and Waiotauru rivers, popularly known as Otaki Forks, is the starting point for many hikes on the western side of the Tararua Range. Once logged extensively and then farmed, the area is slowly returning to its natural state and now offers pleasant sites for picnicking and informal camping. In summer the many pools in the rivers are popular for swimming. Maps and more information are available from the ranger station at the Forks. Access is signposted on SH 1 at Te Horo and on the south side of the Otaki River Bridge. The road finishes 21 km from SH 1, with some narrow sections at the top end where it passes gorged sections of the river.

The main camping areas are beyond the ranger station, a short way up the Waiotauru Valley, by some large pine trees that mark where a school and small settlement once stood. From here there is a choice of short walks, or you can just wander up the valley beside the river where you will find many other pleasant camping or picnic spots.

The main track, to **Field Hut** and **Vosseler Hut,** commences at the footbridge over the Waiotauru River by the ranger station and climbs directly up the spur between the Otaki and Waiotauru rivers. At the beginning, markers point the way across the farmland to the bush edge where the well-established track begins. Field Hut, one of the oldest in the park, is situated just below Table Top and is reached in 2.5 to 3 hours. Above here an extensive area of subalpine leatherwood is passed, dwindling to tussock as Dennan Peak and then West Peak are climbed. Vosseler Hut, reached in 1.5 to 2 hours from Field Hut, lies in a shallow basin on the top of West Peak. In clear weather there are extensive views northeastward along the humped Main Range and Mt. Holsdworth ridge, while to the west lie the coastal plains. Be prepared for cold, wet conditions above Field Hut at any time of the year.

Other tracks from the Forks lead to Waetewaewae Hut, on the upper Otaki River, and Penn Creek Hut, on a tributary stream. Landslides along the steep sides of the Otaki Gorge have made the Penn Creek Track dangerous and the Waetewaewae Track has also been in bad condition, but they may have been upgraded recently. Check at the ranger station.

Lake Papaitonga

Lake Papaitonga is a short distance from SH 1 and is signposted at the corner of Buller Road, about halfway between Ohau and Levin. From Wellington, this is the fourth road on the left after Ohau. Surrounding the lake's shallow waters is a rare remnant of the lowland forest that once covered the sand dunes and plains from Waikanae to Wanganui. Tawa, titoki, and mahoe grow on higher areas, but in low lying areas this changes to kahikatea swamp forest. Very wet areas near the lake edge have a dense covering of flax, hebes, and sedges. Buttressed tree roots, epiphytic kiekie, lianes, and an unexpected lack of light within the forest give the impression of a primeval tropical jungle. Only crocodiles, snakes, and the flashes of brilliant birds are missing. The lake has a colorful history and was once the scene of a plot to kill Te Rauparaha. These days it is home to fifteen species of waterfowl. A short, board-walked track leads through the forest and swamp to lookout points.

WINDSURFING AND SURFING

With its windy climate, Wellington is ideal for windsurfing. The best places around Wellington Harbour are Lyall Bay, Days Bay, Eastbourne, Petone foreshore, and Keo Point near Evans Bay. North of Wellington, Plimmerton Beach and Paremata Harbour on the west coast can be good in the right conditions, and Lake Ferry in the Wairarapa is popular. For further information contact Wellington Sailboard Assn., 66 Lyall Bay Parade, Wellington, Phone (04)3877-964.

Wellington's city beaches are only good for surfing in south or southwest swells, and popular places are Lyall Bay and Houghton Bay. On the west coast, any of the beaches north of Paekakariki are surfable. South of here, Blakes Beach at Plimmerton and Titahi Bay are the only good places in west or northwesterly swell conditions. South or southeasterly swells are required for the Wairarapa beaches to give good rides. Favorite places are around Palliser Bay and toward Cape Palliser; White Rock, and Tora on the southeast coast; and at Riversdale and Castlepoint beaches.

Windsurfing and surfing gear can be bought or rented from the following outlets:

Barton Sail Surf'n Ski, 2 The Esplanade, Paremata, phone (04)2399-369.
Recycled Recreation, 29–31 Jackson St., Petone, phone (04)5682-019.
Southcoast Sail Surf'n Ski, 66 Lyall Bay Parade, Lyall Bay, phone (04)3877-964.
Stunned Mullet, 107 Victoria St., Wellington, phone (04)4997-303.
Wild Winds, 282 Jackson St., Petone, phone (04)5687-546.

DIVING

Almost all of Wellington's southern coast, except Lyall Bay, is good for diving, unless there is a strong southerly swell, which tends to make the water cloudy and conditions dangerous. During southerly conditions the inner harbor or the coast around Makara are best. Marine life is particularly varied and prolific around Island Bay, which makes it an interesting place for snorkeling or rock pool exploration. The water is usually crystal clear and very cold. The western coast between Titahi Bay and Paekakariki is also good, as are the waters around Kapiti Island. On the eastern side, the Cape Palliser coast and Mataikona/Castlepoint areas are considered best.

For more information contact any of the following:

Aqua Ventures, Adrian Van Dooren, 36 Havelock St., Vogeltown, phone (04)3893-727.

Island Bay Divers, corner of Reef St. and The Parade, Island Bay, phone (04) 3836-778.

Underwater Sports, 293 Jackson St., Petone, phone (04)5685-028.

Divers World, 57 Rugby St., Wellington, phone (04)3858-533.

BIRDWATCHING

The best place to see bush birds is **Kapiti Island,** off the Horowhenua coast, which is an important bird sanctuary administered by the Department of Conservation. Permits to visit the island are strictly controlled, and can be obtained through the Department of Conservation, Box 5068, Wellington, phone (04) 4725-821. You will need to apply well in advance, as only a limited number of visitors are allowed each day. The Coastlands Information Center, Paraparaumu, can arrange boat rental to Kapiti Island.

For wading birds and waterfowl, the **Waikanae lagoons and river mouth,** just inland from the south end of Waikanae Beach, are good places. Waimeha Lagoon has a walking track around its perimeter, a boardwalk for access to swampland vegetation, and a blind for observing shy birds, such as the relatively uncommon dabchick, which nests only on the North Island. Access is from Waimea Road or Tutere St. off Te Moana Road.

The shallow waters of **Lakes Wairarapa and Onoke** and their adjacent wetlands are havens for water birds, except in May, when the duck season commences. Western Lake Road from Featherston to Palliser Bay allows access at several points. The northern shore of Lake Wairarapa and mouth of the Tauherenikau River are gained from the Wairarapa Lake Domain, signposted from the Featherston–Martinborough highway. Access to the eastern side of Lake Wairarapa is from Parerata Road which turns off the Featherston–Lake Ferry Road, about 7 km south of Kahutara. About 2 km along Parerata Road, a sign on the left marks a track on the stopbank between Mathews Lagoon and Boggy Pond, two wetland lagoons where bird life is abundant; 4 km farther on, by pine windbreak and a woolshed, another sign indicates access to the lakeshore.

Pauatahanui Wildlife Reserve at the eastern end of the extensive Pauatahanui Inlet also has important habitat for wading birds. Entrance to the reserve is beside the community hall at Pauatahanui Village on SH 58 between Paremata and the Hutt Valley. Paths and boardwalks lead to blinds for observing birds.

USEFUL ADDRESSES

Wellington Public Relations Office, Town Hall, Wakefield St., phone (04) 4735-063.

Lower Hutt Public Relations and Information Centre, The Pavilion, 25 Laings Road, Box 30-771, Lower Hutt, phone (04)5697-428.

Kapiti Coast Promotion Council, Paraparaumu, phone (06)2988-195.

Wairarapa Information Centre, 5 Dixon St., Masterton, phone (06)3787-373.

Department of Conservation, Box 5068, Wellington, phone (04)4725-821; Box 191, Masterton, phone (06)3782-061; Box 141, Waikanae, phone (04)2932-191.

3 THE SOUTH ISLAND

16 ✦ NELSON

LANDSCAPE

Nelson Province is one of those places that has something for everyone. Energetic outdoor lovers will find superb hiking, fishing, sailing, kayaking, rafting, cycling, camping, and botanizing. In summer, the less energetic can just relax and enjoy the fruits of the region. (Almost half of New Zealand's apples and pears are grown here, along with berries, hops, tobacco, stone fruits, and citrus.) And the artistic side of life is represented by dozens of pottery studios, each one offering beautiful, individually styled work.

One of the region's most fascinating aspects is its geology. To the east is the Richmond Range, extending north from Lake Rotoiti and separating Nelson from Marlborough. Rocks of the eastern side of the range are mainly schist, but on the western edge is a narrow band of ultramafic rocks, the Nelson Mineral Belt. Such rocks as gabbro, dunite, peridotite, serpentine, and harzburgite are found here. This distinctive outcrop, which weathers to a reddish-brown color and supports only stunted vegetation, is seen at Dun Mountain behind Nelson city. Similar deposits are found in the Cascade and Red Hills of South Westland. Most of the Richmond Range lies within the Mt. Richmond Forest Park, which is well tracked and offers good hiking. Several rivers flowing westward from the range provide access to the interior and are also pleasant places for picnics and short walks.

Northwest Nelson consists mainly of the jumbled granite ridges of the Tasman Mountains and the fascinating marble peaks of the Mt. Arthur Range, which extends from Abel Tasman National Park to Mt. Owen in the south. Most of the surface rocks in Abel Tasman National Park are granite, but they are replaced in the south and west by a much older belt of marble. Striking outcrops of marble and the steep escarpment on the eastern flank of the Takaka Valley are seen from the road crossing the range to Golden Bay. The marble, formed 500 million years ago, has been eroded by water to form a beautiful karst landscape. The huge 176-m-deep Harwoods Hole, the deepest vertical shaft in New Zealand, and the massive Bulmer and Nettlebed cave systems beneath the Mt. Arthur Range, were all carved by subterranean streams. Bulmer and Nettlebed caves are the largest known in the Southern Hemisphere and are still being explored. The smaller Honeycomb Caves system and Oparara Arch to the west, near Karamea, are similar.

Stretching west of the Arthur Range are the Mt. Arthur Tablelands and the Gouland, McKay, and Gunner downs — elevated tablelands that contrast with the deeply incised hillsides flanking them. These are the remains of an old peneplain that existed 60 million years ago. As the land submerged, it was overlain with rich marine sediments that now form limestone and calcareous sandstone, overlain in turn by mud and more sandstone. At one time these rocks and those of Dun Mountain in the Richmond Range to the east were adjacent to Fiordland, but as movement along the Alpine Fault began, 20 million to 25 million years ago, they were displaced northward to their present position. The land emerged from beneath the sea again 10 million to 15 million years ago, and the last stages of erosion began. Glaciers of the last Ice Age left U-shaped valleys, cirques, and basins, now filled by tarns and lakes. This beautiful, fascinating region is currently contained within the Northwest Nelson Forest Park, but it is being considered for national park status.

Southern regions of Nelson are equally attractive, with clear rivers, beech forests, mountains, and the beautiful twin lakes, Rotoroa and Rotoiti, in Nelson Lakes National Park. Hiking trails lead over grassy river flats and through bush, crossing alpine saddles and passing mountain tarns. Good camping sites, huts, and fishing pools abound. The peaks offer fine climbing for the more serious mountaineer, and there is also a small skifield for fit enthusiasts. For those bent more on rest than action, there is superb scenery.

Lake Rotoiti is the source of the Buller River, a tumultuous waterway that sweeps through 75 km of gorges on its way to the Tasman Sea at Westport. The Buller's Maori name is Kawatiri, meaning "swift and deep," a more fitting name perhaps. Only around Murchison, at the junction of the Buller and Matakitaki rivers, is there much flat land. Here the river's flow is quieter, rippling over open gravel flats between broad terraces of pasture. This calmness is deceptive, as Murchison lies in an area of active faults where blocks of the earth's crust are still jockeying for position. Earthquakes have buckled the land here twice this century, creating devastating landslides that blocked rivers and roads. On a cold, foggy June morning in 1929, a quake rocked the tiny town severely, destroying some houses and burying others under tons of rock and mud. A huge landslide blocked the Matakitaki River, creating a lake that later silted up, and at Whites Creek, where the fault had moved, a giant step 4.5 m high appeared across the road. The displaced Matakitaki River later gouged a new channel to form the Matakitaki Falls. Scars from this quake and another in 1968, centered near Inangahua, can still be seen on the sides of the surrounding hills and through the Buller Gorge. Rockfalls also dammed the Matiri Valley in the ranges south of Murchison, enlarging Lake Matiri and forming other smaller lakes. Behind Lake Matiri is a spectacular landscape of high, rolling limestone tablelands whose intriguing names are Hundred-Acre Plateau and Thousand-Acre Plateau.

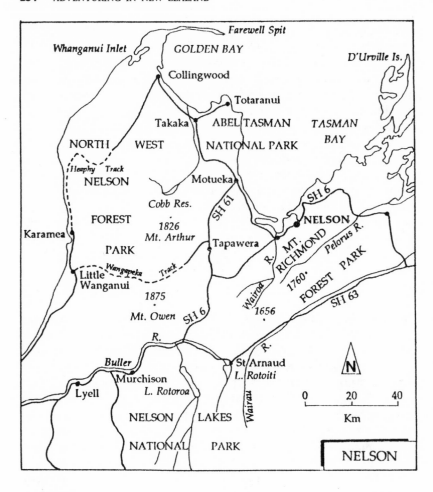

HISTORY

Like many other towns and cities in New Zealand, Nelson was a planned settlement. The Waimea Plains area around Tasman Bay had a mild sunny climate and it was geographically sheltered by mountain ranges to the east and west; many rivers watered the plains, and the harbor would accommodate a sheltered port. Here the New Zealand Company planned to make an agricultural settlement. By 1843 a total of 1,170 50-acre sections and forty-one 150-acre sections had been marked out, and before long the new settlers were farming the land and producing crops. Some of the earliest newcomers were 330 Germans who arrived in 1843 and 1844 on the ships *St. Pauli* and *Skiold;* their descendants still live in the Nelson area. They brought grapevine stock with them that formed the basis for today's wine-making industry.

Known originally was Wakatu, Nelson became a city in 1859, not because it had grown in size but because letters of patent from Queen Victoria made it a Cathedral City. Sited in a commanding position on a hill, with the business center at its base, Nelson's beautiful cathedral still provides a focus for this go-ahead city. Motueka grew to service the orcharding and tobacco- and hop-growing industries, and over the hill, Takaka and Collingwood came into being as settlers attracted by the promise of coal and other minerals moved in. Coal and lime were shipped to Nelson before the discovery of gold created a more lucrative alternative, and as that fizzled the miners were replaced by timber merchants. As the land was cleared, the emphasis switched to dairying, which is still the main industry today.

Most of the land sold to the early Waimea settlers was covered in dense bush, but this was all burned off to prepare the land for farming. In time it became obvious that some areas were no good for farming and these were abandoned. They have since been planted in exotic forests, providing another industry for the region. There was also insufficient land in Waimea for all the new settlers to have farms, and pressure was put on the New Zealand Company to find more land. Meanwhile the company's surveyors were busy exploring the land to the south, and their names—Heaphy, Brunner, Spooner, Barnicoat, Tinline, and Fox—are recorded on many physical features of the region. The Tophouse Pass, leading to the fertile Wairau Plains east of the Richmond Range, was discovered in 1842, but disputes with the Maori over ownership of the Wairau prevented it from being used at the time. The Maori still talked about a large plain to the west, however, and the same year Heaphy, Spooner, and three others went in search of it. They found Lake Rotoiti and followed the Buller River down to the confluence of the Gowan, but found no suitable land.

Heaphy, Brunner, and Fox, with Kehu, a Maori guide, set out again in the summer of 1846 to look for the plains beyond Lake Rotoiti, and this time they explored up the Howard River. After discovering Lake Rotoroa and crossing over to the Tutaki River, they followed the Mangles River down to its junction with the Buller. Also in 1846, Heaphy, Brunner, and Kehu traveled from Golden Bay across to the Whanganui Inlet, then followed the coast down to the mouth of the Arahura River.

In December 1846, Brunner, Kehu, and another Maori set out again on what was to be an epic 18-month journey. Brunner intended following the Buller River to the coast, then traveling along the coast to Milford and back to Arahura before crossing to Canterbury. He badly underestimated the distance and the difficulties. Heavy rain kept them constantly wet, their food supplies ran low, forcing them to live off the land, and flooded rivers halted progress on many days. It was a terrible journey, which Brunner would not have survived if it had not been for faithful Kehu's care. By the time the group returned to Lake Rotoiti in May 1848, sheep were being grazed there.

The early surveyors and explorers knew of the presence of gold in payable quantities in the Wangapeka, Karamea, Takaka, Collingwood, and Buller districts, but the Nelson Provincial Government was not interested in chasing it at the time. They considered the country too difficult, and the distances too great. The small rush to Golden Bay, when gold was discovered in the Aorere Valley in 1856, lasted only three years, during which the population of Collingwood rose to over 2,000. When Gabriel Read found gold in Otago, diggers departed in that direction. Access to the west coast was usually by sea because of the difficult terrain to the south. Consequently the Heaphy and Wangapeka tracks were opened up to provide diggers overland access to the coast. Then, in 1862, gold was discovered in Lyell Creek, a tributary of the Buller, and a new rush started. Access was from the coast by canoe, taking three days up and only six hours down. Some parties attempted to go overland from Nelson, but it was a long, difficult journey. There were tales of fabulous finds, and another rich lode was discovered farther up Lyell Creek by George Zala in 1869. As the town of Lyell grew, with miners returning from the gold fields of the west coast, the need for better access from Nelson became imperative.

A new town, Hampden (now Murchison), had been surveyed in the upper Buller, by Brunner, but it was not until 1876, when a bridle track had been put through over the shorter Hope Saddle route, and a road promised, that it started to grow. Hampden's most colorful resident was an early prospector, George Fairweather Moonlight, who established a bulk store to supply diggers and travelers. He became the first postmaster and unofficial sheriff, a position probably reinforced by his size and strength and American style of dress. His name is recorded at Moonlight Creek, a tributary of the Grey River, where steady gold mining took place for forty years after 1865. Moonlight is credited with the exploration of the Matakitaki Valley and for discovery of the best line for a road down the Grey Valley to the west coast. Once tracks down the Maruia and Grey valleys were opened up, the settlers moved in with their stock.

Gold was not the only mineral to interest prospectors; many searched for copper and chromium. Mining companies set up on Dun Mountain in the Richmond Range as early as 1856 began to extract chromite in the 1860s. They sold it to the American cotton industry for use in a mauve-colored dye. The first railway in the country was built to bring ore down from the mountain to Nelson.

Nelson city's other claim to fame is as the birthplace of Ernest Rutherford, the first man to split the atom. Rutherford excelled at school in Nelson and later went to Canterbury University, where he earned the Master of Arts degree with honors in physics and mathematics. He went on to Cambridge University in 1895, and in 1908 was awarded the Nobel Prize for Chemistry. His theory of the nuclear atom was announced in 1911, but it was not until 1932, with Walton and Crockford, that he was able to split an atom. For this he was made a peer.

◆PLACES TO VISIT AND THINGS TO DO

AROUND NELSON CITY

One of the most popular recreation areas close to the city is the **Maitai Valley,** running up into the hills behind the town; you can walk or drive as far as the **Maitai Dam,** finding many picnic areas and good swimming holes on the way. Walking tracks start from the road end. About 5 km up the valley, opposite the Waahi Taakaro Golf Course, is Sharland Creek Road, with access to **Hira Forest,** where there are more walking tracks. From the city there is a 1-hour round-trip walk to the top of **Botanical Hill,** often called the Centre of New Zealand, as well as longer walks (3 hours or more) in the **Grampians** and **Flaxmore reserves.** Access to these reserves is from Boundary Road or Trafalgar St. South, and a pamphlet explaining them is available. Close to the city center is the pleasant **Queens Gardens,** the **Suter Gallery,** for interesting art exhibitions, and **Cathedral Hill,** where you can easily spend an hour or more.

On the road up the Brook Valley, to the city council's very pleasant motor camp, a sign indicates the start of the **Dun Mountain Walkway,** a 9-km loop taking about 2.5 hours, along a portion of the railway to the chrome ore mines on Dun Mountain. For a longer walk, continue about 1 hour along the line of the railway on a four-wheel-drive road through the bush to Third House, once the site of a maintenance worker's dwelling, at a large, ridgetop clearing. There is now a shelter with fireplaces there.

Tasman Bay is a good spot for windsurfing, and you can rent windsurfers at popular Tahuna Beach. The information center should be able to tell you where you can charter a yacht if you want to sail on Tasman Bay or around the Abel Tasman National Park coastline.

MT. RICHMOND FOREST PARK*
Hacket Creek
Hacket Creek Picnic Area is a popular destination with Nelsonians for day trips into the Richmond Range, and it is also the main starting point for longer trips.

* See also, "Marlborough."

The **Pelorus Track** starts or ends here, and there are short walks to old chromite workings and a waterfall. The picnic area is 27 km from Nelson on the Aniseed Valley Road, which turns off SH 6 just south of Hope.

From the picnic area it's about an hour's walk up Hacket Creek to another picnic area at the confluence of Hacket Creek and Miner River, where three tracks diverge. The main Pelorus Track continues up the true left bank of Hacket Creek to 6-bunk **Hacket Hut** (1.5 to 2 hours) before crossing the ridge and descending to the Pelorus River. The **Whispering Falls Track** lies along the Miner River bed for 10 minutes, then follows terraces before climbing to the left of some limestone bluffs to the base of the falls, which have spectacular travertine formations (30 minutes one way). The track to the **Chromite Workings** follows Hacket Creek for about 120 m, then branches off to the right up Chromite Creek, taking about 30 minutes one way.

Dun Mountain and Rocks Hut
Dun Mountain is reached by first following the Dun Mountain Walkway and then continuing along the track to Third House (see "Around Nelson City"). The round trip walk takes a long day, and a more pleasant alternative might include an overnight stay at the fairly new Rocks Hut en route. From Third House, the well-benched track continues gently upward, still following the railway line, and passing a side track to Wooded Peak, until it leaves the bush for the open scrubby vegetation of the mineral belt. At Windy Point, an obvious corner, the main track turns east to Dun Saddle and the summit of Dun Mountain. The side track to Rocks Hut leaves Windy Corner and descends into a shallow gully before climbing back up to the main ridge near the hut. From Rocks Hut another tracks heads down to Middy Hut on the Pelorus Track.

Wairoa Valley
The Wairoa Valley gives access to huts and tracks in the northern end of the park. To reach it take Lee Valley Road from Brightwater until it joins Wairoa River Road; from here it is 16 km up the Wairoa Valley to a fork in the river. Cross the Right Branch and continue another 5 km up the Left Branch to the road end. The track to **Mid Wairoa Hut** and beyond continues up the true left bank of the Left Branch.

Ben Nevis
At 1619 m, Ben Nevis is a commanding viewpoint. To reach the start of the track, follow Wairoa River Road (see "Wairoa Valley") to the fork of the Left and Right branches. Continue another 2.5 km up the Left Branch and take Boundary Creek Road, which turns sharply right and climbs steeply for 5 km to another carpark. The climb to the open summit through bush and tussock takes 2 to 3 hours, and you will need warm clothes and water.

NELSON LAKES NATIONAL PARK

Maori legend tells how long ago, before the great migration of canoes, a powerful chief named Rakaihaitu came to New Zealand in his canoe Uruao and landed near Nelson. Rakaihaitu decided to look for an overland route through the rugged and unknown interior and set off across the Waimea Plains. Before long he reached the wild Buller River rising from a chain of imposing mountains, and working hard with his *ko*, or digging stick, he dug some huge holes. They soon filled with water and became known as Rotoiti and Rotoroa. Continuing south, Rakaihaitu dug and named more holes, the other great lakes of the South Island, before reaching Foveaux Strait, where he settled.

The high mountains, narrow, steep-walled valleys, and long, deep lakes of the Nelson Lakes region are products of continual uplift and prehistoric glaciation. Huge glaciers once flowed down the Travers and Gowan valleys, scooping out cirques and U-shaped valleys and slicing the ends off ridges. Later, ice retreating left hanging valleys, depressions, and hollows, which filled with water, forming high alpine tarns and Lakes Rotoroa and Rotoiti.

Lake Rotoiti's glacial origins are immediately apparent. On its eastern side, short, truncated spurs drop steeply from the St. Arnaud Range, and to the west the broad bulk of Mt. Robert, at the northern end of the Travers Range, rises steeply from the deep dark waters. The small township of St. Arnaud sits on the moraine left by the retreating glacier, and part way along this, rising from the jumbled rocks, is Black Hill, a roche moutonnée. Other evidence of glaciation is easily seen; Lake Constance and Blue Lake at the head of the west branch of the Sabine River are both dammed by terminal moraines, and the Angelus and Hinapouri tarns on the Travers Range occupy hollows gouged by ice.

Erosion has continued unabated since the glaciers retreated. Forests destroyed by the Ice Age took time to return, leaving mountain slopes unprotected. Also, the fractured nature of the greywacke makes it susceptible to freezing and thawing so that it shatters easily. Huge shingle fans were formed and valleys were filled up as debris was carried down by rivers.

Although the waters were rich with eels, the Maori do not seem to have settled around Lakes Rotoiti and Rotoroa, but they did use them as stopover points between Tasman Bay and Canterbury or the west coast during food gathering and greenstone collecting expeditions. The early European settlers, in their ignorance, contributed to the natural erosion by burning the forests and grazing sheep on the high tussocklands. Early runs often had no boundary fences, and sheep and cattle wandered into the bush and up onto the ridge tops, devouring the succulent herbs and leaving the less palatable tussocks. At one time more than 200 wild cattle roamed the river flats of the Travers Valley. Deer and rabbits followed the sheep and cattle, causing further damage. Repeated burning of some places, such as Mt. Robert, damaged the natural vegetation so much that it may never recover. Few of the early settlers or visitors appreciated the beauty of the lakes, and it was not until the 1930s, when a road reached St. Arnaud, that public interest increased and boaties, trampers, and nature lovers started visiting. In 1956, the area around Lakes Rotoiti and Rotoroa, including the Travers, Sabine and D'Urville valleys, was declared a national park. This was extended in 1983 to include the heads of the Matakitaki and Glenroy valleys.

Apart from a few podocarp trees around the shores of Lake Rotoroa, the forests of the park are almost entirely beech. All four species occur here, with red and silver beech, mixed with some hard beech, occupying lower, warmer areas. Above 1,050 m, silver and mountain beech become dominant. The close canopy of a mature beech forest lets in little light and this, combined with low soil fertility and high altitude, restricts the number of species in the understory. Tree fuchsia, five-finger, horopito, and Hall's totara are common subcanopy species, while the shrub layer includes many small-leaved *Coprosma* and *Cyathodes* species. In damp areas numerous fungi sprout from rotting wood, and the forest floor is thickly carpeted with a rich variety of mosses, ferns, and liverworts. These tend to hide ground orchids, as many, such as the *Pterostylis* species, have small greenish flowers.

One of the beech forest's most notable features is the sooty black substance covering the tree trunks. It is produced by the female sooty beech scale insect, *Ultracoelostoma assimile*, which hides in the bark within a hard waxy cuticle. She drives a feeding tube into the sapwood for sustenance and sends out a long tubular thread. The thread carries the insect's waste products, which form a droplet of sweet liquid, or "honeydew"– an important food for many insects and particularly for birds. Unfortunately, the imported German and common wasps are also attracted to it, resulting in a huge increase in their numbers over the last decade. In places wasps have reached plague proportions and are competing seriously with native birds for food.

Bellbirds, silver-eyes, tui, tomtits, and kaka are found within the beech forests, and above the bushline the kea and the tiny rock wren are at home among the tussocks and scree. The russet-brown kaka rips open rotting wood to get at grubs and beetles, while cousin kea seems to eat anything, particularly trampers' food. The rock wren, while not totally flightless, can only hop and flutter short distances. Paradise shelducks are common throughout the park, usually announcing their presence with loud honking, but the blue duck is seen only occasionally in the heads of valleys. Scaup, or black teal, are seen only around the outlet of Lake Rotoroa.

The valleys of the park are well tracked, offering easy walking for novice trampers, and there are 25 huts and shelters, the largest sleeping 16 and the smallest accommodating only 2. All have bunks and mattresses, but no cooking equipment. A small fee is charged for the use of the huts, and they cannot be booked in advance. During holiday weekends, Easter, and from December to February, they can be full, so that camping becomes not just a pleasant alternative but a necessity. Some of the best extended hikes in the park cross from one valley to another, and these can be as varied and as long as you like. Routes over frequently used passes are marked with cairns and snow poles; others are unmarked; and all can be difficult in winter or adverse weather. Good boots, weatherproof clothing, and a map and compass are necessary for any trip above the bushline, as the weather can be unpredictable.

The park headquarters in St. Arnaud has interpretive displays, maps, handbooks, and pamphlets on walks, and issues up-to-date weather forecasts, hut tickets, and hunting permits. There is also a small visitor center at Lake Rotoroa.

St. Arnaud has hotel and backpackers' accommodation, and there are two campgrounds at Lake Rotoiti. The one at Kerr Bay has toilets and power points only; the other, at West Bay, has showers, toilets, kitchens with cookers, and power points. Lake Rotoroa has a small camping area, with limited facilities, at the north end, and a guest lodge. Camp bookings are through the park visitor centers.

Walks around Lake Rotoiti

There are three short walks close to the park headquarters, all of them taking about 1.5 hours, which provide close looks at glacial formations and their recolonization by kanuka, manuka, and beech forest. Well-formed tracks follow the shoreline on both sides of Lake Rotoiti, and these can be used for short walks or combined to make a full-day round trip. A shorter alternative is to arrange boat transport and walk either of the tracks one way. Small beaches along the eastern side make good picnic spots, and there are many places to cast for trout. During January and February, the scarlet flowers of southern rata make a spectacular sight and liven up the somber green bush.

Mt. Robert on the western side of Lake Rotoiti gives panoramic views and has superb tussock basins and alpine herbs to interest botanists. There are two routes to the top, and these can be combined for a round trip taking about 6 hours. The main track, the well-named Pinchgut, zig-zags up through increasingly stunted beech forest to reach the open tussock basins and the Mt. Robert skifield in about 1.5 to 2 hours. Paddy's Track traverses the open flanks above the lake, climbing steadily to Bushline Hut, with its breaktaking views of St. Arnaud and the northern lake shore. It's a great place to spend the night. From the hut the track continues up the ridge to link with the main track.

A climb to the top of the St. Arnaud Range on the eastern side of Lake Rotoiti takes 5 to 6 hours, but shorter walks can be done on the same track. Views from Parachute Rocks above the bushline are well worth the climb. A short but steep scramble will take you up to the ridgeline, where high tussock basins sprinkled with tarns roll down and away to the Wairau Valley.

Travers Valley

The beautiful Travers Valley is an ideal place for easy tramping. Its tracks will take you through open grassy flats and glades of beech, with many superb camp-sites, before the valley closes in near the confluence of the Arnst River. Travers Saddle at the head of the valley is a popular route to the Sabine Valley. Three streams on the western side of the Travers Valley are tracked, giving access to the basins and peaks of the Travers Range. **Hukere Stream Track** ascends steeply, with the last section through bluffs, to the Angelus Basin and **Angelus Hut** at the edge of a lovely mountain lake. In contrast, the climb up **Hopeless Creek** is on a much easier, well-graded track. Above **Hopeless Creek Hut,** near the bush edge, a steep but well-cairned route leads across Sunset Saddle to the Angelus Basin (7 hours), and there is also access to the easiest routes on Mt. Hopeless. **Cupola Creek,** draining the steep south face of Mt. Hopeless and the east face of Mt. Cupola, is reached by a steep track that climbs beside a gorge so narrow that in one place you can stand astride it.

Walks Around Lake Rotoroa

The dark, somewhat somber waters of Lake Rotoroa have a peaceful, undisturbed quality attractive to fisherfolk. Here, at a lower, warmer altitude are tall podocarps, kowhai, rata, and flax.

    Flowers Bush Walk, a 10- to 15-minute ramble through kahikatea forest at the lake edge is good place to see water birds, and pigeons and tui, which love to feed on the fruits of the kahikatea and miro. The longer **Braeburn Walk** is another place to see birds. The track follows a disused road through superb beech and podocarp forests carpeted with mosses and ferns. It then climbs to a slender waterfall. From a lookout on the **Porika Track,** a four-wheel-drive road used to service the power pylons marching up the ridge, there are extensive views across Lake Rotoroa to the Travers, Ella, and Mahanga ranges at the head. The track around the lake is not particularly pleasant, but the Sabine and D'Urville valleys offer good hiking.

Sabine Valley

Five hours' walking from the head of the lake through beech forest and across river flats brings hikers to the two huts at the **Sabine Forks.** The track up the **East Sabine** continues up the true left bank for an hour or so, passing a very narrow gorge, then crosses and climbs steep slopes to Travers Saddle, taking 7 to 9 hours to reach Travers Hut. The upper valley is untracked.

    At the head of the **West Sabine** are Blue Lake, Lake Constance, the Waiau and Moss passes. Vivid, jewel-like **Blue Lake,** edged with mossy boulders and gnarled bonsai beech trees on one side and golden tussocks on the other, is one of the most beautiful places in the park. Camping is not encouraged here because of the damage it does to the delicate environment and a 16-bunk hut provides warmth and comfort. The frequently used route from Blue Lake across **Moss Pass** to the D'Urville Valley involves a long, steep descent. In winter, ice and avalanches can make the pass dangerous.

A partly cairned route from Blue Lake climbs to Lake Constance, traverses high above the water on the true left (your left as you face downstream), then ascends scree slopes to **Waiau Pass** on the ridge on the far side. The descent to the Waiau Valley is long and steep.

D'Urville Valley

The long, gentle D'Urville Valley offers easy tramping and is a pleasant place to spend a few days. It's an undemanding 4 hours to **Morgans Hut**, through open beech forest and across grassy flats beside the crystal clear river. Side tracks head west to **Tiraumea Saddle** and the Tiraumea and Tutaki valleys, and on to the Mole Tops. **Ella Hut** is another 4 hours upvalley from Morgans Hut, with a short detour about halfway to climb an outcrop of rock for the exciting views down to the river, foaming and crashing between gigantic boulders in a gorged section. The long, steep haul to Moss Pass and the Sabine Valley begins about 30 minutes beyond Ella Hut, and above here the valley becomes steeper and wilder, making for an arduous 3 to 4 hours to the tiny, 2-bunk D'Urville Bivy. The track continues to the bush edge, then peters out among the tussock and boulders of the upper basin, which has passes leading to the Waiau and Matakitaki valleys. Routes over these passes are all long and unmarked.

Matakitaki Valley

Although this is the largest valley in the park, it is probably the least visited. It gives access to the Spenser Range and its beautiful peaks—Gloriana, Faerie Queen, Humboldt, Una, and Enid. Access is from the Tutaki Valley Road, 3 km north of Murchison. From a locked gate at Matakitaki Base Hut there is a 4-hour walk across river flats to dilapidated Downies Hut. The valley narrows above here and the track climbs above a gorge, threading its way around sphagnum bogs and between weather-beaten kaikawaka trees clinging to rock outcrops before descending to the river where it forks. Bob's Hut is about 1.5 hours up the west branch, which gives access to the northern side of Faerie Queen and Gloriana. The east branch also has a hut, about 2 hours up, and from the head there are passes to the D'Urville and a high route to the Waiau Valley.

Skiing

To ski at the small **Mt. Robert Skifield** you need to be both fit and keen, but it does offer a great experience when conditions are right. Getting there involves a 2-hour hike up the steep Pinchgut Track from the end of Mt. Robert Road, lugging your skis on your back. There are 2 lodges for accommodation, 4 "nut-cracker" rope tows, ski rental, and slopes for beginners and the more experienced. Inquiries should be made to **Nelson Ski Club**, Box 344, Nelson. Experienced skiers can tour along the Robert Ridge to the third, fourth, and fifth basins, or continue to Lake Angelus Hut for further adventuring.

Rainbow Skifield, a small commercial enterprise on the east side of the St. Arnaud Range, outside the park boundaries, offers easy skiing and road access.

ABEL TASMAN NATIONAL PARK

By comparison with other national parks, Abel Tasman is small, does not have entirely pristine vegetation, and is somehow—well—different. What it does offer is a superb coastline of bush-fringed, golden-sand beaches and sculptured granite rocks where you can swim, sail, kayak, camp, and hike. For the bush and mountain lover there are beech forests and even an area of subalpine vegetation that is occasionally sprinkled with snow. It's a park where the weather is nearly always congenial, even in winter, and where the only thing that will stop you walking is the tide.

The forests of Abel Tasman National Park suffered badly at the hands of early settlers, who attacked it with saws and fire, and in many places their legacy is gorse- and manuka-covered hillsides. A visitor may wonder why these areas are within a national park, and the reason is that they are being preserved to allow them to return to their former state. The recovery process is slow, and fire is still the greatest threat. After burning, the first plants to colonize were grasses, which was what the settlers wanted as they needed grazing for sheep and cattle. Once the animals were removed, gorse, manuka, and kanuka quickly invaded and formed a dense cover. An introduced species, gorse can rightly be regarded as a horrible, prickly nuisance. Its only redeeming features are that, if left untouched, it provides a nursery for native species and helps fix nitrogen in the soil. The native plants eventually grow over the gorse, and deny it the light it needs to survive. The process is quite rapid in shady gullies and damp sites, but slow where soils are poor and dry.

There are still many large tracts of beautiful forest within the park where good numbers of tui, bellbirds, pigeons, fantails, and white-eyes can be seen. Two birds that don't mind the scrub or grass are the weka and pukeko, both members of the rail family. They are particularly numerous around the campground at Totaranui. Sea birds are plentiful; shags, oystercatchers, herons, and pied stilts feed in the estuaries, while little blue penguins and gannets are often seen on rocky parts of the coast.

One of the most fascinating parts of the park is in the southwest corner known as Canaan, where outcropping marble has been fluted and carved into weird shapes by the action of water. In this karst landscape is Harwoods Hole, a terrifying abyss disappearing into black nothingness. A pebble thrown in takes a long time to hit the bottom.

The park is best known for the easy 3- to 4-day coastal walk between Marahau and Totaranui, and this is widely touted as Nelson's top attraction. Consequently, the **Abel Tasman Track,** as it is known, tends to be crowded with a multinational mix of tourists. If you prefer solitude, you'd do better to avoid it or else walk it in winter. There are many other tracks within the park, all of them offering more challenging hiking than the coastal track. Ten huts are scattered along the coast, and within the park and there are many camping areas. During summer the huts along the coastal track are often overcrowded and it is necessary to carry a tent.

The main campground at Totaranui is reached by road from Takaka. The large grassy area behind a superb beach has toilets, water, fireplaces, cold showers, picnic tables, and a public telephone, but there is no shop, post office, or electricity. Campers need to be self-sufficient. The number of campers is limited, and in summer it is essential to book a space by phoning (03)5288-083.

Further information on the park is available from the Department of Conservation Visitor Centre, Main Road, Motueka, phone (03)5289-117, or in Takaka, P.O. Box 53, phone (03)5258-026. There is also a visitor center at Totaranui. The park map (Infomap 183) and handbook *A Park for All Seasons* give details on tracks and human and natural history.

Short Walks

Around Totaranui. Close to the campground you can take any of several short nature walks for which there are explanatory pamphlets. Other options are to follow the coastal track toward Marahau. One of the prettiest beaches, **Anapai Bay,** is passed on the longer walk north to **Mutton Cove** and **Separation Point.** Another short track, through tall forest that escaped the sawmillers, leads from Pigeon Saddle on the Totaranui–Wainui road to **Lookout Point.**

Around Torrent Bay. Four tracks around Torrent Bay make pleasant side trips from the main coastal track. From the southwest corner, one leads up the Torrent River to **Cleopatra's Pool,** a pleasant swimming hole. Another leads to **Pitt Head,** the site of an old Maori fortification, and to **Te Pukatea Bay,** a beautiful crescent-shaped beach. **Watering Cove,** where D'Urville replenished the *Astrolabe's* water supply, is reached in 45 minutes, crossing a dry ridge where even gorse and manuka struggle to survive.

Canaan Road End. The rough 11-km Canaan Road from near the summit of the Takaka Hill ends at a picnic and camping area, and from here there is a 30- to 40-minute walk to **Harwoods Hole.** Much of the track follows a shallow valley through open beech forest, but the last 10 minutes or so are easy scrambling in a gorge that suddenly ends at the gaping pit surrounded by towering walls. A side track on the right, before Harwoods Hole is reached, leads to a lookout with impressive views from the precipice down Gorge Creek to the Takaka Valley. Here the rocks are jagged, fluted, and jumbled as if churned by a giant hand.

The easiest route to **Moa Park,** the unusual enclave of tussock and subalpine vegetation within the beech forest, is from the end of Canaan Road. Other longer routes start from Pigeon Saddle and Torrent Bay. Moa Park lies in a shallow basin high in the hills and is thought to be a natural phenomenon, not a fire-induced one. One theory for the occurrence of subalpine vegetation at a moderately low altitude is that cold air may be trapped in the basin, creating a microclimate. The walk to Moa Park Hut takes 1.5 to 2 hours, through forests of beech, rata, cedar, and mountain neinei, with views out across the karst landscape and down to the Wainui Valley.

Sea Kayaking

Paddling around the Abel Tasman coastline is becoming a popular alternative to walking the track. Sea kayaks can be rented or you can do guided trips with **Abel Tasman Kayaks,** Marahau, RD 2, Motueka, phone (03)5278-022, or **Ocean River Adventure Co.,** Box 216, Motueka, phone (03)5288-823.

NORTHWEST NELSON FOREST PARK

The complex geology, variety of landforms, and range of altitudes contained within this large park make it a place worth spending more than a casual couple of days. Botanically, it is a fascinating region. During the last Ice Age much of northwest Nelson was a major refuge for plants, and many that survived here were able to recolonize the land after the ice receded. When sea levels were 100 to 150 m lower than they are now, the North and South Islands were joined by a land bridge, and many North Island plants migrated south. Consequently, more than 1,200 native plant species have been recorded here, and of these, 48 are endemic to the region. Others are at their northern or southern limits. The range of forests—from subtropical coastal through to subalpine beech—alpine tussocklands, fellfields (a kind of moor), herb fields, and wetlands, and consequent diversity of ecosystems, supports a good range of bird species and is also important habitat for giant land snails and weta. The fearsome-looking weta, a large flightless insect with long, barbed legs, is considered a relic of Gondwanaland fauna. Introduced rodents have now largely filled the ecological niche in New Zealand forests that wetas once occupied.

A network of tracks and huts gives opportunities for a range of hiking possibilities, from easy short walks around the periphery to demanding overnight or longer excursions into the wild interior. Two of the best known are the Heaphy and Wangapeka tracks. These and many others are a legacy of the search for gold during the short "Nelson Rush." Remains of old workings are still evident in many valleys. Silver was mined in the Wangapeka and Aorere Valley, as well as gold, and in the headwaters of the Little Wanganui and Mokihinui rivers attempts were made to extract copper and molybdenite. Magnetite, chert, and asbestos have been taken from the Cobb region south of Takaka, with the asbestos mine closing only in 1963. The Leslie and Cobb valleys, and many of the tablelands and other tussock-clad areas of high country, were grazed by sheep and cattle around the turn of the century. The cattle were only removed from the Cobb Valley when the Cobb Dam was built, in the early 1950s.

For speleologists, amateur or serious, there is a fascinating underworld to explore. The vast Nettlebed and Bulmer cave systems are still being explored, but others, such as the Honeycomb Caves in the Oparara Valley on the west coast, have guided tours through them. In the same area are the Box Canyon and Crazy Paving caves, and nearer Karamea, the smaller Fenian and Cavern Creek systems, which can be explored by anyone keen enough to crawl in with a good flashlight.

In the Cobb area, 49,000 ha have been set aside for recreational hunting. Pigs, goats, and fallow and red deer are present; permits are obtained from the Department of Conservation.

Pleasant camping areas with limited facilities are found at the Nelson end of the Wangapeka Track, at both ends of the Heaphy Track (Kohaihai and Brown River), and at the head of the Cobb Reservoir. Short walks can be done from all of these.

The park is subject to high rain fall, varying from 5,000 mm annually in the west to 1,600 mm in the east, depending on topography. Tracks and bridges are occasionally washed out, and even when not flooded, all rivers should be treated with respect. In spite of all the rain, some long, high ridges are particularly waterless, and water needs to be carried. Temperatures in coastal areas are generally mild, but snow can fall on high areas at any time of the year. In winter the higher ridges are often snow-covered for weeks at a time.

Just as there are many tracks, there are also many access points, and it is impossible to describe them all here. Some of the more popular areas are mentioned below, but for anyone wishing to visit the area the best reference sources are *The Northwest Nelson Tramping Guide* by Derek Shaw and *Tramping in South Island Forest Parks* by Joanna Wright. The park map has detailed information printed on the back and pamphlets and maps on the Wangapeka and Heaphy tracks and Mt. Arthur Tablelands are available. Other maps covering the park are NZMS 260 series—L25 Kahurangi, M25 Collingwood, L26 Heaphy, M26 Cobb, N26 Takaka, L27 Karamea, M27 Mt. Arthur, and M28 Wangapeka.

Cobb Valley and Dam

This beautiful area offers many easy hikes and great botanizing. The dam lies 28 km up a narrow, winding access road that turns off SH 60 at Upper Takaka, and goes another 8 km around the reservoir to the Cobb Valley. Tracks lead up the gentle Cobb Valley through tussock and bush to the comfortable 20-bunk **Fenella Hut** on Burgoo Saddle. You'll pass several pleasant campsites and the rustic Chaffey and Cobb huts on the way. Fenella Hut is one of the nicest in the park, and it makes an ideal base for day walks to nearby **Lake Cobb, Mt. Gibbs,** and **Waingaro Peak.** Close to the hut is a very deep tarn which is great for swimming in on hot days. Allow 5 to 6 hours from the road end to Fenella Hut.

From the Cobb Dam there is an easy, well-graded track to the **Sylvester Lakes,** which fill glacial cirques in the tussocklands 500 m above the reservoir. Alpine flowers are particularly good here in summer. The short **Myttons Nature Walk** starts from a carpark near the head of the reservoir. Ten minutes up, by Myttons Hut, the Balloon Track branches left and climbs to **Lake Peel** in 2 to 3 hours, then continues to Balloon Hut and Salisbury Lodge on the Mt. Arthur Tablelands. The **Asbestos Track,** the old road to the mine in the Upper Takaka Valley, commences about 3 km above the powerhouse. The first section, to a small waterfall, is an easy 45-minute nature walk, and from here it is a further 30 to 45 minutes to the abandoned mine. Another 30 minutes' climb will bring you to Asbestos Cottage, where Anne and Henry Chaffey lived for 40 years. Built around 1900, the cottage is still usable and has flowers around it planted by Anne. The **Cobb Ridge Track** from the Cobb Lookout leads along the relatively open ridge toward **Mt. Peel,** with good views of the surrounding countryside. It connects with the Balloon Track and Bullock Track from the Takaka River, giving opportunities for a couple of longer round trips.

Mt. Arthur and the Tablelands

The main access point to this area is the **Flora Carpark** at the top of the Graham Valley Road, signposted off SH 61 in the Motueka Valley. From the carpark, at 945 m, there is a network of tracks that can be used for day walks or longer round trips. The **Flora Track** leads to **Salisbury Lodge** on the Tablelands in about 3 hours, passing Flora Hut after 30 minutes and some interesting rock shelters that can be slept in. From Salisbury Lodge there are tracks down to the Cobb Reservoir and Takaka Valley and on to the wilder country of the Leslie and Karamea valleys. Good tracks and huts in the Leslie and Upper Karamea valleys link with the Wangapeka Track.

Ten minutes down the Flora Track the **Mt. Arthur Track** branches left and climbs gently along the ridge for 1 hour through groves of mountain neinei, rough-leaved tree daisy (*Olearia lacunosa*), mountain and silver beech to **Mt. Arthur Hut.** The track continues above the hut, leaving the bush and following the exposed ridge to the summit of **Mt. Arthur** (1,795 m), with fine views out to Tasman Bay and across the Waimea Plains to the Richmond Range. This can be a particularly cold and windy place, even on the best of days in summer. Carry water, as it all disappears underground in this marble country. A route over **Gordon's Pyramid** to Salisbury Lodge is signposted about 40 minutes above the hut; it drops down to cross Horseshoe Basin, with its many sinkholes. Alpine flowers are usually good here as the sinkholes offer shelter and moisture. On the higher, more exposed marble screes are edelweiss, willowherbs, and clumps of vegetable sheep. Both Salisbury Lodge and Mt. Arthur Hut have gas cookers to save the scarce firewood.

Other tracks that can be used to make round trips are those connecting Flora Hut with Mr. Arthur Hut, and Gordon's Pyramid with the Flora Track. The 2-hour climb to **Mt. Lodestone** along the ridge north of Flora Carpark is steep and strenuous but offers rewarding views from the top.

Wangapeka Track

The 50 to 60 km Wangapeka track provides an east-west crossing of the park via the Wangapeka, Upper Karamea, Taipo, and Little Wanganui valleys. Of the 5 main huts on the track, 3 have gas burners for cooking. They are fairly evenly spaced, and the track is usually walked in 3 to 4 days, although extra time allows for side trips or a more leisurely pace. The two saddles crossed by the track are both over 1,000 m, making the Wangapeka a more strenuous hike than the well-known Heaphy Track. A long round trip can be made by combining the two tracks.

The western end of the track starts 8 km up the Little Wanganui River from SH 67. Transport from Karamea can be called for from a telephone 3 km down the road. Access to the Nelson end is from Tapawera on SH 61. A carpark, Department of Conservation Base Hut, telephone, and intentions book are located about a kilometer before the start of the track at the junction of the Wangapeka and Rolling rivers, where there is also a 4-bunk hut and camping area.

The road continues another 4 km up the Rolling River to **Courthouse Flat,** passing two more pleasant camping areas. From Courthouse Flat, once the site of a small town, there are short, interesting walks to old mining sites and the resurgence of Blue Creek from subterranean depths. The Blue Creek walk leads to a restored stamper and has good interpretive signs explaining the many aspects of gold mining. Long, strenuous day hikes can also be made to **Billies Knob** and **Cullifords Hill,** or you can stay overnight at **Granity Pass Hut** and climb **Mt. Owen.** Under Mt. Owen is the Bulmer cave system, the second deepest in the Southern Hemisphere, with 749 m of vertical height. It is also the longest cave system in New Zealand, with 34 km of passages.

Heaphy Track

This popular 77-km track has a wonderful mix of beech forest, open tussock-lands, coastal forest, rivers, and rugged coastline. There are several huts and shelters, which allow it to be walked in 4 to 6 days. Most of the huts have gas cookers and some sleep up to 40 people. They can become crowded during peak times in summer, however, in which case a tent may be preferable. There are telephones at both ends of the track to call local transport operators or for assistance in emergencies. A few places on the coastal section were dangerous in the past during high tides and rough seas, but tracks have now been formed over the bluffs to avoid these. It is, however, a particularly dangerous coast, and you are strongly advised against swimming anywhere in the sea.

Access to the eastern end of the track is at Brown River, 35 km from Collingwood on the Bainham Road up the Aorere Valley. There is a 15-minute nature walk at Brown River, through lush forest with many tall kahikatea, or a longer hike (4 to 5 hours round trip) to **Shakespeare Flat,** where there is some fine podocarp forest and good fishing. The track turns off the Heaphy Track about 4 km from Brown River and reaches the river flat within an hour.

The western end finishes at Kohaihai, 15 km north of Karamea, at a very pleasant Department of Conservation camping area. From the camping area you can zig-zag up the hill behind the shelter to a lookout point, or do an easy stroll around the **Nikau Walk** just across the bridge. The first hour along the main track past **Scotts Beach** makes a pleasant walk, and this can be varied by taking **Fishermans Track,** which drops steeply from the saddle to the southern end of the beach.

Tracks near Karamea

Upper Oparara Valley. The amazing **Oparara Arch** and **Honeycomb Caves** are found in the upper reaches of the Oparara Valley, and nearby are the smaller **Moria Gate** and the **Crazy Paving** and **Box Canyon** caves. Because the Honeycomb Caves are of exceptional scientific value, entry is only by guided tour. Bookings can be made at the Karamea Garage. Skeletons of over 50 different bird species, many of them now extinct, and live frogs, lizards, weta, glowworms, and the rare cave spider *Spelungula cavernicola* are found here.

Access to the area is by a narrow logging road, signposted about 12 km north of Karamea, and it is 16 km to a carpark beside the Oparara River. The Oparara Arch, reached in about 20 minutes by a broad track, is 219 m long, 43 m high and 79 m wide, forming a huge tunnel. Light filters through the shrubs and trees that hang over the entrance, bringing the far end into sharp relief. The picturesque Moria Gate is about 30 minutes downstream from the carpark. The Crazy Paving and Box Canyon caves are a short distance from the Honeycomb Caves carpark a little further down the road. Take a good flashlight and have fun exploring the Box Canyon. It has two smaller entrances besides the one you enter by. A sign on the road also points the way to **Mirror Tarn,** a quiet pool enclosed by tall forest.

Fenian Track gives access to the lower Oparara Valley and Fenian Basin, where there are several small caves worth exploring. Take Oparara Road from Karamea and turn off by the limeworks, continuing on to a parking area by the quarry. About 15 minutes from the carpark a steep side track leads up to the **Top Caves.** It's a further 30 to 40 minutes along the main track to the **Cavern Creek Loop Track,** which passes through **Tunnel Cave** and several smaller caves before returning to the main track. It's a rough, muddy circuit, taking about 45 minutes, and you'll need a flashlight. The main track continues another hour to **Adams Flat,** where there are relics from the gold mining days.

AROUND GOLDEN BAY

It would be easy to spend several days exploring this remote corner of the South Island, even without visiting Abel Tasman National Park, Cobb Valley, or Heaphy Track. Separated from the rest of Nelson by the winding Takaka Hill, it is so peaceful that time seems unimportant. Diversions on the drive over the hill between Motueka and Takaka are the Ngarua Caves, Caanan Road, and Rat Trap Hotel. There are pleasant commercial motor camps around the bay, and if you want real isolation you can drive through to the tranquil **Whanganui Inlet,** with its tiny crayfishing and farming community, and on down the west coast past wild beaches to the Anatori River. If you don't have your own transport, the **Scenic Mail Run** from Collingwood can take you there. There are several pottery outlets between Takaka and Collingwood, all worth a look, goldfields and caves to explore, superb bird life, walks, beautiful beaches, and some unparalleled scenery.

Puponga Farm Park

This combination working farm and recreation reserve at the base of Farewell Spit is open to the public and has walks of geological, botanical, and historical interest. **Cape Farewell** is a magnificent viewpoint, or you can walk down to wild and beautiful **Wharariki Beach,** where the tall stacks of the Archway Islands stand offshore like ships at anchor. There are splendid sand hills here, and at low tide sea caves are revealed. Ask about other coastal walks at the Department of Conservation in Takaka.

Wharariki Beach and the Archway Islands. *Photo by Bruce Jeffries.*

Farewell Spit

Farewell Spit is a nature reserve for the preservation of birds; over ninety different species have been recorded, from kea through spoonbills to sparrows, but the most important are the waders. They come in their thousands each spring, from Northern Hemisphere breeding grounds, to feed in the vast intertidal zone of Golden Bay. Each day as the tide falls they search the sand plain for sandhoppers, mollusks, and small crustaceans; then, as the water returns, they retreat to the spit's low, windswept dunes and scrub to roost. As the southern summer dwindles, the birds prepare to migrate, gathering in huge, excited clouds before their mass departure northwards. To protect the birds, only walking access is permitted, through Puponga Farm Park, and is restricted to a point 2.5 km along the inner beach and 4 km along the ocean beach from the base. The only way to see the spit otherwise is to go with **Collingwood Safaris.** Departure times for the 5-hour trips vary with the tides; bookings can be made through information centers. An excellent pamphlet explaining how the spit is formed, its vegetation, and other aspects is available from the Department of Conservation.

Aorere Goldfields and Caves

These first goldfields of New Zealand were also the first in which sluicing was used and are interesting in that both alluvial and quartz gold occurred close together. Silver and other minerals were also mined here. Access is up the Aorere Valley from Collingwood, turning left at the old Rockville Store, and continuing past the Te Anaroa Caves and Devils Boots on a narrow road through farmland to a carpark. A loop track, taking about 3 hours, passes limestone caves used by the miners and then follows a water race to Druggans Dam before returning past the Slate River Sluicing Co. claim. Take water, as this can be a hot walk, and a flashlight and old clothes for the caves. To get the most out of the walk, take the Department of Conservation pamphlet with you also.

Pupu Springs and Walk

Close to Takaka are the **Pupu Springs**, the largest freshwater springs in New Zealand, with a flow varying between 7.7 and 21 cu m per second. The crystal clear water wells up from the ground in several places that are connected by pleasant short walking tracks through tall pocodarp and beech forest and regenerating manuka, where gold sluicing was once carried out. The springs are fed mainly from the Takaka River, which disappears near Upper Takaka during summer when most of its water is drawn off through sinkholes beneath the gravel bed.

Nearby, at the end of the Pupu Valley Road, is the delightful **Pupu Walk** through an interesting forest of beech and podocarp species mixed with silver pine, mountain cedar, and mountain toatoa. The track follows an old water race built originally for gold sluicing. In places it clings to sheer slopes and is quite an engineering masterpiece. Later, in 1929, a small hydroelectric station was built to take the water.

Anatoki Valley

There are some superb swimming holes in the Anatoki River, and about 5 km up valley from Takaka is Bencarri Farm Park, where you can feed tame eels. They also have llamas and alpacas, and places to picnic and barbecue.

AROUND MURCHISON

The Murchison area tends to be ignored by most travelers on their way from Nelson to the west coast, but it is worth more than a casual glance. The town, although small, is well serviced by main transport lines and has a motor camp, hotel, motel, and cabin accommodations, and banking and shopping facilities. From here the scenic Matakitaki, Maruia, and Tutaki rivers can be explored by road, or you can try gold panning, horse trekking, and white-water rafting. With a dozen rivers within an hour's drive, it's the perfect place to base yourself for trout fishing.

There are tramping tracks at Lake Matiri, in the local ranges, and at nearby Nelson Lakes National Park, and there are easier walkways close to the town. The **Skyline Walk** (1.5 to 2 hours round trip), from the Matakitaki Bridge Scenic Reserve to the skyline ridge above Murchison, gives good views of the town, valley, and surrounding ranges. It starts 1 km west of Murchison at the junction of SH 6 and West Matakitaki Road. **Six Mile Walk** in the Matakitaki Valley is located 10 km south of Murchison on the Maruia Saddle Road. The easy track, taking about 2 hours, starts at the restored Six Mile hydro station and follows a water race built by gold miners through beech and podocarp forest. There is plenty of historic interest here combined with pleasant scenery. **Lyell Walkway** in the upper Buller Gorge visits the remains of historic Lyell township and its gold workings, now being overtaken by bush. The walk starts from the pleasant picnic and camping area beside SH 6.

The local Department of Conservation office (phone (03)5239-106) and Murchison Information and Adventure Centre can give plenty of helpful advice and have pamphlets on walkways.

Transport to Tracks

There are good transport services for trampers from Nelson and Motueka to the eastern ends of the Abel Tasman, Heaphy, and Wangapeka tracks, and to Flora Carpark and the Cobb Valley for walks in the Mt. Arthur area. Bookings can be made at the Nelson Tickets and Information Centre in Trafalgar St. and the Nelson and Motueka information centres. Karamea Motors will pick up from the western ends of the Heaphy and Wangapeka tracks. Phones are located near the trail ends; you can call them at (03)7826-757. Collingwood Bus Services provide transport from Collingwood to the Heaphy Track. Nelson Aero Club have a Nelson–Karamea service, and Heaphy Track Aerotaxi fly between Collingwood and Karamea.

For Nelson Lakes National Park there are daily passenger and freight services from Nelson to St. Arnaud, with Nelson Lakes Transport (phone (03)5211-858), and with Wadsworth Motors, Tapawera, (phone (03)5224-248. Delta Landlines, (phone (03)5781-408), run a bus service between Picton and Greymouth via St. Arnaud.

White-Water Rafting

Nelson's many rivers offer good rafting, from gentle to adrenalin-pumping grade 5 stuff, and options from half-day trips to overnight expeditions with helicopter fly-ins. The most popular for short trips are the Gowan and Buller rivers, with grades to suit most levels of experience. The Karamea is a grade 5 river reached by helicopter, while the Motueka offers a very gentle experience. The following are local operators:

Rapid River Rafting Co., Geoff and Birgit Rowland, Box 83, Brightwater, Nelson, phone (03)5423-110.

Ocean River Adventures, Box 216, Motueka, phone (03)5288-823.

Go West Rafting, Box 99, Murchison, phone (03)5239-315

Trout Fishing

The rivers and lakes of Nelson Lakes National Park are all excellent for fishing, as are the Motueka, Buller, Matakitaki, and other rivers around Murchison. The Wangapeka and Aorere rivers are also worth trying. Most rivers are easily accessible from roads. For help with the best places to go on the Motueka River and elsewhere in Nelson and Westland, contact **Motueka River Guides**, Graeme Marshall Ngatimoti, RD 1, Motueka, phone (03)5268-800. For fishing in the Murchison area, contact **Peter Carty**, phone (03)5239-525, or Moonlight Lodge, Box 12, Murchison, phone (03)5239-323.

USEFUL ADDRESSES

Nelson Information Centre, corner of Trafalgar and Halifax sts., Nelson, phone (03)5482-304.

Nelson Tickets and Information Centre, 143 Trafalgar St., Nelson, phone (03)5484-331.

Golden Bay Information Centre, Willow St., Takaka, phone (03)5259-136.

Department of Conservation Visitor and Information Centre, Box 97, Motueka, phone (03)5289-117.

Department of Conservation, Nelson Conservancy Office, Private Bag, Nelson, phone (03)5469-335.

Nelson Lakes National Park, c/o Post Office, St. Arnaud, phone (03)5211-806.

Abel Tasman National Park, Box 53, Takaka, phone (03)5258-026.

17 ✦ MARLBOROUGH

LANDSCAPE AND CLIMATE

The ferry trip across Cook Strait from Wellington to Picton is many visitors' introduction to the Marlborough Sounds. From Wellington's coast, the peaks of the Inland Kaikoura mountains and lower, more rounded hills of the Marlborough Sounds stand out clearly across the 23-km-wide strip of water. This narrowness causes tidal currents to sweep through the strait at high speeds and also funnels the prevailing westerly winds into a screaming blast that whips foam from the crests of waves, flinging it skyward. Fortunately for travelers, northwest winds don't create too much wave swell, so the trip across the strait in

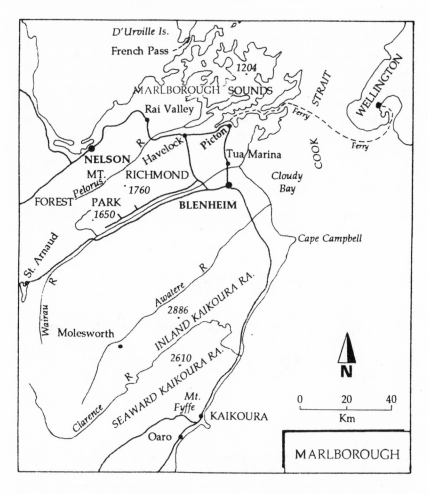

these conditions is usually reasonably smooth. The same cannot be said of a crossing when south or southeasterly winds blow. Originating from depressions far to the south, they create huge swells that travel unrestricted from the Antarctic oceans, causing the ferries to wallow in the troughs and lurch over the crests. Then, unless you are a good sailor, you will probably need seasickness pills.

Once out of Wellington Harbour's narrow entrance and past the treacherous rocks of Barrett's Reef, the ferry turns west and follows the coast. Suburban houses finally give way to steep, brown hills rising abruptly from narrow shingle beaches and rocky headlands before the ferry turns toward the South Island's wild barrier of hills. Heading straight for the rocks it suddenly slips through an impossibly narrow gap and into the tranquil waters of Tory Channel. The ferry then glides smoothly, and for a while it seems as though you can almost touch the hillsides. Before long the channel opens into the broader water of Queen Charlotte Sound, where scrub and bush tumble down to the edge of the clear waters. Small clusters of holiday houses nestle in secluded bays beneath steep hills that rise ever higher as the ferry cruises serenely to Picton at the head of the sound.

The Marlborough Sounds are a continuation of the Richmond Range dividing Marlborough from Nelson, but here the hills are slowly sinking beneath the sea. Separated from Queen Charlotte Sound by a steep-sided neck of land only a few kilometers wide, Keneperu Sound is a large, almost bewilderingly landlocked waterway. Its sheltered and beautiful labyrinth of coves and bays, surrounded by wooded hills that ring with the sounds of bell birds and tui, seems isolated and timeless even though it can be reached by road from Picton. More open to the sea, Pelorus Sound branches into the delightful Tennyson Inlet, which is penetrated in only two places by a narrow twisting road from Rai Valley. Much of this vast maze of drowned valleys, separated by crooked fingerlike ridges, is now part of a maritime park administered by the Department of Conservation.

Blenheim, Marlborough's major town, is set on the flat plains of the Wairau Valley. Here the road divides, east to Christchurch via the Kaikoura Coast, west to Nelson, and south along the Wairau Valley to Lakes Rotoiti and Rotoroa. A cause of much bitterness and disharmony between the Maori and early settlers, the Wairau flows straight along the Alpine Fault east of the Richmond Range to disgorge its contents into Cloudy Bay. The high, steep Richmond Range prevents rain from the west reaching much of Marlborough, and the resulting dry, sunny climate makes the flat plains of the Wairau ideal for growing grapes. Some of the country's best wines are produced here. Much of the Richmond Range is included within the Mt. Richmond Forest Park.

East of Blenheim the countryside changes dramatically to dry, rolling hills rising higher and higher in golden, grassy steps toward the Kaikoura Ranges. The Awatere River begins its journey here, threading its way between dry hills pocketed with oddments of scrub only where trickles of water flow. These are the hills of Molesworth Station, one of the largest and oldest sheep runs in the country.

The vista changes again as the coast is reached, and the road snakes beside the sea at the very foot of high abrupt hills. Only where rivers tumble down from the mountains is there much flat land. It's a dramatic coast of shingle beaches and black rocks fringed with long strands of bull kelp that whip and sway with the ebb and flow of waves. On calm days the sea can be oily smooth; at other times it rages against the rocks, sucking at the pebbly beaches and flinging sheets of spray across the road. At Kaikoura the hills draw back and the coastal plain widens, sloping gently to the steep face of Mt. Fyffe, an outlier of the Seaward

Kaikoura Range. The small protuberance of the Kaikoura Peninsula interrupts the coastline only briefly and forms a sheltering harbor for the town's fishing boats and other craft. To the Maori this was known as Te Taumanu o te waka a Maui–the canoe thwart against which Maui planted his foot while fishing up the North Island. South of Kaikoura, the highway once again hugs the very edge of the land until it turns inland at Oaro.

Behind Kaikoura township and the narrow coastal plain, the eroded Seaward Kaikoura Range rises dramatically from bush-clad lower slopes to a barrier of jagged peaks over 2,500 m high. Hidden from view by the seaward mountains are the higher peaks of the Inland Kaikoura Range–Tapuaenuku (2,886 m) flanked by the Mt. Alarm (2,865 m). Between the two ranges, the Clarence River slices a deep trough across the shingled slopes, following a fault line before cutting its way out to the sea north of Kaikoura.

HISTORY

Abel Tasman sighted the Marlborough Sounds when he anchored his ships in the lee of D'Urville Island and waited out a three-day northwest tempest, but as soon as the weather improved he sailed on without setting foot on the land. It was Captain Cook who discovered the delights of the Marlborough Sounds when he made use of Ship Cove in 1770 to clean his ship's hull and replenish his stores. From a hill on Arapawa Island he sighted the Pacific Ocean through Cook Strait, destroying forever the idea that New Zealand was perhaps part of a great southern continent. Although Cook made four subsequent visits to Ship Cove between 1773 and 1777, he did not explore much of the Sounds. The next recorded visitor, in 1820, was the Russian, Thaddeus von Bellingshausen, who followed Cook's path to his old haunt in Queen Charlotte Sound but added little to existing charts. Seven years later Dumont D'Urville discovered the channel between D'Urville Island and the mainland and made several scary attempts before he was able to sail the *Astrolabe* successfully through. As it was, he was lucky to escape with only the loss of the *Astrolabe's* false keel. Thereafter, the treacherous gap of water was known as French Pass.

From D'Urville's time onward, increasing numbers of whalers came to the Sounds and Cloudy Bay to chase sperm whales in the open sea. One young whaler, Jacky Guard, found himself caught in a storm. Despite all efforts, his ship, the *Waterloo*, was driven closer and closer to the rocks, but just as all seemed lost, it was swept through a narrow passage into a sheltered bay. The party explored their surroundings, and from a low ridge overlooking Cook Strait they saw two huge whales close to shore. Guard surmised, correctly, that the whales passed here regularly, so he lost no time heading to Port Jackson for whaling gear and stores. Within a short time, shore whaling became established and the idyllic Te Awa-iti he had discovered became a rough, evil-smelling settlement nicknamed "Tar White."

The right, or black, whales used Cook Strait regularly on migration and were known to visit the sheltered Sounds and Cloudy Bay to calve. As news of this spread, more whalers, many of them from America, came to Cloudy Bay and it eventually became the greatest whaling port in the world. Unfortunately the slaughter of the right whales was so intense that they were almost exterminated. By the time the first colonists came and British sovereignty was proclaimed, the whaling trade was already declining.

The Sounds, Cloudy Bay, and Kaikoura Coast were well inhabited by Maori when Cook visited. The Kaikoura Coast was particularly attractive, with its rich fishing grounds, teeming bird life both in the bush and at sea; its mild climate, which enabled kumara to be cultivated; and a wealth of timber for houses and pa stockades. Early settlers in the Sounds often found pits and signs of cultivation while clearing the bush, even when it grew right to the water's edge. Legend tells of an early people who were driven out by Te Rapuwai, the first Polynesian Maori, whose ancestors reputedly came from the Tainui canoe. Te Rapuwai were supposed to have been giants, and skeletons up to 2.4 m long have been found, giving credence to the story. The Kaikoura Coast is thought to have been settled by descendants of Chief Waitaha from the Arawa canoe. They and Te Rapuwai were later driven south, as was each successive invading group by another tribe, until the Kai Tahu were able to enjoy about two centuries of peaceful occupation. An influenza epidemic, introduced by whalers, decreased the numbers of Maori living around the Wairau and Kaikoura Coast, allowing them to fall prey to Te Rauparaha. By the time Te Rauparaha had been vanquished, the three or four thousand Maori who had lived at Kaikoura in 1827 had been reduced to seventy-eight.

Te Rauparaha was originally from near Kawhia in the Waikato, but his small tribe was overshadowed by the other bigger Waikato Tribes. He persuaded his people to migrate southward, and after many fights they eventually set up a stronghold on the fertile and almost impregnable Kapiti Island. About 1817, after raiding and defeating tribes of the southern end of the North Island, Te Rauparaha set his sights on the South Island and, with allies from several tribes, he set out across Cook Strait. Armed with guns, his forces moved through the Sounds before proceeding to the Wairau and then down the east coast toward Kaikoura, capturing villages as they went. By 1829 their canoes were just off Kaikoura. The people of Kaikoura Pa were expecting a contingent of relatives from the south, and seeing the canoes, they rushed down to welcome their friends. Taking advantage of that mistake, Te Rauparaha assailed the pa, slaughtering many inhabitants.

Before returning to Kapiti, the invaders made punishing attacks on other pa in the area, forcing survivors to flee. Contingents of Te Rauparaha's kinsmen were left in possession at Wairau and Tasman Bay, and he returned occasionally to visit them, particularly to the Wairau during the season for taking ducks and eels for winter supplies. During one of these visits Te Rauparaha and his men were surprised and overcome by Tuhawaiki, or Bloody Jack, as he was known, a Kai Tahu chief from the Stewart Island region. Te Rauparaha escaped and fled back to Kapiti, never to return, but he still retained ownership of the land around Nelson and Marlborough.

In 1839 Colonel William Wakefield of the New Zealand Company arrived at Ship Cove aboard the *Tory* with a few settlers, and more were scheduled to arrive soon after. It was obvious that there was not enough flat land there to build a settlement, so after a few days the ship was piloted to Te Awaiti in Tory Channel. Ignorant that Cook had already discovered this channel in 1774, the captain of the *Tory* named it after his ship.

Wakefield later made various underhanded land deals with the Maori that ultimately led to disputes and bloodshed. The most famous of these was the Wairau Massacre in 1843; twenty-two Europeans were killed at Tua Marina near Blenheim by a party of Maori led by Te Rauparaha and Te Rangihaeata. The events leading up to the fight were fraught with treachery on both sides, but it was mainly the British who were found to be at fault. The Pakeha settlers demanded justice for the killings, and in return the Maori wanted revenge for their dead—all in all, a nasty situation. The Nelson settlers still wanted land, particularly the Wairau. A later court hearing, in 1845, over ownership of the Wairau, still found in favor of the Maori, and this embittered the Europeans even more. Eventually all Ngati Toa lands as far south as Kaiapoi were bought by Governor Grey for £3,000.

Impatient with the lack of progress over land acquisition, squatters and their sheep had already moved into the upper Wairau Valley from Nelson via the Tophouse Pass. Other high areas of Marlborough were also good for grazing, in spite of the spiny spaniard and tough, spiky matagouri bushes that lamed the sheep and entangled their wool.

Land along the Kaikoura Coast remained with the Kai Tahu and the few survivors of Te Rauparaha's raids, including slaves freed from Kapiti in 1839, who retained unity under Chief Kaikoura Whakatau. Shore whaling was established at Kaikoura by 1842, and within five years the whale numbers had dropped. Seeing his business decline, the owner of the whaling station, Robert Fyffe, introduced sheep to the district and in 1849 applied for a sheep run. Whaling continued until 1921, but with small returns, and the strongly built whale boats were often used for the transport of wool and stores between coastal ships and the growing number of sheep runs. Most of the land was virtually taken illegally from the Maori. The settlers regarded the Maoris' claims as absurd as they seemed to live an almost nomadic life and cultivated only small plots of kumara near their tiny settlements. Dispossession began with the signing of the Wairau Purchase in 1847 and continued in 1859 when more than a million hectares of land from Cape Campbell to the Hurunui River were bought for the paltry sum of £300.

Today the whales are once again earning money for Kaikoura but this time they are not being killed. Whale watching has become big business, and instead of the whalers' harpoons, tourists' cameras are taking the shots. The Kaikoura Coast was once renowned only for its crayfish (kai means "food"; koura means "crayfish"). Now it is a place visitors flock to not only see whales but also seals and sea birds.

◆PLACES TO VISIT AND THINGS TO DO

MARLBOROUGH SOUNDS MARITIME PARK

Marlborough Sounds is composed mostly of sedimentary greywackes and schists, but on the western edge, at D'Urville Island, are two anomalies. One is the appearance of the mineral belt that runs through the western side of the Richmond Range, occurring here as distinct outcrops. The other is the volcanic origin of the dark sea cliffs. Owing to their turbulent position astride two tectonic plates, the rocks of the Sounds, which are on the western side of the Alpine Fault, are exact copies of Otago rocks on the eastern side of the fault. Horizontal movement along this fault has been about 450 km and this, combined with downfaulting, has led to the drowning of valleys, leaving only the tops of ancient mountain ridges and peaks above the sea. In comparison, most of New Zealand is rising, and this is most evident around the Wellington coastline, only a short distance away across Cook Strait.

Tidal flows within the Sounds are the strongest and most varied of any in New Zealand owing to ocean currents flowing up both coasts of the South Island, the topography of Cook Strait, and strong winds. Tides vary throughout the Sounds, and a high tide on the western side can coincide with a low tide on the eastern side, causing a downhill flow of 6 knots on the sea surface. Tide levels also vary considerably, with a 3-m difference between high and low tide in the western reaches of Pelorus Sound and only a 1.5-m difference in Queen Charlotte Sound.

Many islands guard the entrance to the Sounds, the largest being D'Urville on the western side. Others are small, some no more than rock stacks pounded by tidal forces, but their importance to New Zealand's wildlife, particularly some rare life forms found nowhere else, is immeasurable. Besides providing breeding grounds for many sea birds, these rat-free islands are the last sanctuaries for the rare tuatara, Duvaucel's gecko (*Hoplodactylus duvauceli*) and the giant weta (*Deinacrida rugosa*), a huge prehistoric insect weighing up to 30 grams. Maud Island in Pelorus Sound is home to the archaic Hamilton's frog and is also a relocation site for two extremely endangered flightless birds, the kakapo and the takahe. Also found in forested areas around the Sounds, mainly above 300 m, is the large carnivorous land snail, the *Powelliphanta*, which may grow up to 110 mm across. The *Powelliphanta*, with its beautiful, shining brown asymmetric shell, is an efficient predator that feeds on large earthworms, ingesting them by means of daggerlike teeth on a club-shaped tongue.

The sea, of course, is what the Marlborough Sounds are about, and they are a paradise for sea birds, dolphins, fish, shellfish, and boaties alike. Bottlenose and common dolphins are seen regularly, and there is also a small population of Hector's dolphin, New Zealand's smallest species. Gulls, shags, terns, oystercatchers, pied stilts, and herons are common around the inner sounds, but it is on the small islands and rock stacks of the outer sounds that some of the rarer species are seen: sooty and flesh-footed shearwaters, diving petrels, tiny fairy prions, and albatrosses, along with gannets, blue penguins, and the rare king shag. About a million fairy prions, along with petrels and shearwaters, nest on Stephens Island each year within a honeycomb of burrows.

In many areas of the Sounds cleared by settlers, the natural forest cover is regenerating. Its first stages—the manuka/kanuka scrubland, then wineberry/tutu forest—are important for fixing nitrogen in the soil so that climax species in the process of succession can follow. Several plant species are restricted to successional communities, as the mature forest is too shaded. In untouched areas, mature forests retain their original beauty—towering trees are hung with epiphytic orchids, lianes, and perching lilies, casting deep shadows and cool green light. In warm, sheltered gullies, tall podocarps mingle with tawa, kohekohe, and the subtropical nikau palm to form a rich coastal forest. On drier ridges, hard beech predominates up to 500 m. Red beech is the main tree between 500 and 700 m, and above this the cover is mainly silver beech, with some mountain beech, southern rata, and Hall's totara. Only on the 1,203-m summit of Mt. Stokes does forest give way, and here a 2.2 ha of snow tussock and herb field forms a botanical island with some unique alpine plant species.

Forested areas still have reasonably good bird life, in spite of depletion by rats, stoats, ferrets, and cats. Tui, bellbirds, pigeons, tomtits, robins, white-eyes, and fantails are all regularly seen, but particularly intriguing is the flightless weka. It still occurs here in good numbers in spite of disappearing from other parts of the country. Weka are very curious and prone to stealing campers' cutlery and food. They are often seen searching the shoreline for food as well as areas of dense bush and scrub.

Recreational activities in the park are many and varied. There are plenty of camping areas, some accessible only by boat or by walking and others by road. A small fee is charged for their upkeep. Most roads are graveled, winding, and fairly narrow, and although fabulous views and superb scenery are good compensation, it is often quicker to reach a destination by boat. You'll find many water taxis available for private charter from Picton and Havelock. Yacht and launch cruises and fishing trips are available, or you can travel on one of the mail launches when it does its rounds. These services are ideal for people who wish to come and go from points along either of the two main walking tracks. You can also rent a kayak and paddle around the tranquil shoreline. Besides campgrounds, accommodation ranges from cabins to hotels, which will pick up guests from Picton or Havelock. Many have small shops and can dispense diesel fuel and gasoline.

A map is almost a prerequisite for anyone intending to explore the sounds, and Infomap 236 Ed.2, park handbooks, and information on camping areas and tracks are all available from Department of Conservation offices in Picton and Havelock. The Picton Information Centre on the foreshore at Picton is also a good place to find out about transport and things to do.

Places Accessible by Road

French Pass. The 134-km drive from Rai Valley to French Pass, including side roads, is well worth exploring. The road follows a ridge crest for much of the way, with superb views down to Croisilles Harbour and out across Tasman and Golden bays to the west, and to the east, the turquoise bays and coves of Pelorus Sound. The tiny fishing village of French Pass has a small beach, wharf, and waterfront picnic and camping area. You can replenish your gas tank, buy ice cream, have your dive tanks filled, and get transport to D'Urville Island. A short track leads down to a lookout where you can watch the sea rushing through the narrow, rock-strewn gap of French Pass like a noisy river, with numerous whirlpools and eddies sucking and dragging treacherously. Strong winds can turn the sea into a foaming mass of criss-crossing waves.

If it's windy at French Pass there is a nicer camping area back at **Elaine Bay,** a delightful, sheltered cove with a small collection of neat holiday houses. From here you can walk to Tennyson Inlet (6 km) or take the 2-km Piwakawaka Track through pleasant beech forest to another secluded bay where you can collect a feed of mussels at low tide.

Tennyson Inlet has more lovely camping and picnic areas, and you can walk around to Elaine Bay or take the 2-day **Nydia Walk** to Kaiuma and be picked up by boat. The drive in, over Opouri Saddle, passes through some of the best podocarp and beech forest in Marlborough, and from the top magnificent vistas open out toward French Pass and D'Urville Island.

Titirangi Farm Park and Recreation Reserve is located at the outer entrance to the Sounds, 100 km from Havelock at the end of the winding Kenepuru Road. The road starts at Linkwater and follows the length of Mahau and Kenepuru sounds, passing many scenic reserves and campsites, beautiful bays, and the Portage and Te Mahia resorts. It divides at the head of Kenepuru Sound, one branch heading west to the northern bays of Kenepuru and the other climbing through beech forest on the slopes of Mt. Stokes before descending to Titirangi Farm Park.

Titirangi has a camping area, a network of farm roads and tracks, and a fine sandy beach enclosed by headlands that is excellent for swimming. There are several forest areas. The sea-cliffs near the camping ground are among the few remaining natural habitats of the beautiful magenta-flowered *Hebe speciosia*. Public transport to Titirangi is provided by **Marlborough Scenic Tours**, 7 Hampden St., Picton, phone (03)5736-262.

Whites Bay is most easily and quickly reached from SH 1 near Tua Marina, but for views and history, the **Port Underwood Road** is much more interesting. Although long, winding, and dusty, it passes the sites of many old whaling stations. The first telegraph cable to span Cook Strait was brought ashore at Whites Bay, and the small wooden building there, now a museum and caretaker's cottage, was the repeater station. The sheltered, sandy beach is excellent for swimming and the 800-ha bush reserve behind it has many long and short walks through a variety of forest habitats.

Walking Tracks

There are two main walkways in the park and many smaller ones. Hikers can be dropped off and picked up at points along the main tracks by mail boats or by commercial launches from Picton and Havelock. The way is dotted with campsites and there are also a few lodges. Warm clothing and insect repellent should be carried.

Nydia Track. This 2-day track starts at Kaiuma Bay. You can drive the 32 km from Havelock, or you can be dropped off by a boat. The track finishes at Duncan Bay in Tennyson Inlet. The 22 km are usually walked in two stages: Kaiuma to Nydia Campsite (4 to 6 hours) and Nydia to Duncan Bay (5 to 7 hours). From Kaiuma, the track climbs over the 387 m Kaiuma Saddle through scrub and bush to Nydia Bay, then crosses Nydia Saddle (347 m) and descends to Ngawhakawhiti Bay. You may be tempted to spend a night at the campsite on this serene bay, surrounded by lush coastal forest, before you walk the last hour around the coast to Duncan Bay.

Queen Charlotte Sound Walkway. Total walking time for this track from Anakiwa to Ship Cove is about 26 hours, but most people do only sections of it, arranging to be dropped off and picked up by boat. The most popular sections are described below.

Anakiwa to Mistletoe Bay. Most of this 3- to 4-hour walk is through forest dominated by beech, with a pleasant open understory of tree ferns and broadleaf species. There are views down to the sea, and after about an hour a grassy campsite at Umungata Bay is reached. The last hour to Mistletoe Bay is through regenerating forest with good populations of weka and insectivorous tomtits, fantails, and white-eyes. There are two short walks at Mistletoe Bay—the 30-minute Peninsula Walk from the picnic area, and the 20-minute Vogel Track through a stand of regenerating coastal forest behind the foreshore.

Mistletoe Bay to Portage (3 hours). Most of this section follows the top of the ridge between Keneperu, Mahau, and Queen Charlotte sounds with good views along the way from the two windswept high points, both over 400 m high. Most of the forest is regenerating manuka, kanuka, and kamahi, with tangled clubmosses and tough grasses covering the hard dry ground.

Camp Bay to Ship Cove. Allow at least 2 days to enjoy this section. The track starts at Kenepuru Saddle and descends to Camp Bay, where there is a good campsite. From here to Endeavour Inlet takes about 4 hours; then it's another 3 hours to Resolution and Schoolhouse bays, where there are more campsites. Overnight camping is not permitted at Ship Cove, so it is best to make a day trip there from Resolution Bay. The 2-hour walk from Resolution Bay through podocarp and broadleaf forest has superb views across the white-capped waters of Cook Strait to Kapiti Island and the Wellington coast, while the serenity of the cove makes it easy to see why Cook liked it so much and returned so often.

Out on the Water

One of the nicest ways to see the Marlborough Sounds is by paddling quietly around the bays and inlets in a kayak. The **Marlborough Sounds Adventure Company** runs a number of tours, from 2 to 10 days, but if you'd prefer to plan your own trip you can rent a kayak from them. They are located at Mahakipawa on Queen Charlotte Drive, or you can write to them at RD 1, Picton. Phone (03)5742-534. **Topsport Kayaking,** 459 Cashel St., Christchurch, phone (03)3891-789 also rent sea kayaks and run multiday trips around D'Urville Island.

Experienced sailors can rent boats to skipper around the Sounds, but you can also charter a cruise, with someone else taking the responsibility. Both launches and yachts are available. Prices vary according to the season; November to February are the priciset months, when bookings are heaviest. Contact any of the following:

Marlborough Sounds Charters, P.O. Box 284, Picton, phone (03)5737-726 or, after hours, 5736-531.

Charter Link, P.O. Box 292, Picton, phone (03)5736-591, Fax (03)5736-904.

Portage Bay Charters, RD 2, Picton, phone (03)5734-445.
Leisure Launch Charters, P.O. Box 58, Picton, phone (03)5737-925.

AROUND BLENHEIM

Blenheim is mainly a farming center, and activities from here focus mostly on wine tasting, but you can also visit the superb Marlborough backcountry by four-wheel-drive vehicle or raft the Wairau or Clarence rivers. **Billy Tea Tours** offer a variety of day or longer trips throughout the region, combining driving, walking, and bicycling. They operate from the Havelock Youth Hostel; phone Peter at (03)5742-143 or Jon at (03)5742-233. **Molesworth and Rainbow Safaris** take 2-day trips up the Awatere Valley to Molesworth Station, returning via the Clarence and Wairau valleys after an overnight stop at Hanmer Springs. Contact Chris Newcombe, 2 Anglesea St., Renwick, phone (03)5728-022 or 5784-531. The nearby Richmond Range offers hiking, camping, and picnicking, and it's not far south to Nelson Lakes National Park for more of the same amid stunning scenery. (See "Nelson.") The mountains of the Inland Kaikoura Range offer challenges for climbers. Sheltered from the west by the Richmond Range and to the south and east by the Kaikoura Ranges, the town is renowned for its warm sunny weather and has been dubbed the Sunshine Capital.

MT. RICHMOND FOREST PARK

The 180,000-ha Mt. Richmond Forest Park is third largest in New Zealand and is named after a central point on the Richmond Range, which from the Wairau Valley presents a very steep bush-clad flank rising to rocky peaks separated by grassy alpine basins. Much of the range consists of unconnected areas of high alpine tops separated by steep-sided valleys, most of which drain to the west. The rocks making up the mountains are geologically diverse. Schists are found at the southeast end of the park around Mt. Patriarch and the Goulter River, while the western side contains a narrow band of ultramafic rocks known as the Nelson Mineral Belt. (See "Nelson.") The Maori did not use the range much, as their trade routes tended to skirt the high mountains, but they did quarry the hard argillite found there to make tools and weapons. About forty quarry sites have been found here, and the only other place they occur is in Southland. The Europeans found other uses for the rocks, mining copper and chromium in the mineral belt and gold and scheelite at the southern end of the range. Although an exceptionally rich field of gold found in the Wakamarina River in 1860 turned out to be very small, other quartz reefs containing gold and scheelite were discovered in 1870 and several mining operations were set up. The three most successful were in operation until 1923.

Perimeters of the park are forested mainly in scrub and privately owned exotic plantations, but about 85 percent is native beech forest. All five species of New Zealand beech are represented here, in some places growing together, and these, mixed with podocarp species, occupy lower slopes and valleys. Above the bushline, the alpine tussock and herb fields support a rich variety of species, some of which are endemic to the area. The forests provide a range of habitats for numerous introduced and native birds, including kaka, kiwi, and yellow-crowned parakeets, while the rare blue duck is found in several rivers. The carnivorous *Powelliphanta* also occurs here, in beech forests above 760 m.

The park has over 250 km of cut and marked tracks, covering a range of terrain, with huts at convenient intervals. The most popular tracks are the **Pelorus Track** along the Pelorus River (see "Nelson") and the strenuous **Alpine Route** across the range, but there are numerous interconnecting tracks. Most tracks follow ridges and so tend to be waterless, but two, the Wakamarina and Waikakaho/Cullen tracks, follow old benched trails from the mining days. Huts are generally small (about 6 bunks) and do not contain any cooking equipment or utensils.

Sheltered by other major ranges, Mt. Richmond Forest Park generally enjoys drier weather than other South Island mountain regions and rainless periods can last up to 14 days. Like other mountains, however, it also has its bad spells, and it is necessary to be adequately equipped if tramping here, particularly on the open ridge tops, as snow can fall in any season.

Infomap 18 or the Mt. Richmond Park Map (NZMS 274-6) will be necessary for anyone undertaking any extended walks or hikes in the park. These can be obtained from the Department of Survey and Land Information in Blenheim. The following is only a brief guide to the main access areas. Further information should be obtained from the Department of Conservation in Nelson, Picton, or Blenheim. Pamphlets are available for some tracks.

Access to the Marlborough side of the park is from North Bank Road or from SH 6 between Blenheim and Nelson. North Bank Road leaves SH 6 just north of the Wairau River Bridge, 16 km from Blenheim. It gives access to Onamalutu, Fabians, Bartletts, Pine, and Top valleys, Timms Stream, Lake Chalice, Mt. Patriarch and the Goulter River. Public transport is available along main roads around the park, and a TNL/Transpac Company mail truck travels North Bank Road as far as Top Valley each weekday.

Tracks from North Bank Road

Onamalutu Valley. The 11-ha scenic reserve beside the Onamalutu River has a grassed area for picnicking and sports activities and provides access to the Wakamarina Track. There are also camping and caravan facilities, with power points.

Bartletts Creek/Quartz Creek. Turn off 20 km from SH 6 into Fabians Valley Road. Bartlett's Creek Road, which turns right after 1 km, gives access to the Rimu Falls (1 to 2 hours round trip), and the Mt. Royal Track, a 1,200 m ascent to an open summit with good views. There is also access from here to the Wakamarina Track.

Pine Valley turnoff is 25 km from SH 6. From the road end, 3.5 km up the valley, a track leads 1 km upstream to Fishtail Flat camping and picnic area. From here the track to Mt. Fishtail (1,643 m) continues upstream, passing the 6-bunk Pine Valley Hut before crossing the left branch of the stream and ascending the dividing ridge to Fishtail Hut (4 bunks). The summit is reached by climbing directly up from the hut, or via the saddle to the north and then following the ridge toward the southeast. Allow a full day for the round trip and carry water.

The **Top Valley** turnoff is 34 km from SH 6. Top Valley is popular for fishing, camping, and picnicking, and provides short walks as well as access to Lake Chalice, the Goulter Valley, Old Man (1,514 m), Mt. Richmond (1,760 m) and Mt. Patriarch (1,656 m). The climb to **Mt. Richmond** can be done in one day or can include an overnight at the 10-bunk Richmond Saddle Hut. The track starts from the end of Jackson Creek Road, off Top Valley Road. Take Staircase Road, which leaves Top Valley just before the Staircase Stream ford, for tracks to Lake Chalice, Mid-Goulter Hut, and Mt. Patriarch. Staircase Road climbs through pines and subalpine scrub, then continues along the main ridge to Mt. Patriarch. **Lake Chalice** carpark is 12.5 km from Top Valley, and a benched track descends to an 8-bunk hut beside the lake in about 30 minutes. Allow 1 to 1.5 hours for the ascent. Beautiful Lake Chalice was formed by a landslide about 2,200 years ago. The steep track down to **Mid-Goulter Hut** in the **Goulter Valley** starts another 7.5 km beyond the Lake Chalice carpark. The Goulter Valley can also be reached by a vehicle track from Patriarch Station at the end of North Bank Road. Open river flats in this valley make it popular with anglers. The climb to the summit of **Mt. Patriarch** takes about 1 hour from the road end, 26.5 km from Top Valley (the last 5 km are four-wheel drive only). Views over the Wairau Valley and park are superb, as are the alpine flowers in summer.

Waikakaho–Cullen Creek Track

During the 1880s and 1890s this was a gold miners' trail, and its history and existing remains are explained in a Department of Conservation pamphlet. Old drive shafts, chimneys, and evidence of old workings can be seen. As ends of the track are on different roads, it will be necessary to arrange transport unless a round trip is made. This can be done in a fairly long day. Access is from either Waikakaho Road, off the Kaituna–Tuamarina Road on the north bank of the Wairau between SH 1 and SH 6, or from Cullen Creek Road, which leaves the Havelock–Picton Road near Linkwater.

Tracks from SH 6 between Blenheim and Nelson

Wakamarina Valley. Following an old gold miners trail over the Richmond Range to Bartletts Creek and the Onamalutu Valley (see "Tracks from North Bank Road"), this 18-km track can be walked in a day, or overnight stops can be made at either **Doom Creek** or **Devils Creek huts.** There are several possibilities for side trips along the way. Access to the northern end of the track is via Wakamarina Road at Canvastown.

Pelorus Track. This 32-km track leads up the Pelorus River and over the Bryant Range to Hacket Creek and Roding River on the Nelson side. There are 3 huts along the way, and it can be walked in 3 to 4 days. Side tracks give access to Mt. Richmond and to the 20-bunk Rocks Hut near Dun Mountain (see "Nelson"). The Pelorus end of the track is 15 km up Maungatapu Road, which turns off SH 6 north of the Pelorus Bridge.

INLAND KAIKOURA RANGE

Peaks of the Inland Kaikoura Range are generally beyond the average walker, but they offer some interesting challenges to climbers, particularly in winter when they are snow-covered. Temperatures vary from −20°C in winter to over 30°C in summer. In summer the slopes are vast, hot, and composed of very loose rock. These geologically young mountains are still rising rapidly, at a rate that, due to the dry climate, is not balanced by erosion. Although there are no ice glaciers, there are rock glaciers—large deposits of rock scree with frozen cores that cause them to flow. Mt. Tapuaenuku is the easiest of the three main peaks; Alarm and Mitre are more technical climbs due to the steep, loose rock. Access to all three peaks is via the Hodder Valley, a tributary of the Awatere River. It takes 6 to 7 hours to walk up the Hodder, crossing the river innumerable times. The upper section has a narrow gorge and a waterfall which is bypassed on the true right. Contact the **Marlborough Tramping Club,** Box 787, Blenheim, for further information and bookings of Hodder and Murray Adrian huts in the head of the valley.

SEAWARD KAIKOURA RANGE

Rising straight from the sea, these mountains dominate the scenery and strongly influence the weather. Lower slopes of the range and valleys were once heavily forested with podocarp species—miro, totara, matai, rimu, and kahikatea—while higher slopes were almost pure Hall's totara. Some of these forests are preserved in extensive reserves. The subalpine zone has been extensively modified by burning and grazing, but some of the area's more spectacular species, such as the pink broom (*Notospartium carmichaelia*) and rock daisies (*Pachystegia*), are now returning.

One of the more interesting birds found here is the Hutton's shearwater (*Puffinus huttoni*), which nests by the thousands amid the tussocks high in the Kowhai basin each summer. Another is the brown creeper, or pipipi (*Finschia novaeseelandiae*), a small forest bird not found in the North Island. In the South Island, the brown creeper is the main host of the long-tailed cuckoo. The range is also the only habitat of the endangered Kaikoura giant weta, a nocturnal insect that feeds on vegetable matter.

There are many walks in the range and on outlying Mt. Fyffe, and these are fully described in the booklet *Kaikoura Walks and Climbs* by Barry Dunnett, which is available from bookstores and the information center at Kaikoura. Topomaps NZMS 260, sheets 031, P30, and P31, would be useful, and further information can be obtained from the Department of Conservation, Ludstone Road, Kaikoura, or from the information center. Some of the walks are described under "Bushwalks near Kaikoura."

AROUND KAIKOURA

Kaikoura tends to have extremes of climate and can be baking hot one day and very cool the next, depending on the wind direction. Whale watching is the favorite activity here, but you can also swim with seals, go diving, or observe marine life from a glass bottom boat, visit a limestone cave, and take a four-wheel-drive ride or a hike up Mt. Fyffe. More gentle walks can be done in bush on the lower slopes or around the Kaikoura Peninsula, where there are seabirds and seals. Due to the popularity of whale watching, it may be wise to book ahead from Picton, Blenheim, or Christchurch. Information centers in these towns can help you. Seals are seen frequently from the coast road, and if you want to camp along the coast there are Department of Conservation campgrounds at Waipapa Bay, Puketa, and Goose Bay, plus 3 km of more casual sites at Omihi.

Bushwalks near Kaikoua

Hinau Walk. This 45-minute walk through broadleaf forest dominated by large hinau trees starts from a carpark and picnic area at the western end of Mt. Fyffe, 12 km from Kaikoura. From the town center take Ludstone Road, then Red Swamp Road. Turn left into Postmans Road, go to the end and follow the signs.

Fyffe Palmer Scenic Reserve Walks. A network of short tracks wanders through this small reserve on the eastern slopes of Mt. Fyffe to a stand of mature podocarp trees that seems one of the best on the east coast of the South Island. From a carpark at the end of Fyffe Road a marked track leads over farmland to the reserve and a sign. By taking the left-hand track just beyond the sign a loop can be made through the forest, passing a viewpoint and picnic area on the return leg.

Puhi Puhi Reserve. A short bush walk, picnic area, and access to the river make this reserve of lowland podocarp forest a pleasant spot. It lies 5.2 km up the Puhi Puhi Valley Road, just beyond the Hapuku River Bridge, 12 km north of Kaikoura. This is the most southern location on the east coast of the South Island of tawa (*Bielschmiedia tawa*).

Kowhai Valley–Hapuku River. Access to the Kowhai Valley is from the Hinau Picnic Area at the end of Postmans Road. A short side road just below the carpark leads to the river bed. A pleasant day or easy overnight trip can be made up the Kowhai Valley to 6-bunk **Kowhai Hut.** Allow 3 to 4 hours to reach the hut from the Hinau carpark. By climbing the slopes behind Kowhai Hut or the steep spur running northeast to Mt. Uwerau, it is possible to avoid a gorge and enter the picturesque tussock basins of the upper Kowhai Valley, which gives access to Manakau (2,610 m), the highest point on the range, and Uwerau. An alternative 2- to 3-day trip, for more experienced hikers, is to cross Kowhai Saddle and walk out down the Hapuku Valley.

Most travel in the Kowhai Valley is up the river bed, but tracked sections are clearly marked. From Kowhai Hut the route to Kowhai Saddle (2 to 3 hours) is marked by rock cairns, mostly following the steep, bouldery stream bed. A pole marks the start of the final climb to the saddle, and from here there are two routes down to the Hapuku. One descends the very steep water course directly down to the river, and the other sidles east across slopes of Mt. Fyffe before descending an eroding spur. Travel through the scrub below the crest is rough until a track is picked up at the bush edge. This descends through manuka and Hall's totara forest to the river. Across the river a marked track follows terraces on the true left bank before crossing to **Hapuku Hut** (6 bunks) on the true right bank. Allow 2 to 3 hours to reach Hapuku Hut from Kowhai Saddle.

The track continues downstream, crossing the river twice before climbing and sidling high on the true right above a difficult gorge. From where the river is regained, travel is easier in the river bed until the Grange Road ford is reached. Unlike the Kowhai River, places where the track crosses the upper Hapuku River are not well marked, so watch carefully for cairns or orange markers. From the Hapuku Hut to Grange Road allow 3 to 4 hours.

Mt. Fyffe. The 1,602-m summit of Mt. Fyffe provides wonderful views over Kaikoura and the coast and to the mountains behind. In summer the open top sports a mosaic of subalpine scrub, snow tussocks, and alpine flowers. There are several routes to the summit, most of them steep, but the easiest and most popular is along a four-wheel-drive road that climbs the southwest spur from the Hinau Picnic Area (see "Hinau Walk"). It takes about 3 hours to reach Mt. Fyffe Hut (6 bunks) at Tarn Saddle (about 1,097 m), and a further 1.5 to 2 hours to the summit, either following the road or the ridgeline. In winter, if the road is icy, the ridge can be safer. Weather changes on the open upper slopes can be sudden, so take warm clothing.

An alternative, well-tracked and well-marked route follows Fenceline Spur to the summit road and southwest ridge, providing a round trip. A parking area beside the Goldmine Creek ford, on the road to Hinau Picnic Area, marks the start of the track. Follow markers up the creek, then through bush, to gain the spur.

Coastal Walks

Kaikoura Peninsula. The two walks here — Shoreline Walk, around the eastern shoreline, and Cliff-top Walk, which follows the cliff edge — can be linked to form a round trip taking 3 to 4 hours. Both start from a carpark at Point Kean, reached by following the Esplanade about 5 km around the northern shore. From the cliff tops there are spectacular views of the mountains and coastal formations. The wave-cut tidal platforms and offshore rocks are resting places for seals as well as feeding and breeding places for numerous seabirds.

Omihi Lookout Track. A short, easy track (less than 1 hour) to a good lookout point over the coast starts 1 km south of Goose Bay, opposite the northern end of the Omihi Campground. Parts of the track follow an old coastal pack track constructed in the 1860s.

Haumuri Bluff. For anyone interested in geology, a visit to Haumuri Bluff will be very rewarding, as a variety of rocks, belemnite, and other fossils, concretions, and crystals of sulphur and gypsum (or selenite) are found here. The centers of the cannonball-like concretions contain fossils; similar concretions are found at Moeraki, south of Oamaru. You will need a full day for the round trip, and you'll also need to check the tide. From Oaro, where the highway swings inland, follow the railway line around the coast, passing Mikonui Beach and the remains of an old Maori settlement. At the Haumuri tunnel entrance, descend to the beach and boulder hop along the coast, watching for seals and fossils as you go. The last few hundred meters to the bluff can only be reached when the water is at half tide or lower.

Whale Watching

At time of writing, only one company was licensed by the Department of Conservation to conduct 3-hour tours off the coast to view sperm whales, dolphins, and other marine animals. Before more licenses are issued, the whales are being monitored to see whether all the commercial activity is having any negative effects. It is feared that too much attention may drive them away. Sperm whales are seen most often in winter, between April and August, while dusky dolphins are more common during the summer months. Fur seals and sea birds are present throughout the year. A few kilometers off the Kaikoura Coast, the continental shelf plunges to the Kaikoura Trench, more than 1,600 m deep. Upwellings of nutrient-rich water from the trench into the warmer coastal waters supports an abundance of marine invertebrates, which in turn attract fish, mammals, and birds. Whale watching is so popular that you'll be wise to book a trip before you get to Kaikoura. Trips are also subject to weather and sea conditions. Check at information centers or contact **Kaikoura Tours**, P.O. Box 89, Kaikoura, phone (03)3195-045. They are located at the Kaikoura railway station.

If you are in a hurry or feeling extravagant you can hire a helicopter or plane and get a birds-eye view of the great mammals as they rise and plunge in the waves.

Alternatives worth considering, if you can't get to watch whales, are canoe and glass-bottomed boat trips, and swimming, snorkeling, or diving with seals and dolphins. Kayaks and boats can also be rented. Several companies offer these activities.

Fishing

Fishing in Marlborough can be rewarding. The mouths of the Awatere and Wairau rivers are good for sea-run trout, salmon, and kahawai, while the clear green pools of the Pelorus River harbor good-sized brown and rainbow trout. Some of the most beautiful fishing in the district is in the Pelorus. The Goulter River has brown trout only and, although more difficult to reach and fish, is also beautiful. One of the best fly-fishing streams is Spring Creek near Blenheim, but the fish are difficult to catch and patience is necessary. Access is over private property, but permission is usually freely given. Anglers must carry a license and must observe the fishing season, which is October 1 to April 30. Sections of some rivers have extended seasons. Information on this and bag limits for each river are on licenses.

USEFUL ADDRESSES

Marlborough Promotions, Arthur St., Blenheim, phone (03)5784-480, and on the foreshore at Picton, phone (03)5737-513.
Kaikoura Information Centre, 34 Esplanade, Box 6, Kaikoura, phone (03) 3195-641.
Department of Conservation Offices: P.O. Box 32, Kaikoura, phone (03)3195-714; 13 Mahakipawa Road, Havelock, phone (03)5742-019; Box 5, Renwick, Blenheim, phone (03)5729-100; Box 161, Picton, phone (03)5737-582.

18 ◆ CANTERBURY

LANDSCAPE AND CLIMATE

Wide open spaces, tawny hills, neat rectangular fields edged with rows of sheltering pines, broad shingly rivers, and a dramatically wide sky often half-filled with a huge nor'west arch riding the distant snow-capped mountains—all are hallmarks of Canterbury. Filling the eastern seaboard of the South Island, from the rugged Marlborough high country for over 300 km south to the mighty Waitaki River, the irregular parallelogram of Canterbury is very different from the rest of the South Island. Its main feature is a plain, 190 km long by 65 km wide, sloping gently from the coast to about 300 m above sea level where it runs into the foothills of the Southern Alps. The land rises steeply above the plains, in not just one range but several, each roughly parallel to its neighbor, in a broad belt of mountainous country over 50 km wide trending north-south and culminating in the Main Divide. These are old sedimentary rocks, mostly greywackes, but the mountains are geologically young and erosion is rapid.

Between the ranges are wide upland valleys and intermontane basins scooped out by the huge glaciers of the Ice Ages. The basins vary in size and character, some now almost level and covered in undulating tussockland, others filled with lakes as diverse in color and clarity as the sky can be. Largest is the Mackenzie Country, an immense, almost treeless basin of glacial moraine and outwash with three great lakes—Tekapo, Pukaki, and Ohau—fed by rivers from New Zealand's highest mountains. The outflows from these lakes combine to form the Waitaki River, whose waters are now harnessed to provide hydroelectricity. There is an austere beauty in this harsh landscape. In good weather, sunshine gilds the tussocks into golden waves and the pale turquoise lakes glitter like jewels before the high, glaciated peaks of Mt. Cook National Park. When the northwest wind blows, dark clouds pile high to the west, obscuring the peaks. Then the vividness of the lakes is dulled and speckled with caps of white foam, and clouds of fine dust are whipped across the dun landscape. Other similar lakes are Coleridge in the Rakaia Valley and the Ashburton Lakes near the Rangitata Valley.

The broad coastal plain, a product of the young mountains, is a classic example of a piedmont alluvial fan. In places the buildup of silt and glacial outwash carried down and out from the mountains is several hundred meters thick. The formation is particularly apparent when seen from the air. Wide and braided, the snowfed Rakaia, Rangitata, and Waimakariri rivers wear a deceptively stable look during normal flows, but in flood they are savage and menacing. Then the turbid brown flow stretches from bank to bank and the whole mass of gravel and sand can be set in motion to a depth of a meter or more by the speed and volume of water. Early settlers and runholders found these rivers a barrier to travel; sometimes they waited weeks to cross safely. So many drowned that for years drowning was known as the New Zealand death. The snow-fed giants exit the eastern ranges through deep gorges, then cut terraced trenches through the gravels before spreading out toward the coast. Between the big rivers are smaller rain-fed rivers rising in the foothills.

The coastline is mainly low where the gravel plains reach the Pacific Ocean, and here, steeply shelving, long, monotonous stony beaches are raked by dangerous surf. The only places frequented are lagoons at the mouths of the rivers, by anglers who often form long lines when the salmon are running. The salmon were introduced in 1870. North of Banks Peninsula the beaches have finer sand and are safer.

Within this landscape of mountain and plain, Banks Peninsula is a geographical anomaly. Formed of the truncated cones of two volcanoes and once an island, its hills are different from other parts of Canterbury. Deeply eroded valleys fanning outward were drowned when sea levels rose after the last Ice Age and today form sheltered harbors and bays between abrupt headlands and cliffs of dark basalt. Cook thought it was an island and named it after the naturalist Sir Joseph Banks who accompanied him. The error was not discovered until 1809, when Captain Chase tried to sail the *Pegasus* between the "island" and the shore. Only in recent geological times has the island been joined to the mainland by the mass of gravel spreading out from the mountains, and even when the first settlers arrived in the 1850s it was fringed by a wide band of swamps and reedy waterways.

Banks Peninsula has a climate of its own, one that is moister and warmer than that of the plains, enabling early Maori inhabitants to grow kumara on sunny north-facing slopes. Most of Canterbury experiences extremes of climate, with temperatures rising to 30°C or more, especially when the hot, dry northwest winds blow. It lies in the rain shadow of the alps, and although rainfall is fairly evenly distributed throughout the year, the nor'westers have a desiccating effect. A lack of surface water on the coarse gravels of the plains often gives rise to droughts. In winter, frosts are common, and southerly winds can bring sleet and snow to low levels. The hills of Banks Peninsula usually receive a good coating during such storms.

HISTORY

Polynesian seafarers are thought to have made landfall on the Canterbury coast as early as A.D. 950, and during the moa-hunter period, the area was possibly one of the most populated parts of New Zealand. There were several large pa and one, Kaiapohia, near present-day Kaiapoi, was an important center in the greenstone trade. After being processed, the precious stone was exchanged far and wide for cloaks, potted muttonbirds, and other needed items. Bitter fighting during the early nineteenth century within the ranks of the Kai Tahu, the major South Island tribe, decimated the Maori population. Known as the *kai huanga* (eat relation) feud, the fighting disrupted the entire social system and so depleted the strength of the Kai Tahu that they were easy victims of Te Rauparaha's invasions from the north.

After annihilating the inhabitants of the pa at Kaikoura and Omihi, Te Rauparaha moved south to Kaiapohia Pa about 1828, pretending to be interested in trading for greenstone. Forewarned of his earlier savagery, the Kai Tahu feigned friendship and invited eight of Te Rauparaha's Ngati Toa people into the pa, then struck them down. Te Rauparaha withdrew but returned later to exact a terrible vengeance. First he arranged with the captain of the trading ship *Elizabeth* to carry 170 of his warriors to Akaroa Harbour on Banks Peninsula. With the Ngati Toa hidden in the hold of the ship, the captain persuaded the Kai Tahu chief Te Maharanui to come aboard, then took him to his cabin, where Te Rauparaha seized him. Te Maharanui's helpers were also enticed aboard, only to be thrown into the hold. At dawn the raiding Ngati Toa surged ashore and devastated the village of Takapueke before sailing back to Kapiti Island. There Te Maharanui suffered a slow and painful death at the hands of the widows of those killed at Kaiapohia.

Not satisfied, Te Rauparaha returned to Kaiapohia two years later at a time when many Kai Tahu warriors were absent. Most were able to secretly reenter the pa, sited on a peninsula jutting out into a lagoon, during a 3-month siege. During this time the Ngati Toa constructed a ditch across the neck of the peninsula and up to the palisades. Here they piled scrub in preparation to setting the pa on fire. Taking the initiative, the defenders set fire to the pyre first, knowing that the strong northwest winds blowing at the time would blow the flames away from the pa. Unfortunately, as often happens, the strong northwest winds were replaced by a sudden southerly change, which blew the flames back, kindling the century-old wooden fortifications. In the smoke and confusion that followed, the Ngati Toa rushed in and finished the destruction. To complete his triumph, Te Rauparaha sailed across to Akaroa once more and destroyed the remaining Kai Tahu pa at Onawe. Those not killed and eaten were taken back to Kapiti Island as slaves.

Earliest European settlers were whalers who took up residence in the bays of Banks Peninsula in the 1830s. They were followed by a group of sixty-three French migrants aboard the *Comte de Paris* in July 1840. Hoping to set up a new colony for France, the French were dismayed on their arrival at Akaroa to find British sovereignty already being exercised, the Treaty of Waitangi having been signed only a few months earlier. Had they arrived sooner, New Zealand may well have become a French colony. Akaroa still has a strong Gallic flavor, most obvious in its street names and early architecture. Meaning "long harbor," Akaroa corresponds to the North Island name of Whangaroa. In the South Island the Maori *ng* consonant is replaced by a distinct *k* (compare Waitaki and Waitangi, Ngai Tahu and Kai Tahu).

The arrival of the French at Akaroa sparked British interest in the settlement of Banks Peninsula in 1841, but this was forestalled by Governor Hobson, who decided there were already too many undecided claims on the land. In 1843, however, two settlers from Wellington, John and William Deans, transferred their interests to the Canterbury Plains, bringing with them the first cattle, horses, pigs, and sheep.

Port Cooper (Lyttelton) had been considered as a possible site for settlement for some time and was eventually selected for the new Canterbury, originally planned for the Wairarapa near Wellington. Lyttelton's steep hills proved difficult to survey for the proposed town, and an easier, flatter site was chosen over the hills on the edge of the plains. In England, the fifty-three members of the Canterbury Association, many of them clerics or men of upper and aristocratic class, selected migrants to form the new settlement, and on December 16, 1850, the first Pilgrims arrived on the *Charlotte Jane.* They were closely followed by three more ships, and by the year's end, 782 newcomers had been landed.

The Canterbury settlement was envisaged as a closely knit agricultural community, similar to those in England, where the church and traditions of education and class would hold firm. People with capital could form a landed gentry and those without could provide a hard-working peasantry. The plan broke down when Australian squatters, driven across the Tasman by drought, came with capital and bought up large tracts of land. The new pilgrims followed suit and by 1855 the plains and foothills had been leased. Over the next 10 years all land worth stocking, and much that wasn't, right up to the Main Divide, had been taken up. With such a widely scattered pastoral farming community, the church's hold over its flock diminished, and by 1855 the Canterbury Association had ceased to exist. It had, however, done a good job in assisting 3,549 migrants to settle in a new country, allowing them to prosper without burdening them with debt, as was the case of many New Zealand Company settlements. Christchurch is now the South Island's largest city and is often said to be more British than parts of Britain, which is not surprising considering its origins. Indeed, its neo-Gothic cathedral, statues, town square, old buildings, and the willow- and oak-lined Avon River all impart an air of English gentility, but there the similarity ends.

Canterbury's newcomers were faced with a barren, windswept plain, covered in tussock and matagouri scrub. The only patches of bush were along the foothills, where rainfall was higher. Forest that once covered the plains had been destroyed by fires lit by the early Maori, probably to flush out moa. The second transformation began in the 1850s, when the first landholders drained the swamps and established farms on the rich soils near the coast. On bigger sheep runs the natural vegetation was burned to promote the succulent new growth on which the animals thrived. Wool became the province's main export, with excellent profits that set it on the road to prosperity. Wheat grew well on the plains and provided the second biggest export, with bonanza years in the 1880s, until successive crops exhausted the soils. Today, better farming methods and irrigation have restored the former fertility of the soil. The foothills have changed little, except perhaps to show longer erosion scars of grey shingle on their overgrazed slopes. Small towns linked by straight roads dot the plains. Many started as service centers for the scattered farming population and have shrunk in importance and size with the advent of the automobile. The few areas of planted exotic forest have been subjected to damage from the northwesterly gales that sweep across the plains and foothills at times with unremitting ferocity. One of the most successful state forests in the country is the first one, planted at Hanmer in 1902. Some of the earliest plantations there have matured into magnificent exotic forests, which have been retained as a prime recreational area.

Exploration of the foothills and backcountry proceeded as runholders took up vast tracts of land between 1855 and 1860. One of the first to come was Samuel Butler. He had already explored the Waimakariri and Rakaia valleys before going up the Rangitata. As a result of his exploration, Butler bought twenty acres in the Rangitata Valley in June 1860. This was later added to and became the famous Mesopotamia Station. The name can be interpreted as "land in the midst of rivers" or "land between waters." Butler's main claim to fame is his satire *Erewhon* (*nowhere* spelled backwards). The station later became overrun with rabbits, which reduced its carrying capacity from 15,000 to 5,000 sheep. When rabbit killing began in the 1920s, 150,000 were killed in the first year and 100,000 the following year.

The Rangitata Valley had already been explored as far as Forest Creek in January 1855 by Charles Tripp and J. B. A. Acland. Further exploration of the Ashburton Gorge the same year brought them out on the Rangitata riverbed by the Potts River. In 1861, as geologist to the Canterbury Provincial Government, Julius von Haast made a systematic exploration of the headwaters of the Rangitata and named its three big tributaries—the Havelock, Lawrence, and Clyde rivers—after British generals familiar to the public of the time for their exploits in the Indian mutiny.

The Mackenzie Basin was well known to the Maori, who visited it regularly in the warm summer months, first to hunt moa and later to collect other birds that were numerous in the scrub around the lakes and on the broad river beds. Travel was via the Opihi River and either Mackenzie Pass or Burke Pass, or up the Waimate Valley. They built temporary shelters of flax sticks and snow-grass, and many ovens, artifacts, and moa bones have been found. The first settlers were unaware of the vast inland area of grazing land until 1855, when a Scotsman, James McKenzie, was caught near the pass that now bears his misspelled name, driving sheep suspected of being stolen from the Levels, a huge station south of Timaru. Little is known about McKenzie except that he was tall and thin, spoke only Gaelic, and understood little English. McKenzie escaped but was recaptured at Lyttelton and given a five-year jail sentence. He refused to plead either guilty or not guilty and subsequently explained that he had been hired by another man to drive the sheep. His story was generally believed, and nine months later he was pardoned. He subsequently disappeared.

Would-be runholders quickly applied for land and were soon driving mobs of sheep into the Mackenzie Basin. Impenetrable thickets of matagouri scrub and speargrass made travel difficult, and the first act of a new runholder was to fire his land—not just once but many times, to render the tussock more palatable to sheep. Driven by steady northwest winds, the fires often spread to neighboring runs. As the swamps were drained and natural vegetation disappeared, so did the bird life and the seasonal migrations of the Maori. The settlers' first tent dwellings were replaced by low sod cottages that withstood the storms better, but as most were built on the south side of a hill, out of the full force of the wind, they saw little sun in winter. Winters were often bleak, with snow lying on the ground for weeks at a time, and sheep were often buried under snowfalls.

The Southern Alps were generally regarded as an impenetrable barrier beyond which it rained incessantly, and the west coast was considered fit only for a penal colony. The Hurunui river–Harper Pass–Taramakau River route had long been used by the Maori to cross the Main Divide of the Alps to get greenstone, and this was explored first by Edward Dobson, then by Leonard Harper in 1857. Within the next few years a track was cut when these rivers were surveyed as part of the provincial boundary between Nelson and Canterbury and, in spite of its circuitous nature, this formed the major walking access for many years. Other valleys leading to the Divide were also explored for possible passes, but it was not until 1864 that Arthur Dobson, son of Edward Dobson, was requested to look for a shorter route than that over Harper Pass. Arthur and his younger brother, Edward Junior, clambered up the Bealey Gorge and next day, on March 13, 1864, descended a short distance into the Otira Gorge. Further exploration revealed no country suitable for grazing sheep, and their conclusions were that although the new pass presented a shorter route to the west coast, a road would need to be built to get horses through. Nobody was interested in funding an expensive road at that time, but opinion changed swiftly as rumors of gold finds on the west coast drew hundreds of miners through Christchurch.

The obvious route for the miners was the trail over Harper Pass, but it was long and difficult. The Bealey–Otira route was reexamined and, virtually by default for a lack of suitable alternatives, was chosen for a road. Construction of the road over "Arthur's Pass" began immediately, with more than a thousand men engaged in the work over the winter of 1865. In spite of the terrible conditions and an especially bitter winter, the road was completed within a year and traversed by the first Cobb & Co. coach on March 15, 1866. The road was a great feat of engineering, but a financial disaster, consuming most of the provincial government's funds. The west coast could be supplied more cheaply by ships from Melbourne, and less than a single ounce of gold was carried to Canterbury via the road. The passenger coach service established by Cobb & Co. in 1866 continued unbroken for fifty-seven years, until the Otira Rail Tunnel was completed in 1923. As the railway was extended, the coaching leg became shorter, but the terrifying narrow switchback section from the summit of Arthur's Pass to the Otira River was the last to go. Drunken drivers, runaway horses, snow storms, and failed brakes added to the excitement, and once off the pass there were the added hazards of swollen rivers. Mishaps were common but, surprisingly, only one life was lost. Motorists crossing Arthur's Pass today will still find the road exciting.

In contrast to the swift completion of the road, the railway to the west coast was a saga drawn out over almost four decades. The Otira Tunnel took fifteen years to build and was a difficult project. The excessively fractured nature of the rock and constant seeping of water caused problems that were compounded by labor shortages created by the war. But once the tunnel was completed, rail excursions to Arthur's Pass became increasingly popular, particularly with the opening of a hostel in 1926 and the creation of Arthur's Pass National Park in 1929.

Canterbury's other road across the Alps, over the Lewis Pass, also followed an old greenstone trail. It was not completed until 1937, and today is the major highway between the two sides of the South Island. Like the Arthur's Pass Road, the scenery is spectacular, but the gradients are kinder and more suitable for heavy traffic.

Despite the overall impression of being a region of bleak grasslands, Canterbury has some delightful areas of beech forest and alpine uplands. These are preserved within Mt. Cook and Arthur's Pass national parks, Craigieburn and Lake Sumner forest parks, Lewis Pass Scenic Reserve, and other smaller national forests, all of which are superb for hiking, camping, and mountaineering. The multitude of lakes and rivers offer unlimited fishing opportunities and there are several ski areas, some commercial and others privately operated by clubs.

◆PLACES TO VISIT AND THINGS TO DO

AROUND CHRISTCHURCH

The first place all visitors should head for in Christchurch is the **Outdoor Recreation Information Centre,** on the corner of Worcester St. and Oxford Terrace, where information on walking tracks and outdoor activities throughout the South Island can be found. It is probably the best information center in the country. The city has many fine old buildings and statues; pamphlets on two city walks that take in points of interest are available. **Guided City Walks,** taking 2 hours, leave from the Kiosk in the Square at 10 A.M. and 2 P.M. daily. The huge

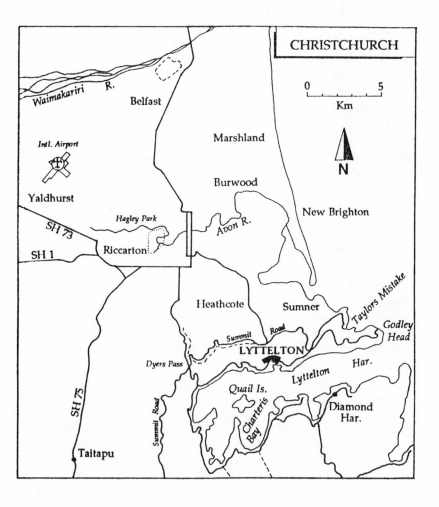

expanse of **Hagley Park** and the **Botanic Gardens,** through which the **Avon River** pursues a gentle course, are a wonderful place for strolling, picnicking, or just relaxing. Canoes can be rented from the **Antigua Boatsheds,** a short distance down stream of the gardens. For those who'd prefer to punt the Avon River in elegance and style, trips depart from the Worcester Street Bridge by the information center. Nearby is the **Canterbury Museum,** which has excellent ornithological exhibits and displays on Antarctica, Polynesia, geology, and colonial times.

Another way to see the city is by bicycle (being flat, Christchurch is a cyclist's city) and you can either rent a bike and do your own thing or go on a 2-hour guided ride with **Garden City Cycle Tours.** They depart from the Arts Center, next to the information center, at 10 A.M and 1 P.M. **Inner City Tours,** run by the City Council's transport section, have a traditional red double-deck London bus to take visitors around the city. It departs from the No. 16 bus stop in Cathedral Square, by the War Memorial, daily at noon, 3, 4, 7, and 8 P.M.

Other walks within the city are at **Horseshoe Lake,** between Marshland and New Brighton roads, at **Bottle Lake Forest** near Burwood Hospital, and at **Riccarton Bush** at Riccarton. On the northeastern outskirts of the city is the 1.5- to 2-hour **Waimairi Walkway,** reached by taking a Rangiora, Kaiapoi, or Belfast bus (numbered 1, 2, 3, or 4) to Darroch St., Belfast. The track starts down Darroch St. and passes through rural and riverbank scenery to a picnic area beside the Waimakariri River. The walk continues up the north side of the river and returns to Darroch St. and the Main North Road.

For the mechanically minded, **Ferrymead Historic Park** on Bridle Path Road, Heathcote, is worth visiting, and the **Yaldhurst Transport Museum** at School Road, Yaldhurst, has vintage cars, motorcycles, horse-drawn carriages, fire engines, farm machinery, and military equipment. Aviation buffs can see military aircraft and memorabilia at the **Air Force Museum** at Wigram.

The suburbs of **Sumner** and **New Brighton,** to the north of Banks Peninsula, have pleasant beaches for swimming. Sumner is tucked in against the lava cliffs of the peninsula and from the end of the beach a walkway climbs the cliffs to **Taylors Mistake,** with grand views north along the coast, before circling back through **Nicholson Park.** New Brighton Beach and its continuation, **North Beach,** usually have good surf, but care must be taken to swim in patrolled areas.

BANKS PENINSULA

You could probably spend an entire holiday on Banks Peninsula, exploring its bays and headlands and walking over the hills. The surrounding waters are a marine mammal sanctuary, whose principal mission is to protect the local population of Hector's dolphin, found only in New Zealand's inshore waters and the smallest marine dolphin in the world. In recent years, so many Hector's dolphins were drowned in fishing nets that there are now severe restrictions on set-netting. Measuring at most 145 cm, Hector's dolphin is easily recognized by its rounded dorsal fin and black, grey, and white markings.

One of the best ways to see the marine life is with **Canterbury Sea Tours,** operated by Anthony Tucker, 8 Nayland St., Christchurch, mobile phone (025) 325-697, or after hours, (03)3266-756. The tours take from 1 to 3.5 hours and depart from the Sumner Boat Club slipway. You can also kayak Lyttelton and Akaroa harbors and the Banks Peninsula coast. Cruises can be one or several days, or you can hire a sea kayak and do your own thing. Contact **Topsport** in Christchurch, phone (03)3891-789.

Lyttelton can be reached from Cathedral Square by No. 28G or 28H buses. Cruises on the harbor leave the launch wharf at 2:30 P.M. daily, or you can catch the harbor ferry to **Quail Island** and **Ripapa Island.** Quail Island has two walkways, the longest taking about 2 hours, taking in secluded coves and views of the harbor. Low, humped Ripapa Island has served as a prison and quarantine station and has a fortress on it, built around 1890 by convict labor to guard the harbor entrance against possible invasion by the Russians. If you want to sail in Lyttelton Harbour, contact Grant Robinson of **Peninsula Charter Yachts,** Box 82, Lyttelton, phone (03)3849-238.

Opposite Lyttelton is the small settlement of **Diamond Harbour,** reached by the No. 28G or 28H buses or by ferry. A 20-km walkway from here, taking 8 to 10 hours, leads to the summit of **Mt. Herbert,** the highest point on the peninsula, and returns through **Orton Bradley Park** to Charteris Bay. You'll need good footwear and warm clothing, as weather changes can be sudden and dramatic. Several easier tracks in Orton Bradley Park lead through bush to surrounding peaks and high points. If you'd prefer to get the views more easily, drive along the **Summit Road.** Start at **Godley Head,** where there is a farm park with walks to old gun emplacements overlooking the entrance to Lyttelton Harbour, and follow the crater rim to **Gebbies Pass.** A right turn here will bring you down to SH 75, which can be followed back to Christchurch through Tai Tapu and the suburb of Halswell, or to Akaroa. Several tours, departing from the information center, take in Lyttelton, Diamond Harbour, Quail Island, Ripapa Island, and Summit Road, and are well worth considering if you have limited time. The crater rim is also traversed by a walkway starting at the **Sign of the Takahe,** now a tea shop but originally planned as a rest house for hikers. The track climbs to the rim close to Dyers Pass Road, and from there can be followed either left or right. The full walk takes several hours, but it can be done in sections, and side tracks lead down to the outskirts of the city. A Department of Conservation pamphlet explaining the walk is available, and city transport buses run from the Square to the Sign of the Takahe.

Beyond the tiny settlement of Motukarara, SH 75 passes the eastern end of **Lake Ellesmere**, a broad, shallow body of water held back from the sea by the long **Kaitorete Spit**. The lake is well known for the number and variety of waterfowl that inhabit its marshy surrounds, and in earlier times it was a valuable source of eels and flounder for the Maori. It's worth making the short detour to **Birdlings Flat**, a wild, bleak spot at the base of the spit where a few hardy fishing families weather the storms that sweep in from Antarctica. It couldn't be more different from Akaroa. The gravel beach is notable for its gemstones. From here, the road follows the shore of Lake Forsyth to **Little River** before making a steep climb to **Hill Top**, where there is a hotel and forest reserve and the first views of Akaroa Harbour. Below is **Barrys Bay**, where a cheese factory produces a delicious range of cheeses, and the Onawe Peninsula, site of the pa sacked by Te Rauparaha. From Duvauchelle, follow the curving harbor to Akaroa.

Akaroa, with its French Riviera atmosphere and seaside cafes, historic buildings, craft galleries, hotels, French street names, and small boats, has a range of accommodation, from budget to luxury, and much to explore. On weekdays, you can get there by InterCity Bus or by the Akaroa Shuttle from the information center. Harbor cruises can be taken on the *Canterbury Cat* to see penguins, dolphins, lava cliffs, and sea caves.

From Akaroa you can walk the 4-day **Banks Peninsula Track** around the coast. The walkway is entirely on private land and a fee is charged (NZ$80 at time of writing). This includes 4 nights' accommodation and transport from Akaroa. You bring your own sleeping bag, clothing, and food, but cooking equipment is supplied and you are guaranteed a bed as only 8 people are permitted per trip. It's a popular walk, and you need to book in advance. Send inquiries to Christchurch Information Centre, or to Banks Peninsula Track, Box 50, Akaroa, or phone (03)3047-612.

A network of minor roads traverses the peninsula to other bays, and another Summit Road follows the crater rim above Akaroa Harbour, with wonderful views on either side. Along here is the track (30 mins.) through a bush reserve to Laverick Peak. **Pigeon Bay** is a beautiful spot with good swimming and boating, attractive old homesteads, and a store built in 1881. Accommodation can be found at the youth hostel, and there is also a very pleasant camping area. The **Pigeon Bay Walkway** follows a grassy vehicle track above the shoreline to near Wakaroa Point, with spectacular views of coastal cliffs across Pigeon Bay. Although mostly at an easy grade, the walk takes about 2.5 hours one way and you'll need to take windproof clothing and carry water.

Okains Bay also has a delightful informal camping ground set among pines beside a sandy beach. There are no power sites but the kitchen and laundry have electricity and are well organized. The small community at Okains Bay used to maintain a museum with excellent exhibits of Maori artifacts and colonial life and also housed a superb war canoe, but unfortunately this was all destroyed in a devastating fire early in 1991. At this stage it is not known how much will be restored. The road between Okains Bay and the small holiday settlement of **Little Akaloa** is particularly scenic. **Le Bons Bay** is another good place for camping and swimming; other attractions are horse trekking and pottery shops.

NORTH CANTERBURY

Along the Coast
Between Kaikoura and Christchurch are several beaches worth investigating. These tend to be missed by visitors as SH 1 passes several kilometers inland. From **Cheviot**, which has a beautiful domain full of old English trees on the site of the homestead of "Ready Money" Robinson, the first settler in the area, it's 8 km to **Gore Bay**, where there is some limited camping and good swimming, surfing, and fishing. A walking track from the picnic area at the south end of the beach climbs through **Gore Bay Reserve** to a high point with views along the coast. The coast road continues steeply around a headland to historic **Port Robinson**, where supplies and sheep were once ferried in and out on lighters, then heads inland to rejoin SH 1. At Port Robinson you can drive down to the beach at beautiful **Manuka Bay Scenic Reserve** where bush comes right down to the beach. From here it's a 2-hour walk along the coast to the mouth of the Hurunui River, or you can take a side road on the way back to SH 1. Just south of the Hurunui River mouth is the lovely **Napenape Scenic Reserve**, where you can camp.

At Motunau, a side road wriggles out to **Motunau Beach**, a small harbor where there is good swimming, fishing, and camping. It's a popular place in summer. South of Waipara, SH 1 swings back toward the coast, and short side roads lead down to good beaches at **Amberly, Leithfield, Waikuku, Woodend,** and **Kaiapoi.** All have good motor camps, and the beaches are excellent for surfing and fishing. The **Pegasus Bay Walkway** starts at Waikuku Beach and follows the coast all the way to Rangiora, with a mix of plantation, sand dune, swampland, and farmland scenery. Needless to say, only short sections are walked at a time.

Toward Lewis Pass
Waipara marks the junction of SH 1 and SH 7, leading to Lewis Pass. Swinging inland, then north again, SH 7 crosses low brown hills and flat plains to beyond Culverden before meeting the Waiau River. As you follow the river through the hills the scenery starts to become more interesting. Keen hikers will sense good country ahead and they won't be disappointed, for they'll find Hanmer and Lake Sumner forest parks and the Lewis Pass Scenic Reserve.

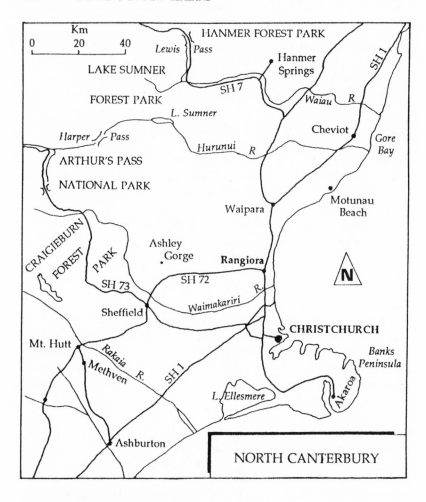

HANMER FOREST PARK

Among New Zealand's forest parks, Hanmer is an oddity in that it has privately managed exotic forests as well as native bush. The park centers around the resort town of Hanmer Springs, situated in a basin below a wall of mountains. Visitors are well catered for here by the many motels and lodges, the three motor camps, thermal swimming baths, and a variety of outdoor activities operators who offer horse trekking, rafting and jet boating on the Waiau River, mountainbiking, four-wheel-drive safaris, hiking, skiing in winter, golf, squash, and tennis. Bikes can be rented at **Rainbow Rent-a-Bike** at the Caltex garage in the center of town or from **Greenacres Motel** for use on specified tracks and forestry roads.

Maps are available from the **Department of Conservation Information Centre** on Jollies Pass Road. Bookings for rafting, jet boat trips, and four-wheel-drive safaris are made at the **Stage Post Gift Shop** or the information center at the **Hanmer Book and Gift Shop** in the town center.

Bird life is reasonably good in the park with kea, pipits, and rock wrens seen on the open tops, and bellbirds, tui, tomtits, fantails, shining and long-tailed cuckoos, South Island robins, and rifleman wrens in the forests. Many introduced birds—chaffinch, greenfinch, red poll, yellow hammer, goldfinch, blackbird, and California quail—are seen in more open areas. Rabbits, hares, possums, ferrets, stoats, red deer, and chamois—all introduced animals—are also present. The chamois are often seen around Mt. Isobel, particularly after a snowfall.

A pamphlet with a map of walks in the area is available from the Department of Conservation; they vary from short, easy strolls through the exotic forests to demanding alpine hikes. Longest is the 4- to 5-hour climb to **Mt. Isobel** behind the town. The walk commences at the Jacks Pass Road carpark and passes through stands of deciduous European and Japanese birches before reaching alpine scrub and grassland. There are panoramic views from the summit, which can be a very cold, windy place, and a good variety of alpine and subalpine plants. The return can be made by the same route or by descending steeply to join the **Waterfall Track** from the end of Mullen Road, then walking back to Jacks Pass Road via Joliffe Saddle and Pawson Road. The Waterfall Track takes about 3 hours, round trip, and entails a steady climb through mountain beech forest to the 41-m-high Dog Stream Waterfall. This also has an alternative return trail to make a round trip. The **Chatterton River Track**, an easy 2.5-hour hike starting opposite the AA Camp in Chatterton Road, follows the river upstream, then returns via the original Jacks Pass Road. Other hikes can be made along the open tops from the summit of Jacks Pass Road.

From Hanmer Springs you can drive along Jacks Pass Road to **Lake Tennyson,** set in a high tussock basin at the headwaters of the Clarence River. The setting is truly alpine and magnificent. The road continues down the Wairau Valley (Marlborough) to join SH 63 just north of Nelson Lakes National Park. Jollies Pass Road passes through Molesworth Station and follows the Awatere River north. Both roads are privately owned and suited to four-wheel-drive vehicles, but they are used increasingly by cyclists. **Trailways Safaris,** based at Hanmer Springs, are licensed to use these roads for four-wheel-drive trips.

LAKE SUMNER FOREST PARK

Lake Sumner Forest Park covers an area of moderately gentle mountain country on the eastern side of the Main Divide between Harper Pass and Lewis Pass.

It shares common boundaries with Victoria Forest Park and Lewis Pass Scenic Reserve to the west and north, and Arthur's Pass National Park to the south. Three species of beech (red, silver, and mountain), with the typical open understory, make up the majority of forest, but toward the Main Divide the vegetation becomes richer and more diverse. Burning, in early times, and grazing have modified the vegetation in some areas, and stock are still run on the valley floors, as these are not included within the park boundaries. The weather is generally drier than in other areas along the Main Divide, and summer snowfalls are usually confined to the tops. Snow remains on the ground above 1,200 m between May and October.

Road access to Lake Sumner is difficult, and the majority of trampers enter the park from the Lewis Pass Road. The most popular hike through the park is up the Hope River and over Kiwi Saddle to Lake Sumner, then up the Hurunui River to Harper Pass. The hike can be continued down the Taramakau River in Arthur's Pass National Park to SH 73 at Aickens. This takes 5 to 6 days, and it should be noted that weather is wetter and terrain more difficult on the western side of the Main Divide once the Taramakau is entered. Maps of both parks should be carried for locating tracks and huts. Public transport is available at both ends of the track. Other tracks lead up the Nina and Doubtful rivers, Deer Valley, and Rough Creek, from the Lewis Pass Road.

The Hurunui–Harper Pass route was used by the Maori to cross to the west coast to obtain greenstone, with the return usually made via the Hope or Amuri passes to the north. The same routes were used by early explorers and later, by miners, to the west coast goldfields, and runholders, moving stock across the Divide. With the decline in gold mining, the tracks fell into disrepair and were not used for decades until contract hunters moved into the area to control the increasing herds of deer.

The Hope and Hurunui valleys offer easy and pleasant tramping through open beech forest and grassy river flats, while easy spurs and side streams, although mostly untracked, give access to tussock basins on the rolling tops. Smaller side valleys also offer good tramping and camping. Huts in the Hope and Hurunui valleys are large, and tracks are easy to follow. **Hope Kiwi Lodge,** a sumptuous abode by trampers' standards, is reached in about 5 hours from the Lewis Pass Highway and makes a good base for day walks in the area. There is a further 5 hours' walking to **No. 2 Hut** and the newer **Hurunui Hut** in the Hurunui Valley, which make good bases for exploring the Lake Sumner area. Huts, numbered 1 to 5, were built on the Hurunui and Taramakau rivers in 1939 with a view to running guided tourist trips in the area, but the advent of World War II called a halt to all activities. More detailed descriptions of the tracks are printed on the reverse of the park map, and further information on the park is available from the Department of Conservation Information Office at Hanmer Springs.

The **Hope River Track** commences at Windy Point, about 6 km above the Hope Bridge where SH 7 enters the Boyle Valley. Look for the Forest Park sign by a gate on the left-hand side. Through the gate a road leads across the scrub-covered river flat to a picnic/camping area beside the Boyle River and a small shelter. A four-wheel-drive track behind the shelter leads to a swing bridge across the Boyle River and track, which climbs brushy river terraces to the bush edge and boundary of the park.

LEWIS PASS SCENIC RESERVE

Above Windy Point, near the junction of the Hope and Boyle rivers, the brown hills of the Waiau Valley are left behind and the scenery changes to dense bush and clear streams and rivers. The road follows the Boyle, then the Lewis rivers, climbing gradually to the pass where the scenery opens out to the peaks of the Spenser Mountains. Between Windy Point and the pass there are two picnic/camping areas, walking tracks suitable for half- or full-day hikes, and the 4- to 5-day St. James Walkway. The large parking and picnic area at the pass has a short nature walk.

St. James Walkway

The 66-km-long St. James Walkway begins and ends on the Lewis Pass Highway, making it an ideal round trip as far as transport is concerned. The scenery is a superb mix of beech forest, river flat, and mountain views. Five huts, each sleeping 20 people, are spaced at easy intervals, allowing the walk to be done by anyone of average fitness. As the track passes through subalpine regions, it is subject to extremes of weather, so warm and wet-weather clothing should be carried. From the parking and picnic area on the pass, the track descends to Cannibal Gorge, or Kapai-o-kai-tangata –"a good feed of human flesh." (There are various theories as to how it got this name.) It then continues upriver to Ada Pass and descends the Ada River to the Waiau Valley. A short distance down the Waiau, the route veers west up the Henry River, then south again over Anne Saddle and down the Boyle Valley to regain the highway. Vehicles are best left at the Education Department Lodge at the Boyle River end of the track or at Maruia Springs Hotel on the western side of the pass, to avoid vandalism. You can either hitch a ride to the pass from here or walk the track in the reverse direction. Many cars stop on the pass, making it easy to get a ride.

Short Walks

Nina Valley. Although the Nina Valley is within Lake Sumner Forest Park it is included here as the valley is suitable for a short walk. The track starts opposite Palmer Lodge (Deerstalkers Assn.), about 10 km below Lewis Pass, crosses the Boyle River on a swing bridge, then follows easy river terraces. After about

40 minutes, some beautiful, deep emerald pools are reached and the track descends for a while to grassy river flats. Lucretia Stream is reached in about 1.5 to 2 hours and a further 30 to 40 minutes of slightly rougher travel brings you to Nina Hut (5 bunks).

Foleys Track and Rolleston Track. These both start by the Lewis Picnic Area 3 km before the pass. Foleys track begins just north of Foleys Creek and climbs directly to the bush edge where a leading ridge is followed to the summit of Travers Peak (6 to 7 hours round trip). Rolleston Track follows part of an old pack track built in the 1860s to the carpark at the pass (1.5 hours one way).

Lookout Track. At the highest point of the road is a small parking area, easily missed if you are coming from the Canterbury side. From here a loop track climbs to a lookout with superb views over Cannibal Gorge, Gloriana Peak, the Freyberg Range, and Maruia Valley (30 to 40 minutes round trip). The energetic can continue upward to the bushline and open tops for even better views.

MID-CANTERBURY

Beyond the plains, where the foothills rise, there is more fine country for hiking, camping, and trout fishing. The best known area is probably Arthur's Pass National Park, easily reached by bus or train, but there are other less obvious places that independent travelers might enjoy. Many of these lie off SH 72, the inland north-south route along the base of the foothills.

Along SH 73 to Arthur's Pass

From Christchurch, SH 73 heads west across the plains to Sheffield, a major junction in the Canterbury highway system, with SH 72 leading northeast to Rangiora and south to Geraldine. Continuing west on SH 73, the road passes through Springfield (campground and motel accommodation here), then leaves the plains and climbs over **Porters Pass**. At 945 m, Porters Pass is higher than Arthur's Pass and in winter is often closed by snow. Nearby **Porter Heights Skifield** is a popular place for family skiing. The road descends to **Lake Lyndon**, a good place for ice skating in winter and fishing in summer, and 8 or 9 km farther on, it passes through a semicircle of hills with remarkable outcrops of limestone. Castle Hill (a station and resort), as the area is known, is a popular base for skiing at the **Broken River** and **Craigieburn** ski areas in the Craigieburn Range. The range rises ahead as a piled mass of forbidding, pink-tinged grey shingle, with fringes of dark bush struggling up from the valley floors, and is just a small part of Craigieburn Forest Park (see below). Other activities at Castle Hill are alpine horse trekking and fishing.

If you find the limestone outcrops of Castle Hill Basin fascinating, watch for the sign to **Cave Stream Scenic Reserve.** Tracks in this small reserve wander around the weird formations, and there is also a 362-m-long cave you can explore, if you have a good flashlight. Two fairly rare plants, cypress whipcord (*Hebe cupressoides*) and Brockie's harebell (*Wahlenbergia brockeie*), occur in the reserve. Only a few kilometers farther on is the entrance to Craigieburn Forest Park and roads to Broken River and Craigieburn ski areas.

The road skirts willow-fringed **Lake Pearson,** shaped like an hourglass, then tiny **Lake Grassmere,** which sit like jewels in the dun-colored landscape. Both lakes are particularly attractive fishing spots as they abound with brown and rainbow trout. Close to here at **Flock Hill Station** you'll find accommodation, horse trekking, and other outdoor activities. After rounding a prominent hill, the Waimakariri River is revealed and the mountains of Arthur's Pass National Park start to unfold before you, but not for long. The wide, shingle-bedded Waimakariri River is crossed and the road enters the narrow **Bealey Valley,** climbing gently through beech forest to Arthur's Pass township. Beyond the tiny settlement, the road narrows and twists, climbing more steeply to the open, tussock- and scrub-covered summit of Arthur's Pass and the boundary between Canterbury and Westland. Below, the narrow defile of the Otira Valley plunges steeply into dark, bush-covered depths, which in summer are ablaze with crimson rata. But that is another adventure.

Along SH 72, between Rangiora and Geraldine

From Rangiora, SH 72 heads southwest directly to Oxford, but a more interesting route is the secondary road on the northern side of the Ashley River through Loburn and Glentui. Along here are access roads to **Ashley State Forest, Mt. Thomas Forest,** and **Oxford Forest,** all of which have picnic and camping areas and walking tracks. Ashley Forest, centering on Mt. Grey, lies to the northeast of Loburn. Pamphlets showing tracks and access roads are available for Mt. Thomas and Oxford forests, which are both administered by the Department of Conservation. At **Ashley Gorge** there is a beautiful campground set in native bush beside the Ashley River. A number of walking tracks through the forest start here, or you can trek into the hills on horseback.

From Oxford, the highway sweeps south across the flat plains to Sheffield, only faltering to dip and cross the Waimakariri River at the narrow **Waimakariri Gorge,** where the broad shingle bed is suddenly constricted by narrow rock walls. This is a good place to try for trout.

South of Sheffield the road continues across the plains at the base of the foothills, passes through the old coal mining towns of Coalgate and Glentunnel, then descends steeply to the **Rakaia Gorge.** From a parking area at the north side of the bridge, a walkway leads 5 km upriver, giving magnificent views into the gorge. The return walk takes 3 to 4 hours, but this can be shortened by taking a jet boat ride one way. The jet boats are locally operated and leave from below the carpark. Across the bridge on the south bank is a camping and picnic area popular with people who come to fish.

The steep narrow road to **Mt. Hutt Skifield,** Canterbury's largest commercial area, is a few kilometers south of the Rakaia Gorge. Mt. Hutt is usually the first ski area in the country to open and often the last to close. International Ski Federation (FIS) races are held here most winters and it also hosted the World Cup races in 1990. There is a range of terrain to suit all skiers, ski rental and instruction, ski tuning and repairs, clothing and accessories shop, cafeterias, and public shelters. Further information on the ski area is available from the Methven Information Centre, the main commercial center for this district, with accommodation and all services.

Staveley and **Mt. Somers,** the next places of interest, are little more than villages but good bases if you're fishing in the region. For its size, Mt. Somers has a lot of accommodation. Behind the two towns, the peak of Mt. Somers rises steeply, forested on its lower slopes and bare and rocky at the summit. Most of Canterbury's hills and mountains are composed of sedimentary greywackes, but Mt. Somers, of more recent volcanic origin, has harder rhyolitic rock. The mountain now forms part of the **Mt. Somers Recreation and Conservation Area** and is traversed by a 2-day walkway. The scenery is a mix of beech forest, subalpine scrub, and high alpine country, with plenty of turbulent streams and grand vistas. The track starts at **Woolshed Creek,** a pretty picnic area on the south side, and finishes at **Sharplin Falls Scenic Reserve** at the end of Flynns Road, Staveley. The walk to the pretty Sharplin Falls takes about 30 minutes round trip. There are also short walks at Woolshed Creek, which is reached by taking Ashburton Gorge Road from the tiny town of Mt. Somers and turning right after about 10 km at a sign marked by two trolley wheels.

South of Mt. Somers, the main highway crosses the Rangitata River to Arundel, where the road to **Peel Forest Park** turns off. Attractive Peel Forest contains a superb remnant of podocarp and rata forest with short walks to huge, ancient trees, waterfalls, and lookouts, and longer, more strenuous hikes onto the open tops. The park's other feature is a large, fully serviced campground set among trees beside the Rangitata River. It's a popular fishing place, particularly during holiday times and at long weekends. Further information on the park and campground can be had by writing to the Department of Conservation, Peel Forest, RD 22, Geraldine.

Geraldine, a pleasant old town with plenty of trees, parks, and an unhurried country atmosphere, is set along the banks of the Waihi River. From here travelers can take SH 79 west to Fairlie and the Mt. Cook region or continue south and join SH 1 north of Temuka.

Ashburton Lakes

Hidden away in the barren, undulating back country behind Mt. Somers are the **Ashburton Lakes**, reached by Ashburton Gorge Road. **Lake Camp, Lake Clearwater**, and **Lake Heron** are good for fishing and are popular recreation spots in summer. In fine, still weather they are supremely beautiful, with the surrounding tawny hills and snowcapped peaks mirrored in their crystal clear waters. In windy, northwest conditions they can be beastly places, but such weather attracts wind-surfing enthusiasts from all over Canterbury, especially at Lake Clearwater. **Clearwater Windsurfers**, 92 Alford Forest Road, Ashburton, have learner's packages available at the lake. Motorboats are allowed on Lake Camp but not on Lake Clearwater, which is reserved for nonmotorized water sports. Lake Clearwater has an untidy conglomeration of holiday cottages and a basic camping area; you can also camp at Lake Camp. Beyond these lakes is **Potts Cutting**, where you can view the head of the Rangitata Valley, the Mesopotamia that Samuel Butler wrote of in *Erewhon*.

Lake Heron also has a basic camping area, tucked into a corner sheltered by willows, where you can watch the rare crested grebe cruise serenely through the water. In winter the Rangitata and Ashburton lakes country is ideal for ski-touring. For all outdoor activities in the area contact Terry King of **Rangitata High Country Adventures**, RD 1, Ashburton Gorge Road, Mt. Somers, phone or Fax (03)3039-727. They specialize in ski-touring, alpine camping and hiking, mountaineering, canoeing, four-wheel-drive safaris, and transport, and they also rent gear.

CRAIGIEBURN FOREST PARK

Craigieburn Forest Park covers 44,000 ha of high country between the Waimakariri and Wilberforce rivers, and includes river valleys forested with beech and high peaks. In winter the main attraction is skiing; in summer there is good tramping and walking. The alpine vegetation and bird life are added bonuses, and in January the beech forests are particularly beautiful, when the parasitic mistletoe produces masses of red or yellow blooms. New Zealand's alpine parrot, the kea, is particularly abundant here. The kea's subtle olive-green coloring splashed with brilliant orange under the wings, cheeky inquisitiveness, comical walk and cocked-head stance make it very appealing. Kea, however, are known to rip the rubber around car windows, tear holes in trampers' packs and clothing, and steal food and shiny or brightly colored objects. These raffish parrots are fully protected, so avoid feeding them and don't try driving them away by throwing stones.

Several walks, from 30 minutes to a full day, start from the visitor center, 2 km from SH 73 on a hill overlooking the forests of Broken River basin, or from **Cave Stream Picnic/Camping Area** beside SH 73. Most tracks are suitable for ordinary walking shoes, and a pamphlet describing them is available from Arthur's Pass National Park Visitor Centre. Broken River and Craigieburn ski areas are small club fields, and some walking is usually involved to get to them. Both are open to the public, but they are usually uncrowded. Rental gear is not available.

The main tramping area is to the west, with the 2- to 3-day **Cass Saddle–Lagoon Saddle** trip the most popular. As the track starts and ends at SH 73 it is an ideal round trip for anyone using public transport. Total walking time is between 12 and 15 hours, with the excellent Hamilton Hut (20 bunks) halfway. Avalanche danger on Cass Saddle in winter makes it more suitable as a summer hike. The track is well marked and is a superb hike through terrain similar to that of Arthur's Pass National Park—but with the advantage of better weather away from the Main Divide. Further information and a pamphlet describing the route are available from the Arthur's Pass National Park Visitor Centre.

ARTHUR'S PASS NATIONAL PARK

This superb alpine park lies mainly in Canterbury but spills over the Main Divide into the west coast. Covering about 100,000 ha, it includes the headwaters of the Waimakariri River and country north along the Main Divide to Harper Pass. The west's moist mixed broadleaf and podocarp forests contrast markedly with the drier beech forests, open river flats, and tussock grasslands of the east. The scenery is spectacular, and there are many interesting and challenging hikes. Most routes travel up rivers and over passes, but a few cross peaks as well. The mountains of the park offer a mix of easy scrambles for beginners and challenging climbs for experienced mountaineers. Huts are strategically placed throughout the park and some are in radio contact with Park Headquarters. It should be stressed that all long hikes require some competency in traveling through alpine country. Many routes follow river beds, and during wet weather rivers can flood. Snowfalls, avalanches, and general bad weather can also cause problems, even for experienced hikers.

Popular 2- to 3-day pass-hopping trips are the Hawdon/Edwards valleys, the Mingha/Deception valleys, and the Binser Saddle/Poulter River/Andrews Stream. The first two are easy enough in good weather; the latter is regarded as the safest, as it does not involve any river crossings. Longer 4- and 5-day alternatives crossing the Main Divide are the Waimakariri/Harman Pass/Taipo River/Carroll Hut trip and that from Aickens on SH 73 to the Lewis Pass Highway via the Taramakau/Harper Pass/Hurunui/Hope rivers (see "Lake Sumner Forest Park"). A week can easily be spent exploring the head of the Waimakariri River. A map of the park is essential, and you can buy or rent one at the park headquarters. You can also rent small portable stoves and buy rain ponchos, if you've come unprepared for the weather.

For casual visitors there are many short walks around Arthur's Pass township and climbs to some of the lesser peaks—Mt. Bealey, Avalanche Peak, Mt. Aicken, and Blimit. Most give easy access to alpine vegetation. A pamphlet with a map and descriptions of these is available. It also gives the location of good camping and picnic places. One of the nicest camping areas is at Klondyke Corner, at the junction of the Bealey and Waimakariri River; the weather tends to be drier and sunnier here than at the pass. Arthur's Pass Village has a restaurant, motel, youth hostel, and backpacker accommodation, and there is a hotel at Otira on the western side of the pass. The park's other attraction is **Temple Basin Skifield,** reached by a walking track from the summit of the pass. Facilities include two club lodges, public shelters, and four rope tows. In summer this is a superb place for alpine flowers and views of the mountains.

Much of the land within the park was set aside for national park purposes as early as 1901 at the instigation of the eminent botanist Dr. Leonard Cockayne, but little happened while the country occupied itself with the building of the railway and Otira Tunnel. Damage to the alpine flora became evident once large numbers of people started visiting on rail excursions, and this so alarmed local residents that they applied public pressure for the park to be established—and it was, in 1929. It was the third in the country, after Tongariro and Egmont national parks, and currently it is fourth largest. Little interest was shown in climbing the mountains until 1912 and 1913, when several, including Mt. Murchison, the highest peak, were scaled. A period of quiet followed, but from 1930 onwards a rush of activity saw every peak ascended by a number of routes.

The park's proximity to Christchurch makes it ideal for weekend visits. Public transport is by the daily Tranz Alpine Express train and by InterCity Bus between Christchurch and Greymouth.

SOUTH CANTERBURY

There is little to excite the adventurous along SH 1 from Temuka to Timaru, or for that matter south to Waimate and the Waitaki River. Inland from Timaru, SH 8 wends its way through Pleasant Point and Cave to **Fairlie,** where it is joined by SH 79 from Geraldine. Both Fairlie and Pleasant Point sit on the banks of the **Opihi River,** which is well known for its fishing. The lower reaches of the Opihi River, below its junction with the Tengawai, are the areas most heavily fished for brown trout, quinnat, salmon, and less frequently, rainbow trout. In the upper reaches and around Fairlie, the main catch is brown trout. The **Opihi River Walkway** on the right bank provides access along two sections

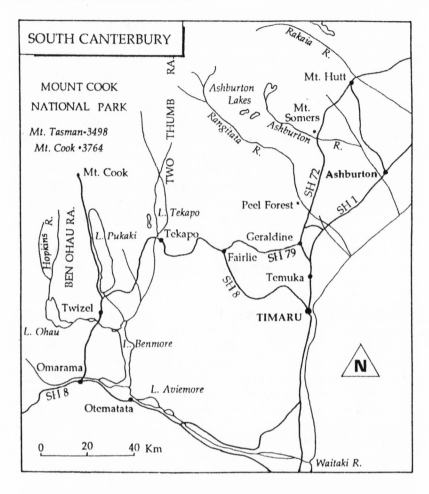

SOUTH CANTERBURY

MOUNT COOK
NATIONAL PARK

Mt. Tasman-3498
Mt. Cook •3764

Mt. Cook

TWO THUMB RA

BEN OHAU RA.

Hopkins R.

L. Pukaki

L. Tekapo

Tekapo

Twizel

L. Ohau

L. Benmore

Omarama

SH 8

Otematata

L. Aviemore

Rakaia R.

Mt. Hutt

Ashburton
Lakes

Rangitata R.

Mt.
Somers

Ashburton R.

SH 72

Ashburton

Peel Forest •

SH 1

Geraldine

Fairlie SH 79

Temuka

SH 8

TIMARU

N

Waitaki R.

0   20   40 Km

of the river, from the Fairlie campground for 3.2 km downstream, and for 12.7 km between Tengawai Road bridge at Pleasant Point, to Arowhenua, on SH 1 about 3 km south of Temuka. The lower walkway can be done in sections as several short side roads off Arowhenua Road (between SH 1 and Pleasant Point) provide access. Fairlie caters well for visitors, and has hotels, motels, a campground, and several restaurants.

From Fairlie the main highway follows the Opihi River up into the hills and over **Burke Pass** (670 m) to the huge Mackenzie basin, with its vastly different scenery. Skiers should watch for the side road to **Dobson Skifield**. Skiing here is mainly for beginners and intermediates on a T-bar, two platter lifts and one fixed-grip tow. Ski patrol, ski school, ski rental, canteen and a day shelter are provided. It's a short drive from Burke Pass to the tiny settlement of Tekapo on the shores of **Lake Tekapo,** where there is hotel, motel, and motor camp accommodation. The simple Church of the Good Shepherd, built of local stone near the lake outlet, is a memorial to pioneer runholders of the Mackenzie Country. Lying at an altitude of 707 m and fed by the waters of the Godley and Macauley rivers, Lake Tekapo stretches for 25 km beneath the slopes of the Two Thumb Range. A road around the eastern side leads to **Lilybank Safari Lodge,** at the confluence of the two rivers. Lilybank is a high country station now catering for hunters and outdoors people. The address is Box 60, Tekapo, phone (03)6806-522.

The gentle slopes of the Two Thumb Range are ideal for the cross-country and telemark skiing trips run by **Alpine Recreation Canterbury,** Box 75, Lake Tekapo, phone (03)6266-736 or Fax (03)6266-765. In winter they are based at **Tekapo Skifield,** an area serviced by one double chairlift, two platter lifts, and one rope tow on terrain ideal for beginner and intermediate skiers. More experienced skiers are catered for with heliskiing in the nearby Richmond Range. Alpine Recreation also do guided climbs in Mt. Cook National Park, crossings of the Copland Pass to Westland, and two high-country walks. One is an easy 3-day walk above Lake Tekapo, and the other is a strenuous 2-day alpine crossing of Ball Pass in Mt. Cook National Park.

Lake Pukaki, lying about 40 km south of Tekapo, is fed by the Tasman River, which drains the Tasman, Murchison, and Hooker glaciers. At its head the magnificent summit of Mt. Cook can be seen in clear weather, standing high among a dozen other snowy peaks. Highway 80 follows the western side of the lake to the Hermitage Hotel and **Mt. Cook National Park.** The main highway continues south through **Twizel,** a town built specifically to service the construction of the giant Benmore Power Scheme on the Waitaki River, and on to **Omarama** and the junction of SH 83 along the Waitaki Valley. Omarama has a range of accommodation and is ideally located for fishing the many lakes and rivers of the district. The town also claims fame as a center for gliding, using the warm northwest winds that blow over the Mackenzie Basin. Two world records have been set here. Highway 83 gives access to the shores of Lakes Benmore and Aviemore and their water-based attractions—fishing, boating, and waterskiing.

The Mackenzie Basin is the only breeding place of black stilts, once the world's rarest wading bird—its numbers were down to 32. A captive breeding program run by the Department of Conservation since 1979 has raised the population to seventy. These glossy black, red-legged birds can be viewed from a blind close to the nesting site by the Ruataniwha Outlet near Twizel by arrangement with the Department of Conservation Information Office at Twizel.

Lake Ohau, the smallest of the three Mackenzie Country lakes, is also the southernmost. It lies, almost hidden, behind the Ben Ohau Range, to the west of Omarama and Twizel. Unlike Lakes Pukaki and Tekapo, its waters are clear, and stocked with trout. High above the western side of the lake, **Ohau Skifield** nestles in an alpine basin reached by a narrow twisting road. The area has three lifts, including the longest T-bar in New Zealand, ski patrol, cafeteria, and heliskiing. Views from the slopes are breathtaking. Accommodation is available at the Lake Ohau Lodge beside the lake, or you can camp at Lake Middleton near the southern end. Access to Lake Ohau is by a side road about midway between Twizel and Omarama.

OHAU FORESTS

Centered around the **Hopkins Valley** at the head of Lake Ohau, is a superb area for tramping, climbing, hunting, fishing, camping, or relaxing. It's equal to anything you'll find further south around Queenstown, Wanaka, and Te Anau. Broad, grassy river flats give way at the valley edges to beech forests, which rise up the valley sides to about 1,000 m, where they merge into a subalpine scrub zone. Above are alpine grasslands, scree, and snowfields. Surrounding peaks rise to over 2,600 m and offer some challenging mountaineering. Within the forests there are good tracks, with footbridges at some of the more difficult river crossings, and huts for shelter, some with gas for cooking. A number of passes between side valleys of the Hopkins and the Ahuriri Valley to the south make good round trips possible. For those with mountaineering experience, passes on the Main Divide give access to the Landsborough Valley. Access is by Lake Ohau Road, around the western shore, through Lake Ohau and Huxley Gorge stations to Monument Hut and picnic area near the bush edge in the Hopkins Valley. A side road lower down the valley leads to another picnic/camping area and tracks up the north and south branches of Temple Stream. Thar, chamois, and red deer are found throughout the area. Two pamphlets describing the Ohau Forests (tracks, huts, picnic areas, tramping routes, etc.), further information, and hunting permits can be obtained from the Department of Conservation, Private Bag, Twizel.

MT. COOK NATIONAL PARK

Although Mt. Cook is primarily a mountaineer's park, it can also be enjoyed for its stunning mountain scenery and alpine vegetation. Walking tracks in the lower regions can be tackled by anyone moderately fit. The park extends along the eastern side of the Main Divide and encompasses the glaciated headwaters of the Tasman and Godley rivers and the high peaks of Tasman, Sefton, Cook, Elie de Beaumont, and many others over 3,000 m high. Mt. Cook (3,764 m) is New Zealand's highest peak, followed by graceful Mt. Tasman (3,498 m). Attempts to reach the summit of Cook began in 1882 with the efforts of the Reverend W. S. Green, from England, and his Swiss companions Emil Boss and Ulrich Kaufmann. They came close to their goal, but it was self-taught local mountaineers Jack Clarke, Tom Fyfe, and George Graham who finally reached the top on Christmas Day, 1894. The summits of Tasman and Sefton were claimed a few weeks later by Swiss guide Mattias Zurbriggen and Englishman E. A. Fitzgerald, a determined pair who made many remarkable ascents. By any standards, the ascents of Cook, Tasman, and Sefton are long climbs.

Mt. Cook National Park abuts Westland National Park along the Main Divide, and one of the most popular transalpine treks between the two is over the **Copland Pass** (2,149), a 4-day trip in good conditions. It should be stressed here that the Copland Pass is not an easy route to the west coast. Ice axes, crampons, and ropes are necessary, and the crossing should only be undertaken by experienced mountaineers. Guided crossings are available.

The park headquarters and visitor information center are located in Mt. Cook Village. From the village you can take enthralling alpine flights over the peaks and valleys and possibly land on one of the larger glaciers or snowfields to experience the silence and grandeur of mountains and the world of mountaineers. Ski-touring is a popular winter activity and, weather permitting, those with limited time can fly to the head of the Tasman Glacier and ski down as far as snow permits. Guided climbs and ski-touring trips are available (see below), and some climbing and skiing gear can also be rented. Previous experience is necessary.

Luxury accommodation is available at the Hermitage, and beds in a lower price bracket can be found at the Glencoe Lodge and Mt. Cook Chalets. The budget-minded can stay in the youth hostel or camp at White Horse Hill nearby. About 20 km before Mt. Cook Village, at Glentanner, there is another fully serviced motor camp. The present Hermitage is the third hotel to be built here. The first, merely a simple, iron-clad sod cottage built in 1884, was replaced by a large elegant structure in 1914. This was destroyed in a spectacular blaze in 1957 and was quickly replaced by the present building.

Being a high alpine area, the weather in the Mt. Cook region can vary by the hour from glorious sunshine to blizzard. Up-to-date weather forecasts are available from the park headquarters and these should be checked before setting out, even on a day walk. All huts in the park are in radio contact with the park headquarters and a regular call schedule is maintained for safety reasons.

Walks in the park vary from the 20-minute **Glencoe Walk** through forest behind the Hermitage Hotel, and the 1-hour stroll in the beech forest of **Governor's Bush,** to a full day hike up Hooker Valley to the glacier terminal. Other options are a 500-m climb to **Sealey Tarns** on the Sealey Range (2 hours one way) and a less strenuous hike to the **Red Tarns** (1.5 hours one way) for glorious views of Sefton and Mt. Cook. The **Kea Point Nature Walk** crosses tussocky river flats and dense subalpine scrub-covered ancient moraines to a viewpoint high on a lateral moraine of the Mueller Glacier. Across the glacier are the awesome ice cliffs and hanging glaciers of the southeast face of Mt. Sefton. From November to January, when alpine flowers are at their best, even the most unbotanically minded person can hardly fail to be impressed. The Mt. Cook lily, a huge white buttercup, is particularly spectacular just before Christmas. Out in the open you'll likely see the rascally kea, diminutive rock wrens, pipits, harrier hawks, and falcons.

From the Hermitage, a side road crosses the Hooker River and travels up the western side of the Tasman Valley to the Blue Lakes carpark. Short walks from here lead to lookout points and the terminal face of the glacier. All around is a desolate scene of grey moraine debris, but this is compensated for by the wild grandeur of the mountain setting.

Information on climbing in the Mt. Cook region should be sought from any of these sources:

New Zealand Alpine Club, South Canterbury Branch, Box 368, Timaru.
Alpine Recreation Canterbury, Box 75, Tekapo, phone (03)6266-736, or Fax (03)6266-765.
Alpine Guides (Mt. Cook), Box 20, Mt. Cook, phone (03)4351-834.
Peak Experience, 9 Euston St., Christchurch 4, phone (03)3482-373.

RAFTING AND JET BOATING

Jet boats were specifically designed for travel on Canterbury's braided rivers where conventional boats couldn't go, and their use has steadily expanded. Many jet boating companies operate in Canterbury, offering rides on the Waimakariri, Rakaia, and Waiau rivers. Some rides are good value, but others are expensive for the length of time spent on the river. It will pay to find out just what you are going to get for your money. The most interesting sections of all the rivers are around their gorges, where they cut through the foothills. Most jet boat operators do salmon fishing as a sideline and advertise widely through local information centers. Several Canterbury rivers are used for rafting, and most are in the grade 1 and grade 2 category. Exceptions are the Hurunui River, below Lake Sumner, at grades 1–3, and the Rangitata River at grade 5.

USEFUL ADDRESSES

Outdoor Recreation Information Centre, Box 3057, Christchurch, phone (03)3799-395.

Department of Conservation:

Canterbury Conservancy Office, Private Bag, Christchurch, phone (03)3799-758.

Hanmer Springs Visitor Centre, Box 6, Hanmer Springs, phone (03)3157-128.

Arthur's Pass National Park, Box 8, Arthur's Pass, phone (03)3189-211.

Mt. Cook National Park, Box 5, Mt. Cook, phone (03)4351-819.

Twizel Information Centre, 34 Glenbrook Crescent, Twizel, phone (03)4350-802.

19 ◆ OTAGO AND SOUTHLAND

LANDSCAPE AND CLIMATE

Otago stretches south from the Waitaki River in a contrasting mix of land forms. From a narrow, moist coastal plain the hills rise steeply to a high, arid plateau rolling inland to the great glacier-carved basins filled by Lakes Hawea, Wakatipu, Te Anau, and Manapouri. Tussock-covered hills behind Dunedin, only a few kilometers from the sea, mark the edge of an open brown landscape of high, dessicated country. The Pisa, Dunstan, Rock and Pillar, Raggedy, and Rough ranges line up across the province in endless rows of rolling hills divided by wide flat valleys. Dramatic outcrops of schist give character and wild beauty to these treeless hills, where only short grasses and small spiky shrubs survive. The geology is a legend of violent upheaval and gradual erosion. This part of the land began its genesis 250 million years ago as sludge on the ocean bottom. Intense pressures transformed the sludge to rock, which was later uplifted as a broad plateau of schist. Little happened until about 5 million years ago, when the Alpine Fault started to twitch and heave. Pressure from the west, where the land was buckling up into peaks, caused the plateau to break into a series of schist blocks with steep, dramatic scarps on the western flanks and gentle slopes to the east.

Dunedin is spread over steep hills and valleys at the base of the Otago Peninsula, but here the rocks are different. Like Banks Peninsula to the north, the Otago Peninsula has volcanic origins. It formed as a shield volcano with its center near Port Chalmers. Eruptions were in three phases, the last stage laying down the basalt that covers Swampy Summit, St. Clair Hill, and Mt. Cargill. In the 10 million years since volcanism ceased, erosion has worn away stream beds and created valleys that have been drowned by rising sea levels to form Dunedin's harbor and other inlets. The volcanic remains became an island, which has since been rejoined to the mainland by a tombolo of schist sand carried seaward by the Clutha River.

Rich rolling farmland around Milton and Balclutha, and the broad plains of Southland, give the high inland plateau a gently sloping southern edge: rivers and ample rainfall prevent the droughts that give Central Otago its characteristic dryness. The rivers are all excellent for trout fishing and are often considered the best in the South Island. Between these fertile plains and the sea, on the southeast corner of the South Island, is another area of rugged country where parallel ridges trend southeast-northwest. Known as the Catlins Coast, this superb area of forests reaching down to curving golden-sand beaches is one of the least well known of the South Island's many scenic attractions. Along this rugged, ragged coastline are reefs, rock stacks, cliffs up to 200 m high, sheltered coves, sea caves, river mouths, and tranquil estuaries where seabirds, seals, and bush birds thrive unmolested by the pressures of human population.

Stewart Island is different again, with an intensely ragged coastline and more rolling topography studded with outcrops of granite. The dense bush and wild nature of this third, almost deserted, portion of New Zealand have resisted people's attempts to tame it. A mild, damp climate nourishes the forests, providing food and shelter for numbers of bush birds, while warm ocean currents supply abundant sustenance for marine organisms, which in turn feed seals, whales, and seabirds. With little intrusion by humans, Stewart Island remains one of the last major strongholds of New Zealand wildlife.

HISTORY

Early Polynesian inhabitants knew well the rich food resources of Stewart Island and the Catlins Coast—the fish, eels, flounder, whitebait, seals, penguins, bush birds, and moa. Many ancient campsites have been discovered, and from excavations it seems that settlements at Pounawea on the Catlins Coast were first occupied in the twelfth century. The inhabitants lived on a diet of moa flesh, seal, whales, birds, and fish, butchering the carcasses with massive flake knives. By 1450, moa were becoming scarce, and by 1650 they were almost extinct. Shellfish, which were not eaten previously, became an important part of the diet; campsites were smaller; and there were fewer people in the region. By the end of the 1600s most campsites had been abandoned and were overgrown with trees. Excavation of later sites has revealed different tools, more use of greenstone, and signs of a life style more like that of the Maori, but how these changes came about is not known.

The original tribes of Otago and Southland—the Rapuwai, Waitaha, Mamoe, and Tahu—later coalesced to form Kai Tahu. A population of between one and two thousand Maori inhabiting the Otago Peninsula and coast when the first sealers and whalers arrived was drastically reduced by intertribal fighting and introduced diseases, such as measles and influenza, by the time of Dunedin's formal settlement in 1848. Otago was named after a Maori village near the end of the Otago Peninsula; the word is a corruption of *Otakou,* which commemorates Takou, a tribal ancestor. Otakou had once been a very large village, but its population in 1848 was only 110 people.

James Cook reached the southeast corner of the South Island late in February 1770, and for almost a week bad weather drove him 200 km off the coast. What he and his crew did see was an abundance of whales, seals, and penguins. They anchored off Ruapuke Island, which they named Bench Island because of its shape, at the eastern entrance to Foveaux Strait, then sailed around the bottom of Stewart Island and up the coast of Fiordland. Thirty years later, in 1804, Captain Oben Folger Smith landed a sealing gang at Port Pegasus on the south coast of Stewart Island and then explored north. Smith confirmed what Cook's officers had suspected—that a channel existed between the mainland and the southern land they had sailed around. He named it Smith's Strait, but the information was suppressed because at the time it was illegal to catch seals in that region. A full description was not supplied for another five years, when Captain John Grono sailed to Sydney with 10,000 seal skins taken from the area. Grono renamed the channel Foveaux Strait, after Major J. J. Foveaux, Governor of Sydney, who may have supplied him with the information in the first place.

Sperm whales had been hunted in these southern waters for thirty years, since the arrival of the *William and Anne* at Dusky Sound in 1792. During the 1820s the right whale became the target; its baleen or whalebone was "right" for boned corsets, used by women to obtain a desirable hourglass figure. Shore stations appeared on the south coast around 1829, and for the next fifty years the whaling industry boomed. Generally, relations between the Maori and whalers of the south coast were good, mainly through the offices of one man, James Caddell. In contrast, there had been much animosity between the Maori and the early sealers, who were notorious for their cruelty. Caddell was only 16 in 1810, when he and five others were sent ashore at South Cape on Stewart Island to look for whales. The group was attacked by Maori, and only Caddell was spared because a young girl had thrown a cloak over him and claimed his life as her privilege. She was Toki-toki, daughter of a chief. After adapting to the ways of his captors, Caddell married Toki-toki and was later tattooed and made a chief. He grew up with Tuhawaiki, who later became paramount chief of the South Island and, because of their friendship, Caddell was able to act as interpreter and intermediary in deals between the whites and the Maori.

As a boy, Tuhawaiki was known as Jacky Snapper, but through his association with the rough sailors and whalers he learned to use the colorful adjective "bloody," hence his nickname, "Bloody Jack." In spite of his nickname, Bloody Jack was a peaceful character known to be shrewd, highly intelligent, and straightforward in his dealing with the Europeans over land sales. One of the first areas sold was Preservation Inlet in Fiordland in 1829 for a whaling station. The price was 60 muskets, which Bloody Jack used to rid the South Island of the scourge of Te Rauparaha.

By 1829 Te Rauparaha had suppressed the northern half of the South Island. Determined that he should come no further south, Bloody Jack and his warriors, armed with muskets, paddled 1,000 km north to Marlborough and landed in 1833 on the south side of Cape Campbell. Here they learned that their enemy was expected to arrive soon at Lake Grassmere to hunt paradise ducks. With a handful of picked men, Bloody Jack hid in flax on the shores of the lake and waited. Te Rauparaha soon appeared, and as his boat was beached, he noticed a line of footprints that Bloody Jack had deliberately left. Outraged that a poacher should be on his private land, Te Rauparaha rushed into the flax followed by his dog and a few men. Unfortunately, the dog sensed the hidden intruders and warned Te Rauparaha, but not before Bloody Jack was able to launch an attack. Seeing he was outnumbered, Te Rauparaha fled for the beach, with Bloody Jack so close on his heels that he was able to grab Te Rauparaha's cloak. Like a slippery eel, Te Rauparaha managed to wriggle out of the cloak and made for one of his waiting canoes, which was then paddled swiftly away.

Undeterred, Bloody Jack pursued the fleeing Te Rauparaha and administered a crushing defeat at Port Underwood in the Marlborough Sounds. Te Rauparaha again escaped unharmed to his stronghold on Kapiti Island, never to return to the South Island. To avenge this insult, he sent one of his generals, Te Puoho, down the west coast to attack Bloody Jack on his rear guard. In an amazing outflanking movement, Te Puoho and his men battled down the west coast and through the Haast Pass, annihilating the occupants of all small villages along the way lest they warn Bloody Jack. By 1837 they had traveled down the Mataura River and taken the village at Tuturau. Here they rested, sated with victory and human flesh. Unbeknown to Te Puoho, a few Kai Tahu had escaped to tell Bloody Jack, who immediately assembled every warrior and advanced up the Mataura Valley to Tuturau, arriving at night. The following dawn, Bloody Jack stalked Te Puoho and shot him as he sat outside his hut. In contrast to the tactics of Te Rauparaha and his henchmen, Te Puoho's followers were spared, but Te Puoho's head was stuck on a pole and his body rolled in a mat and burned in his hut.

Even before the Treaty of Waitangi was signed in 1840, Bloody Jack had sold off large blocks of land, including Milford Sound, Bluff Harbour, and a large piece of the south coast. When the Treaty eventually reached the South

Island it was Bloody Jack who signed on behalf of all the South Island peoples. One of the oldest towns in the South Island was Bluff, founded in 1824 when James Spencer landed there to establish a supply depot for whaling ships, which were coming in increasing numbers. A house and gardens were built, and later a fishing station, which employed twenty-one men. News of a great catch of whales off the mouth of the Mataura River brought whaling ships from Great Britain, France, and America, and among them was whaler Johnny Jones, who later became the most famous whaling magnate in New Zealand. Jones arrived in 1835 and decided that this was where his fortune was to be made. After purchasing large tracts of land from Bloody Jack, he had whaling stations set up at Bluff, Riverton, and as far north as Waikouaiti, where he settled. The one at Bluff was established by William Stirling in 1836. Riverton was at first called Jacobs River Station, and soon became a pleasant village with whitewashed huts and enclosures of corn and potatoes. The pleasant atmosphere is still retained today in this town of neat cottages and stately houses along the estuary of the Jacobs River, where fishing boats tie up at the wharves.

Exploration inland didn't take place until 1850, when W. J. Hamilton, a surveyor with the New Zealand Company, and Captain John Lord Stokes, master of *HMS Acheron*, which was doing a coastal survey of New Zealand in 1850, traveled overland from Bluff to Riverton and Otautau. After returning to the Oreti River estuary, they headed northeast over the Waihopai Plains to the Mataura River, which they crossed, then made their way to Dunedin. They were pleased with the land they had seen, described by Stokes as the "prairie land of the Middle (South) Island," as it looked suitable for farming and settlement. Stokes ascertained that the Maori were willing to sell "Murihiku," the whole southern region of the South Island except Stewart Island and Ruapuke Island, and consequently W. B. Mantell was appointed to negotiate the purchase. Over the next three months, Mantell traveled by foot and by boat, making an exhaustive survey, laying out native reserves, and carrying out a census of the population. The purchase of Murihiku was finalized in 1853 for the paltry sum of £2,600. Mantell is better known as the man who first reported the rare, new bird species *Notornis mantelli*. The Maori had long known of its existence near Lake Te Anau and called it takahe, but it was not seen again until rediscovered in 1948.

Invercargill's first settler, an Irish whaler named John Kelly, arrived from Bluff in 1856 and set up house on the estuary of the Oreti River. Kelly was soon followed by other settlers, and the town's population swelled slowly but steadily as graziers moved inland across the plains. News of gold in Central Otago brought many new arrivals to augment the ranks for a short time, and being the closest access port to the goldfields around Wakatipu, also increased Invercargill's importance as a supply town for meat and other food and for working bullocks. After 1864 Bluff became the principal port for the district, but Invercargill remained the main center for the steadily growing farming community.

New Edinburgh (Dunedin) was a settlement planned as a joint venture between the New Zealand Company and the Free Church of Scotland, with the first 344 settlers arriving on the *John Wickliffe* and *Philip Laing* in March and April 1848. By the following year's end, another 700 had arrived, many of them Scottish. About two thirds of the population were Presbyterian, but this was soon to change, and within two years the Scots were a minority. Such was the fervor of the first Scottish settlers, however, that they stamped their character on the new settlement by naming it Dunedin, a Gaelic form of Edinburgh, and copying many of the old city's street names. Development of the new town was slow, as the site was hilly and steep, and as the population grew it became divided over the issue of whether squatters were suitable citizens. Some saw them as being undesirable because of their lack of affinity to the church; others agreed with the squatters, who saw good grazing for sheep, and felt that the future lay with the pioneering runholders. In the end the squatters won out and the burgeoning woolly empires were legalized.

For a few years the farmers had the place to themselves; then came news that was to change the face of Otago. Thomas Gabriel Read, a veteran of the California goldfields, had discovered a rich deposit of gold in the hills behind Lawrence and almost overnight, Gabriel's Gully, as it became known, was flooded with miners. Read made his find public in a letter to the *Otago Witness* in July 1861, and for this he was later rewarded by the provincial government. He continued prospecting for them for a few years, then returned to Hobart and died in 1894, a pauper in an old men's home. Gold production at Gabriel's Gully boomed and peaked at 5,660 kg in 1862, but within four years it had slumped to a tenth that amount. It continued to decline until the late 1930s, when it finally ceased.

A year after Read's discovery, American Horatio Hartley and Irishman Christopher Reilley dumped the equivalent of 40 kg of gold on the counter of Dunedin's gold receiver and started a new rush. The gold had been found in the Dunstan district, now Clyde, Cromwell, and Alexandra. The first prospectors to follow Hartley and Reilley faced terrible hardships getting to the new site and were dismayed and angry when they saw the Clutha River. At normal flow it is a big, mean river, but in full flood, as they saw it, it looked like an impossible place for gold. Besides, they were used to digging for gold. Under threat of being lynched, Hartley took a pan, waded into the river and filled it with gravel from the bed. The pan glinted with gold, melting the anger into astonishment. Within weeks two canvas towns had sprung up to house, feed, and entertain the 4,000 miners, and a weekly coach service from Dunedin was established.

Within six months the population of Otago more than doubled. Half the influx was single men from Victoria, Australia. By 1863 there were an estimated 24,000 people working in the goldfields, and Otago had more than one-third of New Zealand's white population. Two years later the rush was all over and the rural population had dwindled to 7,000. The first miners used only shovels and tin dishes to swill the alluvial gravels on the surface; later, more sophisticated machinery was used to extract deeper deposits. Over 8,000 km of gravity-fed water races were built, and sluices with high pressure jets replaced the diggers' spades. Explosives and giant rock-crushing batteries and stampers did the jobs of thousands of picks. The old dish and cradle were replaced by huge dredges, and by 1903 more than two hundred of these machines were carving their way through the gold-bearing gravels of Otago and Southland, causing even greater devastation of the landscape than the sluicing had done.

By the late 1860s a new rush to the west coast goldfields took the majority of miners out of Otago; the machinery was left to rust, and the old gold towns became ghost settlements. Of those who stayed, some continued mining but others put the water races to use for irrigation and founded one of Central Otago's major economic activities – orcharding. Dunedin, however, was never the same after Gabriel Read's discovery; it changed from a staid provincial capital to a bustling outpost. Businesses flourished, and by 1874 the town's population, 18,500, was larger than Auckland's 12,700. To stress the importance of education, the town's early leaders founded Otago University in 1878, the first in the country. The original slate-roofed bluestone building still stands, surrounded by many modern structures erected to keep pace with the growing number of students who today breathe an air of youthfulness into the otherwise somber city.

✦PLACES TO VISIT AND THINGS TO DO

AROUND DUNEDIN

Otago Peninsula
One of Dunedin's big attractions is its easily accessible wildlife. **Taiaroa Head** at the top of the Otago Peninsula is the only place where the **royal albatross,** the world's largest seabird, nests close to civilization. Parent birds arrive late in September to prepare for nesting in November. Incubation of the one egg takes eleven weeks, and the duty is shared by both parents. After it hatches, the chick is guarded constantly for the first 39 to 40 days by one of its parents while the other searches for food. After this it is left to fend for itself at the nest while both parents go out to collect food. At 100 days, the chick is a large ball of fluffy white down and can consume up to 2 kg of solid food at a time. At about ten months the chick is fully fledged. It wanders from the nest, testing its wings,

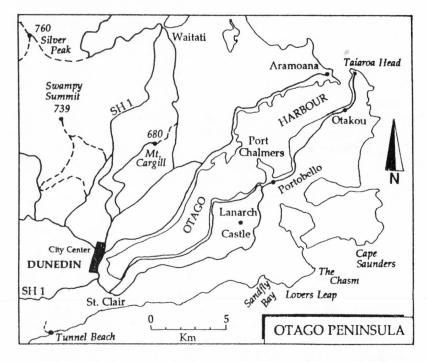

OTAGO PENINSULA

and eventually, with the aid of a strong wind, is able to fly from the cliffs. It will wander the oceans for three to six years before returning to its birthplace to seek a mate for life. The parents, having successfully raised a chick over a period of 300 days, will take a year's spell at sea before returning to breed. Public viewing of the birds is strictly controlled and bookings must be made, either through the Dunedin Visitor Centre or the **Trust Bank Royal Albatross Centre,** phone (03)478-0499.

Historic **Fort Taiaroa** with its Armstrong disappearing gun, can also be visited after seeing the albatrosses but bookings need to be made in advance and the cost is extra.

You'll need at least a day to explore the peninsula thoroughly. The **Portobello Aquarium** on the harbor side is operated by the University of Otago and is open daily from November to February inclusive, and all weekends, from noon to 4:30 P.M. It specializes in marine life of the region. On the ocean side of the peninsula are **Lover's Leap** and **The Chasm,** two spectacular fissures in the sea cliffs caused by wave action and the collapse of sea caverns. The 45- to 60-minute round trip walk starts at the end of Sandy Mount Road, a popular place at weekends for hang-gliding and remote-control model airplane flying. **Cape Saunders** is a magnificently wild, windswept spot with huge black basalt cliffs fringed with tendrils of brown kelp. Within a white picket fence on the hillside beside the lighthouse, stand the lonely gravestones of Thomas and Ellen Henaghan, who died at 1 and 2 years of age, within four months of each other in 1863 — mute testimony to the hardships of living in this inhospitable place. On a fine day, the coastal views are spell-binding and seals can be seen lolling in rock pools or basking and playing at a sheltered beach below the cliffs.

Sandfly Bay on the west side of Sandy Mount is a wildlife reserve where you may have the luck to see the rare hoiho, or **yellow-eyed penguin,** come ashore at dusk. After spending the day at sea, the hoiho scrambles from the waves and clambers up steep sand dunes to its nest. It is the world's rarest penguin, and sadly, numbers have declined steadily in the last few years to the stage where it is now a very endangered species. The short track down to Sandfly Bay starts at the end of Sealpoint Road and leads down to the beautiful pale beach backed by huge sand hills. Rock pools at the end of the beach invite exploration.

Guided tours to view the peninsula's wildlife can be arranged through the information center. All tours include some walking, and you need to bring wet-weather gear and warm clothing. Dunedin's climate is notably variable and un-predictable. Another way to view Otago Harbour and the seals and birds at Taiaroa Head is to take a harbor cruise on the *MV Monarch* or a sail on the *Southern Spirit.* Both boats depart from the Rattray St. Wharf, close to the InterCity bus terminal. **Surf Rafting Dunedin** operate from St. Clair Beach, a popular surfing venue on the south side of the peninsula. As well as providing the thrill of motorized rafting in the surf, they will take you out to White Island and explore other parts of the dramatic coast. Bookings for all boats can be made at the information center.

The northern arm of the peninsula is also worthy of exploration. **Port Chalmers** has many historic buildings, and you can continue on to **Aramoana,** a sleepy seaside village beside a huge sandbar that juts into the harbor entrance. Aramoana has achieved notoriety on a number of occasions; it once declared itself an independent state, strongly protested at being used as the site for an aluminum smelter, and more recently, in 1990, it was the scene of tragedy when a gunman went berserk and killed eleven residents. The mudflats protected by the Aramoana spit are a good place to view wading birds.

City Walks

The high tussock-covered ridge tops and areas of bush around Dunedin's perimeter are superb areas for walking, whether for the views, scientific interest, or just fresh air. Well-marked walkways leading to high points and along ridges are easily accessible by public transport. The most popular are the **Mt. Cargill, Organ Pipes,** and nearby **Grahams Bush walks,** with their bush, subalpine scrub, geological formations, and views over the Otago Peninsula and city. The Organ Pipes are a spectacular outcrop of columnar basalt on the slopes of Mt. Holmes. The **Pineapple–Flagstaff** walk climbs to rolling, tussocky hills behind the city for views over the city and peninsula and the high arid hill country to the west. The walk can be extended to **Swampy Summit** and on to the **Silver Peaks**, an area of high country to the north of the city. Take warm and weatherproof clothing on these tracks, in case of weather changes.

South of the city, the short **Tunnel Beach** walk gives views of spectacular coastal cliff formations and a beach that can only be reached by a tunnel through the cliffs. Leaflets giving details of all walks are available from the information center and the Department of Conservation, 77 Stuart St., Dunedin.

Museums and Places of Historic Interest

Fine old stone buildings, many of them dating from the last century, give Dunedin an old world character. Most famous of all is probably **Lanarch Castle** on the peninsula. More accurately a baronial hall than a castle, it was built in 1871 by William Lanarch to provide a fitting abode for his wife, the daughter of a French duke. At that time this extravagant and ornate building was the utmost in sophistication in a fledgling city. Many of the materials used in its construction were imported from Europe. The building has a checkered history and today is a tourist attraction offering accommodation ranging from budget-priced bunks to luxury rooms. **Olveston** is another grand home, this time in Jacobean style, filled with antiques and other treasures collected by its former owners. Bookings to view Olveston can be made at the information center. The **Early Settler Museum** has displays depicting Dunedin in the last century, while the **Otago Museum** specializes in New Zealand's natural history and Maori heritage.

For a trip into the past combined with scenic beauty, take a 4-hour ride on the **Taieri Gorge Excursion Train** through the rugged Taieri Gorge. The old railway has numerous tunnels and magnificent stone viaducts built by Victorian engineers. The line extended to Cromwell and played a major part in the development of Central Otago, moving thousands of tons of produce and livestock, until it was closed for economic reasons in 1990. The section of railway between Dunedin and Middlemarch has since been purchased by Dunedin City Council with funds raised by the community and has become New Zealand's longest private railway. Departure times are available from the information center.

EXPLORING THE GOLDFIELDS

Many of the old historic sites have been preserved to show a cross-section of Otago's goldmining era and are administered by the Department of Conservation

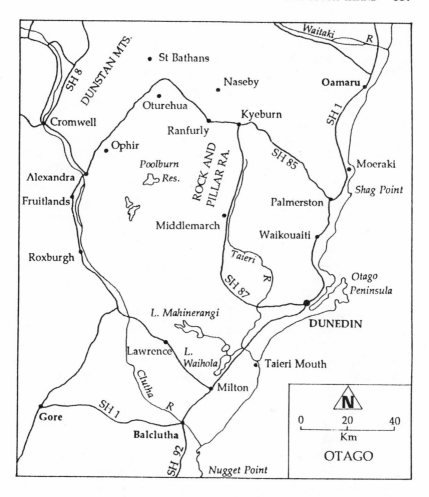

as the **Otago Goldfields Park**. Most sites are along the main highways linking Dunedin and Queenstown, and a pamphlet describing their whereabouts and history is available. Along these roads are towns born of the gold days where you will find old pubs and restaurants built of stone, nostalgia-filled museums, rebuilt mining settlements, monuments, and replica shops recreating the character of the gold days. All sites are signposted. Most of the towns offer a choice of accommodation, from campgrounds to hotels and motels, and have gasoline and food supplies. A highlight each year is the Goldfields Heritage Celebrations, held for ten days in November, centering on a horse-drawn gold coach that travels the routes taken by the miners.

Along SH 85—Palmerston to Alexandra

Once known as the Pigroot, probably as an allusion to its quality, although many pigs were found throughout the area, SH 85 through Ranfurly is today an excellent road over mostly easy country. In summer the dun-colored countryside appears drab and burned dry by the hot sun, but in autumn and winter deciduous trees flame with golden color and glitter with hoar frost. A detour off SH 85 at Kyeburn will bring you past the sluiced cliffs and heaped tailings of the **Kyeburn Diggings** to **Danseys Pass,** with its hotel built in the 1880s. Now restored to its former glory, it offers accommodation and refreshments. An alternative route is from Duntroon on SH 83 up the Waitaki Valley. **Naseby** is a friendlier place these days than when 4,000 miners lived there and worked without shelter on the exposed treeless plains. Exotic forests have softened the harsh countryside and the town is now a popular holiday village where you can explore historic sites, walk in the forest, swim or fish in lakes in summer or skate on them in winter. Hogburn Gully, where gold was struck about 1 km from the town, was never a spectacular goldfield, but it provided good rewards for those who worked hard for many years. When mining finally ended in the 1940s, Naseby's townsfolk were sustained by work on the forests.

At Idaburn there are two routes to choose from. Continuing along SH 85 you'll find the loop detour to **St. Bathans,** where you can enjoy a beer in the original Vulcan Hotel. Other old buildings still standing are the Post Office, Gold Office, and Public Hall. A 120-m-high hill once stood at St. Bathans but was carved away by miners, leaving a 69-m-deep hole, which has since filled with water and formed **Blue Lake** as testimony to their efforts.

An alternate route is through the small farming center of **Oturehua,** famous for its winter Brass Monkey Motorbike Rally. Hardy motorbike enthusiasts from all over meet on hoar-frosted farmlands to swap tales and warm themselves by blazing fires. Long woollen undies are essential. Nearby is the **Golden Progress Quartz Mine** site and the only remaining poppet head in Otago. The road continues past the **Idaburn Dam,** a popular ice-skating spot, and on down the Idaburn Valley, before crossing the Raggedy Range and descending to **Ophir** in the Manuherikia Valley. Rustic one-street Ophir was once called Blacks Diggings. All its buildings seem to incorporate the stone remains of an old miner's cottage and the Post Office, built in 1886, still opens on weekday mornings.

Alexandra

Alexandra stands at the junction of the Manuherikia and Clutha rivers in a basin ringed by mountains. It's a place of extreme temperatures—searing heat in summer and cold clear weather in winter. New Zealand's coldest temperatures have been recorded around here, and the town's average annual rainfall is only 30 cm. The first gold dredge was invented in Alexandra, starting a new boom in gold mining in the 1890s, which revived the town. At one stage 150 dredges worked the Clutha and Manuherikia rivers, clanking and rattling throughout night and day. Now only piles of tailings remain, the most recent being from the Clutha dredge, which worked the Earnscleugh flats until 1964.

Starting at the early pioneers' cemetery in Graveyard Gully, just over the Shaky Bridge across the Manuherikia River, you can follow an old bridle trail down the true left bank of the Clutha to the **Roxburgh Gorge,** where there are stone huts, mine shafts, water races, and bits of machinery scattered over hillsides covered in wild thyme. There are many other walks around the town and surrounding district that take in places of historic interest.

Alexandra's other attractions are the **Blossom Festival,** held the fourth week in September, and ice skating on the **Manorburn Dam,** daily from June to September (skates can be rented), or you can watch the locals curling, a traditional Scottish game a bit like bowls on ice. Many old roads and tracks wind among the local hills, and if you want to do some exploring, contact **Central Otago Off Road Adventures,** Box 99, Alexandra, phone (03)4489-428. The Roxburgh Gorge is a favorite with canoeists, and you can rent canoes or do day trips with **Roxburgh Gorge Canoe Adventures,** phone Alexandra (03)4486-360. Both the Clutha and Manuherikia rivers are good for fishing, as are the many irrigation reservoirs (Poolburn, Upper Fraser, and Conroys) in the district.

Only 10 km up the Clutha River from Alexandra is **Clyde,** once the center of the Dunstan goldfields and now overshadowed by the monumental Clyde Dam. Stone buildings dating back to the 1860s line the streets of this historic town, offering accommodation and fine food. Down valley from Alexandra, about 12 km along SH 8, you'll find **Fruitlands Gallery,** once a pub supplying weary travelers and now a restaurant and craft gallery. The stone building, constructed in 1866, has been restored. Close by, about 1 km up Symes Road, is **Mitchells Cottage,** a fine example of Shetlands Island stonemasons' handiwork. From Fruitlands you can take four-wheel-drive trips to the tops of the local mountains.

Lawrence and Waipori

It was close to Lawrence that Gabriel Read made his exciting discovery, but, passing through the sleepy town today it is hard to imagine that 10,000 people rushed here to find their fortune. From the town, signs indicate the way to **Gabriel's Gully** and **Blue Spur,** where New Zealand's first hydraulic elevator was used to raise gold-bearing gravels. There is little to see nowadays, although extensive water races and cuttings are still visible. Displays in the Lawrence Museum give a good idea of how the place once looked. From Lawrence a very scenic drive back to Dunedin can be made along the **Waipori–Lawrence Road,** passing **Lake Mahinerangi,** which covers the site of another boom town. There are two historic reserves here. One is the OPQ mine, site of the first underground quartz mine in Otago, and the other includes excellent examples of complex water distribution systems of races, reservoirs, and aqueducts. The road continues through the **Waipori Forest,** where there are walking tracks and picnic areas, and rejoins SH 1 near Dunedin Airport. Near Berwick watch for signs to Ducks Unlimited Sinclair Wetlands, which attracts indigenous and exotic waterfowl. Species seen here include blue ducks, New Zealand scaup, shoveler ducks, brown teal, and fernbird.

ALONG THE NORTH OTAGO COAST

South of Oamaru, SH 1 runs inland for 34 km before swinging back to the coast at Hampden, where you can join dozens of other tourists in viewing the famous **Moeraki Boulders.** Lying scattered along the beach like giant marbles, these spherical concretions up to 2 m in diameter are still in the process of weathering out from the grey siltstone cliffs where they were formed. At the southern end of the beach, the small fishing village of Moeraki huddles beneath a sheltering headland. Moeraki was one of the first places in North Otago to be settled when a whaling station was established there in 1836. From the village you can drive out to the lighthouse at **Katiki Point** for good fishing and views and a chance to see seals, penguins, and other wildlife. The pale curve of Katiki Beach sweeps southward to **Shag Point,** the site of a coal mine for 100 years until the 1960s and another place to see wildlife. Mine shafts ran out under the sea and from the point, reached by a rough road, coal seams can be seen exposed in the cliff faces. Boat tours around this exciting section of coast can be made with **Moeraki Nature Tours,** 2 RD, Palmerston, phone (03)4394-864.

An interesting alternative to SH 1 along this stretch of coast is **Horse Range Road,** which travels inland through **Trotters Gorge,** where there is a grassy picnic area surrounded by native bush and flanked by huge limestone cliffs. Horse Range Road turns right off SH 1 a few kilometers south of the Moeraki turnoff and rejoins it at Palmerston.

The main highway continues inland from Palmerston and reaches the coast again at **Waikouaiti,** site of whaler Johnny Jones's northernmost station and once Otago's principal port. Today it is a pleasant holiday village and a good place to watch for wading birds. **Karitane,** just to the south, is another beautiful seaside village, where there is good swimming, boating, and fishing. For more superb coastal views, continue around the coast from Karitane and rejoin SH 1 near Waitati.

BALCLUTHA TO INVERCARGILL
VIA THE CATLINS COAST

At Balclutha you have a choice of routes. If you are in a hurry to get to Invercargill, continue on SH 1 through Gore. If you have time, take SH 92 and explore the spectacular **Catlins Coast**. The Catlins region is made up of a number of forests interspersed with farmland in the valleys and several scenic reserves. The landscape is characterized by a parallel series of hill chains whose ends are exposed to the erosive forces of the sea, resulting in the formation of high cliffs and features such as the Nugget Point sea stacks. Between the rugged headlands are golden-sand beaches and estuarine river mouths. Rainfall along this coast is frequent and temperatures are generally cool, as it is exposed to the south, but the bonus is a forest cover that is rich in species.

The majority of forest is podocarp hardwood, with rimu and kamahi or rata at higher altitudes, and in places there are pure stands of silver beech, growing to its southerly limit. In summer, when the rata blooms, the forests are ablaze with red. The diversity of habitats and richness of the forests ensures an equally rich wildlife. Seabirds, waders, and bush birds are all well represented, as are marine mammals.

Today's forests are mere remnants of the "Great Tautuku Forest," which once covered the east coast of the South Island. Some valleys and headlands had been cleared with fire by the early Maori, but destruction accelerated once the Europeans arrived. The first were the sealers, who established a base at Molyneux in 1810, then the whalers, with stations at Waikawa, Molyneux, and Tautuku in the 1830s. A large block of land was purchased from the Maori in 1840 by Captain Edward Cattlin (note the spelling), but the first tract was not leased until 1854. The new runholder, James Brugh, soon set up a sawmilling industry in the district with a water-powered mill running at Glenomaru by 1858. By the early 1900s, thirty mills were operating, shipping timber to Dunedin and Invercargill from the Catlins and Waikawa harbours. As the easily logged timber supplies dwindled, so did the number of mills and the associated shipbuilding industry, to be replaced with dairying on the cleared areas. Most farms did not prosper, and over the following years people gradually drifted away from the area. Today there is still a small amount of sawmilling on private land and the dairying is being replaced with beef and sheep farming, but the population is sparse and scattered.

The first detour (strongly recommended) is to **Kaka Point** and **Nugget Point**. Kaka Point is a small seaside holiday village with a fine beach and pleasant motor camp set near bush at the back of the town. The road continues around the coast past Willsher Bay and Nugget Burn fishing village, then climbs steeply inland to **Roaring Bay** and the **Nugget Point Lighthouse**. From the parking

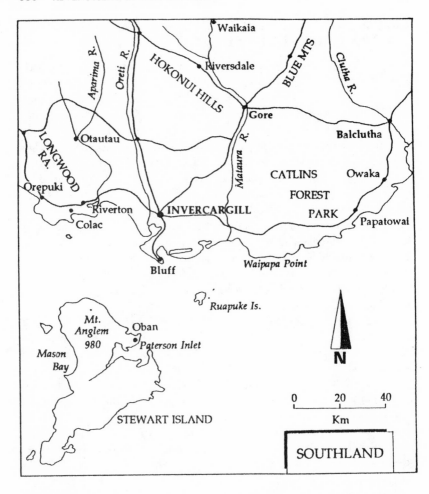

area above Roaring Bay a track leads down to a blind where you can view yellow-eyed penguins at dusk and dawn on their daily trek to and from the sea. They nest in the wind-shorn scrub and forest on the headland. The Maori name for Roaring Bay was Hakapararaoa, meaning "tall trees cut low"—a very fitting name.

A walking track leads out to the lighthouse and a viewing platform on the windswept headland. Below are sheer cliffs and a line of steep rock stacks jutting out into the ocean, each one the perch of hundreds of seals and seabirds. Species seen here include fur seals, elephant seals, Hooker's sea lions, Australasian gannets, Stewart Island and spotted shags, blue penguins, and sooty shearwaters. Nugget Point is the only area in New Zealand where fur seals, Hooker's sea lions, and elephant seals coexist and is also the only mainland site where elephant seals breed. These enormous animals are usually seen between mid-October and mid-November on the beach below the lighthouse. The vegetation at Nugget Point is an unusual mix of salt-tolerant plants and species more commonly associated with alpine regions. The Nuggets daisy (*Celmisia lindsayii*), a mountain daisy found only on the windswept Catlins cliffs, occurs alongside the forget-me-not (*Myosotis rakiura*), the native carrot (*Anisotome lyalli*), celery (*Apium prostratum*), and spinach (*Tetragonia trigyna*). On the most exposed sites are blue shore tussock (*Poa astonii*) and the succulent iceplant (*Disphyma australe*).

From Willsher Bay, Karoro Creek Road leads back to SH 92 and **Owaka** where the Department of Conservation has an **information and visitor center** for the **Catlins Forest Park**. Maps and guides to walks and places of interest along the coast south of Owaka are available here. Many of the walks in the Catlins Forest Park are short. If you drive from one to the next, you can do most of them in a day, but it is worth spending a longer time exploring the beaches and more remote spots. If you are planning to spend a few days in the area, Owaka is a good place to stock up on gasoline and food.

There are excellent campgrounds with all facilities at **Papatowai** and **Pounawea,** and several other camping areas with limited facilities are scattered throughout the park. The **Tawanui** camping area beside the **Catlins River** is a particularly pleasant spot. From here, access roads and gentle walking tracks run up the river, which is good for fishing. **Purakaunui Bay** is another gem. There are coastal and bush walks at Pounawea, Papatowai, **Tahakopa Bay,** and **Tautoko Bay.** It's worth waiting for low tide to visit the spectacular **Cathedral Caves** at the northern end of **Waipati Beach.** The two connecting caverns looming 30 m high are hung with coastal forget-me-not and small ferns. At high tide the sea crashes against the base of the cliffs and sweeps in and out of the caves, making them inaccessible. Don't miss **Lake Wilkie** either. A five-minute amble will bring you to a viewpoint over this little "bog lake" overhung with tall southern rata. At a boardwalk on the lake edge, the infilling process of the lake and forest succession are explained. When the rata trees are flowering the reflections are magnificent.

The petrified forest at **Curio Bay** is another place you can only appreciate fully at low tide. It is signposted off SH 92. Although this fossilized forest is not the world's oldest, it is one of the most extensive and least disturbed. The forests grew 180 million years ago, on the edge of the ancient supercontinent Gondwanaland. There were no birds yet, but the first land animals were appearing. The trees were subsequently destroyed by volcanic activity, and buried by sediments, which eventually hardened to rock. Only in the last few million years have these rocks been thrust to the surface and eroded by the sea to reveal the hard, silica impregnated tree stumps and logs. Fur seals, Hector's dolphins, and yellow-eyed and Fiordland crested penguins are all seen around Curio Bay.

There are sheltered campsites (with toilets and showers) tucked in among the huge flax bushes on the windswept headland that separates Curio Bay from **Porpoise Bay.** The sandy beach at Porpoise Bay is good for swimming and surfing, and dolphins will sometimes approach and swim alongside people who are floating quietly. Other sheltered camping areas nearby are at the **Waikawa Domain** and at the **Waipohatu Recreation Area** just off the Haldane–Curio Bay Road.

Waipapa Point, another magnificently wild place, is pounded relentlessly by the swells of the southern ocean. Otara Reef, lying about 1 km off the dune-backed beach, was the scene of one of the worst civilian maritime disasters in New Zealand when the SS *Tararua* ran aground in misty weather in 1881 and 132 people died. Instead of heading for the open sea, the lifeboats made for the shore, only to be smashed on the rocks. Some passengers stayed with the ship for another twenty-two hours but were drowned when it finally broke apart and the hull overturned. The bodies of 65 of the victims are buried in the sand hills in a cemetery known as **Tararua Acre.**

AROUND GORE

Southland's second largest town, Gore, sits between hills on the broad plains of the Mataura Valley. Once a bleak, treeless, and windswept place, the swamps and tussocklands have since been converted to lush farmland. Huge forests covered these plains in prehistoric times, leaving large deposits of lignite coal and gigantic stumps buried in the swamps. Charred logs found east of Gore are perhaps a legacy of the "Great Fire of Tamatea," which Maori tradition tells us swept over much of Otago and Southland many centuries ago. Gore grew, slowly at first, at the Long Ford, a place where the Mataura could be crossed safely by miners on their way to the goldfields at Waikaia, Nokomai, and Wakatipu. The town surged ahead once the rail link with Invercargill was opened and farms were put up for sale.

Gore's biggest claim to fame in the past was the illicit whiskey, or "Hokonui," produced there during the prohibition years, between 1903 and 1954. The name originated from the nearby Hokonui Hills, where moonshiners operated their stills. Incredible efforts were made to conceal the stills, and smoke from the fires was often piped several kilometers underground through the bush to conceal its source. Close to Gore, a remnant of the bush that once covered the Hokonui Hills is preserved as **Croydon Bush Scenic Reserve.** There are several access points, but the main one is **Dolamore Park,** where there are pleasant bush walks, picnic areas, and a campground administered by the Gore District Council.

North of Gore are the Blue Mountains and Waikaia Forest, two attractive areas for camping, fishing, hiking, and hunting. The **Blue Mountains** lie close to Tapanui and are a popular place for hunting fallow deer and pigs. Beech forest clothes the flanks of the hills below tussock-covered ridge tops sprinkled with tarns and alpine bogs. From the Whiskey Gully Picnic Area at Tapanui, the **Whiskey Track** climbs steeply to several spectacular waterfalls and out onto the open tops where there are panoramic views. North of Tapanui on SH 90, more good camp sites can be found at Black Gully.

 Waikaia Forest is reached by turning off SH 94 at Riversdale and traveling north to Waikaia. Continuing on the same road for another 26 km will bring you to **Piano Flat,** where a concert was once played for the gold miners. Now the grassy river terraces surrounded by beech forest make ideal camp and picnic sites. There are several short loop walks in the forest, or you can follow the **Waikaia River Track** (4.5 hours round trip). From the river track another path climbs to **Titan Rocks,** an impressive lookout on the tussocky tops (a full day, round trip). The bush here is a good place to see robins and parakeets. Other activities in the forest are fishing, hunting for red deer, orienteering, and horse trekking.

INVERCARGILL AND THE SOUTHERN COAST

Invercargill's flat, tidy squares laid out on the river plains surrounding the New River estuary are not particularly inspiring, but the city has an excellent visitor information center in Dee St. where you can get timetables and prices for get-ting to Stewart Island, and find out about other local attractions. Near the center of town is the very pleasant **Queens Park** and recently modernized **Southland Museum,** with good displays on the sub–Antarctic islands. The town's main swimming and surfing area is at **Oreti Beach,** an immense sweep of flat sand curving west to Riverton. At low tide, cars can drive safely on the hard sand. It's a popular spot for surf-casting and for netting flounder. The drive out to Oreti Beach takes you through **Otatara** and **Sandy Point Domain,** a superb recreation area with a campground; walking tracks through native bush, pine forest, and sand dunes; and a choice of estuary or surf beaches for boating, fishing, and other water sports. The estuary is notable for the number of wading and migratory birds that roost or feed within its sheltered confines. **Thomson's Bush,** a remnant of the great forests that once covered the site of Invercargill, is another pleasant place close to town, with picnic areas by the Waihopai River and ram-bles under huge, ancient trees. It's just a few kilometers north of the main post office, off Queens Drive.

 From Invercargill, SH 1 continues south for another 30 km to end at Stirling Point, **Bluff.** A signposted turnoff at Greenhills, before Bluff, points the way to **Omaui Reserve,** once the old pilot station for ships entering the New River estuary and now a pleasant coastal reserve of rock pools, sandy beach, and regener-ating bush. In spring and summer, when clematis and rata are blooming, this is a particularly beautiful drive. Directly across the entrance to Bluff Harbour is the Tiwai Point Aluminum Smelter, where bauxite, shipped from Australia, is processed using low-cost electricity from the Manapouri Power Scheme in Fiordland. Stirling Point was first a whaling station, established by William Stirling in 1836, and later the pilot station for vessels entering the harbor. From the carpark, the **Foveaux Walkway** follows the coastline for 6.6 km to Ocean Beach, ending by the freezing works. On fine days, from lookout points above the rocky, wave-swept coastline, the views include Ruapuke Island, once the stronghold of Bloody Jack, paramount chief of the South Island, Stewart Island, and the headlands of Riverton, Colac Bay, and Wakapatu. Branching off the coastal walk after about 1.5 km, the **Glory Walk** leads back up Bluff Hill through bush to a carpark at the end of Gunpit Road. The dense podocarp and hardwood forest, strung with entanglements of supplejack and harboring resident bush birds, is an absolute contrast to the coastal vegetation and scenery. Streets can be followed back to Stirling Point to make a round trip taking 1 to 1.5 hours.

Awarua Bay, an eastern extension of Bluff Harbour, is popular for windsurfing, and the adjacent Awarua wetlands are good places to see waterfowl and some unusual and varied plant communities. More information on the wetlands is available from the Department of Conservation, Invercargill.

SH 99 reaches the coast at the pleasant fishing town of Riverton. From town you can drive out to the **Riverton Rocks** and **Howells Point,** where there are good picnic areas and beaches for swimming. The coastal scenery is gentle, passing the broad arc of **Colac Bay** with its small community of craftspeople. Shops here sell pottery, woodwork, handweaving, and jewellery made by local people. The northern end of the beach is a great place for shell collecting, while the southern end has good rock pools. Continuing around the coast, side roads lead down to **Wakapatu,** and other small bays good for fishing, before reaching **Orepuki** at the eastern end of the great Te Waewae Bay. Across Te Waewae Bay, beyond the Waiau River, the hills and mountains of Fiordland rise in a dark, forbidding mass.

Inland the scenery is dominated by the distinctively rounded, bush-clad slopes of the **Longwood Range,** the southern slopes of which were mined extensively for gold by Chinese diggers who stayed on after the main gold rushes had faded. The old dams, sluice pits, and water races they constructed can still be seen; to view them, contact the McKays at Midland Farms, Colac Bay, phone (03)234-9004. There is some pleasant walking and camping in the Longwood Forest, inland from Riverton. The main area is the **Pourakino Valley,** reached by taking the road from Riverton to Otautau and turning off to Ermedale. Take Ermedale Road and turn right into Harrington Road. Along here within the beech forest there is a large, grassy picnic/camping area and a map-board with details of the **Pourakino Walkway** and other tracks. The walkway can be followed either 2.5 km upriver or 6 km downriver, through beech forest that can be scarlet with mistletoe flowers in summer. There are brown trout in the Pourakino River and access is good from the walkway.

STEWART ISLAND

On clear days, this third island of New Zealand stands out clearly across the waters of Foveaux Strait, but when strong westerly winds blow, whipping spray from the caps of waves, it becomes but a distant hazy smudge. Named after William Stewart, an officer of the *Pegasus*, which surveyed the island in 1809, Polynesian mythology tells us that *Rakiura*, the Island of the Glowing Skies, was the anchor stone of Maui's canoe (the South Island). The glowing skies are thought to refer to the Aurora Australis, the Southern Lights, occasionally seen from here. Roughly triangular in shape, Stewart Island is part of the roof of a large intrusive granite mass lying mainly beneath the sea south of the South Island. Emergent areas form part of Fiordland, Stewart Island, the Snares Islands and other sub–Antarctic rocks and islets. Millions of years ago the whole region was an almost flat land surface. Since then it has warped and tilted and much has submerged. Present-day topography is of ice-smoothed granite domes protruding above undulating bush-covered ridges and deep harbors and inlets, formed when rising sea levels flooded ancient valleys. Within the harbors are sheltered crescents of golden sand protected by rugged, rocky headlands. Surrounding seas are crystal clear and rich in marine life, influenced by a warm flow from the Australian Current, which modifies the otherwise cold southern waters.

Despite its southerly position, Stewart Island's climate is generally mild, but damp, with frequent winds blowing coolly from the southwest and more warmly from the northwestern quarter. The mild temperatures and high rainfall permit a rich forest cover dominated by kamahi, miro, thin-barked totara, and rimu, all hung with perching plants and orchids. Southern rata is common near the coasts but, surprisingly, there are no beech trees. Subcanopy trees include broadleaf, lancewood, various species of coprosma and tree ferns, and a rich assortment of ferns in damp gullies. The coastal fringe consists largely of muttonbird scrub (*Senecio reinoldii*), grass tree (*Dracophyllum longifolium*), and the coastal tree daisy (*Olearia angustifolia*).

Bird populations on Stewart Island are good and have remained relatively unaffected by changes on the mainland. There are multitudes of seabirds, and in the bush, parakeets and kaka are common. Kiwi still occur in good numbers and, unlike other areas, they can be seen here during the daytime. In remote areas, the rare kokako and kakapo still survive, but in very low numbers.

Comparatively few Maori made Stewart Island their home, but several small adjacent islands were the scenes of annual migrations by southern tribes of the South Island, who came seeking supplies of muttonbirds (grey-faced petrel, *Pterodroma macroptera*), a favorite food. Sealers and whalers settled around Paterson Inlet because of its many safe anchorages and gradually intermarried with local Maori so that by the end of the nineteenth century full-blooded Maori were outnumbered by people of mixed heritage. When not engaged in whaling activities, most settlers ran livestock or grew gardens. Almost inevitably, sawmills began operating about 1861 and continued for thirty years. With the ready supply of timber, an associated shipbuilding trade grew steadily. About the same time a fish-curing station was established at Port William and deep-sea oysters were discovered. The island also saw a minor gold rush toward the end of the 1800s, most of it associated with tin mining activities. Ironically more gold than tin was won by the miners. By 1870, Halfmoon Bay was a small but active township based on timber and fishing industries. Whaling, established in the 1820s, lasted fifty years, but gradually petered out as whale numbers fell. A renewed demand for whale products during World War I brought Norwegian whalers to Paterson Inlet in the 1920s and saw the establishment of the Rosshavet Whaling Co. From their base here they operated two factory ships and five chasers in the Ross Sea until the late 1930s. Little farming was attempted because of the terrain, climate, and rapid regeneration of the bush on cleared areas. Today the small population of part-time fishermen and retired people is centered in the island's only town, **Oban**, at Halfmoon Bay. The only other industry is tourism.

Apart from Oban and a small area around the southeastern corner, the whole of Stewart Island is administered by the Department of Conservation as **Rakiura Park**. There are many short walks around Oban and Halfmoon Bay and a network of tramping tracks traverses the northern half of the island, with huts at comfortable intervals. The southern half is an untracked wilderness. The most popular long hike is the circuit around the northern coast which takes a week to complete. A side trip can be made to the summit of **Mt. Anglem** (980 m), the highest point on the island and extra time should be allowed to include a visit to **Masons Bay** on the west coast, a huge surf beach backed by sand dunes, where kiwi can be easily seen. Huts and tracks are heavily used during summer holiday periods and there is a limit of two consecutive nights in each hut. At these times it's an advantage to have a tent and a small cooker. All huts have mattresses, but you need to be self-reliant in food and cooking equipment. You will also need good boots, warm clothing, and wet-weather gear. Two booklets on the walking tracks are available from the Department of Conservation Visitor and Information Centre, Box 3, Stewart Island. One gives information on hiking tracks and huts and the other includes short walks and general information.

Accommodation in Oban is limited and needs to be booked ahead to be guaranteed. A list and description of places to stay is available from the Department of Conservation or the Invercargill Information Centre. These vary from high-priced hotels to a backpackers' lodge. There is also a campground with rental caravans, and several residents offer reasonably priced homestay accommodation. Food is expensive on the island. **Southern Air** fly daily between Invercargill and Oban, or you can cross Foveaux Strait on the ferry from Bluff (**Stewart Island Charter Services**), which goes two or three days a week, depending on the season. The 20-minute plane flight is much more expensive than the 2-hour boat ride, but if you are prone to sea-sickness it is probably a better choice. Foveaux Strait is a notoriously rough stretch of water. Boats can be chartered from Oban for fishing, sailing, wildlife viewing, or transport to tracks, and there are also minicoach tours and cruises on Paterson Inlet.

FISHING

Otago and Southland pride themselves on having some of the best fishing waters in the South Island—both sea and trout fishing. The entire coast from Oamaru south is good, but parts of it are fairly wild and could be dangerous. Check with locals as to where the best spots are and what to watch out for. Catch limits are usually well signposted at popular spots. Among the many large rivers in Southland, the Mataura and its tributaries and the Oreti, Waiau, and Aparima rivers are reckoned to be the best, but you can try almost anywhere. Around Alexandra, try the Clutha or Manuherekia rivers. A favorite spot is the river junction just below the Clutha Bridge; others are the many irrigation reservoirs around the district—Poolburn, Upper Manorburn, Butchers, Fraser, and Conroys dams. Information centers in all towns are usually happy to put you on the right track, or you can hire a fishing guide. Both Mataura and Riverton information centers have lists of local guides and their phone numbers.

WILDLIFE TOURS

Catlins Wildlife Trackers, Fergus and Mary Sutherland, Box 2192, South Dunedin, phone (03)4552-681 (evenings). Two-day tours of the Catlins region from Dunedin, with homestay accommodation.
Wildsouth, Box 199, Mosgiel, phone (03)4897-322, Fax (03)4894-038.
Nature Quest New Zealand, Box 6314, Dunedin, phone (03)4898-444.

USEFUL ADDRESSES

Department of Conservation: Otago District Office, Box 5244, Dunedin, phone (03)4770-677; **Murihiku District Office,** Box 743, Invercargill, phone (03)2144-589; **Rakiura District Office**, Box 3, Stewart Island, phone (03)2191-130.

Visitor and Information Centers: Dunedin Visitor Centre, 48 The Octagon, Box 5457, Dunedin, phone (03)4743-300; Southland Promotions, 82 Dee St., Box 705, Invercargill, phone (03)2186-091; Alexandra and Districts Information Office, Tarbet St., Box 56, Alexandra, phone (03)4489-515.

20 ✦ FIORDLAND AND THE SOUTHERN LAKES

LANDSCAPE AND CLIMATE

Fiordland and Mt. Aspiring national parks, and Lakes Wakatipu, Wanaka, and Hawea are part of Otago and Southland provinces, but they are dealt with separately here as they form such a distinct region, both geographically and from a visitor's point of view. Scenically, this is one of the most spectacular parts of the South Island, or even New Zealand, and it is well publicized overseas. Consequently, it is also one of the most heavily visited. For the outdoor adventurer, it's an absolute paradise. On the famous Milford Track or equally beautiful and popular Routeburn or Kepler tracks you can hike in beautiful valleys and cross alpine passes surrounded by snowy mountains. Those not into strenuous hiking can fish in gin-clear streams, rivers, and lakes, camp on grassy river flats, explore old gold towns, jet boat and raft some exciting rivers, bungee jump, ride helicopters, horse trek, ski in winter, or just enjoy the magnificent vistas of lakes, bush, mountains, deep glaciated valleys, and plunging waterfalls.

Part of the magic of this southwestern corner is its contrasting landforms and climates. The eastern edge, around the townships of Wanaka, Queenstown, Cromwell, and even Te Anau, tends to be dry—a golden landscape of high rocky ranges whose sides have been smoothed by the passage of great glaciers that carved the deep basins now filled by lakes. As rainfall increases toward the west, so does the vegetation, from open beech forests to the dense entangled bush of Fiordland, with its thick ground cover of spongy mosses and ferns, perfectly designed to soak up downpourings of rain. A look at rainfall figures for the region tells a compelling story. Milford Sound, an exceptionally wet place by any standards, receives about 7,200 mm of rain annually, yet at Cromwell, just over 100 km directly east, only about 300 mm fall. Even at Lake Te Anau there are marked differences. Te Anau township on the eastern edge of the lake receives about 1,100 mm, while the western shoreline is drenched with 1,700 mm. When a light drizzle falls at Queenstown there is often heavy rain at the head of Lake Wakatipu.

Mythology tells us that the southern lakes were dug by the great *ko*, or digging stick, of that early explorer, Rakaihaitu, who arrived on the Uruao canoe. Rubble from his excavations created the mountains. Wakatipu, a contraction of Whakatipua, meaning "the trough of the demon," attained its shape differently. The demon was Matau, a bad fellow who was compelled to sleep when the west wind blew. One day Matau captured a chief's daughter. Her father gave chase and eventually caught up with Matau when the west wind rose and he was forced to sleep before he could reach his lair. A huge fire was lit next to the sleeping Matau and as the flames reached higher, fed by his body fat, the demon drew his knees up in pain and his body sank deeper and deeper into the melting earth, creating the deep trough in the shape of a bent figure. Only his heart was left unburnt and this continues to beat, causing the lake to rise and fall rhythmically.

It was the Maori god Tu-te-Rakiwhanoa who created the fiords of the south. Appalled by the impenetrable wall of rock facing him, he decided to breach the mountains and let the sea run in. Starting from the south he began to chop with such vigor and enthusiasm that his exertions caused the land on which he stood to separate from the mainland, thus forming Secretary and Resolution islands. His first efforts were clumsy, leaving many chips, which became islands, but as he proceeded northward his work improved until by Milford he could make a straight, clean-sided cut. In all the fiords, Tu-te-Rakiwhanoa provided a pass to the interior, but at Milford he was called away before he could do the job. A minor god, Ruru, took over, but being inexperienced he cut too steep a wall at the base of the Homer Saddle. Realizing his mistake, Ruru turned to the Mackinnon Pass and this time started at the top, with the result that the debris fell down to widen the base. His labors completed, Tu-te-Rakiwhanoa then rested at Milford, where he was visited by the goddess of Death. She brought not death but a worse fate, for she liberated mosquitoes, sandflies, and fleas with instructions to multiply and spread.

HISTORY

The Southland Maori visited Fiordland in summer to obtain the prized greenstone, and fur seals and seabirds, whose flesh was preserved in fat inside bags made from blades of bull kelp. These were laboriously carried over the Mackinnon Pass or up the Hollyford Valley, then transported by canoe across Lake Te Anau, and finally floated down the Waiau River on rafts made from bundles of dried flax stalks. At times moa were hunted around the inland lakes; when they disappeared, smaller birds such as takahe, kakapo, kiwi, weka, pigeon, and kaka were taken. The surplus flesh was preserved and the feathers used for decoration. During these visits, the travelers used caves or overhanging rocks for shelter, or constructed small conical huts of sticks covered with foliage.

Otago Maori used the Haast Pass as a route to the west coast to obtain greenstone, and there were small villages at Hawea and Wanaka in 1836 when Te Puoho, Te Rauparaha's offsider, brought his war party through to take revenge on Southland's Bloody Jack. Most of the inhabitants were killed and eaten, but one small boy escaped to warn relatives living by the outlet of Lake Hawea. While most fled over the Lindis Pass to the east coast, a few remained and attempted unsuccessfully to ambush Te Puoho, who continued on to Tuturau, where he was eventually killed by Bloody Jack.

The coast of Fiordland was noted by Cook on his first visit to New Zealand in 1770, but he did not make landfall there until three years later, when he returned from Antarctic waters. This time the sheltered waters of Dusky Sound made a welcome haven for the crew, who had been 123 days at sea. Five weeks were spent repairing the ship, replenishing water and food supplies, exploring, and recording the flora and fauna. One of Cook's midshipmen, George Vancouver, returned to Dusky Sound in 1791 in command of the *Chatham* and *Discovery* and stayed three weeks, completing Cook's mapping of the fiord. The next visitor was the *Britannia* in 1792, which left William Leith and a gang of eleven sealers in Dusky Sound. During their ten-month stay before being picked up, Leith's men collected 4,500 seal skins, constructed a sizeable house, and almost completed a 16-m boat. Two years later, one of the gang returned to Dusky Sound aboard another *Endeavour*, which, soon after leaving Sydney, was found to be leaking badly and to have 46 stowaways on board. On reaching Dusky Sound, the *Endeavour* was pronounced unseaworthy and was already partially stripped when a storm drove her onto rocks. A companion vessel, *Fancy*, had insufficient room for the 244 castaways, so work began on the completion of Leith's vessel and the conversion of a lifeboat for a sea voyage. After 5 months, the new vessel, *Providence*, finally set sail for Norfolk Island accompanied by the *Fancy*. The longboat followed later, leaving behind 35 men who remained marooned another 12 months before they were rescued in 1797.

Interest in sealing around the New Zealand coast increased during the early 1800s after Australian sealers had almost wiped out the Bass Strait seal colonies. Camps were set up around the Fiordland coast and southern islands and the slaughter was so great (one vessel returned with a cargo of 60,000 skins) that the seal stocks were almost depleted by the 1820s. Attention then turned to the whales, which had been seen in great numbers, and in 1829 land in

Preservation Inlet was sold to Peter Williams, who set up a substantial whaling station. The sixty muskets received by the Southland Maori for this land were used to defeat the invading Te Rauparaha. With the inevitable decline in the whaling industry, the station at Preservation Inlet was deserted by 1838 and, except for surveys by Captain Stokes of *HMS Acheron* in 1851, there was little further activity on Fiordland's coast for the next twenty years.

Coal was the next resource to attract attention, but attempts to recover it during the 1860s were unsuccessful. Payable gold was found on Coal Island in Preservation Inlet in the late 1880s, and over the next few years there were miniature rushes as new alluvial finds were made. Mining was extremely difficult in this precipitous and densely forested country, where high rainfall regularly flooded streams and creeks, destroying days of patient work. The site was also extremely isolated but this did not deter the hopeful. Before long, Cromarty, originally set up as a fishing village for Scottish immigrants, became a busy mining town, and at the Wilson River, east of Puysegur Point, Te Oneroa mushroomed with boarding houses, shops, a hotel, and private dwellings. By 1894, a railway had been completed between Cromarty and the Wilson River, and a 5-headed stamper was installed, which worked night and day. Another 5-headed battery was installed later, and although a total of over 347 kg of gold were recovered, all was abandoned by the turn of the century to be overwhelmed by the bush, silence, and isolation once more.

The same year that the *HMS Acheron* made its survey, C. J. Nairn and W. H. Stephen left Riverton on the Southland coast to explore inland. A week after setting out, they caught their first glimpse of Lake Te Anau from the slopes of the Takitimu Mountains, and a few days later they reached the shores of Lakes Manapouri and Te Anau. Within a few years sheep runs had been set up at both lakes. Further exploration was made in 1852, when Nathaniel Chalmers, guided by Reko, an old Maori from Tuturau, made a desperate journey inland in search of more grazing land. They saw Lake Wakatipu from the slopes of the Remarkable Range and crossed the Kawarau River by a natural stone arch, since collapsed. The travel was extremely tough, through dense matagouri and spaniard scrub, which ripped Chalmers' clothes to shreds. He was wearing sandals made of flax and cabbage tree leaves and as well was suffering from dysentery. By the time they reached Lakes Wanaka and Hawea, the exhausted Chalmers could not go on, so they returned down the Clutha and Kawarau rivers on a raft made of flax, a terrifying ride in the fearsome upper gorges.

The shores of Lake Wakatipu remained unvisited until 1854 when John Chubbin, John Morrison, and Malcom Macfarlane, after battling the scrub, finally stood at the water's edge surveying the scene. A match, dropped casually by one of the group when lighting a pipe, set the matagouri scrub and grass ablaze, forcing the party to retreat into the lake with their horses and stand in cold water for three hours while the fire burnt itself out.

Further exploration inland was done in 1857 by J. T. Thomson during a marathon survey of the south, in which he covered 2,400 km, mainly on foot, and produced a remarkable map of Otago and Southland. Like Nathanial Chalmers's journey, it was desperately hard travel, living off damper—a flour and water dough cooked over an open fire—and tea and sleeping on the ground. Later the same year, Thomson headed inland up the Waitaki River in search of the pass spoken about by the guide Reko. He discovered it and named it Lindis Pass. From a high point farther west he was able to see Lakes Hawea and Wanaka and a mountain to the west standing high above the others. He named it Mt. Aspiring.

Wakatipu was visited again in 1859 by a highlander, Donald Hay, who explored the shores by flax raft in the depths of winter. The same year, William Rees and Nicholas von Tunzelmann fought their way up from Moeraki and over the Crown Range through the terrible speargrass and matagouri. After exploring the lake, the pair returned to Dunedin to claim their sheep runs—Rees on the site of the future Queenstown and von Tunzelmann on the far side. To stock the runs, sheep had to be driven 130 km from Oamaru, a three-month journey over high passes, through scrub-choked valleys and across swift rivers. By 1861, 3,000 sheep had reached the site of Queenstown and had been taken up the lake in the whaleboat *Undine*, which had been dragged all the way from Invercargill by bullock team.

William Rees's peaceful life was shattered when news of rich finds of gold in the Arrow River leaked out. Rumors had persisted for some months in 1862 that William Fox, a veteran of both the California and Victoria goldfields, was onto a good find. He was seen occasionally in Dunstan selling large quantities of gold, but always managed to give his followers the slip. One group "hunting the Fox" stumbled on gold in the Cardrona Valley, and although claims were worked there until the late 1870s, they were overshadowed when Fox's secret was finally revealed, sparking a rush larger than all the previous ones. From being a farmer, Rees was forced to become provisioner and ferryman to the thousands of diggers who flocked to Lake Wakatipu, and the station homestead became the nucleus of today's town. Shortly before the rush started, Rees had applied to purchase the land around the homestead, but this was now refused and as well, the entire pastoral lease of 450,000 ha of land was canceled. Queenstown was surveyed and in just one day of sales the government recouped the £10,000 compensation it had paid Rees. Across the lake, von Tunzelmann had little better luck; he was eventually eaten out by rabbits.

The miners were thorough in their search of the Queenstown area and made extraordinary journeys to the head of the Shotover River. The Bullendale quartz reefs were found on Mt. Aurum and there were incredible finds such as the one at Maori Point, where two Maori boys went to the rescue of a dog swept down the river. By nightfall they had collected 11.35 kg of gold from the crevices in the rocks. Although usurped for a while by the Klondike, over the years the Shotover yielded the greatest quantity of gold, earning itself the title of the richest gold-bearing river in the world.

Queenstown's fortunes have never really looked back. Described by a miner as a "town fit for a queen," its gold now comes as tourist dollars. As far back as 1888, when the Milford Track was opened, Queenstown was seen as a place to recuperate from or to prepare for the rigors of the walk. With its bracing climate and marvelous scenery it was known by the 1930s as Southland's Riviera. Those who built holiday homes then are today sitting on property worth small fortunes.

Wanaka's prosperity came not from gold but from the timber on the shores of the lake. In the bleak Dunstan goldfields, where a miner's essential tool for washing gold-bearing gravel was a wooden cradle, timber was a scarce and expensive commodity. Big waterwheel-powered sawmills sprang up in the Matukituki and Makarora valleys and timber was floated across the lake, then down the Clutha. Navigating the rafts of wood down the river was exceedingly dangerous and difficult, and if the landing place was missed, there was no choice but to shoot the rocky Cromwell Gorge.

Timber also played a role in the development of Tuatapere, near the mouth of the Waiau River. Once Hugh Erskine, the first settler to the area, had proved the value of the land for farming when cleared of bush, the sawmillers soon followed. Working their way west, they slowly cleared the forests between Orepuki and Tuatapere which, with the arrival of the railway in 1909, became a major sawmilling center. Tuatapere's fortunes remained high until very recently, when pressure from environmental groups forced the government to almost totally ban the logging of native timber. One of the largest timbermills in the country was at Port Craig, at the western end of Te Waewae Bay, where from the sea edge magnificent stands of primeval forest ran back into the hills. Much of the forest was rimu, occurring in huge stands of tall straight-boled trees, and its potential was recognized by Dan Reese of the Marlborough Timber Co. Reese took up 1,620 ha of the Waitutu forests fronting the sea and extending west to the Wairaurahiri River, flowing from Lake Hauroko. The block contained an estimated 14 million cu m of millable timber.

Initially a small mill was set up at Port Craig to provide timber for houses, stores, and huts as well as a dance hall and billiard room. Then the most up-to-date machinery was brought in from America and a wharf was built to receive coastal steamers, which carried timber to northern ports. Output climbed to

21,240 cu m of timber a month, with a record 21,778 cu m in May 1928, the largest output for any mill in New Zealand. Like so many other boomtowns in Fiordland, Port Craig was doomed, and in spite of a bright-looking future, prices for timber fell during the Depression years. Although much of the magnificent Waitutu Forest was cut, vast areas were left untouched and can be enjoyed today.

✦PLACES TO VISIT AND THINGS TO DO

FIORDLAND NATIONAL PARK

Fiordland National Park is not only the largest National Park in New Zealand but one of the largest in the world. First impressions are of narrow valleys, sheer mountains towering skyward, waterfalls, thundering rivers, lush forests cloaked in mosses and ferns, dark mysterious waterways, and an overpowering sense of human puniness. In Fiordland, nature has the upper hand and any attempts to conquer or subdue this landscape are overcome by the powerful forces of weather and water. Thanks to modern transport it is possible to enjoy this wilderness in a way the first visitors never could have imagined as they struggled through entanglements of wet bush and scrub, sat out torrential rain in meager leaking tents or draughty rock shelters, and risked life and limb crossing swift rivers. Nowadays good tracks lead up valleys and over passes, and there are comfortable huts to sleep and dry out in; helicopters and float planes can reach previously inaccessible areas, and comfortable buses cruise smoothly in a few hours to Milford Sound, reachable only by sea until the route over the Mackinnon Pass was rediscovered in 1888. But the weather still dictates whether you will reach a destination or even see anything. Torrents of rain can wash away bridges and hillsides; avalanches thundering off the sheer mountainsides often block the Milford Road in winter; at times the scenery is hidden by a thick blanket of cloud. Such is Fiordland, but then it wouldn't be the place it is if it weren't for the weather. On wet days the sight and sound of hundreds of cascading waterfalls is as awesome as the mountains and fiords in fine weather.

Most activities in Fiordland center around hiking, fishing, sightseeing, or boat trips on the lakes or fiords, but one of the more unusual activities is diving. When cruising over the calm, inky-dark waters of the fiords, it is hard to imagine that the abundance of flora and fauna above water level is almost equally matched below the surface. Surprisingly, the steep rock walls of the fiords, in places plunging more than 450 m before levelling to the flat basin floors, are a unique marine habitat.

The extremely high rainfall in fiordland causes a huge runoff. Fresh water, stained dark by tannins leached from the forest humus, flows into the fiords

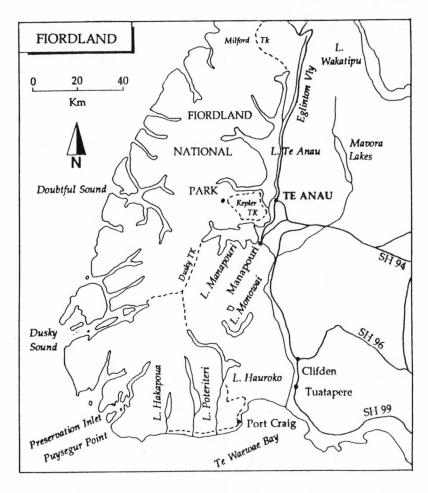

and forms a layer over the sea water. This prevents seaweeds from growing around the low-tide mark and the dark color allows insufficient light penetration to support algal growth. Below the layer of fresh water, the seawater is calm and clear and relatively warm, with an annual temperature range of 11°–15°C, the smallest range anywhere in New Zealand. Below a depth of 5 m the rock walls support extremely diverse communities of marine organisms, many of which are rare and only found in very deep waters elsewhere. Between 5 m and 15 m depth are thick encrustations of sponges, tubeworms, colonial sea squirts, soft corals, and file shells, which are fed on by a variety of sea urchins, starfish, snails, and sea slugs. Below 15 m, in perpetually gloomy but clear water, are large sponges, sea squirts, red hydro-corals, black coral, gorgonians, and brachiopods. Fish are also plentiful, and at least fifty species have been recorded in the top 45 m, including subtropical, temperate, and deep-water species.

The wide range of ecosystems within Fiordland—coastal to alpine, open river valley to lake, and dense rainforest to open beech forest—produces a good variety of habitats for birds. Little blue and Fiordland crested penguins are common on the coast and in the fiords, while river mouths attract shags, white-faced herons, and kingfishers. Oceanic birds such as albatrosses, mollyhawks, sooty shearwaters, and petrels are more likely to be seen outside the fiords. Most of the main lakes have mallards, grey ducks, and scaups, and pairs of crested grebes are occasionally seen. Flocks of paradise shelducks are common in open river valleys, but blue ducks will only be seen in fast-flowing mountain rivers. Bellbirds, grey warblers, fantails, rifleman wrens, silvereyes, brown creepers, and yellow-breasted tits are common in most bush, but yellow-heads, robins, and yellow-crowned parakeets prefer drier red beech forests. Tui, kaka, and pigeons seem to prefer mixed lowland forest, where there is more fruit and nectar. Above the bushline, the tiny rock wrens, friendly kea, and occasional pipits are about the only flying birds, but weka and South Island brown kiwi are also found in subalpine grassland. The rare, flightless takahe, or *Notornis*, is found only in the Murchison and Stuart mountains on the western side of Lake Te Anau, and efforts are still being made to save the species from extinction. The kakapo, a huge flightless parrot once so common in Fiordland that its strange booming call kept settlers awake, is now extremely rare.

The main cause for the decline of takahe and kakapo has undoubtedly been the introduction of rats, stoats, and ferrets, but deer can also be blamed as they compete for food. This is especially true for the takahe, which feeds selectively on the basal portion of the leaves of tussocks and mountain daisies. Deer were first liberated in the area in 1901 and found the vegetation much to their liking. Neither water nor mountains impeded their movement, and by 1931, deer numbers had risen so high that government shooters were employed. Because of the vast areas of difficult terrain, and problems of access, the cullers had little impact, and it was not until a commercial market for venison was established in the late 1950s that deer numbers in easily accessible areas started to decline. From the mid 1960s, helicopters were used to hunt deer, giving access to the most difficult areas and allowing carcasses to be transported easily. The peak came in 1974, when twenty-four helicopters worked out of Fiordland and 18,000 deer were shot. As deer farming was introduced, the capture of live deer replaced the shooting, and numbers are kept under fairly good control. Several methods of capturing the deer were used, all of them improvements on the first method—jumping from the helicopter onto the animal, then wrestling with it until it was tied up. The commonest method today is the net, fired over the deer at short range from a gun to completely entangle and immobilize it.

Fiordland's fame has always stemmed from the undeniable beauty of **Milford Sound** and the famous **Milford Track**, usually described as the "finest walk in the world." These, however, are only two of many attractions. Each lake has its own beauty, each walking track its vistas, changing vegetation, mountains, and wild rivers.

✳ **Lake Hauroko** breathes moodiness and mystery and with a depth of 462 m, well below sea level, is New Zealand's deepest lake. It is often considered Fiordland's finest lake, but is probably the least visited.

In spite of environmental degradation caused when its level was raised 2.5 m in 1925, **Lake Monowai** still has charm and is popular with anglers because of its abundance of rainbow trout. One of its more unusual residents is the crested grebe, which nests in floating islands of rushes and waterweeds near the shore.

Lake Manapouri, the second deepest lake at 440 m, has a complicated shoreline and numerous islands, which give its peaceful waters a mysteriousness that whispers of hidden places. Water from Manapouri is used to provide hydroelectric power for the aluminum smelter at Bluff. The giant power station is underground, and the water used is carried out to Doubtful Sound. When it became known during construction of this power project that plans included raising the lake level by 8.5 m, public support changed to anger. Mindful of the mess made at Lake Monowai, the Save Manapouri Campaign in 1970 presented the largest-ever petition to Parliament. The unsympathetic response from the National Government was enough to contribute to its defeat in the 1972 election and cause the incoming Labour Party to promise not to raise the lake level, ever. The powerhouse and **Doubtful Sound** can only be visited with organized tours.

Like Fiordland's other lakes, **Te Anau** has many moods, appearing calm and benign one day, then cold and inhospitable the next. With its four arms reaching deep into the mountains, it is deceptively large. At 352 sq km and 417 m deep, it is New Zealand's second largest lake and the largest in the South Island. On the western shore, between the south and middle fiords, are the extensive Te Ana-au Caves, whose name, which means "swirling waters," bespeaks the river that rushes through them. The caves were spoken of in Maori legend but remained undiscovered by Europeans until 1948. Today they are a major tourist attraction. The lake's name derives from theirs.

Don't expect to find solitude at such well-advertised attractions as Milford Sound and Doubtful Sound, or on the main hiking trails. If you do, you'll be disappointed. At the same time, don't be put off. They are easy to get to and are popular for the very reason that they are so spectacular. If you have your own transport, you can largely avoid the hordes of tourist buses that travel the road to Milford Sound each day and can enjoy the sights at your leisure. Another way to avoid the crowds and enjoy this spectacular park is to take a cruise with **Fiordland Cruises** c/o Post Office, Manapouri. They do 2- and 3-day cruises on Doubtful Sound, 6-day cruises around Doubtful, Dusky, and Breaksea sounds, or can be chartered for game fishing or diving in the fiords.

Basic camping and picnic areas are located at or near the ends of access roads to Lakes Hauroko and Monowai and along the Eglinton Valley. The park has more than sixty huts and over 500 km of tracks. Some huts around the shores of lakes are accessible only by boat and are popular with hunters and anglers. A fee is charged for the use of huts, and the only ones that can be booked are those on the **Milford Track.**

The park headquarters and visitor center are located at Te Anau township, on the edge of Lake Te Anau, and here you can get maps and all information on tracks in the park. Te Anau has all services and a range of accommodations and restaurants to satisfy the tourist demand. For those who want to tramp and fish, perhaps the most important shop in town is the Te Anau Sports Centre, which rents hiking clothes and equipment and also sells all other necessities for outdoor survival.

HIKING IN FIORDLAND

Around Te Anau
Although the town lacks short walks, you can always amble along the waterfront, which is pleasant, and take in **Ivan Wilson Park** and the Department of Conservation's **Wildlife Centre,** where you can see takahe, weka, kea, morepork, and other native birds. For half- or full-day walks close to town, the **Kepler Track** is the best place. From the Control Gates at the lake outlet the track can be followed in either direction. To the right, it follows the lakeshore for 5.6 km before starting to climb to Mt. Luxmore; **Dock Bay** is reached in about 30 minutes, and **Brod Bay** in another hour. Both bays have picnic and camping areas. Going left will take you along a pleasant terrace above the Waiau River. An alternative is to drive to **Rainbow Reach** (12.6 km from the park headquarters), and join the track. From here **Shallow Bay Hut** (6 bunks) on Lake Manapouri is reached in just over an hour, or you can continue another 20 minutes to **Moturau Hut.**

Around Manapouri
If you get a dinghy from the Manapouri Store and cross the Waiau River, you'll find the **Circle Track,** a 3- to 3.5-hour circuit through a variety of bush with good bird life. From high points there are excellent views of Lake Manapouri and Mt. Titiroa, a prominent peak to the south. A longer circuit (5 to 7 hours) or overnight hikes can be made via the tracks to **Hope Arm** and **Back Valley**

Huts or to **Lake Rakatu**. Another attractive walk, accessible by boat, is the **Stockyard Cove Nature Walk** near the mouth of Hope Arm.

Along the Road to Milford

From Te Anau, the road to Milford first crosses the undulating scrub-covered countryside on the east side of the lake, then passes Ten Mile Bush before reaching Te Anau Downs, the departure point for boats taking walkers to the start of the Milford Track. The road now enters the beautiful **Eglinton Valley**, with its tall, open beech forests and occasional grassy river flats giving glimpses of the Earl Mountains at the head of the valley. Toward its head, as the valley narrows, the road passes Lakes Gunn and Fergus before reaching The Divide (531 m), the lowest east-west pass in the Southern Alps. The Routeburn Track starts here and a good walk can be made on the first section to **Key Summit** (2.5 to 3 hours round trip) for superb views of Mt. Christina, the Hollyford Valley, and the adjacent Darran Mountains. A slightly longer walk can be made by continuing on to the first hut at **Lake Howden** before returning to The Divide.

From The Divide, the road descends to the Hollyford Valley and the junction of the Hollyford Valley Road. About 1 km down the valley you'll find the carpark and track to **Lake Marian,** a beautiful alpine lake surrounded by spectacular mountains. The well-graded track climbs steadily for over an hour to reach the bush edge and a grassy picnic area beside the lake. The Hollyford Road continues down valley for another 16 km to the start of the Hollyford Track, passing Murray Gunn's Camp, with its store and quaint huts. A fascinating museum of Fiordland history and memorabilia collected by Murray Gunn and his father Davy has unfortunately been destroyed by fire. Murray is a rather taciturn fellow, but if you stay at his camp you may get him to open up and tell you some of the history of the area. The family ran cattle in the lower Hollyford for years.

The Milford Road continues up the Hollyford, across bouldery, scrub-covered river flats and massive avalanche fans (the road is often closed here in winter), heading toward an imposing dark wall of rock, a dead end it seems. Just before the Homer Tunnel, at the last patch of bush, a small side road on the right crosses the bouldery stream bed to the Homer Huts and the track to **Gertrude Saddle**. This is perhaps one of the best walks in the park, and in spring and summer it is an outstanding area for alpine flowers. The track follows the flat floor of the Gertrude Valley, then climbs past waterfalls and over ice-smoothed rock slabs to a tussock-covered saddle. The views of surrounding peaks and glaciers of the Darran Mountains and down toward Milford Sound are stupendous. Allow 2 hours or more to reach Gertrude Saddle.

Much of the Milford road was constructed during the Depression years of the 1930s under a government work scheme, and from The Divide, a pack track continued up the Hollyford for another 10 km. Access to Milford was over the Grave–Talbot Pass. This involved climbing to Homer Saddle and ascending a steep rock ridge, known as Talbot's Ladder, before descending the cliff face above the tunnel portal on the Milford side by wire ropes—a route used by the mail carrier for many years! The Homer Saddle was discovered in 1889 by William Homer, who, convinced a road to Milford was possible, suggested that a tunnel be put through the rock wall. His idea was at first dismissed, but later investigations showed it was feasible and work commenced in 1935. For the workers, the conditions were severe and the pay meager. Rainfall averaged 6,350 mm annually, and in winter there were heavy snowfalls and the constant threat of avalanches. The men lived in canvas tents close to the tunnel site, where no sun shone for six months of the year. Avalanches took their toll, killing a tunneller and injuring several others in 1936, and even reinforced shelters built out from the tunnel portal proved no protection. In spite of the difficulties and hardships, "hole through" was achieved by 1940. Work was then delayed by World War II and by further avalanche damage to the tunnel approaches in 1945, but in 1954 the first car was finally able to drive through.

The unlined tunnel descends at a grade of 1 in 10, and from the Cleddau portal the road drops 700 m in 9 km between the sheer rock walls of the Cleddau Canyon, running through subalpine scrub and then bush to the valley floor. It's an awe-inspiring place, and even more so when the rain pours down and the mountainsides shed curtains of water. About halfway down the Cleddau, a short walk leads to the **Chasm**, a spectacular slot through which the river roars and thunders before plunging over a lip of rock. Milford Sound is best appreciated from the water, and cruises run regularly. The 16-km-long sound, named by whaler John Grono after his birthplace, Milford Haven, in Wales, reaches its greatest depth (265 m) off Mitre Peak, which soars to 1,692 m. Across the water the Bowen Falls hurtle 165 m into the sea from towering cliffs, which are dwarfed by the sheer magnitude of the surroundings.

Milford, now a fishing port and tourist center, was first settled in 1878 by Donald Sutherland, a veteran of the goldfields and North Island campaigns against the Maori. He loved the solitude, and with his dog, John O'Groat, spent months exploring and digging for gold. It was during one of these exploratory trips up the Arthur Valley in 1880 that Sutherland and his companion John Mackay discovered first the Mackay then the Sutherland falls and most likely saw and even climbed the pass discovered later by Quintin Mackinnon. A collection of small thatched huts built by Sutherland and dubbed "City of Milford" provided accommodation for the occasional explorers, painters, and photographers who visited, and then for the first tourists over the Milford Track. Today, guided walkers stay in the Milford Hotel. Independent walkers can find budget accommodation at the Milford Lodge, a short distance along the Milford Road; book by writing to Box 10, Milford Sound, or phoning/faxing (03)2498-071.

Dozens of tour buses travel between Te Anau and Milford every day that the road is open. One company carries mountain bikes on its bus so you can cycle the downhill bits and better appreciate the gradients. Most tours include a boat trip on Milford Sound or can be combined with a scenic flight.

The Milford Track

Opened in 1889, the Milford Track has felt the passage of hundreds of feet since Quintin Mackinnon guided the first tourists over the pass that bears his name. For many years the track was controlled by the Tourist Hotel Corp., and independent walkers were not allowed on it, but this changed in 1966. Currently, over 8,000 independent and guided trampers walk the track each year. It is the only track for which you must make a booking, and numbers are limited.

The 53-km walk takes 4 days and is renowned for its magnificent scenery, particularly the 580-m-high Sutherland Falls. It is also well known for rain, and you can expect snow at any time of the year, particularly on the Mackinnon Pass. Good boots, warm clothing, and rain gear are essential. **Independent walkers** must pay a permit charge (NZ$82.70 in 1991). Transport charges are another NZ$71.00 or so. As an independent walker, you carry all your own food, clothing, and cooking equipment. Huts contain stoves, mattresses, and drying rooms. **Guided walkers** stay in different huts and take an extra day for a boat trip on Milford Sound. Food, transport from and back to Te Anau, and hot showers are provided, and you only need to carry a small daypack. The cost at time of writing was NZ$1,125.00 per person.

For bookings and further information write to the Te Anau Resort Hotel, Box 185, Te Anau, phone (03)2497-411, Fax (03)2497-947.

Kepler Track

The Kepler Track, opened in 1988, is regarded as a fairly strenuous walk requiring above average fitness and some experience, as one day's walking is above the bushline over exposed country. Since its opening, the 67 km, 4-day round trip has been very popular, particularly over the Christmas–New Year holiday period. The three 40-bunk huts, serviced with heating, gas cooking and lighting, mattresses, running water, and flush toilets, are often filled to capacity. Hut wardens are in residence from early November to late April. One reason for the track's popularity is its proximity to Te Anau and the fact that transport is not required to get to the track end. The scenery includes lake and riverside beech forest, open hillsides with alpine vegetation, and glacial valleys.

The first and last days of the walk can be shortened by using the **Kepler**

Shuttle transport to Rainbow Reach and **Sinbad Cruises'** yacht *Manuska* to return across the lake from Brod Bay. Check times at the Te Anau Motor Park or at the main wharf.

Routeburn Track

For scenery and popularity, the Routeburn Track rivals the Milford. From the Main Divide on the Milford Road the track climbs steadily along the flanks of the Humboldt Mountains, past beautiful Lake Mackenzie, to cross the range at Harris Saddle (1,277 m). Views west across the Hollyford Valley to the spectacular Darran Mountains and east of the peaks of Mt. Aspiring National Park are superb before the track descends through a picturesque alpine basin to the Routeburn Valley and the head of Lake Wakatipu. The track can be walked from either end, and 3 days are usually taken. Several side trips are possible and many people commencing the walk at the Glenorchy end return via the Greenstone or Caples Valley tracks. Transport to and from both ends of the track is supplied by InterCity, Backpacker Express, and the Magic Bus Company.

For guided walks of the Routeburn Track, write to **Routeburn Walk,** Box 568, Queenstown, phone (03)4428-200, Fax (03)4426-072, or **Te Anau Hotel,** Box 185, Te Anau, phone (03)2497-411, Fax (03)2497-947.

Hollyford Track

Less popular than the three tracks discussed above, perhaps because it does not traverse alpine country, the 60-km Hollyford Track follows the Hollyford River down to the sea at Martins Bay, where for a time in the 1860s and 1870s there was a small settlement. Views of some of Fiordland's loftier peaks more than compensate for the lack of high country walking, and there are good opportunities for fishing in Lakes Alabaster and McKerrow and at the coast. Martins Bay has a seal colony and the chances of seeing Fiordland crested penguins and dolphins are good. The lush, mixed lowland forests, lake, estuary, and coastal environments provide a diversity of habitats and bird life is correspondingly varied. Four days are usually taken to reach Martins Bay, but there are several huts along the walk so it can be more leisurely and longer with side trips. The return is usually made the same way or you can arrange to fly back by float plane. A longer and more difficult alternative for experienced hikers is to continue on to Big Bay and return to the Hollyford via the Pyke Valley. Tents are needed on this section.

Guided trips to the Hollyford Valley include jet-boating sections of the Hollyford River and Lake McKerrow, minimizing much of the walking, and fly-out options. Write to **Hollyford Tourist and Travel Co.,** Box 205, Wakatipu, Central Otago, phone (03)4423-760, Fax (03)4423-761.

Dusky Track

For seasoned and competent trampers, the Dusky Track offers a challenging experience in some of Fiordland's more remote and rugged country. The track commences at West Arm, Lake Manapouri, and follows the Spey River to its head before crossing Centre Pass and descending the Seaforth River to Supper Cove in Dusky Sound. The Department of Conservation keeps a dinghy at Supper Cove, so you have the chance to go out and catch your supper. A return can be made by the same route or you can arrange to fly out by helicopter or float plane. Many parties retrace their steps part way up the Seaforth, then cross the Pleasant Range and descend the Hauroko Burn to Lake Hauroko, making a trip of 8 days or more. Boat transport across Lake Hauroko must be prearranged but there are regular boat services across Lake Manapouri to West Arm. It should be stressed that you need to be fit to do this walk and that the track is not a well constructed path. Difficulties often involve flooded streams and rivers.

Other Walks and Hikes

All long hikes (except the Dusky Track) and short walks mentioned above are on well-constructed tracks suitable for most people. There are, however, many other tracks and routes in the park that more intrepid and experienced adventurers might enjoy. Some are suitable for long day hikes or overnight excursions, but for all of them you will need a map and advice from park staff before setting out. Tracks lead up most side streams of the Eglinton Valley, many of them from camping areas, and two are particularly interesting. The track to **Dore Pass** makes a good day trip.

A round trip up **Hut Creek** and over **U Pass**, returning via **Mistake Creek**, can be done in one day (9 to 10 hours) or as an overnight trip. Both valleys have well-marked tracks to the bush, but from there on you must find your own route.

The more masochistic might enjoy **Moraine Creek** in the Hollyford Valley, which gives access to the spectacular central Darran Mountains. The hard granite of the Darrans offers some of the finest rock climbing in New Zealand, and until Moraine Creek Hut was destroyed by an avalanche, the valley was a popular venue for climbers. Since then the track has become somewhat overgrown but is well marked. Users need to be prepared to negotiate many windfalls and thick fern, which frequently obscure the track, but the rewards are good as the views and camping in the upper valley are excellent. From the upper flats a sparsely marked and difficult-to-follow track leads up through scrub on the true left to the edge of the moraine wall above Lake Adelaide. Cairns mark a route over the huge boulders of this ancient moraine to a view point, or you can continue around the true left side to a bivy rock at the head of the lake. From the carpark near the end of the Hollyford Road, allow 3 or 4 hours to reach the first river flats, another 2 to 3 hours to the top of the moraine, and a further 2 to 3 hours to the bivy rock.

Teal Bay Hut on the shores of Lake Hauroko is reached by an arduous 9-hour hike, which can be continued over the Hump Range to Te Waewae Bay on the south coast. (See "Waitutu Forest.") Huts on the shore of Lake Monowai and in the hills to the north can be linked during a 2- to 3-day hike.

MAVORA LAKES PARK

The Mavora Lakes lie between Lake Te Anau and Lake Wakatipu near the head of the Mararoa River, in a trough carved by an Ice Age glacier. To the west are the Livingstone Mountains and to the east the Thompson Mountains, products of massive uplifting. Access to the lakes is signposted off SH 94 between Te Anau and Mossburn. The South Mavora Lake and lower end of the North Lake are surrounded by beech forest, which gives way to vast tracts of tussock and scrub in the upper reaches of the Mararoa. Pleasant camping and picnic areas at the road end by North Mavora Lake make the area popular with anglers, mountain bikers, canoeists, and trampers. There is no public transport, but **Inderland Cruises** (132 Te Anau Terrace, Te Anau) bring sightseeing groups here.

From the North Mavora Lake you can walk through to Lake Wakatipu in 3 to 4 days. The route follows a four-wheel-drive track around the North Lake and across open country at the head, then continues north up the Mararoa River. A tributary of the Mararoa, the Pond Burn, is followed to a low saddle connecting it with the Pass Burn, a tributary of the Greenstone, and the route then joins the Greenstone Track in its last stages to Lake Wakatipu. Public transport is available from the road end at the Greenstone Valley. There are 3 huts along the 51 km route, each with 8 bunks, mattresses, running water, and flush toilets, but no cooking facilities. Portable stoves must be carried. To avoid conflict with stock management, the track is closed and the huts are kept locked between May and the end of October. Get further information about this route from the Department of Conservation at Te Anau or Glenorchy before you use it.

WAITUTU FOREST

This southern corner of Fiordland is usually overlooked by tourists and New Zealanders alike, perhaps for no better reason than it is overshadowed by its large neighbor, Fiordland National Park. There may not be an immediate landscape of snowy mountains, deep lakes, and waterfalls on the track to **Port Craig**, but the magnificent bush and coastal scenery, combined with the area's history make it a place well worth visiting. The coastal track was constructed in 1897 to service the settlements of Cromarty and Te Oneroa at Preservation Inlet, and later a telegraph line was installed as far as Puysegur Point. There is also the **Hump Track,** cut in the late 1800s to the top of Hump Ridge to provide access for sheep grazing and now used to reach Teal Bay Hut on the shores of Lake Hauroko. The alpine tarns, granite outcrops, and views over Foveaux Strait and the forests surrounding Lakes Poteriteri and Hauroko from the Hump are spectacular and memorable.

Access to the Waitutu Forest is from Tuatapere: turn left into Papatotara Road after crossing the Waiau River and, after 6 km follow signs to Bluecliffs Beach. The road ends 21 km from Tuatapere. Cars can safely be left with the local farmer who lives a short distance along the road that heads steeply uphill by the road end carpark.

From the carpark follow the remains of the road for 7 km around the coast, and the beach, where it's easier, to the Deerstalkers' Assn. Hut by the Track Burn. To reach the **Hump Track,** backtrack about 200 m and follow the side road heading uphill along the main ridge system. From a sign indicating the start of the track, there is a steep, 2- to 3-hour climb to a 6-bunk Deerstalkers Hut near the top of the ridge.

The **Port Craig** track continues around the coast, in places along the beach. Blowholes Beach, reached after about 1.25 hours, has pale golden sand and good campsites, although water is scarce. There are often deer tracks on the sand and you may see Fiordland crested penguins or seals. In some high seas the offshore rocks produce spectacular spouts of water, giving the beach its name. At the western end of Blowholes Beach, Breakneck Creek enters the sea at a rocky point requiring a high scramble to pass, and from here the track continues about 500 m inland. At low tide in calm sea conditions there is marvelous walking for another 3.5 km along sandy beaches and rocky shelves to the Whata, site of a food store in early days. You'll find plenty of mussels on the rocks to collect for dinner. A steep headland with sea caves makes travel beyond the Whata difficult, but if you look upward, at the corner where a small stream enters, you'll find a marker indicating the steep scramble up to the main track, with an easy 30- to 40-minute walk through tall forest with many ancient rata trees to Port Craig Hut, once the school and now the only building left. Remains of other buildings can be found among the regenerating bush, and a side track passed just before reaching the hut leads down to the old wharf and remains of old trolleys.

The track continues past Port Craig to the Wairaurahiri River and on to the Waitutu River, which drains Lake Poteriteri, and Big River, draining Lake Hakapoua. There are 12-bunk huts at the Wairaurahiri and Waitutu rivers. The section between Port Craig and Wairaurahiri Hut is easy walking along the old tramline and takes about 4 hours. After about 1.5 hours, the turnoff to Sandhill

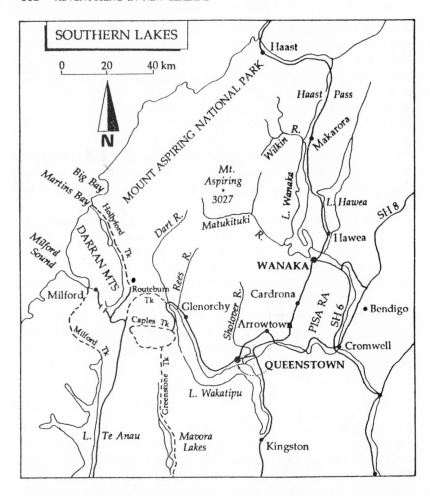

Point is reached. This historical reserve is thought to be the most western stopping point used by the Maori on journeys to Lake Hauroko because of the abundant fish and shellfish found here.

Beyond Sandhill Point the track crosses Maori-owned land, which has been extensively logged, and walkers are requested not to leave the track. There are four viaducts, built in the 1920s, along this section, and the largest one, over the Percy Burn, at 36 m high and 124 m long, is one of the biggest wooden viaducts in the world still standing. There is another 4 to 6 hours of walking between Wairaurahiri and Waitutu huts, through virgin stands of rimu and silver beech in one of the largest expanses of temperate rainforests in the country. Big River is another 5 to 7 hours away through more beautiful forest.

An excellent way of making a round trip in this area is to travel to Wairaura-hiri Hut by jet boat, via Lake Hauroko and the Wairaurahiri River, then walk back along the track. The river falls relentlessly from the lake to the sea, making for very exciting travel. This is also the route used for Tuatapere's "Wild Challenge," a one-day multisport event that involves canoeing across Lake Hauroko and down the Wairaurahiri, running the track, and cycling to Tuatapere. For the jet boat, contact Val MacKay of Lake Hauroko Tours, Box 13, Tuatapere, phone (03)2266-681. Further information on the tracks is available from the Department of Conservation, Box 29, Tuatapere, phone (03)2266-607.

MT. ASPIRING NATIONAL PARK

Here is another incredibly beautiful area of glaciated mountains and river valleys just asking to be explored. The park, established in 1964, covers 287,205 ha along both sides of the Main Divide between the northern edge of Fiordland National Park and the Haast River. Access is from Queenstown, Wanaka, and SH 6 over the Haast Pass. Much of the interior is very rugged and mountainous and of interest mainly to mountaineers, but there are plenty of places for easier walks and extended hikes. Most mountaineering is centered around majestic Mt. Aspiring (3,027 m), the highest peak outside Mt. Cook National Park, and surrounding peaks at the head of the Matukituki Valley. There are also challenging peaks to the north around the Wilkin Valley, and in the south, Mt. Earnslaw (2,816 m), between the Rees and Dart rivers at the head of Lake Wakatipu, is another testing climb. Permanent snow lies above 2,000 m and there are more than 100 glaciers of varying sizes. Glacial and hanging valleys, cirques, and lake basins are numerous.

Lying as it does along the Southern Alps, the park is subject to the usual extremes of mountain weather. Rainfall is much heavier in the west and in alpine areas, and often exceeds 5,000 mm annually. Eastward there is a sharp drop in rainfall and humidity, and corresponding increases in sunshine and temperature. Vegetation patterns reflect the rainfall, with dense rainforests and scrub carpeted with mosses, ferns, liverworts, and lichens on the western side of the Divide, and open beech forests on the eastern side. Birds are plentiful, with migratory and shorebirds on the river flats, bush birds in the forests, and kea and rock wrens above the bushline.

The Haast Pass (562 m) was long known to the Maori, but it was January 1863 before James Cameron discovered the route. Later the same month, Julius von Haast and four companions struggled to the west coast and back in ceaseless rain. A track was formed and from late last century cattle were driven over, but building of the road did not commence until 1929, and it was not until 1960 that Haast and Wanaka townships were linked. The final gap between

Haast and Paringa on the west coast was not completed for another five years. The drive over the Haast Pass along the northern edge of the park enables all travelers to experience its variety and beauty, from western rainforests to the open valleys, grassy riverflats, and beech forests in the east.

Headquarters for Mt. Aspiring Park are located in Wanaka township, and there is another Department of Conservation information center at Queenstown; field stations are located at Glenorchy and Makarora. The best-known walk in the park is the Routeburn Track from the head of Lake Wakatipu to The Divide on the Milford Sound road, and this is described under "Fiordland National Park." Other long hikes crossing from one valley to another are the Rees–Dart, Greenstone–Caples, Matukituki–Rees or Dart, and Wilkin–Siberia–Young. InterCity, Backpacker Express, and Magic Bus provide regular services from Queenstown to the Routeburn, Greenstone, Rees, and Dart tracks between November 1 and May 31. Glenorchy Holiday Park operate an on-demand service at other times.

Rees and Dart Valleys

The 50-km round trip through the Rees and Dart Valleys takes about 4 days, but an extra day is usually added to visit the Dart Glacier. There are 3 huts, and a reasonable standard of fitness is required. The Rees Saddle on the Forbes Range between the two valleys is normally closed by snow between May and November. Most people start the walk up the Rees Valley, as the ascent is more gradual.

Greenstone and Caples Valleys

Tracks in these valleys provide a low-level alternative to the Routeburn Track or are used in conjunction with it. The gentle Greenstone Track (29 km) can be walked at any time of the year, while the Caples (21 km) is usually closed by snow on McKellar Saddle from late May to October. Both tracks have 2 huts and usually 2 days are required for each, or 4 days for the round trip. Guided walks through the Greenstone are available with **Greenstone Valley Walks**, Box 568, Queenstown, phone (03)443-7805.

Matukituki Valley

The Matukituki Valley flows into Lake Wanaka from the west and provides easy access to the mountain heartland. From Wanaka the road is good as far as Glendhu Bay, then becomes more rutted as it heads up the valley. Views become more exciting as the valley swings northwest and include the peaks of Mts. Aspiring and Avalanche by the time Cameron Flat, opposite the confluence of the East Matukituki River, is reached. Cameron Flat is 47 km from Wanaka and it is possible to drive another 6 km, fording a couple of streams that can become impassable after heavy rain, to Raspberry Flat.

A hiker on Mt. Aspiring. *Photo by Bruce Jeffries.*

High cliffs guard the entrance to the **East Branch,** reached by fording the river and following the road to Aspiring Homestead. There is pleasant walking for 2 to 3 hours to Junction Flat, where there are good views of Mt. Avalanche, Moncrieff Peak, and the Pope's Nose. The river's deep pools offer good fishing. From Junction Flat, another hour up Kitchener Creek will bring you to Aspiring Flat below the 610-m walls of the Kitchener Cirque, plunging sheer from the Bonar glacier above. Passes at the head of the East Matukituki to the Wilkin Valley are difficult and dangerous.

From Raspberry Flat in the **West Branch** there is easy walking over undulating river flats and terraces for 10 km to the Alpine Club's **Aspiring Hut.** Above are the glistening peaks and glaciers at the head of the valley. Below Aspiring Hut, on the west side of the valley, steep slopes lead to Cascade Saddle, which can be used as a route to the head of the Dart Valley. The slopes below Cascade Saddle can be deceptively dangerous when wet or snow-covered and have claimed more than one life. Arawata Saddle, closer to the head of the Matukituki, gives access to the head of the mighty Arawata Valley in South Westland.

For a pleasant half-day walk from Raspberry Flat, follow the stream opposite to its upper basin below the glaciers of Rob Roy Peak. The Matukituki River is bridged near this stream and a track climbs up through bush on the true left side to the bush edge. Above here you can wander as far as you like, but on a warm summer day it's pleasant to just sit and watch the blocks of ice break off the glacier and avalanche down the cliffs.

Matuki Services (15 Norman Terrace, Wanaka, phone (03)4437-135) provide minibus transport from Wanaka to Raspberry Flat and back on a regular basis from mid-December to the end of January, and a weekday service in conjunction with the school bus run at other times of the year. Bookings can also be made in Wanaka at the Kaleidoscope Bookshop, phone (03)4438-540; Wanaka Youth Hostel, phone (03)4437-405; Wanaka Booking Centre, phone (03)4437-277; and Wanaka Bakpaka, phone (03)4437-837.

Makarora Valley

From Wanaka, SH 6 passes through Hawea township, which has a nice campground, and follows the steep and rather barren western side of Lake Hawea. At The Neck, a narrow pass between Lake Hawea and Lake Wanaka, a side road leads to **Kidds Bush**, a lakeside camping and picnic area. The main road continues around the east side of Lake Wanaka before entering the Makarora Valley, the lower part of which is farmed. Makarora has a shop, an information office, and an excellent campground with cabins and motel units, which makes a good base for exploration in the valley. Between here and the Haast Pass (18 km) there are more good campsites at **Cameron Flat, Pleasant Flat,** and **Davis Flat**. There are short and long walks from Makarora, and most of the tributary valleys of the Makarora River have tracks to their upper reaches. While most are for experienced trampers only, some are suitable for short walks. A booklet describing these tracks is available from the Department of Conservation at Wanaka or the Makarora Field Station.

One of the easier tracks leads to the lower part of the **Blue Valley**. Take the short walk to the translucent **Blue Pools** (10 minutes), where you will probably see trout swimming, and continue up the track from the bridge. The climb around the lower gorge is reasonably gentle, and in an hour or so you will reach Camp Flat, a pleasant spot for lunch or camping.

The **upper Makarora Valley**, with its long grassy flats leading to an impressive basin beneath Mt. Brewster, is particularly beautiful and makes a good place for a 3-day hike. The track starts at the Davis Flat carpark, crosses the river, then climbs steeply beside the Stewart Falls to sidle high above the Makarora Gorge before descending to the first river flat. Makarora Hut (4 bunks) makes a good base from which to explore the upper valley.

Wilkin Valley

The Wilkin Valley, a major tributary of the Makarora, is exceedingly beautiful and is easily accessible. Bird life is good, and if you fish you will find the pools in the swift blue-green river very rewarding. Most folk avoid walking the lower river flats, which are grazed, and the sometimes tricky crossing of the Makarora River, by taking a jet boat ride from Makarora to **Kerin Forks Hut** (10 bunks). From here it's another 6 hours on an easy track through beech forest and across river flats to **Top Forks Hut** (16 bunks) at the junction of the north and south branches. Above the forks the dark bluffs of Mt. Ragan tower 1,500 m. The south branch leads to a difficult and dangerous crossing to the East Matukituki, which is not recommended. The **north branch,** with Lakes Diana, Lucidus, and Castalia, hanging glaciers on the flanks of Mts. Castor and Pollux, and spectacular alpine scenery, is a superb place for a day walk. Also worth exploring is the **Wonderland Valley,** which enters from the north below Top Forks Hut. Although there is no marked track up the valley, access on the north side is reasonable, in places following parts of an old cattle track. Peaks along the western side of Wonderland Stream have the evocative classical names of Juno, Perseus, and Vesta.

The **Siberia Valley,** entering the Wilkin at Kerin Forks, is another superb place to spend a few days. The Wilkin River is crossed to reach Siberia Stream and the track to **Siberia Hut** (10 bunks), which climbs steeply on the true left and sidles high to avoid a gorge before reaching Siberia Flats, where there is a small airstrip. Siberia Hut is further up the river flats. Excellent day trips can be made from Siberia Hut to the head of the valley and to **Lake Crucible,** an alpine lake nestled high under Mt. Alba. Experienced trampers can return to the Makarora via **Gillespie Pass** and the **Young Valley.** The 3- to 4-day Wilkin–Gillespie Pass–Young trip is one of the best in Mt. Aspiring National Park.

InterCity buses pass through Makarora daily on the Haast–Wanaka run. **Haast Pass Tourist Service,** based at Makarora, operate the jet boat and also fly parties into Siberia Flats. Their **Siberia Experience** is a superb day trip that involves a flight to Siberia Flats, a walk down to the Wilkin River, and a return to Makarora by jet boat. They also do exciting scenic flights over the Mt. Aspiring region, to Mt. Cook, and to Milford Sound. Their address is just Makarora, via Wanaka, phone (03)4438-372.

Queenstown

There are so many exciting things to do in Queenstown that it is hard to know where to begin. The town is geared up for tourists and has a range of accommodation, from budget to luxury, shopping malls, pleasant cafes, good information outlets, and good transport connections. Fantastic scenery and wild rivers combined with a fascinating history leave no excuse for being bored. You can jet boat or raft the Shotover and Kawarau rivers, and this can be combined with helicopter rides and bungee jumping, all in one day, if you have the nerve and necessary cash. You can even float down the Kawarau with a mini surfboard or kayak and canoe the rapids. The Kawarau is quieter than the technically more difficult Shotover River. Rides on the Shotover end by shooting through the 170-m-long Oxenbridge Tunnel, built by Ned Oxenbridge and his relatives. Their idea was to divert the river so the bed could be worked for gold. It took three years to blast the tunnel through solid rock, and when finished, the end was over a meter above the river level. Other things to do in Queenstown are horse trekking along old gold miners' trails, guided motorcycle adventure touring, mountain biking, and parapenting. Windsurfers, catamarans, canoes, kayaks, dinghies, and Zodiac rafts can be rented from **Frankton Beach Hire** in summer, if you'd rather do your own thing on the lake. In winter there is ice skating and ice hockey at the local amusement park.

More sedate activities include cruising on the *TSS Earnslaw,* a grand old steamer that first started plying the waters of Lake Wakatipu in 1912. She was built in Dunedin and brought in pieces by train to the railhead at Kingston, where she was reassembled. Until the road to Glenorchy was opened in 1962, the *Earnslaw* carried sheep, mail, and stores to stations near the head of the lake. Destined for the scrap heap by the late 1960s, she was saved by a band of enthusiasts who saw her tourist potential, and is now operated by Fiordland Travel. The *Walter Peak Catamaran* also does trips across the lake to Walter Peak Station, or you can sail on the twin-masted schooner *City of Dunedin.*

There is very pleasant walking along the lake shore to **Frankton Beach,** and this can be continued to the **Kawarau Falls** dam and bridge, built in 1924 to control the river flow so that miners could get at gold in the river bed. The expensive scheme was a failure, and during the few times the river level fell, the bottom was found to be choked with mining debris. Other short walks close to town are the **One Mile Creek Walkway** (1 hour round trip) and the **Sunshine Bay Track** (1 to 1.5 hours round trip). The **Queenstown Hill Walkway** from the top of Edgar St. is a steady 1-hour climb through mostly exotic forest to an open rocky top with a panoramic view of the lake, town, and mountains. For more sensational views, ride the gondola to **Bob's Peak** directly behind Queenstown. The energetic can continue on to **Ben Lomond** (1,750 m) for views extending to Mts. Cook, Aspiring, Earnslaw, and Aurum. The climb takes nearly 4 hours and can be started from town or from Bob's Peak. Take warm clothes and water; in winter, boots and ice axes are necessary. Different views are had from the **Coronet** and **Remarkables ski fields. Lake Alta** at the Remarkables area is an excellent place for alpine flowers and is reached by about 30 minutes' walking. If you follow the ski lift tows up to the right behind the lodge, you'll find a lookout point on the main ridge with bird's-eye views over Lake Wakatipu. **Double Cone,** above Lake Alta, is very steep near the top, but rewards with even better views.

Skippers Canyon has sensational scenery—a mix of deep gorges between rolling, tussocky hills dotted with craggy outcrops and tall shaftlike tors of schist, all grey and gold, barren and forbidding. It was a terrible place for the miners who worked here in winter when river levels were low, fighting frostbite, malnutrition, snowfalls, and floods. The road to Skippers turns off the Coronet Peak Road and is no place for nervous drivers. It twists and turns around narrow, blind corners for many kilometers to the Skippers Suspension Bridge, where the daring do their bungee jumping. Built in 1901, the spectacular bridge is 105 m long and stands 69 m above the Shotover River. At the roadend, the **Mt. Aurum Recreation Reserve** has pleasant picnic areas and easy short walks around the site of the old Skippers township. Longer hikes follow old miners trails to the Bullendale Reef mines and sites at Dynamo Creek. There are huts at these sites and a fascinating 2- to 3-day round trip can be made exploring the rugged country the early pioneers had to contend with. More information on the area is available from the Department of Conservation. If you don't want to tackle the road yourself, there are daily tours.

Arrowtown is another interesting place to spend half a day. Many old buildings in the main street have been restored and there is an excellent museum. At the top end of the main street, where it swings down to a picnic area beside the Arrow River, are restored buildings from the Chinese mining settlement. Several walking tracks start from the picnic area, the main ones being the **Sawpit Gully Track**, an 8-km loop, and the **Big Hill Track** to **Macetown**, an old gold town. The 27-km Big Hill Track takes 4 to 5 hours to walk one way. It was once the only route to Macetown. It was icy and dangerous in winter, so fell into disuse once the road up the Arrow Gorge was put in 1884. The road can be walked in about 3 hours and is still usable by four-wheel-drive vehicles. Some buildings have been restored, but there is little left of isolated Macetown now except the sweet briar (planted by miners as a source of vitamin C) and the poplars, sycamores, cottonwoods, and hawthorne, which blaze with color in autumn. The town site and road are part of the Otago Goldfields Park, and guidebooks are available from the Department of Conservation. To explore all the relics and historic sites requires more than one day. Excellent guided tours to Macetown, which includes gold panning, are run by **Nomad Safaris**. These are good value, and reservations can be made with any booking agent in Queenstown, or phone Nick Duncan at (03)4426-699.

Along the road to Glenorchy, signs indicate walks and places of interest. **Moke Lake** is a pleasant peaceful place for picnicking and fishing, and you can walk back to Arthur's Point via the Moonlight Track. Opposite the Moke Lake turnoff are Seven-Mile Point and the 6-km return, **Wilsons Bay Track**. About 1.5 km past Wilsons Bay you'll find the track to **Lake Dispute**, another good spot for swimming and fishing (1 hour round trip). At the Twelve Mile Creek Bridge a sign points the way to **Mt. Crichton**, a long hike passing disused mining sites, which rewards with excellent views over Lake Wakatipu.

Glenorchy came into existence when scheelite was discovered in the local hills and mining camps sprang up at Paradise, Sylvan Lake, and several creeks along the Rees and Dart valleys. The town has a motor camp, pub, visitor center, and booking office, where you can inquire about horse treks, four-wheel-drive trips, tramping tracks, and jet boating trips. One of the best value trips is the **Dart River Jetboat Safari**, a 5.5-hour excursion that takes you as far as it's possible to navigate up the Dart River. It's an exciting ride, and the scenery is superb. Gold was also mined above the Rees Valley at the **Invincible Mine**, which operated between 1882 and 1889. It had a 10-stamp battery and an unusual set of berdans (the cast-iron bowls for grinding the ore). The track is signposted along the Rees Valley and it takes about an hour to climb to the mine site, with wonderful views across to Mt. Earnslaw and the Rees Valley below.

Short walks in the lower Dart Valley are to **Turner Creek** and waterfall (40 minutes one way), and a 1.5-hour climb up **Glacier Burn** to a basin on the slopes of Mt. Bonpland, both tracks starting off the road to Kinloch. The track to **Sylvan Lake** (2 hours round trip) starts off the road to the Routeburn Track. There is good fishing at Sylvan Lake and also at **Diamond Lake** near Paradise. Camping areas will be found at Diamond Lake and Kinloch.

OVER THE CROWN RANGE

SH 89 linking Queenstown and Wanaka over the Crown Range is much shorter than SH 6, but not necessarily any quicker. The Queenstown side is very steep and unsuitable for caravans and the top section is often closed during winter by snow and ice. From the turnoff on SH 6 the road zig-zags steeply to Crown Terrace before leveling off to give views over the Arrow Valley. Along here you may see people parapenting, a colorful sight as they float down to the flat land below. If you'd like to try this sport, contact **Max Air Parapentes**, Box 738, Queenstown, phone (03)4437-770, or any booking office in Queenstown.

Above Crown Terrace the road continues its steep climb to the crest of the range at 1,120 m above sea level. By walking 200 m up a track here there are more impressive views over the Kawarau Valley and back to Queenstown. The descent is much more gradual, down the **Cardrona Valley** where miners once tried their luck, leaving piles of tailings and water-sluiced cliffs. As the valley flattens out, signs mark the roads to **Cardrona Skifield** and the **Nordic Ski Area.** Just past these is the **Cardrona Pub,** which is well worth stopping to visit, either for refreshment or historical reasons. Built around 1870, it is one of the few buildings remaining of the gold town that once had three thousand inhabitants.

The old pub served the traveling public until 1961, when its license was revoked, and it stood then as a sad and silent reminder of the old times. New owners have lovingly restored the pub and given it a new lease on life; the outside still wears a decrepit air, but inside you can enjoy a drink or meal in fine surroundings.

CROMWELL AND THE KAWARAU GORGE

To drive along SH 6 through the wild Kawarau Gorge is to appreciate just how difficult it was for early travelers to reach Queenstown and why the climb over the Crown Range was preferable, even in winter. The water foams and churns through the hostile rock canyon that was only crossable at the Roaring Meg Power Station, where boulders could be jumped by the stout-hearted. Even when a track was put through, the potholes and pits made the journey a drawn-out endurance test. The old **Kawarau Suspension Bridge** adjacent to the present steel arch bridge, was, at the time of its construction in 1880, a model of design and workmanship. The steel ropes, suspended over towers of locally hewn schist, are individually anchored and have an inward curve to provide stability against crosswinds. Toward the lower end of the gorge, a footbridge leads to the **Kawarau Gorge Mining Centre,** where you can learn how the miners won and lost their fortunes, and try panning for gold yourself. You can see tracks through old diggings, tunnels, tailraces and shafts, a 5-stamp battery, miners' crude shelters, and a hydraulic monitor and elevator.

The rock-strewn slopes of the gorge give way to flat terraces of the Clutha Valley, where you'll see numerous fruit stands, before Cromwell is reached at the junction of the Clutha and Kawarau riverrs. The setting is barren but wildly beautiful, with the Dunstan Mountains to the east and smooth Pisa Range to the west, lit with fruit blossoms in spring and the blazing colors of exotic trees in autumn. Controversy over increased costs of the Clyde Dam and the loss of historic sites and orchards around Cromwell through flooding when Lake Dunstan was filled in 1992 has been bitter and long. An audiovisual presentation on the dam project can be seen at the Cromwell Information Centre.

Close to Cromwell there are many old gold town sites worthy of exploration. **Bendigo** seems full of ghosts, with its crumbling buildings and deep mine shafts set in a wild rocky landscape dotted with sweet-smelling thyme. You can drive to Bendigo but probably need four-wheel-drive to continue up the steep track to the mines at **Logantown** and **Welshtown,** where there are more buildings in better condition. Alluvial gold was found here in 1862, but it was not until the following year that miners arrived, after Thomas Logan discovered some of the richest exposed quartz reefs in the country, high up in the mountains above Bendigo Creek. **Bannockburn** also has many old buildings and close by there is a walk through the old workings at deserted **Stewart Town.** The treeless

landscape of hostile cliffs and yellow clay escarpments scarred by sluicing is swee-
tened only by the fragrance of wild thyme. Tours of the high country around
Cromwell, old gold towns, and other historic sites can be arranged through the
visitor center.

WANAKA

Wanaka lacks the stir of touristy Queenstown; its atmosphere is more gentle,
more relaxed. Until 1940, the town was called Pembroke after the Earl of Pembroke, who was Colonial Secretary in 1855. The present name is a corruption
of Oanaka, meaning "the place of Anaka," a chief who used to fish in the area.
The low annual rainfall—only 650 mm—and the sunny climate, proximity to
several ski areas, and opportunities for fishing and boating, make it particularly
attractive in both summer and winter. The town has a good range of places
to eat, sleep, and shop, along with all other facilities.

A pleasant 20-minute stroll around the lake edge will bring you to **Eely
Point** and it's another 40 minutes to the outlet and the Clutha River. Wide
four-wheel-drive tracks beside the river make for easy walking and good fishing
access for 5 km to Albert Town. Walking in the other direction from the wharf
for 30 minutes brings you to **Wanaka Station Park,** and in another 30 minutes
you'll reach the track to **Waterfall Creek.** Behind the town, the rocky hump
of **Mt. Iron,** a roche moutonnée smoothed by the glacier that carved out the
lake's basin, gives good views. The well-graded track starts a couple of kilometers out of town on SH 6 and takes about 1.5 hours round trip. A more strenuous full-day hike can be made to **Mt. Roy** (1,585 m) for breathtaking views
over the lake and mountains. The track starts 8 km along the road to Glendhu
Bay and is closed in October for lambing season.

Jet boats operate on the Clutha River or you can skim over the lake and
up the lower reaches of the Matukituki River in a Hovercraft. Fishing trips,
backcountry four-wheel-drive trips, kayaking, mountain biking on the Pisa Range,
guided hiking, rafting on the Clutha River, kayaking on the Motatapu River
and windsurfing are all available from Wanaka.

SKIING

Several downhill ski areas are located within an hour's drive of Wanaka and
Queenstown. There are also a nordic ski area close to Wanaka and options for
heliskiing. The **Mt. Cook Line** offer good-value 7-day ski holiday packages that
include airfares from Auckland, ski passes, and accommodation. Further information is available from travel agents.

Coronet Peak, only 18 km from Queenstown, has varied terrain and is often regarded as one of the best ski areas in the Southern Hemisphere. The field has a vertical drop of 428 m, is served with two chairlifts, a T-bar, and two poma lifts, and is rated as 15 percent beginner, 45 percent intermediate, and the rest advanced and expert skiing. Facilities include ski rental and repair, retail shop, ski school, cafeteria, and licensed restaurant. There is also night skiing on selected nights.

Remarkables, a 325-m vertical drop, has three chairlifts serving three distinct areas and is rated as 30 percent beginner, 40 percent intermediate, and the rest ideal for advanced skiers looking for challenges. This high alpine area also has some excellent cross-country and telemarking terrain. All facilities are available.

Cardrona, located 26 km from Wanaka above the Cardrona Valley, is spread over three basins and has three chairlifts, providing an uphill capacity of 6,000 skiers per hour. The field has a 390-m vertical drop and over half the terrain is suitable for intermediate skiers, making it an ideal family area. Facilities include ski rental, ski school, ski patrol, and cafeteria.

Treble Cone, located 28 km from Wanaka, has one chairlift, two T-bars, one platter lift, and one fixed-grip learners tow. The alpine terrain, with magnificent views over Lake Wanaka, has some exciting runs for advanced skiers, some regarded as the best in the country. The vertical drop is 660 m and rating is 15 percent beginner, 45 percent intermediate, and 40 percent advanced skiing. Facilities include ski school, ski patrol, heliskiing, and cafeteria, but no ski rental.

Pisa Nordic Range is the country's newest commercial area and is located 26 km from Wanaka on the Pisa Range, opposite Cardrona Ski Area. It has 25 km of groomed cross-country trails, with terrain suitable for first-time Nordic skiers through to advanced telemark skiers. Facilities include ski rental (both track and skating skis), ski school, ski patrol, day lodge, and cafeteria. Accommodation huts are available for overnight ski-touring trips, but reservations are essential. Contact **Nordic Ski Area,** Cardrona Valley, Private Bag, Wanaka, phone (03)4437-542 or Fax (03)4438-161.

Harris Mountains Heliski has bases in both Queenstown and Wanaka and operates in the Harris and Buchanan ranges around Lake Wanaka, and Remarkables, and South Harris Mountains from Queenstown. They cater for all ages and abilities. The Wanaka operation offers single-run helilifts through to 13-day packages. Further information is available from Harris Mountains Heliski, Box 177, Wanaka, phone (03)4437-930; or Harris Mountains Heliski, Shotover St., Queenstown, phone (03)4426-722.

Southern Lakes Heliski operates principally in three areas: Coronet Peak and the Remarkables, Thompson Mountains, and Richardson Mountains, with runs suitable for beginners through to experts. Write to them at Box 426, Queenstown, phone (03)4426-222.

USEFUL ADDRESSES

Department of Conservation: Corner of Ballarat and Stanley sts., Box 811, Queenstown, phone (03)4427-933; Fiordland National Park, Box 29, Te Anau, phone (03)2497-921; Mt. Aspiring National Park, Box 93, Wanaka, phone (03)4437-6600.

Queenstown Promotion Board, Box 353, Queenstown, phone (03)4427-440, Fax (03)4427-441.

Wanaka Promotion Assn., Box 147, Wanaka, phone (03)4431-233.

21 ♦ WESTLAND

LANDSCAPE AND CLIMATE

Westland is a wild, verdant province where the mountains seem to rise with incredible steepness from a meagre coastal strip bordered by long, surf-pounded gravel beaches. Currents along the shore are strong, building long shingle spits that impound the flows of rivers and streams and form quiet, sheltered lagoons rich in plant and animal life. Where offshore reefs provide good anchorage for bull kelp and other algae, seals find food and basking places, their numbers now increasing again after near annihilation by nineteenth-century sealing gangs. Much of the coastal plain is built from the moraines of massive glaciers that once flowed into the sea, or from debris carried from the mountains by fast-flowing rivers. Swamps and lakes are numerous, some filling hollows left by retreating ice, others created by the damming of rivers. Many swamps, known locally as pakihi, have human origins, having formed after forests were cleared. The high moisture content of the soil limits the number and variety of soil organisms, and retards decomposition of vegetable matter, causing it to collect in a peaty layer above the mineral soil. Other swamps have formed on the oldest moraines, where the soil is poor from heavy leaching and bad drainage over long periods of time. Most lakes are home to introduced trout and the native whitebait, or inanga (*Galaxias maculatus*), which spawns in estuarine rushes and grasses on riverbanks during high spring tides and then dies. The eggs remain high and dry until the next spring tide, two weeks later, when they quickly hatch and are washed out to sea, to return to the rivers again next spring. When the whitebait are "running," locals are out in force with nets to catch the tiny delicacy.

Beyond the coastal plain, the mountain wall is abrupt, a maze of tortuous gorges, precipitous bluffs, icefalls, and valleys. Uplift of the Southern Alps has been so rapid that erosion has been unable to cut the slopes back to a more normal angle. From the 3,000-m summits of the Main Divide, the Tasman Sea appears a mere stone's throw away. Lush primeval rainforests cloak the lower hills and mountain slopes, giving way to dense, tangled subalpine forests of stunted tree daisies, *Dracophyllums*, mountain ribbonwoods, and shrubs with twisted, gnarled trunks. Above the scrub, tussock and herb fields mingle with boulders and scree slides tumbling from rocky peaks, snowfields, and glaciers. Along this western side of the Main Divide most of the rock is schist, formed when the original greywacke and argillite sediments were subjected to pressure and heat. Layers of minerals give the schist a flaky appearance, and it glitters with mica and flakes of feldspar and quartz. Subsidiary ranges in the north, composed of granite, have a more complicated history and a diversity of rocks that differ in age and structure. Here also are coal deposits, formed from peat swamps that were buried by sediments when the seas invaded the land 50 million years ago.

Squeezed between the mountains and the sea, Westland is subject to intense weather contrasts and is well known for its "wet coast" weather. Less well known is the fact that a high number of sunshine hours are also recorded, more than Southland or coastal Otago receive. It is just that when it rains here, it really rains. An overnight deluge in January 1991 dumped 257 mm (9 inches) of rain at Franz Josef. Downpours such as this are common and can last for days; almost 3 m of rain fell during one 72-hour storm in March 1982. Frontal systems bringing strong westerly winds and rain can follow one another for days on end, particularly in spring, and there are many tales of climbers being trapped for up to nine days by storms. Clearing comes when the wind becomes more southerly. In contrast, when storms run up the east coast, the weather in Westland is fine and clear. Approaching fronts are preceded by northwest winds and fine high clouds that gradually thicken and darken, so that the mountains stand out clearly. Before long, masses of low ragged clouds roll in from the sea to enshroud everything in mist and rain. Rainfall is higher nearer the mountains and the coast is often sunny when the mountains are cloaked in mist and drizzle.

HISTORY

None of the early navigators sailing along the coast of Westland mentioned sighting Mts. Cook and Tasman, probably because they were under cloud, and the peaks were first noted by Captain Stokes of the *Acheron* in 1851. The Fox and

Franz glaciers remained unseen and unknown until their existence was recorded in the log book of the *Mary Louisa* in 1859. Nineteenth-century sealing parties from Fiordland apparently cared little what lay inland, unless shipwreck forced them to take note. In 1857, a group of seven survivors from the *Pacifique* walked from the Cascade River in South Westland to Nelson, completing the first unintentional traverse of the coast by Europeans, but leaving little detail of their journey. Cook's description of the Westland as "an inhospitable shore, unworthy of observation except for its ridge of naked, barren rocks covered with snow" was more or less confirmed by Charles Heaphy and Thomas Brunner, who spent many arduous weeks in early 1846 looking for land for settlers. Brunner's epic 18-month journey down the Buller and west coast in search of a route to Canterbury or Otago ruined his health and failed in its objective.

Few Maori lived on the coast, as kumara could not be grown south of the Buller River. Most settlements were small coastal villages that worked greenstone in the winter after storing food during the summer. The main source of greenstone was the Arahura River near Greymouth, but it was also found as far south as Jackson Bay. For almost a decade after Brunner's visit the coast's solitude remained intact until explorations by James MacKay and Leonard Harper revived interest. Harper, with Maori guides, crossed from the Hurunui Valley in Canterbury to the Taramakau Valley on the west coast. In 1859, MacKay, a young Scot, followed Brunner's footsteps and negotiated with the Maori of Mawhero Pa on the south bank of the Grey River for the sale of land. The Maori were understandably reluctant to sell land that held greenstone but when it was agreed that reserves would be set aside, the deal was clinched—at £300. Samuel Mackley, who had witnessed the deal, immediately took up land in the Grey Valley and became the first settler. Others followed but confined themselves mainly to the Buller and Grey regions.

Greymouth became a settlement in 1863 when a government depot was established near Mawhero Pa to facilitate a survey of Westland. The decision to close this depot in 1864 had already been made when a letter was received from Albert Hunt, claiming a £1,000 reward offered by the Canterbury Provincial Government for finding payable gold reasonably accessible to Christchurch. At that time Westland was part of Canterbury, but Hunt's claim did not meet the requirements of being reasonably accessible. Gold had also been found near Greymouth by two Maori while searching for greenstone, and when news got out, the rush started, with 16,000 miners arriving in 1864. The first prospectors followed rivers toward the mountains, then gold was discovered on the beaches. By 1866, Okarito had 1,250 people while another 2,500 worked the Three Mile and Five Mile beaches to the south. Gillespies Beach, named after its first successful prospector, became another large center. The finds were beyond belief; one party of four retrieved 50 kg of pure gold dust in three months.

The beach workings soon fizzled out, but were replaced by sluicing, then suction and bucket dredges, none of which was particularly successful, although the last one at Gillespies Beach remained working until 1946 and repaid all capital and even some dividends. The settlement at Gillespies Beach has now gone except for a few cottages, but it formed the basis for a small farming community that slowly spread up the Cook River.

Fabulous finds were also made at Kaniere, Ross, Waimea, and in the Callery Gorge near Franz Josef. In one week in 1896, four miners took 6.5 kg of gold out of the Callery, a fearsomely wild, damp canyon that seldom sees the sun. Hokitika, Greymouth, and Westport sprang up as ports for ships bringing supplies to the smaller mining settlements, and, as farmland and timber milling replaced the mining, have continued as service centers. Hokitika, no more than an indefinite name on a map in 1864, was within three years the busiest port in the country. The waterfront was crowded; ships and vessels four deep were turned around in two days. In one five-day period, forty-two boats crossed the bar and a record nineteen either left or entered on one other day. Many ships never made it across the bar and up the narrow S-shaped channel to the wharves. In a light breeze, a sailing ship could not maintain sufficient steerage through the breakers to round the corner of the spit and would founder. Rollers would then lift the vessel bodily onto the beach where waves would pound it to pieces. Crowds gathered at the river mouth to watch ships "running the blockade" and to plunder any that didn't make it. As the number of wrecks increased, Melbourne insurance companies raised premiums until they were five times the rate for vessels trading between Melbourne and Brisbane. The port was finally closed in 1954 and today only a few piles remain.

The mouth of the Buller River was a good natural anchorage, and Westport became a distribution center for gold rush settlements at Charleston, Brighton, and Addisons Flat. It was first sited on the northern spit, but continual flooding was a problem. Finally, when the river changed its course during one immense flood, swept through the town and carried four hotels out to sea, the site was changed. Westport's real wealth, however, was from the coal that Heaphy and Brunner had found during their exploration. Much of it lay above 600 m on the ranges behind the plain north of Westport, and early mining attempts at Mokihinui and Ngakawau failed because of transport difficulties. A railway was built from Westport to Ngakawau in 1876–77 to bring coal to the port, and in 1878 the first serious attempts were made to mine the high-level deposits. The Denniston Incline, a self-acting haulway in two stages, was built to convey the coal down the escarpment to the railway below. Its steepness made it an engineering feat that attracted worldwide attention. As overseas export demands increased, production rose to 348,335 tons in 1910. When demand fell, production declined steadily, but Denniston still produced an average of

202,137 tons annually until 1931. By the time it closed in 1967, a total of 12,600,000 tonnes of coal had been carried down the Incline.

Denniston township, which once had a population of 2,000, is now almost a ghost town. Coal is still mined on the high plateau but is carried down the road in trucks, and the miners prefer to live down at the coast, where the climate is kinder. Coal from the nearby opencast Stockton Mine is carried down to Ngakawau by an 8-km overhead cable way.

Greymouth also gained wealth from the coal mining industry when gold mining waned. Remains of the Brunner Mine can be seen along both banks of the Grey River a couple of kilometers above the town. When it closed in 1906, the Brunner Mine had produced almost 2.2 million tons of coal. Other mines were located at Blackball, further up Grey Valley, but these have also closed. Today Greymouth is the largest town on the west coast.

South Westland still remains largely untamed. Even the few farms on the flats of some of the bigger rivers have a rough look about them, as though the bush was never properly cleared in the first place. With annual rainfall in this region around 4,500 mm (177 inches) and a corresponding growth of vegetation, farmers have a hard job keeping their land clear. The early geologists—Gerhard Mueller in 1864, Julius von Haast, and J. R. Hackett in 1868—did geological surveys as far south as the Cook River, and Haast had crossed over the Haast Pass to the west coast in 1864, but exploration of the rest was mainly through the efforts of one man, Charles Douglas. Charlie Douglas explored every river between Ross and Big Bay, often with no companions other than his pipe and one of several dogs that could catch kakapo, weka, and other birds for the pot. Between 1889 and 1903 he produced hundreds of detailed reports of previously uncharted land. It was extremely hard work in difficult country and hardships of earlier journeys caused Douglas to suffer from painful rheumatism on later trips. A well-educated man, Douglas was, however, philosophical about the hardships and seemed to enjoy the solitude and discomfort of exploration. He never learned to swim, yet survived forty years of crossing New Zealand rivers when hundreds of others drowned—saved, perhaps, by his reasoning that you took more risks if you knew how to swim.

There is little evidence today of old towns and mining operations; most have been reclaimed by the ever-encroaching bush, which made life difficult for the farmers following on the heels of the goldseekers. Clearing the land was backbreaking work, first cutting down forest trees, then burning repeatedly to clear regenerating scrub. Isolation, heavy rain, and swamps contributed to the misery of the early farmers. Access was extremely difficult, whether by sea or land. After landing at Hokitika, travel was along the beaches, and fording the rivers and passing the bluffs between the beaches was fraught with risk. The climb over was often difficult and dangerous; the alternative was a dash around the bottom at low tide. Many drowned, and the New Zealand Death accounted for 47 percent of all fatalities during the country's early years. With the increase in farming, and tourism, to view the Fox and Franz glaciers, there was a need for better access, and the beach route was slowly replaced by a road, built by gangs of ex-diggers. By the 1880s it had reached Franz Josef, but beyond was still a rugged wilderness traversed only by a primitive track.

There was limited farming around the Haast River for many years, and a small settlement at Jackson Bay. Created in 1875 as a timber milling and fishing village with the potential for agriculture, the Jackson Bay settlement was a dismal failure. The road over the Haast Pass was extended, and a wharf was built in 1937 to bring in construction equipment, but it was too late to save the town. Haast township was established as a Ministry of Works depot and was serviced by plane for many years. Work on the road was interrupted by World War II, and it was not until the Haast River was bridged and the final 56 km between Haast and Paringa completed that South Westland lost its isolation.

◆PLACES TO VISIT AND THINGS TO DO

SOUTH WESTLAND

Haast and Jackson Bay

Entering South Westland via the Haast Pass is a dramatic introduction to this uncompromising, untamed region, which has recently been declared a World Heritage Site on account of its majestic scenery, diverse forests, and wildlife. From the top of the pass the descent is reasonably gentle until you reach the Gates of Haast, where the river plunges through a narrow defile choked with massive schist boulders. The difficulties of making a road through here can be easily imagined. At the lower end, Pleasant Flat makes a good stopping place, and before long there are views north up the mighty Landsborough River to Mt. Hooker and other snowy peaks. Beginning its journey near Mt. Sefton in Mt. Cook National Park, the Landsborough flows parallel to the Main Divide for over 50 km before swinging west to join the Haast River on its final run to the Tasman Sea. If you have time, stop at the Roaring Billy Falls carpark where a short walk through tall forest will bring you to the edge of the river and a view of the Roaring Billy Falls as they thunder and cascade down the hillside opposite.

Haast township is small but has hotel accommodation, garage services, and a new visitor information center. The main road continues north, across the 732-m Haast Bridge, which stands 3 m above the highest recorded flood level and is designed for a flood flow of 400,000 cu m per second. The road to Jackson Bay turns south by the bridge and crosses scruffy country to the small

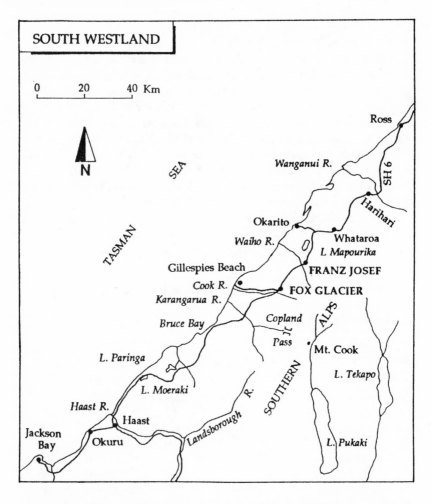

SOUTH WESTLAND

settlement of Haast Beach where there are motels, a general store, and service station. If you are looking for the Haast Motor Camp, which offers good, clean budget accommodation, you'll need to continue on to **Okuru** to find it. Opposite the camp is the delightful 15-minute **Hapuku Bush Walk,** with boardwalks into the estuary and through dense podocarp rainforest. The estuary is a good place to see wading birds and the unusual forest, thick with ferns, lianes, and kiekie, stands with its roots semipermanently in water.

The road south is surprisingly good and straight, through tall forests of kahikatea and rimu, to the **Arawata River** where, after crossing the bridge, it makes a sharp turn right. The **Cascade Road,** which heads straight ahead from the bridge, goes to the Cascade River and Red Hills area, a recent addition to

Mt. Aspiring National Park. There are good camping and picnic sites along this road and a lookout just beyond the **Martyr Saddle** gives superb views of the ultramafic Red Hills. The track to **Lake Ellery** (30 minutes one way), starts 3 km along the road and follows the quiet, dark-colored outlet stream through podocarp forest struggling to grow in the poor soil here.

About 1 km past the Arawata Bridge on the Jackson Bay road, a sign marks the 10-minute stroll into idyllic little **Lake Mary**. The small cluster of fishermen's houses at **Jackson Bay** are tucked against the bush behind the wharf, the sheltered beach, and the visitor information kiosk. In the future, the **Smoothwater Track** will start here rather than at its present location, 1 km back along the road. The track was originally constructed as a road to the Smoothwater part of the 1875 special settlement, where twelve German and Polish immigrant families once attempted to wrest an existence from the bush. On reaching the Smoothwater River, the road continued upstream to the settlement site. The river can be followed down, with several crossings, to Smoothwater Bay where you'll quite likely see Fiordland crested and little blue penguins and seals (3 hours round trip to Smoothwater Bay).

Between Haast and Ross

North of Haast the main highway continues through dense rainforest along the edge of the coast, with spectacular views of wild seas pounding the cliffs at **Knights Point** before it turns inland to **Lake Moeraki**. Beside the tranquil lake is the **Lake Moeraki Wilderness Lodge,** offering high-class accommodation and activities for natural history buffs. Although they accept casual guests for overnight stays, the proprietors, Anne Saunders and Dr. Gerry McSweeney, who are both ardent naturalists and conservationists, prefer groups or guests wishing to stay longer so they can show them the superb wildlife and bush of the region. For further information, write to Private Bag, Hokitika, phone (03)7500-881 or Fax (03)500-882.

Lake Moeraki is considered one of the best trout fishing waters on the west coast and its surrounding bush is particularly good as it has not yet suffered damage from possums. Starting by the lodge, the 30-minute **Munro Walk** passes through outstanding podocarp forest to a beautiful secluded bay where Fiordland crested penguins breed in winter. The promontory to the north can be crossed, using a rope, to reach a long, broad beach that provides good walking and beachcombing.

Before reaching **Lake Paringa**, another good place for casting a lure, you'll pass the sign indicating the **Haast to Paringa Cattle Track**. Prior to the opening of SH 6 in the 1960s this track was used by stockmen to drive cattle from southern valleys to markets at Hokitika. The 32-km track takes 2 to 3 days to walk, but a shorter excursion (2.5 to 3 hours round trip) can be made to Blowfly Hut beside the Moeraki River.

North of Lake Paringa, the bush is suddenly left behind as the road skirts the edge of **Bruce Bay,** a wild desolate beach where the surf casually tosses ragged tree trunks onto the gravel, and the constant west wind stunts the rimu forest and trims its foliage in a close-cropped cut. The beach is a good spot to find polished and rounded stones of white quartz. This view of the sea is all too brief and the road heads inland once more to the few houses at Jacobs River, through more tall forest and across enclaves of farmland to **Fox Glacier** township. At the northern end of town you'll find the Fox Glacier Visitor Centre, where you can pick up information on Westland National Park. The Hobnail Coffee shop in the middle of town is another good place to find out about commercially operated activities within the park.

Only 23 km separate Fox Glacier from **Franz Josef,** but this portion of road includes two steep, twisting sections of hill. Most cyclists find this bit fairly devastating after the generally flat travel on either side. The Waiho River is crossed by a suspension bridge, the existence of which has become increasingly threatened in recent years. With each flood, ice-borne gravels from the Franz Josef Glacier are swept downstream and are gradually raising the riverbed beneath the bridge. The riverbanks upstream are eroding, and recent floods have carried water and chunks of ice to decking level, threatening to sweep the bridge away on several occasions. Locals say it is only a matter of time before the inevitable happens. Like Fox Glacier, Franz Josef has a range of accommodation and services for visitors.

Beyond Franz Josef, the landscape becomes a little tamer, but no less beautiful, as the road skirts **Lake Mapourika** and **Lake Wahapo** to reach the small timber towns of **Whataroa** and **Harihari.** If you turn into Wanganui Flat Road at the south end of Harihari, then take La Fontaine Road, you'll end up near the mouth of the Wanganui River and the start of the **Harihari Coastal Walkway.** Using part of the old Wanganui Coastal Pack Track, the walkway skirts the estuary of the Wanganui River, partly on boardwalks and partly along terraces, before climbing to the Doughboy, a rock promontory giving spectacular views over river estuaries, bush, and river flat to the Southern Alps. Bird life on the estuary is good, and so is the fishing, particularly for whitebait, when they are running. The small huts along the riverbank near the start of the track are where whitebaiters stay during the season, each position jealously guarded. It takes about 45 minutes to reach the Doughboy and another 45 minutes to reach the Poerua River; when the tide is low, a round trip taking 2 to 3 hours can be made.

Lake Ianthe, another beautiful bush-fringed lake typical of Westland, is passed before reaching the historic gold mining town of **Ross.** There are two walkways at Ross, both taking about 1 hour round trip, to restored mining apparatus, water races, and hand-stacked tailings. The goldfields at Ross were particularly rich; it was here that a fist-sized nugget of gold weighing over 2.8 kg was found in 1909. If you'd like to try your luck, you can pan for gold in the creek or buy a bag of gravel to wash. The town's story is told in displays in the small museum, housed in a historic cottage. More quartz mining sites can be seen on Mt. Greenland (904 m) behind the town, which is reached by a steep four-wheel-drive track. This is a full-day walk for the fit and keen.

WESTLAND NATIONAL PARK

Westland National Park is one of those rare places that encompasses all life zones from sea level to permanent ice and snow, thoroughly deserving its status as a World Heritage Site. There are not many national parks in the world where you can stand on a beach and view seals and penguins, walk in rainforest, and touch glacier ice all in one day, but Westland is one of them. The Fox and Franz glaciers are dynamic bodies of ice, moving forward or retreating in amazingly short periods of time depending on the accumulation of snow in the névés during preceding years. At present, both glaciers are generally retreating and have been doing so for the last century. The fascinating story of that movement over thousands of years is imprinted on the land in the form of ancient moraines, kettle lakes, ice-smoothed rocks, and trimlines. Forest succession is another story, clearly related here as plants recolonize the land left bare by retreating ice.

The earliest stages can be seen on ice-scraped boulders and rock surfaces. Grey-colored lichens form a crust on the surface, while moss spores lodge in crevices where dust has collected. Able to survive out of water because of the wet climate, the algae *Trentepohlia* spreads across rock surfaces, giving them a brilliant orange-red color. First colonizers of the moraine gravels are grasses, willowherbs, and scabweeds, which are closely followed by nitrogen-fixing tutu and broom. After about ten years, enough humus collects to support germination of *Coprosmas*, *Hebes*, tree daisies, and toetoe grass. Within fifty years these early colonizers begin to be suppressed by rata, kamahi, and broadleaf, which will form a tall forest. It will be another hundred years or more before the first podocarp species begin to become dominant.

With its great range of altitudes and environments, the vegetation of the park is correspondingly varied and diverse. The best-drained fertile soils support forests of matai and totara, now a rare forest type, as most has been cleared for farming. Less fertile coastal hillslopes and old moraines have forests of rimu, kamahi, and rata, and where drainage is poor, the tall, straight-boled kahikatea flourishes. Epiphytic orchids, ferns, and lilies are numerous, and vines of bush lawyer, supplejack, rata, and kiekie form dense walls of foliage. On the forest floor, tree ferns, mosses, and ground ferns grow in profusion. Forests of rata and kamahi cover extensive areas of the park, growing on the steepest slopes up to 1,000 m. There is usually a scattering of Hall's totara throughout, and in cold, frost-prone sites toward the bushline, the conical mountain cedar, or kaikawaka, makes an appearance. As journals of the early explorers testify, the subalpine forests can be amazingly thick and difficult to move through, consisting mainly of resilient flowering tree daisies, mountain neinei, and shrubs of *Dracophyllum longifolium* and *D. uniflorum,* with erect needlelike leaves. In erosion-prone gullies and at the bushline, groves of deciduous mountain ribbonwood form a more open forest with a ground cover of tall, bristly shield ferns.

The same range of altitudes and environments also provides a good variety of habitats for birds, and most mainland species are found within the park. Of the bush birds, the South Island brown kiwi, now rare throughout the South Island, is confined to forests south of Okarito, but its cousin, the great spotted kiwi, can often be heard at night. The many lakes and lagoons are frequented by waders and waterfowl, with two notable specialties — the kotuku, or white heron, and the royal spoonbill. While not rare worldwide, the white heron (*Egretta alba modesta*) is relatively uncommon in New Zealand, and the only nesting site is near Okarito. This is shared with a small number of royal spoonbills.

The park headquarters is at Franz Josef and information on tracks, weather, and road conditions is available here and from the visitor center at Fox Glacier township.

Around Fox Glacier and Franz Josef

Without a doubt the park's biggest attractions are the Fox and Franz glaciers, which tumble awesomely from their snowy birthplace, at around 3,000 m, to 300 m, where there are dense rainforests. There are walking tracks to the snouts of the glaciers, but if you want to go up on the ice you need to do it with a guided group. To get a bird's-eye view of the ice, take a helicopter or ski plane flight from Fox Glacier township. For a closer look at a glacial river, you can raft the Waiho River, a fast, exciting ride; bookings can be made at the **Glacier Rafting Office,** Main Road, Franz Josef, phone (03)7520-763. A more sedate pursuit available is horseback riding along the river flats and bush toward the coast with Susan Miller of **Waiho Stables,** Franz Josef, phone (03)7520-747 or 7520-786. Bicycles can be rented at Franz Josef and Fox Glacier if you don't have car transport to get up to the glaciers or tracks.

Many short walks start from the roads leading up to the glaciers and from the townships of Fox and Franz. These are all well signposted and described in pamphlets. Longer, more strenuous hikes with great views of the ice and peaks are the **Roberts Point** and **Alex Knob tracks** at Franz Josef, and the **Cone Rock** and **Mount Fox tracks** at Fox. One of the most popular short walks is around **Lake Matheson** in the Fox Valley, where you are almost guaranteed to get perfect reflections, including the mountains if they are visible. The track is very easy and is boardwalked most of the way to prevent wet feet, except in exceptional circumstances. Even better views are had from **Lake Gault,** a kettle lake on the ancient moraine above Lake Matheson.

Gillespies Beach

Gillespies Beach provides a totally different experience to the glacier and mountain environment and is a wonderful combination of wild sea coast, bush, history, and lagoon. The remains of old gold dredges can be seen and you can walk north along parts of the old coastal pack track to view a seal colony. Even if the tide is wrong and you don't see the seals, the view from the high point is grand in fine weather. A longer alternative is to follow the pack track north to lonely **Galway Beach,** where driftwood lies in piles beneath ancient moraine cliffs. The southern end of Gillespies Beach is also littered with the skeletons of forest giants, contorted and broken by the immense forces of the flooded rivers that rooted them out and bore them to the sea. An old road leads to a viewpoint on **Otorokua Point** (30 to 40 minutes one way) or you can walk beneath the cliffs at mid-tide to a huge beach of flat schist pebbles and the outlet of the Cook River. Other things to do at Gillespies Beach are fossicking for gemstones (and maybe a speck of gold) and camping at the picnic area at the northern end.

Copland Valley and Track

An overnight or 3-day hike up the **Copland Valley** offers an unusual sort of experience. You won't need to struggle as Charlie Douglas did when he first explored the valley, looking for an easy route to the Canterbury side of the Alps, but you will need to be reasonably fit and be prepared for rain and wet feet. The valley's main attractions are the superb alpine scenery and natural hot pools at Welcome Flat, where you can soak yourself while viewing the jagged Sierra Range across the river. A crossing of the **Copland Pass** (2,150 m) is best done from east to west and should only be undertaken by experienced parties equipped with ice axes, crampons, and ropes. Guides and rental equipment are available from Alpine Guides (Westland) at Fox Glacier or Alpine Guides (Mt. Cook) at the Hermitage. The Copland Valley track begins about 26 km south of Fox Glacier on SH 6, just north of the Karangarua road-bridge. Public transport is available with InterCity buses. There are 2 huts in the valley, at Welcome Flat (30 bunks) and at Douglas Rock (16 bunks), and a hut warden is usually in residence over the summer. The 17 km from SH 6 to Welcome Flat Hut takes about 6 hours, crossing open river flats to the confluence of the Copland and Karangarua rivers, then alternating between river terraces and bouldery riverbed to Architect Creek. Above here, the track climbs steadily, sidling above a gorge. The 7 km between Welcome Flat and Douglas Rock take another 3 hours, crossing a series of river flats before climbing around the upper gorge.

The crossing of the Copland Pass from Douglas Rock to Hooker Hut in Mt. Cook National Park takes 10 to 12 hours. Further information on the track should be obtained from the Department of Conservation at Fox Glacier or Franz Josef.

Lakes Mapourika and Wahapo
These two attractive lakes adjacent to the main road between Franz Josef and Whataroa are notable for good trout and salmon fishing. Both lakes are surrounded by forest and have high numbers of grey ducks and mallards, New Zealand scaup, paradise ducks, and black swans. The rare crested grebe is also seen here. Basic camping areas and picnic sites are located at McDonald Creek by Lake Mapourika, and at Lake Wahapo along the old road.

Okarito
Once important as a gold mining center, Okarito is now better known for the birds that feed in the lagoon, wild seascapes, and panoramic views of the Southern Alps. The broad, shallow expanse of **Okarito Lagoon** is a wildlife refuge and is the main feeding ground for the rare white heron and royal spoonbill, which breed by the Waitangiroto River to the north. The present small settlement of Okarito is reached by a side road off SH 6 between Franz Josef and Whataroa. There is hotel, motel, and backpacker accommodation in the vicinity and a pleasant campground by the beach at Okarito. From the road-end there are walks to **Okarito Trig** (1.5 hours round trip) where you look down on the lagoon and across miles of virgin forest to the mountains while to the south the coast stretches hazily away in a mix of beach, lagoon, and headland. At low to mid tide it is possible to walk south around the coast to **Three Mile Lagoon** (1 hour one way) or you can take the slightly longer pack track over the Kohuamarua Bluff through low wind-shorn forest of rimu, rata, and silver pine. From Three Mile Lagoon you can walk, in another hour or so, to **Five Mile Lagoon**, where hundreds of miners worked the sands for gold in the 1860s. The bluff at the south end of Three Mile can be rounded at low tide. Don't attempt to cross the lagoon mouths; quicksand and tide rips are not just unpleasant surprises—they can be extremely dangerous.

Visiting the White Heron Colony
Entry to the white heron colony is strictly controlled, and the easiest way to get there is with **White Heron Sanctuary Tours**, Box 19, Whataroa, phone (03)7534-120. The tours, which use a jet boat, take approximately 2 hours and take place during the nesting season between November and February. Private parties can go there, provided they first obtain a permit from the visitor center at Franz Josef. Visitors must give 24 hours notice and must be accompanied on the tour by the colony warden. There is a fee for the permit, the warden's

time, and use of the boat to the colony. A private visit also involves a 2.5- to 3-hour walk down the Waitangitaona River to reach the warden's hut. Instructions on how to get there are issued when you get your permit.

Mountaineering and Ski-Touring

The vast névés of the Fox and Franz Josef glaciers give access to many peaks along the Main Divide and are also popular in winter for ski-touring. Many parties fly in by skiplane or helicopter and make Pioneer Hut, at 2,400 m in the head of the Fox Glacier, a base for extended trips. Vagaries of weather and prolonged storms, added to the isolation of the area, make all mountaineering activities potentially risky. Scheduled daily radio contacts with huts relay weather forecasts and keep tabs on the whereabouts and intentions of climbing parties. However, all parties need to be prepared to descend on foot, and this can be difficult, depending on the state of the Fox and Franz glaciers at the time. Guiding services are available from Alpine Guides (Westland), Box 38, Fox Glacier, phone (03)7510-825 or Fax (03)7510-857.

CENTRAL WESTLAND

Central Westland, around the towns of Hokitika and Greymouth, includes many gold mining sites and walkways. Both towns have all services and a range of accommodation. The motor camp at Hokitika must be the most uninspiring in the country as far as scenery goes, but it has reasonably good facilities. Greymouth is the larger of the two towns and has less of a wild feel about it. Northbound travelers have a choice of routes beyond Greymouth. The most scenic is the coastal route (SH 6) through **Punakaiki** and the edge of **Paparoa National Park** to Westport. The route using SH 7 to Reefton then SH 69 to Inangahua, while shorter and easier, misses the scenic Buller Gorge but gives access to the **Lewis Pass** and **Victoria Forest Park,** where there are some interesting mining sites and good walks.

Around Hokitika

The first stop in Hokitika should be the information center in Sewell St., where you can pick up the town's information brochure. This lists local craft outlets for greenstone jewelery and ornaments, woodwork, weaving, handspun sweaters, pottery, artwork; local rafting, horse trekking, and canoeing operators; hunting guides; and locations of walking tracks. Bookings for adventure activities can be made at the information center. The Department of Conservation, also located on Sewell Street close to the information center, has brochures on local walkways and historic gold towns.

The West Coast Historical Museum in Tancred St. is worth a visit if you are spending time in the town. It has displays of relics from the gold mining

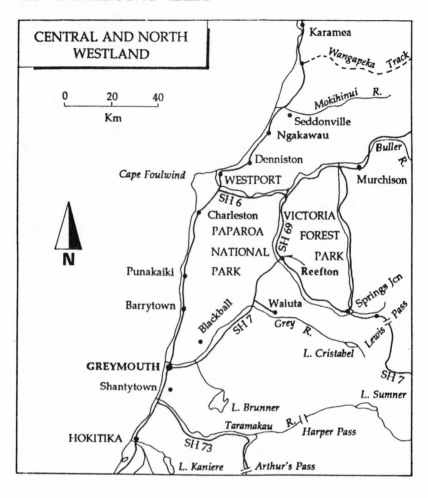

CENTRAL AND NORTH
WESTLAND

0   20   40
Km

N

Karamea

Wangapeka Track

Mokihinui R.

Seddonville
Ngakawau

Denniston

Buller R.

Cape Foulwind

WESTPORT

Murchison

SH 6

Charleston

VICTORIA

PAPAROA

SH 69

FOREST

NATIONAL

PARK

Punakaiki

PARK

Reefton

Barrytown

Blackball

Waiuta

Springs Jcn

SH 7

Grey R.

Lewis Pass

L. Cristabel

GREYMOUTH

SH 7

Shantytown

L. Sumner

L. Brunner

Taramakau R.

Harper Pass

HOKITIKA

SH 73

L. Kaniere

Arthur's Pass

era, Maori greenstone artifacts, and a small working model of a gold dredge. A 20-minute audiovisual program tells the story of exploration of the west coast and the gold rushes.

Lake Kaniere

Lying 18 km east of Hokitika in a trough left by a departing glacier is beautiful Lake Kaniere, surrounded by unspoiled native bush, a popular place with locals for fishing, camping, walking, and water sports. The road from Hokitika reaches the lake at its outlet, where there are views of surrounding mountains; a picnic area here has an information kiosk and a peak indicator. Starting at the picnic area, the **Water Race Walkway** follows a water race for 7.5 km down to the hydroelectric power station passed on the way up. The track is well graded and takes about 3 hours one way; return transport or a pick-up needs to be prearranged. A short distance around the lake to the right is **Sunny Bight** picnic area and the short **Kahakitea Forest Walk.** At the end of the road is the start of the **Lake Kaniere Walkway,** a 13-km track around the western shore taking about 4 hours. The track passes through a variety of forest types and gives access to good beaches for swimming and fishing; Lawyers Delight Beach near the southern end of the walkway has a small 4-bunk hut. In summer the forest is often brightened with the red of flowering rata. The southern end of the track is signposted on the Kaniere–Kokatahi road.

Along the eastern shore is the delightful short walk to **Canoe Cove,** and **Hans Bay** where you can picnic and camp. The start of the climb up to **Mt. Tuhua** (1,125 m), which gives superb views over the alps and coast, is near here. The round trip takes about 7 hours, and you'll need boots and warm clothing; it should not be attempted in bad weather. Further around the lake another short track leads to the beautiful **Dorothy Falls,** and at **Geologist Creek** there is another grassy camping area. The route to **Mt. Brown,** a high granite peak overlooking the lake, starts near here. Again it's a 7-hour round trip hike, and you'll need boots, warm clothing, and fine weather. The return drive to Hokitika can be made through Kokatahi.

Lake Mahinapua

This delightful spot is reached by turning off at the south end of the Hokitika River Bridge at Kaniere township, following the river to the coast, then going south along the coast. At Mananui there is a short walk through coastal bush to the sea, and you can slake your thirst, or stay, at the rustic Mahinapua Hotel. Nearby is the entrance to the **Mahinapua Walkway,** following an old logging tramline for 5.5 km through native and exotic forests to SH 6. Details of other short walks in the vicinity are displayed at the large picnic and camping area at **Shanghai Bay.** SH 6 can be regained by continuing south through Ruatapu.

Goldsborough

Nothing remains today of this once bustling gold town. A number of walking tracks to old workings wander through the surrounding bush, and a pamphlet describing these and the town's history is available from the Department of Conservation. The walks vary from 5 minutes to a full day, most of them leaving from a picnic and camping area where the town once stood. Access to the area is via the Stafford–Dillmanston Road, 10 km north of Hokitika on SH 6.

Around Greymouth

Greymouth has a good visitor center, located in the Regent Theater at the western end of MacKay St., and it doubles as an outlet for Department of Conservation information on historic gold town sites, gold panning sites, and walkways. As might be expected, the choice of accommodation is greater here than in Hokitika, with several hotels and lodges, motels, backpacker lodges, and two motorcamps to choose from. The town also has a full range of banking services, which you won't find elsewhere on the west coast. For surfing and windsurfing, head for Cobden or Seven Mile beaches.

Shantytown
Shantytown could be one of those tourist traps you wish you'd never visited, but it isn't. It is an excellent replica of a typical west coast mining town around the turn of the century. Restored buildings and genuine furniture and articles of everyday life give a good picture of how places that have since disappeared must have looked. The town is set in native bush and has its own short railway and steam train ride to a gold claim, panning site, and working sawmill. The road to Shantytown is well signposted, 8 km south of Greymouth. By continuing past Shantytown another 17 km, following signposts, you'll come to **Woods Creek Track**, a 1-km loop through tailings and past tunnels, dams, and water races. The tunnels are up to 100 m long and can be explored with a flashlight.

Lake Brunner
A popular haunt of the boating and fishing fraternity, Lake Brunner can be reached from the Arthur's Pass Road (SH 73) by turning off near Jacksons, or from SH 7 between Greymouth and Reefton, by turning off at Stillwater. Accommodation is available in **Moana** at the northern end of the lake, either in the Moana Hotel, which also has cabins and backpacker rooms, or at the Moana Camping Ground. More up-scale accommodation can be found at the Lake Brunner Sporting Lodge at Mitchells on the southern edge of the lake. Fishing and pleasure cruises are available, or you can hire a dinghy, from the Moana Hotel. If you want to go sailing on Lake Brunner, or gold panning or rafting in the area, contact **Off Beat Tours**, phone (03)7324-842 or 7324-705.

Croesus and Moonlight Tracks
The Croesus Track, from Blackball in the Grey Valley across the Paparoa Range to Barrytown on the coast, follows an old miners' route. It used to be walked in one long day, but a new modern hut provides good overnight accommodation for a 2-day trip, giving time to explore the many side tracks to old mining sites on the Blackball side of the range. Blackball township grew as coal mining became established in the area around 1890, eventually taking over from the gold mining operations. The Depression years forced a return to gold prospecting between 1929 and 1935, and this was followed by dredging, until 1953. With the closing of the Blackball coal mine in 1964, the town's population dwindled, but today it is making a small comeback; the Blackball Hilton offers backpacker accommodation.

The Moonlight Track starts in the Moonlight Valley behind Atarau and leads to old workings and eventually the top of the Paparoa Range. Moonlight Creek was named after the prospector George Moonlight, who discovered gold here in April 1865 and started a rush of 300 diggers. The early rush soon slowed, but for the next forty years, steady amounts of gold were retrieved by up to a hundred men, much of it in good-sized nuggets. The most notable was one of 2.476 kg, found by Peter Passeni in 1916. There are two picnic and camping areas in Moonlight Creek, and the public are permitted to pan for gold in marked areas. To reach Blackball and Atarau from Greymouth, take SH 6 north, turn right immediately after crossing the Cobden Bridge over the Grey River, and take the road through Taylorville.

Point Elizabeth Track

One of the nicest walks close to Greymouth is the Point Elizabeth Walkway, following an old miners' trail along the coast between Cobden and Rapahoe. Along the well-formed, northern end of the track, dense coastal bush of nikau palms, tree ferns, rimu, matai, and rata, festooned with kiekie and supplejack vines, forms a sheltered canopy along the cliff tops, giving way to matted wind-shorn vegetation, then dramatic views of the wave-swept coastline at Point Elizabeth. In bad weather, the contrast is dramatic between the quiet, sheltered forest sections and the exposed cliffs where the wind roars and the sea pounds furiously against the rock stacks off Point Elizabeth. The southern end of the track, beneath the Rapahoe Range, is rougher and much more exposed to the elements; views from the cliff tops are impressive. The 5-km track can be walked from either end, taking about 2 hours one way, but return transport or a pick-up needs to be prearranged. A very pleasant shorter walk can be made along the northern section of the track, from Rapahoe to Point Elizabeth, either return-ing the same way or, if the tide is low and the weather fine, by the beach. A ladder down the cliffs at Point Elizabeth gives access to the beach, but you need to be sure you won't be trapped by a rising tide. To reach the northern end of the track, take SH 6 and turn left before crossing the bridge over Seven Mile Creek at Rapahoe.

Nelson Creek

Reached by turning off SH 7 a kilometer or so north of Ngahere, Nelson Creek is another of those boom-and-bust gold towns where you can wander around the old workings on a network of tracks. A small community still lives here, patronizing the local shop and hotel, and you can camp and picnic at the recrea-tion area.

Around Reefton and Springs Junction

Reefton is one of those funny little towns you could easily bypass, but it makes a good base for fishing, hiking, or exploring the many gold mining sites in

Victoria Forest Park. The place still has an old gold town flavor about it, and you can stay in one of the vintage hotels or in a modern motel. For budget travelers, the motor camp is pleasant and has good facilities. Springs Junction has one motel. Basic camping areas are at Marble Hill, sited a few kilometers from Springs Junction along SH 7 toward Lewis Pass, and at Slab Hut Creek, 10 km south of Reefton on SH 7. The Department of Conservation maintains a field base in Reefton where you can pick up pamphlets, maps, and advice on walking tracks in the Lewis Pass area and Victoria Forest Park, some of which are described below. There is also an unattended information booth at Springs Junction.

Lake Daniell
Lake Daniell is a pretty, bush-girt body of water popular for trout fishing or just relaxing. The hut at the south end of the lake sleeps 32 people and is reached in 2 to 3 hours by an easy, well-graded track through majestic red beech forest. The track starts from the Marble Hill Camping area east of Springs Junction.

VICTORIA FOREST PARK

Victoria Forest Park covers 180,000 ha of mountain land to the east and south of Reefton and is notable for its good fishing rivers, bush, gold, and coal mining sites. It straddles the Maruia River and is bounded to the west by the Inangahua River, to the north by the Buller River, and to the south by the upper Grey River. The forests are a mix of beech and podocarp species, with a rich under-story of tree fuchsias and shrubs, and a ground covering of mosses, lichens, and ferns. Toward the bushline, *Dracophyllum* species form a distinctive band, with some huge specimens of mountain neinei; mountain ribbonwood and *Olearia* fringe some alpine basins. Above the forests, tussocks and alpine herbs cover slopes smoothed and carved by Ice Age glaciers; U-shaped hanging valleys and small cirques now filled with tarns are legacies of colder times. Unlike the schists and greywackes of the Southern Alps, rocks of the Victoria Range between the Maruia River and Inangahua River are granite, with reefs of gold-bearing quartz and coal. The variety of forests provides a good range of habitats for bush birds, with bellbirds and robins being particularly common. Brown creepers are seen near the bush edge, and kea and rock wrens inhabit the open mountain slopes. Blue ducks occur in the upper reaches of streams and rivers, and areas of pakihi swamp provide good country for fernbirds.

    While miners rushed to other parts of Westland in the mid-1860s, few ventured far inland to the Reefton area. All this changed when gold-bearing reefs were discovered in Lyell Creek in the Buller Valley and at Murray Creek, near Reefton. To mine these reefs, heavy machinery was required, necessitating a lot of capital and the use of extensive labor for the construction of tunnels, tracks, and tramways. Stamper batteries and boilers were brought in, with great difficulty, to crush the ore, and towns grew to support the mining communities. Of the many towns, Reefton became the main center and survives today. After the initial early find, more reefs were discovered at Big River and Merrijigs, and later still at Kirwans Hill in 1896 and at Waiuta in 1905. Waiuta was the richest and was worked until 1951. Over the 80 years of mining in the district, more than 62,000 kg of gold were extracted. Many mining companies made good profits, while others foundered through bad management and bad luck. As the reefs were worked out and the companies folded, the equipment they had brought in with such difficulty was abandoned and remains on site, slowly being reclaimed by the bush.

The onset of gold mining brought a boom in timber milling and coal mining; timber was used for mine props, tramway sleepers, and fluming for water races, while the coal provided fuel for the mining operations. Both coal mining and timber milling continued when gold mining ceased. Many of the old mining tracks and tramlines have been restored to provide easy access to historic sites, while other, more rugged tracks give access to places more of interest to nature lovers. Although sheltered from the full brunt of the prevailing westerly winds by the Paparoa Range, Victoria Forest Park still receives plenty of rain. Rainfall varies considerably, depending on proximity to the Main Divide; Reefton receives about 1,840 mm while Lake Cristabel on the flanks of the Alps receives 4,000 to 5,000 mm annually. Because of the park's sheltered inland position, frosts and valley fogs are common in winter.

If you are interested in the gold mining history of the area there are several short walks at **Murray Creek,** just 2.7 km out of Reefton at Blacks Point. These range from 10 minutes to 2.5 hours, through lovely beech forest. **Larrys Creek Track** provides another easy 2- to 3-hour walk through exotic and beech forests to one of the earliest quartz goldmining sites; the clear, swift-flowing Larry River is good for fishing. Access is 16 km north of Reefton off SH 69. **Alborns Coal Mine Walk** is an easy 90-minute loop track through the machinery and workings of a mine that first developed in 1880 to supply coal to gold mining operations, then continued production until a lack of workers forced its closure in the mid-1950s. The track starts 9 km along Soldiers Road, off SH 7 just south of Reefton.

Waiuta

Now a ghost town, Waiuta is a fascinating place to explore. The town grew around the Blackwater Mine and by the mid-1930s had a population of over 600. Most of the quartz from the Blackwater Mine was taken along a tunnel from the vertical mineshaft out to the banks of the Snowy River, where it was crushed by huge water-driven batteries. Another shaft, the Prohibition, was sunk on a hill above the town and at 879 m became the deepest in New Zealand, with more than a third of it below sea level. Enough rich quartz to keep the mine going for years remained untouched when the Blackwater shaft collapsed, letting poisonous gases and water into the Prohibition workings. With profits already falling because of fluctuating world markets, the company decided against making repairs and the mine closed abruptly, in mid-1951. Only five dwellings remain of the once large town, and four of these are still inhabited. Interpretive signs and photographs show how the town once looked and tracks lead down to Snowy Creek where the foundations of the battery and old cyanide tanks remain. You can camp at Waiuta or stay in the 30-bunk **Waiuta Lodge**, which is run by the Department of Conservation. Bookings are essential, through the Department at Reefton (P.O. Box 100, phone (03)7328-391), and you need your own food and sleeping bag. The road to Waiuta leaves SH 7 21 km south of Reefton.

Big River Track

Big River was another gold mining town where men toiled to bring in heavy machinery and worked the quartz reefs for 62 years, only to abandon all eventually to the bush and birds. You can drive there on a rough four-wheel-drive road from near Reefton, or make an interesting 2- to 3-day hike along the old track from Waiuta, staying overnight or longer at the large and comfortable Big River Hut overlooking the town site. The well-graded track is signposted past Waiuta (see above) on the road to the Prohibition Mine, and it takes 4 to 5 hours to walk the 11 km to Big River. A day can easily be spent around the town site visiting the old boiler house, dam site, winding plant, and magnificently restored poppet head. If you don't want to return the same way and can arrange transport, you can walk out to the Inangahua River and SH 7, passing many more interesting sites and relics along the way. The distance is 11 km and takes about 5 hours. The Inangahua River can be forded if it is low, or you can continue down a track on the true left bank to a swingbridge.

Kirwans Track

This provides a 2- to 3-day round trip to the site of an opencast quartz mine where the ore was transported down the mountainside to a stamper by aerial ropeway. The track starts at the site of the former mining town of Capleston at the end of Boatmans Road, 10 km north of Reefton on SH 69. The first day entails a long climb (6 to 7 hours) to the new, 20-bunk Kirwans Hut at the bush edge on Kirwans Hill. Views from the hut and from the tussock-covered top of Kirwans Hill (1,297 m) are superb, taking in the Inangahua and Grey valleys, Victoria and Paparoa ranges, and the Main Divide as far south as Mt. Cook. The next two days are easier and involve a descent below the open-cast workings and line of the collapsed aerial ropeway to Kirwans Creek and the

Montgomerie River. Montgomerie Hut (6 bunks) is reached in about 4 hours from Kirwans Hut, and from here it is a 12-km walk along a four-wheel-drive track through red beech forest and open grassy river flats to Gannons Bridge. A return to Capleston can be made from Gannons Bridge by a track (1 hour) that climbs to a fire break, then descends an overgrown face of gorse and manuka to Boatmans Creek. Alternatively, it is 5 km down Gannons Road to SH 69 and another 3 km to Reefton.

Lake Cristabel
This superb lake, nestled in beech forest against the Main Divide at the head of the Blue Grey River, is notable for being free of introduced fish and forms the core of Lake Cristabel Ecological Reserve. The Blue Grey River is a clear, rushing stream that offers good fishing. Lake Cristabel Hut is reached by about 6 hours' walking. More experienced trampers can return over Robinson Saddle and down the Robinson River, taking 3 days for the round trip. There are 2 huts in the Robinson Valley: Mid Robinson, with 6 bunks, and Top Robinson, with 12 bunks. Tracks up the Blue Grey and Robinson Rivers both start on Palmer Road, which turns off SH 7 on the outside of a hairpin bend, 4 km from Springs Junction toward Reefton. For permission to cross private property, to the start of the Robinson Track, apply to the Farm Manager, Blue Grey Farm, Private Bag, Reefton, phone (03)5238-892.

Rahu Saddle Tracks
Several tracks suitable for half- and full-day hikes start off SH 7 between Reefton and Springs Junction, near the Rahu Saddle. All are signposted, but the small signs are very easily missed. The **Klondyke Track** and **Klondyke Spur Track** both start from a gravel side road on Rahu Saddle, the latter climbing steeply to the bushline and on to a trig point at 1,540 m. The Klondyke Track follows the Rahu River to a basin at the bushline where alpine tarns lie below towering granite cliffs. A round trip can be made by climbing up any of the side gullies to join the Klondyke Spur Track. The **Mt. Haast Track** starts from a carpark just above the upper Inangahua Bridge and climbs steeply to the bush edge. From here, an unmarked route to the summit lies up the right-hand ridge. Pyramid-shaped Mt. Haast has good alpine herb fields and provides spectacular panoramic views in fine weather. About 1 km down the road from the Mt. Haast Track carpark, on the opposite side of the road, **Lake Stream Track** leads to a 2-bunk hut in a pretty tussock clearing near the bush edge. As the walk takes 3.5 hours one way, it could be worth considering as an overnight trip; excellent campsites, alpine tarns, and mountain scenery make it worthwhile. The **Duffy Creek Track,** starting at Duffy Creek bridge, leads in about an hour to a clearing that becomes a swamp or a small lake, depending on how much rain has fallen recently. It's a pretty spot in fine weather, when you can see the granite bluffs

at the head of the creek, but there's little to see on a wet day except the lush mosses and ferns. The track tends to be boggy and crosses masses of jumbled and twisted tree roots, making for difficult walking, and in one section, through a jumble of boulders and stumps, track markers are hard to follow.

PAPAROA NATIONAL PARK

The majority of visitors to Paparoa only see the fascinating "Pancake Rocks" and blowholes at Punakaiki before moving on to their next destination, not realizing that there is a wonderful area of limestone karst country waiting to be explored. The park is small and relatively undeveloped compared to other national parks, but the tracks it has enable everyone to enjoy the spectacular scenery of limestone bluffs, gorges, wild coastline, and warm rainforest. Formed millions of years ago under the sea floor, the limestone beds have been raised to form a strip of karst country between the granite peaks of the Paparoa Range and the coast. Rivers flowing off the Paparoa Range have cut deep, narrow gorges through this belt, and in some places disappear underground for long distances before reappearing. Young caves and cave systems, fluted rocks, potholes, arches, and dolines lie concealed in the rich vegetation nourished by a warm, damp climate. Along the coast, the layers of sediments, welded together by calcium over long periods of time, can be clearly seen. At Dolomite Point, acid waters from flax bogs have eaten into the limestone, sculpting it into distinctly layered pinnacles and blocks. In other places along the coast, where the sediments were coarser and less calcium carbonate was available to cement the grains together, soft sandstones have formed.

Bird life within the park is varied, with seabirds and bush birds represented. The park is the only place where the Westland black petrel (*Procellaria westlandica*) breeds in New Zealand, in an area covering around 7,000 ha. Largest of the burrowing seabirds, the Westland petrel is totally different from the black petrel (*Procellaria parkinsoni*), which nests only on islands of the Hauraki Gulf. Since large-scale fishing commenced in the region in 1966, providing the birds with an easy diet of fish waste, the Westland petrel has doubled its numbers. The birds nest in winter and most of the dozen or so nesting colonies are within the park and are strictly protected. However, a few are on private land and these can be visited with **Paparoa Nature Tours**, Box 36, Punakaiki.

Information on the park and walking tracks is available from the small visitor and information center on the main road at Dolomite Point. Next to it are tearooms and a small shop, an excellent craft shop, and a restaurant. Almost all tourist buses and public transport stops here. Accommodation in Punakaiki is limited to one small motel and the motor camp, which has cabin accommodation. The motor camp, sited next to the beach, is very pleasant and has excellent facilities; it also is very popular during summer. The nearest other accommodation is the hotel and tavern at Barrytown to the south, or at Charleston to the north, where there is a motel and campground. Canoes can be rented at Punakaiki for a paddle up the Porarari River.

The **Dolomite Point Walk,** opposite the visitor center, gives access to the Pancake Rocks and blowholes, which perform best at high tide when there is a westerly swell. Although the track takes only 10 to 15 minutes to walk, a much longer time is usually spent watching the sea surging in and out of holes and caverns, dashing against the cliffs, or spouting through the famous blowholes.

Porarari River Track

For spectacular gorge scenery, walk about an hour up the lower **Porarari Gorge** as far as the junction of the Inland Pack Track. The Porarari River Track continues upriver on the true left for about 15 minutes until opposite Cave Stream. Here you must cross to continue up the benched track on the true right bank, reaching a good viewpoint over the upper Porarari Gorge in about 1 hour. For a longer round trip of about 3 hours, take the Inland Pack Track over a saddle and down to the **Punakaiki River.** Across the river a rough road leads out down the true left to the main highway, about 1 km south of the visitor center. This walk can be done in reverse, but at present is best done as described. The Inland Pack Track is muddy, and a crossing of the Punakaiki River at the end gives a chance to clean boots and legs. There are plans to upgrade the track and a new one will be cut on the true right of the Punakaiki River to avoid the river crossing.

Inland Pack Track

Built around 1867 or 1868 to provide an easier and safer route than the coastline, this makes a good 2- to 3-day hike, or sections of it can be done as day hikes. Even though it involves many river crossings, the Inland Pack Track was the major route for travelers until 1927 when the coast road between Punakaiki and Fox River was constructed. The southern section of the track between the Punakaiki River and Porarari River is described above. The middle section, from the Porarari River to Bullock Creek, can be done as a 5-hour loop walk from Punakaiki. At present the Porarari River is forded about 100 m above the junction of the Pack Track and Porarari River Track, but there are plans to build a bridge near here. On the opposite bank, the track continues through tall silver beech forest, in an area liberally pocked with concealed potholes, to an old logging road at Bullock Creek Farm. Follow this road to a signposted junction (2 hours from the ford) and a return can be made down the road back to the main highway.

To continue on the Pack Track, follow signs to a ford over Bullock Creek and cross farmland to the bush where a track leads to Fossil Creek. Descend

Fossil Creek to Dilemma Creek (3 hours). Grassy flats here make good campsites, and others can be found at Bullock Creek near the ford. The next section, down Dilemma Creek, involves many river crossings and should not be attempted in heavy rain as there is no way out of the canyon. The Fox River is reached in about 1 hour 15 minutes, and a signposted track will be found on the true left at the confluence with Dilemma Creek. This stays fairly high above the river, then descends to a ford and continues on the true right bank to the main road (2 hours). A tent and spare food should be carried when walking the Inland Pack Track, as all rivers can become impassable after only short periods of heavy rain, and no attempt should be made to cross them.

Fox River

A hike along the Inland Pack Track can be combined with exploration of the **Fox River Caves** and a visit to the **Ballroom Overhang**. If starting from the main road, the caves are above the true right bank about 30 minutes beyond the first ford. You'll need a good flashlight for the caves; the lower one is suitable only for experienced cavers past the first 50 meters. To reach the amazing Ballroom Overhang, continue up the Fox River above the junction of Dilemma Creek, crossing the river about 5 times. Side streams around here with arches, overhangs and tunnels, and beautiful mossy banks are also worthy of exploration.

Truman Track

Even if your visit to Paparoa National Park is brief, try not to miss the short walk along the **Truman Track** to the **Te Miko Coast**, about 2.5 km north of the information center. The bush is a superb example of coastal rainforest, with tall podocarp species and gnarled rata giants overtopping nikau palms, five-finger, broadleaf, treeferns, and entangling supplejack and kiekie. A fine example of how rata uses a host tree to reach daylight can be seen a few minutes along the track, where one is engulfing a huge matai tree. The edge of the forest is abrupt and gives way to salt-tolerant coprosma shrubs and flax, then salt marsh vegetation. At low tide it is possible to wander along the beaches beneath the huge overhangs and wave-cut ledges of the sandstone cliffs. Early travelers using the Maori trail along this coast scaled the cliffs here on a flax and rata vine ladder. This was replaced by a chain ladder with wooden rungs, but continual use by gold miners soon broke the rungs, leaving only the bare chains to shin up and down.

AROUND WESTPORT

The area around Westpost is usually referred to as the Buller Region, after the river that so affected the region's history. With coal and timber production falling in recent years, the town has also declined, and now relies more and more on tourism. It has all services, a number of motels, hotels, and two motor camps, one out at Carters Beach and the other within walking distance of the center of town. If you are planning to go up the coast toward Karamea, stock up on food and other essentials here; shopping in Karamea is limited. The same applies if you intend to spend time in Paparoa National Park.

In town, you can wander along the wharves and watch the fishing boats unloading or the locals whitebaiting if it's "the season." There is good swimming, surfing, and fishing at **North Beach,** near the eastern breakwater at the river mouth, and at **Carters Beach,** 4 km to the south of town. The **Coaltown Museum** in Queen St. has excellent exhibits on the coal mining industry, particularly of Denniston and its famous Incline. When you see the size of a full coal wagon at the museum, and later visit Denniston and see the Incline, it's impossible to not be impressed.

Seals can be seen near **Tauranga Bay,** just south of **Cape Foulwind.** A walkway crosses farmland along cliff tops from the Cape Foulwind lighthouse to Tauranga Bay, taking about an hour one way. Coastal views north and south and inland to the Paparoa Ranges are good, as is the immediate coastal scenery. If you are short of time, drive to Tauranga Bay. The seal-viewing platforms are then only a 5-minute walk away. Tauranga Bay is good for surfing, and rock pool investigation at low tide. Just south of the peninsula from Tauranga Bay is **Nine Mile Beach,** another popular surfing venue, and at the road end the **Okari River** is a good spot for windsurfing at high tide and for whitebaiting in season.

Tiny **Charleston** with its one motel, tearooms, store, and campground, was reputed to have had 101 hotels between 1866 and 1869. There is plenty of history here, as a wander around the local cemeteries will show. The pakihi swamp around Charleston is raised beach, and this was worked extensively to retrieve gold. The few remaining workings now lie concealed in the scrub, but you can see how gold was produced in the old days by visiting **Mitchell's Gully Gold Mine,** a working mine using old methods and machinery. The town is said to have been named after Captain Charles Bonner, skipper of the ketch *Constant,* who braved great dangers to bring food to thousands of starving miners who'd been marooned here by gales and flooded rivers. Looking at Constant Bay today, it is hard to imagine that ships once squeezed in and moored to rings set into the rocks on either side. The bay was much deeper then, but tailings from the mining operations raised the sea bed and rendered it too shallow by 1879 to use as a port.

A fantastic limestone cave system in the nearby **Nile,** or Waitakere River, can be explored with **Norwest Adventures,** 41 Domett St., Westport, phone (03)7896-686 or 7898-922. They run a variety of caving trips, including underground rafting, all of them exciting and guaranteed to get the adrenalin buzzing.

Their other specialties are helitreks into the Paparoa Ranges and abseiling adventures. They can also arrange jet boating, horse trekking, and white-water rafting trips.

WESTPORT TO KARAMEA

The coast north of Westport is one of those out-of-the-way places usually seen only by trampers getting to or from the end of the **Heaphy** or **Wangapeka** tracks. It has a wonderful feeling of being off the beaten track that is not felt elsewhere on the coast. Heading north from Westport, the first place you'll come to is **Waimangaroa,** at the foot of the Denniston Incline. If you've already visited the Coaltown Museum in Westport, a visit to **Denniston,** perched on the edge of a high, exposed plateau, will complete the picture of early coal mining. The town is still inhabited but has an abandoned air, with its ramshackle buildings, rusting car wrecks, and remains of the Incline machinery. Excellent interpretive signs explain how the Incline worked. You can either drive there on the road snaking up the escarpment or follow the **Denniston Walkway** from the end of Conns Road, Waimangaroa. The 5-km walkway, taking about 3 hours up and 2 hours down, follows the old bridle track, constructed when the custom of riding up and down on the coal wagon proved too dangerous. The best views of the Incline are had from the top.

Four kilometers north of Waimangaroa, a sign points to the **Britannia Track** leading to the Britannia Battery and other gold mining remnants. You can pan for gold in the stream beside the carpark. The next town is **Granity,** which runs into **Ngakawau** and **Hector** where the aerial ropeway bringing coal down from the Stockton open-cast coal mine ends. Turn right just before the bridge at Ngakawau and past the coal load-out station for the start of the **Charming Creek Walkway.** The walk follows the old Charming Creek Railway through the spectacular lower Ngakawau Gorge, where the river foams between huge boulders beneath high bluffs. The railway, put in to bring coal down from the Charming Creek Mine near Seddonville, clings to the side of the gorge, climbing at a steady gradient and passing through tunnels and natural arches. After about an hour's walking a suspension bridge and short side track to the **Mangatini Falls** are reached. The falls are very impressive when seen close up or from across the river. The original suspension bridge collapsed in 1934 under the weight of a heavy rake of coal trucks but was replaced in an incredibly short time by men working in three shifts. This meant men being suspended over the swift torrent even at night. Across the present, newer bridge, the railway enters another long tunnel, which opens out to a view up the canyonlike gorge. The scenery changes as the railway enters Charming Creek and the site of Watson sawmill. A return can be made from here or you can continue along the railway, through overgrown farm country to the remains of the Charming Creek Mine. The complete walk is 10 km one way, taking 2.5 to 3 hours.

At the Mokihinui River the road turns inland. Surfcasting, trout fishing, and whitebaiting are good in season around the mouth of the river. There is a motor camp here but it has a neglected appearance, perpetuated by the neighboring houses and car wrecks. If you are looking for accommodation, head up valley to **Seddonville**, where there is a comfortable motor lodge and a motor camp. The camp is in the disused school, and as well as being clean and tidy, it has all facilities, and bunk rooms sleeping four people, at incredibly low rates. The **Chasm Creek Walk** beside the Mokihinui–Seddonville Road takes about 10 minutes and in that short time it passes mossy banks and cuttings, two bridges, and a tunnel, with magnificent views of the river.

Leaving the Mokihinui River behind, the long ascent to **Karamea Bluff** brings views out to the coast. The descent through rata and kamahi forest to **Little Wanganui**, where there is another hotel and campground, is more gentle, passing the track to picturesque **Lake Hanlon** (50 minutes round trip) on the last downhill stretch. To reach the start of the Wangapeka Track, turn off by the bridge over the Little Wanganui River. The first part of the **Wangapeka Track** to Little Wanganui Hut makes a good day walk.

Karamea is another 18 km up the coast across a coastal plain. Before crossing the Karamea River, you'll pass the side road to Karamea Motor Camp. It is not very modern, but the cabins and facilities are clean and adequate, and the setting is pleasant. You can also camp in the rather barren domain in town, or use the bunkhouse; the key is available from the tearooms, which also serve as an information office. The Karamea Tavern also has budget accommodation, or you can go more up-market and stay at the Karamea Township Motels. A pleasant grassy camping area with basic facilities is maintained by the Department of Conservation at **Kohaihai** where the **Heaphy Track** starts. Kohaihai is at the end of the road, 15 km north of Karamea. Information on the Heaphy and Wangapeka tracks and other local walks is available at the Department of Conservation, located on the corner opposite the tearooms, service station, and police station.

Most of the bush country north and west of Karamea is included in **Northwest Nelson Forest Park**. It contains some exciting limestone country with notable features such as the amazing **Oparara Arch** and **Honeycomb Caves**. These and the **Cavern Creek Caves** on the **Fenian Track**, and **Crazy Paving** and **Box Canyon Caves** are all described in the section on Northwest Nelson Forest Park in "Nelson." There are other easy, short walks at Kohaihai and along the start of the Heaphy Track. If you want something more strenuous and adventurous, you can climb **Mt. Stormy** (1,080 m) to the southeast of Karamea. It's a full-day hike, with rewarding views up and down the coast and over the park. The track starts 5.5 km up Arapito Road on the south bank of the Karamea River by a shelter and notice board. Permission to cross the private farmland is obtained by asking at Mr. Le Brun's farmhouse or by phoning Karamea (03)7826-809. From the notice board follow the old road south to the range, then markers to the bush edge and Elford Creek. The track follows the true left bank for 2 km, the true right for another 1 km, then climbs a steep, narrow spur to the bush edge. Easy tussock slopes lead to the summit.

Transport to the start of the Heaphy Track, and other tracks, can be arranged with David and Carol Higgs, **Karamea Motors,** Bridge Road, RD 1, Westport, phone (03)7826-757. Air taxi services are arranged through the Karamea Tavern. There is public transport every weekday between Karamea and Westport with **Cunninghams Coaches,** 179 Palmerston St., Westport, phone (03)7897-177.

OTHER ACTIVITIES

Westland has some exciting white-water rafting on the Buller, Karamea, and Mokihinui rivers; horse trekking; some gentle canoeing on lakes; underground rafting; and caving. Goldpanning is fun, and places where you can legally pan or dig for gold are set out in a Department of Conservation pamphlet. Many sites have picnic and camping areas and hiking tracks.

Trout fishing is excellent, and with so many lakes, rivers, and streams to try, any advice here would be superfluous. Information on season, bag, and size limits in Westland is available from the West Coast Fish and Game Council, Box 179, Hokitika, phone (03)7558-456. The adventure tour operators listed below offer a range of activities and can be contacted for further information.

Buller Adventure Tours, SH 6, Westport, phone (03)7897-286; rafting, jet boating, horse trekking, gold panning, hunting, fishing, and canoeing.

Norwest Adventures, 41 Domett St., Westport, phone (03)7896-686 or 7898-922; caving in Paparoa National Park, helifishing, hiking, hunting, underground rafting, gold fossicking.

Franz Josef Glacier Guides, Main Road, Franz Josef, phone (03)7520-763; glacier excursions and mountaineering, backcountry hiking and hunting.

South Westland Paddle and Saddle Safaris, Peter and Ruth Salter, Waitaha Valley, RD Ross, South Westland, phone (03)7554-182; horse trekking along beaches and through bush, and Canadian canoe trips on lakes, or a combination of both.

Scenic Rafting Hokitika, C. Adams, Kaniere Road, RD 3, Hokitika, phone (03)7557-114; rafting on the Hokitika River and Canadian canoe trips on Lake Mahinapua.

USEFUL ADDRESSES

Department of Conservation: Box 47, Karamea, phone (03)7826-852, Fax (03)7826-639; Box 357, Westport, phone (03)7897-742 or 7897-743, Fax (03)7898-003; Box 100, Reefton, phone (03)7328-390 or 7328-391; Punakaiki Field Centre, Box 1, Punakaiki, phone (03)7311-893; Westland National Park, Box 14, Franz Josef, phone (03)7520-796; Private Bag, Hokitika, phone (03)7558-301, Fax (03)7558-425; Haast Field Centre, c/o Post Office, Haast, phone (03)7500-809.

Westport Information Centre, Brougham St., Westport, phone (03)7896-658.

Greymouth Information Centre, Regent Theater, Mackay St., phone (03)7685-101.

Hokitika Information Centre, Sewell St., Hokitika, phone (03)7558-321, Fax (03)7558-026.

22 ◆ THE CHATHAM ISLANDS

LANDSCAPE AND CLIMATE

Lying deep in the South Pacific, 768 km south east of Wellington, are the windswept Chatham Islands, an isolated and relatively forgotten part of New Zealand that is sufficiently eastward to have its own time zone (45 minutes ahead of mainland New Zealand). To avoid placing them in a different day, the International Dateline deviates from 180 degrees longitude here. Of the ten islands in the group, only Chatham and Pitt islands are inhabited, and only by about 750 people. The largest island, Chatham, is roughly one-third the size of Stewart Island and knucklebone-shaped, its center filled with a shallow lagoon. Most of the land is gently contoured and grazed by sheep, but the coastline is rugged, its majestic cliffs and blow-holes contrasting with long sandy beaches. Volcanic peaks, peat bogs, and patches of dense forest add to the variety. Lying mid-ocean, the Chathams are exposed to the southern elements of wind and rain, but have a surprisingly temperate climate—12°C–18°C in February and 6°C–10°C in July on average. It can even reach 24°C at times in summer. Rain falls on about

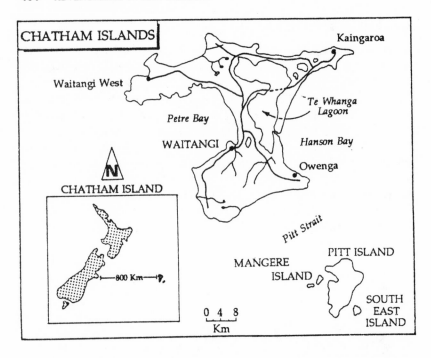

135 days of the year, depositing around 900 mm annually, and clear skies are recorded on about 60 days a year. The wind blows almost constantly from the west, often with considerable force!

Bird life is abundant and includes eighteen species unique to the islands. Many of these, such as the Chatham Islands black robin, are on the rare and endangered list and are found only on the small, outer islands that are not open to the public. Marine life is also abundant and most of the islands' inhabitants earn a living by fishing. Crayfish are caught in large quantities, and there are also scallops, oysters, and paua (abalone) for the taking; flatfish and eels are prolific in the lagoons.

Waitangi, the only town, has one hotel and one motel, two shops, a post office, a four-bed hospital, a museum, and one policeman who also acts as customs officer. There are about 180 km of roads on Chatham and 13 km of roads on Pitt Island, but no public transport. Vehicles can be rented in Waitangi. Pitt Strait, between Chatham and Pitt islands, is frequently dangerous, with mountainous seas, and the usual way to get across is by air, a 15-minute flight by three-seater Cessna 180.

HISTORY

Earliest inhabitants of the islands were the Moriori, who lived in peaceful isolation for around 700 years until 1791, when Lieutenant Broughton arrived aboard the *Chatham* on a voyage between Australia and Tahiti. Broughton is said to have proclaimed the islands British, marking the beginning of change. Fighting broke out between the sailors and Moriori, with one local being killed, an event marked by a memorial near Kaingaroa, but afterward relations remained cordial. A decade later, the sealers arrived to slaughter seals that were vital to the Moriori way of life. They were followed by whalers from Europe and America, who established shore stations and brought with them deadly diseases. In 1835, the first Maori arrived from the mainland, looking for more land following intertribal warfare. Many of the pacifist Moriori were slaughtered or taken as slaves, and by the 1860s their numbers had dropped from about 2,000 when Broughton arrived to about 160. As a people they were doomed, and the last full-blooded Moriori, Tommy Solomon, died in 1933.

There is more history here than on many parts of the mainland. Much of it, such as the rock carvings and unexplained tree carvings, remains enshrouded in mystery; of the rest—the shipwrecks, missionaries, whalers, and other inhabitants—there is ample evidence.

GETTING THERE

The only way to get to the Chathams is by air, from either Wellington or Christchurch, aboard a Safe Air Argosy geared more for mail and freight than for tourists. It does have thirty Boeing 737 seats and is air-conditioned to provide some comfort for passengers on the three-hour flight. Bookings are made through travel agents and Air New Zealand Offices in New Zealand or overseas.

Commercial tours to the Chathams are taken by only one company, **Southern Heritage Tours,** run by Rodney Russ, a former wildlife officer who worked on the mission to save the Chatham Islands black robin in the 1980s. The emphasis of these tours is on the cultural and historical background and outstanding wildlife of the islands. Russ also runs tourist expeditions to the sub–Antarctic islands. Further information is available by writing to him at Box 22, Wakari, North Canterbury.

THINGS TO DO

Hiking
The numerous beaches are great for beachcombing, shell collecting, and watching penguins and seals, and there are endless walking opportunities, particularly

around the rugged southern end of Chatham Island. As most of the land is privately owned, permission must be obtained from landowners first, but this is usually readily given.

Diving

Clear water, abundant marine life, and many shipwrecks make this a great place for diving. You will have to take your own equipment, though, and organize dive trips through local fishermen.

Horse trekking

The Rekohu Pony Club meets fortnightly at Te One, and you can hire ponies for trekking.

Birdwatching

Endless opportunities exist for observing seabirds, waders, bush birds, waterfowl, weka, and pukeko on Chatham and Pitt islands. Rangatira (South East) and Mangere islands are wildlife sanctuaries, and visitors are not normally permitted to land, although you could check with the Department of Conservation in Wellington. Further information is available from the Department of Conservation Field Centre, Box 14, Waitangi, Chatham Islands, phone (03)3050-098.

Fishing

Surfcasting and line fishing from rocks is good from many areas, and there is excellent netting for flatfish in the lagoons. Permission to cross private land is necessary. Six crayfish, with a minimum tail size of 13.5 cm (6 inches), and 10 paua per person per day can be taken.

APPENDICES

♦SELECTED READINGS

Environment

Allison, K. W., and Child, J. *Mosses of New Zealand.* University of Otago Press, 1971.

Ayling, T., and Cox, G. J. *Collins Guide to Sea Fishes of New Zealand.* Auckland: Collins, 1982.

Beatson, D. *The New Zealand Weather Book.* Christchurch: Whitcoulls, 1985.

Chinnock, R. J. *Common Ferns and Fern Allies.* Mobil New Zealand Nature Series. Wellington: A. H. and A. W. Reed, 1981.

Cockayne, L. *New Zealand Plants and Their Story.* Wellington: Government Printer, 1967.

Cooper, D. *A Field Guide to New Zealand Native Orchids.* Price Milburn, 1980.

Dennis, A., and Potton, C. *Images from a Limestone Landscape.* Nelson: Craig Potton, 1987.

Doak, W. *Fishes of New Zealand Region.* Hodder and Stoughton, 1972.

Enting, B., and Molloy, L. *The Ancient Islands.* Port Nicholson Press, 1982.

Gage, M. *Legend in the Rocks: An Outline of New Zealand Geology.* Christchurch: Whitcoulls, 1971.

Gibbs, G. W. *New Zealand Butterflies.* Auckland: Collins, 1980.

Harris, G., and Hasler, G. *A Land Apart: The Mount Cook Region.* Wellington: A. H. and A. W. Reed, 1980.

Lentle, R., and Saxton, F. *Red Deer in New Zealand.* David Bateman, 1991.

Maddock, S. *Islands of the Gulf.* Auckland: Collins, 1966.

Mark, A. F., and Adams, N. *New Zealand Alpine Plants.* Wellington: A. H. and A. W. Reed, 1900.

Poole, and Adams, *Trees and Shrubs of New Zealand.* Wellington: Government Printer, 1979.

Potton, C. and Wood, P. *Yesterday's New Earth: New Zealand's Geothermal Landscape.* Nelson: Craig Potton, 1990.

Readers Digest. *Readers Digest Complete Book of New Zealand Birds.* Sydney: Readers Digest, 1985.

Robb, J. *New Zealand Amphibians and Reptiles.* Auckland: Collins, 1980.

Salmon, J. T. *Native Trees of New Zealand.* Wellington: A. H. and A. W. Reed, 1980.

Soons, J. M., and Selby, J. M. *Landforms of New Zealand.* Longman Paul, 1982.

Stevens, G. *New Zealand Adrift.* Wellington: A. H. and A. W. Reed, 1980.

History

Bates, A. P. *The Bridge to Nowhere: The Ill-fated Mangapurua Settlement.* Wanganui Newspapers, 1981.

Beaglehole, J. C. *Life of Captain James Cook.* London: Adams and Charles Black, 1974.

Beaglehole, J. C. *The Voyage of the Endeavour.* Haluyt Society, 1955.

Brailsford, B. *Greenstone Trails: The Maori Search for Pounamu.* Wellington: A. H. and A. W. Reed, 1984.

Charles, A., and Begg, N. C. *Port Preservation.* Christchurch: Whitcombe and Tombs, 1973.

Grady, D. *Perano Whalers of Cook Strait.* Christchurch: Whitcoulls, 1978.

Hall-Jones, J. *Fiordland Explored.* Wellington: A. H. and A. W. Reed, 1976.

Hall-Jones, J. *Goldfields of the South.* Invercargill: Craig Printing, 1982.

Maning, F. E. *Old New Zealand.* (reprint) Golden Press, 1980.

May, P. *The West Coast Gold Rushes.* Pegasus Press, 1962.

McKenzie, A. *Pioneers of Martins Bay.* Christchurch: Whitcombe and Tombs, 1970.

Pascoe, J. (ed.). *Mr. Explorer Douglas.* Wellington: A. H. and A. W. Reed, 1957.

Potton, C. *Tongariro: A Sacred Gift.* Nelson: Craig Potton, 1987.

Sinclair, K. *History of New Zealand.* London: Allen Lane, 1980.

Smart, J. J., G., and Bates, A. P. *The Wanganui Story.* Wanganui Newspapers, 1972.

Outdoor Guides

AA Guide to Tramping and Bushwalking in New Zealand. Auckland: Landsdowne Press, 1988.

AA Guide to Walkways: North Island. (rev. ed.) Auckland: Landsdowne Press, 1987.

AA Guide to Walkways: South Island. (rev. ed.) Auckland: Landsdowne Press, 1987.

Burton, R. and Atkinson, M. *Trampers Guide to New Zealand's National Parks.* Reed Methuen, 1987.

du Fresne, J. *Tramping in New Zealand.* Lonely Planet, 1990.

Dunnett, B. *Kaikoura Walks and Climbs.* Nikau Press, 1988.

Logan, H. *Mount Cook Guidebook.* New Zealand Alpine Club, 1982.

Murray, K. W. J., and von Kohorn, R. S. *A Cruising Guide: Cape Palliser to Marlborough Sounds and Tasman Bay.* Steven Williams, 1982.

Nicol, E., and Nicol, J. *Tramping in North Island Forest Parks.* Auckland: Heinemann Reed, 1991.

Pickering, M. *New Zealand's Top Ten Tracks.* Auckland: Heinemann Reed, 1990.

Ringer, B. *Guide to Cycle Touring in New Zealand.* Hodder and Staughton, 1990.

Shaw, D. *Golden Bay Walks.* Nikau Press, 1988.

Shaw, D. *Northwest Nelson Tramping Guide.* Nikau Press, 1991.

Sumner, T. *Buller Walks.* Nikau Press, 1989.

Temple, P. *Shell Guide to the Copland Track.* Christchurch: Whitcoulls, 1985.

Temple, P. *Shell Guide to the Heaphy Track.* Christchurch: Whitcoulls, 1985.

Wright, J. *Tramping in South Island Forest Parks.* Auckland: Heinemann Reed, 1990.

◆COMMONLY SEEN BIRDS
Asterisk indicates introduced species.

Penguins
Blue Penguin, *Eudyptula minor*
Fiordland Crested Penguin, *Eudyptes pachyrhynchus*

Tube-nosed Seabirds
Southern Giant Petrel, *Macronectes giganteus*
Grey-faced Petrel/Muttonbird, *Pterodroma macroptera gouldi*
Fairy Prion, *Pachyptila turtur*
Sooty Shearwater, *Puffinus griseus*
Fluttering Shearwater, *Puffinus gavia*
Common Diving Petrel, *Pelecanoides urinatrix*

Gannets and Cormorants
Australasian Gannet, *Sula bassana serrator*
Great Cormorant/Black Shag, *Phalacrocorax carbo*
Little Black Cormorant/Little Black Shag, *Phalacrocorax sulcirostris*
Pied Cormorant/Pied Shag, *Palacrocorax varius*
Little Pied Cormorant/Little Pied Shag, *Phalacrocorax melanoleucus*
Spotted Shag, *Stictocarbo punctatus*

Herons
White-faced Heron, *Ardea novaehollandiae novaehollandiae*
Reef Heron, *Egretta sacra sacra*

Swans and Ducklike Birds
*Black Swan, *Cygnus atratus*
Paradise Shelduck, *Tadorna variegata*

*Mallard, *Anas platyrhynchos platyrhynchos*
Grey Duck, *Anas superciliosa superciliosa*
Scaup/Black Teal, *Aythya novaeseelandiae*

Hawks/Falcons
Australasian Harrier, *Circus approximans*
New Zealand Falcon, *Falco novaeseelandiae*

Quail and Pheasants
*Brown Quail, *Synoicus ypsilophorus*
*California Quail, *Lophortyx californica brunnescens*
*Ring-necked Pheasant, *Phasianus colchicus*

Rails and Coots
Weka, *Gallirallus australis*
Pukeko, *Porphyrio porphyrio melanotus*
Australasian Coot, *Fulica atra australis*

Waders and Gulls
South Island Pied Oystercatcher, *Haematopus ostralegus finschi*
Variable Oystercatcher, *Haematopus unicolor*
Spur-winged Plover, *Vanellus miles novaehollandiae*
Banded Dotterel, *Charadrius bicinctus*
New Zealand Dotterel, *Charadrius obscurus*

Wrybill, *Anarhynchus frontalis*
Eastern Bar-tailed Godwit/Kuaka,
 Limosa lapponica baueri
Knot, *Calidris canutus*
Pied Stilt, *Himantopus himantopus
 leucocephalus*
Black-headed Gull, *Larus dominicanus*
Red-billed Gull, *Larus novaehollan-
 diae scopulinas*
Black-billed Gull, *Larus bulleri*
Caspian Tern, *Hydroprogne caspia*
Black-fronted Tern, *Sterna albostriata*
White-fronted Tern, *Sterna striata*

Pigeons
*Feral Pigeon, *Columba livia*
New Zealand Pigeon, *Hemiphaga
 novaeseelandiae*

Parrots and Parakeets
Kaka, *Nestor meridionalis*
Kea, *Nestor notabilis*
*Eastern Rosella, *Platycercus eximius*
Yellow-crowned Parakeet, *Cyanoram-
 phus auriceps*

Cuckoos
Shining Cuckoo, *Chrysococcyx lucidus
 lucidus*
Long-tailed Cuckoo, *Eudynamys
 taitensis*

Owls
Morepork/Ruru, *Ninox novaeseelandiae novaeseelandiae*

Kingfishers
New Zealand Kingfisher, *Halcyon
 sancta vagans*

Wrens
Rifleman Wren, *Acanthisitta chloris*
Rock Wren, *Xenicus gilviventris*

Larks
*Skylark, *Alauda arvensis arvensis*

Swallows
Welcome Swallow, *Hirundo tahitica
 neoxena*

Pipits and Wagtails
Pipit, *Anthus novaeseelandiae*

Accentors
*Hedgesparrow, *Prunella modularis
 occidentalis*

Warblers, Thrushes, and Allies
Fernbird, *Bowdleria punctata*
Brown Creeper, *Finschia novaeseelan-
 diae*
Whitehead, *Mohoua albicilla*
Yellowhead, *Mohoua ochrocephala*
Grey Warbler, *Gerygone igata*
Fantail, *Rhipidura fuliginosa*
North Island Robin, *Petroica aus-
 tralis longipes*
South Island Robin, *Petroica australis
 australis*
Tit, *Petroica macrocephala*
Pied Tit, *Petroica macrocephala toitoi*
*Song Thrush, *Turdus philomelos
 clarkei*
*Blackbird, *Turdus merula merula*

Silvereyes
Silvereye, *Zosterops lateralis lateralis*

Honeyeaters
Bellbird, *Anthornis melanura*
Tui, *Prosthemadera novaeseelandiae*

Buntings and Finches
*Yellow Hammer, *Emberiza citrinella
 caliginosa*
*Chaffinch, *Fringilla coelebs gengleri*

*Greenfinch, *Carduelis chloris chloris*
*Goldfinch, *Carduelis carduelis britannica*
*Red Poll, *Carduelis flammea cabaret*

Sparrows
*House Sparrow, *Passer domesticus domesticus*

Starlings and Mynahs
*Starling, *Sturnus vulgaris vulgaris*
*Indian Myna, *Acridotheres tristis*

Magpies
*Australian Magpie, *Gymnorhina tibicen*

◆LESS FREQUENTLY SEEN AND RARE OR ENDANGERED BIRDS

Kiwi, *Apteryx spp.*
Yellow-eyed Penguin/hoiho, *Megadyptes antipodes*
New Zealand Dabchick, *Podiceps rufopectus*
Crested Grebe, *Podiceps cristatus australis*
Royal Albatross, *Diomedea epomophora*
Mottled Petrel, *Pterodroma inexpectata*
Chatham Island Taiko, *Pterodroma magentae*
Cook's Petrel, *Pterodroma cookii*
Chatham Island Petrel, *Pterodroma axillaris*
Pycroft's Petrel, *Pterodroma pycroft*
Broad-billed Prion, *Pachyptila vittata vittata*
Westland Black Petrel, *Procellaria westlandica*

Buller's Shearwater, *Puffinus bulleri*
Hutton's Shearwater, *Puffinus huttoni*
King Shag, *Leucocarbo carunculatus*
White Heron, *Egretta alba modesta*
Blue Duck, *Hymenolaimus malacorhynchos*
Banded Rail, *Rallus philippensis*
Spotless Crake, *Porzanza tabuensis plumbea*
Black Stilt, *Himantopus novaezealandiae*
Fairy Tern, *Sterna nereis*
Kakapo, *Strigops habroptilus*
Red-crowned Parakeet, *Cyanoramphus novaezelandiae*
Black Robin, *Petroica traversi*
Stitchbird, *Notiomystis cincta*
Saddleback, *Philesturnus carunculatus*
Kokako, *Callaeas cinerea*

◆COMMON PLANTS

Trees
Beech: Silver Beech, *Nothofagus menziesii*
  Red Beech, *N. fusca*
  Mountain Beech, *N. solandri var. cliffortioides*
  Hard Beech, *N. truncata*
  Black Beech, *N. solandri*
Bog Pine, *Halocarpus bidwillii*
Broadleaf, *Griselinea littoralis*
Cabbage Tree, *Cordyline australis*
Mountain Cabbage Tree, *Cordyline indivisa*
Five-finger, *Pseudopanax arboreus*
Hinau, *Elaeocarpus dentatus*
Kaikawaka, *Libocedrus bidwillii*
Kahikatea, *Dacrycarpus dacrydioides*
Kamahi, *Weinmannia racemosa*
Kanuka, *Leptospermum ericoides*
Karaka, *Corynocarpus laevigatus*
Kauri, *Agathis australis*
Kohekohe, *Dysoxylum spectabilis*
Kotukutuku, *Fuchsia excorticata*
Kowhai, *Sophora tetrapetala* and *S. microphylla*
Mahoe, *Melicytus ramiflorus*
Matai, *Prumnopitys taxifolia*
Miro, *Prumnopitys ferruginea*
Mountain ribbonwoods, *Hoheria lyalii* and *H. glabrata*
Mountain Neinei, *Dracophyllum traversii*
Neinei, *Dracophyllum latifolium*
Nikau, *Rhopalostylis sapida*
Pepperwood/Horopito, *Pseudowintera axillaris*
Pigeonwood, *Hedycarya arborea*

Pohutukawa, *Metrosideros excelsa*
Pukatea, *Laurelia novae-zelandiae*
Puriri, *Vitex lucens*
Southern Rata, *Metrosideros umbellata*
Swamp Maire, *Syzygium maire*
Rangiora, *Brachyglottis repanda*
Rata, *Metrosideros robusta*
Rewarewa/Honeysuckle, *Knightia excelsa*
Rimu, *Dacrydium cupressinum*
Tanekaha, *Phyllocladus trichomanioides*
Taraire, *Beilschmeidia taraire*
Tawa, *Beilschmeidia tawa*
Toatoa, *Phyllocladus glaucus*
Toro, *Myrsine salicina*
Totara, *Podocarpus totara*
Hall's Totara, *P. cunninghamii* (formerly *P. hallii*)
Tree Daisies, *Olearia spp.*
Tutu, *Coriaria arborea*
Wineberry, *Aristotelia serrata*

Tree Ferns
Mamaku/Black tree fern, *Cyathea medullaris*
Katote/Soft tree fern, *Cyathea smithii*
Ponga/Silver fern, *Cyathea dealbata*
Wheki/Hard tree fern, *Dicksonia squarrosa*
Wheki-ponga, *Dicksonia fibrosa*

Vines and lianes
Clematis, *Clematis paniculata*
Bush Lawyer, *Rubus cissoides*
Kiekie, *Freycinetia banksii*
Supplejack, *Ripogonum scandens*

In the Shrub Zone
Flax, *Phormium tenax*
Mountain Flax, *Phormium colensoi*
Inaka, *Dracophyllum longifolium*
Manuka, *Leptospermum scoparium*
Matagouri, *Discaria toumatou*
Mountain Inaka, *Dracophyllum
    recurvum*
Hebe, *Hebe* (numerous spp.)
Coprosma, *Coprosma* (numerous spp.)
Mountain Toatoa, *Phyllocladus
    aspleniifolius var. alpinus*

Snowberry, *Gaultheria spp.*
Snow Tussocks, *Chionochloa spp.*
Speargrass, *Aciphylla spp.*
Sun Orchids, *Thelymitra spp.*
Toetoe, *Cortaderia richardii*

In Swamps
Bog Umbrella Fern, *Gleichenia
    dicarpa*
Raupo/bulrush, *Typha orientalis*
Wire Rush, *Empodisma minus*

◆GLOSSARY

New Zealand Words and Expressions

bivy rock a large overhanging rock under which you can camp or bivouac

boaties people who mess about in boats, either sailing or motorized

braided rivers rivers where the flow is split into many separate channels

campervan small van fitted out for living in, a small R.V.

carpark parking area

crèche day nursery

dairy factory place where milk is processed into cheese and milk powder

damper unleavened bread made from flour and water and cooked over an open fire

dear expensive, costly

domain park or recreation reserve

dunny pit toilet

fair dinkum genuine, true

fellfield upper level of the alpine vegetation zone generally consisting of small herbs and scattered tussocks

fossick to rummage, search about

Gondwanaland the ancient supercontinent that existed in the Southern Hemisphere up to Triassic-Jurassic times

greywacke sediments deposited in ancient ocean basins and subsequently hardened to greyish rock

Infomaps maps published by the Department of Survey and Land Information

motorway freeway

petrol gasoline

poled route route (over open country) marked with poles

return trip a trip to a specific destination and back again by the same route

river flat flat area of land beside a river

round trip a trip to a specific destination and back again by a different route

run (sheep run) large tract of land leased from the government for grazing sheep

run holder person who holds the lease to a run

sealed road paved road (signs saying Seal Ends indicate that the paved surface ends)

slip landslide

spur a ridge projecting laterally from a mountain or mountain range

surfies addicts of surfing

take aways food to go/take out/carry out

tar-sealed road paved road

tarn pond or small lake

ton metric ton (1000 kg)

torch flashlight

track trail

trig a trigonometrical survey marker

true right or true left the right or left side when facing downstream or downhill

walkway special designation for some trails

whitebait the edible young of a native freshwater fish

Maori Words and Expressions

When saying Maori words, pronounce each syllable separately. When there are two or more vowels together, each is sounded separately. Vowel sounds are:

A as *ar* in far
E as *ea* in feather
I as *ee* in feet
O as *aw* in paw; never as *oh*
U as *oo* in moon

The consonants *ng* and *wh* often appear together. Pronunciation varies between districts. *Ng* can be sounded as the *n* in *singing* or just as *n*. *Wh* can be sounded as *f*, as *h*, like *w* on its own, or sometimes like *wh* as in *where*.

aroha love

haere ra farewell

haere mai welcome

haka a challenge, chant

hapu subtribe

hangi food cooked in the traditional way

hongi to rub noses (meaning "to share breath")

ika fish

iwi tribe

iti small, little

kai food, to eat

kainga village

kaumatua old man, elder (male)

kia ora hello (means "may you be well")

korero talk

kuia old lady, elder (female)

kumara sweet potato

kuri dog

mana prestige

manga tributary or stream

manuhiri visitors, guests

marae sacred ground in front of the whare tipuna

maunga mountain

mere club, usually made of whalebone or greenstone

moana sea

ngati the people (of)

nui large, big

o of, or the place of

pa fortified village

Pakeha Europeans, white people

po night

powhiri a formal welcoming ceremony

puke hill

puku stomach, belly

rangatira chief or person of high status

rangi sky

roto lake

tane man, husband

tangata person

tangata whenua people of a particular place

tapu sacred

te the

tena koe hello! (greeting one person only)

tipuna ancestors
umu an oven (a hole in the
  ground in which hot rocks
  were placed)
utu revenge, price
wahine woman, wife

wai water
waiata a song, to sing
waka canoe
whanau family
whare house

◆CONVERSION TABLES:
AMERICAN STANDARD AND METRIC MEASURES

	American Standard	Metric	
Mass	1 ounce	28.3	grams
	1 pound	454	grams
	1 stone	6.35	kilograms
	1 ton	1.02	tons
Length	1 inch	2.54	centimeters
	1 foot	30.5	centimeters
	1 yard	0.914	meters
	1 mile	1.61	kilometers
Area	1 acre	0.405	hectares
	1 square mile	2.95	square kilometers
Volume	1 pint	0.568	liters
	1.76 pints	1	liter
	1 gallon (imperial)	4.55	liters

Temperature Degrees Fahrenheit $= \dfrac{9 \times {}^\circ C}{5} + 32$

$\dfrac{5({}^\circ F - 32)}{9}$ = Degrees Celsius

There is an easier but less accurate way to do temperature conversions: To change Fahrenheit to Celsius, subtract 30 and halve the remainder; thus for 60°F: 60−30=30, half of 30=15° Celsius. To change Celsius to Fahrenheit, double the degrees Celsius and add 30; thus for 10°C: 10+10=20, 20+30=50°F.

INDEX